LIVE | DEAD

MISSIONARY GOD, MISSIONARY BIBLE

A ONE-YEAR, MISSIONS-CENTERED, CHRONOLOGICAL READING OF THE BIBLE

— *DICK BROGDEN* —

Published by Abide Publishers
1600 N. Boonville, Suite B&C, Springfield, MO 65803

Cover design, typesetting, and interior design by Lucent
(www.lucentdigital.co).

Unless otherwise specified, Scripture quotations used in this book are from
the New King James Version®. Copyright © 1982 by Thomas Nelson.
Used by permission. All rights reserved.

Scripture quotations marked (NASB) are taken from the New American
Standard Bible®, Copyright © 1960, 1962, 1963, 1968, 1971, 1972, 1973, 1975,
1977,1995 by The Lockman Foundation. Used by permission.

THE HOLY BIBLE, NEW INTERNATIONAL VERSION®, NIV®
Copyright © 1973, 1978, 1984, 2011 by Biblica, Inc.® Used by permission.
All rights reserved worldwide.

Unreached people group statistics from Joshua Project.
joshuaproject.net

ISBN: 978-1-952562-05-1

Printed in the United States of America

DEDICATED TO PASTOR-TEACHERS

ELI, MARK, JIM, CHAD, ROB, DAVID, AND ROD
AND AN ARMY OF BROTHERS AND SISTERS LIKE THEM

*To all the shepherds who live and burn for the glory of God
among all nations and lead their flocks towards this glorious flame.*

INTRODUCTION

This book is a result of a prayer and strategy session in Dubai in 2018 with the elders and leaders of the Live Dead movement. We discussed how there needs to be a push-and-pull effect in mobilizing missionaries to make disciples and plant churches among the unreached. On the one hand, missionary speakers can pull, inviting the body of Christ to come join them in pioneer fields. On the other hand, pastors and teachers can push, stirring their flocks and followers to seriously obey Jesus' command to make disciples of all nations.

From that discussion I saw the opportunity to add another resource to the growing library of works on a biblical theology of mission in the hope that it would aid pastors, teachers, mobilizers, intercessors, and obedient disciples everywhere to passionately proclaim that missions is the center of God's heart and the organizing theme of the whole Bible. The book endeavors to prove its title: God is indeed a missionary God and the whole Bible His missionary message.

Missionary God, Missionary Bible is a one-year devotional based on a chronological reading plan. Each day includes a Scripture reading, a devotional explaining how the reading is missions applicable, and an unreached people group to pray for. Day by day the case builds, and the message is reinforced over and over: *He who is holy delights to be our God. We are to be His holy people that He might dwell among us. His glorious presence will wholly bless us in order that all nations, every distinct people group, might be likewise blessed.* This grand plan, centered on and culminating in Jesus as Savior, Lord, and eternal King over all nations, is what our faith, our Father, and our future is all about. Generally, in the body of Christ the "all nations" as central to the end game is forgotten or neglected. Neither God nor His Bible lets us underemphasize how central *all nations* are to His overall plan.

In this devotional, I often refer to peoples and places by their current geographical names and contexts, knowing this is anachronistic since various peoples of varied religion have lived in these places over time. For example, Temites do not necessarily equate directly to Saudi Arabians, nor Job from Uz (likely in Edom, located in what we now call Jordan) to current Jordanians. My point, however, is to emphasize that God intends to receive global, not parochial, glory, so I will combine the past and the present to show that God has been, and will be, glorified everywhere, among every nation.

So let it be, and so shall it be done. God will be glorified in every people group and then He will come again in power and glory. It is for this joy we labor while it is day.

DICK BROGDEN

Jeddah, The Kingdom of Saudi Arabia
August 2020

"*There is a ripple effect to the gospel that's inevitable. There's a ripple effect to true grace. It doesn't lead us to only sit and contemplate what happened to us. It leads us to proclaim what's happened to us—and what can happen to anybody and everybody on the planet.*"

OSWALD CHAMBERS

JANUARY

JANUARY 1: SO IT WAS IN THE BEGINNING

TODAY'S READING: GENESIS 1–3

"[God] has an inexhaustible enthusiasm for the supremacy of his name among the nations."

JOHN PIPER

God is a missionary God, and the Bible is a missionary book.

From Genesis to Revelation the Bible presents God's goal: representatives of every tribe, tongue, people, and nation glorifying Him, enjoying Him forever.

Missions is not a theme introduced in the New Testament, it is *the* unifying theme of the Scriptures. "The fact remains that the goal of the Old Testament was to see both Jews and Gentiles come to a saving knowledge of the Messiah who was to come. Anything less than this goal was a misunderstanding and an attenuation of the plan of God. **God's eternal plan was to provide salvation for all peoples"** (emphasis mine). The opening chapters of Genesis are "decidedly universal in scope," with Adam and Eve being the original human couple not assigned or restricted to any one ethnicity.

In the same way that the Spirit of God hovered over what was without form and void, so God's Spirit now hovers over all the peoples of earth, including the 7,000 people groups yet to be reached with the gospel. In the same way that Adam was made in God's likeness, so too are the Arabs, Malay, Turks, and Somali. In the same way that Eden encompassed rivers in Arabia (see Gen. 25:18) or India (Pishon in 2:11), Sudan (Gihon in 2:13), and Iraq (Hiddekel and Euphrates in 2:11, 14), so too will the Spirit flow to all nations of the earth. In the same way that Adam and Eve sinned, so too did the curse spread to all humans everywhere, and in their seed, so too will all nations be blessed.

Genesis 3:15 "guaranteed that the coming man of Promise, from the male line of Eve, would once and for all settle the issues that the sin of Adam and Eve had raised." So it was in the beginning—God's plan to redeem all peoples of the earth, for He is the desire of all nations. So it has been and is now—He is the conquering seed. So it shall be in the end—we shall be like Him, representatives of all tribes, tongues, peoples, and nations around the throne (Rev. 5:9, 7:9)—worshiping the Lamb, reinstated in His love. Maranatha! Let it be.

PRAYER FOCUS: *Southern Pashtun Afghanistan (Evangelical: 0.01%)*

JANUARY 2: ALL NOAH'S SONS

TODAY'S READING: GENESIS 4-7

"This is the grand purpose for which we were created: to enjoy the grace of Christ as we spread the gospel of Christ from wherever we live, to the ends of the earth."

DAVID PLATT

The Genesis record is a historical one; salvation history unfolds in the context of the whole earth and all the nations. Eve knew there was a problem. She understood a divine answer would come from her seed, and so she said in Genesis 4:1, literally, "I have brought forth a man, even the Lord." "Eve thought that the birth of her first son would be the answer to the promise of Genesis 3:15, and that this male descendent would be divine.... While her instincts were correct, her timing and identifying abilities were not." The fullness of time had not yet arrived. Cain was not the Messiah, but he would serve in other ways. From his line would come the development of cities, nomadic pastoralists, music, and metal workers.

Most importantly, Cain illustrated that there is a brotherhood of man and that we are responsible for one another. We are responsible for one another's blood physically as Abraham Lincoln soberly reminded a divided nation when framing civil war as God's judgment on slavery: "Every drop of blood drawn by the lash shall be paid by another drawn with the sword." We are responsible for one another spiritually. Believers who have received salvation must broker it to their brothers of every race who have not.

Genesis does not allow us to escape the interconnectedness of the peoples of earth. The genealogy of Adam in Genesis 5 is echoed by the Sumerian King list in southern Mesopotamia. The listing is of the kings of Sumer and Accad with a flood account and similar long reigns before the flood and shorter spans after. The flood itself is echoed in the Near East tales of Gilgamesh and Atrahasis. Humanity has a common start and a common problem—we are all wicked and every thought of our heart is evil continually. We have fallen together and we will be rescued together. Shem, Ham, and Japheth all had to be rescued in the same ark. All Noah's sons, Jews, Arabs, Ethiopians, Iranians, Turks, Egyptians, Somali, Berbers, Tuaregs, Germans, Koreans, Finns, and Indians were rescued by the same cross.

PRAYER FOCUS: *Gorani of Albania (Evangelical: 0%)*

JANUARY 3: A PROMISE MADE

TODAY'S READING: GENESIS 8–9

"Jesus did not say, 'Go into all the world and tell the world that it is quite right.'
The Gospel is something completely different. In fact, it is directly opposed to the
world."

C. S. LEWIS

The flood was universal. *All* the high hills under the whole heaven were covered. *All* flesh died. *All* in whose nostrils was the breath of life died. We have flood stories from the time of Ammisaduqa (King of Babylon, 1646–1626 BC). In that story, the Mesopotamian gods destroyed humans because they were noisy. I guess sin bothers the heart *and* ears of God. The Gilgamesh flood story (King of Uruk, around 2600 BC) is allegedly related by flood survivor Utnapishtim from the edge of the world. The point here is, the flood affected all men everywhere; it was not a particular or parochial event—the flood was an all nations judgment requiring an all nations cure.

When the ark docked between Turkey and Armenia, God gave universal promises and proscriptions. First of all, God showed He was for population growth, telling us all to be fruitful and multiply in all the earth and that all men (black, white, red, yellow, brown, and any other combined hue and race) are made in His image. Second, God promised regularity to all men of all races: "While the earth remains, seedtime and harvest, cold and heat, winter and summer, and day and night shall not cease" (Gen. 8:22), which is where our great hymn "Great Is Thy Faithfulness" gets its lyrics. Finally, the covenant, signified by the rainbow, was "between Me and you and every living creature of all flesh" (Gen. 9:15). The whole earth was to be populated from the sons of Noah and the rainbow was the sign that all those tribes and tongues were in covenant with God.

Every time we see the rainbow of the gay and lesbian community, whether a flag, bumper sticker, or t-shirt, we should both wince and warm—wince because they haven't understood the lesson of the flood, and warm because the promise of the rainbow includes them (as well as Buddhists, Muslims, Hindus, animists, and secularists) and *all* who will repent. The rainbow does indeed stand for inclusion and universalism—the biblical style—which says all men and all women of all orientations and races are sinful and will be judged by a holy God *and* all men and all women of all orientations and races can escape judgment if they will repent.

When the eight survivors emerged from the ark, God made a promise to dwell in the tents of Shem. "This promise to 'dwell' was most encouraging, for it assured mortals that despite God's transcendence He would come to planet earth to take up residence." That God picked the Semites and started with an Iraqi named Abraham is startling and purposeful—as we shall see.

PRAYER FOCUS: *Algerian, Arabic-Speaking of Algeria (Evangelical: 1.48%)*

JANUARY 4: TAKING UP HIS NAME

TODAY'S READING: GENESIS 10–12

God intentionally made the different languages and cultures and races of the earth, and God intentionally placed these peoples in specific and spread-out locations. In this period (Early Bronze Age, around 3000 BC), we have record of peoples settling as far away as Spain (Tarshish in 10:4). In Erech, or present-day Iraq, we have the first public architecture, cylinder seals, and the origin of both urbanization and writing. In Egypt, the 365-day calendar is adopted, the great pyramids built, copper pipes manufactured, government centralized, and both oars and sails employed. From Spain to Iraq to Egypt, the peoples of earth are both advancing and desiring to make a name for themselves.

God objects to the self-aggrandizement and declares that blessing will come His way through His vessel, and He chooses a Hebrew (the ancient term was "Habiru" and meant a person in flight or those in armed gangs) to be the instrument of blessing. The Great Commission of the Old Testament is found in Genesis 12:1–3. Because this text is so critical, let me quote several parts of Walter Kaiser's thoughts on this passage.

"In Genesis 12:1–3 [God] repeats five times his determination to 'bless' Abraham, his seed, and all the families of the earth…. [Abraham] was not to be singled out as one of God's favorites whom he would spoil rotten with gifts…. Everything he was given was a gift to be shared for the enrichment of others.

"The Hebrew phrase used for 'all the people/families' is **kol mispehot**, a phrase that is rendered in the Greek translation of the Old Testament as **pasai hai phulai**, meaning 'all the tribes' in most contexts…. Therefore the blessing of God given to Abraham was intended to reach smaller people groups as well as the political groupings of nations…. God's gift of a blessing through the instrumentality of Abraham was to be experienced by nations, clans, tribes, people groups, and individuals. It would be for every size group, from the smallest people group to the greatest nation.

"In fact, the word given in Genesis 12:3 that in Abraham's seed all the nations of the earth will be blessed is equated with the sum and substance of the 'gospel' in Galatians 3:8. Therefore, without a doubt we are at the center of what is at the core of the gospel and mission in both Testaments. The word to Abraham was meant to have a great impact on all the families on the face of the earth in all ages: a high and lofty missionary teaching, if there ever was one."

The whole purpose of God was to bless one people so that they might be the channel through which all the nations of the earth might receive a blessing. Israel was to be God's missionaries to the world—and thereby so are all who believe in this same gospel.

Mankind need not make a name for itself. Rather, we are invited to the blessing of taking up the Name above all names for our own.

PRAYER FOCUS: *Azerbaijani of Azerbaijan (Evangelical: 0.22%)*

JANUARY 5: THERE IS BUT ONE

TODAY'S READING: JOB 1–4

"Never pity missionaries; envy them. They are where the real action is—where life and death, sin and grace, Heaven and Hell converge."

ROBERT C. SHANNON

Job is thought by most scholars to be a contemporary of Abraham or possibly to have lived shortly after Abraham. Like Abraham, Job's wealth was based on accumulated animals and Job worshiped God directly without the intermediary of a priest. Uz is an uncertain location, but most likely located in Edom, what is today the southern sector of Jordan. Job's friend Eliphaz is thought to be Palestinian, and his friends Bildad and Zophar from Arabia. The Sabeans were probably from Yemen and the Chaldean raiders were likely tribes from Northern Arabia (or Saudis). Ezekiel referenced Job from Babylon (Eze. 14:14, 20) and made him real to the exiles outside Israel as they share in Job's sorrows. The story of Job played out before an international audience. In our current geography Job the Jordanian lost all he held dear to Saudi and Yemeni raiders, was dis-comforted by his Palestinian and Saudi friends, and understood only by a refugee population in Iraq.

Larry J. Waters in his article "Missio Dei in the Book of Job" says: "Besides displaying one man's faith in God in times of suffering, the Book of Job also has a **'missionary' purpose. That is, a believer's suffering should be viewed, as seen in Job's experience, as a witness not only to God's sovereignty but also as a witness to His goodness, justice, grace, and love to the nonbelieving world.** Yet in studies of Job God's redemptive purpose and action in relation to missions is rarely addressed. Often the purpose of the Book of Job is seen simply as concerned with the sovereignty of God and man's response to His will. But the book is also part of the progressive revelation of God's purpose and mission, so that the book is, in a sense, missional and evangelistic. That is, as believers undergo undeserved suffering, they are witnesses to nonbelievers of God's goodness, justice, grace, and love" (emphasis mine).

The wisdom (or philosophy) of the day was that good things come to good people and bad things to bad people. If something bad happened to you, you deserved it. Counter to this wisdom, Job prefigured the suffering servant as he wrestled with the knowledge that a bad thing happened to a good person. God used this story to prepare the world for bruising His own Son for the redemption of all peoples. A very good God will do a very bad thing to a very good Son for the very good good of very bad humans. It was mind-blowing then as it should be mind-blowing now. Job is the scandal of the cross played out before representatives of various nations. "Whoever perished being innocent?" Eliphaz asked in Job 4:7. There is but one: Jesus.

PRAYER FOCUS: *Arab, Bahraini of Bahrain (Evangelical: 0.9%)*

JANUARY 6: THE WATCHER OF MEN IS WATCHING

TODAY'S READING: JOB 5-8

"He is no fool who gives what he cannot keep to gain what he cannot lose."

JIM ELLIOT

I am often amused by those who underline in their Bible or quote authoritatively expressions from Job's friends. Certainly, there is truth in their harangues, but it is twisted truth. Wisdom requires us to exegete context and even pre-suppositional logic. The same is true for our approach to the Scriptures broadly. The context for the Bible is a missionary hearted God determined to be glorified by every people group on earth. Every truth of every line of every chapter of every book of the Bible must be approached from that pre-suppositional starting point.

Eliphaz made a brave run at truth in Job 5, but he failed, for he lost the big plot: God allows bad things to happen to good people so that God will be glorified by all men everywhere, by all peoples through all time. Job found his friend's half-truths as unhelpful and disappointing as a river bed without water, such as the Tema of Job 6:19, which incidentally was located in Saudi Arabia. These rivers, dry when needed most, were also a source of despair to the travelers of Yemen. Tema sat at the center of Arabian trade routes and members of many nations competed there to control the market for incense. The peoples of the earth are never far from the heart and Scripture of God.

Job turned the wonder of Psalm 8:4 ("What is man that You are mindful of [honor] him....") into the worry of that responsibility. It would be nice to have honor without assignment, but God never blesses without expecting us to pass blessing on. Echoing Genesis 12, Job was blessed to be a blessing, even to those not within his family or nation, and he was un-blessed to do the same. Job's un-blessing was intended to display God's glory broadly. Whenever we shirk responsibility for the unreached, whenever we do not pass on blessings, something shifts off center within us. We don't know what that is at first, but we know something is wrong. If God's missionary Spirit lives within us and we are not acting missionally, we are spirit-sideways and we feel it before we understand it.

If you are unsettled, if something in your soul is not quite aligned and you sincerely can't think of any sin of commission or omission, if you are asking in honesty with Job, "Have I sinned? What have I done to You, O watcher of men," perhaps the answer is centered on the mission of God—or the lack of it. Maybe what you have done to God is kept His blessings away from all nations by hoarding them. Perhaps the Watcher of men is watching you to see if you will bless the nations.

PRAYER FOCUS: *Shaikh of Bangladesh (Evangelical: 0.0%)*

JANUARY 7: NOTHING TO DO WITH US

TODAY'S READING: JOB 9-12

"If a commission by an earthly king is considered an honor, how can a commission by a Heavenly King be considered a sacrifice?"

DAVID LIVINGSTONE

Zophar seems harsh to us as he tells Job that God has given him "less than [his] iniquity deserves" (Job 11:6). Ancient wisdom had a cut-and-dried view of good and bad. If good things happened to you, you deserved them because you were good. If bad things happened to you, they happened because you were bad, so shut up and take it because you probably deserved worse. "Ancient people believed that the gods governed the universe based on some principle of right and wrong. They were confident that pious acts would result in well-being, but aware that wrong doing would result in misfortune or distress. When misfortune struck, they would consult the gods to discover the cause of their misfortune. If innocent, they would seek divine justice from the gods. So, Job, not understanding why he must suffer, calls on God, 'Show me why You contend with me'" (Job 10:2).

The problem of suffering is one that all peoples of earth have puzzled over. But what if like Job and his friends, we all start from the wrong assumption? What if our suffering is not about us? Ultimately, we all think we're the center of the universe; more so, we think the most important bilateral relationship in history is ours and God's. But what if my suffering has nothing to do with me? What if my suffering is all about God and others? What if my suffering reflects the suffering servant who innocently paid the price for others? What if God thinks beyond just the two of us?

Job trembled before a God who—counter to the wisdom of that day and this day—does what He thinks is just for all whether or not that act seems good to a single man. Tiring of the narrowness of his friend's understanding, Job unwittingly referred to gospel realities: We all look up at the same stars; God's glory shakes the earth; the earth and all peoples are under the wrath of God; no one is righteous; God will incarnate and mediate between God and man; and all nations are under the judgment of God. The Bible story is that neither my suffering nor God's salvation are about me; my suffering and God's saving are intended for all the peoples of the earth. We err with Job when we put ourselves at the center of any difficulty or any deliverance.

Let God be exalted and His glory cover the earth. Let *all* the peoples praise Him.

PRAYER FOCUS: *Drukpa of Bhutan (Evangelical: 0.0%)*

JANUARY 8: RATTLING OUR LITTLE BUBBLE

TODAY'S READING: JOB 13-17

"We must be global Christians with a global vision because our God is a global God."

JOHN STOTT

The gospel is hard to contain. The gospel was not designed to be held within one nation, one people, or one person. The gospel has this bursting, spreading, growing attribute intrinsic to its essence. God designed the gospel to be borderless, unrestrained by either the problems or prejudices of man. The book of Job is seemingly about suffering, injustice, confusion, and questioning, yet all through its chapters, the gospel bubbles and bursts out, the gospel universal in scope.

You can easily picture Jesus going over these expressions of Job as He hung on the cross: "Though He slay me, yet will I trust Him" (13:15); "I know that I shall be vindicated" (13:18); "if a man dies, shall he live again?" (14:14); "He pierces my heart...He pours out my gall on the ground" (16:13); "o earth, do not cover my blood" (16:18); "my friends scorn me, my eyes pour out tears to God" (16:20); and "He has made me a byword...in whose face men spit" (17:6). Prophetically, Job spoke of the cross, the meeting place of all peoples.

What's really going on in Job is God bursting from the confines of man's preferred definition. The God of glory refuses to be limited by my prejudiced definition of His character. Job's friends could not conceive of a God broader than their narrowness. Job in raw honesty was wrestling with the radical concept that God is above the wisdom and ordered world that was known and conventional. As is the gospel. It is above and beyond our comfort; it cannot be contained in one people; and it must burst away from our "surly bonds" to all.

Job 15 begins to repeat the arguments of earlier chapters, but now the gloves are off and it gets more personal and biting. Because Job pushed back against accepted wisdom, his friends (and tradition, way of life, and comfort itself) are threatened. If there is indeed another way of understanding God, humanity, and the world, then our little experience of the cosmos can be rattled. Missions rattles our little bubble. Missions precludes our view of life and the world from us being the most important ones and forces us to a God-centered view of the world, a view dedicated to *every* people and nation having a place at His table. For those used to the best portion and home-cooked meals, this can be a grievous threat. We all tend to settle on a comfortable view of God, and God shakes us so He might use us to shake the nations.

PRAYER FOCUS: *Bosniak of Bosnia-Herzegovina (Evangelical: 0.03%)*

JANUARY 9: SUFFERING PRECEDES GLORY

TODAY'S READING: JOB 18–20

"When Christ calls a man, he bids him come and die."

DIETRICH BONHOEFFER

In Greek mythology, Pluto was the God of the netherworld, ruling below the earth. In Ugaritic myths, Mot was the god of death, the king of terrors that Bildad referenced in Job 18:14. All peoples are terrified of hell, and all peoples dream of the milk and honey of paradise. The global and timeless question is how heaven is gained and hell escaped. In Job's day, the prevailing wisdom was that if you were evil, you would first suffer in this life and later suffer anguish hell. The logic was, "If I suffer, I must have done something wrong." Job served us all because he realized that perhaps we suffer because we have done something right.

I met a new follower of Jesus this week. He is from Saudi Arabia. I'll call him Mohammed. Recently, Mohammed, with some trepidation, called his brother and revealed his new faith. Mohammed's brother was shocked, alarmed, and warned him that he would one day stand before Allah and face the consequences. Thankfully, Mohammed's brother did not threaten to level those consequences himself, but the reality is that Mohammed will indeed soon face persecution for his decision. Mohammed will suffer for what he has done right.

Perhaps we should read Job 19 through the lens of a brave Saudi deciding to follow Jesus and suffering for it. That Saudi can easily say with Job: "He has removed my brothers far from me, and my acquaintances are completely estranged from me. My relatives have failed and my close friends have forgotten me.... My breath is offensive to my wife, and I am repulsive to the children of my own body.... I arise, and they speak against me.... All my close friends abhor me, and those whom I love have turned against me.... Why do you persecute me...." (vv. 13–14, 17–19, 22). Those who follow Jesus and suffer for it know deep inside they have done something right—and they have Job to thank for this awareness.

Men and women like Mohammed who follow Jesus and pay the price for it can also follow Job to hope: "For I know that my Redeemer lives, and He shall stand at last on the earth, and after my skin is destroyed, this I know, that in my flesh I shall see God" (vv. 25–26). Today, Job speaks to the brave and suffering for Jesus' sake in both affirmation and hope: "You have done nothing wrong, and at the last you will see God." It's not a little bit of hell now and a lot of it later (like Job's friends thought). And it's not a little bit of heaven now and a lot of it later (like the heresies of our day). The sober reality for the follower of Jesus is a little bit of hell now and a whole lot of heaven later. For Christ and Christian, for the godly and righteous, suffering always has and always will precede glory.

PRAYER FOCUS: *Brunei Malay of Brunei (Evangelical: 0.05%)*

JANUARY 10: DOOMSDAY IS COMING

TODAY'S READING: JOB 21-24

"We talk of the second coming; half the world has never heard of the first."

OSWALD J. SMITH

All cultures and all peoples share the common idea of a day of reckoning. All cultures eventually decline, and all societies have some type of prophecy, mythology, theology, or belief of an end to the world as it's known. Frustration with the wicked thriving in this world is universally balanced with an expectation of doomsday. One day the wicked will get what they deserve. Job put it this way: "For the wicked are reserved for the day of doom; they shall be brought out on the day of wrath" (Job 21:30). Job told himself, his friends, and us that this life and this history of the world will never see lasting justice. We might as well get used to dealing with injustice frequently (without resigning ourselves to it), for lasting justice will only come on doomsday, on the day of wrath.

The day of wrath is terrifying because every honest person realizes he nurtures a bit of his own evil within. It is one thing to cheer on doomsday because the wicked—some heinous other people out there—get what they deserve on that day. It's another thing to cheer on your own doom. Job wrestled with this tension. He wanted the obviously evil to be dealt with severely, but what does that mean for me, for us, the quiet and surreptitiously sinful? Job said of God and that day of doom: "He performs what is appointed for me.... Therefore I am terrified at His presence; when I consider this, I am afraid of Him, and the Almighty terrifies me" (23:14–16). And we all should likewise be terrified.

The Bible story is a missions story. The missions story is an eschatological story. There is an end coming to life on this world as we know it. This world and our human history are going to end calamitously on a day of doom, a day of judgment. On that day, the wicked will finally get what they deserve. And all the righteous will cheer on that day. But those cheers are restrained and ultimately self-silenced by all the honest righteous because they must confess they have a little bit of ugly in them. The terror of God we wish on others is the very terror we deserve ourselves.

Missions cannot be removed from the Second Coming, but the Second Coming is both a day of joyful justice and wrathful doom. The sober Christian cannot think of that day without both crying and laughing. It is this sobriety that urgently launches the missionary out to the peoples of the world shouting out a message of warning and invitation: "Doomsday is coming. It is a great and terrible day. It will cause joy and tears. Come stand with me under the loving protection of the One who has swallowed the wrath of God for us all. Come worship with me the One whose mercy protects us from the justice we plead for, the very justice we deserve."

PRAYER FOCUS: *Jula, Dyula of Burkina Faso (Evangelical: 0.02%)*

JANUARY 11: STANDING WITH JOB

TODAY'S READING: JOB 25-28

"Evangelism is when the Gospel, which is good news, is preached or presented to all people."

BILLY GRAHAM

The wisdom of the day in the time of Job was pretty pessimistic concerning the ability of man to interact with or understand God. Bildad bluntly called man a maggot and, intriguingly, "the son of man" he termed a worm (Job 25:5–6). Ancient wisdom considered life after death to be a dark and miserable watery place under the earth, which they called "Sheol." In Mesopotamian understanding, the deities Nergal and Ereshkigal hung the dead on butchers' hooks. In Syria-Palestine, the deity Mot was hungry to eat the living. Because there was no hope after death, long life became desirable, and the heroes (the righteous) of the Old Testament were the long-lived rich, those who experienced good things because they hung on to their integrity as long as they lived.

Into this somewhat dark picture are gleams of prophetic gospel hope. Job said, "By His Spirit He adorned the heavens; His hand pierced the fleeing serpent. Indeed, these are the mere edges of His ways" (26:13). Looking back to Eve's promise and looking forward to the promise of the Spirit, Job's heart knew there was more, so much more to understand. Job did not reject the wisdom tradition entirely but sought a more complete and nuanced application. Something in Job's spirit wondered if God could be known, and if in knowing Him, life on earth would be revealed as more complex than "good things happen to the good, and bad things to the bad."

Job wondered aloud if some things only made sense to God and inferred that the wisest thing we can do is trust that God is wise. Job stood on the edges of the ways of a magnificent God and concluded: "God understands [wisdom's] way, and He knows its place.... Behold, the fear of the Lord, that is wisdom, and to depart from evil is understanding" (28:23, 28).

We all stand in a world—no matter our nation—confused about death. We are surrounded by men and women who either fear, misunderstand, or deny the afterlife. Not much has changed in the last 5,000 years. We stand with Job (further along, thanks to the cross) in understanding the ways of God and in hope. We can endure bad things because we know that in this life bad things happen to good people. We can endure unimaginable things because we know that there is a better life to come.

It is incumbent on those so enlightened to spread the good news. There are yet 7,000 unreached peoples still deathly afraid of their Nergal, Ereshkigal, or Mot. Let's publish the good news of a God who loves us and wants to commune with us forever. He wants a feast for us and prepares a table for us—and He has no desire to eat us.

PRAYER FOCUS: *Khmer of Cambodia (Evangelical: 1.9%)*

JANUARY 12: IMPOSSIBLY MORE

TODAY'S READING: JOB 29-31

"Some wish to live within the sound of a chapel bell; I wish to run a rescue mission within a yard of hell."

C. T. STUDD

Job, battling the prevailing wisdom of his time and his own fears, had inklings that there must be more. He fretted about the passing of time. The inexorable march toward death scared him as it does so many of us who claim to believe in eternal life. More terrifyingly, life as it continued became more troublesome and difficult, and Job pined for the good old days: "Just as I was in the days of my prime, when the friendly counsel of God was over my tent" (Job 29:4).

Not only does later life involve more pain and suffering, for Job it also involved taunting and mocking. There was the certainty that death approached ["For I know that You will bring me to death, and to the house appointed for all living" (30:23)] and the terrified uncertainty of what that meant ["For destruction from God is a terror to me, and because of His magnificence I cannot endure" (31:23)]. Almost plaintively, Job listed all that he had done right, starting with making a covenant with his eyes, and included a litany of other right acts he had performed. Again, we see a searching longing for more than what is offered.

And there is. The gospel always offers more. Jesus always offers us more.

The different fears and hopes of different cultures help us appreciate the full gospel. Because Greek and Roman tradition is so influential in Western thinking and theology, those from the West tend to focus on the forensic view of the gospel: We were guilty, and Jesus declared us innocent. Those from Africa, Asia, and Latin America who deal daily with destructive demons appreciate the power dimension of the gospel: Fear bound us, and Jesus gives us power over Satan. Those from cultures like Job (i.e. Semitic cultures) are thankful for the relational components of the gospel: Shame ostracized us, and Jesus gives us honor.

Job's words are at an end, but God's words are just beginning. When we come to the end of ourselves and when guilt, fear, and shame overcome us, we stand with Job at the mere edges of God's grace. There is more, impossibly more, than we could ask or think. Let us sally forth from that discovery to the gates of hell and proclaim the good news globally—innocence for guilt, power for fear, and honor for shame.

PRAYER FOCUS: *Baggara, Shuwa Arab of Chad (Evangelical: 0.4%)*

JANUARY 13: CHALLENGE THE HALF-WRONG
TODAY'S READING: JOB 32–34

"I have but one passion: It is He, it is He alone. The world is the field and the field is the world; and henceforth that country shall be my home where I can be most used in winning souls for Christ."

COUNT NICOLAUS LUDWIG VON ZINZENDORF

An intriguing if mysterious figure now enters the story of Job: a young man, Elihu, whose name intriguingly means "My God is He." Just as intriguingly, the Buzites were most likely from Northern Arabia, a land described as full of snakes and scorpions. Elihu was a rather smug little lad whose scholarship was matched only by his arrogance. Elihu castigated Job's friends for being unreasonable and without answers, and he condemned Job for being unwise and speaking without knowledge. In contrast to his lacking elders, Elihu was fairly confident that he understood God's character and ways. Elihu was smart enough to be half-right. But the trouble with being half-right theologically is that it usually means you have God disastrously wrong.

Elihu was right that God is greater than man and Elihu was right that God "if He should set His heart on it, if He should gather to Himself His Spirit and His breath, all flesh would perish together, and man would return to dust" (Job 34:14–15). Elihu was right about God's transcendence, power, authority, and majestic sovereignty. But in not knowing God's tenderness, mercy, love, compassion, and immediacy, Elihu got God wrong—for a half-right view of God is fully idolatrous.

False religions have God half-right. Islam is right that God is transcendent, but Islam denies the incarnation, that God was made flesh. Islam gets God tragically wrong. What is most important, therefore, in missions and gospel proclamation to God's beloved peoples of earth is not where we agree, but where we disagree. If we only spend our time affirming points of agreements with those who hail from non-Christian faiths, we only reinforce their errant and idolatrous views of God. The most loving thing we can do in missions is to winsomely and passionately engage others on where the Bible differs with their view of God—and particularly their view of Jesus as God.

A good missionary does not waste much time agreeing with idolaters. A good missionary is so zealous for the true nature of God. He or she does not congratulate the half-righters, but instead challenges the half-wrongers to repent and bow before the God who is both transcendent and intimate, both loving and angry with sinners every day, both holy and kind.

PRAYER FOCUS: *Han Chinese, Xiang of China (Evangelical: 1.9%)*

JANUARY 14: RIGHT-MINDED, RIGHT-HEARTED

TODAY'S READING: JOB 35–37

"Pray as though everything depended on God. Work as though everything depended on you."

AUGUSTINE

Elihu, being half-right about God, had God horribly wrong. Elihu intoned that God is great (true) and that we do not know Him (false) in Job 36:26. Elihu said that God is awesome in majesty (true) and that we cannot find Him (false) in Job 37:22–23. No Christian and no missionary can afford to be half-right about God, especially as we are charged with presenting the fullness of God to the nations.

Job is a missionary book. Even Elihu in his youthful arrogance was aware that God is at work across the peoples of the earth, his speech being full of global references: "For by these [God] judges the peoples... He sends it forth under the whole heaven, His lightning to the ends of the earth.... He seals the hand of every man, that all men may know His work.... that they may do whatever He commands them on the face of the whole earth" (36:31; 37:3, 7, 12). Elihu, this young, arrogant pre-Saudi, recognized that God intends to be worshiped and glorified by all the peoples of earth. Which brings up Elihu's second error. He was right in much that he said, but because he said it from an arrogant posture ["one who is perfect in knowledge is with you" (36:4)], he lost his audience. Elihu's arrogance restricted his truth from being heard—as can tragically be the case in missions.

When we as missionaries go out among the nations with the right view of God but the wrong view of ourselves (one who is perfect is with you!), we do incalculable damage to the gospel. Yes, the missionary task is to speak towards the fullness of the character of God. Yes, the missionary task is to confront idols and the deceptions of Satan. Yes, the missionary task is to be passionately against the things that infuriate and insult the holiness of God. And yes, the missionary task is to speak truth with both fire and lowliness—a combination most difficult for the young and most impossible in our own strength.

Good missionaries, good Christians are both right-minded and right-hearted. Good missionaries are courageous enough to speak for God and humble enough to learn from those enslaved in the very idolatry the missionary opposes. Good missionaries are lowly enough to glean from the very ones they harvest.

PRAYER FOCUS: *Comorian, Ngazidja of Comoros (Evangelical: 0.24%)*

JANUARY 15: ENDING WITH A BANG

TODAY'S READING: JOB 38-42

The book of Job culminates as it started: God is so much bigger than any of us individually and God will be inclusively worshiped by every people group on earth. God refuses to be limited to my individual understanding of Him. God refuses to be limited to my individual preferences about how He should work and who He should bless. God refuses to allow me to put either my fortune or misfortune at the center of the world—whatever happens to me of good or evil is for the glory of God and the benefit of others. In the beginning all the sons of God shouted for joy and at the end God's creative will shall be seen and done to the ends of the earth. In the middle there are things we cannot know or do or even understand—least of all the majesty of heaven. What we can be sure of is that everything under heaven is God's—every animal, nation, person, and people—and God will do with His own what He jolly well pleases.

It's when we argue with God about His passions that we get in trouble and are vile. We want to contend, correct, and condemn God. The legal among us don't like His mercy on all peoples, and the loose among us don't like His judgments on all nations. God resolutely sets out to bless all nations of earth, and we just as resolutely resist His orders. In our little rebellious hearts, we think that God is wrong to tell us to go, that He is wicked to tell us to suffer, that He is wasteful to tell us to die, and that He is wanton to tell us to lavish His love on the violent, resistant, and proud. God blithely ignores our questions and simply says that He alone can make great Leviathans into great servants. He alone can, does, and will transform serpentine Sauls into apostolic Pauls. Our missionary God will use all men to reach all men.

And thus, the book of Job ends with a missionary bang. An inclusive God demands we have inclusive hearts. It was no accident that Job lived in present day Jordan and had enemies from present day Yemen and friends from present day Saudi Arabia. It was no small thing that the fortunes of Job were restored and amplified when he prayed, forgave, and loved again these rascally Arabs. Like Abraham, Job was resourced to bless the nations and peoples of the earth and restored to do the same. Job was to speak the truth that God must always be the center—both of our joy and our sorrow—and that everything that happens to us is for the purposes of God. Job reminds us that obedience must often precede understanding and that we best love God when we trust Him. On a final harmonious note, showing that God allows enmity neither between the peoples of earth or the genders of society, Job's daughters are as his sons: they share in the blessings and the responsibilities to see God glorified in all things, places, peoples, times, and ways, always.

PRAYER FOCUS: *Malinke, Ivorian of Cote d'Ivoire (Evangelical: 0.4%)*

JANUARY 16: GOD HIMSELF WALKED

TODAY'S READING: GENESIS 13–15

"God's work done in God's way will never lack God's supplies."

HUDSON TAYLOR

It was a dizzying, crowded, and technologically booming time. Drains, sewers, and pottery were being developed in Crete. Egypt launched a postal system. Babylon was using soap, and cities were flourishing in Lebanon, so it was timely to have soap on the scene. A confusing array of tribes, peoples, and places surround Abraham and Lot—with Iranians causing the most trouble. God delivered these nations into Abraham's hands, yet through Melchizedek He was quick to remind Abraham that war only serves to make peace and that all things and peoples belong to God. People are after all the greatest of God's treasures—a point He will shortly, dramatically demonstrate to Abraham.

In that day covenant relationships were verified by public ceremony. The Hittites (who hailed from present-day Turkey) had a ceremony that purified their soldiers after a defeat. "The troops are required to perform the ritual 'behind a river,' where a man, a goat, a puppy, and a small pig are cut in half. The sections, thus divided, are arranged oppositely parallel on one side and the other…fires are lit on both sides of the arranged pieces. Then the troops are obliged to pass between the fires and are sprinkled with water upon reaching the bank of the river."

Biblical covenants had similarities to the above but were different on key points. In Genesis 15:3, Abraham, bearing the disappointment of unfulfilled promises, asked the Lord in essence: "Are You sure? Will You really bless *all* nations through my seed? For I have no child, and no natural heir. God, do You really intend to bless all peoples?" God told Abraham to bring a cow, a goat, a ram, a turtle dove, and a pigeon. These animals were cut down the middle, separated on the path, and then God Himself walked in between the bloody pieces, appearing as a flame of fire.

In the usual covenants of the time, the lesser (or vassal) promised a litany of services to the greater (or suzerain), and by walking over the blood, the lesser demonstrated his fate should he not fulfil his oath. In this startling contextualization of "cutting the covenant," the great God of all power walked over the blood, saying in effect: "He would die before He would allow His covenant with Abraham to fail." And that is exactly what God did. God died to fulfil His promise that representatives of every people group on earth would be brought into His family. "I am sure, Abraham! I am so sure that I promise by My Calvary blood. I promise that I will bless all peoples of earth." If God would promise and generously pay such a price for the nations, should we not also in the same spirit and for the same cause be just as liberal? We should, and so by His grace we shall be.

PRAYER FOCUS: *Somali, Issa of Djibouti (Evangelical: 0.12%)*

Though much has been made of Sarah's haste in pushing Hagar on Abraham, not much has been made of the reality that Hagar was Egyptian. Thus, Abraham's first son (by Sarah's choice) was half "foreigner." Perhaps this is why God called Sarah "mother of nations, kings of peoples" (Gen. 17:16), for multi-racial families are a wonderful demonstration of God's heart.

Hagar was instructed to submit to Sarah. That command is ironic in that "Islam" literally means "submission," and Arab Muslims broadly consider Ishmael to be their ancestor. In effect, Islam was told early on to submit to the Lord's plan for salvation, a plan that must pass through Isaac, and ultimately through Jesus. God said to the sons of Ishmael, pre-Muslims, early on, "I have heard you, I have seen you, and I will bless you, and you will belong to Me along with representatives of all nations who submit to Me."

God's plan is not complicated. In John 15, Jesus said He no longer calls us servants (*doulos*), but friends (*philos*), and God never hides from His friends what He is doing (Gen. 18:17). Over and again "what God is doing" is reinforced in the Scripture as centered on blessing all peoples of the earth. Genesis 18:17-19 being no exception (emphasis mine): "Shall I hide from Abraham what I am doing, since Abraham shall surely become a great and mighty nation, **and all the nations of the earth shall be blessed in him?** For I have known him, **in order** that he may command his children and his household after him, that they keep the way of the Lord, to do righteousness and justice, **that the LORD may bring to Abraham what He has spoken to him**."

It's all about the glory of God among all peoples. The context of this passage is God destroying Sodom (or sparing it if He can find ten righteous there), and the point of this passage is God's heart to mercy all penitent peoples. God bluntly said to Abraham and to us: "I want you to know what I am doing. I am judging and mercying all peoples of earth. Abraham, I know My people *in order* that they lead their children and household, keep the way of the Lord, do righteousness and justice *in order* that I fulfil what I promised you—all people groups have opportunity to be saved in Jesus."

What is the goal of godly parenting and obedient children? *All peoples receive Jesus.* What is the goal of our Christian holiness? *All peoples receive Jesus.* What is the goal of acts of social justice? *All peoples receive Jesus.* God doesn't hide the main point of what He is doing from His friends. Friends of God align everything they do around that main point. A missionary God and a missionary Bible demand our missionary participation.

PRAYER FOCUS: *Arab, Sudanese of Egypt (Evangelical: 0.26%)*

JANUARY 18: GETTING EXTREME

TODAY'S READING: GENESIS 19–21

God will destroy what is wicked. God will consume and punish. God will rain fire and brimstone on the earth. God will turn disobedient housewives into a pillar of salt. And God will do this even when men in all of our fallen intelligence protest: "Surely God must be joking! Surely hell is not real. God is not angry, and punishment is not eternal. Surely God is more balanced than that" (see Gen. 19:14). But God is not balanced. Neither is He moderate. And neither is missions. Missions talks about hell and heaven, judgment and mercy. Missions understands it is loving to warn and hateful to pretend that God's extremes cancel each other out.

Those who have not grown up in a communal culture cannot fathom Lot offering up his daughters to rapists to protect his guests. Those who have not grown up in an individualist culture cannot fathom how you would ever let those to whom you have offered hospitality lack or suffer. It was not that Lot hated his daughters. It was that Lot loved both honor (his family) and hospitality (his guests) with extreme passion. When both honor and hospitality were threatened, Lot was stuck in an impossible dilemma, so God rescued him in mercy. Lot's problem was that fear led him to folly as did a little fermented wine. Abraham, too, allowed fear to almost bring harm on the ones he was meant to love and bless. Abimelech was a Philistine, a righteous one, and of God-endorsed integrity, but he almost lost his life and all hope of children due to Abraham's fear.

Four thousand years later, the sons of Abraham are still afraid of the Philistines, and through our fears we damage both them and their children. Abraham had a fearful reluctance to tell the truth—because of what the truth would cost him. That reluctance almost led to the death of others who ask in essence: "Why do you hate us so much? Your lack of truth is actually a lack of love that leads to our death!" (see Gen. 20:9). Our reluctance to tell the gospel truth (due to the fear of what it will cost us) still leads to death— for every two seconds of silence from the church, someone globally dies eternally.

Missions is extreme. It guarantees death and life. If we don't speak the truth, the unreached die. If we do speak the truth, we die (minimally to self, possibly more), but Philistines live. We shockingly stand with Lot knowing that either our guests or our family will pay an impossible price. And an extreme God steps in to help us. Our sinless and holy God died for sinners, morally declaring it's not a big deal for us sinners to die for others, too. Not if we believe in extreme love. Not if we believe in an extreme God. If the blessing of father Abraham is going to "life" the unreached of Eritrea, some sons and daughters of Abraham will have to love them enough to speak truth and pay some cost.

PRAYER FOCUS: *Tigre, Eritrean of Eritrea (Evangelical: 0.06%)*

JANUARY 19: FATHERS AND SONS TOGETHER

TODAY'S READING: GENESIS 22-24

Historians estimate that the Pythagorean theorem was discovered around 1900 BC, concurrent with the life of Abraham. It's almost as if God is helping us see that (His blessings on His children)^2 + (His Spirit)^2 = (His glory among all peoples)^2. Sarah died and Abraham the Iraqi haggled with Ephron the Turk for a piece of land in Palestine using contractual means established in northern Syria for a burial site, then he sent his oldest servant back to eastern Turkey to find an Iraqi bride for Isaac. Family, life, death, a little bit of math, and economics all converged in the context of diverse nations back then—as it should be now.

Speaking of death, there was the little matter of child sacrifice. Child sacrifice was normal to pagan worship in Abraham's day, and tragically it has become normal in our day, too (abortion is nothing but a sanitized modern edition of murdering our own children and future). Three times Abraham said, "Here I am," and all three were in context of relationship between father and son. After Isaac the son asked the pivotal question about the lamb, Abraham the father gave the prophetic answer. Then we have a most beautiful prophetic picture: "So the two of them [father and son] went together" (Gen. 22:8). Indeed, they did—all the way to Calvary.

God then spoke with missionary thunder: "Now that I know that you fear God, since you have not withheld your son, your only son, from Me.... Because you have done this thing, and have not withheld your son...I will bless you. In your seed all the nations of the earth shall be blessed, because you have obeyed My voice" (vv. 12, 16–18). The missionary spirit is Father and Son agreeing together to go to the cross for the sake of all nations. The missionary spirit is fathers and mothers across the globe commissioning their sons, their only sons, to take up crosses and preach the gospel among unreached peoples.

And not just sons. Laban and Bethuel release their sister and daughter: "Here is Rebekah...take her and go...as the Lord has spoken" (24:51). It wasn't easy, and when the cost and immediacy of sending began to hit home, the loving senders wavered: "Then they called Rebecca and said to her, 'Will you go with this man?' And she said, 'I will go'" (v. 58). Rebecca had her own "here I am" response. "And they blessed Rebekah and said to her: 'Our sister, may you become the mother of thousands of ten thousands'" (v. 60).

And so it is whenever parents and families stand crying in airports or kneel in suddenly quiet living rooms with tears in their eyes and pain in their hearts. God looks down at those who have entered into His pain and pleasure and He whispers over them tenderly, "I am Jehovah Jireh. I am the Lord who provides."

PRAYER FOCUS: *Somali of Ethiopia (Evangelical: 0.03%)*

JANUARY 20: BIRTHRIGHTS AND BOWLS

TODAY'S READING: GENESIS 25-26

"Every great movement of God can be traced to a kneeling figure."

D. L. MOODY

Abraham took a third wife named Keturah. Since 1 Chronicles 1:32–33 calls Keturah a concubine, some rabbinical commentators think she was the same person as Hagar. The connection is unlikely as her sons are listed in the text as Zimran, Jokshan, Medan, Midian, Ishbak, and Shuah, while Hagar's son is listed as Ishmael.

Abraham sent Keturah's sons east and possibly south. Keturah's nationality is uncertain, but the African writer Olaudah Equiano thinks eighteenth century English theologian John Gill was right when he posited that the Africans were her descendants. Abraham died, and Isaac and Ishmael came together to bury him, for brothers should always unite when things really matter—and what really matters to God is missions. For all that divides us, God's glory among all peoples is the one thing that can bind us together. Ishmael headed to Havilah, which some think is Bahrain and others Somalia, one writer even suggests Zimbabwe.

Isaac's wife Rebecca was barren, but God heard her cries, only for her to have a difficult pregnancy. She agonized to God: "Why am I like this?" (Gen. 25:22). God's mission answer was: "Two nations are in your womb" (v. 23). Difficult pregnancies are so we give birth to nations. We may lose the plot of the story, but God does not. He is fixed, single-eyed on His glory manifest among all peoples. It's why He gives us children (whether those babies are humans or ministries), and God expects us to pass on His plan to our progeny.

Esau as the firstborn son was first in line to extend God's glory to the nations, but he sold that right for a bowl of lentil soup. God repeated to Isaac the plan given to Abraham: "In your seed all the nations of the earth will be blessed" (26:4). Esau was the seed of Isaac and Abraham. Esau's birthright was being first in line to bless the nations—this was what Esau despised. When we are not first to give to missions, not first to pray for missions, not first to go as missionaries, when we are not focused on the glory of God among all unreached peoples, we despise our birthright. The great gift of our spiritual inheritance is that we are invited into the mission of God, the mission to see Him glorified globally, by every people group. Let's not sell that birthright for a bowl of lentil soup.

PRAYER FOCUS: *Berber, Kabyle of France (Evangelical: 1.5%)*

JANUARY 21: THE GATE OF HEAVEN
TODAY'S READING: GENESIS 27–29

Twenty times between Genesis 27:1 and 28:1 the verb "blessing" is used. When reading the Bible with a missiological lens, it is impossible to read the word "bless" outside the context of God's covenantal promise to Abraham: Blessed to be a blessing to all nations of the earth. Genesis 27 is not a tale of Esau as victim of Jacob's deception; it is a tale of Esau's villainy. Isaac wanted to bless Esau, but it doesn't matter how many "here I am" commitments (v. 1) you throw around if you are cavalier about God's inheritance—blessing all nations.

The tale of Jacob and Esau is not the tale of scheming, but the tale of judgment. You can't scheme against God and succeed. When you are cavalier or disobedient about God's intention to be glorified among every people on earth, His blessings will evade you no matter how hard you try to please Him in other arenas. It's all too easy to blame others for the loss of blessing when we must really first examine our hearts—have we despised or ignored God's plan for the nations? To neglect or evade the passions of God is to forfeit His blessings.

Likewise, it is not about parental blessing either. Some of us will never get the blessing of our earthly parents to leave home and venture to the unreached. Our lives will testify over time that when we pursue God's passion for the nations, blessing comes directly to us from the hand of God no matter how hurtful the actions of our natural family. At the end of the day, we seek and will receive the blessing of God through Abraham, Isaac, and Jacob: "May God Almighty bless you, and make you fruitful and multiply you, that you may be an assembly of peoples" (28:3). When we bless the nations, we continue in the blessing of God Almighty.

Lest there be any doubt about the grand purposes of God in Jacob's mind or ours, God opened the heavens and told Jacob again: "And in you and in your seed all the families of the earth will be blessed" (v. 14). God's missionary grit was then guaranteed: "I am with you and will keep you wherever you go…for I will not leave you until I have done what I have spoken to you" (v. 15). When faced with the fire of missions that is God's heart, we can but respond with Jacob: "The Lord is in this place.... This is…the house of God…and this is the gate of heaven" (vv. 16–17).

Everything we do, including who we marry and the children we bear (Gen. 29), should be centered around the mission of God. When we come face to face with our awesome God, we cannot separate that grandeur from His burning passion to redeem for Himself peoples of every tribe, tongue, and nation. God said to Jacob, "I am with you and will use you to bless the nations," and Jacob says to us: "This is the gate of heaven." This passion should consume our waking hours and infiltrate our sleep. To live at the gate of heaven is to live and die for the gospel reaching all peoples of the earth.

PRAYER FOCUS: *Mandingo, Mandinka of Gambia (Evangelical: 0.97%)*

JANUARY 22: OR ELSE I DIE
TODAY'S READING: GENESIS 30–31

Out of envy Rachel cried out: "Give me children, or else I die" (Gen. 30:1). Not coincidentally, it's the same language John Knox prayed: "Give me Scotland, or I die!" Rachel, of course, wanted physical children, for they gave honor, prestige, and security. In an age and location (not dissimilar from some places globally today) where there were no retirement provisions or planning, children were the promise for today and the security of tomorrow. In Rachel's case, especially compared to Leah, she had no current honor and no long-term retirement provision. The names of the boys encapsulate the big picture struggle: Son, Heard, Attached, Praise, Judge, Troop/Fortune, Happy, Wages, Dwelling, and He Will Add.

We compare ourselves to others regarding physical accruements and security. We judge ourselves according to what others have and we do not—we fixate on the physical treasure. God, too, looks at treasure, but His riches are souls, disciples from all nations. God is looking for mothers and daughters, fathers and sons who will cry out to Him in desperation: "Give me Germany, give me Somalia, give me an unreached people in northern India—or else I die." God delights in children so focused on His passion for every tribe and people that they think of nothing else, that they don't want to live unless His glory is revealed and embraced by the unreached.

There are, of course, right and wrong ways to pursue God's glory among all nations. Rachel stole the household gods when Jacob stole away from Laban. This theft was not simple idolatry, but a power grab. "Information gathered from one ancient tablet found at the 2nd millennium BC city of Nuzi suggests that, at times, household gods were used as evidence of family leadership." Rachel wanted her husband to have more than goats and sheep; she wanted him to be tribal chief. God, however, is not interested in mixing missions with the politics of power. God's missionary example is to give up power, to avoid politics, to take up the towel, and to lay down our lives.

Inherent to God's desire to bless all cultures, nations, languages, tribes, and peoples of earth is God's delight in the redeemed aspect of them all. Laban was an Aramean, which is also translated "Syrian." Aramean states never ascended politically to the power of Babylon or Assyria, but their language endured beyond those of other Mesopotamian kingdoms. Eighteen hundred years after Laban, Jesus spoke Laban's language, Aramaic. Jesus does indeed want to redeem the daughters and sons of every people, yet in His affirmation of godly aspects of all cultures, He modeled and expects us to respectfully ransom in such a way that rejects false gods while retaining what is culturally distinct and beautiful. Let's lay the power down and take the language up. Careful missionary contextualization can lead to the modern Labans who likewise kiss their sons and daughters, bless them, and send them on their gospel way.

PRAYER FOCUS: *Turk of Germany (Evangelical: 0.00%)*

JANUARY 23: LIMPING ON

TODAY'S READING: GENESIS 32–34

Jacob didn't feel worthy to carry God's missionary baton. God revealed the master plan regarding His glory among the nations to Jacob, and now Jacob carried two internal stresses: he felt unworthy and he fretted that his brother would eliminate him. Jacob, like Abraham, struggled to connect the dots ("I just don't see how God will use me and my limitations to bless the nations!") and had to wrestle this through with God. Blessing had been promised—a blessing inextricably linked to the nations—and Jacob had to hold onto that promise, not letting go of God until he had peace it would be fulfilled. That peace has to be wrestled for alone. No one can tell another what his/her role will be among the nations; whether to go or to send (or to do both) is between each one and Jehovah.

Jacob obtained both his peace and his limp. Jacob realized he saw the face and heart of God, and in aligning his will to God's will, life was preserved. Limps remind us with whom we wrestled and what God's bigger picture is, and they remind us that God's will ultimately links to the broadest blessing. Gaining God's missionary heart always marks us; something we thought we needed must be lost if we are going to walk in His ways.

Jacob also laid down the desire for physical blessing and security. I imagine that realizing he could get along without two strong legs taught him he could get along without his accumulated wealth. He said to his brother: "Please, take my blessing that is brought to you, because God has dealt graciously with me, and because I have enough" (Gen. 33:11). On the heels of a wrestle for the heart and mission of God, this sentiment is not just about physical wealth. Jacob was saying that God's will and purpose are enough and that carrying God's missionary baton—even with a limp—was more than enough.

God is looking for those who can overlook offense in order to make Him famous among the nations. A leading cause of missionary attrition is the inability to overlook hurts received from brothers (sisters, leaders, friends, disciples, colleagues, local partners) in the work. Many missionaries limp home; they do not limp on. The princes of God [for that is what God now calls Jacob (35:10)] are those who limp on after offense and who cause no offense to the nations.

The Dinah incident displayed the un-missionary heart of Simeon and Levi, a heart that held onto offense and in angry hurt kept the nations out of God's family. Shechem, imperfect yet honorable, wanted to marry into God's family and to bring his whole tribe with him, but two of Jacob's sons could not countenance a walk with that ignoble limp. Unable to absorb offense, they made their father (and our Father) obnoxious among the nations. To be faithful sons and daughters of the Father is to overlook offenses—from within and without—absorbing them and limping further down the path, determined at all costs to make room for all God's peoples to inherit all God's blessings.

PRAYER FOCUS: *Mamprusi, Manpelle of Ghana (Evangelical: 0.20%)*

JANUARY 24: KEEP THE MAIN THING, THE MAIN THING

TODAY'S READING: GENESIS 35–38

Because we humans have short memories, God takes pains to remind us over and over that His eye is singularly focused on blessing all nations. The patriarchs tended to be hardheaded, so God repeatedly told Abraham, Isaac, and Jacob what the main thing was, and through them God reminds us to keep the main thing the main thing. God returned Jacob to Bethel, the place where Jacob first received the plan to bless all nations, the house of God, the gate of heaven. There God sang the same song over him: "'Your name is Jacob; your name shall not be called Jacob anymore, but Israel shall be your name.' So He called His name Israel. Also God said to him: 'I am God Almighty. Be fruitful and multiply; a nation and a company of nations shall proceed from you, and kings shall come from your body'" (Gen. 35:10–11).

Jacob was blessed and had his name changed to remind him and all his descendants that Israel was blessed so that all nations would be blessed. We should not be able to read about Old Testament Israel, or the modern-day nation state, without Jacob's story pounding in our heart. It's not about our limps, our resources, our parent's favorites, our families, or even us. It's about the promises of God to redeem for Himself men and women from every nation. It's about our princely privilege in singing this song with our King.

In Genesis 36, Esau and friends spread out as chiefs and kings, and Jacob and sons began to quarrel. Joseph unwisely shared his princely vision with his less-than-enthusiastic older brothers, and we have a multinational summit. Pre-Islamic Ishmaelites (from Saudi Arabia, 37:28) returning from Gilead (northern Jordan, 37:25) purchased a slave from some pre-Jews and gave him a free lift to Egypt, which at that time a Semitic people known as the Hyksos likely ruled. It might seem chaotic, but those who know how the story ends know that God always has the glorious saving of lives in mind.

In one final, shocking incident before this act ends and we traipse down to visit the superpower of the day, Tamar enters the story. God included this X-rated tale because He wanted us to remember that a Canaanite prostitute is in the genealogy of Jesus (Matt. 1:3) and that the gospel story is ever centered on the inclusion of all peoples. Judah visited his Adullamite friend and fell for the Caananite daughter of a man called Shua. Three sons followed, as did two deaths, the last one because Onan wickedly wanted pleasure without responsibility. God considers it wicked when His representatives enjoy the pleasures of the nations without taking up the responsibility of the nations. If we love Ethiopian food, but do nothing to reach the Oromo; if we love to travel to exotic places, but never bear witness to frontier peoples; if we tap our foot to Swahili music, but ignore the Muslims of the Swahili coast; or most alarmingly, if we live a nice cozy international life, but never become fluent in local language or embedded with local culture and friends, then we are probably just as wicked as Onan.

PRAYER FOCUS: *South Asian, General of Greece (Evangelical: 0.70%)*

JANUARY 25: BAKERS, BUTLERS, AND BUSINESSMEN

TODAY'S READING: GENESIS 39–41

Zaphnath-Paaneah was a pretty good businessman, perhaps the first to use his business sense for the cause of God's global glory. He knew how to ride bull and bear markets. He invested shrewdly and leveraged his wealth for even greater wealth and wider global impact. We know him, of course, by his birth name: Joseph. Joseph found himself in Egypt at a time the Hyksos likely ruled. The Hyksos were a blend of Semitic Asians who took advantage of a fragmented Egypt around 1800 BC to invade and rule for 100 years. Having a Semitic Pharaoh probably helped a Semitic problem solver get the second-in-command gig. What was more helpful to Joseph's business rise was the clear, observable reality that God was with him. Both Potiphar and prison keeper noticed God was with Joseph and so gave him responsibility. Whatever blessing God gives us in business, management, leadership, or wealth management is given so the nations of the world see it and recognize the hand of God. To abuse the favor of God and the trust of the nations by plundering the assets we were invited to steward (i.e. Potiphar's wife), God counts as wickedness. We are careful stewards, not rapacious pirates.

The people of God should be the best businesspeople on the planet—because we work hard, are informed, advance through merit, *and* have the Spirit of God empowering us, not because God endorses our laziness, ignorance, or nepotism. If all have the same education and the same opportunities, if all work hard, if all work with integrity and collaboration, but some have the Spirit of God in them, it is evident who will rise to prominence before the powerbrokers of earth. God intends for His businesspeople to create and grow wealth for one singular purpose: His glory among all nations, the preservation of life, and the advance of the gospel to every tribe, tongue, people, and nation.

God is yet looking for Josephs—men and women He can trust with wealth and influence because He knows they will use that trust to extend His glory to all peoples. If you have been gifted in business, if the Spirit of God in you has given you an "unfair" advantage in the marketplace, it is because He wants to use your gifts globally. God's Spirit in God's people in business is for one of these reasons:

- That you use your skills to support yourself as a missionary among an unreached people. Your business will grant you access to places and peoples others cannot engage.

- That you use your skills to make a way for others as representatives and employees of your company to enter countries and contexts where they cannot obtain visas, that they may stand before the peoples of that nation on credible footing to proclaim the gospel.

- That you give extravagantly, ridiculously, and generously to sustain boots-on-the-ground missionaries who need your monthly support.

PRAYER FOCUS: *Fula Jalon of Guinea (Evangelical: 0.00%)*

JANUARY 26: WEIGHING THE RISK

TODAY'S READING: GENESIS 42–45

"A young man should ask himself not if it is his duty to go to the heathen, but if he may dare stay at home. The command is so plain: 'Go.'"

LOTTIE MOON

Joseph legitimately took on the interests of his host nation. He learned the local language and observed their customs. When we take the time to learn the ways of other cultures (whether we visit them or they visit us), we reflect the heart of our God, a God who is above nationalism and who is interested in only one party's greatness: His own, Himself. Celebrating other cultures respectfully is actually reveling in the God who made us harmoniously different.

As Joseph thrived in Egypt, Jacob languished in Canaan and Reuben had to explain to his anxious father that sometimes you need to risk precious lives to save others. Missionary families know that sons and daughters must be commissioned to difficult places at cost—costs ranging from loneliness to martyrdom. The very possibility of loss can be crippling, yet even our military, police force, coast guard, and firefighters know that life must be risked in order for life to be saved. Disjointed in our day is that it's considered heroic for the military to serve in Afghanistan, Somalia, and other nations of dangerous instability, but foolish to send our missionaries to those very same places. It is currently honorable to die for flag and country, and almost dishonorable to die for souls and the King.

Risk, cost, loneliness, slavery, and prison are all intended by God for saving lives. For the God of nations, the God far above nationalism, the lives He longs to save are red, yellow, black, brown, and white. "Do not therefore be grieved," Joseph said, "for God sent me before you to preserve life.... And God sent me before you to preserve a posterity for you in the earth, and to save your lives by a great deliverance" (Gen. 45:5, 7). God ever thinks globally. God saves us that we might be His agent of saving others. God blessed Abraham so that through Abraham all nations might be blessed. God stewarded Joseph through slavery and prison, allowed him to learn and appreciate other cultures, and empowered him to help another nation be great, all so that lives will be saved—lives in Egypt, lives in Canaan, and lives from all the other grain-seeking nations of the world.

God intends for His glory in His people to be on display, not that we brag but that we can further bless. God intends for His people to receive the best of the nations—not their money or lands, but their people—and we do not receive them as servants, but as sons, brothers, fathers, and friends. Whatever our journey, from pit to prison, God wants His people to live interculturally for His glory and for the salvation of many lives.

PRAYER FOCUS: *Fulani, Fulakunda of Guinea-Bissau (Evangelical: 0.28%)*

JANUARY 27: THE SAME RESPONSIBILITY

TODAY'S READING: GENESIS 46-47

"Do you know that nothing you do in this life will ever matter, unless it is about loving God and loving the people he has made?"

FRANCIS CHAN

Israel offered sacrifices to the God of his father Isaac. This family worship reflects the continuity in the blessing to Abraham: there is an expectation that all the sons of Abraham will bless the nations of the world. God's blessing is always linked to responsibility, and He unfailingly gives to us so that we have resources to give to others. All the patriarchs repeated the expression "here I am!" (Gen. 46:2); all the prophets lived or spoke it (Isa. 6:8); and we should constantly repeat it. The whole context for this "here am I" refrain is to hear again God's heart for all nations, and the entire expectation is that we spring into obedient going. Jacob/Israel was instructed to go to Egypt; it was all part of the grander plan. In the same manner, God continues to send us into the nations in order to make us a blessing. That commission is likewise always accompanied with the promise that He will go with us.

Wherever spiritual Israel went, God blessed. The youthful Pharaoh's wonder at wrinkled 130-year-old physical Jacob escaped royal lips and he blurted out: "How old are you" (Gen. 47:8). In a harsh age where life was short, young Pharaoh assumed God must have blessed Jacob and thus submitted to blessing. Ordinarily, the greater blessed the lessor, but in this case age and some intuitive recognition that Jacob was intimate with God allowed the most powerful ruler in the known world to want what Jacob offered. It's a fertile scene for our imagination—a wrinkled and frail old man (with all the promise and power of the Godhead) lifting his hands to bless the young, virile ruler of earth's most fearsome nation. It is prophetic, of course. God intends through the mouths and proclamation of His prophetic people to bless all the nations of the earth—great and small, strong and weak, old and young. That little incident, no doubt played out in a great hall of power, is played out today in little huts and hovels all across the globe. Other Jacobs, other Pharaohs; same God, same glory.

The missions template is simple and clear. God is focused on blessing all nations through Abraham's seed. All Abraham's seed is heir to this responsibility. We go to the nations with the promise of God's presence. The indelible presence of God upon us opens the hearts of the peoples of all nations that we might open our mouths to declare the heart of God. Not much has changed in 3,800 years. God is still sending Abraham's children to the nations. He is still promising them His presence. He is still expecting them to open their mouth and proclaim. He still uses pits, prisons, and princes to save both the Pharaohs and the poor. Same God, same glory, same gospel, same grace, same go.

PRAYER FOCUS: *Brahmin of India (Evangelical: 0.01%)*

JANUARY 28: THE COMING OF THE END

TODAY'S READING: GENESIS 48–50

"The Bible is not the basis of missions; missions is the basis of the Bible."

RALPH WINTER

Jacob inserted into his own eschatology the central nugget that Shiloh will come from the house of Judah and to him shall be the obedience of the people. The same sentiment is echoed in Romans three different times when Paul talks about "the obedience to the faith of all nations" (Rom. 1:5; 5:19; 16:26). As Genesis comes to a close, Jacob prophetically opens our eyes to the promise of Jesus in Matthew 24:14 (this gospel of the Kingdom will preached to all people groups and then Shiloh will come) and Revelation 5:9 and 7:9 (around the throne of the King at the end of it all—or better put, the beginning of it all—men and women from every tribe, tongue, and people will worship).

Along the way, we can't lose the big plot in the smaller pains. God weeps when we miss the big picture because we're so focused on particular problems. It was not about Joseph being spoiled. It was not about Joseph being thrown in a pit, falsely accused, stewing in prison, or even creating wealth for Pharaoh. It was always about life being saved. It was always about God's promise to Abraham running unbroken and unhindered through time and place—all the way until Shiloh comes.

Joseph remembered the big picture and held steady to the reality that "God meant it for good, in order to bring it about as it is this day, to save many people alive" (Gen. 50:20). There is no place for hand-wringing about our culture or our times or the state of the world. Our sovereign God has taken all that was meant for evil and re-purposed it for good in order to bring things about as they are this day, to save many people alive, to save some from every people of earth.

As Joseph came to the end of his race, he reminded all who follow that the baton must be continually passed: "I am dying; but God will surely visit you, and bring you out of this land to the land of which he swore to Abraham, to Isaac, and to Jacob" (v. 24). And thus, Genesis ends as it began—not about land, but about God's promise to bless every people, every nation on earth through Abraham and his seed. Joseph reminded his brothers and children that every generation inherits this promise and this responsibility. We are to be the brokers of God's blessings in Jesus to every people group on earth—and then Shiloh will come. Even so, Lord Jesus, come.

PRAYER FOCUS: *Sunda of Indonesia (Evangelical: 0.05%)*

"This generation of Christians is responsible for this generation of souls on the earth!"

KEITH GREEN

Exodus means "the road out." Israel as an extended family that started with seventy persons multiplied, thanks to the midwives who feared the Lord, for God loves those who save other lives at risk to their own. It should always be kept in mind that the multiplication and fruitfulness of Israel was a promise, a promise linked to the responsibility to be a blessing to all nations. Christopher Wright has excellent summary thoughts on the metanarrative of missions as revealed in Exodus. "There is a kind of push and pull effect motivating God's action. On the one hand, he is pulled down by human cries to rectify injustice on earth. On the other hand, he is driven forward by his own declared intention to bless the nations and fulfill his covenant to Abraham. Both of these continue to be prominent themes in the way the Old Testament subsequently uses the exodus story as a model for understanding the character and action of God....

"YHWH is the exodus God. YHWH is that God who sees, hears, and knows about the suffering of the oppressed. YHWH is the God who hates what he sees and acts decisively to bring down the oppressor and release the oppressed so that both come to know him, either in the heat of his judgment or in glad worship and service. YHWH is the faithful God, who calls to mind the things he promised, the purposes he has declared, the mission to which he is committed. YHWH is the God who will not stand by to watch these great goals snuffed out by the stubborn recalcitrance of genocidal tyrants."

God is indeed "driven forward by his own declared intention to bless all nations," so let us likewise drive. All peoples will come to know God, "either in the heat of his judgment or in glad worship and service," so let us labor that the nations be glad. God will not stand by to "watch these great goals snuffed out," so let us not align with and not resist God's passion for all nations. Recalcitrance to get on board with God's missionary heart didn't go so well for Pharaoh, and it won't go well for us.

Wright points out that though what happened in Exodus was "a unique and unrepeatable event in the history of Old Testament Israel, it also stands as a paradigmatic and highly repeatable model for the way God wishes to act in the world, and ultimately will act for the whole of creation. The exodus is a prime lens through which we see the biblical mission of God." Exodus then gives all nations hope, for what God did for Israel (bring them out of bondage to Pharaoh) He promises to do for every people group (bring them out of the bondage of sin). God's road out has lanes for all peoples.

PRAYER FOCUS: *Persian of Iran (Evangelical: 1.90%)*

JANUARY 30: ON MISSION WITH GOD

TODAY'S READING: EXODUS 2–3

How delightful that when Moses needed refuge, he ran to Saudi Arabia! Moses named his son Gershom ("an alien there"), reminding us God's heart and home has always been open to immigrants and refugees. Moses' rash action from a pure motive necessitated his flight. Some interpret Moses looking "this way and that way, and when he saw no one" (Gen. 50:12) not as being sneaky, but as being frustrated. No one was doing anything to help an obvious need, so he jumped in. All young missionaries should remember that neither the wrath nor rush of man accomplishes the purposes of God. Well-meaning but misapplied zeal led Moses to Saudi Arabia. But God overruled, for it was there that God chose to reveal and repeat Himself.

The Bible drums away into our thick skulls that God is a missionary God. God called Moses and Moses responded in classic missionary form: "Here I am." God identified Himself as the God of Abraham, Isaac, and Jacob three times, the God who will bless every people group on earth. God prefigured the incarnation in saying, "I have come down to deliver" (Exo. 3:8). God said that *He* would send Moses to bring all His people out. God assured Moses: "I will certainly be with you" (v. 12). It was all about God and His missionary heart. God would bless this growing Syrian family, deliver them from Egypt, and take them to Palestine, the land of the Canaanites, Hittites, Amorites, Perizzites, Hivites, and Jebusites, all for the glory of His name. God sends us from the nations to the nations—sometimes as refugees and immigrants.

God also clearly linked His covenant name to missions. "I AM WHO I AM," God said to Moses, "and you shall say…'I AM has sent me to you'" (v. 14). This holy name, YHWH, is how God wants to be represented forever, and God links that name to being the God of Abraham, Isaac, and Jacob (i.e., the God who blesses so that all the people groups of earth may be blessed).

Christopher Wright points out that "once YHWH appears as a character in the drama, we become aware of a further dimension. The Israelites' slavery to Pharaoh is a massive hinderance to their worship and service of the living God, YHWH. One way the story makes the point is a simple play on a single Hebrew verb and noun. 'abad means to serve—that is to work for another; 'aboda means service or slavery… But the same words can be used for worship, the service of God. And of course, Israel's destiny was to serve and worship YHWH…and Pharaoh was preventing both."

YHWH is the God who sees, hears, and knows. YHWH is the God who remembers His covenant to Abraham. The Hebrew word for remember (zaakar) "denotes a thoughtful consideration of something one has deliberately called to mind with a view of taking action on it." God is resolutely committed to saving the lives of His children. But He does not save them empty-handed. God saves His children so they can join Him in His joy: plundering hell to populate heaven, a heaven He designed to be multi-racial, multi-cultural, multi-ethnic, multinational, and multi-glorious.

PRAYER FOCUS: *Arab, Iraqi of Iraq (Evangelical: 0.20%)*

JANUARY 31: LET GOD'S PEOPLE GROUPS GO

TODAY'S READING: EXODUS 4–6

Signs, miracles, and wonders are always linked to messages that need to be believed—they are not about power, but proclamation. God gave Moses signs that he might be believed and that the people might believe in the God of missions, for that was what the repeated reference to Abraham, Isaac, and Jacob implied. God's covenant to Abraham and his seed was centered on all nations being blessed. Despite Moses' insecurities he was told to go and to speak; commands Jehovah still issues today. And many of Moses' mentees still respond: "Oh my Lord, please send by the hand of whomever else" (Exo. 4:13). This angered Jehovah then, and it angers Him now.

What God did for Israel in Egypt, He intends to do for all nations. God looks down on the affliction and groaning of Muslims, Buddhists, Hindus, Sikhs, animists, pagans, and secularists and grieves over their bondage. He determines to send His servants; He promises to be with their mouths and teach them what to do; and He warns that He will use whatever force necessary to bring liberation. We are to open our mouths, speak for Jehovah, and address the religious Pharaohs of our day with the assertive demand: "Let My people go!" God has ordained a remnant from every people to be redeemed and satisfied in Him. God has promised that from every nation, tribe, tongue, and false religion there will be men and women around His throne, fulfilled in worship, satisfied in the presence of Jesus.

This declaration, this demand of *"Let's God's people groups go!"* is to be shouted by all God's people in unison. We shout from our knees and we shout in prayer. Central to the work of missions is the banding together in the Spirit of all God's people, lifting our voices with those around the world and across time, demanding that Pharaoh release God's peoples. Prayer needs no passport and no financing. Humble prayers in humble homes by humble fathers and mothers in front of their children are part of the global demonstration on behalf of those in the bondage of false religions. John G. Paton was an incredibly fruitful missionary to the (then) cannibal islands of Vanuatu. He went because of his father's prayers: "My father's prayers impressed me deeply. When, on his knees with all of us kneeling around him in family worship, he poured out his whole soul with tears for the conversion of the heathen world…. As we rose from our knees, I used to look at the light on my father's face and wish I were like him in spirit, hoping, in answer to his prayers, I might be privileged to carry the blessed Gospel to some part of the heathen world."

We are all to partake in Jehovah's mission. We are all to demonstrate and demand the release of the captives. We can all bend our knees and petition heaven for the nations to be redeemed. God promised this heritage to Abraham and we are Abraham's sons and daughters. On our knees let us pass on this glorious inheritance to our children. Do not rob your children of their share in Abraham's blessing because you refused to use your voice to call out in prayer daily for the liberation of all peoples.

PRAYER FOCUS: *Jew, Israeli Sabra of Israel (Evangelical: 0.06%)*

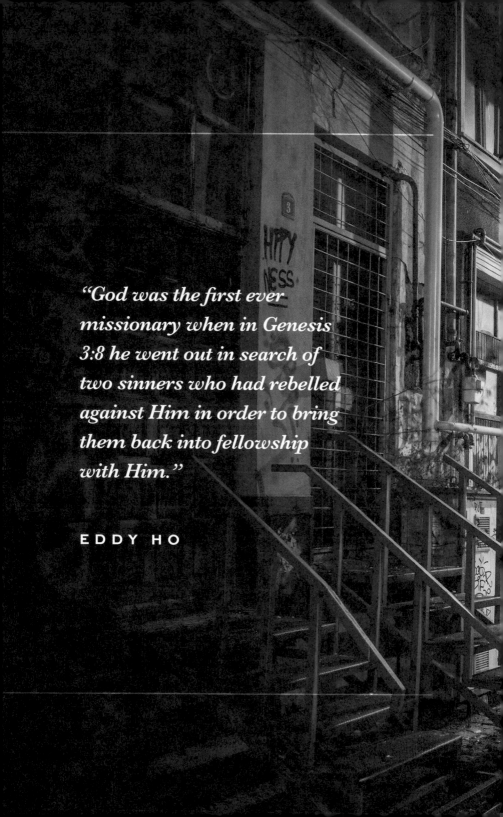

"God was the first ever missionary when in Genesis 3:8 he went out in search of two sinners who had rebelled against Him in order to bring them back into fellowship with Him."

EDDY HO

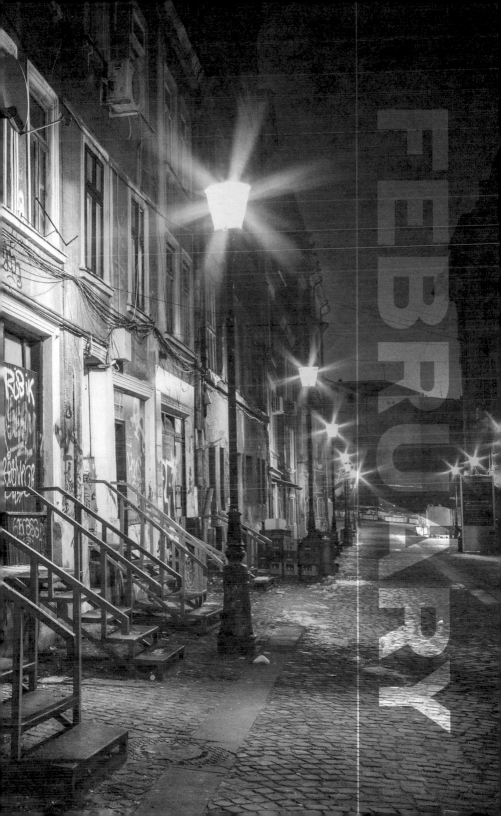

FEBRUARY 1: THE SUPERHERO

TODAY'S READING: EXODUS 7-9

"Every missionary I know is extraordinarily ordinary. Everything they do,
they do by the grace of God."

MATT CHANDLER

Superhero and superpower showdowns enthrall us because the fate of the world is at stake and huge egos and weapons collide before our eyes in the struggle for supremacy. But they're all child's play compared to the show that went down in Egypt. The god of Egypt defied the God of heaven and it became a throwdown. The plagues dramatized the politics of power better than any movie or missile crisis.

Pharaoh stuck his tongue out at God saying in Exodus 5:2: "Who is the LORD [Jehovah].... I do not know the LORD [Jehovah], nor will I let Israel go!" Pharaoh claimed he did not know who God was, therefore he would not obey. God took up the thrown gauntlet and proceeded to educate Pharaoh with a series of power encounters. The lessons and plagues ascended in both importance and inconvenience. Christopher Wright puts it this way: "Israel's primary source of knowing YHWH to be the one true and living God (**the God**) was their experience of his grace in historical acts of deliverance. But those acts of deliverance for **Israel** meant judgment on their **oppressors**. These enemies too would come to know God but they would know him as the God of justice who could not be resisted with impunity... The exodus narrative has as its major plot, of course, the deliverance of Israel from their oppression under Pharaoh. It also has as its major sub-plot, however, the massive power encounter between YHWH, the God of Israel, and Pharaoh, king (and god) of Egypt—and all the other gods of the Egyptians. The trigger for this subplot is the fateful refusal of Pharaoh to recognize YHWH as having any jurisdiction in his territory."

Jehovah emphatically demonstrated that He had all jurisdiction (power and authority) in Egypt and in all the earth among all peoples, and He clearly wanted Pharaoh, all kings, and all of us to know that the reason for all this power being flung around was that His name may be proclaimed in all the earth: "The Egyptians shall know that I am the LORD [Jehovah]"; "that you may know there is no one like the LORD [Jehovah] our God"; "in order that you will know that I am LORD [Jehovah] in the midst of the land"; "that you may know that there is none like Me in all the earth"; and "for this purpose I have raised you up, that I may show My power in you, and that My name may be declared in all the earth" (7:5; 8:10, 22; 9:14, 16). Wright succinctly says: "Clearly, the motivation from God's point of view was not only the liberation of his enslaved people, but this driving divine will to be known to all nations for who and what he truly is. The mission of God, to be known, is what drives this whole narrative." Any power we have, then—whether power of wealth, power of intellect, power of persuasion, power of time, power of creativity, or any other power—must diligently be used to make Jehovah known, glorified, and worshiped by every tribe, tongue, and people in all the earth.

PRAYER FOCUS: *Arab, General of Italy (Evangelical: 0.06%)*

FEBRUARY 2: WHEN GOD SAW THE BLOOD
TODAY'S READING: EXODUS 10–12

The plagues ascended in drama and damage, each one destroying the illusionary power of false Egyptian gods. Christopher Wright rightly writes "the emphasis of the story as the suspense builds is that YHWH is not merely intent on liberating slaves but on reclaiming worshipers…. The exodus demonstrates who is truly God. YHWH stands alone and incomparable." Jehovah was establishing Himself above all gods and above all false worship. Pharaoh was preventing true worship, and as God will be worshipped by all peoples, He would not let little pretending gnats thwart His global purpose, so God said in Exodus 12:12 (NIV): "I will bring judgment on all the gods of Egypt. I am the LORD [Jehovah]."

God judging all false gods and God destroying all who resist His global worship gives us a beautiful, sobering advance view of the gospel. It is, after all, God who saves us from God. God says to us all: I will bring one more plague. I will go out into the midst of Egypt; and all the firstborn in the land of Egypt shall die. I will pass through the land of Egypt and will strike all the firstborn. I will execute judgment (11:1, 4–5; 12:12). And He did—the Lord struck the Egyptians and all the firstborn. The Lord does His own killing (see 13:15). He does not send the devil to do His "dirty work," and it was the blood of the lamb that saved the people from God's wrath. For the blood did not save them from Pharaoh or Pharaoh's armies (that deliverance came later), but the blood saved them from the destroying hand of God. When God saw the blood, He passed over. For the gospel is simply this: The love of God saves us from the wrath of God for the joys of God.

A further beauty of the Exodus story is that God never has had and never will have favorites. The blood is color blind, ethnic blind, gender blind, age blind. All who shelter under the blood from the wrath of God enjoy His love in the present and His eternal joy. "Should the question be raised as to the effectiveness of all these demonstrations of the power of God in the plagues and the crossing of the Red Sea, the answer is available to us. When Israel left Egypt, a 'mixed multitude' or a group of 'many other peoples' went out with them (Exod. 12:38).… Many Egyptians were more than merely impressed by what they saw and heard. They were some of the first fruits of the work of God in their midst." God's destroying wrath and His covering love were not singularly aimed at nor restricted to the Israelites or the Egyptians. What happened at that specific time for those specific people was a microcosm of God's redemptive work in history, a prefigurate of the blood of Jesus shed on the cross and of Jesus absorbing the wrath of God for us all, and a prophecy that one day around God's throne, there will indeed be a mixed multitude—and that multitude will include the Japanese.

PRAYER FOCUS: *Japanese of Japan (Evangelical: 0.30%)*

FEBRUARY 3: KNOWING GOD

TODAY'S READING: EXODUS 13-15

"Missions is the overflow of our delight in God because missions is the overflow of God's delight in being God."

JOHN PIPER

The God of wrath lovingly led and lit His people out of bondage. Because God usually doesn't lead us along conventional paths, others seek to attack what God is doing. Every danger and every criticism should be seen as an opportunity for God to gain glory.

In Exodus 14, God twice stated: "The Egyptians will know that I am the LORD [Jehovah]" (vv. 4, 18). "There can be little mistaking the fact that the word 'know' here connotes more than a mere cognitive awareness of who God is. It expresses a desire that the Egyptians might themselves come to a personal and experiential knowledge of who Yahweh is. God would proclaim his own name among the Gentiles, even if the Israelites were not outgoing in their witness." God is always calling the peoples of earth to Himself, even when we run from those very peoples in fear. The whole process in Exodus was intended to turn God's people from serving *and* fearing the nations so that God could use them as His instruments of blessing to those nations. "The following months and years would see Israel on a steep learning curve, but by the end of it their worldview would be changed forever. They would know who was truly God in Egypt (and everywhere else)."

Glimmers of this confidence emerged from the song of Moses. The people of God raised their heads as the shame and fear rolled off with the waters of the receding sea. They had just seen the strongest army of the day with the best technology of the time completely overwhelmed with one breath of God. And so they sang, that Jehovah was their God and they would praise Him. They sang that Jehovah was their father's God and they would exalt Him. This reference to lineage—all the way back to Abraham—was of course linked to God's promises to Abraham. The God of strength was the God of glory was the God of wrath was the God who would send His fear and dread ahead of His people into Palestine and Jordan and all nations of the world.

In the understanding of the day, each city/nation had a territorial god who fought for their principality and subjects. "Terror, or fear, was assumed to be separate substance which went before the deity, defeating enemies before the god arrived." Jehovah obliterates all tribal gods and indeed His terrifying and wooing Spirit goes ahead of us in missions to all corners of the world. God's representatives can walk into the Jordans of the world, look confidently and graciously into the eyes of temporal monarchs, and boldly proclaim the gospel because the Spirit of God already invaded and inspired reverence. Our ambassadorial role is merely to find those that Jehovah has already conquered.

PRAYER FOCUS: ***Arab, Jordanian of Jordan (Evangelical: 0.30%)***

FEBRUARY 4: BATTLE TOGETHER, BETTER TOGETHER

TODAY'S READING: EXODUS 16–18

A missionary reading of the Bible acknowledges that Abraham was blessed to be a blessing to all the peoples of the world and that all who are spiritual sons of Abraham have the same mandate. Israel as a nation then was brought out of Egypt so they could fulfil God's plan.

The road out of bondage (to carry Abraham's mandate) usually lacks water, bread, and meat. The road to blessing the nations is arduous and lacks the conveniences of home. All those who walk towards the nations stub their toes, forget their prior woes, and seriously question whether the price required to reach the inconvenient lost is worth it. Enemies steal into that deliberative process, adept at turning God's missionaries against each other. The biggest challenge on the road to blessing the nations invariably becomes infighting and complaining about our friends and leaders (Exo. 17:4). One of the first commitments missionaries must make is that they will not allow infighting to take them off the blessing trail. That commitment connects to a trust in God to provide the necessities—physical, emotional, and relational.

A second commitment missionaries must make is to depend on prayer (17:11). Samuel Zwemer said, "The history of missions is the history of answered prayer...it is the key to the whole missionary problem. All human means are secondary," and J. Oswald Sanders said, "[Prayer] is fundamental, not supplementary.... All progress can be clearly traced back to prevailing prayer." Oswald Chambers famously said: "Prayer does not equip us for greater works—prayer is the greater work...but remember that it is prayer based on the agony of Christ in redemption, not on my own agony.... When you labor at prayer, from God's perspective there are always results. What an astonishment it will be to see, once the veil is finally lifted, all the souls that have been reaped by you, simply because you have been in the habit of taking your orders from Jesus Christ."

A third commitment missionaries (and all men and women) must make is to never attempt to thwart God's missionary purposes. Amalek tried to wipe out Israel and God went to long-term total war against him. The logic is simple: God's people have one purpose—to bless all people groups on earth. If God's people are eliminated or restricted, God's peoples do not receive the blessing of God. God will then go to war with whoever tries to stop His blessing of all peoples going forward. The sentiment seen on a bumper sticker of "whoever messes with Israel messes with God" is right, but that's not referring to a pagan political entity that itself resists the deity and authority of Jesus. Biblically understood, the "don't mess with Israel" sentiment refers to anyone who works against God's purpose to bless the Kazakh with the gospel. Stand against the missionary purposes and people of God, and you will see Jehovah Nissi unfurl His battle banner. He will go to war with you from generation to generation. It's more productive to fight for God than against Him.

PRAYER FOCUS: *Kazakh of Kazakhstan (Evangelical: 0.07%)*

FEBRUARY 5: GOD'S MOVABLE TREASURE

TODAY'S READING: EXODUS 19–21

I don't believe we can improve on Walter Kaiser's explanation of Exodus 19:4–6: "The election of Israel, far from meaning the rejection of the other nations of the world, was the very means of salvation of the nations. Election was not a call to privilege, but a choosing for service. As such, the priestly character of the nation of Israel came into view almost from the beginning of her existence as a nation. The people were to be God's ministers, his preachers, his prophets to their own nation as well as to the other nations.

"[In this text, 'possession' is translated from the Hebrew word *segulla* which] referred to property that could be moved as opposed to real estate that could not be moved. Accordingly, Israel was to be God's 'jewels'…his special treasure above all his other possessions. But they were to be treasures that he could move around and disperse as he pleased.

"A second role that Israel was to play was that of been a 'kingdom of priests' to God. This phrase is best translated as 'kings and priests' or royal priest to God. Here is where Israel's role and function on behalf of the kingdom of God is made explicit if it was ambiguous previously. Her role as a nation was a mediatorial role as they related to the nations and people groups around them…. Unfortunately for Israel, when this ministry for all the believers was opened to them…they turned back from so awesome a task…. But what was rejected at this moment was never disposed of, but simply delayed in his fullest expression until New Testament times. It was not scrapped: it remained God's plan for believers.

"A third function was preferred to the nation: they were to be a 'holy nation'. This meant they were to be 'wholly' the Lord's…. The truth is that the Old Testament word 'holy' meant 'set apart wholly for God's use.' This nation was to be set apart not only in their lives but also in their service. Through them all the families of the earth were to receive the blessing God had in store for all who believed.

"As God's special movable treasure, his royal priests, and a nation wholly dedicated to him, Israel was to assume two relations: one side toward God, their King and the other side toward the nations and people groups on earth. They were to be a nation for all times and for all peoples—distinctly marked and challenged to serve. Alas, however, Israel missed the prize of her high calling and acted selfishly on her own behalf only. Thus, while carrying a portfolio of the coming Man of Promise and the Seed by which all the world would be blessed, she myopically declined, for the most part, to carry out her high calling as the channel through which the grace of God could come to all the nations."

We now in our age are God's movable treasure. If He should transfer us to Somalia, it is our delight to go. We are His royal priests. We are to represent God to Somalis through proclamation and to represent Somalis to God through prayer. We are to be wholly His. Every part of us aligned with His passion to be glorified by Somalis. God forgive our myopia. God grant we rise to the privilege He offers us.

PRAYER FOCUS: *Somali of Kenya (Evangelical: 0.09%)*

FEBRUARY 6: THE INVITATION OF JEHOVAH

TODAY'S READING: EXODUS 22–24

God did not begin to make things up on Mt. Sinai. Previously, He asked the Sabbath to be honored, and the precedent for that went all the way back to creation and God's example. Murder was taboo since Cain. Much of the structure of the law given from the mountain echoed the Code of Hammurabi (1792–1750 BC), and the format of "if…then" (called case law) was common to other cultures of the period. The fact that the Sinaitic law was similar to other codes of the day—which is far from being problematic—is evidence of law and truth coming from a common origin and heading to a common climax. These commonalities are direct evidence of a literal Adam, and a common ancestry and understanding that all truth is God's truth. The commonalities prophesy and morally endorse a final eschatological judgment of all mankind—by the only One wise and true enough to make and uphold these universal laws.

Both God's truth and God's salvation are universal. "One demonstration of the Law given through Moses is to favorably demonstrate life in **the fear of the Lord….** This distinctive way of life was a means of instructing the nations. The entire covenant at Sinai should be understood as a treaty deliberately enacted according to the prevailing treaty format of the day: a sovereign king entering into a covenant with a vassal…. Since holiness necessarily involves separation to the purposes of God, it follows that God was revealing His will that Israel bless the nations by both proclaiming His covenant to them and interceding on their behalf."

Since Jehovah is King of all the earth, King of all peoples, He expects and desires to have similar relationship with them as He had with Israel. Israel was the example, the shining light to the nations: Look how wonderful it is to serve Jehovah! Look how fulfilling it is to fear the King of kings! God's blessing on Israel was intended to provoke a holy jealousy, to exemplify to the nations how sweet covenant relationship with the one true God was. All nations are invited to taste and see that Jehovah is good—even North Korea, especially North Korea.

This invitation of Jehovah is not one to be negotiated or taken lightly. The God of Mt. Sinai should not be provoked. He sends His fear ahead of Him, and He is a consuming fire. This God of fear and fire makes no covenant with false gods and will overthrow all false religions completely. The missionary call is an inclusive and universal one, even as it is an uncompromising one. All (Amorites, Hittites, Perizzites, Canaanites, Hivites, and Jebusites) are welcome, but all must come bowing and all must check their idols at the door. We fall with no conditions at Jehovah's feet—He does not fall at ours.

PRAYER FOCUS: *Korean of North Korea (Evangelical: 1.56%)*

FEBRUARY 7: TABERNACLE WITH GOD

TODAY'S READING: EXODUS 25–27

"Missions is not the ultimate goal of the church. Worship is.
Missions exists because worship doesn't."

JOHN PIPER

God's great desire is to dwell among humanity (Exo. 25:8). The purpose of the desert tabernacle was a resting place for Jehovah in the middle of His people. The imagery in Exodus of Jehovah living in the middle of His people, providing food and water for them, enjoying their company and deigning for them to enjoy His is rich indeed. It broadcasts what God wants and will affect for all peoples. His joyful self at the center, and all of life enriched as a result. God dwelt in the desert tabernacle. God became flesh and "tabernacled" with us. God will come again in glory that we may forever tabernacle with Him in all the delights of our permanent heavenly home.

It is fascinating that the ark (the presence of God in the midst of the tabernacle) was at once dangerous and comforting. Approach or touch the ark unworthily and die. Yet the ark was covered by the mercy seat, and it is from the mercy seat that God communes with us. It is terrifying to live in the reality that to approach the presence of God unworthily and without propitiation (i.e., His wrath appeased) is deadly. It is stupefying that the very same presence protects and embraces us; God's presence is both shelter and shade. "Christ also is a shade giving comfort and shelter. He shelters us from outward wrath, and gives comfort for inner weariness.... When the heat of God's wrath is ready to scorch the soul, Christ shades the soul from its heat. Under the shadow of His wings we sit down quietly, safely, because we put our trust in him. And all this we do with great delight."

John Piper is right: "Missions exists because worship doesn't." Missions is a thing of earth; it will not exist in heaven. God is the center of eternity, everlastingly beautiful. "Once again we are driven back to see how important it is to ground our theology of mission (and our practice of it) in the mission of God and in our worshipping response to all God is and does. From that perspective, we are advocates for God before we are advocates for others." Before we go to the nations, we go to the presence of God. Before we give out gospel glory, we feast on the gospel feasts ourselves. Our going to the nations is because we lost ourselves in the love of God, and wondrously smitten we advocate for Him to those starving for affection. We shout of the God of mercy to those who only know the God of wrath.

Carl Braaten wrote, "God and not the church is the primary subject and source of mission. Advocacy is what the church is about, being God's advocate in the world. The church must therefore begin its mission with doxology, otherwise everything peters out into social activism and aimless programs." Thus we praise. The people of a glorious God encounter Him, cannot contain Him, and advocate for Him to the nations of the world. God tabernacles with us that the nations might tabernacle with Him.

PRAYER FOCUS: *Albanian, Kosovars of Kosovo (Evangelical: 0.20*

FEBRUARY 8: OUR DAILY MARCH TO THE CROSS

TODAY'S READING: EXODUS 28–29

"Since God is a missionary God, God's people are a missionary people."

EDDY HO

What God did for Abraham was a microcosm of what He wants to do for the world. What God did for Israel in both ceremony and civic life was a picture, an announcement of what He wants to do for all nations. When Aaron the high priest entered the presence of God, he did so with the names of the tribes of Israel over his heart. This is a beautiful picture of God carrying all the tribes and tongues of history in His heart. He is not willing that any of them should perish. He guarantees that representatives of every one of them will be around the throne.

"It was to be God's covenantal presence in Israel that would mark them out as distinctive from the rest of the nations. This would be the purpose of the tabernacle… The very purpose of redemption was so that God would dwell with his people." God's great passion is for all nations, and His requirement for relationship is that those nations are holy. By nature God cannot fellowship with what is vile, and by nature all the tribes of history are vile, so God provides our holiness at immeasurable cost. By His glory God sanctifies what is soiled. By His altar God consecrates what is crooked. God so aches to live in intimacy with His people that He willingly absorbs the horrific price required.

Exodus 29:46 says, "They shall know that I am the LORD their God, who brought them up out of the land of Egypt, that I may dwell among them." Jesus wants to live and abide with us more than we want to live and abide with Him. The greater cost of communion was paid on the cross, but lesser bills are due daily. To live in intimacy with Jesus, we must constantly submit to His refining fire. Selfishness must be repeatedly burned off of us and out of us. Daily we must march our hearts to the cross; we must lay our wills on the altar; and we must pick up our cross and follow—for Jesus carried His cross, not ours.

When God's people submit to God's purifying processes, they begin to shine, and that luster creates a holy jealousy in all who observe. A holy God intimate with a holy people is a relationship so beautified that those in false relationships cannot help but long for what they see. God's purification process in you is intended to have such an evangelistic effect. Embrace your fire, your altar, your cross, your trial, your cleansing, your daily dying, for it is beautifying your communion with God so that others from all nations may desire what you have. What God is doing in you and for you, He wants to do for others. Your submission to the painful process will bless far more than you, for even your purging is not really about you. It is for the glory of God among the nations— this is ever the way of our Father.

PRAYER FOCUS: *Arab, Arabic Gulf Spoken of Kuwait (Evangelical: 0.53%)*

FEBRUARY 9: WE ARE ART TO BE VIEWED

TODAY'S READING: EXODUS 30–32

"God uses men who are weak and feeble enough to lean on him."

HUDSON TAYLOR

It is beautiful—and typical—of the God of the nations that the holy anointing oil and the incense of His temple could only be made by compounding spices from a variety of nations. The oil of the tabernacle was made from liquid myrrh, sweet-smelling cinnamon, cane, cassia, and olive oil. The incense was an equal multi-national collection of stacte, onycha, galbanum, and pure frankincense. These spices were gathered from Palestine, Arabia, India, and, in the case of onycha, the Red Sea, and they were compounded according to the "art of the perfumer" (Exo. 30:25). What a beautiful picture of God, the perfumer who crushes different people together so that their aromas influence one another with the total sweetness being greater than the sum of the parts.

It does not take long, however, for human aromas to stink, and Moses was not long on the mountain before Aaron and friends made their own stench by compounding their own concoction, weakly explaining, "I cast [their gold] into the fire, and this calf came out" (32:24). God was not amused. In fact, He was angered and told Moses that He would wipe out His chosen people and start all over again. Moses appealed the decision and "based his appeal (among other things) on the grounds that God had a reputation to think of. What would the nations (especially the Egyptians in that context) think of YHWH as God if he first delivered Israel from Egypt and then destroyed them in the wilderness…? They would think that YHWH was either incompetent or malicious. Is that the kind of reputation YHWH wanted? The name (reputation) of YHWH among the nations was at stake in what God did **against** His own people, just as it was involved in all that he did **for** them."

What God does to us in mercy or in punishment is meant to be publicly viewed and "the clear assumption underlying this bold intercession is that whatever God does to His people in anger will be as visible to the nations as all that he did for them in his compassion." God displays both His blessing love and His discipline love openly. Our lives are not to be about us, lived out in private and for self-glory. Our lives are to be about God, lived out in full view of the nations and for His name's sake. We must relinquish all rights to our own lives, even the right to be loved or corrected privately. God used Israel to display the fullness of His character to the nations. He wants to use us in similar fashion. We are His workmanship. He puts great care into our crafting, for He intends His art to be viewed by all that He might be further praised and desired.

PRAYER FOCUS: *Kyrgyz of Kyrgyzstan (Evangelical: 0.65%)*

FEBRUARY 10: MAKING HIM KNOWN
· TODAY'S READING: EXODUS 33-35

There is a fine line between art and idolatry. God is pro art, giving artists the Spirit of God in design. God fills artisans with skill so that their creations may glorify the Creator globally.

The problem with art is that it is easily perverted. Some give Aaron's artistry the benefit of the doubt: "In the ancient Near East, bulls, as well as other animals, were sometimes intended not as an image of the deity itself, but as mounts for the god who was understood to be present." Perhaps Aaron's compromise was to craft an image on which the uncarveable Jehovah could "sit." But even if the intention was good, the compromise was still idolatrous. We must not call idolatry "art," and if the art is perverse or indecent, it's idolatry and it ticks God off. What makes God especially upset is if places of worship become places to perform our "sacred" arts. When music and speaking in the church become performance based—showcasing the creature in the very place God alone is to be honored—we have crafted idols. We may profess that it's merely a "bull" for the Lord to sit on, but that would be…well…bull.

God was so angered that He threatened to abandon Israel, but thankfully, Moses interceded. The first intercession was missional, for "the kind of response expected from YHWH's elect [is] that the divine blessing may be mediated to the nations.… That is to say, we learn the missional significance of intercessory prayer." Moses reflected to God the divine heart for all nations to be blessed—what the early intercession of the Bible was based on. In effect, Moses asked God to stay the course in the divine plan to use Abraham's seed to bless all nations.

The second intercession was just as vital and missional. God offered to help Israel go on into Canaan and fulfil His promise to Abraham. But God said this would be done with His help, not His presence. God was offering His power without His person, miracles without intimacy, victory without relationship. Moses would have none of it: "If Your Presence does not go with us, do not bring us up from here. **For how then will it be known that Your people and I have found grace in Your sight…"** (Exo. 33:15–16, emphasis mine). Moses understood that God's blessing was to be found and lived in among the nations, in integration with them, an integration that avoided compromise. God expects us to live holy and wholly among the nations in such a way that *He is known.* Home for the people of God is not to be a seclusion or sequestering away from the different peoples of the earth. Canaan's land was the people of God (wherever they are), marked by His presence, surrounded by the nations. This was why God plunked Israel down in the middle of the pagan, powerful nations of Moses' day. This is why He plunks immigrant Buddhist Lao in our neighborhoods, Arab Muslims in our workplaces, and Hindu children in our schools. Jehovah wants the nations to see that when we are with Him, our faces shine. It's a daily reminder that His presence is life.

PRAYER FOCUS: *Lao of Laos (Evangelical: 1.9%)*

FEBRUARY 11: MOVABLE ARKS

TODAY'S READING: EXODUS 36–38

"Lost people matter to God, and so they must matter to us."

KEITH WRIGHT

God puts wisdom and understanding in gifted individuals so they can beautifully represent a beautiful God in all the earth. There are many similarities between the contents of the tabernacle and the artifacts used in pagan worship. Egypt's religion, for example, had an ark, as did Babylon—but with critical differences. For example, the cherubim on the ark were not images of God, but rather divine attendants. Other arks provided idolatrous images or etchings of gods, but Jehovah's ark was a symbol of the invisible presence of God.

The ark was built for travel, having gold rings through which long poles were inserted. The symbolic ark, representing the very real presence of God, was intended for portability. The presence of God cannot be contained in one place or by one people, but surges across the nations, seeking worshipers. We can adorn, but not restrict, the presence of God. When we apply our God-given art, talent, design, and craftsmanship to physical matter creating beauty, we merely point to Him who is most beautiful, who is beyond imagination. Art captures inadequately He whose beauty we cannot tame or record—and that beauty is meant to travel.

The beauty of who God is, adorned by the devoted gifts of His people, is to be carried to all the world and every people group through every vocation. It is a misconception to say that only those with gifts of rhetoric and formal teaching are qualified for missions. While all are called to make disciples through preaching (evangelism), teaching (discipleship), healing (praying for the sick), and praying (believing in faith for miracles), this does not mean that all need to have the public gift of apostle, pastor, teacher, evangelist, or prophet. God wants to use athletes, musicians, artists, lawyers, doctors, plumbers, shepherds, farmers (who understand the laws of sowing and reaping better than anyone), police, engineers, and even (incarnate) carpenters to make His glory known.

In the work of global missions, we are far from the blessed problem of the people bringing "much more than enough for the service of the work which the Lord commanded us to do" (Exo. 36:5). The Lord of the harvest commanded us to make disciples of all the nations, all the unreached peoples of earth. Counting varies, but there are probably still 7,000 unreached people groups globally, and some of those groups number in the millions. We still need hundreds of thousands, if not millions of missionaries, of every gift, every talent, every age, every race. Men and women full of God's creative wisdom in their craft, making God beautiful as they carry His presence, as His movable ark to the unreached peoples of the world. Will you not be His Spirit-filled ark and artist in Lebanon?

PRAYER FOCUS: *Kurd, Kurmanji of Lebanon (Evangelical: 0.01%)*

FEBRUARY 12: CARRY THE NATIONS

TODAY'S READING: EXODUS 39-40

The lesson of Exodus is that Jehovah delivered His children out of bondage and brought them into the blessedness of His presence. In Genesis, Jehovah brought Abraham out of Syria and into the blessedness of covenant relationship with the express purpose of all people groups of earth following suit. Exodus continued this metanarrative, for what Jehovah did for Israel (the physical sons of Abraham), He wants to do for all peoples (the spiritual sons of Abraham). We cannot forget this foundational truth when reading the Bible: God's acts for Israel and in Israel were pictures and prophecies of what He wants to do among all peoples of earth. God wants to bring men and women of every people group out of bondage and into the glorious and fulfilling liberty of His presence.

When Aaron the priest entered the presence of God, with the names of the sons of Israel engraved on his ephod, that was a missions act of intercession. The sons of Israel were blessed and empowered for the singular purpose of being a demonstration and channel of God's love for all nations. We cannot read or understand any biblical reference to Abraham, Israel, or blessing outside the foundational hermeneutic of missions. God will bless Abraham's spiritual children (of every people group) through Abraham's spiritual seed (the Lord Jesus). What God did for Israel, He wants to do for all. When Israel's sons were carried on the shoulders of an intercessor into the presence of God, they entered His presence in advance hope for us all.

On the crown of the priest was the dedication: holiness to the lord (Exo. 39:30). At the head of our thoughts, face forward in our global journey, is the sanctification of all the peoples of earth to Jehovah—the God of Abraham who will at all costs redeem men and women of every race and tribe to Himself. We should not be able to enter the presence of God privately, nor gather together as the redeemed in small or large settings, without carrying the peoples of earth on our shoulders in prayer and global devotion to Jehovah stamped on our foreheads. Our dedication to the Holy One is inextricably linked to His goal of being worshiped by every tribe and tongue. As saints holy to the Lord, our central question when we gather must always be, "Who is not yet here?"

Aaron and sons ministered to the Lord as an advance deposit of global worship. When in holiness Aaron and sons worshiped Jehovah, glory filled the tabernacle. If this was true for the small proto-worshipers, just imagine the glory cloud when God's purposes on earth are done! Imagine the soul-bursting reality when it's not just Israel, but representatives of every tribe and nation, made holy by the Lamb, worshiping with full-throated praise.

Today as you singularly enter God's presence, carry the nations on your prayer shoulders. Join your heart to the heart of the Father and ask Him to bring His lost ones home. This week as you join the saints in holy worship, look forward with joy to that great glory burst when all are assembled and the heavens shake with multilingual praise.

PRAYER FOCUS: *Gola of Liberia (Evangelical: 0.82%)*

"The mark of a great church is not its seating capacity, but its sending capacity."

MIKE STACHURA

The book of Leviticus is named after the order of priests—Levi and sons. The book of Exodus reveals that God appointed a priestly role to Israel as a nation, and Leviticus fleshes out what that means exactly. "It is…richly significant that God confers on Israel as a whole people the role of being his priesthood in the midst of the nations. As the people of YHWH they would have the historical task of bringing the knowledge of God to the nations, and bringing the nations to the means of atonement with God…. Just as it was the role of the priests to bless the Israelites, so it would be the role of Israel as a whole ultimately to be a blessing to the nations."

In the mercy of the Lord there is provision for our unintentional sins. If a person, whole congregation, ruler, or any of the common people sin because they were ignorant of one of God's command, there is a path forward, a path that includes repentance and restitution. It is not uncommon for Christians who awaken to God's great heart for unreached peoples and for missions to feel guilt—guilt because they haven't been functioning in their priestly role for the nations. Many have served Jesus for years but have done so myopically, focused on their needs, community, or country. When the great missions heart of Father God bursts over us and we lift our heads to the magnitude of unreached peoples in the world, we are first clouded with shame. We did not sin intentionally against God's great heart and purpose, but we sinned all the same. We have been unknowingly selfish and ingrown. We have been unknowingly parochial, not global. We have been large in our own eyes and small towards God's glory among all peoples. When we awaken to the unintentional sin of neglecting God's great missionary purposes for every unreached people, let us both repent and make restitution. Laying our lives on the altar of sacrifice for God to use for His global glory among all peoples is a pleasing aroma to Him and the only acceptable way forward.

Though the book of Leviticus was probably written in the short period of about six weeks between the completion of the tabernacle and the Israelites' departure from Sinai (Exo. 40:17, Num. 10:11–12), it can seem like forever when wading through a reading of the laws and sacrifices. As you wade through Leviticus, do it with the joyful reminder that you spiritually are a priest and you stand in Abraham's and Levi's lines with a two-fold task—to represent Jehovah to the nations and the nations to Jehovah. Read Leviticus prayerfully asking what the Lord of harvest requires you to sacrifice toward this great glory, the glory of God among Libyan Arabs and all unreached peoples.

PRAYER FOCUS: *Arab, Libyan of Libya (Evangelical: 0.04%)*

FEBRUARY 14: WE ARE ALL PRIESTS

TODAY'S READING: LEVITICUS 5–7

When you read the Bible missiologically, it is enthralling, especially chapters detailing the role of priests. Is there anything more invigorating than having the assignment of representing Jehovah to the nations and the nations to Jehovah? "The priest was an intermediary and, therefore, had a mission between God and men. If we apply this concept to Israel as a people, it suggests that Israel is also an intermediary between God and the nations…. Israel's privilege is one of service. Israel was taken from among the nations to be at the service of the nations. Israel is a mediator. She must bring mankind closer to God, pray to God for mankind, and intercede for mankind…. Her service to God is in the name of others. But Israel also brings God closer to men, by bringing them God's revelation, his light, and the good news of salvation."

Reading Leviticus with the eyes that we, the priestly spiritual sons of Abraham, have the most important job on earth as God's ambassadors to unreached peoples, missional applications leap out at us from every chapter. Granted, Leviticus has a contextual application of how a certain people in a particular period in a specific place deal with sin, yet it's not disassociated from God's overall aims. Thus, we can draw applications for today and tomorrow:

- **5:1** *"If a person sins in hearing the utterance of an oath, and is witness…if he does not tell it he bears guilt."* We have heard God's oath to bless all nations through His people over and over. If we don't witness, we will bear guilt.

- **5:7–11** *"If he is not able to bring a lamb, then…two turtle doves or two young pigeons but if he is not able to bring [birds]…then he shall bring a [tiny bit of] flour."* No economic bracket is excluded from reconciliation from God. No tribe will be lost. No people group neglected. The gospel is for all strata of all ethnicities in all nations.

- **6:13** *"A fire shall always be burning on the altar; it shall never go out."* God's fiery passion to redeem men and women from every unreached people group through history is never extinguished. His heart burns with eager intensity, ever brighter and stronger for all nations to be redeemed and reconciled to Him.

- **7:10, 21** *"Every grain offering…shall belong to all the sons of Aaron, to one as much as the other… and who eats the flesh of the sacrifice of the peace offering that belongs to the Lord, that person shall be cut off."* Serving God's passion by making Him famous is our sustenance and life. Is there anything better than assisting the gospel to go where it has not gone? That is life-giving to both giver and receiver. Yet, glory and credit for life must only go to God. No sender and no goer can take credit for the miraculous movements of life among unreached peoples.

The Levites remind us that we are all priests. We who have been redeemed have the unparalleled privilege of representing Albanian Macedonians to God, and God to Albanian Macedonians.

PRAYER FOCUS: *Albanian, Macedonian of Macedonia (Evangelical: 0.00%)*

FEBRUARY 15: A CAUTIONARY TALE

TODAY'S READING: LEVITICUS 8–10

"To know the will of God, we need an open Bible and open map."

WILLIAM CAREY

The Urim (light) and Thumim (completeness) were the two parts of the lot connected to the high priest's garments. A lot was something that helped determine God's leading, and with only two components, ostensibly one was "yes" and the other "no." How marvelous that God's "yes" brings light and His "no" makes us complete. Just as viable is the counter reality. Perhaps when God says no, we see better (light) and when He says yes, we are fulfilled (complete). Either way, both the "yes" and "no" of God are beautiful.

When it comes to God's purposes in the world, we are to take our questions to His presence. We do that individually (Lev. 8:35) and we do that corporately (9:5). When we allow God to choose for us, when we submit to His choices and like it, then the glory falls. God's choices all through the Bible center on His passionate desire to redeem to Himself members of every people group on earth. It is in this course of action (His and ours) that He receives glory. It is why He ordains and equips priests. Aaron, ordained and equipped, lifted his hand to bless the people. Fidelity to the big picture makes it impossible to read about blessing without reference to God, Abraham, and the nations of the world, and it is impossible to participate in blessing all peoples of the world without both the glory of Jehovah appearing and the fire of Jehovah falling. What can we do but shout and fall on our face!

Leviticus, however, includes a cautionary tale for those who light their fire from sources other than where Jehovah concentrates His. Nadab and Abihu offered profane fire and were roasted for their impertinence. Jehovah explained their fate simply: "By those who come near Me I must be regarded as holy; and before all the people I must be glorified" (10:3). It's stunning. If God's priestly sons do not glorify Him before all the people, then He is dishonored and disregarded. It's sobering. If we devolve worship (in its fullest expression is every tongue and tribe praising Jesus together) into a ritualistic, ethnocentric, and self-serving exercise that does not glorify the God of all peoples before all peoples, then we, too, will burn, no matter from what family we hail.

Today's reading ends with stringent missional intolerance. Aaron's sons did not glorify God before all people. God's anger consumed them. Aaron was not allowed to grieve. If our lives and worship, our ministries and churches, our prayers and purses do not glorify God before all peoples, then God will burn them down or up, and He won't allow us to grieve them. God sends light and completeness to those who truly worship by glorifying Him among all peoples, and He sends the fire of death to those who don't.

PRAYER FOCUS: *Yao, Muslim of Malawi (Evangelical: 0.50%)*

FEBRUARY 16: SAFE FROM THE SWAMP
TODAY'S READING: LEVITICUS 11–12

As God transitioned and prepared His people to be a light to all nations, they would travel through territory where some foods would be advantageous and some abominable. There is speculation on what made some foods unclean, but no definitive answers. One suggestion is that the unclean foods were identified by improper or irregular locomotion. A more likely scenario is that a large group of travelers needed to eat what would keep the travelers healthy. The real point is linked to the key missionary skill of distinguishing between principle and application. The principle is that we stay pure, holy, and healthy so that we might vigorously pursue the mission aims of God. The application may vary (i.e., our diet or external forms and approaches), but God gets to call what is holy, holy. And God calls missions holy, so we do what we must to stay wholly on point.

God also reminds us that He is holy *and thus* we should be holy (v. 44). God did not bring us out of bondage so that we defile ourselves in new contexts. God brought His people out of a double bondage: physical slavery and spiritual idolatry. To be taken out of Egypt is to be taken out of the influence of false religion. When we come to Christ, we leave all former, vile religions. We can't stay in old religions and be loyal to Jehovah; we can't remain a part of what defiles us.

Historically, circumcision reinforced the necessity of physically and noticeably identifying with Jehovah. Yes, the indicator was discreet, but it was permanent and even initially costly. The modesty of location in circumcision was never intended to imply that Jehovah could be followed secretly or in isolation. Just the opposite. To follow Jesus must be done in company, publicly and at cost, by abandoning all false and former religion. The great God of glory who allowed His Son to shamefully writhe in naked pain on the cross does not allow secret believers. One can't be a secret believer and be a proclaimer, witness, soul winner, or missionary. Secret faith is selfish, corrupted faith. Public faith is refined, corrected, and enhanced by solidarity with others. Yes, discretion is called for, and modesty and humility only adorn our beliefs, but we are to be public witnesses, heralds, announcers, and representatives of the King. We are to be marked by Him, noticeably different than the false religions we were saved out of.

Jehovah is neither capricious nor purposeless in His boundaries. He wants us near enough to the lost that He can use us to save lives and far enough from evil to avoid being sullied or poisoned. Think of the lost from all peoples of the world, sinking in the toxic swamp of false religion. In that swamp is every kind of filth and predator. The mission heart of God wants us close enough to that swamp to reach in and grab a beloved friend or family member and far enough away on solid ground, safe from slipping into that evil again. God's Leviticus boundaries are missionary in this very sense.

PRAYER FOCUS: *Malay of Malaysia (Evangelical: 0.52%)*

FEBRUARY 17: GOD'S MATCHMAKERS

TODAY'S READING: LEVITICUS 13-15

Leviticus 13 and 14 address leprosy on people, clothes, and houses. Leprous clothes probably referred to infestation and leprous houses probably to decay formed by fungus, mildew, mold, or dry rot. Regardless, the whole reason for the laws of leprosy and bodily discharge is explained in Leviticus 15:31: "Thus you shall separate the children of Israel from their uncleanness, lest they die in their uncleanness when they defile My tabernacle that is among them." God's great missionary heart is to dwell with those He created and loved. God condescends to live with men and He is determined to live joyfully with men and women of all races and peoples. God by nature cannot condescend by compromising His holiness, and He knows His holiness would consume us, so He makes provision for our filth by eradicating it.

All the imagery of Leviticus is centered around the spiritual concept of priesthood. Leviticus 13 and 14 dwell more on the priest than on the leprosy. In these two chapters the words "leper," "leprous," and "leprosy" are mentioned thirty-four times, which is significant, but that pales compared to the eighty-three times "priest" is referenced. Leviticus is the story of a royal priesthood, a people who are to represent God to all the unreached peoples of the world and to advocate to God the desperate leprosy of those bound in sin and the evil of false religions. The function of both the Levites for Israel and the church today is as representative of Jesus our great High Priest.

John Owen, the Puritan chaplain to Oliver Cromwell, recounted the wonder of our High Priest not just being a mediator, but a husband: "Christ gives himself freely to us to be our Christ, our beloved, to fulfill all the purposes of his love, mercy, grace, and glory.... The Lord Jesus Christ, then, was set up and prepared to be a husband to his saints, his church. He undertook the work of Mediator for which he was especially filled with the Spirit. As Mediator he purchased for his people grace and glory. Now he offers himself to them in the promises of the gospel, making himself desirable to them.... And when they agree to receive him, which is all he requires or expects from them, he enters into a marriage contract to be theirs forever. On the saints part, all that is required is their free, willing agreement to receive, embrace and submit to the Lord Jesus as Husband, Lord and Savior, to abide with him, subject their souls to him to be ruled by him forever."

How assuring to be married to our High Priest! How comforting to know that the one who makes mediation for us is our husband! It is this covenantal love that the "unwed" Maldivian is dying to know. As Jehovah's priests today, we are to love unreached peoples in marriage covenant commitment. We are to arrange marriages between the nations and the great Lover of their souls who also happens to be their faithful and compassionate High Priest. Industrious matchmakers in the Maldives are long overdue.

PRAYER FOCUS: *Maldivian, Malki of Maldives (Evangelical: 0.00%)*

FEBRUARY 18: WE MUST PURSUE PURITY

TODAY'S READING: LEVITICUS 16–18

The Day of Atonement was the most important day of the whole year. Jehovah instructed Moses that the high priest should not come at just any time into the holy of holies; he should come but once a year only. This "once a year only" was indicative of the "fullness of time" when global atonement would be made for all peoples. It is also indicative that in this most critical passage on atonement, God takes pains to mention four times (Lev. 16:29; 17:8; 10, 12) that all are invited, even strangers. The God of all the nations makes it clear from beginning to end that all peoples are part of His atoning plan.

Scriptural images of atonement include Socinian (atonement as example), moral influence (atonement as love), governmental (atonement as justice), ransom (atonement as victory), and satisfaction (atonement as propitiation)—all have valid aspects. The heart of atonement, however, is expressed in this passage—the one day of the year where everything stopped and all Jehovah's people focused singularly on God's wrath being appeased through penal substitution. Because the penalty for sin was death and no man or woman could bear the penalty, Jehovah transferred the guilt onto the scapegoats—one was sacrificed on the altar and the other released into the wilderness. In this action we see both propitiation (the slain goat appeased the holy wrath of Jehovah) and removal (the released goat carried the sins far away).

Smack in the middle of the wonder of atonement, Jehovah not only insists on reminding us that the provision is for all peoples, but also that His people cannot be like all peoples. No more sacrifices should be offered to "goat idols" (se'irim). The Israelites were prohibited from sacrificing to these goat idols, these demonic/devilish evils. The people of God were not allowed to imitate the idolatry of Egypt or Canaan or of any nation where they would be commissioned. The people of God were called out from the nations and commissioned into the nations to be unlike the nations.

It is not coincidental that on the heels of atonement being provided for all peoples comes the stringent warning against sexual sin, so prevalent among all peoples. Leviticus 18 warns against any sexual perversion including homosexuality and abortion. God calls these practices perverse and warns that they defile the land to the degree that the land itself will eventually vomit out the practitioners. God's missionary people are to be holy and sexually pure. God will not countenance sexual sin among missionaries. God will not listen to missionary prayers from perverted intercessors. God will not bless missionary dollars from unclean hands and hearts. God's missionary people live in an age that worships the goat-idols, that bows before the demons of sensuality. There must be nothing of that practice or spirit about us, not if we are to represent Jehovah to the nations. If God's missionary people are involved in anything sexually unholy, He will vomit us out of His missionary team. We cannot with God's favor communicate atoning truths if we do not live them daily.

PRAYER FOCUS: *Bambara of Mali (Evangelical: 1.10%)*

FEBRUARY 19: UTTERLY UNIQUE, NOTICEABLY DISTINCT

TODAY'S READING: LEVITICUS 19–22

"To belong to Jesus is to embrace the nations with him."

JOHN PIPER

Leviticus 19 begins with God telling Moses to tell the people that they should "be holy, for I the LORD your God am holy" (v. 2). God then proceeded to lay out moral and ceremonial*laws, all based on His character. Over and over again God stated the reason for the rule as being: "I am the Lord." We do what we do to look like Jehovah. "YHWH is not simply one of the gods of the nations, and not even like them…. For Israel to be holy then meant that they were to be a distinctive community among the nations…. Or to be more precise, Israel was to be YHWH-like, rather than like the nations. They were to do as YHWH does, not as the nations do. Israel was to respond to their redemption by reflecting their redeemer. In doing so they would not only prove their own distinctiveness from the nations but also make visible YHWH's difference from the gods of the nations. And that, as we remind ourselves so often, was their very reason for existence, their mission. If the people of Israel were to be God's priesthood in the midst of the nations, then they had to be different from the nations."

Everything about the Bible centers on God's plan to love and be glorified by all the nations. Jehovah repeatedly includes the stranger in His requirements and restrictions, for God's gospel has ever been universal. What appears to be boring text on rules and regulations is in reality an exhilarating call to live in such a *distinctive* way that all peoples of the world become consumed with a holy jealousy for the Jehovah we reflect. What can be twisted into legalism is actually a law of fruitfulness. If we will live, think, talk, and act like Jehovah, the result will be that all peoples of the earth will want that light and life they see in us—*because it's different.*

Israel in Leviticus "was called to embody and demonstrate all this uniqueness in practical, ethical distinctiveness from all other nations (18:1–5). In all these aspects the relationship between God and the historical Israel of the Old Testament period was unprecedented (he had done nothing like this before) and unparalleled (he had done nothing like this anywhere else)." God did through Israel what He now does and wants to increasingly do through the church. In unprecedented and unparalleled ways, God wants us to live holy lives right in the middle of unholy peoples and unholy places. If we don't live holy lives before and among the nations, then Jehovah reserves the right to forcibly eject us (20:22). Let's display God's holy goodness and glory. Let's live utterly uniquely among the nations. Let's live noticeably distinct lives totally *other* than the wasted, selfish, lewd life offered globally. Let's stop trying to look like the nations; let's look different. Let's live holy. Mauritania is a good place to start.

PRAYER FOCUS: *Moor of Mauritania (Evangelical: 0.10%)*

Mark Levitt and John Parsons posit that Leviticus 23 is the single chapter of the entire *Tanakh* (Old Testament) that sums up everything. They believe that God's eternal plan—from chaos to eternity—is ingenuously revealed through the nature and timing of these feasts of the Lord.

- **Passover (*Pesach*):** God saves us from God for God. Those under the blood of the lamb are saved from the destroying wrath of God.

- **Unleavened Bread (*Chag HaMotzi*):** Unleavened bread eaten on the go symbolizes a holy life, fueled by abiding communion with Jesus, the bread of life.

- **First Fruits (*Reshit Katzir*):** A celebration of resurrection, God bringing the spring harvest after winter's death, a looking forward to the resurrection at the end of time.

- **Pentecost (*Shavu'ot*):** A celebration of the summer harvest, the feast required two loaves baked with leaven, a symbol of Gentile union with Jew in the family of God.

All these feasts have been fulfilled in Jesus, but the feast of Trumpets, Atonement, and Tabernacles are pending.

- **Trumpets (*Yom Teru'ah*):** Trumpets declared liberty and victory. Historically, the high priest blew the trumpet, and the people would stop harvesting and come to worship. So shall it be for us. We will harvest among all peoples until the great High Priest blows the trumpet and calls us all home to worship around the throne.

- **Atonement (*Yom Kippur*):** Contextually a day to afflict one's soul, we of course cannot atone by works or wailing for anything we've done. We can only accept grace. A day is coming—the great and terrible day of the Lord—when judgment and affliction will fall.

- **Tabernacles (*Sukkot*):** Historically a remembrance that God provided a home in the wilderness, this feast reminds us we are pilgrims and heaven is our ultimate home.

Repeatedly throughout Leviticus 23, God pointed out that these feasts were not for one particular tribe or one generation; that harvest was to include the strangers among them; and that Israel was brought out of the bondage of one nation to become a holy nation so that all nations might enjoy the feasts of the Lord.

We perch now between the times. The Messiah of *all* peoples has come, died, resurrected, and given us His Spirit so we can harvest from all nations. We plunge into the harvest field, ears waiting for the trumpet, knees knocking because of what that means for the unrepentant, and hearts longing for our heavenly home and eternal feast. It is incumbent upon us that someone tells the unreached of Mayotte that they are invited, too.

PRAYER FOCUS: *Comorian, Maore of Mayotte (Evangelical: 0.12%)*

FEBRUARY 21: DON'T PLAY FAVORITES

TODAY'S READING: LEVITICUS 24–25

Bi-racial marriage is not problematic for God. After all, Moses married both a Saudi and a Sudanese. What is problematic is anyone of any race disrespecting the God of all races and His variegated children. Lest there be any doubt that Jehovah's heart, purposes, and statutes are global, for all peoples, He said: "You shall have the same law for the stranger and for one from your own country; for I am the LORD your God" (Lev. 24:22). Jehovah is no tribal deity with a favorite people: He chose a weak, insignificant child as an example of His grace to all His children. He chose a foolish, recalcitrant runt as an example of His strength to all His beloved. Jehovah chose Israel to bless all nations, but this does not mean they have special laws or allowances. The perfect Parent loves all His kids.

The laws revealed to Moses are said by some to copy the Code of Hammurabi. Hammurabi was a Babylonian king (1792–1750 BC) whose code stated that if a citizen injured another citizen's eye or tooth, "his eye shall be destroyed" or "his tooth shall be knocked out." As all truth is God's truth, I find it highly unlikely that God plagiarized Hammurabi for any of the good things humanity has implemented. More likely, from Adam on down, God injected and leased His wisdom to those with ears to hear. Jehovah loves to share truth with all His children; what He doesn't like is when *we* play favorites with truth or law.

Laws that required eyes for eyes and ears for ears seem primitive, barbaric, and retaliatory. In historical context the strong and powerful over-punished criminal offenders. Old Testament law was a corrective to the corrector, a loving God setting boundaries for punishments. Jesus then took it a step further—not only should we keep our mean streak in check, we should develop our compassion. Any laws or systems that unfairly persecute and punish a subsector of society or a race different than the majority power holders are anathema to God. The compassionate heart of God for all peoples and demographics is repeated in the laws of Jubilee, Sabbath, property redemption, lending, and service. The Jubilee laws were to protect the nation against a few families or sectors becoming ridiculously wealthy and corrupt, essentially enslaving the poor. Lord Acton's principle about "power corrupting" has ever been true, and Jehovah is not a fan of corruption, nor of power concentrated in the hands of a few.

What is true for citizens is true for cities, states, nations, and churches. Blessing is given to be given, not to be hoarded. Wealth is given to be disbursed, not to enshrine the possessor in power. When churches give to missions, to the spread of the gospel to peoples on earth that have never heard of the spiritual wealth found in Jesus, those churches are blessed. When churches (or families, societies, or nations) send no gospel relief to the nations or spend disproportionately and indulgently on themselves, they violate God's laws and will soon face His justice.

PRAYER FOCUS: *Mongol, Khalka of Mongolia (Evangelical: 1.90%)*

FEBRUARY 22: CHOOSE TO THRIVE

TODAY'S READING: LEVITICUS 26-27

"Is not the commission of our Lord still binding upon us?
Can we not do more than now we are doing?"

WILLIAM CAREY

The Bible is a missionary book, revealing and reminding us that God is a missionary God. The shocking ease with which we forget that missions is the organizing theme of the Bible should give us compassion for the people of God throughout history. We cannot cast stones at those who held to vital truth longer than we have. Over and again we must march our hearts and understanding to the missionary heart of God as revealed in His Word.

The missionary motif in Leviticus is that because God is holy, He cannot live among the perverse or the unclean. The overall purpose of the sacrificial system was to keep the people in a status that would allow the presence of God among them. If the people became unclean, God would not live with them. If God would not live with them, they would not be blessed. If they would not be blessed the nations would suffer. "Holiness and cleanness were the preconditions of the presence of God. And the **presence of God** was the mark of **Israel's distinctiveness from the nations.** And Israel's distinctiveness from the nations was an essential part of God's mission for them to the world. So we can see that even something so esoterically Israelite as their Levitical, ritual, and sacrificial system reflects the fundamentally missional orientation of Israel as God's holy and priestly people, embodying the presence of God in the midst of the nations."

Lest we forget what God emphasized in Leviticus, the book ends with a thunderclap of missional clarity. At the close of Leviticus, God mentioned His covenant over and again: He will look favorably and make fruitful, multiply and confirm His covenant. He will remember His covenant with Jacob, Isaac, and Abraham. He will remember the covenant of their ancestors whom He brought out of Egypt in the sight of the nations. The language (blessing, fruitful) and motive (the nations might see and likewise be blessed) of covenant is the gist of God's missionary passion. We are His holy people that He might use us for His holy purpose: the redemption of every tribe, people, tongue, and nation.

Jehovah delights to bless us with His presence, to walk and dwell among us, to set us free to fulfill His covenantal promises to all people. The warning is that if we walk counter to God's plans and break covenant by not focusing our lives on blessing all nations, then God will be a terror to us, set His face against us, and walk contrary to us in fury. Interestingly enough, if we don't carry God's blessing to all nations, He finds ways of scattering us there to perish. I don't know about you, but I'd prefer to thrive in Morocco while publishing the gospel rather than perishing there because I didn't give heart, soul, and strength to God's glory among the unreached.

PRAYER FOCUS: *Moroccan, Arabic-Speaking of Morocco (Evangelical: 0.08%)*

FEBRUARY 23: GOD WILL BE GLORIFIED

TODAY'S READING: NUMBERS 1–2

"The evangelization of the world waits not on the readiness of God but on the obedience of Christians."

BILL M. SULLIVAN

Accepting the early date for the Exodus, Israel likely reached the plains of Moab (southern Jordan) around 1406 BC. Canaan needed to be conquered, and conquest demanded armies, and armies demanded organization. A census is an official count of a population, used to assert governmental power, raise taxes, or pull together an army. Jehovah spoke to Moses and told him to take a census to pull together all those able to go to war. War loomed as Canaan must be conquered and kept. Historians tell us that Pharaoh Amenhotep II led two campaigns into Canaan from 1405–1403 BC.

The name for the book of Numbers in the Hebrew Bible is "In the Wilderness." It was in the wilderness that Israel organized to travel and fight. Some of the grumbling introduced in Exodus hit a crescendo in the wilderness and God once again showed that complainers don't inherit the promised land. God's missionary assignment proved harder than anticipated as whiners don't make warriors. God would train and use Israel to bring His judgment on the nations of Canaan, but the process required they learn a lesson. "The lesson Israel had to learn from this signal part of their own history, however, was far from comforting. The fact was that if God could use Israel as the agent of His judgment on wicked nations, he could rapidly apply the same principle in reverse to Israel itself…. YHWH could use Israel as the agent of judgment on other nations; he could equally use other nations as the agent of judgment on Israel."

The Pentateuch drips with missions richness. Numbers as a book includes more priestly instructions, a census or two, laws and regulations, and narrative. These seemingly disjointed components harmonize when we remember the Bible is a missionary book and God is a missionary God. Everything God does in human history drives at His redemptive work that will be efficacious for every people group on earth. God organizes, trains, and equips His people so that we may be agents and warriors for His glory in all the earth. When we align with (giving to, praying for, and going in missions) and organize around (robust sending structures which prioritize church planting among the unreached) His battle plans, He blesses us. When we fearfully (focus first on those at home), selfishly (decry partnership with the wider, global body of Christ), or queasily (recoil from His wrath, judgment, holiness, and power) shrink back from blessing the nations, then God uses the nations to judge us.

God *will* be glorified in the nations. Our choice is whether we participate in that as a vessel of honor or whether God uses us as an example of what not to do. We can be either His ambassador or His exile to the Makonde people of Mozambique. Ambassadors tend to have a broader, more joyous assignment.

PRAYER FOCUS: *Makonde of Mozambique (Evangelical: 0.50%)*

FEBRUARY 24: WE ARE TO BE MOBILE PRIESTS

TODAY'S READING: NUMBERS 3-4

Pastors Rob and Justin have an incredible vision for their church: To send 500 missionaries. We were all in Cairo, standing around the grave of William Borden, the young missionary from a wealthy family who died in Egypt as he was preparing to reach Muslims in China. Right there, our friend Omar challenged Rob to send 500 missionaries, and Rob felt the Holy Spirit awaken that vision within him. A few years later, Rob's church has mobilized over 100 missionaries and continues to steam ahead towards the goal. Recently, I was in another meeting with Rob where he mused out loud: "I wonder if, after we have sent our 500th missionary, we should just shut our doors and send all our people to other churches, because we did our job." We were all a little stunned, and no doubt the Lord will lead and guide at that time, but the very fact that Rob was thinking through his ecclesiology with a missionary lens was invigorating. That's how we're supposed to think through the Bible.

In Numbers 3 and 4 are the organization and duties of the priests, the sons of Levi. Priests had the function of representing God to the people and the people to God; they served as a living reminder that God wants all His people to serve in that role of a mediator to the nations. Israel was to be holy so that the Lord could use her to win the nations to Himself. We can't read any passage in the Bible about priests without thinking of 1 Peter where we're called a holy and royal priesthood (1 Peter 2:5, 9). Peter was writing to followers of Jesus (Jews and Gentiles, v. 10) scattered across Turkey and in persecution. Priests live holy lives so that the Holy One lives among them so that the unholy nations are attracted to His light and life.

Levitical organization in Numbers then brims with missiological challenge and encouragement. The Levites were one tribe of Israel, one tribe of twelve. Would it not be holy and royal if we sent one missionary for every twelve members of each church? Rob, Justin, and their church are not the only ones to be blessed with the joy of sending. The Levites were organized by task: Kohath, Gershon, and Merari were all divisions of Levites with different roles. How beautiful that missionary teams have space (and need!) for different roles. Not all have the gifts of Paul. Every missionary team needs someone good at business, someone fervent in prayer, someone gracious in hospitality. How informative that all the priests were expected to be mobile—all had to take their holiness on the road. The gospel is made to travel.

Myanmar today is full of priests—the wrong kind. May someone reading these words feel a priestly call. May the Spirit rise up within you and may you yield to His passion for Jesus to be glorified among the Burmese, not clothed in Buddhist orange, but clothed in dazzling righteousness and love.

PRAYER FOCUS: *Burmese of Myanmar (Burma) (Evangelical: 0.08%)*

FEBRUARY 25: WHEN WE LIVE HOLY LIVES

TODAY'S READING: NUMBERS 5-6

God's covenantal promise is simple: I will be your God, you will be My people, I will dwell with you, and I will bless you to be a blessing to all the nations. This simple covenant is the baseline for God's relationship with mankind. Every law, commandment, precept, and narrative of the Bible underlines this covenant. God uses all kind of pictures, metaphors, events, people, and teachings to reinforce this essential commitment.

Marriage is a picture of God's missional covenant. God is the husband, and His people are the bride. We are to be faithful to the covenant, under the authority of our Husband, aligned with His passions, contributing to His purpose. If we are unfaithful, we will be cursed, shamed, and judged. When we enter into a covenant with God, He lays out the marriage principles: I will be your Husband, you will be My wife, I will dwell with you, and we will together bless the unreached peoples of earth. And we the bride say, "Amen, so be it" (Num. 5:22). To break any component of the covenant is to commit spiritual adultery. When we, the church of God, do not align all our strength, will, energy, and focus on making disciples of all nations, we are adulterous. Our illicit lovers may be big buildings, fancy programs, slick performances, popular books, catchy worship songs, peppy conferences, or a thousand other gilded ministries, but they are betrayers all the same if we are not faithful to the missionary heart of our Husband.

Numbers 6:8 reveals another picture—the Nazarite who was separate to the Lord all the days of his life. When a Nazarite dedicated himself to wholly serve God's purposes, he agreed to wholly abstain from wine (even grapes, grape juice, and raisins were avoided). Nothing even close to the forbidden was considered. They made the same covenant: You are my holy God, I will be Your holy servant, Your holy presence will dwell with me, and I will be Your holy blessing to all the peoples of earth. Missionaries are today's Nazarites—the men and women of every nation who consecrate themselves to being holy that the God they revere may be made holy globally. In that endeavor they say "no" to good things that God may do great things. The Nazarite spirit also lives on in the generous businessman who says, "My business is holy unto the Lord," wholly given over to use its profits for missions. The Nazarite spirit is strong in our retirees who on their knees pray that the Holy Spirit is poured out among unreached peoples. The Nazarite spirit flows through the church pastors, elders, and deacons who keep their vows by leading their whole congregation to God's passion for His own glory among all peoples of earth.

When we live holy lives, the Lord indeed blesses us, keeps us, and makes His face shine upon us, and He is gracious, smiles upon us, and gives us peace. All those blessings have a reason—that we carry them to Nepal and disburse them to the uttermost parts and peoples of earth.

PRAYER FOCUS: *Chhetri of Nepal (Evangelical: Unknown)*

FEBRUARY 26: A JOYFUL PARADE

TODAY'S READING: NUMBERS 7-9

Numbers 7 looks like a numbing, repetitive procession of priests, each giving the same thing: platters, bowls, pans, bulls, lambs, and goats. The tragedy for many readers of the Bible is that when they lose the metanarrative, they lose the meta-joy. Because the Bible relays the plans and purposes of our missionary God, we must always keep in mind the big picture if we are to enjoy the big thrill.

There is purpose in everything recorded for us—and it's not to put us to sleep. "The list of gifts presented to the Lord is highly formal and ceremonial (Num. 7:12). It resembles Egyptian pictures dating from 2650 BC that show servant after servant presenting trays of offerings to the temple. The ceremonial repetition produces an effect of order and abundance." Priests bringing their offerings to the Lord, one after another, lavishing on Jehovah the best that they have, is a picture of the greatest offering that a royal priesthood can give to the King. One day around the throne, God's people will walk towards it, hand in hand with representatives from the nations: John Paton with former cannibals from the New Hebrides; Hudson Taylor with the Chinese; Adoniram Judson with Burmese; David Livingstone with Africans; and Samuel Zwemer with Arabs. Men and women in joyful parade presenting to Jesus the gift He most treasures—souls. The presenters will be of every race: African missionaries presenting Russians, Arab missionaries presenting Afghani, Indian missionaries to Dubai presenting Emirati, Swedish missionaries presenting Turks, and Latino missionaries presenting Indonesians. Abundant harvest, abundant joy.

Jehovah sets apart a priesthood within a people. This election is precious; it's a microcosm of what God has done and is doing globally. He is setting apart a priesthood from every people for Himself. God looks over the diversity of our world and says of some Somali, "They shall be Mine!" God looks at war-torn Afghanistan and says of some specific Pashtun, "They shall be Mine!" God weeps over Mindanao and declares over radical Muslims there, "They shall be Mine!" God mourns over the darkness of Nepal and assures us that some of those Buddhists, "They shall be Mine!" Of Spanish secularists, Nigerian animists, and American pagans, the Lord thunders: "They shall be Mine!" What comfort to the priestly people of God. He has appointed us to go find, through preaching, those that will be His.

God is relentless in His inclusion, and He won't let us forget the unreached either. Numbers 9 relates the second Passover. Because the Passover was so critical, those that missed it in the first month were permitted to celebrate it the second month, included in that second chance were the strangers dwelling among the Israelites. Another opportunity to be covered by the blood, another opportunity for the strangers to join in, "one ordinance, both for the stranger and the native of the land" (v. 14). And so the pillar and cloud lead us on, native and stranger together, Moroccan Berbers and European Dutch walking hand in hand in their ordered turn.

PRAYER FOCUS: *Berber, Rif of Netherlands (Evangelical: 0.10%)*

TODAY'S READING: NUMBERS 10–11

"'Not called!' did you say? 'Not heard the call,' I think you should say."

WILLIAM BOOTH

"So they started out for the first time" (Num. 10:13). It's fascinating that the very first time the presence of God as connected to the tabernacle moved, Moses invited an Arab from Saudi Arabia along. Moses says to his father-in-law, a Midianite (Midian is present-day Saudi Arabia): "We are setting out for the place which the Lord said, 'I will give it to you.' Come with us, and we will treat you well; for the Lord has promised good things to Israel" (v. 29). How glorious! Jehovah declared He will be Israel's God; Israel covenanted to be His people; Jehovah descended to "tabernacle" with men; together Jehovah and Israel will bless the nations; Jehovah gave the commission to go; and Moses invited a Saudi! Makes you want to do handstands! God's great missionary heart on display. Indeed, "rise up, O Lord! Let your enemies be scattered" (v. 35). Let any who hate this great passion and plan of God flee away.

Intriguingly, right after Moses invited along an Arab, the people complained. This may be incidental, but it's certainly indicative. To invite along the "other" is always uncomfortable. To include other races and traditions in the household of faith always means a ceding of power and preference. Let us not forget that those who complain about the uncomfortable commission of God face His consuming fire. The context centers around difficulty and the deprivation of luxuries (in this case, food), but the wider context cannot be ignored. Sandwiched around the complaint about delicacies was the invitation Moses gave a Saudi to enjoy the good things God promised and the pouring out of the Spirit, including on two people outside the camp. "In an interesting historical note…two elders, Eldad and Medad, prophesied as the Spirit rested upon them 'in the camp' (v. 26) rather than around the Tent of Meeting with the rest of the seventy, where the Spirit had come upon them for that purpose (v. 16.) But Moses refused to rebuke the prophetic manifestation of the two. Instead, seemingly anticipating the great day later prophesied by Joel, Moses said, 'I wish that all the Lord's people were prophets and that the Lord would put His Spirit on them' (11:29). Later this would take place as God's chosen means for accomplishing His mission."

The people complain and face God's wrath in between two "out-of-camp" experiences: Moses inviting a Saudi into the blessings of God and God pouring out His Spirit away from the centered tabernacle. Surely this is didactic, not accidental. God wants the other included. He wants to pour His Spirit out on all flesh. He pours the Spirit out on the guys outside the house, the Gentiles (there were Arabs at Pentecost, too; see Acts 2:11), so that the gospel can go to every people by every people. Saudis, Arabs, and all nations are invited to travel with the glory and blessings of God. How marvelous! How wonderful! And my soul shall ever sing. Now if only I can find some Hausa to sing with me!

PRAYER FOCUS: *Hausa of Niger (Evangelical: 1.60%)*

FEBRUARY 28: GOD OF GENTLE INCLUSION
TODAY'S READING: NUMBERS 12

Moses' first wife was from Saudi Arabia (Midian). In Numbers 12:1, he married a Sudanese woman and it created consternation. We are familiar with the story of Aaron and Miriam's dissension, but we usually fail to connect that dissension to missions resistance. Here is how the text (vv. 1–2, emphasis mine) reads: "Then Miriam and Aaron spoke against Moses because of the Sudanese whom he had married; for he had married a Sudanese woman. **So they said,** 'Has the Lord indeed only spoken through Moses?'"

The objection to Moses being the spokesperson for the mission of God linked directly to his marriage with a Sudanese. What seemed like a family squabble for power was sparked by and rooted in God's prophet including the nations in his nuclear family. In essence Miriam and Aaron said: "Well, Moses can marry a Saudi and Sudanese and be a living example of God's mission. But that's just his perspective and his error! Being mission centered, being focused on the inclusion of all peoples in the plan of God is one way to live and speak, but it is narrow, problematic, and uncomfortable. Besides, God has not only spoken that way; there are other options—our preferred ones that are disconnected from the Sudanese and the Saudi and all the peoples of the earth. You don't have to listen to the God of Moses, the God of Gentile inclusion. We speak against that. We speak for another way of living and viewing the world."

It's worth noting that this attack against Moses resulted in Miriam becoming white with leprosy. God became so irritated with this small, provincial thinking, He was so angry against this racism and rebuttal of His heart for all peoples that he cast Miriam out of the camp. The irony is profound. An angry God punished the racist who rejected the black wife of Moses with white leprosy and banished her from the camp. In effect, when we want to speak against the inclusion of all peoples in the family of God because of our prejudice, when we want to keep them out of the "camp," God gets so irritated that He gives us a taste of what exclusion feels like.

God clearly made Himself known to Moses, and Moses was faithful in all God's house. Surely it was not coincidental that Moses, the law broker, the humblest man alive, the man chosen to lead God's people out of Egypt as a declaration of God's glory to all nations, married a Saudi and a Sudanese. Think of it. This living demonstration that God—in the private life of His most trusted servant—loved and blessed all the people groups of the earth. Surely the siblings' objection to Moses' inclusion of the nations as their reason for dissent was not accidental. God wants us to see that spiritual leaders resisted and resented intimate diversity in the household of faith. Let us be warned. The penalty for non-compliance with the missionary plans, purposes, and prophets of God is to get leprosy and to be thrown from the camp. If we don't welcome the nations into God's house, God will give us a punitive taste of what it feels like to be outcast on the outside looking in.

PRAYER FOCUS: *Fulani, Nigerian of Nigeria (Evangelical: 0.26%)*

FEBRUARY 29: THE EARTH SHALL BE FILLED

TODAY'S READING: NUMBERS 13–14

Before Israel was assigned to conquer Canaan, Canaan was a collection of different city-states. These city-states morphed into Egyptian provinces after 1504–1492 BC when Pharaoh Thutmose I established unstable control in Palestine. These provinces were better organized and defended on the west side of the Jordan, which is probably why the Israelites began their conquest on the eastern bank. Different ethnicities lived in the land and are often in the Bible lumped together as "Canaanites."

Moses gave a command to the spies to determine how the land can be conquered. The spies encounter Nephilim.[1] There is some mystery here, but what is certain is that the land was inhabited by entrenched strongmen that had to be driven out. Ten men trembled; in their quaking they forgot their assignment was not "if," but "how." Jehovah is not asking us to investigate "if" we should send missionaries to North Korea, Saudi Arabia, or Libya—He is asking us to figure out "how." When God made this request, the people cried like babies, preferring to return to slavery over making Jehovah famous among all peoples. First, Miriam and Aaron resisted Gentile inclusion and attacked Moses. Then the people faltered at large when told to glorify Jehovah among all the nations of Canaan's land and complained against Moses. There has ever been too much crying and complaining when God's people are told to magnify Him among all peoples. Our reading in Numbers emphasizes these points:

• We are not asked how difficult missions is. We are not asked to do this work *only if* the opposition is weak and no sinister human/demonic hybrid forces are arranged against us. We are asked to investigate *how* to do missions in difficult places.

• We were designed to overcome. Caleb yelled out: "Let us go up at once and take possession, for we are **well able** to overcome it" (Num. 13:30, emphasis added). In more measured and statesman-like terms, Joshua said: "If the Lord delights in us, then He will bring us into this land.... Only do not rebel against the Lord, nor fear the people of this land, **for they are our bread**" (14:8–10, emphasis added).

• Any worry about being victims and our children suffering is ridiculous. God says that our children will be victors, entering and knowing the land that we despised. If we blame our disobedience on pretending to do the best for our children, our children will one day call us cowards.

• Missions includes prophetic intercession and the understanding that the nations watch everything that God does to His people—both acts of anger and mercy. All that God sends our way—blessings or banes—is a message to the unreached peoples of our time.

Most wonderful of all is the combination of God's mercy and missions. When God's people falter, He mercifully forgives them, yet stays true to His own mandate. This is the message of Numbers and the mandate of the church: the Urdu of Norway shall see and be conquered by the glory of God—as will all the earth.

PRAYER FOCUS: *Urdu of Norway (Evangelical: 0.00%)*

"*To stay here and disobey God—I can't afford to take the consequence. I would rather go and obey God than to stay here and know that I disobeyed.*"

AMANDA BERRY SMITH

MARCH

MARCH 1: OUR CLEAR WORK

TODAY'S READING: NUMBERS 15; PSALM 90

L ost in the slog of the laws of Numbers can be the beauty of sweet sacrifice. Six times in Numbers 15, sacrifices are described as a "sweet aroma." When men and women walked in God's way because they were passionate about His desire to be glorified by all peoples, it was a perfume pleasant to Jehovah. Lost in the slog of the litany of tasks in daily living can be the purpose for which we remain on earth—that Jehovah is known and worshiped by all peoples. When our daily acts of service and sacrifice are linked toward the great passion of God, then even menial things are a pleasing aroma to heaven.

The Bible cannot cease from reminding us that God intends every people group to enjoy Him forever, and it cannot get away from including the nations in the humdrum of daily living. When God gave Moses instructions about sweet aromas, He included the strangers. The nations, too, offered sweet aroma, "just as you do" (Num. 15:14). One law and one custom were for all. One law for the native-born and the stranger. The nations were to enjoy the same privileges and to endure the same punishments as the Israelites, and their daily sacrifices yielded the same sweet aroma to God. It is hard to refrain from weeping when we read in the Bible the constant and insistent delight of our Lord in including all peoples in His family.

God's people were commanded to use tassels as a memory aid for Scriptural truth. These twisted, knotted threads on their clothes reminded the people of God's commands. So must we ever find ways in daily life to remind us not to get lost in routine, but to lift up our eyes to God's great purposes for His glory among all peoples. Maybe it's a screenshot of Matthew 28:18–20 on our cell phone, maybe it's computer screensaver showing a picture of a mosque, temple, or shrine—something that reminds us every day that all our ways must line up with God's commands.

Psalm 90 is a psalm of Moses. We picture him in the wilderness, homeless, on mission for God, exhaling: "Lord, You have been our dwelling place for all generations" (v. 1). We hear him admitting that God's wrath and holiness are terrifying. We agree with the request to be satisfied early with mercy, and we join our hearts to Moses' prayer: "Let Your work appear to Your servants, and Your glory to their children" (v. 16). This psalm is likely written at the same time God reminded Moses: "All the earth shall be filled with the glory of the Lord" (Num. 14:21). Thus, Moses closed his psalm with: "Let the beauty of the Lord our God be upon us, and establish the work of our hands" (Psalm 90:17). The Lord's work is clear—for His glory to cover the earth and include all peoples. Our work is clear—to be glory bearers to the uttermost.

PRAYER FOCUS: *Arab, Omani of Oman (Evangelical: 1.20%)*

MARCH 2: SEEKING INTERCESSORS

TODAY'S READING: NUMBERS 16-17

Aaron got a taste of his own medicine when the same sentiment he expressed against Moses was then leveled against him. Korah, Dathan, Abiram, and 250 leaders rebelled against Moses and Aaron and accused them of taking too much upon themselves. The charge was connected to calling, for the rebels thought they were holy enough to perform the priestly function. It appears the rebels once again lost the big picture, and in so doing rebelled not against Aaron, but against the passions of God. What was the big picture? Jehovah promised to be Israel's God and to live among them. That covenant promise required Israel to be holy so God could dwell in their midst and bless them to be a blessing to all nations of the earth. Holiness had a fixed focus beyond ritual cleansing, for it was intended as the empowerment to bless nations with the glory of God. This is why the Spirit of God is called the Holy Spirit, not so God's people can be quarantined in church buildings or safe little Bible studies, but so we are fit to proclaim God's glory in all the earth.

This misguided power grab of Korah and friends did not end well—the earth swallowed some, fire consumed others, and wrathful plague destroyed the rest. Evidently, God doesn't take it too well when anyone suggests a deviation from His passions. This sobering story has applications for missions: When we forget the mission of God, we tend to misjudge the motive of our leaders (Num. 16:3); when we are dissatisfied with our role in missions, our ambition leads to complaining (vv. 8–11); when we do not have the patience to see God's purposes prevail among the nations, we easily slip into rebellion (vv. 12–14); and rebellion leads to the destroying wrath of God on us, which severely hampers our ability to be intercessors going forward (vv. 32, 35, 46)!

Perhaps the most precious missions takeaway from this story is the reaction of Moses and Aaron. Moses and Aaron responded to the folly of their followers with an interceding heart. And once again God's missionary heart and nature was exposed and highlighted as the center of the narrative: "the God of the spirits of all flesh" (v. 22). This is the center of it all—God loving, redeeming, sanctifying, and blessing *all flesh*. He is the God of *all* peoples, nations, tribes, and tongues. God absolutely loves it when His priests reflect His own heart back to Him. A second time God threatened to consume, and Moses and Aaron again fell on their face and interceded. God is the God of all flesh. God is not willing that any perish. God wants *all* 414 unreached people groups of Pakistan to be saved from the wrath to come. God is looking for men and women, who will not grumble, judge, or seek a title or more noticeable position, but who will fall as intercessors on their faces and weep for those billions still under the looming wrath of God.

PRAYER FOCUS: *Jat (Muslim Traditions) of Pakistan (Evangelical: 0.00%)*

MARCH 3: DEMONSTRATE INTIMACY

TODAY'S READING: NUMBERS 18-20

As Levites, Moses and Aaron were given the priestly honor of representing the purposes of Jehovah and the responsibility of acting out those purposes in Jehovah's manner. They were given the priesthood as "a gift for service" (Num. 18:7). In fulfilling Jehovah's mission, however, their service was never to replace intimacy with Jehovah Himself (v. 20). No part of the Levite tribe was to inherit land. Their inheritance was to be something much more meaningful—the Lord would be their portion and inheritance. Service that took priests away from intimacy with God was a service in which God was not pleased. True then, true now.

Numbers now heads to a conclusion and the drama therein is whether or not the new generation would believe God and believe what their fathers believed. Neither Moses, Aaron, or Miriam (The Big 3) would set foot in the promised land because they did not believe God, they did not hallow Him in the eyes of the children of Israel. In one way that was harsh, but in another way, it made complete, justified sense. The Big 3 dying in the wilderness is only sad when we misunderstand the biblical narrative: It's not about land for a particular people; it's about the glory of God in *all* the lands of earth. What is most important to God concerning His people is whether or not they walk with Him faithfully in the world. He knows that His presence is our great reward.

We can't fall on our faces before the glory of God in private and then misrepresent Him publicly before people. It's not about being busy and successful for Jehovah; it's about being so intimate with Him that others desire that same intimacy. This was why Jehovah was angry with Moses. He did not represent His Lord well, and he misused the spiritual power that his intimacy with God provided. Moses' service moved God away from who He is because Moses was doing in a carnal manner what God wanted. The water still came from the well, and the problem was solved, but it was not solved in a way that glorified Jehovah. Therefore, in winning, there was loss. In a way, God had mercy on Moses by taking service away, for service was not what delighted Moses most—God was.

The peoples of earth are ever being thought of, and we are ever to display how to interact with and obey God. The king of Edom followed all that happened to Israel and knew all that God did to deliver them. What God does in His people, He does as an example for all the nations to see, whether blessing or punishment. The greatest thing we can do as missionaries among the unreached Maranao is to live among them in such a way that it's evident Jesus is our great reward and inheritance—not service or land. The greatest thing we can do as followers of Jesus in our home society is to live in such a way that demonstrates to the watching unsaved that lasting satisfaction is found only in intimacy with God Himself.

PRAYER FOCUS: *Maranao, Lanao of Philippines (Evangelical: 0.23%)*

MARCH 4: THE DONKEY TALKS

TODAY'S READING: NUMBERS 21–22

God's plan for human history as revealed in the Bible is to redeem men and women for Himself from every people group on earth. God enacted this plan by choosing an Iraqi immigrant to bless, promising that through Abraham's seed all the people groups on earth will be blessed. God warned Abraham's descendants that blessing and cursing were indivisibly attached to His plan: To participate in God's plan would be to receive blessings that we bless the nations, and to reject or resist God's plan would be to receive curses for our selfish disobedience. God blesses and curses according to the level we buy into His missions heart.

Balak was confused. He thought Balaam had the power to bless and to curse. An 8th century BC inscription from Jordan confirms that Balaam was a renowned prophet. But the power to bless and to curse is not the proprietary power of prophets, but of Jehovah God. "Though Balaam was a pagan soothsayer (Josh. 13:22), the Lord's self-disclosure to him and the oracles he delivered are remarkable in their insight into God's blessing upon Israel. This is especially significant in the light of the function of the blessing and cursing provisions of the Abrahamic covenant.... Abraham was blessed that he might bless all nations. Had Balaam succeeded in cursing Israel, the nations would not have had the blessing of revelation even then being mediated to them through Israel, nor would they have had the hope of sharing in the blessing promised through the seed of Abraham, the Messiah. So in the attempt to hire Balaam, Balak king of Moab was challenging, albeit unwittingly, the entire promise plan of God."

God will not allow His promise plan to be challenged. God's plan will go forth and God's invitation to all nations and peoples will be proclaimed, even if He must use donkeys to do it. Balaam doubly erred: He was willing to curse God's people (and in effect curse all peoples of the earth), and he was willing to do that for money. This was so perverse to the Lord that He sent an angel to kill him, and it was one donkey talking to another that saved Balaam.

The sobering truth in this power is that God finds perverse any who would work against His plan to bless all nations, especially if selfish gain is part of the package. If we refuse God's missionary call on our life to go and proclaim Him among all nations because we want to make money and live a comfortable life in our home country, we are perverse. If we hinder God's missionary plan by the sin of omitting to sacrificially give to missions, if we give only from our excess, if our houses are built while God's name among unreached places has nowhere to dwell, we are perverse. If we, stubborn as donkeys, refuse to speak up for Jesus among the unreached Arabs of Qatar, we are perverse. And if we *are* speaking up for Jesus among the unreached, we probably shouldn't take much pride in that either. Rather, we should probably just remember that God has spoken through donkeys before.

PRAYER FOCUS: *Arab, Arabic Gulf Spoken of Qatar (Evangelical: 0.08%)*

MARCH 5: IF THE PAGANS CAN ALIGN THEIR WORDS

TODAY'S READING: NUMBERS 23-24

When Balaam refused to curse Israel, he said he cannot curse whom God has not cursed. He also saw a people who lived apart from the nations and mentioned that the dust of Jacob cannot be counted. Balaam's citing of "a people dwelling alone" was a reference to them being a holy people "commissioned to be God's people on behalf of God's earth which is God's." This priestly role, repeatedly referenced in Leviticus and Numbers, is to underline that "Israel as a kingdom of priests is Israel committed to the extension throughout the world of Yahweh's presence." The God of mission will use His missionary people to declare and carry His glory to all peoples of earth. Balaam lost the power struggle with God. Then Balaam, in acknowledging the dust of Jacob, conceded that a missionary God will indeed be glorified by all peoples everywhere. God's purposes cannot be stopped; they must be blessed if we are to stay on the right side of Jehovah. "Balaam's oracle does not quite express the universality of the climax of the Abrahamic covenant, but it certainly is an echo of that text. His refusal to curse Israel may have been under divine constraint, but there was an element of self-preservation in it too. The distinctiveness of Israel's role among the nations is also referred to, as is the expectation of their numerical growth like 'dust'—a clear echo of the part of God's promise to Abraham (Gen. 13:16). And, finally Balaam probably echoes the final line of Genesis 12:3 by wishing to be like Israel…. Balaam's next oracle is even more emphatic in affirming the blessing of God on Israel, which no human sorcery can reverse (Num. 23:18–24), and his third oracle virtually quotes God's words to Abraham (Num. 24:9)."

Even false prophets understand God is a missionary God who blesses His people to be missionary. If pagan prophets can stand and align their words to this overriding passion of God, should not true prophets thunder this message through every medium and faithful preachers teach these precepts in every sermon? "YHWH had promised that Abraham's family would become as numerous as the grains of sandy soil in the land (Gen. 13:16, 28:14); Balaam testifies that this has come about (Num. 23:10). YHWH had promised that people would pray for blessings like Abraham's (Gen. 12:3). Balaam does so. (Num. 23:10)" Let's not abdicate the testimony of missions or the prayer for blessing on the nations to rocks and trees, donkeys and pagan prophets. Let's exercise our privilege and let the Tatar know that blessings in Christ are stored up waiting for them. John Goldingay points out there is one more critical aspect to the unfolding events, writing that "the story needs to transition back from deliverance talk to blessing talk. Israel's story (the world's story) is not ultimately about deliverance but blessing." It's wonderful to be delivered and protected, but God did so for a reason: that all the unreached peoples of earth would be blessed by the heavenly presence of God living among them.

PRAYER FOCUS: *Tatar of Russia (Evangelical: 0.49%)*

MARCH 6: STAND GUARD

TODAY'S READING: NUMBERS 25-27

There are both external and internal threats to God's mission. Unfortunately, the internal attacks often prove as effective as the external. The external threat to God's people and plan was Balaam's curse. God neutralized that attack and even turned it into a blessing. We know from Numbers 31:1–16, however, that Balaam slyly used sexual temptation to do from within what he failed to do from without.

In short order, the Israelites began to "commit harlotry with the women of Moab" (Num. 25:1), bow down to their gods, and arouse the fierce anger of God. "The Israelites who joined in the feast not only ate the sacrifice, but also 'bowed down' to the Moabite gods (25:2). The men had not just gone along with the women for sexual favors and a free meal; rather they had joined the local cult.... For worshipping gods other than Israel's God, the punishment was death (25:4) leaving the corpses of the offenders exposed was a practice used also by the Assyrian armies. It both disgraced the dead and served as a warning to other." So disgusting was this mess of sexual immorality and spiritual idolatry, Moses ordered the offenders to be hung in the sun. The people wept in shame and sorrow. All but one. One Israelite was unrepentant, and in fact, explicitly perverse; so Eleazar ran him and his Moabite partner through with a spear, stopping the plague.

God will always (eventually) bring sexual sin into the light, for sexual sin is an especial threat to the mission of God. God wants to dwell with His people, and His covenant requires a holy people. When sexual sins are not dealt with violently (quickly, openly, decisively, severely), they tend to spread. When sexual sin spreads, God will not dwell with or bless His people. When God does not bless His people, the nations become disadvantaged. Sexual sin in God's people, in His church, has a domino effect that negatively affects missions. And God actively attacks all that adversely affects missions, whether that enemy is a seductive prophet or a sensual priest.

God is so grieved when women are seen as objects rather than as equal partners in His great redemption plan. Not a man who resisted God's plan to possess Canaan remained, but those men had daughters. They appealed to Moses to be given a possession with their brothers. Moses consulted God and was reminded that the Lord is God of the spirits of all flesh and He wants all men and women to have a part in His plan. Some of the best missionaries in history have been women; some of the best missionaries today are women. God seeks men and women marked with His Spirit. He wants them to live in purity. He wants them to demonstrate to the men and women of Saudi Arabia that women are not objects, but they are cherished as equal partners in the great plan of God. Let all men and women stand guard that God's mission does not survive external curses only to be felled by internal perversity.

PRAYER FOCUS: *Arab, Saudi, Najdi of Saudi Arabia (Evangelical: 0.12%)*

"Love is the root of missions; sacrifice is the fruit of missions."

RODERICK DAVIS

As we read through Numbers, "it is not an outlandish idea to think that the Lord was simultaneously extending the offer of salvation to others during the Old Testament in addition to Israel." A loving God wants to dwell with His holy people that they may be a channel of His presence to all peoples of the earth. All peoples satisfied in Christ is the endgame and it began from the first verses of the Bible. Therefore, when we read about sacrifices, we look past ritual worship and the cleansing from sin to the purpose of that holiness. The feasts and sacrifices of the Old Testament were all aimed at creating, maintaining, and enlarging the intimacy between God and His people that all peoples may likewise be blessed. A metanarrative understanding of missions then makes a reading of daily sacrifices come alive. What God ordained regarding the daily sacrifices on Mount Sinai for a sweet aroma foreshadowed the great offering of men and women redeemed that we can bring to Jesus.

Is there a more pleasing daily aroma wafting up to the throne than the daily coming to Jesus of men and women around the globe, incense from every nation and every people? How pleasant that aroma must be when it ascends from a resistant people like the Wolof of Senegal. Rare aromas can be especially delightful. We no longer offer lambs and grains upon physical altars, we now offer sacrifices of praise. How pleasant those praises when they spring forth in the tongues of unreached peoples.

Leith Anderson speaks of our longing to have witnessed the day of Pentecost, a day when 3,000 people from many different nations of the world were saved, nations that today offer pitifully little praise. We wonder where that glorious Spirit outpouring is today. Leith points out that *daily* in our time more than 3,000 people are saved. As you read these words right now, someone is being redeemed and the angels praise the Savior. By the time this day is done, 3,000 people from around the world—maybe even from the Wolof—will have come to Jesus. When we get to heaven, Leith posits, it may not be us running up to Peter to ask what the day of Pentecost was like. Peter may run up to us and ask, "What was it like to live in the last days? What was it like when the sacrifices of God's people yielded a Pentecost-like harvest every single day? What was it like for the Spirit to be poured out on all flesh and to be surrounded by the ascending aroma that so gladdened the heart of God?"

There are Old Testament sacrifices we do not make today, and the daily pleasing aroma of souls being saved will likewise come to an end. Missions is a thing of earth; it will not exist in heaven. But what a joy that we can send this sweet perfume up daily. Lord, may a family from the Wolof that turns to You today be our global sacrifice and pleasing aroma to You.

PRAYER FOCUS: *Wolof of Senegal (Evangelical: 0.00%)*

MARCH 8: WE ARE THE CHURCH MILITANT
TODAY'S READING: NUMBERS 31–32

It's interesting that Jehovah described Moses' death as being "gathered to his people" (Num. 31:2). Moses' tribe was the "church at rest"—the redeemed who preceded him to his heavenly home. Those of us still living as pilgrims, strangers, and aliens here on earth are not yet with "our people." Let not the prejudices of earth make us forget to what people we permanently belong: "We're the people of God, called by His name, called from the dark, and delivered from shame. One holy race, saints everyone because of the blood of Christ, Jesus the Son."

We who yet live and follow Jesus are called the church militant. We still war for nations, just not with physical weapons. Longstanding abuse of military power makes us shy away from some of the great hymns of a militant church, hymns we should sing again with vigor: "Stand up, stand up for Jesus! The trumpet-call obey; forth to the mighty conflict in this His glorious day! Ye that are His now serve Him against unnumbered foes; let courage rise with danger and strength to strength oppose."

In Numbers, physical nations were conquered as a sign that the one, true, holy God would reign in all the earth. The conquest and capture of Midianites was a two-fold demonstration and prophecy: God *will* be glorified in all the earth, and He *will* indeed capture the hearts of men and women from every nation. That capture will be complete; men and women must come into union with God on His terms. We are to be a multi-cultural people, but we are also to have united hearts that fear God's name (Psalm 86:11). Moses gave instruction that only what can be purified by fire or water is what can be brought into the fraternity of the King. This people (militant and at rest) is our primary family, and it is a multinational family worth fighting for.

Reuben and Gad decided to settle in northern Jordan, and Moses made sure they were not checking out of God's passion, which would arouse God's wrath. God will be glorified in every nation, and men who wholly follow the Lord understand that. Men who do not pursue the glory of God among every nation are called a brood of sinners. It's wartime, and brothers go to war until all of God's people are represented in His kingdom.

It is in context of going to war for the glory of God among all nations that this oft quoted truth was said: "Be sure your sin will find you out" (Num. 32:23). If you do not fight for the glory of Jesus among the nations of the world, you sin, and that sin will be exposed and the wrath of God will judge you. Your lot may be on this side of Jordan or that side, you may be assigned to stay in your home country or to go overseas, but all the brothers must fight for God's glory among the nations, and some of those brothers and sisters must fight in Serbia.

PRAYER FOCUS: *Bosnia of Serbia (Evangelical: 0.03%)*

MARCH 9: GOD'S STRATEGY, OUR STUPIDITY

TODAY'S READING: NUMBERS 33–34

"It is our confidence in the sovereign grace of God that gives us any hope of success in missions."

KEVIN DEYOUNG

Strategic thinking and Spirit empowerment in missions go hand in hand. I, as a Pentecostal missionary, have always been friends and partners with Southern Baptist missionaries. A friend once joked that if all the Pentecostal zeal could be linked with all the Baptist strategy, we might very well be onto something. The history of missions is littered with missionaries doing stupid things and God overcoming them. Yet, if God can use our stupid ideas, think of what He can do with our smart ones. The review at the end of Numbers reminds us that God is orderly and strategic. He did miracles in the wilderness. He parted the Jordan and brought down Jericho's walls. But He also made Moses create a list of all the starting points and campsites and He gave detailed instructions about borders and boundaries.

God gave thorough details (i.e. strategy) about what must be done in order for His name to be glorified. God's people were to drive out, destroy, demolish, dispossess, and dwell. Now I doubt Jehovah is as fond of alliteration as the King James translators were, but He was clear: Whatever is of sin and false worship must go. If we do not drive out all that is ungodly, He will do to us as He thought to do to them. God in this way plays no favorites—all must obey and all must be holy if they are to live under the blessing of the Most High.

Applying these lessons to missions today, the people of God must be completely dedicated to declaring the glory of God among all peoples in God's way and spirit. God must be faithfully and fully represented. Syncretism is not a faithful representation of God—it's one of those stupid ideas for which God has no patience. After the Passover, God brought the children of Israel "out with boldness in the sight of all the Egyptians" (Num. 33:3). This statement is repeated throughout the Pentateuch, for God wants the nations to know who He is and that they are invited to join Him. God brought His people out boldly, for He expects the Passover redeemed of the nations today to also come out boldly. All that is false about other religions must be driven out, destroyed, and demolished. If we are syncretistic, we will first be harassed by lesser powers and ultimately judged by God.

In missions, we must be careful that pseudo-compassion does not lead us to think what is stupid is smart. The nations must boldly come out of their false religions and be displayed as a testimony to other peoples of the glory, power, and wisdom of God. We do the Tamil who have left India to live in Singapore no favors if we encourage them to stay within Hinduism. We set them (and ourselves) as opposed to God. God has boldly brought many peoples out of bondage before. He is looking for volunteers to help Him do so again among the Tamil.

PRAYER FOCUS: *Tamil (Hindu Traditions) of Singapore (Evangelical: 0.80%)*

MARCH 10: AFFIRMATION OF EQUALITY
TODAY'S READING: NUMBERS 35-36

Cities of refuge were protection against vendettas or private revenge and they guaranteed that the community of people (when guided by God) were the only ones with the gathered wisdom to apply the most drastic punishment. In the same way that the Spirit of God in the people of God makes us moveable temples (God sends His Spirit into the world through a multitude of carriers), so, too, in our day are God's people movable cities of refuge. The accuser and destroyer of souls hounds the lost from every people unmercifully, and there is no sanctuary. Who can escape the demons that pass through walls and glide over borders? None but the redeemed, for the fiends of the devil have no authority to penetrate the hearts of the saints. God sends His people out into all the earth as moveable temples (that the unreached might find salvation) and as moveable cities of refuge (that the unreached might find sanctuary).

Whatever your political opinion of affirmative action, it's intriguing that God is intentional about maintaining an environment where diversity can flourish. When we read the end of the Bible, which is the beginning of eternity, we see men and women of every tribe, tongue, people, and nation around the throne. It is clear that the goal of God in history is not a number, but an inclusion. God is not aiming for unanimity of one race or people; He is aiming for the ultimate inclusion of representatives of every race. Every race, culture, people, language, and tribe that God created *will*, by His sovereign power, be represented in heaven.

Pictures of this wonderful and intentional inclusion were given as Numbers concludes. Concern was raised that if ladies married outside their tribe, over time property would be lost to other tribes, with the result that some tribes would become dominant and others fade out. God's solution was to make provision that every tribe's inheritance be preserved, and the means was that women could choose their mates as long as they chose someone from their tribe. The implications that ring across the centuries are empowering: It's an affirmation of the equality of women with men. It's an affirmation that God loves the unique races and cultures. He does not want our differences erased or boiled down to some boring uniformity. And it's an affirmation that every race, people, language, and tribe are wanted in God's heavenly house.

In this sense Numbers ends as the Bible ends: Every tribe with an enduring place in God's land. Every people with an eternal place around God's throne. Let us be diligent to always keep this inclusive passion of God before us. Let's celebrate the tribes. Let's remember that they combine to make one beautiful family of God. Let's live out that unity now on earth as an invitation to that great family reunion above—a union and reunion without end. Will someone please let the Kuranko know they are missed? We don't get to start the party until they join us.

PRAYER FOCUS: *Kuranko of Sierra Leone (Evangelical: 0.00%)*

MARCH 11: WE SEND AND GO AGAIN

TODAY'S READING: DEUTERONOMY 1–2

*"Do not underestimate what God can do when the church is sending
and workers are going to people who need the gospel."*

DAVID PLATT

The book of Deuteronomy is essentially three sermons from Moses. These sermons were a long time coming. The trip from Horeb to Kadesh Barnea was only an 11-day trip that in reality took 14,600 thirsty days (40 years). Joshua, Caleb, and Moses were the only warriors left standing, witnesses to the wrath of God on those who refused His mission. What God did to and through His people He did as a sign of what He would do to and through all the nations of the earth. Moses began his last series of sermons by bringing attention back to how all things began: We are to leave what is familiar and go. We are to fulfil the promise God made to Abraham, Isaac, and Jacob. Israel taking the land is necessary for the physical presence of God among a holy people and is representative that God will love-conquer all peoples of earth. Everything that the Israelites did in conquering nations physically, then, is exemplary to us regarding what Jehovah wants to do now, through us, to all the people groups of earth.

Look, the Lord our God has set the peoples of the world before us. We are to go to them. The same Jehovah that promised to bless those nations through Abraham's seed, Jesus, is with us. We should not fear or be discouraged. Let us send missionaries and overcome our excuses to make Jesus famous in all lands and among all peoples. Some of us won't go to unreached peoples because we are rebellious. Some of us go and complain all along the way because our ideal of what missions would be like gets crushed. Some of us go and don't stay because we became discouraged. And to us, even down through the years, Jehovah speaks through Moses: "Do not be terrified, or afraid…. The Lord your God, who goes before you, He will fight for you…" (vv. 29–30).

It's not an easy thing to be a missionary to the Somali people. The Somali are one of the giants of our day, fiercely resistant to the Lord and His redemption plan. If we don't reach them, our children will rise up and call us cowards and possess Somalia for Jesus. If we try to reach Somalis in our own strength or in ways not blessed by the holy, truthful Spirit of God, He will not be with us. The odds against reaching Somalis are so great that there is no way we can succeed unless God fights for us. And when we fail, when missionaries retire, flee, desert, or die, God says: "Get up and go again. This time, be careful to attack only where I say and to partner well by not meddling in what I assigned to others" (2:2, 4–6, 12). So, we pick up the pieces of broken missionaries and missions, and we send and go again. As we set our faces resolutely to meet God, as He fights to win the hearts of the Somali, we feel Him smile as we join our feeble steps to His grand ones.

PRAYER FOCUS: *Somali of Somalia (Evangelical: 0.00%)*

MARCH 12: ARE WE WILLING?

TODAY'S READING: DEUTERONOMY 3-4

The Lord fights for us as long as we fight for His glory among all nations. As soon as we start fighting for our own glory or against our brothers, we have no guarantee of God's protection. God says in effect, "Enough of that! You will not inherit the land." God's mission is about God, not Moses and not me. The very fact that God denied Moses entry into the land of promise is testimony that God has no favorite son or people. God is the center of the gospel, the mission, and the glory, and He will use all who understand and rejoice in this beauty. God advises us to live in this wisdom in the sight of all the peoples of earth, that they, too, desire the beauty of Jehovah.

Israel's exceptionalism was quite different from the current version of American exceptionalism (i.e., our own national interests first). "It would be quite wrong to construe the affirmations of **Israel's** uniqueness as tantamount to an absence of involvement by YHWH in the affairs of **other** nations. On the contrary, it was part of the bold claim of Israel that YHWH, their God, was the supreme mover on the stage of international history…the claim was that YHWH was in fact the sovereign God of all the earth, ruling the histories and destinies of all nations. And in **that** context of universal involvement with **all nations**, YHWH had a unique relationship **with Israel**." It is the simple Abrahamic covenant, a covenant God will not break. We are blessed with knowing Jehovah in order that we are a blessing to every people on earth.

The "covenantal and missional logic" in chapter 4 runs on grand loop: Israel was summoned to live in wholehearted obedience to God's covenantal law when they took possession of the land (vv. 1-2); failure to do so would lead to the same fate that befell those seduced into idolatry and immorality by the Moabites at Beth Peor (vv. 3-4); covenant loyalty and obedience would constitute a witness to the nations whose interest and questions will revolve around the God they worship and the just laws they live by (vv. 5-8); this witness, however, would be utterly nullified by Israel going after other gods, and so they must be strenuously warned against that through reminders of their spectacular past and warnings of a horrific future if they ignore the word (vv. 32-38); they then would need to demonstrate their acknowledgement of all these things in faithful obedience (vv. 39-40); and therein was their future security as a people, and thereby also was their mission as the people chosen by God for the sake of His mission (v. 40).

Moses' reminder to us is that there is no one like our God. The question, however, goes beyond knowing to sharing: Are we willing to share God's heart for all people groups of earth by going, loving, and dying among the half million Hindi in South Africa who don't know our incomparable Jehovah? Are we willing to risk people going to hell because we did not live holy lives, therefore Jehovah did not live among us, therefore there was nothing exceptional about us to draw the Hindi to Jesus? God forbid.

PRAYER FOCUS: *Hindi of South Africa (Evangelical: 0.60%)*

MARCH 13: DON'T LOSE THE WHY

TODAY'S READING: DEUTERONOMY 5–7

"You can give without loving. But you cannot love without giving."

AMY CARMICHAEL

God made a covenant with Father Abraham to bless all nations, but at Sinai, Moses reminded us all: "The Lord did not make **THIS** covenant with our fathers, but with us, those of us who are here today, all of us who are alive" (Deut. 5:3, emphasis mine). What God expected of Abraham, He expects of us. What God promised Abraham, He promises us, that it might be well with us and our children forever. God wants the wellness of His presence among us that His blessings might extend to all His nations.

My friend Kevin says people lose their way when they lose their why. When Jehovah unveils the greatest commandment, we lose our way, even in love, if we forget why. We are to love the Lord our God with all our heart, so that His holy presence can dwell with us, so that we may experience the fullness of His blessing (*shalom*), so that He might use us to bless all the unreached peoples of the world. We love Him because He has redeemed us to be His agents of redemption. He has disposed of others, so that we can be a holy people, a special treasure above all the peoples of the earth, because He loves us and wants to keep His promise to Abraham to bless all the peoples of the earth.

Historical Israel was special for the same two reasons we are special: They were small and weak, and they were loved. That love has a why. "The election of Israel, therefore, was not tantamount to a rejection of the nations, but explicitly for their ultimate benefit. Election is missional in its purpose. If I might paraphrase John, in a way he probably would have accepted, 'God so loved the world that he chose Israel.'" God so loved the Arab Sudanese Muslim that He saved and blessed us, that we might bless Sudanese Arabs. We bless best by gospel proclamation in the heart language of God's Sudanese Arab sons and daughters, so they can hear that their Father misses them and that He has devised ways to bring them home.

Every time we revisit the Ten Commandments, we should read them through a missional lens. Our morality is based on God's missionary character. The "why" of what we do—why we love, why we obey, why we are ethical, why we are industrious, why we are kind, why we are respectful—every "why" of life is based in the great metanarrative of the Bible, the great missionary heart of God, so that a holy God can live among us, so we can receive and extend His blessings, so that every tribe, tongue, people, and nation may come taste of His sweetness and enjoy Him forever. God loves us, and we love Him, that many Sudanese Arabs might love and be loved with us.

PRAYER FOCUS: *Arab, Sudanese of South Sudan (Evangelical: 0.40%)*

MARCH 14: USE YOUR STRENGTHS OR LOSE THEM

TODAY'S READING: DEUTERONOMY 8–10

God tends to test our memory. He humbles us and leads us through difficulties so that what is unimportant fades and what is critical remains. What is critical to God is that all nations experience His redemptive love. To forget what is most important to God is to forget Him. God intends for the difficulties and advantages of life to drive us towards His missions heart.

Why does God give us power to get wealth? That He might establish the covenant He swore to our fathers. What did He covenant with our fathers? To bless them, to make them a blessing, to bless all the people groups of earth through them. If we forget that, we forget the Lord our God. If we forget that our wealth is for the singular purpose of God's glory among all the nations, He won't ask us to steward it long. If we forget that God wants us to be holy so that He might woo the nations to Himself, it won't be long before we realize that in being like the nations, we lose our distinctive, our blessing, and the presence of Jehovah—in effect, we lose it all. Why does God take wealth away? To remind us that we are to use our wealth to win the nations, not to join them.

Why does God make us strong? That His mighty power in us might win unreached peoples to Him because He is a consuming fire. Why does God make us weak? Why does He set us up against peoples greater and mightier than we are? That His mighty power in us might win the warriors to fight for Him. God makes us wealthy or poor, weak or strong, wise or foolish, healthy or sick so that "He may fulfill the word which the LORD swore to your fathers, to Abraham, Isaac, and Jacob" (Deut. 9:5). It is all about the God of missions. God chose our gender, personality, race, and socio-economic status for one purpose: His glory among all nations. God did not choose us because of any worth on our part; we like Israel have no inherent goodness that makes us useful. "Deuteronomy 9 makes the surprising case that Israel has no legitimate claim to the land at all. She has no greater righteousness than the nations. Indeed, the chapter stresses that if anybody deserved to be destroyed, it was Israel." Bluntly, we use our strengths for Jehovah's fame among the nations or He removes His blessing on them. Wonderfully, we give Jehovah our weaknesses and He magnifies Himself through them among all nations.

No matter our status, there is one attribute of Jehovah we can all share: His compassion for the lost. Moses assumed a role initiated by Abraham and completed by Christ: a priest and prophet who prays. Prayer needs no skill, visa, education, or natural strength. We can pray from prison, our sick bed, and hospice or heaven. When we intercede for the redemption of God for the Moroccan immigrants in Spain, the Father who listened to Moses will surely listen to us for the saving of lives.

PRAYER FOCUS: *Moroccan, Arabic Speaking of Spain (Evangelical: 0.05%)*

MARCH 15: BIGGER AMBITIONS THAN A BACKYARD GARDEN

TODAY'S READING: DEUTERONOMY 11–13

"Tell the students to give up their small ambitions and come eastward to preach the gospel of Christ."

FRANCIS XAVIER

The Lord has so much more for His people than to just live, work to provide for families, in order to raise godly children, so that *they* can live, work to provide for their families, in order to raise godly grandchildren, so that *they* can live, work, provide, raise godly great-grandchildren and so on until Jesus comes. What kind of small-minded and numbing cycle is that? Yet, it is the ambition of so many of God's own. God has bigger ambitions for us. God wants us to live our lives out for His glory in such a way that will impact the peoples of earth.

In Deuteronomy, God told His people that He was taking them to a different reality. He was taking them to a land where the harvest would be so much bigger than a little vegetable garden watered "by foot" (Deut. 11:10). Greg Beggs once painted the picture of a little humble Israelite slave, just back from work on Pharaoh's buildings, wearily standing on a tiny plot framed by an irrigation channel of simple earth. With his foot, the farmer squiggles a little path through the soft dirt mound for the creeping water to enter another tiny patch of tomatoes. It's not bad to block and open a little channel with your foot for vegetables, but God has a much grander vision. God took that slave people and said, "I am going to plunk you down as an example in the center of the great civilizations of the day. Though you are weak and feeble tomato farmers pushing soil around with your feet, I am going to give you a land and a platform that will yield bountiful harvest. I will bless you and increase you so that all the nations of the world sit up and notice, so that they will see what you have and desire it, so that they will realize what you have is the blessing and favor of God Most High!" God has a much grander vision for us than just farming the fruit of our little family generation after generation, beautiful as it is for a family lineage to be redeemed. God's vision for our farming is that our harvest will include the nations.

Moses instructed his children that if they obeyed God's commands, it would go well for them and their children. God's consistent command from the garden to this generation has been to go forth and multiply. God never tires of calling His children to higher ambitions, to link our vision to His, a vision that sees a harvest from every tribe, tongue, people, and nation. The greatest gift we can give our children is not a comfortable life. The greatest inheritance is to give our children their heavenly Father's missionary heart. God will be much more glorified if you raise your progeny to fluently proclaim Christ in the Tamil tongue among the Sri Lankan Moor Muslim people than if you teach them to live an indulgent, visionless, backyard garden kind of life.

PRAYER FOCUS: *Sri Lanka Moor of Sri Lanka (Evangelical: 0.00%)*

MARCH 16: NEVER LOSE THE WHY

TODAY'S READING: DEUTERONOMY 14–16

Why do the children of God rejoice at funerals and have no fear of death? Because we know God chose us to be with Him, and whoever was sad about going home? Moses reminds us that we are God's movable treasures, His jewels that He wants to carry around and display. Beauty does no good when it's sequestered, so God unveils His beautified children as an invitation to all the peoples of the earth: *Come and be made beautiful, too!*

Why do the people of God eat healthy and refuse what undermines physical strength? Because we know our holy God wants to dwell among us, so we must be holy—whole in body, mind, and spirit. When God dwells among us, there are enough resources to wholly meet the needs of the whole earth. When we are healthy and whole, God is extending an invitation through us to a watching world: *Come and be made whole, too!*

Why do the families of God live generously, respect the Lord by tithing, and provide liberally for all we employ? Why do we take care of immigrants from the unreached nations of the world alongside the poor and bereaved of our own communities? Because when we live generously, both physically and spiritually, God blesses us with more, so that we can give more. God wants His children to have the capacity to be a physical and spiritual blessing to the unreached peoples of the world, like the Saramaccan, an unreached animist people in Suriname. When the nations of the world see the generosity with which our heavenly Father meets our needs, God is extending an invitation to the Saramaccan: *Come and be taken care of, too!*

Why do the people of God take time every year to remember what God has done? Why do we often stop to remember that God delivers us from sin, that God harvests worshippers out of every nation, and that God came down to live among us that we might eternally live with Him? Because God wants the 3.15 billion unreached peoples of the world to know that they are redeemable, that no tribe or people is excluded, and that the pain of this life is temporary. We have a perfect heavenly home waiting. Through our feasts God calls to the nations of the word: *Come and be rescued, too!*

Why do the communities of God insist on just systems and judges without bias? Because God is impartial, because He loves the whole world, because He will judge the whole world, because justice is a good thing when wielded by Him who is full of grace and truth. Justice on earth is a reminder that the great day of judgment is soon to be upon us and that those who have made peace with the court of heaven can rush towards that court with joy. Justice through God's people to God's people for God's people is an invitation to all nations: *Come and be acquitted, too!*

Everything God does in His people on this earth has a reason. Let's not lose the why.

PRAYER FOCUS: *Saramaccan of Suriname (Evangelical: 0.80%)*

Missional Moses was preaching away to his people, a people who were both a family and an army. Moses, heir to Abraham, had not forgotten the purposes or covenantal promises of Jehovah: We are blessed that all people groups of the world would be blessed. We must live in such a way that Jehovah can abide among us, and when we do so, we receive and pass on Jehovah's blessings to His great delight and our further benefit, and that of the whole world. In his speech, Moses laid out principles of missionary leadership, principles practical for his context and for today's ongoing work among the unreached.

1. Missionary leaders make better decisions when they are responsible for the consequences of those decisions. Witnesses who condemned others to death were to be the first to take up stones and enforce the punishment. There is no room in missions for executives to hide behind their decisions, remote from the field in their ivory palaces. Every missionary leader should be a disciple maker.

2. Missionary leaders are not to abuse their positions by amassing physical, relational, or financial resources for themselves. Subtle is the shift between kingdom good and personal advancement.

3. Missionary leaders are most fruitful when they remember the Lord is their inheritance. When we are consumed with legacy, we focus on programs over the presence of the Lord and end up losing both.

4. Missionary leaders need to guide their colleagues to a robust, non-compromising missiology that makes no room for syncretism. There are abominations that we are not appointed to partner with, adapt, or mimic. The "no" of missionary leadership is as important as the "yes."

5. Missionary leaders need to use their pulpit cautiously. To use position to speak presumptuously will not end well for speaker or listener. But the leader who speaks what God puts in his mouth, however unpopular, will give life.

6. Missionary leaders need to empower second chances for their hardheaded missionaries who make mistakes as well as for their tender-hearted missionaries who get chewed up by the hardheads.

7. Missionary leaders deal quickly and ruthlessly with those who cause disunion. False witness and division are evil, and we should have a zero-tolerance policy for those who do not follow the dictates of Matthew 18 for peacemaking and reconciliation.

8. Missionary leaders need to appoint missionaries who are unafraid to take on overwhelming odds and who are not afraid to die. In leadership, it is better we find the unafraid (of impossibilities or death) and position them for battle. We need missionaries who trust the Lord is with us and fighting for us despite appearances to the contrary.

9. Missionary leaders need to have a sanctified ruthlessness. In order to have a single eye, some things can't be allowed to live or breathe. A tender toughness to recognize spirit-led deaths allows the focus of Spirit-led life and growth.

10. Missionary leaders need to have a sanctified conservationism. Not all the trees of a local culture have to be destroyed.

PRAYER FOCUS: *Beja, Bedawi of Sudan (Evangelical: 0.00%)*

MARCH 18: WE ALL ARE CLOSEST

TODAY'S READING: DEUTERONOMY 21-23

The anguished cry for help of a woman being sexually assaulted is the same word used to describe the anguished cry of the Israelites in bondage in Egypt (Deut. 22:24, 27; Exo. 2:23). It was a cry of pain, terror, and desperation; it is the cry of the unreached peoples of the world. An isolated woman under attack becomes panicked as there is no one nearby to help and rescue seems a forlorn hope. This kind of cry is more a lament than appeal, for deliverance seems impossible. So it is for the unreached. At least the lost in lands filled with Christians have some hope that their cries will be heard, but who will hear the cries of 11 million Arab Syrians?

In ancient Israel, there were specific provisions for a murdered body found in a field. In that communal society, if the one responsible was unknown, the whole nation was guilty and a sacrificial cow had to be offered by the closest community. In essence, the "we don't know who did it" defense will not hold up before the penetrating gaze of the Judge of all nations. Jehovah gave a communal responsibility to preserve life, so when life is lost, we are all responsible. So, who is responsible for the 11 million Arab Syrians who lie dead and dying in our global fields? Who is closest? We all are.

Moses thundered along in his sermon reminding God's people and us that God's ambassadors to the nations must have a collective conscience and responsibility, must take care of women and the vulnerable, must maintain justice, must model obedience and deal quickly with rebellion, must avoid communal defilement by dealing sternly with gross sin, must be proactively kind, for we are our brother's keeper, must save life, and must be pure. All these "musts" would have the beautiful result of a holy God dwelling among a sanctified people. This blessed cohabitation would have the direct intention of modeling a family that all peoples of the world would admire and pursue.

Holiness and missions in the Bible also cohabitate. God relinquishes neither His demand for purity in His family and house *nor* His desire that representatives of all peoples be included. This was why some were excluded and Egyptians were allowed, even up to the third generation. What seemed inconsistent was, in fact, divine balance. God was not capriciously denying the Ammonites and Moabites to favor the Edomites and Egyptians based on race; God was saying that all are welcome, but on His terms. Those that come in and those sent out must all come and go on God's terms. When we are sent out on mission, we must keep ourselves from every wicked thing, for the Lord our God walks in our midst to deliver our enemies to us. Thus, our camp must be holy. Missions is holy, sacred to God. Missions is God's passion and the organizing theme to the Bible. Missions will only go forth when a holy people follow a holy God that calmly insists on only allowing the holy into His assembly. If we love the God of missions, our first steps must be towards the altar that will burn all that is unholy out of us.

PRAYER FOCUS: *Arab, Syrian of Syria (Evangelical: 0.16%)*

MARCH 19: REDEEMED TO BE A REDEMPTION AGENT

TODAY'S READING: DEUTERONOMY 24–27

Deuteronomy is a reminder of the central points of the covenant between God and man. On the cusp of entering the promised land, on the eve of going on into glory, Moses used his last words to remind his people of what was most vital. They were to constantly remember that they were redeemed. They were to constantly remember who redeemed them. They were to constantly remember that the One who redeemed them wanted to use them as His agent of redemption among all peoples of earth.

But you shall remember that you were a slave...redeemed (Deut. 24:18). Missionary zeal flows from a gratefulness that we are under the blood of Jesus, safe from the wrath of God, saved from God by God for God. What we announce to others is alive because we have experienced it. We announce redemption because we can't stop singing the song of the redeemed. We push past barriers and fear because we can't get over what Jesus has done for us.

But you shall remember...the Lord your God redeemed you (v. 18). Jehovah is not like the other gods. Jehovah comes near, tabernacles with man, and talks with man face to face. Jehovah is holy and demands His people be holy. All the laws and guidelines are for a beautiful purpose—that we can be a people that holy Jehovah can walk among, live among, and bless. The rituals, sacrifices, regulations, and rules are not burdensome to us then, for they help us live in community in such a way that Jehovah can live with us.

But you shall remember that you were...in Egypt (v. 18). The story of Jehovah coming down to redeem and live with men was played out before the nations. The people of God were redeemed out of Egypt, and as such they were ever to remember the nations. They needed to remember the stranger when they harvested their fields and their olive trees. When they gathered grapes, they should remember the other ethnicities around them because they were once slaves in Egypt. The connection to Egypt was really a connection to the whole narrative, a remembering of the why, and the why, good or bad, was played out in front of the nations.

The Bible is relentless. It will not let us forget that God is a missionary God and desires us to be a missionary people. We are instructed that when we have finished our normal worship, we are to tell the Lord we have not forgotten the stranger nor His commandments which are ever linked. We can then in confidence know that God will look down from heaven as we ask for the blessing of our fathers. When we remember well, God too remembers His promise of blessing: He will be our God. We will be His holy people. He will live among us, and He will bless us to bless all the unreached peoples of earth. Let's sing the songs of redemption today over us and over the Hakka of Taiwan. Let's sing for the four million who have yet to lift their voices.

PRAYER FOCUS: *Han, Chinese, Hakka of Taiwan (Evangelical: 0.42%)*

MARCH 20: IT'S ALWAYS ABOUT THE NATIONS
TODAY'S READING: DEUTERONOMY 28

Blessings in the Bible are related to the great covenantal promise that God made to Abraham in Genesis 12. Again and again, the Bible returns to this central theme: Father Abraham and all we his children live under this promise, and if we scorn it, this curse. Moses brought this second sermon to an end by reminding us that to walk in obedience to the commands of God is to be overtaken by blessings and to walk in disobedience is to be overtaken by curses, *and* both blessings and curses are connected to the nations.

In Deuteronomy 28:9, we are to be the holy people that Jehovah can live among and bless in order to bless all peoples, and if we do that, "then all the peoples of the earth shall see that you are called by the name of the LORD" (v. 10). Why? To die of envy? No! That they might be redeemed, too. In verse 12, we are told that God will open the treasures of heaven for us, blessing the work of our hand. Why? So we get rich and fat? No! That we can provide for many nations in their time of need. It's always about the nations. The biblical blessing can never be removed from the promise of Abraham. Whatever blessing we receive is a stewardship. God's blessings are to be used to bless all the people groups of earth by giving them opportunity to come live with our Jehovah.

Just as blessings (when we obey Jehovah) affect the nations, so do God's curses (when we disobey Him). If we are not holy, we in effect kick Jehovah out of our neighborhood and having lost Jehovah's presence, we have lost all—not least the power to bless the nations. Now, we become a curse even to them. We become troublesome to all the kingdoms of earth. Not only will we have boils and tumors and be plundered continually, but we will be stricken with madness and blindness. How can we possibly be a blessing to seven million Tajik in that condition?

The consequences of being a perverted, disobedient people are disastrous globally. All power to bless is gone. All hope of redemption, snuffed out. It is one thing to forfeit our own eternity, but how severe will our judgment be when we stand before the King and face the consequences of not being God's agent of blessing to unreached people groups of earth? There is consequence to hoarding God's blessings due to selfish fear or to squandering them due to arrogant disobedience. Moses warned those who despised blessing that their sons and daughters would be given to another people and their eyes would fail with longing for them all day long. The God of blessing asks that we joyfully send our sons and daughters as missionaries to difficult places and unreached peoples. I am convinced of the sober reality that in our age, the nations will have our children one way or another—either as slaves or as missionaries. I'd rather my sons go to Tajikistan carrying the blessing of Father Abraham, not carrying the curses of a father who would not commission them to spend their lives that the unreached might be redeemed.

PRAYER FOCUS: *Tajik of Tajikistan (Evangelical: 0.06%)*

MARCH 21: EXACTLY WHAT IS MOSES SAYING

TODAY'S READING: DEUTERONOMY 29–31

"I have but one candle of life to burn, and I would rather burn it out in a land filled with darkness than in a land flooded with light."

JOHN KEITH FALCONER

Moses began the last sermon of Deuteronomy, the last public address of his life, by summing up what was most crucial. He reminded the Israelites that they have entered into the covenant and oath of God in the very same way that God covenanted and made oath to Abraham and the fathers. The tripartite formula was simple: I will be your God; you will be My holy people; and I will dwell among you to bless you and make you a blessing to all the unreached peoples of earth. This is the message of the Bible, the heartbeat of God, the lens with which we must view the world, history, and the days to come.

Moses indicated the universality of this hermeneutic when he commented that this covenant included those not present on that particular day (Deut. 29:14–15). Reaching backward to Abraham and the patriarchs, reaching forward to the prophets, Christ, and the church, Moses declared that God's will for the world always plays out in the context of all nations. He could not stop talking about the nations because God can't stop thinking about them and He will never stop loving them. God is so committed to being worshiped by every ethnic group that He will make it possible whether or not His people are compliant. If we submit to God's great passion, He blesses us, and His blessing spreads to all the earth. If we rebel against God's great passion, He curses us, scatters us to all the earth, and uses that negative example to get His invitation across. God will include all the nations, all the peoples of earth in His family, and the invitation will go through His people. Whether that invitation is a joyful one or a scary one is up to us. God's goal is to rejoice over us and our obedience, even as He rejoiced over our fathers, but His grand purposes will advance even if we get petulant and disobedient.

God's life in His people was never intended to be an insular circle of blessing. God's love for His people was never intended to be confined to one family or nation. The whole reason God ransomed and redeemed Israel from Egypt was that it be a shining example to the nations, a witness to what God will do for all of them. The whole reason God has redeemed us is that He can use us to take that redemption glory to the uttermost parts of the earth. The greatest danger of wrath from God may not be the sins of commission; it may very well be the disobedience, the non-compliance, the non-sending of missionaries to the Swahili Muslim coastal peoples of East Africa and beyond. Could it be that Moses bluntly says to us over the years, "Life is to participate fully in God's missionary plan to be glorified by all peoples, and death is to do anything lessor, anything otherwise." I think that's exactly what he's saying.

PRAYER FOCUS: *Swahili of Tanzania (Evangelical: 0.80%)*

MARCH 22: THE BLESSING OF JOYFUL PARTICIPATION

TODAY'S READING: DEUTERONOMY 32–34; PSALM 91

"If the Great Commission is true, our plans are not too big; they are too small."

PAT MORLEY

As we end our missiological traverse of the Pentateuch, it's fitting to remember that the story therein frames the metanarrative of the Bible. The Psalms, some scholars say, are divided according to the five books of the law. Some consider Deuteronomy 32 to be "Romans in a nutshell." Evidently, Paul drew deeply from the whole book and ended his magnificent epistle by quoting directly from that chapter. Moses sang and taught one last song in Deuteronomy 32, knowing that we best remember truths when put to music. To punctuate God's passion, Moses' last words in his last song, which is the last point of his last sermon, were these: "Rejoice, O Gentiles with His people.... He will provide atonement for His land and for His people" (v. 43). With one last thunder, Moses laid out the heart of God: God will redeem for Himself people out of every tribe, tongue, people, and nation for their great eternal joy and His great eternal glory. Then Moses gathered himself and died.

God's Old Testament dealings with non-Israelites can seem contradictory. On the one hand, He extended blessings to them; on the other hand, He seemed intent on wiping them out. On the one hand, the nations seemed the recipients of His blessing through His instrument Israel, and on the other hand, the nations were the instrument of God to judge His own. Moses reminded the people of God of the great privilege they had been given—to extend God's fame to all the peoples of earth—*and* he foresaw that they would fail spectacularly. But because God by nature cannot be defeated, Moses prophesied that God would even use our failures for His trans-national glory.

In God's wonderful wisdom, the blessing and cursing, life and death, exile and return, redemption and atonement for Israel is ever linked (past and present) to the same being done for all the nations of the world. The simple and repeated message of the Pentateuch is threefold: (1) God chose Israel to be His covenantal holy priesthood among the nations; (2) this choosing was evidenced by the awesome wonder of God living among His people (which was the singular difference between them and all the peoples of the earth, *and* the source of their power and witness); and (3) the failing of Israel to be holy, to cherish the presence of God, and to bless the nations ironically led to the nations being included, not dooming them to exclusion. These principle understandings shape the rest of the Bible story, even the theology of Jesus and Paul.

May God grant us eyes to see, ears to hear, and wills to obey. May we choose the life and blessing of joyful participation in the great mission of God.

PRAYER FOCUS: *Thai, Central of Thailand (Evangelical: 0.27%)*

MARCH 23: TO CANAAN AND THE UTTERMOST PARTS OF THE EARTH

TODAY'S READING: JOSHUA 1-4

"God's part is to put forth power; our part is to put forth faith."

ANDREW A. BONAR

Joshua presents us with three major principles for a people in covenant with the God of mission.

God's manifest presence accompanies those who advance toward His kingdom according to His will. The Lord Himself appeared to Joshua and promised His presence. God promised to never leave Joshua and to be with him wherever he went. "Under Joshua, God's covenant people advanced boldly to accomplish the mission of their God and King; they moved in assurance that the manifest presence of God was among them. God's promise to Joshua would later provide the basic wording for Jesus' assurance to His disciples when He sent them on His mission": "And lo, I am with you always, even to the end of the age" (Matt. 28:20). The people of God entered Canaan with inferior equipment and untrained men, yet they had the secret sauce superpower—the presence of Almighty God. "Remember in any age, people called by God's purpose can be sure that God's manifest presence will go with them. Those advancing in mission are never alone."

All true victories in the kingdom of God are done with the blessing of the nations in view. Twice Joshua 3 referred to God as "the Lord of all the earth" (vv. 11, 13). Jehovah was (is) not a local deity; He was (is) Jehovah everywhere over all peoples. This truth is repeated in Joshua 4 when the Jordan River was parted, for Jehovah commanded the waters of Egypt and Palestine, and Jehovah was to be glorified in all lands by all peoples. Jehovah had the nations in mind when He led Joshua into Canaan. "Specifically, the conquest of Canaan under Joshua's leadership grew out of the Abrahamic covenant. God, having dealt with all nations, made Abraham the center of His purposes." God wanted a base of operations and He chose Canaan. From there, God promised His presence to all who obey His commission.

It is necessary to allocate kingdom tasks to God's people and make the people accountable for their completion. It is God's nature to entrust human beings, those He created, with specific missions as means toward the accomplishment of His grand design for history. God does this amazingly, knowing how frail and faithless we human messengers can be. We will visit this concept again as much of the book of Joshua is given to the details of allocation. For now, let us marvel, not analyze. God has given to weaklings and human "hobbits" the responsibility of making Him famous among ten million Muslim Tunisians and all the unreached peoples of earth. God entrusted this mission not to angels, not to super-apostles, but to us weaklings. So, if you are weak, you are qualified, and Tunisia awaits.

PRAYER FOCUS: *Arab, Tunisian of Tunisia (Evangelical: 0.00%)*

MARCH 24: ONLY GOD GETS THE GLORY
TODAY'S READING: JOSHUA 5-8

It will be impossible to reach 56 million Turks unless powers greater than ourselves are in the fight. The lesson of Joshua is that God fights for us and there are forces at war we cannot see. When missionaries enter new lands, God went ahead of them and battles have raged in the heavens long before they arrived to "save the day." Joshua got a bit of a wake-up call in this regard. He thought he was the first one in, that he was pretty central to the invasion plan. Seeing a warrior in front of him, Joshua asked the obvious question but received a surprising answer—that God is not for or against us. God is for God, and the question rests on whether or not we fall on our face and take off our shoes before Him.

Missionary service has some treacherous ground. Joshua was not actually in charge because the battle was not actually his, but the Lord's. Joshua and friends didn't even have to fight; they just walked in circles, for the unseen forces did all the heavy lifting. God gave the city over to Joshua, and God was to receive all the credit. The "accursed" things mentioned in the text (Josh. 7:1) were of two varieties: either things destroyed or things dedicated to God. The purpose was the same: to show who the real conquering warrior was. Not Joshua, not you, not me, but God. When the citadel of Islam falls in Turkey, it will be God who did it. We walk in circles a few times, and unseen powers bring the walls down. The treacherous ground, then, was when Achan took something that belonged to God. Achan took some of the accursed (dedicated to God) treasure. When missionaries take credit for what God does, we take of the accursed things, and God will not share His glory with another. For missionaries to glory in their going, for senders to glorify in their giving, for intercessors to glory in their praying is to steal something devoted to God and to bring curses on ourselves. When marshalling to war, we, like Joshua, need to fall on the ground and ask the General of angel armies: "What does my Lord say to His servant" (5:14)? The message for those who have obediently enlisted in the Lord's army focused on reaching unreached peoples with the gospel, is the same now as it was then: Only God gets the glory. Any attempt to steal (or share) in the glory that results will be met with stones and fire and a burial under the curse.

Missionaries are ever in danger of exaggeration, fabrication, and glory shifting. Knowing humility is a virtue, we become adept at the glory share or the secret stash. We don't brazenly take of the accursed thing, we just bury it in our heart. When we do, we find the Lord of hosts is against us in that situation. We lose the battle at Ai and Ankara, and all advance of the kingdom halts until all stolen glory is returned to the King. What is needed today are men and women who will go to the Turks to give glory to Jesus, not to take it.

PRAYER FOCUS: *Turk of Turkey (Evangelical: 0.00%)*

MARCH 25: ADDING DAGGER TO SWORD

TODAY'S READING: JOSHUA 9–11

Partnership is essential to missions. The American church cannot reach unreached peoples by itself. We were not the first to engage in missions and we won't be the last. Americans, however, do not have a corner on the market as far as hubris goes. No one nation can reach all the nations. It is as unwise to say, "The Africans are the answer!" Just as it is to think the Latinos, Arabs, or Asians are the future of missions. The unfinished task will only be accomplished when all nations send missionaries to all nations.

Non-partnership is also essential to missions. Who we *don't* align with is just as important as who we do align with. Our "no" is as important as our "yes." Our "no" may be required for strategic partnerships. We say "no" to partnership because that union would dilute the specific task God has called us to. There are some cases when the godliest thing we can do is to agree to work in our respective corners of God's field. As critical as partnership is, God does not ask us to partner willy-nilly. There must always be parameters and an assurance of like precious faith. We *must* "ask counsel of the Lord" (Josh. 9:14). Joshua and the leaders made this classic error with the Gibeonites. They made an agreement based on appearances, not on the Lord's call to work together.

In mission partnerships, two essential reactions can mislead or oppose us. One is deceit (Gibeonites in vv. 22–24) and the other is assault (king of Jerusalem and friends in 10:1–5); both reactions are based on fear. Fear is the real enemy of mission partnership. Fear can lead us to seek alliances we should avoid or to resist or attack those alliances we should make peace with. This fear is usually connected to jealousy or anxiety about being overlooked or left behind. By all means, let us partner, for we will not see God's glory among the 4.7 million Turkmen if we don't work together. But let our partnership decisions not be based on fear; let them be based on the counsel of the Lord.

A second beautiful reality of mission partnership is that our essential union with each other is based on partnering with Jehovah: He the senior partner, and we the lads and lassies He allows into the fray. It is a bit of a mystery why God includes frail humans in His mission. After all, consistently "more die from the hailstones than the children of Israel kill with the sword" (v. 11). God's part is so much bigger than man's part whenever peoples are saved. God indeed fights for us and does most of the work, yet not in a way that our little contribution is unneeded or insignificant. In partnership with God regarding mission, there is mystery. God doesn't need us, yet He chooses to need us. God could save the nations without us, yet if we decline partnership, there is a deadly cost paid by the unwarned (Ezekiel 3 and 33). I cannot logically or emotionally settle the justice or terror of someone going to hell because of my disobedience, so my determination is to make that question redundant by obedient participation in mission. I will draw my little dagger and lend it to God's almighty sword.

PRAYER FOCUS: *Turkmen of Turkmenistan (Evangelical: 0.00%)*

MARCH 26: A CALL TO ARMS

TODAYS' READING: JOSHUA 12-15

Every generation has kings to conquer. This is not just because the task is unfinished or because some of our ancestors failed to obey. Both are true. It is also because we were made for battle. Yes, it's true there is land yet to possess and land yet to conquer. Yes, it's true there are 7,000 unreached people groups who do not yet glorify *the* King. But there is more to conquest than completion of the task: We were created to be fulfilled when we work for what is glorious. Fighting is part and parcel of winning. There is no fun in wins without fights.

The greatest inheritance we can give our children and disciples is the commission to fight for the glory of God in all the earth. If the inheritance we leave behind is a challenge and not a check, we will do more for the souls of those we love than if we left them a fortune. To leave a legacy that removes fight and invites corruption is no kindness at all. We were created to derive joy from battle, not from retreat. Rest is delicious when it is a reprieve from battle, not when it is a retreat. Rest is not an abdication from fighting; it is a pause so that we can fling ourselves into the fray with even more zest and joy. Our greatest inheritance is a call to arms for the eternal souls of unreached peoples. As the family of God, as the army of the Lord of hosts, we have been given a precious double inheritance: the summons to battle and the gift of God's presence. Oh, how blessed are the children of God—our inheritance is God and His fights! As parents and grandparents, let us pass *that* blessing on, and not the corruptible inheritance of so much money our children and grandchildren forget how to battle. Let us pass on the inheritance of the presence of Jehovah and a delight in spiritual war.

Battle calls are not just for the young. Caleb was feisty when he was young *and* when he was 85. His strength and appetite for war did not diminish as he aged. Battle calls are not just for males. Caleb's daughters were feisty in their own right. If you're a single man, the best way to prove your manhood is to go on the warpath for the glory of God for the nations. Caleb's feisty daughter's hand in marriage was earned by a man who proved he could fight on the frontier. Those men who dedicate themselves to fighting for God's glory among the frontier peoples of earth will have no problem finding godly, feisty wives.

It should be self-evident that the militarism Jesus calls for is not physically coercive crusading, for the weapons of our warfare are not carnal. Grandmas can kneel next to grandkids and do battle for the Aringa of Uganda. Sons can join fathers and grandfathers as missionaries to the unreached. Mothers can teach daughters how to fight for all that is pure, so that all of life can be a winsome invitation to the nations to find sanctuary, meaning, fulfilment, and beauty in identifying with Jesus. Young and old, we have a beautiful inheritance—the God of all the nations. He is ours, and we most fully have Him when we fight for all the peoples He died for.

PRAYER FOCUS: *Aringa of Uganda (Evangelical: 1.50%)*

MARCH 27: MIRACLES, MAIDENS, AND MOUNTAINS

TODAY'S READING: JOSHUA 16–18

In missions, many breakthroughs are miraculous. God does it. God works unexpectedly to do something we could not do or something we never even considered. Missions, the advancement of God's glory and gospel to all peoples of earth, does not always go easily. There are some places and peoples that still hold out against the invasion of God's love and truth. And I'm sure Joshua could relate. In Joshua 16:10, it is recorded: "And they did not drive out the Canaanites who dwelt in Gezer; but the Canaanites dwell among the Ephraimites to this day." There are some peoples and places of this earth as dark and lost now as they were hundreds of years ago. History and the biblical record tell us that Gezer was not overcome until Pharaoh (perhaps Siamun in 978–959 BC) conquered it and gave it to Solomon as a wedding present (1 Kings 9:16). If Joshua began the conquest of Canaan around 1400 BC as commonly thought, this means one stubborn little town held out for over 400 years.

Essentially, the people of God did not take Gezer. God gave it to them and God used an Egyptian Pharaoh as the giver. Over and again in missions there are breakthroughs by miracle. God's people didn't do anything. God just gifted through an unusual way or person. It is important that we do wise things in wise ways, yet wise and gritty action doesn't automatically mean breakthrough. Sometimes we wait 400 years and then God grants a miracle.

In missions, many breakthroughs are at the hands of maidens. Zelophehad had no sons, but he did have magnificent daughters: Mahlah, Noah, Hoglah, Milcah, and Tirzah. These daughters stood on the promises. They went to Joshua and reminded him that Moses promised an inheritance. These marvelous maidens remind us of Lillias Trotter, Lilian Trasher, Gladys Awlyard, Lottie Moon, and an army of other magnificent women who pioneered the gospel and carried the glory of God to distant peoples. Both single and married, the women of God have done as much—if not more—to take the gospel to the unreached than men have. To the shame of the church, there are still roughly seven missionary women to every missionary man. To the glory of God, missions has not faltered through the centuries because women stood and answered the missionary call regardless of what the men did.

Missions requires taking the forests and the mountains. In a delightful and penetrating exchange, the children of Joseph complain that their assignment is too small, but double-tongued (or perhaps weak-hearted) they don't want the difficult assignment. In a play on words, they consider themselves a great people, and Joshua, perhaps with a twinkle in his eye, said, "If you are so great, go take the mountains" (see Josh. 17:14–18). Jesus with a twinkle in His eye yet asks the strong and numerous churches: "How long will you neglect to go and possess the land" (18:3)? Or in another paraphrase: "If you're such hot stuff, why have you done so little for My glory among unreached peoples?"

PRAYER FOCUS: *Tatar, Crimean of Ukraine (Evangelical: 0.10%)*

MARCH 28: SHIPS MOORED IN FOREIGN LANDS
TODAY'S READING: JOSHUA 19–21

God commanded Moses to establish cities of refuge and Joshua implemented this obedience. The city of refuge concept had precedent in other cultures and contexts. "A Sumerian incantation hymn dedicates a temple…. The temple is described as the 'house of refuge, wide house of the protective deity.' As described in the Sumerian hymn, this house of refuge functioned as a 'far off ship moored in a foreign land'…. It was designated for 'that person who in his own village, any man could cut him down.'" There is uncanny similarity to certain contexts around the world where a profession of faith in Jesus and obedient discipleship to Him makes a person fair game for any who would want to harm or kill him. The haunting beauty of a "far off ship moored in a foreign land" nicely pictures those who have followed Jesus, hiding in Him when no place left in their own country is safe for them.

Great evils and great tragedies (like great blessings) are not physically restrained. Harm cannot be avoided through geography or wealth. Cancerous cells or demons are not intimidated by any race or person. From some things, there is no place to hide. The man being persecuted because he is the first believer in Jesus from that people or the only believer in a family realizes quickly that there is nowhere to run other than to Jesus. When we are unsafe in our own land, when the danger is our own family, when there is physically nowhere to go, we run to our "ship moored in a foreign land." We run to our ark who is a Person, not a place. In missions, the people of God have a responsibility to give shelter to those who have nowhere else to go. This does not mean extraction, for how will the church ever be built if everyone leaves? It means the body of Christ mooring its ships in difficult harbors, taking on risk and suffering along with the persecuted, providing family, care, and the presence of Jesus when it can be found nowhere else. We take the cities of refuge to the nations. We anchor our boats in the city ports and inland harbors of Emirati Dubai and Abu Dhabi.

Once all the land was allocated (assigned for conquest), Joshua himself was given a portion. The work of making disciples among unreached peoples is for all—leaders included. Let us all take some land. Let our leadership footprint be smaller. Let all travel, and let all teaching, leading, and training come from working models. And let the big rock of every missionary be a city of refuge for the unreached. If all of us in missions make it our priority to make disciples, then it will be for us as it was for the conquerors of Canaan (Josh. 21:43–45): The Lord will give to us all that He swore to give our fathers. Not a man will stand against us. The Lord will deliver all the unreached peoples to us as our inheritance. Not a word of God will fail, nor any good thing which He has promised. All will come to pass.

PRAYER FOCUS: *Arab, Arabic Gulf Spoken of UAE (Evangelical: 0.30%)*

MARCH 29: WE ARE WITNESSES

TODAY'S READING: JOSHUA 22-24

*"Every saved person this side of heaven owes the gospel
to every lost person this side of hell."*

DAVID PLATT

The missionary call is a collective one, given to the whole body of Christ. The church exists for missions, and missions is the collective assignment of the church. As the brotherhood of believers, we then have a joint responsibility to keep each other focused and obedient. Joshua commended the Reubenites, Gadites, and the half tribe of Manasseh because they stuck with their brothers and remained dedicated to the big picture even though their land was gained (see Josh. 22:5–6). When these two and a half tribes crossed to the east side of the Jordan River, they erected an altar of witness. This altar caused consternation and nearly a civil war. The tribes on the western side of the Jordan misunderstood it; they thought the eastern tribes gave up on the assignment and removed themselves from the covenant with Jehovah. Those on the east explained: "We are still on board" (see v. 27). Relieved to hear this, the western tribes calmed down and the altar was named "Witness." What a great name for the symbol of what we are committed to do.

Missions is a collective assignment. If we don't finish the task, the Lord will hold us all responsible. If we don't preach the gospel in all the world to every people group, then we're all culpable, even if some of us obeyed while others rebelled. Disobedience by one part of the body signals demise for us all. This is why brothers keep brothers on point. If we truly love the other, we won't quietly stand by as they make decisions that will destroy their souls. To see one member disobey spells doom for us all. In missions this is doubly true as we can't fulfil this grand assignment without every member of the body fully engaged.

Both Joshua the book and Joshua the leader come to an end, and in the final speech Joshua rehearsed the big dream, the covenant made with Abraham, the metanarrative of the Bible: "You choose how you are going to live your life. I know what family I belong to, the family of Abraham. My family was given the privilege of God being our God, we being His people, His presence dwelling among us, His blessings pouring over us, and His goodness extending to the ends of the earth. You choose if you are going to maintain this collective family calling. But I have made my choice. I stand with my fathers. I and all my children will serve the God of missions. We will live and die for His glory in all the earth" (see Josh. 24:15–18). The people responded in chorus that they too would serve the God of missions saying, "We are witnesses" (v. 22). So Joshua released them, each to their own inheritance: to win the nations for the glory of God. Joshua and Jesus—same name, same commission, same last words: You are witnesses. Go glorify God among all unreached peoples.

PRAYER FOCUS: *Gujarati of United Kingdom (Evangelical: 0.03%)*

MARCH 30: THE WAY BACK TO THE FAVOR OF THE LORD

TODAY'S READING: JUDGES 1-2

When Joshua led the people of Israel into Canaan, they were outclassed. Canaanite towns had public drainage systems and houses with paved floors. Canaanite culture was sophisticated with fancy pottery, detailed art, and exquisite jewelry. Archeology shows Israelite towns to be simple, comprised of houses with uncut stones and no mortar. As the time of the judges opened, "the Israelites were poor, oppressed, and threatened by the superior cultures of their new neighbors; they were barely clinging to existence." The Israelites, a loose confederation of independent tribes, entered Canaan in force during a time when the power of that day's superpowers (Egypt and Assyria) were at ebb tide.

Two things kept the confederation together: worship and war. In worship, the Israelites gathered around the ark, usually at Gilgal or Shiloh. In war, when there was an existential threat, a warlord rose to call the tribes together to fight. The threat of extinction had to be strong enough, and the warlord charismatic enough to forge unity. The book of Judges is not so much about leaders that were judges (essentially, they were warlords who then tried their hand at administration only to fail), but about the Lord judging Israel when they wandered away from His mission. A missionary God and a missionary Bible insist on the nations of the world as central to the story. If Israel would not glorify God among the nations, then God would use the nations to remind His own people of His glory and nature. Judges 1 recounts the effect of not glorifying God among the nations. By not completely driving out the nations, Israel then became bound by them. We either win the nations or they win us. Our mission is to invite the nations to join Jehovah, and the blessings that result from our obedience are the most convincing invitation. We are not to leave Jehovah to join the nations—that blesses no one.

The Angel of the Lord appeared and reminded the wayward people of God what the main plot of the story was: God came down to save them out of the nations to keep His promise to Abraham and the fathers. When we realize this path is lost, we should join our fathers and weep, for the unavoidable result is that the hand of the Lord will be against us for calamity wherever we go, whatever we do. When we do cry, the Lord raises up warriors who remind us that it's about God's glory among the nations, and they lead us back to the covenant. When God tests us, it centers around His covenant and the nations. We cannot escape the biblical reiteration of God being a missionary God and God's people being a missionary people and missions being centered on all nations of earth glorifying Jehovah.

In our declining churches, we long for revival. We see that we have lost the faith and fervor of our fathers. The way back to the favor of the Lord for us is the same as it was for the people of God in the time of the book of Judges—a rededication to the glory of God being manifested and demonstrated among the nations of the world. Either we go to war for the glory of Jesus among unreached peoples or He uses those people to judge us.

PRAYER FOCUS: *Jew, English Speaking of United States (Evangelical: 1.60%)*

MARCH 31: WEAPONIZING HOSPITALITY

TODAY'S READING: JUDGES 3-5

The events in the book of Judges are thought to have occurred over roughly 400 years (around 1406 to 1050 BC). It is difficult to know the precise period as several judges served specific tribes and some overlap to their activity is likely. What we do know is that after Joshua died, things deteriorated quickly, and the life of Israel spiraled downward in cycles of apostasy, oppression, supplication, and deliverance.[1] Seven such cycles of oppression and deliverance occur between Judges 3 and 16. Each story is unique and in its own way, missionally didactic.

Othniel teaches us that when the Spirit of the Lord comes upon us, there is always a physical consequence. In his case, the Spirit sent him to war, but in all cases, there is an initial physical consequence to Spirit filling. We will see this throughout the book of Judges and on into the New Testament. When the Spirit fills us, the result is always that we have a dynamite effect on the nations. Encounters of the Spirit that are gluttonous, secret, or retiring in their self-absorption are far from the intent of the God who sends us to war. **Ehud** teaches us that secrets never tend to be positive. Not to be confused with mystery, secrets almost always destroy. God is not about keeping news secret. God is all about us opening our mouths and boldly speaking truth in love. Boldness is not an enemy to discretion; it is merely a commitment to the God of light and truth. In missionary living there should be no secrets or questions of blurred identity about us. If we are not known as proclaimers of the gospel, we are not doing our job. We do not bring life; rather, we aid death. **Shamgar** teaches us that God can do mighty things with little weapons and **Barak** teaches us that God sometimes deploys great forces against us so He can win greater glory. In taking God to unreached peoples, God continually uses the unknown, simple, hardworking men and women who labor on the back side of deserts or far sides of mountains in such obedience that God gains great glory and 600 men and more are defeated by Jehovah's love.

Deborah teaches us that God is no respecter of persons. God will use young and old, male and female, and if we shrink back from participation in God's battle to win the nations to Himself, it is our loss, not His. God will ever get glory. **Jael** teaches us that God can use housewives to do what strong men fail to do. Many are the spiritual battles won because wives and mothers, who may not have the public gifts, time, or desire of their husbands, have weaponized their hospitality. They have prayed with tears as they stood at the kitchen sink or sung in the Spirit as they held crying toddlers. They have hosted local guests and friends generously at every hour, visited neighbors and cried when friends endured agonizing loss, and opened their mouths with little words of witness and giant expressions of kindness to discouraged team members. Housewives in mission among unreached peoples have won more battles than may ever be known. Deborah and Jael weaponized their femininity and hospitality, and God was glorified among the nations. Let there be many more.

PRAYER FOCUS: *Uzbek, Northern of Uzbekistan (Evangelical: 0.01%)*

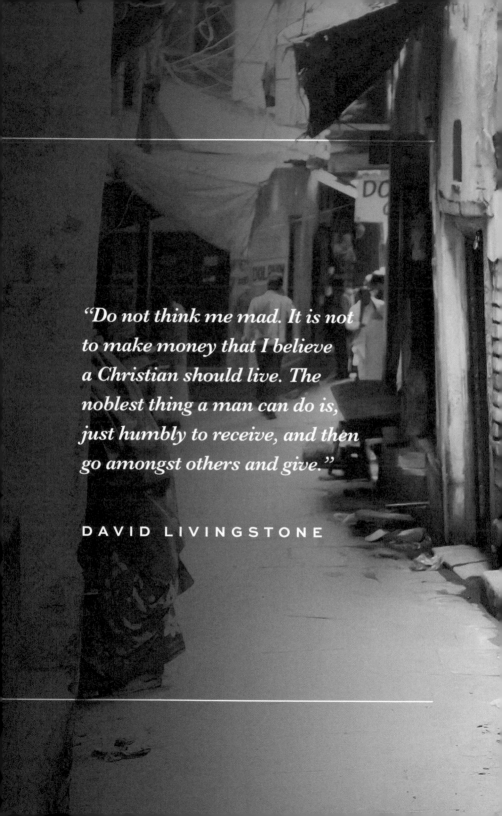

"*Do not think me mad. It is not to make money that I believe a Christian should live. The noblest thing a man can do is, just humbly to receive, and then go amongst others and give.*"

DAVID LIVINGSTONE

APRIL

APRIL 1: REVIVAL WILL COME IF

TODAY'S READING: JUDGES 6–7

"The command has been to 'go,' but we have stayed—in body, gifts, prayer, and influence. He has asked us to be witnesses unto the uttermost parts of the earth… but 99% of Christians have kept puttering around in the homeland."

ROBERT SAVAGE

An honest survey of today's church landscape regretfully reveals a body in decline. We are not healthy—and we know it—and all our protests to the contrary ring hollow. We have the same blind, complaining question of Gideon: "If the Lord is with us, why then has all this happened to us? And where are all His miracles" (Judges 6:13)? And God reminds us that He is not at fault. He brought us out of Egypt to be our God, to dwell among us, and to bless us that we might bless the nations. Our undoing is in its reverse: We do not bless the nations, so we lose the blessing of God, so we start complaining. The way out of our general church demise is the same way it was for Gideon and friends—tear down idols and win glory for Jehovah among all the world's unreached. The church has no right to complain if she will not obey God's commands. This was cure for Gideon and the commission of Jesus, and it is our cure today.

For revival, we have to destroy the family idols. Gideon's father set up an idol to Baal. Baal was referred to as the storm god. Gideon tore down his image, and Gideon's father said that if Baal is so strong, he can plead for himself. Gideon's name is changed to Jerubbaal, meaning, "let the storm god plead for himself." Before we storm against the nations, we must face the wrath of forsaking the things at home that bring us comfort but are idolatrous. Anything that brings prosperity, protection, growth, or even safety but is not of Jehovah must be broken down. In breaking our idols of program and performance, we will find we didn't actually need them—they can't defend themselves or their existence. The next step to revival is to be filled anew with the Spirit. True Spirit fillings have physical consequences, and the way back from church decay includes mobilizing the church to go to mission. Revival actually doesn't happen around altars—but around Midianites.

The famous lesson of Gideon is that God will not share His glory with anyone—not missionaries and not the church. God will reduce us until we are small enough in our own eyes to ensure He gets all the glory. Maybe revival tarries because we are too big, too brash, too arrogant, too ambitious. Maybe God is waiting for barley loaves and men and women so weak they get down on their faces just to survive. Our churches are in trouble. But it's not because God has left the building, it's because we abandoned the mission. Revival will come—it must come—but it will come to the people who break the family idols, who are small in their own eyes, who get down on their faces in desperation, who, full of the Spirit, mobilize others to battle, and who take up God's fame among the Tay of Vietnam and all unreached peoples. We will be revived if we will be God's missionary people.

PRAYER FOCUS: *Tay of Vietnam (Evangelical: 0.20%)*

APRIL 2: THE GLORY GAME

TODAY'S READING: JUDGES 8-9

Amending President Truman's quote, it's amazing what we can accomplish when we *do* care who gets the credit. Because Gideon knew the glory belonged to Jehovah, he was able to placate petty grievances by laying down any credit to himself to honor those of his brothers. "God has delivered into your hands," he deftly responded to jealousy, giving glory to God for using others (Judges 8:3). That is excellent missionary statesmanship: simultaneously giving God glory, crediting the contribution of others, and marginalizing our role in any of the global gains. Gideon's humility was not hard to find, given what he just experienced. Three-hundred warriors killed 120,000. There remained 15,000 enemies and the 300 were "exhausted but still in pursuit" (v. 4). Gideon kept fighting and attacked "while the camp felt secure" (v. 11).

Missionary lessons abound: We will always be outnumbered. We will not always be well supported. We pursue when exhausted. We give God glory and others credit. God wins the day. Then the real battle begins. Gideon returned from God's magnificent victory and the spoils of victory became a snare. He refused one trap [rule for him and his sons (v. 23)] but succumbed to others—riches and reputation, collecting wealth for himself to make an ephod, a public memory to what he did. When we send our representatives to battle for God's glory and God uses their weakness for magnificent movements of peoples to Jesus, we often misinterpret their God-used weakness for natural strength. The snares of rule, riches, and reputation have shipwrecked many of God's humble warriors. When we ask missionaries to rule, we remove some of the best workers from the field and stick them in administrative roles. When missionaries are fruitful, we have a dangerous habit of asking them to circuit preach in churches and shower them with accolades and offerings. Every missionary appreciates affirmation and the finances for the work, but the addictive, deceptive aspects of praise and plenty cripple the soul. We turn our best hired hands (laborers on the ground) into hired guns (fundraisers in the pulpit).

The children of our naïve actions are squabbling rivals, each one scrambling in their ambition to lead the kingdom we created together. If we twist missions into another performance of the charismatic in our churches rather than into a quiet obedience in the unseen fields of the world, we have asked our Gideons to rule over us. All too often in Christianity and missions, we lose the battle right after we win it. When we are humble, God does magnificent things through us among the nations. We then get proud and elevate those God used to a place that destroys them and us. How much better to live outside the limelight like a brother now serving in the West Bank. He has been there for four decades, and because he shuns the "glory game," God can trust him with fruitful missionary activity. There are many more like him. They take no glory. They make no ephods. They accept no accolades. They refuse all titles. They just keep winning the unreached to Jesus. Lord of the harvest, raise up more. And let not our raising them to prominence undo them and us.

PRAYER FOCUS: *Arab, Palestinian of West Bank & Gaza (Evangelical: 0.04%)*

APRIL 3: SERVING MAMMON

TODAY'S READING: JUDGES 10–11

God loves monogamy. He wants to be our only love, our only God, in holy matrimony with one pure, holy bride. How heart-rending to the Husband, then, when His bride has multiple affairs. When we, the bride of Christ, are unfaithful to our Husband, we not only break His heart, we also remove ourselves from His plan. We can no longer be trusted to bless the nations of the earth. The spiritual infidelity of the church leads to the spiritual poverty of the unreached.

The children of Israel served the Baals and the Ashtoreths—multiple gods and multiple betrayals. God's people were serial adulterers. Not content with one betrayal, they (we) continually broke God's heart and assaulted God's mission plan. "By worshiping the Baals and Ashtoreths of Canaan, the Israelites were following the normal religious traditions of their day. They would have learned from the indigenous population that these gods were owners of this land and needed to be worshiped in order to prosper there." The Israelites wanted food, shelter, provision, and security, so they gave into the pressure and allure of prosperity. As the centuries rolled by, man became no wiser, just more sophisticated. We still adulterate with Baals and Ashtoreths—we call them dollars, euros, and yen. The modern Christian's syncretism is not so crude as to have physical idols in our homes. We set our idols up in IRA accounts, storage units, and house-sized cottages on the lake—there we bow. Our first energy and our true worship—as evidenced by where we spend our time, how little we give to missions, and what motivates us—is to mammon, not to Jehovah. A litmus test on our devotion to Jehovah is if we serve mammon or if we use it to serve God's mission purposes in all the earth. We pass or fail that test on whether we give to missions from our abundance or our lack. We can take no comfort in a generosity that doesn't hurt or cost us.

The great Giver of heaven longs to hear His people cry: "We have sinned against You, because we have both forsaken our God [and His mission] and served the Baals [of mammon]" (Judges 10:10). Unfortunately, in Judges that cry was only heard after all prosperity and security were lost and the people had nowhere else to go. A great tragedy of human history is we tend to not call on the Lord until we have violated His intimate covenant and experienced His anger. It doesn't *have* to be this way, but it usually is. One of the great deceptions of human society is that our children justify the pursuit of security, riches, power, and status. We rationalize our idolatry by telling ourselves it will be better for our children. The story of Jephthah's daughter corrects us through her mouth: "If you have given your word to the Lord, do to me according to what has gone out of your mouth, because the Lord has avenged you of your enemies, the people of Ammon" (11:36). A pure child rejoiced that God's purposes were accomplished among the nations. Our children prefer the glory of God among the nations to their personal security. Don't hide your idolatry behind your children. The Spirit of God in your children wants you to use all you have for the glory of God among the nations.

PRAYER FOCUS: *Saharawi of Western Sahara (Evangelical: 0.00%)*

APRIL 4: GOD SEEKS OCCASIONS TO MOVE

TODAY'S READING: JUDGES 12-15

The inability of the Ephraimites to pronounce their "sh" sound came with great consequence. Their resulting "sibboleth" (versus "shibboleth") led to 42,000 Ephraimites being killed (Judges 12:6). The tragedy of brothers killing brothers has implications on missions. So easily brothers "kill" brothers in places of extreme service. The competition, jealousies, or petty grievances between mission entities, ministers, and organizations severely limits our ability to take and hold kingdom ground among the unreached. There are enough human resources available in the global church for us to reach every unreached people on earth. The tragedy is that either we do not go, or if we do, we squabble. It's hard to win the nations when constantly fighting a civil war. Despite our frailties and follies, God still seeks "an occasion to move" (14:4) among the nations. God's regular global method is His Spirit coming on ordinary, flawed men and women. As is the normative biblical pattern, when the Spirit of God comes upon us, there is a physical evidence, an action of consequence.

The Spirit of the Lord came mightily upon Samson to the extent that he physically ripped apart a lion "though he had nothing in his hand" (v. 6). Applying this principle to missionary service, it is upon the nothing in man that God builds His greatest works. It is through the weak, foolish, and poor that God delights to move in power. There are two great enemy lions to the missionary: the spirit of "I know" and the spirit of "I can." These enemies must be ripped apart without mercy, for the missionary that God can trust is the one who says, "Lord, I don't know what to do, but my eyes are on You," and "Lord, I cannot do this in my own strength, but with You all things are possible."

The Spirit of the Lord came mightily on Samson again, this time with the physical consequence that thirty Philistines were killed, while their clothes were preserved enough to give away as gifts (v. 19). That must have been some finessed fighting—slaughtering without soiling. Robust missionary work among the nations is not crude. The Spirit's power and wisdom are needed to know which elements of clothes and culture to retain and which elements to abandon and even destroy. Imperialism and syncretism are two sides of the same coin: one the result of arrogance, the other of accommodation. It's easy to look back and say that slavery, foot binding, and widow burning were despicable evils, but looking forward, we need the Spirit's powerful help to contextualize without arrogance or accommodation.

One more time the Spirit of the Lord came mightily upon Samson. The ropes on him fell off like flax burned in fire and the bonds broke loose from his hands. Truly, where the Spirit of the Lord is, there is liberty. Some things can only be broken or burned by Spirit fire. There are demonic strongholds, deceptions, perversions, and darkness so entrenched over time and so wickedly restrictive that only God can overcome them. The Spirit must break the bonds. There is nothing for us to do but believe. A second reality concerning the breaking of bonds is the danger that follows victory. We are often most vulnerable just after God breaks through and uses us in some small role. May the Spirit of the Lord who helps us win the war also help us win the peace.

PRAYER FOCUS: *Arab, Northern Yemeni of Yemen (Evangelical: 0.00%)*

APRIL 5: GOD'S EXTREME MEASURES

TODAY'S READING: JUDGES 16–18

A missionary God will be glorified among all peoples with or without human compliance. God's joyful preference is to see His children join Him in His missionary passion; but if we refuse, it does not alter His mission or His goals. It is similar to godly parents. We have no greater joy than when our children serve Jesus with us; but if they don't, despite our sorrow over their disastrous choices, we will still serve the Lord. Our ultimate joy is not in whether or not our children participate with us in serving the Lord; our ultimate joy is in serving the Lord ourselves. The same is true for God. His ultimate joy is not in us, nor in our service; His ultimate joy is in Himself and in His mission purposes for the whole creation. The theme running through Judges is this very reality: There is joy in serving Jehovah and glorifying Him among the nations, but if that joy is forfeited, God will still glorify Himself.

It is theologically true that God is just as glorified in His judgments as in His mercy. A judge is good only if he or she both vindicates the innocent *and* condemns the guilty. No glory of God is lost when He judges from His holy throne. God is just as glorified when He consigns the unrepentant sinner to hell as when He graces the repentant sinner to heaven. There is no glory to God if He would allow the wicked into His holy heaven. When God judges His judges because they do not represent Him well, He is glorifying His holy character. When God judges the nations because they do not bow at His majestic feet and receive His offered clemency, He is eminently glorious. God will ever and always be glorified no matter how humans react to Him.

That act of glory simultaneously ended the life of God's representative, a life of mixed results, for no tool of Jehovah is exempt from holy living. Samson died with the Philistines because neither glorified Jehovah as they should. There is one non-negotiable standard for all men, saved and lost—the glory of God. Whoever dishonors the Lord will eventually have the roof fall on their heads. Interesting to note, Samson's death had a greater impact than his life.

The word "Nazarite" means "one who is consecrated (or separated or devoted) to something." A Nazarite was one who had taken a vow to the Lord. What a tragedy to see Samson so conflicted and wholly devoted to unholy women that there is no mention of his heart for Jehovah. Samson had all the external strength and charisma of a devotee, but none of the internal character that sought the glory of God. The lesson of Delilah's scheming is that nothing put on us can bind us. The only thing that can bind us is that which is taken because we gave it away—namely, our intimate covenant with God. Samson was living a charade, and his last attachment to glorious devotion was his obedience to not cut his hair. With his hair shaved, gone was the last vestige of any diminishing glory that he voluntarily gave Jehovah among the nations. So, the fearsome principle was applied: Because Samson did not voluntarily glorify his Lord before the non-people of God, his Lord took extreme measures for the honor of His own name, no matter the price to His servant or His people.

PRAYER FOCUS: *Pashtun, Southern of Afghanistan (Evangelical: 0.02%)*

APRIL 6: THE UNIMAGINABLE REQUEST

TODAY'S READING: JUDGES 19-21

Judges ends with one of the stranger sequences of the Bible: A man stole from his mother. For his confession he was rewarded with an idol. The idol was then used to lure a priest of the Lord into private service. That priest was then forcibly commandeered to serve a wayward tribe. Another priest of the Lord took a concubine and offered her up to be raped by lewd men to save himself from molestation. She died, and he cut her into pieces. The tribes of God went to war and the good guys got pounded, but then the bad guys were virtually wiped out. Finally, the remaining few bad guys were allowed to kidnap the other guys' wives. Hollywood writers have nothing on the real events of Judges, and the whole story unfolded because God's people did not glorify God among the nations. Each one did what was right in his own eyes and no godly leadership called them back to holy glory.

The loose confederation of Israelite tribes was only united by God, and when their devotion to God receded, so did their unity and their ability to glorify God among the nations. More glory was forfeited among the nations when the Benjaminites turned out to be more perverted than the Jebusites. God's people were meant to live in holy relationship to Jehovah as an invitation to the nations; instead, they fell into sins even more disgusting than their wicked observers. And as is so sadly often needed, even today, the only recourse for God and His glory was for Him to use the wicked to destroy the wicked. Summoning up a memory of devotion, the Israelites agreed that the men of Gibeah had gone too far. Benjamin defended the wicked (what a shame when our loyalty trumps our integrity), and death reigned. The Israelites did many things right in this passage and still suffered loss. They wept, fasted, and sat before the Lord, inquired of Him and asked if they should press on after great losses, and God told them to "go."

God ever seems to make that request: "Go!" Even when we have suffered unimaginable loss, even when He knows the price of redemption is the death of His Son, even when He knows that the price of the unreached around the throne is the suffering witness of the saints. We are not that different from the Israelites at the end of Judges. We have drifted from our devotion. We have concentrated more on the glory of the church than on the glory of God. We are waking up to that egregious error, and as the body of Christ we are repenting and turning our eyes again to unreached peoples and dedicating ourselves to glorifying God among the most difficult places and most resistant peoples of earth. As we press forward in this obedience, many of our missionaries will die, and many of our local partners will be tortured and killed. The real question is, what we will do next? When we take unimaginable losses, when some of our best are struck down for doing right, for pursuing God's glory among the nations, what will we do then? Will we still send? Do we have the collective will to fight on? When this inevitable cost in these last days is levied, God grant us grace to sit before the Lord, weep, seek His counsel, hear Him once again say "go," and then once again obey.

PRAYER FOCUS: *Berber, Kabyle of Algeria (Evangelical: 1.80%)*

APRIL 7: A LOVE STORY
TODAY'S READING: RUTH

The events in Judges transpired over 400 years. Spun together, the tales make it appear as if this was a constantly chaotic period. The reality was, in the middle of the wars and intrigue was much normal, daily, boring life. The story of Naomi, Ruth, and Boaz took place in the middle of the era described in Judges, and in the book of Ruth, we take a collective breath and enjoy a romance. We remember that crops were planted and harvested, deals struck at the city gates, marriages celebrated, children born and raised, and tears shed at funerals. Immigration took place, and Israelite civilians traveled to Moab and intermarried. Life was 99.99 percent normal.

"Ruth is a small but amazing book, and it is also a great poetic love story. Even the number of words are counted and balanced artistically in the Hebrew text.... Ideas are balanced, names have meaning, vivid language is used, and wordplays make the writing beautiful. However, there is more to Ruth than beautiful writing. The theology of the **missio Dei** is also present.... Ruth the Moabite widow made a powerful declaration here about her faith in God. She wanted the God of Naomi the Israelite to also be the God of Ruth the Moabite. Ruth was considering the kingdom of God and wondering if her nation could be blessed as well."

Isn't it amazing that the God who said He didn't want a Moabite in His sanctuary for ten generations (Deut. 23:3) is the same God who goes out of His way to bring a Moabite home to Israel, link her to a sad widow, and marry her to an older, shy bachelor? God twinkles through Ruth, sparkling with His inclusive nature. "In Ruth, the narrative looks toward the Davidic kingdom through the historical lens of a kinsman-redeemer acting on behalf of a Gentile woman.... In this way, Judges and Ruth are connected to both their Genesis antecedents and the Davidic kingdom that follows." How beautiful are the redemptive themes of the gospel scattered through Ruth: The book ends by listing the foreign women in the bloodline of Jesus: Syrians, like Rachel and Leah, Canaanites like Tamar (a prostitute), and Ruth the Moabitess. God is the great Kinsman-Redeemer who sacrifices Himself to bring all the nations home.

By bringing a foreigner home, sharing life, food, and fellowship with her, Naomi's actions were a microcosm of God's actions, for she in effect brought home the Messiah. How ironic for Naomi to wail in bitter agony, "I went out full, and the LORD has brought me home again empty" (1:21), when by bringing home Ruth, Naomi brought us King David, the most beautiful psalms, and ultimately the King of Kings! In the grand scheme of things, a husband and two sons were a small price to pay on that return. Many have sacrificed much—much more for much less. I do not denigrate the widow's pain or the pain when parents bury children. I am only saying that Naomi's pain became the joy of the world, and it all came as a result of bringing a Moabite widow into the family. What might happen in our time if we bring the Azeri into our homes?

PRAYER FOCUS: *Azerbaijani, Azeri Turk of Azerbaijan (Evangelical: 0.15%)*

APRIL 8: A MOTHER'S PRAYER

TODAY'S READING: 1 SAMUEL 1–3

The book of 1 Samuel is the transition from the wild, wooly period of the judges to the monarchy. First Samuel "begins not with a king, but with the imposing figure of Samuel. Samuel is priest and prophet and judge, indeed everything except king." Samuel was this extraordinary combination of roles, critical in helping a rascally, divided people transform into a regional power. But the Samuel books are not about Samuel; in fact, they open with the remarkable figure of his mother Hannah. Hannah was exemplary for several reasons. First, she understood God's sovereignty. She was barren because "the LORD had closed her womb" (1 Sam. 1:5). Mocked by a rival wife, Hannah was at peace with the sovereignty of God. The single most important quality that assures missionary grit is when we believe God is sovereignly good in all that He allows and ordains. We may never know which it is, but those who believe all things pass through the hands of He who loves us are unshakable.

Second, Hannah understood how to pray. Year by year, weeping in anguish, continuing to pray before the Lord, pouring out her soul, ever trusting, she knew "for this child [she] prayed, and the LORD [had] granted [her] petition which [she] asked of Him" (v. 27). Hannah modeled the travailing prayer that God would love to see repeated in global missionary praying. Hannah's heart was for a physical child, and oh, that the mothers (and fathers, sons, and daughters) today would have that same intercessory anguish for children! Oh, that missionaries would year by year, in weeping and anguish, ever believing, continually pour out from the soul and bombard heaven for our inheritance— sons and daughters from unreached peoples.

Third, and to me most wonderful of all, Hannah understood that all of life was about the glory of God in all the earth among all the nations. Think of her, an uneducated, poor wife from a little village in Palestine. A second wife, a nobody, illiterate and simple, humble and quiet. Until she opened her mouth to pray. Then she transformed into a lioness of God, and cosmic confessions coursed from her spirit: "No one is holy like the LORD.... The pillars of the earth are the LORD'S, and He has set the world upon them.... From heaven He will thunder…[and] judge the ends of the earth. He will give strength to His king, and exalt the horn of His anointed" (see 2:1–10). From the heart of this humble, illiterate mother came expressions of a glorious God who will be exalted in all the earth.

Contrast her with the sons of Eli who as priests should be all about the glory of God to the ends of the earth and a holy people being a light to all nations. Instead, they squabbled over the best cuts of meat and lost sight of what God wanted to do globally. So it is today— prominent ministers squabbling over pensions and prestige, while simple mothers raising the prophets, priests, judges, and missionaries of tomorrow bring the saints and angels of heaven roaring to their feet as their private prayers rend the heavens and bring the glory down. It is those prayers from hidden Hannahs all over this earth and all through time that have birthed the "here I am" of their Samuels. Truly, God does hear when these mothers of Israel pray.

PRAYER FOCUS: *Persian of Bahrain (Evangelical: 0.80%)*

APRIL 9: RAISE MY EBENEZER
TODAY'S READING: 1 SAMUEL 4–8

Israel made a mistake common to many idolaters: they assumed an artifact had the power of the deity it represented. They took the ark of the covenant to war and whooped and hollered so loud the earth shook. They even momentarily intimidated the Philistines who assumed similarly that "God [was] in the camp" (1 Sam. 4:7). This assumption proved false when 30,000 foot-soldiers on "God's" side perished and the ark of God was captured. Obviously, God was not with them or in the ark.

We look disapprovingly at the hicks of the Old Testament who fell for this folly without realizing we have contemporary idols of our own. Now we worship worship. We have our fog and light machines. We convince ourselves (and maybe a few others) that God is in the camp. Then we go to spiritual war and get decimated. We worshiped the creation, not the Creator. We bowed before the artifact, not the Architect. For years the church worshiped faith. Then we worshipped worship. Now we've graduated to worshiping preaching, and I assume we will eventually get our doctorates by worshiping prayer. All these worships are idolatrous.

God has ever looked for a people who would have no idols whatsoever. Modern anthropologists criticize those who condemn idol worship for not understanding that the idolater is not worshiping the idol, but the god the idol represents. Old Testament prophets, however, understood this perfectly and condemned idol worship because the false god being worshiped had no power to save either the idol nor the idolater. False gods tend to go missing when idolaters need them most. Biblical prophets made fun of the supposed gods who couldn't even defend their own representative images, let alone their worshippers. So bluntly put, all idols and arks will fail us. When we worship faith, worship, preaching, or prayer, we wake to find them all fallen over with broken head and hands. We deceive ourselves by thinking we worship Jehovah when really we have slipped to worshiping the beautiful (but not divine) means by which God gave us to worship. Faith is not the savior, Jesus is the Savior. Worship is not the deliverer, Jesus is the deliverer. Preaching is not the solution, Jesus is the solution. Prayer is not the answer, Jesus is the answer. The nations of the world, every false religion, all have faith, worship, preaching, and prayer. But they don't have Jesus.

Samuel used the lesson to remind the people to put away all foreign gods and to glorify Jehovah alone. They did, and then the Lord thundered with a loud thunder against the Philistines and they were subdued. In other words, God was glorified amongst the nations only when His people stopped worshipping worship (also faith, preaching, and prayer) and again glorified only Him. It's the same with us. Then, and only then, will we see that God helps us. That's when we will be able to "raise our Ebenezer" in the sight of all the peoples of earth, including the 294 unreached peoples of Bangladesh. Ichabods (departed glory) can only be followed by Ebenezers (the Lord's help) among the nations when we purely worship Jesus and carefully avoid worshipping what so beautifully can represent Him and what so wonderfully ushers us into His presence.

PRAYER FOCUS: *Namassej of Bangladesh (Evangelical: Unknown)*

APRIL 10: THE WEAKLINGS
TODAY'S READING: 1 SAMUEL 9–12

There are two different lenses with which to view the monarchial period in Israel. One is "prophetic" (the lens of Samuel and Kings) and the other is "priestly" (the lens of Chronicles). The books of Samuel and Kings are mostly concerned with prophets and prophecy, which is why when we are introduced to Saul, one of the first things we see him do is speak under the power of the Spirit (1 Sam. 10:11–14). The reason Saul appeared on the stage is directly connected to the Bible's metanarrative of missions: Jehovah told Samuel "in his ear" (9:15), "You shall anoint [Saul] commander over My people Israel, that he may save My people from the hand of the Philistines; for I have looked upon My people, because their cry has come to Me" (v. 16). When God saves His people from the nations (in this case, the Philistines), it is as always both a demonstration of and an invitation to the one true God.

From the beginning of the monarchy it's clear God destined this turn of events for His glory among all peoples. God picked from the smallest tribe to fill the most insecure man with His Spirit, so that the ongoing plan could unfold, only to the credit of Jehovah. Kings and kingdom people are for one purpose: *that God's great name would be exalted in all the earth among all peoples.* God was pleased to make Abraham His friend, to make Abraham's sons and daughters His people, to make you and me His treasured, moveable priests for this reason. In making Jacob into Israel and Saul a king, Jehovah determined to get all the glory by choosing the smallest and weakest to manifest His glory among all nations. God did not choose the superpowers of the day—He chose the weaklings. God's choice of Saul is a microcosm of the grand design—the smallest tribe, the most insecure leader. For it's not about the fame of Saul's name or to magnify Benjamin as a tribe, it is about the great name of Jehovah among all peoples.

The choosing of Saul and Israel (i.e., weaklings) to manifest the glory of God globally gives hope to all of us who know we're small. It's not the mighty in their own eyes that God uses, but the meek. Perhaps the reason we are not used greatly is because we think too highly of ourselves. Perhaps the reason we don't see miracles, signs, and wonders in America is because God knows we will want a share in the glory. Perhaps God is not using us right now in dramatic ways among unreached peoples because we are spending too much time and energy making our name great—not His. Perhaps God is not using us for His name's sake because we are chasing empty things that cannot profit or deliver by allowing the nations to influence us, rather than by living so dramatically differently from them. Not fooled, God demurs. What a shame that our ambition veils the glory of God. What a shame that the name of Jehovah is not yet known and talked about by the Turks in Belgium because we are too busy talking about our own.

PRAYER FOCUS: *Turk of Belgium (Evangelical: 0.07%)*

APRIL 11: THE SPRIT TO FIGHT

TODAY'S READING: 1 SAMUEL 13–14

God uses the weak and overwhelmed to win improbable victories (and many souls), and He does this so all the glory goes to Him. Jonathan is my favorite Old Testament character and a great model for missionaries, and we can revel in the spirit of Jonathan and aspire towards it in our assignment to see God glorified globally.

Jonathan had half as many men as his father the king, yet he went on the attack while his colleagues and countrymen hid, fled, trembled, or scattered. From the beginning, Jonathan had the missionary spirit of "go": "Come, let us go!" he said to his armorbearer (14:1, 6, 10), for the missionary is never content to stay where all is safe. Jonathan had a specific goal for his go. His reference to the uncircumcised was not a racial slur, but a missional challenge. Circumcision was the sign of covenant with Jehovah. To be uncircumcised was to be unsubmissive to the King of glory, and the missionary heart of Jonathan would not countenance that indignity to His Lord. Those devoted to their Lord desire all glory and honor be given to Him by every people and every tongue; wherever that honor to the King is absent, there is work to be done, war to be waged. In our day, we must cast our eyes across the span of nations and ask: What knees are yet unbowed, and what hearts yet uncircumcised? Who does not yet honor our King? Then we must go to those peoples and lands and do something about it.

Jonathan was so dedicated to the glory of Jehovah among the uncircumcised (the nations) that he needed no guarantees. Jehovah's honor was worth dying for. Jonathan's countrymen were trembling and hiding, and his father blundering, so Jonathan, in desperate times, realized the best thing to do was attack, even if it went poorly for him. He said to his armorbearer, "It may be that the LORD will work for us. For nothing restrains the LORD from saving by many or by few" (14:6). That beautiful spirit lived out today is the young man in rural America or Sweden, Kenya or the Philippines, Paraguay or Jordan, who turns to his pregnant bride and says: "Come on! Let's go to North Korea. It *may* be that the Lord uses us to see one person come to Jesus. For nothing restrains the Lord from saving, whether by many or by few."

Jonathan was the visionary, but mission visionaries need someone to rush to battle with them and clean up their messes. Jonathan's armor bearer shared in the "go" spirit saying, "Go then; here I am with you, according to your heart" (14:7), and this priceless team member harvested those that Jonathan mowed down. One of the most precious missionary determinations of Jonathan and his armor bearer was that they determined to fight for God's glory among the nations—it was just a matter of where. Jonathan said in effect: "If they come down, we will fight. If we go up, we will fight" (vv. 8–10). Fighting is not the question; the question is just geography. In our age the God of all peoples has brought Hausa to Benin, Syrians to Sweden, Turks to Germany, and Arabs to America, and the missionary spirit has determined to win them for God's glory. Whether that fight takes place in Saudi Arabia or South Dakota, it doesn't matter—the missionary spirit is to fight.

PRAYER FOCUS: *Hausa of Benin (Evangelical: 0.05%)*

APRIL 12: FOR WHOM DOES YOUR HEART BURN

TODAY'S READING: 1 SAMUEL 15–17

"If ten men are carrying a log—nine of them on the little end and one at the heavy end—and you want to help, which end will you lift on?"

WILLIAM BORDEN

Goliath was raining down curses on the people of God, and David understood what these insults actually attacked—the honor of Jehovah. When Jehovah's warriors cowered in fear, it made Jehovah look weak, and the Spirit of Almighty God in David couldn't stand it. The fire burned within, and David succinctly gave the reason for victory over the giant (who stands as a representative of the nations of the world): "that all the earth may know that there is a God in Israel" (1 Sam. 17:46). "The purpose of David's victory is not simply to save Israel or to defeat the Philistines. The purpose is the glorification of Yahweh in the eyes of the world.... David is the one who bears witness to the rule of Jehovah. In so doing he calls Israel away from its imitation of the nations and calls the nations away from their foolish defiance of Yahweh. In a quite general sense this is a 'missionary speech' summoning Israel and the nations to fresh faith in Yahweh." The trajectory of David's stone followed the flight path of biblical revelation, a trajectory that "is primarily about the knowledge of who God is, YHWH's demonstration of his deity to the nations." There is a didactic missionary purpose in this favorite Bible story of a flattened Goliath: When it comes to the glory of God, all giants and all nations are the underdog, and they don't stand a chance.

Often overlooked due to its close proximity to the David and Goliath narrative is the story of Saul and the Amalekites. It ended the same—the glory of God among the nations—but that glory was achieved through loss and lesson, not victory and vindication. Saul was instructed to completely annihilate the Amalekites. Because Saul disobeyed this command, the Lord rejected him as king and tore the kingdom from him. Again, let us be clear: Saul lost the kingdom because he did not completely annihilate the Amalekites. Samuel's explanation was as clear as David's: "Now the LORD sent you on a mission, and said 'Go, and utterly destroy the sinners, the Amalekites and fight against them until they are consumed. Why then did you not obey...'" (1 Sam. 15:18). Saul was sent on a mission. He was told to "go." Saul was to radically obey God among the nations, to take drastic action, to ensure that God was completely and comprehensively glorified. Both the Amalekites and Goliath were to be completely overwhelmed by Jehovah *at the hands* of the people of God. Saul was not radically attendant enough to God's glory—and he lost the kingdom. David overflowed with zeal for the glory of God—and he was made king.

We now neither bear the physical sword of Saul nor swing David's sling, but the glory of God among the Monpa of Bhutan is still in question. Is there a David reading these words whose heart so burns that Bhutan know "there is a God in Israel" that his or her feet will run towards that goal?

PRAYER FOCUS: *Monpa of Bhutan (Evangelical: 0.00%)*

APRIL 13: CONSUMED WITH GOD'S GLORY

TODAY'S READING: 1 SAMUEL 18–20; PSALM 11, 59

Some think when Saul offered David his armor, it was more a test of heart and ambition than a well-intentioned gesture of help. "Positions of authority in the ancient world were marked by formal insignia, or by special clothing. Even more important, the ruler's weapon, usually a sword, was seen as a gift of the deities and a mark of their favor toward the bearer as the legitimate ruler. So when Saul offered David his armor, he would have been understood by Israelite culture as offering David his own position as king of Israel. The transfer of clothing signified a transfer of status.... Saul's sword was the mark of his position as defender of Israel; when the sword was given to David, Saul's kingship went with it. But David could not wear the armor or the sword; he was not ready to rule, even though he already had the favor of God and the courage to defend Israel."

When David refused the armor, he indicated his ambition not to rule. He had bigger giant fish to fry. David was consumed with God's glory, not his own. Jonathan repeated the gesture giving David his robe, armor, sword, bow, and belt. While Saul's sincerity ebbed and flowed, Jonathan was constant. David and Jonathan were kindred spirits in this essential glory: Neither one of them wanted a title or a position; all they wanted was to fight for God's fame in all the earth. If the world is to be won for Jesus, then we are to have this same spirit, ambition, and fire—the ambition for God's glory among all the nations.

The superscriptions at the beginning of each psalm are helpful, for they refer to the event or context to which the Israelites applied the psalms. The superscript of Psalm 59 refers to Saul's jealous rage and murderous attempts on David's life. Saul was jealous for the kingdom that Jonathan bequeathed and David did not covet. David responded to the assassination attempt by saying: "You therefore, O LORD God of hosts, the God of Israel, awake to punish all the nations.... And let them know that God rules in Jacob to the ends of the earth" (Psalm 59:5, 13). Even when fleeing his father-in-law in the middle of the night, David's soul could not escape the big picture: the nations submitting to the glorious rule of God. All David cared about was that Jehovah ruled among the nations to the ends of the earth. This is the missionary heart and spirit.

The missionary spirit does not worry about title or position, prestige or status. All the missionary thinks about is if God is glorified, ruling, and reigning in Bulgaria. The missionary spirit doesn't desire recognition or rule, title or throne, position or prestige. The missionary spirit just wants to see Jesus embraced by Turkish Muslim immigrants globally. No one who truly knows the weight of the crown will in their right mind desire it. The missionary spirit just wants to fight for the glory of God among the unreached peoples of earth where the souls are most bound, and the danger greatest.

PRAYER FOCUS: *Turk of Bulgaria (Evangelical: 0.01%)*

APRIL 14: THE MOST BEAUTIFUL PRAISE

TODAY'S READING: 1 SAMUEL 21–24; PSALM 34, 56

"Missionary zeal does not grow out of intellectual beliefs,
not out of theological arguments, but out of love."

ROLAND ALLEN

We cannot escape the reality that the drama between Saul and David played out before the nations, whether the Philistines, Moabites, or Edomites. Tragically, energy that should have been spent on missions was spent on infighting. God allowed the kingdom of Israel because He wanted it to be an invitation, a displayed relationship so life-giving between Israel and Jehovah that holy jealously would stir all the nations to know Jehovah themselves. But instead of focusing on this kingly mission, Saul spent his energy trying to find and kill David, hardly making union with Jehovah appealing to the nations. Instead of glorifying God among the surrounding nations or developing justice and peace as God's holy example, Saul toggled back and forth between fighting Philistines and fighting David. What might Saul have done if he had trusted David and concentrated on developing Israel? What might we do as the body of Christ if we spent less time fighting with one another and instead concentrated all our prayers, emotional energy, finances, and personnel on glorifying God among the nations? The unreached remain unreached, not because there are not enough gospel resources available globally, but because those resources are not singularly applied to harvest. They are divided—some for gospel advance and some for self-protection (at best) and civil war (at worst).

If Saul was causing international shame, David was at least trying to lift global praise. The superscript of Psalm 34 says that David wrote it when he pretended madness before Abimelech. The seeming tension resulting from the text in 1 Samuel 21:10–15 calling the Philistine king "Achish" is resolved when we realize that "Abimelech" was the title for Philistine kings—literally meaning "my Father, the King." The beauty of David's feigned madness was in the content of his praise. David was fleeing for his life. His leader wanted to kill him. He had no safe place in his own nation to rest and had to beg at the gates of his mortal enemy. He must pretend that he had lost his mind with no shred of dignity left and his life reduced to shame. And in that context David's spirit and character soared as he opened his mouth and declared: "I will bless the LORD at all times; His praise shall continually be in my mouth… Oh, magnify the LORD with me, and let us exalt His name together" (Psalm 34:1, 3). And so it is around the world, through history, and in times of duress, the most beautiful praise is when men and women surrounded by and isolated among the peoples, whether hostile or curious, lift their eyes off their pain and sorrow and declare, "I will bless the Lord at all times," and invite the Fulani, "Magnify the Lord with me!"

PRAYER FOCUS: *Fulani, Gurmanche of Burkina Faso (Evangelical: 0.23%)*

APRIL 15: NO PLACE IS SAFE

TODAY'S READING: PSALM 7, 27, 31, 52, 142

"Where does your security lie? Is God your refuge, your hiding place, your stronghold, your shepherd, your counselor, your friend, your redeemer, your Saviour, your guide? If He is, you don't need to search any further for security."

ELISABETH ELLIOT

David was not yet king. In fact, he was running for his life. He sent his family as refugees to the nation of present-day Jordan and he fled to the nation of Philistia. He hid in caves and in the wilderness. In all his hiding and fleeing, David learned that shelter and safety were not found in a place. There is no safe nation, for there is no sin-free nation. David discovered the only safety was (and is) in a person—in God. There were (and are) no guarantees for any place on earth. In Psalm 27, David said: "One thing I have desired of the LORD, that will I seek: That I may dwell in the house of the LORD all the days of my life, to behold the beauty of the LORD and to inquire in His temple. For in the time of trouble He shall hide me in His pavilion; in the secret place of His tabernacle He shall hide me" (vv. 4–5). God's pavilion could be Gath. It could be a cave in the wilderness. It could be field or forest, prison, or the eventual palace. The geography doesn't matter, for as David reminds us, God is our rock and our fortress, and He will hide us in the secret place of His presence. We can send and go to the most volatile places and peoples of earth because of this assuring truth: Our *place* of refuge is not in a Western, developed suburb sanitized from all disease and walled off from all criminals. Our place of refuge is in a person, in God Himself, for all other refuges fail us.

In the ebb and flow of world history (directly linked to the redemption narrative that biblical missiology explains), there is no enduring physical refuge. Nations that make Jehovah their God enjoy His blessings. He lives among them and uses them to bless others. When those nations rebel (as they always do), the blessing is removed and the slow decline of cultures unfolds. Prosperity shifts to those who will use it for the glory of God—wittingly or otherwise. David put it this way: "So the congregation of the peoples shall surround You; for their sakes, therefore, return on high. The LORD shall judge the peoples; judge me…" (Psalm 7:7–8). David knew that all the nations will be judged according to whether they knew and obeyed Jehovah, whether they lived holy so He could live among them, whether they blessed others with what Jehovah provided. David knew that Jehovah is a just judge and angry with the wicked every day. That's the real danger. For neither our safety nor our destruction is a place or a human. Our protection and our demise are found in Jehovah. Our fate depends on whether or not we obey God to bless the nations. Our times are in His hand. May He save us for His mercy's sake. May He use us to offer His shelter to Vietnamese and Cambodians as their recent history shows that geography offers no shelter. Maybe we can be used to help them find their rock.

PRAYER FOCUS: *Vietnamese of Cambodia (Evangelical: 0.17%)*

APRIL 16: A WAR OF WORDS

TODAY'S READING: PSALM 120, 140–141

God has primarily committed the communication of His truth to preaching; that's preaching in the sense of all God's people clearly verbalizing and explaining all the gospel in all places through all mediums among all nations. An essential reason for this commitment is to make sure the locus of attention and glory is on God, not on projects, personalities, people, or programs. And this reality has led to a furious war over words. Tongues are lifted in acrimonious strife, accusation, confusion, distraction, and distortion globally. In every nation and false religion, there is a cacophony of lies, distorted truth, veiling, mocking, twisting, suppression, and oppression of words of life and beauty.

The psalms in today's reading relate to the season in which Saul maligned David, supposed friends betrayed him, and real friends said things that hurt. In that distress David cried out to the Lord and said, "Deliver my soul, O LORD, from lying lips and from a deceitful tongue" (Psalm 120:2). It's not clear if David needed sanctuary from the tongues of others or his own. It was probably both, for we damage as much with our tongues as we help. We, too, need to deliverance from our own lying lips and deceitful tongue. This is why David prayed, "Set a guard, O LORD, over my mouth; keep watch over the door of my lips" (141:3). Christians can be both the best and worst representatives of Christ. Our mouths bring Him much glory, and just as often bring much shame, and as faithful channels of our hearts, they reveal the ugly within us to the world.

Public tongues in our home cultures are increasingly combative, perverse, self-centered, deceitful, and poisonous. The rhetoric in the nations of the earth is increasingly partisan, tribal, defensive, and fearful. We do spiritual battle for the King among all the nations of the world, equipped with our main weapon of preaching, yet every vile word known to man fills the airwaves. The noise of the battle of words is so great it's nearly impossible to get a fair hearing, even if we've overcome the internal vice of a bifurcated heart which funnels mixed messages from our mouth. Spiritual warfare is perhaps not so much about casting demons from those writhing at our feet, but more about "destroying speculations and every lofty thing raised up against the knowledge of God, and…taking every thought captive" (2 Cor. 10:5 NASB).

The battle for the heart, soul, and heads of the Fulani in Cameroon is not the battle of swords or spears. It is the battle of words, truths, ideas, and concepts of sin and salvation. This is why we need the practical skill of speaking the heart language and the spiritual skill of taking every thought captive. We need God to protect our minds if He will be able to trust our tongues. There is a vicious war for the glory of God being waged, and it is a war of words. Christians and missionaries have a stewardship duty to sharpen their weapons, to practice with them, and to use them wisely. As our words are so precious, so finite in number, let's commit them all to the King and His gospel. Let our words be few and focused, pure and piercing, prophetic and loving, anointed and fearless.

PRAYER FOCUS: *Fulani, Adamawa of Cameroon (Evangelical: 1.30%)*

APRIL 17: OVERFLOWING WITH GENEROSITY

TODAY'S READING: 1 SAMUEL 25–27

The generosity of Jehovah towards Abraham was linked to blessing the nations. God indeed prospered Abraham, but with the very specific intent that all peoples of the world would notice and be attracted to the God who so comprehensively blessed. Abraham was to be both recipient and dispenser of God's blessings, as were Nabal and Saul, as are we. To receive generously without passing it on in such a way that affects more than our own, without investing our wealth in such a way that makes God globally glorious, is to be ungrateful and to ultimately lose it all. God's generosity is contingent on us acting in like manner.

Nabal was indeed a fool, for he did not pass on what God provided. He lived in prosperity, which God allowed, but with no intention of passing it on, which God abhorred. David exhibited God's inherent disgust with those who were blessed but did not bless and he set out to punish the ungenerous fool. Abigail entered the scene and stole the show. She is a Proverbs 31 woman: beautiful and wise, quick-thinking and acting in crisis, and generous, humble and spunky, prophetic, astute, moral, and cautionary. So stunning was Abigail that she stopped a wrathful king in his tracks and all he could do was sputter blessings. Nabal's lack of generosity incurred the scorn of the people, the wrath of the king, and the loss of his life. Abigail's overflowing generosity led her to intimate union with the king. And so it will be with us: A lack of generosity with the blessings of God is foolishness and leads to death. Generosity used to wash the feet of those who battle for God's glory leads to joy with the King and to a beautified bride.

We give because God is a giver and He wants us to look like Him. Our primary motive for generosity is that that we look like our heavenly Father. This giving includes honor to our leaders and opportunity to our followers. Abigail wisely instructed David not to take vengeance into his own hands. How fortunate she inspired this grace right before David was positioned to harm Saul. David realized the Lord would strike whoever needed to die, and Saul realized he had been a fool and erred exceedingly. Saul had the same lack of generosity that Nabal had. God generously gave authority to Saul, but Saul hoarded it jealously, wouldn't pass it on, and as a consequence, lost it all. How different were David and Abigail—giving, blessing, releasing, and honoring. David generously provided for the kingdom, generously honored others, and generously yielded the kingdom. When he lapsed (ungenerously taking a friend's life and wife), death and disaster resulted. No one is exempt from being generous, and no one is exempt from the judgment of God when ungenerous. All of us are meant to steward God's generosity to us for His glory among all the peoples of earth.

PRAYER FOCUS: *Punjabi of Canada (Evangelical: 1.50%)*

APRIL 18: AT THE MERCY OF THE NATIONS

TODAY'S READING: PSALM 17, 35, 54, 63

The Philistines were a sea people that inhabited the coastal plain along Israel's southwest Mediterranean coast. Philistia was comprised of five major cities, each with a leader or king, with vassal cities all around. The Philistines' constant encroachment from the coastal plain up towards the hill country of Judea was the cause of ongoing tension and war with the Israelites. With the long-running, life-and-death animosity between these two nations, it's shocking that David was forced to go to Gath for shelter. It would be like Churchill asking Hitler for sanctuary in Nazi Germany in 1941. For a year and four months, David was exiled to the homeland of his mortal enemies, wrestling every day with sadness and shame.

It was from Gath that precious truths from the psalms emerged: "Let my vindication come from Your presence" (Psalm 17:2). "Keep me as the apple of Your eye; hide me under the shadow of Your wings…from my deadly enemies who surround me" (vv. 8–9). "Fight against those who fight against me" (35:1). "I will give You thanks in the great assembly; I will praise You among many people" (v. 18). It was from the Judean desert when David was either hiding in the wilderness or being betrayed by the Ziphites to Saul that we get these beautiful verses: "Behold, God is my helper" (54:4). "O God, You are my God; early will I seek You. My soul thirsts for You; my flesh longs for You in a dry and thirsty land where there is no water" (63:1).

After fifteen years in Sudan, my wife and I could truly confess that we needed Sudan more than Sudan needed us. It is true that God sends His people to the nations and uses us there for His glory, but along the way of lifting Jesus up in difficult places, we find Jesus uses those difficult places to make Himself incredibly sweet to us. It was as a shame-filled refugee that David realized the Lord was his vindication. It wasn't until enemies surrounded David that he realized he was the apple of God's eye. It was while living in Philistine territory that David determined he would give thanks in the great assembly and praise God among all the peoples. If David had not spent time at the mercy of the nations, he would not have as deep an appreciation for the mercy of God.

We go to the nations hoping to bless and then are sweetly surprised to find that God uses the nations to bless us. Thirsty lands and dangerous contexts are unimaginable blessings, for they show us what we really want and *who* we really want. When all dignity, strength, capacity, and resource are stripped away, we are finally alone with God Almighty. We have nowhere else to go, and we find Him immeasurably sweet. We find that He delivers us from all trouble. We find that being delivered from all trouble is a heart and spirit deliverance, not necessarily a no pain, no problems, no disappointment guarantee. We need the difficulty of serving among the nations to open our eyes to how sweet Jesus is, to help us see that He is all we really want, all we really need, and all we really have to give to the peoples of the earth.

PRAYER FOCUS: *Fulani, Bagirmi of Central African Republic (Evangelical: 0.03%)*

The text details the international realities of the moment on the day that David became king. The Philistines were once again invading Israel, conveniently removing King Saul, his sons, his armorbearer, and all his men from the picture and leaving the way open for David to be crowned. Meanwhile, the Amalekites (who, with their camels, ranged from Sinai to northern Arabia) attacked David's camp, and an Egyptian provided vital information for war. For David, this particular day, this day of Saul's death, included the Philistines releasing him from fighting for them, winning his family and possessions back from the Amalekites, and having the threat of Saul removed once and for all. Psalm 18 likely refers to this consequential period as it was written to celebrate the day that David was delivered from all his enemies and from Saul.

It is impossible to comprehend the story of David's ascension to the throne of Israel outside the context of global consequences. The nations were part and parcel of the ascension; their fate was linked to David's rule. In the short term, God continued His covenantal mission promise to Abraham. In the long term, from David's seed will come the divine God-man who will tabernacle with us and deliver us from sin. David's rule was not just about a tiny people on a tiny sliver of land, somehow surviving between the superpowers of then and now. David's rule was about all the nations, all the Gentiles hearing the praise of Jehovah, every people group bowing before God's Messiah who is David's seed.

It is impossible to comprehend God's perspective of any promotion, advance, or leadership position granted to us outside of these same global implications. Did you just get pregnant? That child is intended by God to have some impact on the nations. Did you just get a raise? That blessing is intended by God to have some part in God's global glory. Did you just get elected foreman, sergeant, chair, president, or director? That position is not for your glory, but for the fame of Jesus, and not just locally (school, business, civic body, national entity), but globally. Whenever God gives us a leadership position, it's never about us and it's never confined to just a parochial blessing. God advances us locally that He might be praised and worshiped globally. Our task is to see how every leadership opportunity is to be leveraged to make much of Jesus everywhere.

The tragedy of Saul's ending, confused and afraid, was inevitable from the moment he thought his leadership position was something to preserve, rather than something to give to God's global glory. What might have happened among the Philistines for the glory of God if Saul was not threatened by David, if he did not care how God was glorified or through whom? When we view our positions or promotions selfishly and jealously, we abuse them, and we violate the reason God granted them to us. God's blessings have ever and always will be intended for His glory amongst all peoples of the earth. We only retain the blessings we give away, and this is most true as regards the gospel and all nations.

PRAYER FOCUS: *Kanembu of Chad (Evangelical: 0.00%)*

APRIL 20: PILGRIM'S PROGRESS

TODAY'S READING: PSALM 121, 123–125, 128–130

The psalms of ascent were used by pilgrims from Israel and beyond, up from the low coastal plains to the mountains of Judea that surrounded Jerusalem. Some of the psalms are attributed to David and they certainly reflect this season of his life. From the coastal exile of Philistia and the desert harshness of fugitive existence in the wilderness, David ascended to the throne, up to Jerusalem to rule.

In the larger sense, we too ascend from the dusty plains of earth towards heaven's higher ground. The biblical theology of missions includes apocalyptic eschatology. The King of kings is coming back to rule and reign. There is a great and terrible day of the Lord. There will be a resurrection of the living and the dead. There is an eternal heaven and hell. All nations will be represented in the King's eternal heaven. History itself is climbing the hill of time to that great and terrible day when the trumpet sounds and the Son of Man descends in glory. Every day that passes brings us closer. Every trial that assails us, we step higher. Every people group reached with the gospel, we draw nearer. Every prayer, martyr, sacrificial dollar to speed the light is a step of ascent, and we draw near in these last days to the temple mount. Whether it was David ascending to the throne, the Israelites ascending to the temple, missionaries extending the gospel into the heart of unreached places and peoples, or the body of Christ ascending to the day of the Lord, we all press forward, and all pilgrims can take comfort in the psalms of ascent.

"[God] will not allow [our] foot to be moved" (**Psalm 121:3**). Some versions say, "He will not allow your foot to slip." We lift our eyes up to the hills that hold danger, murderers, and thieves. Where will our help come from? Certainly not the mountains. As the pilgrims drew near Jerusalem, their bodies were tired, their legs weary from travel. Sometimes the path twisted around ravines and loose gravel made the way dangerous. It could have proved terrible to slip at the wrong moment. God responds to this danger by saying He will not allow it. To the pilgrim God promises that when we are tired and most vulnerable to temptation, He will not let us slip.

"He who keeps you will not slumber" (**v. 3**). At the end of a long day, camp was set up, a simple meal prepared, and the pilgrims bedded down for an uncomfortable night. They took turns to keep watch for bandits and wolves that lurked just beyond the safety of the firelight. It was not unusual for a bone-weary traveler to fall asleep at his post. If he did, the thieves would steal in and plunder. God responds to this danger of pilgrimaging with those who fail us and with us who fail others by saying that He will never fall asleep or fail us

"The sun shall not strike you by day, nor the moon by night" (**v. 6**). There was a belief common in Palestine that exposure to the moon could make you loony. Our English word "lunatic" comes from "lunar" or moon. Some travelers believed constant exposure to the moon affected one's mind. God responds that He will protect our minds. Day and night, God will get us home safely. God will be with us when we are sent out and when we come in. God will protect His pilgrims from all evil.

PRAYER FOCUS: *Hui of China (Evangelical: 0.01%)*

APRIL 21: WE DON'T CELEBRATE DEATH

TODAY'S READING: 2 SAMUEL 1-4

*"Obedience to the call of Christ nearly always costs everything to two people—
the one who is called, and the one who loves that one."*

OSWALD CHAMBERS

As 1 Samuel ends, Saul was told that the kingdom was taken from him because he did not execute God's wrath on Amalek. The first verse of 2 Samuel notes that David returned from slaughtering the Amalekites on the day that Saul died, the day that he became king. That slaughter was in direct obedience to the commands of God. It's fascinating (and intentionally recorded) that the kingdom was lost and gained in proportion to obedience regarding the Amalekites. God's favor and wrath always stay connected to whether or not we glorify Him among the nations.

David never celebrated the death of Saul, and we should never celebrate when God's judgment falls on the nations or on those who lead. Judgment on us all is inevitable as the purpose of godly judgment is the eradication of evil so that what is pure might thrive. If God destroys a civilization or an institution or a civic leader so that God's people and purposes go forward, we do not gloat even if we are grateful. Rather we stand with David at that funeral and choose to remember the good days and the good things of the person, place, or leader. In fact, David went on to call Saul beloved and pleasant while he lived, conveniently forgetting the spears he dodged. This spirit allows missionaries and local believers who have been persecuted or imprisoned in a local context to sincerely love and cherish what is good about the locus and locals of their place of languish. God's missionary people do not make a habit of calling down fire from heaven.

What made David a man after God's heart was his constant concern for the name and fame of God among the nations. This passion erupts through the whole book of Psalms and was espoused at the death of Saul: David always wanted Jehovah to look good, David always wanted the nations to be attracted to Jehovah, and David wanted good things to happen to God's people as a light and testimony to the goodness of God. Likewise, if we are to be men and women of God's own heart, we must be concerned with how every victory and defeat is interpreted by the nations. We must desire that whether we experience pain or pleasure the result is that God looks good internationally. Our sorrow is not wasted if it somehow is used to bear testimony to the goodness of God. When a missionary family buries their child on the field, living and grieving among their adopted unreached people, and through their tears point their cultural comforters to Christ, that family lives for the glory of God in grief. We do not seek or desire sorrow, but we can welcome it when it leads to Jesus being made beautiful before unreached peoples.

PRAYER FOCUS: *Han Chinese, Hakka of China, Hong Kong (Evangelical: 1.50%)*

APRIL 22: THE LEAST WE CAN DO

TODAY'S READING: PSALM 6, 8–10, 14, 16, 19, 21

"Do we claim to believe in God? He's a missionary God. You tell me you're committed to Christ. He's a missionary Christ. Are you filled with the Holy Spirit? He's a missionary Spirit. Do you belong to the church? It's a missionary society. And do you hope to go to heaven when you die? It's a heaven into which the fruits of world mission have been and will be gathered."

JOHN STOTT

In the Psalms, there are more references to the nations than there are actual psalms. "It is a profound fact that 'the hymn of praise is missionary preaching par excellence' especially when we realize that such missionary preaching is supported in the Psalms by more than 175 references of a universalistic note relating to the nations of the world…. Indeed the Psalter is one of the greatest missionary books in the world." The great song book of the people of God has stanzas in every hymn about the nations and God's glory in all the earth. Almost every psalm has a reference to God's activity among the nations. It may be blessing or wooing, conquest or judgment, but over and over again the psalms underline that God is a missionary God who blesses His missionary people to bring all the peoples of earth to the blessings of their God.

In Psalm 6, David reminds us that God will be glorified among the nations regardless of their response. God is just as glorified when nations refuse His love and face His wrath as when they accept His mercy and receive His joy. In Psalm 9, we are reminded that God's judgments will equally apply to all the peoples of earth. God intends to make very clear His magnificence in all the earth, thus the sobriety and urgency of the missionary mandate to go into all the world and urge the nations to flee the wrath to come. In Psalm 10, we are reminded that Jesus shall rule "where'er the sun doth his successive journeys run" and for all time. In Psalm 14, we are encouraged that God will bring His elect out of every nation and send His elect from Zion into all the world to every people as agents of salvation. In Psalm 16, we are exhorted to join in with God's love for all His global beloved. In Psalm 19, we are challenged that if the glory of God is so clearly expressed in the heavens, should He not be more glorified by the crown of His creation—by men and women of every race? And in Psalm 21, we are sobered: God will destroy all those who rebel against His rule and reject His mercy.

Truly, the book of the Psalms resounds with God's plan and passion for every people group to know, praise, and glorify Him. Surely, the very least we can do is sing about His glory in all nations every time we open our mouths to praise.

PRAYER FOCUS: *Han Chinese, Cantonese of China, Macau (Evangelical: 1.26%)*

APRIL 23: UNSTOPPABLE GLORY

TODAY'S READING: 1 CHRONICLES 1–2

"His authority on earth allows us to dare to go to all the nations.
His authority in heaven gives us our only hope of success.
And His presence with us leaves us no other choice."

JOHN STOTT

The books of Chronicles are a review of Israel's history through the lens of the priests. These genealogies are missionary oriented because they clearly link humans to God's majestic plan, a plan that began with Adam, was covenanted to Abraham, and prophesied through David. In fact, Abraham and David figure prominently in all critical biblical genealogies, including those of the Gospels. Chronicles begins with a list of nations, similar to Genesis 10 and 11 where God listed all the different ethnicities of earth He would bless through Abraham's seed. God's global heart is demonstrated here, and we should read these lists with wonder, not boredom, for they remind us that God is passionate about every unique culture and every individual person. Strange names and places are comforting, for they assure us that the great God of glory has a plan for our nation, our tribe, and our person, and if no one else knows or remembers us, Almighty God does and will. And the Lord doesn't want us to forget that the ones that scare us are actually family members. Edomites, Moabites, Ishmaelites, Midianites, and Egyptians are all part of our family tree (and they often are more scared of us than we are of them).

As in the genealogies of Jesus in the Gospels, the Chronicles genealogies take care to remind us of the inclusive nature of our heavenly Father. David came from Judah's line; thus, we are reminded that the sons of Judah were born to him by the daughter of Shua, the Canaanitess, and by Tamar, also from Canaan, who employed prostitution in order to gain her child. The mention of Boaz implies the outsider widow named Ruth, as well as David's sisters and an Ishmaelite.

The God of all peoples tolerates no racism in His children. God reminds us that His kingdom plan includes and centers around every tribe, tongue, and people group worshiping Him. It's ironic that Western peoples feel we have more affinity with biblical figures than Arabs, Africans, or Asians, when in reality our cultures are more distant than theirs. We joined the family much later than the peoples of the Fertile Crescent, so we should have a little bit of humility regarding our family history. Perspective of our past not only helps us stay lowly; it also helps us stay faith-filled when faced with the decline and decay of our home culture. Our home culture has no corner on the market regarding the presence or favor of God. God's powerful, intimate blessing descended on cultures older than ours before we existed, and He always has a remnant. As our culture collapses, we can be certain that God's kingdom is unstoppable. The glory will find an obedient, holy people elsewhere, and the mission of God will steam on to its irrepressible conclusion: a throne room and throng, all colors, ages, peoples, and songs, and one Lord.

PRAYER FOCUS: *Comorian, Ndzwani of Comoros (Evangelical: 0.24%)*

APRIL 24: THIS IS US,
THE REDEEMED OF THE NATIONS

TODAY'S READING: PSALM 43–45, 49, 84–85, 87

The very poor memory of man combined with the very constant rebellion against what we do remember repeatedly leads us to disaster. And repeatedly, God offers us the joy of His presence. The Most High God pursues us. He desires to be our God, and all that He asks is that we be His holy faithful bride. If we will be His, He will live with us, bless us with His presence, power, and provision, and use us to bless all the peoples of earth. The folly in man fixates on the provisions, forgets the Provider, and abandons the purpose; and the result is, we lose both the provision and the protection. The cries in the psalms result from this plight, for to abandon the purposes of God to selfishly focus on His pleasures is to lose His presence—and that is to lose all. When God's people selfishly withdraw from blessing the nations, God responds by scattering them to the nations.

God will use us to reveal His glory among the nations, either through prosperity because in holiness we have been faithful or through pain because in selfishness we have been false. "Shame accompanies the experience of defeat and applies even to those who are not personally responsible for what happened." As a collective body we were commissioned to lift up Jesus among all peoples. If this is not happening, we together bear shame. We are all responsible for aborted babies in our nation, for prayerlessness in our churches, for unreached peoples who receive no gospel witness. We are all responsible to repent and to work together "that glory may dwell in our land" (Psalm 85:9). For surely then His salvation is near. And if we don't collectively repent, we will collectively be punished.

All is not lost, for in His mercy, God still woos us. He is fairer than the sons of men, and from that beauty, the peoples fall under Him and are won to His heart. He responds with the affirmation: "The LORD loves the gates of Zion.... The LORD will record, when He registers the peoples: 'This one was born there'" (87:2, 6). In the expansive heart of God, His intention is that "Zion will become a multinational community of people from many nations, all of whom will belong to YHWH, and therefore they will be rightly counted as belonging to Israel. God Himself will dwell in the midst of 'you', Zion of the nations… The identity and membership of Israel have thus been radically redrawn by YHWH himself. It is no longer Zion **and** the nations but Zion inclusive of the nations."

The psalms are not just songs—they are missionary anthems. These anthems remind, warn, encourage, and inspire us. Hearts swell and eyes mist as we remember that it's not us and them, Zion and the nations. The Zion of God is *us, the redeemed of all the nations*. We look with eyes of faith at a South Asian Hindu family in the Congo, and we sing by faith over them: "These ones were born in Zion!"

PRAYER FOCUS: *South Asian, General of Democratic Republic of Congo (Evangelical: 0.04%)*

APRIL 25: PRAY THE PRAYER

*"The motto of every missionary, whether preacher, printer,
or schoolmaster, ought to be 'Devoted for life.'"*

ADONIRAM JUDSON

❝Now these were the kings" (1 Chr. 1:43) becomes "now these were the sons of David" (3:1). The books of Chronicles were written after the Jews returned from exile in Babylon. They were concerned to show continuity with their pre-exilic family. The best way to do so was through genealogies. "Genealogies recorded the continuity of families through the disaster of exile and beyond. To show an unbroken family line with Judean ancestors before the Exile became a way of establishing continuity and thus claiming a proper role in the postexilic society." The priority then was on position (can you be a priest?) and property (can you regain your family land?). Lost along the way was the overarching passion of God. "The genealogical list of 'the sons of David' (1 Chr. 3:1) subtly supported the restoration of a Davidic king in postexilic Jerusalem. The Exile happened, yet the descendants of David should still be the rightful rulers of Israel. The Davidic Genealogy (1 Chr. 3:1–24) reminded the readers that God was not yet done with the line of David in Israel." The larger passion was not centered on a specific people having a specific piece of real estate, nor a specific family getting to rule that little sliver of land. The larger passion was that *that* specific people and king would be used to mediate all the royal blessings of God to all the peoples of earth. Jehovah's kings ruled Jehovah's people so that Jehovah's blessings might permeate all nations of earth. The God of the Bible is not concerned about who gets to be priest or potentate as an end; rather all positions and all properties are intended to be means for the nations to be won to Jehovah.

The reason we read Chronicles at this point in the chronological reading of the Bible is that though it was written after the exile, its early chapters describe the settling of Canaan and the establishment of priests and kings. In Judah's line we encounter Jabez who asks for blessing, enlarged territory, and God's helping hand, presence, holiness, and purposes (4:1–9). These are missionary descriptions, set in a litany of names to remind us of the main point. Whenever we read the word "bless" in the Bible as referring to something received from God, we must read it through the lens of God blessing Abraham to bless all nations. No blessing of God is meant to be terminal; all blessings are meant to pass through our hands to others, to unreached peoples. Likewise, enlarged territory is not for despotic rule; all expansion of authority is ambassadorial for God's people—we are to represent the King to all nations. The cries for God to dwell among us as His holy people are eternally linked to His purposes in all the earth—not to cause pain, but to give gospel life. Jabez directly prayed the tripartite formula: Be my God, dwell with me, make me your holy representative, and let me pass on the blessings of union with the one true God. When we pray these missionary prayers, God delights to grant what we request (v. 10).

PRAYER FOCUS: *Jula, Dyula of Cote d'Ivoire (Evangelical: 0.00%)*

APRIL 26: START REMEMBERING

TODAY'S READING: PSALM 73, 77–78

"If you are sick, fast and pray; if the language is hard to learn, fast and pray; if the people will not hear you, fast and pray; if you have nothing to eat, fast and pray."

FREDERICK FRANSON

Israel was promised through Abraham that they would be blessed to be a blessing. As a royal priesthood, they were to both intercede and to rule under God's smiling sovereignty, and in their prosperity all the nations of the world were to see how beneficial it was to live as sons and daughters of Jehovah. This was the plan. But along the way it did not seem to be working. Holiness and consecration, and justice and integrity often led to poverty and being taken advantage of. Conversely, wickedness and corruption seemed to reward the evil. The sadness of cleansing their hearts and living in innocence seemed to be in vain. God seems to not bless us but strangely bless the ones who disobey and scorn Him. The reality of life as we know it is too unfair and painful to think about until we go to the sanctuary of God, for there we see their end.

Where we get in trouble is when we fixate on one day or too short a period of time. The God of missions is the God of history. God's purposes move inexorably forward, despite the appearances of one day, the setbacks of one year, or the losses of a century. Ever onward, God works for His own glory among all peoples of the earth, and sometimes the sum span of one person's 70 years coincides with a setback that is 100 years long. If our lives are all we have to judge God's mission by, many of us would not have much to shout about. But when we lift our eyes off ourselves and go into the presence of the God who is outside of time, when we open our Bibles and look back to Abraham and forward to the trumpet sounding, when we fill our hearts through reading the testimonies of history and our ears with the triumphs of God's team around the world, then we understand. God is indeed winning, and there is no contest. My little heart and flesh in my little corner of the battle may fail, *but God* is the strength of my heart and my portion forever, and He is resoundingly winning the nations to Himself. It is good for me to draw near to God and to trust Him, that I may declare His works and His wins.

Psalm 77 frames the mercy of God in missionary boundaries. Have His promises failed? Has God failed to keep His word to bless all peoples of earth by blessing His own holy people? When all seems bleak as if God has forgotten us, we handle the disappointments of life by remembering Him. We look at the bigger picture. "Surely I will remember your wonders of old…and talk of Your deeds…. You are the God who does wonders; You have declared Your strength among the peoples" (vv. 11–15). If you feel forgotten, start remembering. Remember what God has done through history among the nations.

PRAYER FOCUS: *Cypriots, Turkish of Cyprus (Evangelical: 0.26%)*

APRIL 27: LET'S GO TO WAR IN SONG

TODAY'S READING: 1 CHRONICLES 6–7, PSALM 81

God's purposes triumph either in the nations or through the nations. Either God's missionary people receive God's blessings and carry them to the nations, or God has His people carried to the nations to use their plight to showcase His glory. It's interesting that the text lists music ministers directly after the verses describing Nebuchadnezzar carrying God's people to exile. We all get to sing, and whether those songs be celebratory victory chants or funeral dirges depends on our missionary obedience. Worship is a primary means of warfare. When surrounded by lostness, one of the best things we can do is lift our voices in praise, for praise pushes back darkness and wins battles. Because worship is warfare, it is critical we sing well. Singing well means (a) we sing Scripture, (b) we avoid an overuse of first person pronouns when we sing, (c) we specifically mention the names and specific titles of our God, (d) we sing songs simple and memorable enough that everyone can sing without instrument or professional singer, (e) we sing without performing or drawing attention to ourselves, and (f) we repeatedly sing the great redemption themes (like those found in many of our great hymns). Let's go to war in song!

The Chronicles genealogies are fascinating for their inclusion. Reading through them to discover the illuminating side commentary invigorates, for over and over again we see that God is interested in foreigners and the marginalized, daughters and sisters, warriors and sons of warriors, and leaders. God's missionary plan is that all people of all peoples will take the glorious gospel to all people of all peoples. God is sending the young and old, male and female, rich and poor as missionaries. God is sending Latinos, Europeans, Africans, Arabs, Asians, Americans, and every combination thereof to represent Him among unreached peoples. Missionary qualification is judged by the internal content of character, fidelity to the Scriptures, and obedience to the Spirit, and not by the color of external skin. All God's children are invited to lift their song among the nations.

Psalm 81 instructs the variegated people of God to shout joyfully to the God of Jacob. The superscript of the Psalm indicates this hymn was composed on an instrument of Gath, a Philistine city. How beautiful that Jehovah taps His toe to ethnic music. On a redeemed instrument the people of God recalled what God did in Egypt when His people were surrounded by a language hard to understand. With Jehovah filling us with Himself, with a steady diet of His presence, we can overcome all nations and enemies, and His love can win the hearts of all the peoples of the earth. But, alas, though He would have fed us with the finest of wheat and satisfied us with honey from the rock, we stubbornly refused to sing His songs and refused to walk in His missionary ways.

God is a singer. In C. S. Lewis' *The Magician's Nephew*, Aslan represents the Creator who sings a new world into being and into beautiful order. God sings over the nations, and He asks us to sing with Him. The great conductor of heavenly choirs enjoys the enthusiastic anthems when all His people shout and sing. Yet with His divine ear He wistfully notes the ongoing absence of Afar voices and instruments.

PRAYER FOCUS: *Afar of Djibouti (Evangelical: 0.00%)*

APRIL 28: SPARKLING VETERANS

TODAY'S READING: PSALM 88, 92-93

The psalms are helpful missionary ballast. When we set sail to obey the command of God to preach the gospel in all the earth making disciples of every people, we start that journey sparkly. Many are the "shiny" missionaries we have seen disembark to their port of entry with new clothes, fresh hope, big dreams, and joyful expectation. Around month three, the romance is gone. Around month six, leaders once revered are revealed as humans with smelly feet of clay. Around year one, loneliness and culture stress seem insurmountable. After two years, they manage to speak the local language at a fourth-grade level with a speech impediment and find themselves wondering if the McDonald's back home has a janitorial position open and muse about the best way to get an honorable discharge. At that point, they read Psalm 88 and find themselves agreeing more and more with the melancholic sons of Korah: crying day and night, full of troubles, no strength, cut off, in the depths, afflicted, shut up, and wasting away. Contrary to the testimony of missionary lions, their particular missions history is that of *unanswered* prayer; all they can think is that "loved ones and friends have been put far from [them]" (v. 18).

The elder veterans can inspire the young ones when they shine forth the joyful triumph of the Lord in the battle for His glory in all the earth. Something spiritually invigorating is imparted when Jesus-loving warriors shine and sparkle after years of service. How depressing is the grumpy veteran and how glorious and gladdening is the scarred-up man or woman who limps into the room but leaps in the light. When a veteran of missions, ministry, and Jesus-centered living who is unaware and oblivious to their obvious wounds rubs joy on all they meet, power and hope surge through every level of our ranks. We need to hear our living saints testify: "I am anointed with fresh oil. My eye has seen my desire. I have flourished and grown like a cedar in Lebanon. I am bearing fruit in old age. I am fresh and flourishing. The Lord is my rock and there is no unrighteousness in Him" (see Psalm 92:10–15). Everyone knows that life, ministry, and missions are brutally hard, so what we don't need are grumpy, bitter veterans. We need men and women who shine with the joy of the Lord's favor because they fight His battles, not despite the battles.

Lord, grant to us the veteran voices who agree with Psalm 93 that the Lord reigns on a throne established in eternity and that our Lord on high is mightier than the noise of many waters. If you are a veteran soldier of Christ, find a new recruit today and sparkle at them, look them in the eye, and tell them that if they persevere, God will indeed use them to win the Romani gypsies of Egypt to His joy. There's no need to talk about scars. Rather, let's talk about God's triumphs. Let's sow hope and faith that the same God with the same glory will do it all again.

PRAYER FOCUS: *Romani, Domari of Egypt (Evangelical: 0.64%)*

APRIL 29: THE MISSIONARY CHIEFS OF STAFF

TODAY'S READING: 1 CHRONICLES 8-10

The genealogies in Chronicles begin with Adam, focus on the priests, and end with Saul. The chronicler did not spend a lot of time on the negative aspects of Saul, his family, or even David's sins, preferring a more positive narrative that centers on the temple and priestly duties. In the final genealogy which ends with Saul's death, Saul's son Ishbosheth is listed as Esh-Baal and his grandson Mephibosheth is listed as Merib-Baal. The names have the same root, and it appears the writer of the book of Samuel exchanged the Canaanite word for God, "baal," with the Hebrew word for shame, "bosheth." How sad that the legacy of Saul became a shameful one. Because he did not faithfully pursue God's passion in dealing with the Amalekites, he was deemed unfaithful and so God killed him. Judah fared no better and was, in turn, carried away to Babylon for its respective unfaithfulness. God is pretty serious about His covenant relationship with His people. He will be our God, He will live among us, we will be His holy missionary people, and He will bless us so we bless all nations—or else He kills us and sends us to Babylon. This is the harsh Old Testament rendering, yet God has lost none of His fiery passion for His own glory among all peoples in our day.

Speaking of fiery passion, the Levites tended the fires of sacrifice and all the worship of the temple. These were then intended to keep God's people holy, sanctified to His missionary purposes in all the earth. First Chronicles 9:17–27 details the interesting role of the Levitical gatekeepers. "Gatekeepers played very significant roles in a temple centered society with crude locks and keys…. A significant role for the gatekeepers was their control of the temple offerings and payroll…a responsibility that included distributing allotments by divisions…persons of great integrity were needed to ensure the proper financial care of the temple and its personnel." No wonder the text describes the gatekeepers as able men whom the Lord was with, and who held a trusted office. It's not that different today. God has able men and women globally with the integrity He can trust with wealth. Money so easily corrupts, and there are few God can trust to give much to, few He knows who will give much away both wisely and strategically. In the ongoing pursuit of the global worship of Jesus by every tongue and tribe, there are many roles to play, and all of them need funding. In practical terms, someone must oversee the treasury of God's house and ensure it is directed towards the last, least, and lost. God's missionary will is empowered when God's missionary businesspeople are favored and trusted with God's missionary wealth. Faithful gatekeepers seek out people groups like the Beja and get behind missionaries called to take the gospel to them. These "missionary chief of staff" givers are central to the Great Commission. Bless them, Lord, to be a blessing to all the peoples of earth.

PRAYER FOCUS: *Beja, Hedareb of Eritrea (Evangelical: 0.00%)*

APRIL 30: THE CHOICE
TODAY'S READING: PSALM 102-104

It's pretty intuitive that God by definition must have universal worship. If indeed He is God, then all peoples from all places in all the creation must worship Him and be only fully satisfied in and by Him. You can't be God and not have universal scope, whether that be power, knowledge, presence, or worship. If God will not be glorified everywhere by everyone in everything, then He is no true God. The wonder of free will must be interpreted through its limited period of operation—we can choose to worship God now, but the day is coming where every knee will be compelled to bow and every tongue confess that Jesus Christ is Lord to the glory of God the Father. Because God by definition is worthy of universal worship, it is academic that the course of history marches toward that end. All the peoples will praise Him—it's just a matter of time. We can resist this inevitable future, but it is futile resistance. We can rebel against this certain end, but frankly, that means we align with the devil and his demonic host, and at the end of the beginning (when King Jesus returns), those efforts are overwhelmingly defeated. We can worship other things, but that only disappoints now and eternally, or we can "sing praise to the Lord as long as [we] live" (Psalm 104:33).

The wonder is not so much that the God of glory, the God so worthy of worship allows humans a period of choice. The wonder is that this awesome Lord does not consume us for rejecting and disrespecting Him. Perhaps the definitive description of God in the Old Testament is found in Psalm 103: "The LORD is merciful and gracious, slow to anger, and abounding in mercy.... The mercy of the LORD is from everlasting to everlasting" (v. 8, 17). The fact that God is slow to anger indicates that anger is a legitimate, wonderful, and necessary part of being God. It reminds us that one day indeed sinners will "be consumed from the earth" (104:35), but first there is a season of grace where mercy allows escape from deserved wrath. How foolish, even wicked, is the suggestion that God is harsh to unleash His wrath. This line is a slap in the face to the Lord of mercy. We should not wonder at the God who destroys; rather, we should marvel at the God who saves.

We live in the age of incredible mercy. God created mankind and gave us all the privilege of will, which everyone living and dead has abused in order to worship self and a range of idols, causing great pain. God should destroy us all, but God astoundingly declared a fixed period of amnesty, a time to have His people announce God's mercy to all the peoples of earth. The Lord of mercy blessed Abraham so that the not-yet established six million Oromo of Ethiopia would be warned to flee the wrath to come, to take advantage of God's amnesty, and to remember that "the LORD has established His throne in heaven" (103:19). Missions is both blessing God now and announcing a period of God's merciful amnesty globally so that all peoples can bless Him eternally.

PRAYER FOCUS: *Oromo, Hararghe of Ethiopia (Evangelical: 0.05%)*

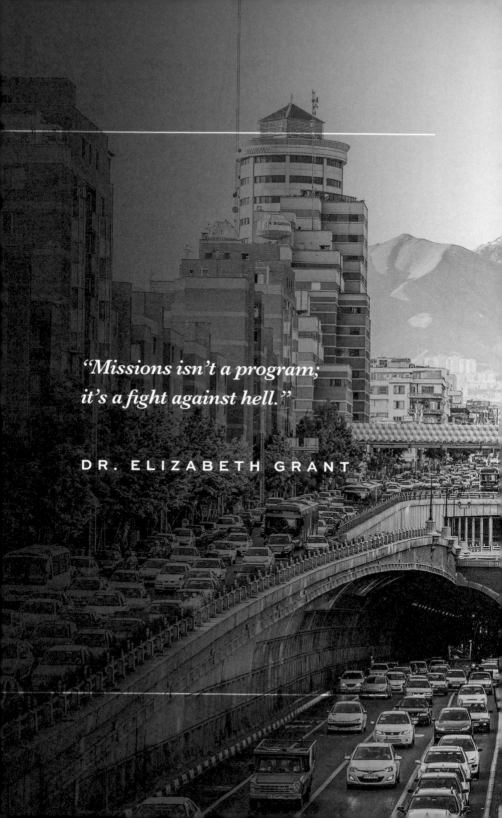

"*Missions isn't a program;
it's a fight against hell.*"

DR. ELIZABETH GRANT

MAY 1: SALUTING SENDERS

TODAY'S READING: 2 SAMUEL 5; 1 CHRONICLES 11–12

In today's reading, David was made king by all the tribes of Israel, and the record of Chronicles lists every tribe having representatives who wanted David to be king. This mixed multitude included members of every tribe, different nationalities, and a dizzying array of families. Revelation 5:9 assures that all families of earth will welcome back King Jesus. The strange tribes at the end of each day's devotional reading are today's families—each one will be around Christ's throne. In the meantime, all of God's family is needed to take the gospel to all the world.

Once crowned king, David consolidated his people, ruling from Hebron for seven years before taking Jerusalem. Entrenched on top of a fortified mountain, the Jebusites taunted David, thinking they were so established that David would never conquer the city. It's an oft-repeated mistake. The Algerian Arabs who immigrated to France might seem entrenched in Islam, and they may even taunt the God of missions saying: "The gospel will never come in here. Even our weakest are stronger than that!" It may be that what David did to defeat the Jebusites is what God will do to win Algerians. The people of Jerusalem had dug through rock to a water source and David used this Jebusite-made shaft for surprise access into the city. What helped the Jebusites resist invasion became the means of their defeat. The Lord in His wisdom is able to take that which unreached peoples have used to resist His advance and turn it into the means of His access into their hearts.

Once David took Jerusalem, the Philistines came after him. Once the gospel starts to penetrate an unreached people, demonic attacks increase. The devil is not concerned about ineffective churches or missionaries and is surprisingly content to leave them alone, to let them muddle on in their ineffectiveness. Once we start to make disciples that make disciples, the forces of evil marshal against us. David wisely asked advice of God; God told him to attack and God broke through. A second battle opportunity came up, and David again sought the Lord. God told him to circle around and wait for the sound of marching in the tops of the trees. Sometimes we quietly climb shafts, sometimes we boldly take things head on, and sometimes we circle around while God sends angel armies to march on tree tops. Let's stay creative in mission. Let's keep asking God's advice.

As soon as David took Jerusalem, he built "the Millo." It's not clear what "the Millo" was, though archaeology has revealed terraces built into the steep eastern slope of the city, serving as retaining walls supporting the buildings above. Whatever the wars for God's glory among the nations, David needed a secure home base, a solid sending structure. So it is today. The innovative structures that send missionaries are critical to conquest and are often the unsung heroes of the missionary story. If you are a sender, I salute you. You are the foundation on which every missionary stands. We are one army; together we rise or fall.

PRAYER FOCUS: *Algerian, Arabic Speaking of France (Evangelical: 0.10%)*

MAY 2: FIGHTING FOR RARE UNITY

TODAY'S READING: PSALM 133

"The true greatness of any church is not how many it seats but how many it sends!"

UNKNOWN

Through a missiological lens, an alternate reading of Psalm 133:1 would be: "Behold how good and how pleasant it is when brethren plant churches together in unity." Note that someone very familiar with the pain of disunity penned this psalm. David's father and brothers did not think highly of him. His king doubted his loyalty and repeatedly tried to kill him. His first wife was given to another man. David betrayed and divided a friend from his wife. One son tried to take the kingdom from him, while another raped a relative and was murdered by a third. David's nation was divided before, during, and after his reign. This psalm is a deep longing from one who knew how precious unity was, and how damaging and painful was its lack. A man of blood, David did not often live in the blessedness of true unity.

This is the central warning of the psalm. Unity is as rare as the once-in-a-lifetime anointing of the high priest or as rare as a heavy Mt. Hermon dew falling on the much lower, more arid Mt. Zion. With this simple foundation reminding us that true unity is astoundingly rare and with a stated qualifier that the focus of missions is the priority of making disciples and planting churches among unreached peoples, I share some partnership convictions: *If we are not desperate for partnership with God,* we haven't understood our weakness. Real partnership is based on being desperate for God *before* we are desperate for God. *If we are not desperate for partnership with others,* we have not understood missions. If our missionary activity is only in contexts where we do not acutely feel the need for partnership, then we are under-challenged and not engaged where the battle is fiercest. If we can handle our assignment alone, then our vision is too small and our goals too cowardly. *And if we do not understand that we must fight for partnership,* we do not understand its power or the devil's hatred of it. We must fight through the idea that partnership is about receiving and remember it's in giving that we receive. We must fight through the perceived threat that partnership will harm our longevity and security. We must fight through the inconvenience that partnership demands. We must fight through denominational concerns to face the battlefield joy of unlikely "foxhole companions." We must fight through the agonizing pain of betrayal and disappointment.

If we do not understand the commanded blessing of partnership, we will miss out on the beauty of what God will do in these last days. We know how it all ends, for the Revelation 5:9 vision is the culmination of partnership: every tribe, tongue, and nation around the throne. How we get there is important to Jesus. Jesus knows how difficult, rare, and precious real partnership is, so when He sees it amongst us, when He sees the self-denying, others-centered cost we paid to fight for partnership that He be glorified globally, He delightedly rises from His throne and unleashes blessing.

PRAYER FOCUS: *Fulani, Fulakunda of Gambia (Evangelical: 0.05%)*

MAY 3: HOW TO BE ABHORRED BY GOD

TODAY'S READING: PSALM 106–107

The history of redemption from Egypt is often repeated, as in Psalm 106, with different nuances underlined. If God visited His chosen people to save them once, He can do it again, so that blessing is gained and glory shared with others. The tragedy of the human element in this ongoing story is that blessings always corrupt us. The progression is simple. We start physically and fiscally unable to help ourselves. From that helplessness we cry out to the Lord who in mercy saves, blesses, counsels, and comforts us. Those blessings are always given so we will bless all peoples in His name. And we may start out doing so, but time and temptation take our eyes off the nations and off our need for God. Physical needs made us spiritually desperate and dependent on Jesus for everything. Physical blessings make us spiritually slothful, and the very consequences of God's blessings pull us away from Him as we no longer acutely sense our need for Him. We keep Him on retainer as an insurance policy for all the provisions that wealth cannot supply. We forget God our Savior, the God who did great things in Egypt, wondrous things in the land of Ham, and awesome things by the Red Sea.

Not only do we forget the Unforgettable One, we also take up the wicked ways of those we live among, horrifically sacrificing our sons and daughters to demons. Since Roe vs. Wade in 1973, more than 50 million babies have been murdered. How many missionaries were murdered in their mother's wombs? How many astute businesspeople gifted in creating wealth to give to missionary work among the unreached were slain before they drew a breath? How many billions of hours of intercessory prayer have been lost because men and women who would have stormed heaven for the sake of those who have never heard were never heard themselves? Make no mistake, the consequence of disobeying God's commands to live as a holy missionary people never only affects us—it also eternally impacts all the nations of the world. The doom of any nation that rebels against God is sure. That fact that God allows any good to come from a nation that has brutally murdered 50 million children can only be explained by His unfathomable mercy and the fact that a remnant still lives for His glory among the nations. Secular America scorns Jesus-centered and gospel-preaching missionary activity today. Ironically, that activity may be the only reason God has not destroyed this land.

Psalm 107 echoes Psalm 106. It repeats the refrain that those who despise the Most High's counsel will be brought down to hard labor with none to help. However, Psalm 107 gives hope that God's mercy endures forever. If we will repent, God will yet forgive our wicked ways. If we will exalt Him in the assembly of the people, He will yet bless and multiply greatly. The Psalms remind us that God has never wavered from His purpose: to be glorified by and to satisfy every people group on earth. God blesses His children that live and die toward that end. Those that forget, ignore, or oppose our missionary God, alongside those who kill His present and future workers, He abhors.

PRAYER FOCUS: *Azerbaijani of Georgia (Evangelical: 0.00%)*

MAY 4: TWIRL IN SINCERITY

TODAY'S READING: 1 CHRONICLES 13–16

"God cannot lead you on the basis of facts that you do not know."

DAVID BRYANT

David was angry because he "was afraid of God that day" (1 Chr. 13:12). The trouble started when David wanted to bring the ark of the covenant to Jerusalem. The idea wasn't wrong, but the process was. David didn't carefully follow God's instructions to have Levites who were sanctified fulfil the task. Further, Uzza unthinkingly assumed God needed help and for his assumption was killed. No one gets to disrespect God, especially those who serve Him. In their sincerity, David and all Israel played music and sang with all their might, but Uzza was still killed. Even in the best of times, when we are sanctified and have done all things according to the good pleasure of God, we still can't contain Him. God will always break out against anything or anyone that tries to restrain Him.

Shockingly, sincerity is not enough in the heart of worshipers if their praise does not honor God. For too long we in the church have hidden behind "sincerity" as a justification for worship that is actually ignorant and unpleasant to God. We jump around, work up a sweat, and sing at the top of our lungs, but if it only feels good to us while burning a few calories and yet still ignites the anger of the Lord, then eventually someone will die. What if our sincere worship in song and music is offensive to God because it's not specific enough? A church of sincere worshipers sang four songs one Sunday. Three of the four songs never specifically mentioned God. The first song was about freedom and could have been sung at a civil rights rally. The second song was about rivers and creation and could have been sung by a Hindu or a secular environmentalist. The fourth song was so generic that a Muslim could have sung it completely in line with Koranic teaching. None of the words were bad—just general. I wonder if God would have been more pleased if the lyrics specifically glorified the uniqueness of the God of the Bible and the unique person and work of the Lord Jesus Christ? There was a second noticeable absence from the mouths of these sincere worshipers: It was a missions service and there was nothing sung about the glory of God among all peoples. If the worship lyrics in our churches is disconnected from the heart of God for unreached peoples and the lost globally, no matter how many lights we flash, is He really pleased?

David was shocked that the sincerity of Israel's corporate worship didn't make up for their absent theology. He recalibrated, corrected sanctification and scope, and brought the ark to Jerusalem. He didn't lay down sincerity, though. He danced with all his might and the music soared again, and he delivered a psalm (1 Chr. 16:8–36). He twirled into Jerusalem in both sincerity and sanctification. I'm not much of a dancer myself, but I don't mind if you are as long as you press beyond sincerity to specifically praising the God of the Bible (Father, Son, and Spirit) and include in your enthusiasm God's great missionary heart for all the nations.

PRAYER FOCUS: *Turk of Germany (Evangelical: 0.00%)*

Sometimes the evidence needs no explanation. If we compiled the word-for-word missionary citations from the handful of Psalms in today's reading into one collection, the resulting song would sing unadorned over the nations and over those who lay down their lives to take up the glory of God among the nations.

Blessed is the man whose delight is in the law of the LORD. He shall be like a tree planted by the rivers of water that brings forth its fruit in its season, whose leaf also shall not wither, and whatever he does shall prosper.

Why do the nations rage, and the people plot a vain thing? The kings of the earth set themselves, and the rulers take counsel together, against the LORD and against His Anointed. He who sits in the heavens shall laugh; then He shall speak to them in His wrath: "Yet I have set My King on My holy hill of Zion. Ask of Me, and I will give You the nations for Your inheritance, and the ends of the earth for Your possession." Now therefore, be wise, O kings; Be instructed, you judges of the earth. Serve the LORD with fear, and rejoice with trembling. Kiss the Son, lest He be angry, and you perish in the way.

LORD, who may abide in Your tabernacle? Who may dwell in Your holy hill? He who walks uprightly, works righteousness, speaks the truth in his heart, does not backbite with his tongue, does no evil to his neighbor, does not take up a reproach against his friend, despises evil, honors those who fear the LORD, swears to his own hurt and does not change, is generous and incorruptible. He who does these things shall never be moved.

They pierced My hands and My feet; they look and stare at Me. They divide My garments among them, and for My clothing they cast lots. But You, O LORD, do not be far from Me; O My Strength, hasten to help Me! Save Me from the lion's mouth. I will declare Your name to My brethren; in the midst of the assembly I will praise You. All the ends of the world shall remember and turn to the LORD, and all the families of the nations shall worship before You. For the kingdom is the LORD's, and He rules over the nations. They will come and declare His righteousness to a people who will be born.

Let God arise, let His enemies be scattered. The LORD gave the word; great was the company of those who proclaimed it: "Kings of armies flee" when the Almighty scattered kings. You have led captivity captive; you have received gifts among men. Blessed be the LORD, who daily loads us with benefits, the God of our salvation! Kings will bring presents to You. Envoys will come out of Egypt; Ethiopia will quickly stretch out her hands to God. Sing to God, you kingdoms of the earth.

God is a missionary God. We are His missionary people. The Bible is a missionary book. The Psalms are our missionary hymnal.

PRAYER FOCUS: *Gonja, Ngbanyito of Ghana (Evangelical: 0.50%)*

MAY 6: THE CHARTER FOR ALL HUMANITY

TODAY'S READING: 2 SAMUEL 6-7; 1 CHRONICLES 17

God's promise to Abraham and to David are the two pivotal covenants of the Old Testament. They are, of course, missionary covenants that give us the riverbanks for a biblical theology of mission all the way through the Scriptures, and they are why Matthew opens his Gospel by linking Jesus to these two patriarchs. If you want to summarize the Bible and its missionary heart in three names, it would be Abraham, David, and Jesus. To know how their stories interact in covenant with Jehovah and the nations is to know all. God's covenant with David is so critical and so essential to understanding the Bible.

When David mentioned to Nathan that he wanted to build God a house (2 Sam. 7:2), "God promised to make a 'house' that is, a dynasty, out of David…. Moreover the 'Seed' to whom David looked and trusted for his salvation, would now come from [David's] own body…. God would also grant him a throne and a kingdom that would last forever. It was in the midst of all these surprise announcements that the overwhelmed David went in, sat before the Lord, and exclaimed, **'Who am I, O Lord Yahweh, and who is my family, that you have brought me this far? And as if that is not enough in your sight, O Lord Yahweh, you have spoken about the future of the house of Your servant. And this is the charter of humanity, O Lord Yahweh.'"**

The translation of David's words in bold above is Walter Kaiser's, and Kaiser points out two fascinating aspects of these verses (2 Sam 7:18–19). First, the use of "Adonai Yahweh" (Lord God) was the expression used when God had promised Abraham "a seed," showing that these two covenants are linked. Second, the phrase translated "charter for humanity" is critical, and other translations (using "is this Your usual way of dealing with man") miss the point. David used the word *torah* (law) here and is not asking a question but making a statement. An astonished David remarked back to God: "This is your outline/law/decree/charter by which You have established Your plan for all humanity!" David realized that "this charter of humanity" was in reference to "the seed" of which he would combine with Abraham to father (Matt.1:1), the seed that God would use to save representatives of all nations on earth.

No wonder David sat down stunned in the presence of Jehovah. David had offered God plans for a temple of brick and stone, and God had given David *the* plan, the charter, for how God would interact with all humanity—every tribe, people, and nation. That plan would flow through David's "seed" and include every ethnic group, every unreached people, and every demographic in every era of history. In awe and anticipation, because he could hardly stand the wait, David would sing about that hope of all nations in most every psalm. Let us read the Psalms then in the same key of joyful missionary hope in which they were written.

PRAYER FOCUS: *Mandyak, Manjaco of Guinea-Bissau (Evangelical: 0.84%)*

MAY 7: OPEN YOUR MOUTH

TODAY'S READING: PSALMS 89, 96, 100–101, 105, 132

"The Great Commission is the Great Adventure of Christianity."

RON LUCE

The mission priority on preaching, proclaiming, teaching, and making disciples of all unreached peoples is not original to the New Testament—it has been the heart of God from the beginning of time.

Walter Kaiser says that Psalm 96 is one of the great missionary psalms, for the psalm's author ordered the Jewish people to both praise Jehovah and to proclaim His salvation and glory among the nations. "The Hebrew word for 'proclaim'…is the Old Testament equivalent of the New Testament **euangelizomai**, 'to bring good news,' 'to announce glad tidings', or to 'announce the gospel'. As most know, the 'announcement of good news' in the New Testament is applied to the finished work of Christ on the cross. And here it is expressly applied to the call to announce this same news about the Messiah to the nations and peoples of the world."

God's covenant with David established that the Lord would establish His seed forever and that seed would be the Messiah whom all nations would worship as He would rule forever. All lands and peoples are to come before the Lord with a joyful shout. All the sons of Abraham and David share in the same big idea: We are to praise the Lord and make known His deeds among all the peoples of earth. The missionary people of God are to sing out the songs of the Lord and to speak out the gospel from day to day among all unreached peoples, for all the peoples of earth are to glory, worship, sacrifice, and welcome the judgments of the one true God, Jehovah. "The context demands that God's character…and his conduct…be 'declared'…universally and internationally…. Israel, along with the new converts from all the earth, are to 'preach'…that 'Yahweh reigns' and that he will come to 'judge the peoples with equity'…. Thus, praise of God preceded preaching, but both were part and parcel of Israel's witness to the nations. The point is that there was a call for an **active** witness… by Israel to the Gentiles."

The application for us is threefold: First, we must be a people of praise. We must open our mouths in private and public and magnify Jesus; we cannot invite the nations to do what we do not practice. Second, we must go. The center for evangelism can be neither in the church building nor the homeland; it must be in the marketplace and among the nations. Third, the heart of missions is the verbal proclamation (teaching, preaching, proclaiming) of the gospel, the making of disciples, and the gathering of those disciples in indigenous churches. All other (good) things are but means to this end.

PRAYER FOCUS: *Maninka, Eastern of Guinea (Evangelical: 0.00%)*

MAY 8: THE ONLY TRUE POWER

TODAY'S READING: PSALMS 25, 29, 33, 36, 39

"I have seen, at different times, the smoke of a thousand villages—villages whose people are without Christ, without God, and without hope in the world."

ROBERT MOFFAT

In the Psalms, our missionary God has provided us with a great missionary hymnbook. "Most Christians who read the Psalms say they are about the troubles we face in life and how God helps us in them. While the Psalms do discuss how God helps us in our troubles, to miss the **missio Dei** [mission of God] in the Psalms is to read them blindly. In the Psalms we find the nations, the peoples, the ends of the earth, the nobles of the nations, the coastlands, the distant shores and more...."

There is a theology intrinsic to the Psalms, says Christopher Wright, the theology that Old Testament monotheism is directly connected to and centered on God's sovereign rule over all peoples and all nations. He broadly outlines this Old Testament monotheism in these terms: The Lord alone is Creator, owner, ruler, judge, revealer, lover, savior, leader, and reconciler because in relation to the heavens, earth, and all the nations, the Lord made them, the Lord owns them, the Lord governs them, the Lord calls all to account, the Lord speaks the truth, the Lord loves all He has made, the Lord saves all who turn to Him, the Lord guides the nations, and the Lord will bring peace. "Ultimately, we pay the cost of putting ultimate trust in what can never deliver ultimate security. Ultimately, it seems, we never learn that false gods can never fail to fail. That is the only thing about a false god you can depend on. By contrast, after magnificent reflections on the sovereign power of the Lord and his word in redemption, creation, providence and history, the author of Psalm 33 warns us against investing our hope for salvation anywhere else."

India has over 2,000 unreached people groups. There is no hope for India outside of the sovereign Lord and His uncompromising gospel. The pantheon of gods has failed. The litany of human cures has faltered. The thousand mission projects, programs, and businesses cannot save or redeem one soul. The billions of dollars in government spending, foreign aid, and social programs have not provided answers or eternal help. There is only one hope for salvation for the unreached of India: the God of the Bible and the faithful undiluted gospel message. And what is true for 59 million Brahmin Hindu is true for us: We have nowhere to go, nothing to trust, and no one to save other than Jehovah. Let us not make gods of our plans, projects, dollars, and programs. God, through Christ, is still the only true power of the gospel.

PRAYER FOCUS: *Brahmin of India (Evangelical: 0.01%)*

MAY 9: GOD'S RISKY, COSTLY PRESERVATION

TODAY'S READING: 2 SAMUEL 8–9; 1 CHRONICLES 18

Chronicles is the G-rated version of David's life. Written by priests who were concerned to show David in the best possible light, Chronicles makes no mention of Bathsheba, the civil war with Absalom, or the fact that David slaughtered two thirds of the Moabite army he captured. The record of David's life in 1 and 2 Samuel is for the more mature reader. David came to the throne when the nation was in jeopardy. Saul's son Ishbosheth was an uninspiring ruler, cowed by the Philistines who thought they had David in their back pocket. David disabused them of that notion in quick succession driving the Philistines from Israel, defeating Ammon across the Jordan, Edom to the southeast, and the Aramean (Syrian) kingdoms who stretched from Damascus to beyond the Euphrates. "In typical fashion, though, the biblical history pays scant attention to such feats of arms. Instead, the text focuses on David's behavior while his armies were off at war—especially on his affair with Bathsheba." God's glory among the nations is so easily sullied by our moral laxity at home. May Jesus help us to do nothing at home or abroad to divert attention from His mighty deeds among the nations. For if we do, God's glory will be forgotten and our scandals will get the press.

David's legacy does include many intentional acts of glorifying Jehovah. He took the shields of gold that belonged to the Syrian kings, the silver, and bronze, and dedicated them to the Lord. While David was intentional in not taking what was God's (gold or glory), he stumbled at taking what belonged to man (i.e. the wife of one of his mighty men). In missionary endeavor we must be doubly on guard for the thief within us all. We tend to be more vigilant to not take credit for what God has done and less careful to give credit to our brothers and sisters for what they have done. Mark the missionaries who never talk of their exploits and always praise their colleagues—they are missionaries after God's own heart. Remember, the chief sign of a glory thief is to talk much of oneself.

When David's heart was right, the Lord preserved him wherever he went. In Christ's service, it is not centrally about place or location but about God's glory. We as the body of Christ have the stewardship responsibility to identify the places where the gospel has not gone and focus our attention there. But the accompanying reality is that there are many such places and God is with us wherever as long as He is glorified. Our identity is not inextricably bound to one location or one role. What matters is that wherever we go, God is glorified, and thus, He preserves us wherever we go. Preservation does not mean missions is risk-free or cost-free; it means God's glory is maintained and His gospel advances no matter the cost. We can't historically make a case for the total immunity from pain for God's messengers. What we can know for sure is that when we live in God's holiness and when we glorify Him wherever we go, He wins souls to Himself for His own glory, but always with risk and cost to the messenger.

PRAYER FOCUS: *Java Pesisir Lor of Indonesia (Evangelical: 0.01%)*

MAY 10: USE YOUR WEALTH

TODAY'S READING: PSALMS 50, 53, 60, 75

Psalm 67 employs an interesting use of God's name. Rather than the covenantal name between Israel and God (Yahweh/YHWH), the title *Elohim* is used. This is the name used when one must express the Lord's relationship to all people, nations, and creation. The psalms in today's reading use Elohim as well. The sentiment of God's missionary heart expressed in the Psalms is the same theme started in Genesis with the blessing of Abraham. It is the chosen people of God praying: "May God be gracious to us and bless us fellow Israelites. May He increase our families, making them large and spiritually prosperous. May our crops increase and produce bountifully and our flocks show marked enlargement. May all of this and more happen so that the nations may look on us and say that what Aaron prayed for, and by way of God's blessing, has indeed occurred. The very bounty of God demonstrates that God has blessed us. Accordingly, may the rest of God's purpose come to pass as well, that in the blessing of Israel all the nations of the earth might be drawn to receive the message of God's salvation as well."

This is the biblical message of prosperity: it is not wealth to be lazy, selfish, and indolent, living lives removed from the poor and the lost, but wealth of the world to use on mission for God. Psalm 50 states that the rising sun of the fire of God will come out of Zion and go into the whole earth judging all the people, and that every beast of the forest, the cattle on a thousand hills, all the birds of the mountains and wild beasts of the field are His. God looks across the world to find those He can trust with wealth, those who realize the money is to be applied for the glory of God among every nation. For not only is the wealth of all creation God's, so are the peoples. The blessings of God—wealth, resources, and power—to the people of God are given for the same reason today as they were when the Psalms were written. The people of God are not blessed because we are better than others. The people of God are blessed so that the nations might know the ways of God in the earth, so that the ends of the earth would fear Him. It stunned the Israelites and it should stun us: Any wealth we have is for God's glory and goodness to be revealed among all peoples.

There are 16,000,000 Azerbaijani Muslims in Iran who are spiritually poor—that's more than all the Azerbaijani in Azerbaijan! God has given wealth to His people for the very specific reason that it be used to help these people become spiritually rich. If God has given you physical riches, He did not do it for you to retain them for yourself and your children. Rather, He did it that you use them to help Him bring His lost Azerbaijani children home.

PRAYER FOCUS: *Azerbaijani, Azeri Turk of Iran (Evangelical: 0.15%)*

MAY 11: AT WAR AGAINST IMPOSSIBLE ODDS

TODAY'S READING: 2 SAMUEL 10; 1 CHRONICLES 19; PSALM 20

Much damage occurs when we don't assume the best. David out of kindness sent a delegation across the river to Ammon to mourn the passing of a friend. The new regime assumed the worst and it led to war. The new king of Ammon departed from his father's kindness, moving beyond just being guarded to being insulting. First, he misunderstood. Then he exacerbated the situation with his reaction—he shamed the delegation by cutting off their beards and clothes. A beard to the Israelites of David's day was a sign of status, representing maturity, dignity, and wisdom. To dishonor David's representatives was to dishonor David, and it led to needless war. Countless is the waste by missionaries, ministers, and followers of Jesus because first we assumed the worst and then reacted poorly, shaming the other through our dishonor. Of course, the great shame in internecine fighting is that the real battles for the glory of Jesus among all peoples are hindered, or even abandoned.

When we diligently do not allow ourselves to be offended, we can concentrate on the valid battle, which usually requires our full attention as the odds are against us. With 3.15 billion people collected in 7,000 unreached people groups with no clear exposure to the gospel, we have enough to do without fighting ourselves. Joab surveyed the landscape and saw "the battle line was against him before and behind" (2 Sam. 10:9), so he chose some of Israel's best and put them on the frontlines. There is a disturbing trend in missionary appointment—the sending of amateurs. The deterioration of our sending cultures as we descend into secular darkness leads us to panic and to ask our best Paul and Barnabas to stay in the home church of Antioch and to send to Cyprus and Asia Minor only our young ministers that won't hurt us too badly if they left. How antithetical to the spirit of Acts 13 which was in turn the Spirit of the Father who sent His Son, His only Son, His very best. With the size and scope of the task that remains, we too must send our very best seasoned warriors to the front.

Our reading today details how the Syrians and Ammonites arranged themselves in battle array before the city gates. Cities were fortified by stone walls with gates largely made of wood. The gate was the most vulnerable part of the defenses, the most heavily defended, and the most complicated. If we are going to win the nations to Jesus, we will have to take the gates. We can be encouraged that where the heaviest defense is, the greatest vulnerability is also. All too often missionary strategy avoids the apparently most difficult and dangerous places, but that is where we must fight, for the massed opposition is actually the indication of the access point to that culture and people group. We must focus our best where the enemy is strongest, for behind that resistance lies the path to the heart of the culture and people.

The missionary spirit is to be un-offendable with one other, un-divertible from where the darkness is deepest and the battle fiercest, and unshakable in the source of our help. We go to war against impossible odds. We go to win 3.15 billion unreached to Jesus from Iraq and elsewhere.

PRAYER FOCUS: *Arab, North Iraqi of Iraq (Evangelical: 0.20%)*

MAY 12: THE SACRED DIGNITY

TODAY'S READING: PSALMS 65-67, 69-70

"Seek each day to do or say something to further Christianity among the heathen."

JOHNATHAN GOFORTH

The premise of a missionary reading of the Bible is that God is good and glorious, worthy of all worship, great in mercy and holiness. Our majestic God created humans of every variety and made us to be fully satisfied only by being in relationship with Him, a relationship defined by worship and friendship. That we can be friends with the God we worship is a delightful mystery that only eternity will fully explain. This God of wonders blesses us, and "the only proper response to blessings and benefits received at God's hand was worship and obedience. That was another core belief in Israel. But if that was true for them, then it must also be true of all nations because they too came under the sphere of God's blessing. Indeed, Israel's own praises for blessing received had a missional edge, in reaching out in proclamation to the nations. And so there is a range of texts anticipating the praise of the nations, and a few that speak of their obedience as well.... The theme of the worship of the nations being offered to YHWH, God of Israel, occurs from the beginning to end of the Psalter...."

Historically, God's blessing was bestowed on Abraham, then Isaac, Jacob, and the Israelites as "the firstfruits of God's wider harvest among all nations on earth." The Bible is the story of this passed-on blessing that is centralized in Jesus (the seed of Abraham), and the Psalms envision "a whole earth and all its peoples now gladly affirming Yahweh's sovereignty and gratefully receiving from Yahweh all the blessings of a rightly governed creation." This wonderful Jewish hymnbook (Psalms) reverberates with the harmonic prophesies of what God is going to do for and through *all* the peoples of earth. Most striking of all in the Psalms of today's reading is Psalm 67 which in particular reveals the universal scope of worship for Jehovah. The author takes the Aaronic blessing and rewrites it. Instead of "Jehovah" blessing "you" (the particular Jewish people), the psalm wondrously declares "Elohim" will bless all the nations through blessing "us." "This Psalm is a prayer for salvation in the widest sense, and not for Israel only, but for the whole world. Israel's blessing is to be a blessing for all men. Here, in particular, the psalmist does more than adopt the Priestly formula (Num. 6:22-27); he claims for Israel the sacerdotal dignity, Israel is the world's high priest... If Israel has the light of God's face, the world cannot remain in darkness."

We have the sacred dignity of knowing the one true God and of making Him known to all the peoples of earth. We have the sacred privilege of bringing the lostness of the nations to the throne in prayer. We have the sacred duty of sending and going to the most unreached peoples and places of earth singing: "God be merciful to us and bless us...that Your way may be known on earth, Your salvation among all nations. Let all the peoples praise You.... Oh, let the nations be glad and sing for joy.... God shall bless us, and all the ends of the earth shall fear Him" (67:1-4, 7).

PRAYER FOCUS: *Arab, Palestinian/Israeli of Israel (Evangelical: 1.85%)*

MAY 13: ROOFTOPS OF SIN

"If missions languish, it is because the whole life of godliness is feeble.
The command to go everywhere and preach to everybody is not obeyed until the will
is lost by self-surrender in the will of God. Living, praying, giving and going will
always be found together."

A. T. PIERSON

We were designed for battle and created to fight for the glory of God among all peoples. When we take our eyes off the war for God's glory among all peoples, we are prone to stupid, selfish, and sinful things. When energy intended for battle lies listless at home, it leads us to the rooftops of sin. To lay down the fight for God's glory globally is slowly and surely to climb the steps of lust toward what we should not have.

David's army was fighting for the glory of God across the Jordan River. David's inactivity led to misplaced energy and all kinds of devilish damage. Never again would there be the joy of unsullied obedience. Forgiveness would be sought and given but what was done could not be undone. David's first sin was against God, but he certainly sinned against his own mighty man, his brother-in-arms, Uriah the Hittite. Uriah refused to participate in David's sin. I'm pretty sure Uriah knew what David was trying to do; thus, he had extra motive not to go home, not wanting to validate or participate in the deception and sin. Yet, his primary point is well-taken, even for us 3,000 years later. The God of glory has deployed His army of salvation into all the world. Those called to send and support from the home base must join the army in living in a wartime mentality. We can't pretend there is no war, we can't live as if it's peacetime. It's wartime, and all who claim allegiance to the King must live with a wartime mentality, no matter their assignment or geography. To ignore the war for souls through a withdrawn or self-serving lifestyle is the sin of omission that leads to all kinds of damaging sins of commission. We cannot live smugly—being faithful to our wives, providing well for our children, and never committing any sexual sin like David—if we are doing all these while ignoring the global conflict to reach the unreached. *Both* the inaction of living like there is no global war for God's glory among the unreached *and* the action of applying wasted war energy on selfish sins are *equally* displeasing to the Lord.

The 1 Chronicles account of this event whitewashes it, not detailing David's sin but concentrating on David's presence at the ceremonial taking of the city. The chapter is a sad indicator of what can happen in missions and ministry when leaders who live selfish lives ascend the grand stage to take credit for what anonymous soldiers paid for in sweat and blood. I write this as one of the pompous: God forgive us all for taking credit from those on the ground who labor under such duress so loyally. Chapter 20 lists the giants slain and victories won, and the silent condemnation is the absence of David. Yes, roles change, but we should never stop fighting for souls. Any leader in any position should continue to win souls and make disciples. When we stop fighting for Jesus, we start sinning against Him.

PRAYER FOCUS: *South Asian, General of Italy (Evangelical: 0.50%)*

MAY 14: DAVID'S REPENTANCE— A MISSIONARY APPEAL

TODAY'S READING: PSALMS 32, 51, 86, 122

Our readings today center on David's prayers for forgiveness and deliverance. There is a special type of agony when you realize you're the bad guy and you've caused pain. It's one thing to pray for the Lord to deliver you from the bad guys. It's another thing entirely to pray that the other guys will be delivered from you and your sin. It is this agony that led David to weep: "My sin is always before me. Against You, You only, have I sinned" (Psalm 51:3–4). David certainly sinned against Uriah, the honor of the nation, and the royal throne, and even against Bathsheba, but all those sins pale in comparison to the hurt David caused Jehovah. David's greatest violation of trust and the greatest offense was against the Lord. It was doubly painful as David was so intimate, so close to God.

We find a missiological underpinning in David's prayer for forgiveness. As David cried out for mercy, He acknowledged Jehovah: "Among the gods there is none like You, O LORD.... All nations whom You have made shall come and worship before You, O LORD, and shall glorify Your name. For You are great and do wondrous things; You alone are God" (86:8–10). Jehovah is both incomparable (there is none like Him) and transcendently unique (there is no other god); therefore, Jehovah cannot be just Israel's God but must be the God of all the nations. When David repented of the heinous crimes of adultery and murder in light of this uniqueness of Jehovah and established that all sin is first committed against God, he was in fact establishing the universality of sin against the God of Israel, the universal need for all peoples to be reconciled to the God of Israel, and the universal urgency that all nations be told this. Even David's repentance is a missionary appeal. What was true for David is true for all men of all cultures of all places—their sin is a grievous offense to the God of Israel and they must be reconciled to this one true God by the means He has established or perish. The missionary message then is to be sure that all peoples of earth know who they must confess their sins to if there is to be any hope of forgiveness and reconciliation with the only true God.

Our sins and failures can indeed lead us back to the beauty of who the God of Abraham, Isaac, and Jacob is. To receive atoning pardon from Him whom we have so painfully wronged is a beauty beyond description. The next time you sin and receive pardon, remember that the One who has forgiven you is not your personal God—He is the God of all the nations and peoples of earth. Remember that the unreached don't know who they have sinned against, don't know they are under wrath, don't know how to repent or to whom. Remember that they have no hope unless you or someone you send lives out before them who to repent to, how to repent, and how to walk in forgiven freedom.

PRAYER FOCUS: *Okinawan, Ryukyuan of Japan (Evangelical: 0.15%)*

MAY 15: HE DEVISES THE WAYS AND MEANS

TODAY'S READING: 2 SAMUEL 13–15

No good thing comes from passive resistance to the missionary plan of God. The turning point for David and his kingdom was the Bathsheba incident. David's passivity led to immorality and murder, which in turn opened the door for even more damaging immorality and murder (incest and fratricide). It's daunting to look at the rage of the nations and tempting to avoid the thick of the fray, but it's delusional to think we can escape the conflict or remain neutral as the great powers collide. God is at war for the hearts and souls of men from every tribe, tongue, people, and nation. We must actively fight with Him, lest our passivity lead to home front disaster. Lounging around home didn't end well for either David or Amnon.

Incest led to murder, and murder led to one of the great missions truths of David's story. Absalom was banished and then allowed to return to Jerusalem after Joab used a hypothetical tale in the mouth of a wise woman. Trapping David through emotional appeal, the wise woman uttered the timeless truth, unwittingly prophesying the gospel: "God does not take away a life; but He devises means, so that His banished ones are not expelled from Him" (2 Sam. 14:14). How beautiful is this gospel truth—that God devises means to save life. God's immutable laws must be upheld: A holy God must punish sin with death; a holy God cannot allow sinful men into His presence; a holy God must destroy all sin in fiery wrath; and a holy God must banish the sinful offender from His sacred presence. All this must be done, and yet God devises means for the impossible to happen—to bring His lost ones home. God devising means for the lost to be found is ever the gist of missions. William Carey, revolting against the missions passivity of his day, insisted that the church intentionally create mission sending structures so that the gospel might be sent to unreached peoples. The link between Joab's meddling in the mouth of a wise old mother in Israel, William Carey and the modern missions movement, and the 2.7 million Palestinian Arab Muslims in Jordan is God devising means to bring His banished ones home.

David's sin meant he must leave home, hounded by his own flesh and blood. Exiting the city of Jerusalem, David granted grace to his loyalists, telling them they need not be banished with him, but the Cherethites and Pelethites demur (ironically, these two peoples are from Crete and Palestine). David's son was trying to kill him while his own mercenary troops from other nations preferred banishment and risked their own lives to keep him safe. Even the Gittites from the Philistine capital of Gath (ground zero for David's sworn enemies) refused to leave David's side. A foreigner swore loyalty not just to David, but to Jehovah, the God of Israel, and that foreigner was from Gath—a proto-Palestinian of the same people we pray for today. Surely God finds ways to bring His lost ones home!

PRAYER FOCUS: *Arab, Palestinian of Jordan (Evangelical: 0.30%)*

MAY 16: LAMENT TO JOY

TODAY'S READING: PSALMS 3–4, 12–13, 28, 55

"What can we do to win these men to Christ?"

RICHARD WURMBRAND

The psalms are generally either hymns of praise or songs of lament that lead to trust. In the general order of the book, the laments lead to the praises. Of the first forty-two psalms, over twenty-two are laments. This movement from woe to joy does not necessarily reflect the trajectory of David's life; due to his own failings and sin, his later years held more sorrow than his former. Not all the psalms have a detailed superscription. Psalm 3 does, and we may assume many of these other lament-filled psalms were from similar times. David struggled with the pain and anguish of hurt, betrayal, and loss, especially as life drew to a close, though what is beautiful about each of these hymns that start with lament and end with trust is their missionary orientation. "The language of complaint, protest, and baffled questioning is...prominent in the psalms—right at the heart of Israel's worship of YHWH.... For among the things Israel knew about itself...was that it held its own faith **in trust for the world.** Israel's God was God of all the earth. Whatever was true for Israel was true for all. Whatever Israel struggled with would be a problem for all. There is then an implicit missiological dimension to the ruthless honesty in Israel's testimony." The cross examination that happened in Israel (and can be read in the psalms) was not "a safe intramural exercise for Israel"; rather they were "issues with which Israel [struggled] for the sake of the world."

With Absalom threatening him, David took his mournful band (which included non-Israelites) across the Jordan River. The questions he struggled with concerning the character of God were struggled through on foreign soil, away from home. It was in Moab or perhaps Edom that David cried and agonized his way to trust: "But I have trusted in Your mercy.... The Lord is my strength and my shield; my heart trusted in Him, and I am helped.... The Lord shall save me...I will trust in You" (13:5; 28:7; 55:16, 23). All these declarations from David are made while running for his life (from his own son!) in a foreign land. David struggled through, from sorrow to praise, for the sake of the nations, for all those in the grip of sin's consequences, for all those in pain who long to be saved. We, too, struggle through our pain, questions, hurts, betrayals, and unimaginable losses not just for our own souls, but so that we can with conviction and compassion help the Uzbek of Kazakhstan do the same. We, too, hold our faith in trust for the good of the rest of the world. God can handle our laments, but for the sake of the nations, let us with David wrestle to trust.

MAY 17: GOD-APPOINTED OPPOSITION

TODAY'S READING: 2 SAMUEL 16–18

God allowed the kingdom of Israel to be an example as He intended it. Jehovah would be the God of the nation, the nation would be His holy people, and Jehovah would live among them, as an invitation to the nations. The energy spent on civil war then is doubly tragic; not only does the family kill its own, it also mars the invitation to the nations. David's latter reign serves as a warning to the body of Christ today: What happened to him and his family will happen to us and ours if we turn from the glory of God among the nations to self-indulgent living at home. This tragic season in Israel holds several lessons applicable to missions.

Opposition in missions is often God-appointed. Shimei, a Benjaminite from the house of Saul, had reasons to curse David. Shimei might not have had the right heart, but there was some truth in his criticisms (2 Sam 16:5–8). David was indeed a man of blood and indeed caught in his own evil, reaping what he sowed. The Lord was punishing David for his sins. It is my experience in both leading and following to reap everything I sowed. Whenever I sowed disloyalty, undermining speech, betraying behavior, or unfaithfulness as relates to friends or leaders, I reaped the same, and just as painfully. The Lord uses critics to show us our own hearts, even if what they say is not fully true, informed, or even fair. There is almost always a germ of truth in what our critics shout at us. The wise leader will humble himself and look for the truth embedded in every oppositional interaction.

We can't do God's mission in ways that displease Him. Joab was one of the more complex characters in David's era. On the one hand, he seemed fiercely loyal to David; on the other hand, he "repeatedly [acted] on his own initiative, even against David's express wishes." Sometimes in our zeal for God's honor, we defend Him (or attack in His name) in ways that do not please or honor Him. Good missionaries remember that God can defend His own name, and we must not pursue His honor in dishonorable ways. Good missionaries have no zeal to defend their own name; they have David's demeanor, not Joab's jealousy.

One great sadness to God's heart is the infighting that destroys missionary union on the field. When Ahithophel gave cunning advice to Absalom about killing his own father, he shrewdly depersonalized his murderous suggestion: "I will strike only the king" (17:2). Ahithophel did not say "your father" or "David"; he just vaguely listed the monarch who allegedly was the hindrance to peace. How often the enemy of unity (a prerequisite for mission advance) deceives us by suggesting we depersonalize our interaction with colleagues. Rather than seeing them as brothers in the fight for faith among the unreached, we turn them into villains, problems, and obstacles whose removal we falsely think will be the solution. How often missionaries assassinate their own—murder assisted by hiding behind depersonalization, murder we'd dare not enact if we looked them in the eye and treated them as we want to be treated.

PRAYER FOCUS: *Oromo, Garre of Kenya (Evangelical: 0.01%)*

MAY 18: LAUD THE GOD OF WRATH

TODAY'S READING: PSALMS 26, 40, 58, 61-62, 64

"Missions isn't a program; it's a fight against hell."

DR. ELIZABETH GRANT

Part of the missionary message is that the whole world, every people, is under the destructive wrath of God. The inescapable reality is that the character of God includes a destructive anger against what is wicked. The passions that rise within us against abuse and injustice are sourced in the nature of God who is slow to anger, but rightly angry. We cannot offer a diluted gospel to the nations, a gospel that does not confront wickedness, a gospel that does not warn the unreached to "flee the wrath to come." Missions is this strange and wonderful representation of the full-orbed character of God. He is indeed angry at sin and sinners and He does indeed find a way for mercy to triumph over judgment. The good news is insensible outside of the bad news, and part of blessing God is proclaiming His terrors.

The psalmist returned to the theme of righteous indignation over and over: "The wicked are estranged from the womb; they go astray as soon as they are born, speaking lies.... So that men will say, 'Surely there is a reward for the righteous; surely He is God who judges in the earth'" (Psalm 58:3, 11). We have so mismanaged anger (for the wrath of man does not accomplish the righteousness of God) that we have lost the ability to purely channel the wrath of God (which does accomplish His righteousness). There is a time and place to rebuke the nations, to call down fire on Sodom, and to warn Nineveh that God does judge all the earth. A missiology devoid of threat, judgment, anger, and alarm is a false missiology, one that certainly does not represent the great passions and realities of who God is, nor one He wants His missionaries to communicate. We do the nations no favors when we tell them distorted lies. To pretend that no judgment looms or that no wrath gathers is an offense to the Lord of heaven and earth and a distortion of His character. As part of the missionary message, we must warn: "But God shall shoot at them with an arrow.... All men shall fear, and shall declare the work of God.... The righteous shall be glad in the LORD, and trust in Him. And all the upright in heart shall glory" (64:7, 9-10). True declaration, gladness, and glory can only follow appropriate fear.

When we rightly praise the Lord, that praise includes His wrath, judgment, undiluted holiness, unapproachable transcendence, and immutable will. What type of praise makes the nations fear? Praise that includes lauding the God of wrath. There is no place for the messenger to be embarrassed by the message or the character of the Master. When praise begins with the fear of God, the crescendo into love then broadcast into the great assembly is both priceless, unparalleled, and universal. We can cry from among the nations at the ends of the earth, and we can invite all unreached peoples to join us.

PRAYER FOCUS: *Thai, Central of South Korea (Evangelical: 0.40%)*

MAY 19: SINGLE-EYED FOCUS

TODAY'S READING: 2 SAMUEL 19–21

"The will of God—nothing less, nothing more, nothing else."

F. E. MARSH

The gospel determines who our friends are. Jesus, his face set like flint, was single-eyed on the reason He came to earth. Nothing and no one could deter or distract Him from giving His life for sinners. Given that focus and fact we are called to share it; nothing and no one should distract us from giving our lives so the lost may be saved. It's in this context we are told to "hate" our families—not in the sense of wanting to destroy them, but in the sense that our true family are those who share a single-eyed passion for the glory of God among all unreached peoples, so that we can all go home.

Joab told David that in mourning the death of his son Absalom, he was loving his enemies and hating his friends and was in danger of losing the kingdom. David was not allowed to prioritize his own flesh and blood over the good of the kingdom; neither can we. The good of the King and His glory among all nations has a higher priority than what our natural family thinks. This is not a call to dishonor parents and loved ones; rather it is a call to honor the King and the gospel above all else. David's friends were literally those who gave themselves to fight and die for the kingdom, not the family who wanted to take the kingdom away. Our friends are those who fight with us for King and gospel. May God grant they be our blood kin.

When David returned to Jerusalem, he met Mephibosheth and asked, "Why did you not go with me?" Mephibosheth presented the evidence that he did *indeed* go with David in the only way he knew how, showing by the neglect of his body that he did not rejoice at not being able to go. God clearly commanded us to go to all the nations with the gospel message. If we do not go, there should be some material evidence that we wanted to go (i.e. a self-denial that produced much prayer for the unreached, many funds for missionary support, and many disciples who went in our place). The friends of God show that they are with Him in all His travels and trials, even if they can't physically be there.

When Sheba rebelled, the Cherethites and Pelethites stood firmly with David. These non-Israelites whom David befriended when he was a refugee among the Philistines were more loyal than David's son or his people. They formed his personal guard, had his complete trust, and helped establish Solomon at David's command. David's best friends and most trusted companions were foreigners, not family. Truly, God's missionary work is a multinational collaboration, a family more intimately linked by gospel DNA than by skin or blood.

The King of glory and His gospel must determine who our friends are and where our loyalties lie, and a single-eyed focus on Jesus being glorified in Kuwait among the Najdi Arabs will lead us to make friends of those who share this sacred passion.

PRAYER FOCUS: *Arab, Saudi-Najdi of Kuwait (Evangelical: 0.00%)*

MAY 20: STAY SMALL

TODAY'S READING: PSALMS 5, 38, 41-42

David's charm is in how he, for the most part, saw himself as small. The king cried out to the King, his God. Surrounded by fawning and flattery, David never lost sight of who the real Royal was and never lost a sense of complete dependency. By some, missionaries are scolded, but in the narrow subset of evangelical, mission-minded churches, missionaries tend to be lauded. How easily we forget that our assignment is part of God's mission and slip into thinking that we have a major role to play. In reality there is only one central figure. When we lose the perspective of how small we are in God's big missionary plan, we lose some fear for God Himself. We take too much credit and blame on ourselves. David stayed small and stayed reverent: "In fear of You I will worship toward Your holy temple" (Psalm 5:7). A healthy respect of the Lord not only keeps us from presumption; it also keeps us from pessimism. Not only are we horrified at taking any glory, but we are also happy to sit back and let God work out the difficult details. We don't strive and strain for attention or for vindication. We work hard in our corner of the field, but let God shoulder the pressure. Being small does not mean being unimportant. Small parts play big roles as long as they stay content and small in their own eyes.

It is interesting and arresting that in the psalm of laments, when David was ashamed of his own failings and reeling from the failings of others, there is a missionary subtext throughout. After bemoaning the betrayal of his son, David said: "Blessed be the LORD God of Israel from everlasting to everlasting! Amen and Amen" (41:13). David was literally running for his life, surrounded by a multinational band, and he praised saying, "Blessed be Jehovah Elohim of Israel forever. Let it be, let it be!" The universal undertones are dramatic. The God of Israel is the God of the nations is the God of Israel forever and ever. Let it be so! How can we but add our amen? David's life is an ongoing reminder that no joy (victory) and no sorrow (defeat) is ever purely personal or isolated from what God wants to do among all peoples of earth. It's not about us. Our victories and defeats are not about us. Missions is not about us. What joy there is in staying small! What joy there is in preserving God as big before all the peoples of earth!

Lest we forget, missions is a thing of earth. Missions is not our joy and not our fulfilment. Going is not our reward, and sending is not our fulfilment. Praying is not our joy, and giving is not our ultimate purpose. All these are beautiful means, rewarding, fulfilling, joyous, and purposeful means, but *just* means, not ends. The end is the presence of Jesus and satisfaction in the glory of God. The end is smallness in union with He who is ever and increasingly great. This is why we state with little David and every demographic through history: "As the deer pants for the water brooks, so pants my soul for You, O God" (42:1).

PRAYER FOCUS: *Uzbek, Northern of Kyrgyzstan (Evangelical: 0.26%)*

MAY 21: WE'LL SING THE OLD, OLD SONGS

TODAY'S READING: 2 SAMUEL 22–23; PSALM 57

"If the Great Commission is true, our plans are not too big; they are too small."

PAT MORELY

The last words of David revealed his simplicity. We find David endearing, even in his faults, because he was uncomplicated, childlike without being childish. There was no guile in him, just passion. As his life closed and his voice sang his last song, he pointed us to the missionary heart of God one more time.

It doesn't seem that David considered himself first a warrior, a man of blood. Even though much of what we know of him was battle related, David's last words revealed that he saw himself in a different light: "Thus says David…the sweet psalmist of Israel: 'The Spirit of the LORD spoke by me, and His word was on my tongue. The God of Israel said, the Rock of Israel spoke to me…" (2 Sam. 23:1–3). It seems David took the most joy in that God spoke to him, that he spoke to God, and that God spoke through him. The Hebrew Bible "associated David with 73 psalms, later translations increase the number…. The Dead Sea Psalms Scroll claims that David wrote 4,050 psalms and songs, all given him by divine inspiration from the Lord." We think of David as a warrior; David thought of himself as a worshiper.

David's worship has constant missionary themes. Second Samuel 22 records David's thoughts for the Lord on the day the Lord delivered him from "all his enemies" (v. 1). This song mirrors Psalm 18 in which David sang about his deliverance from Saul, but the addition of "all his enemies" leads scholars to believe this was David's last song to go with his last words. If that is true, then we cannot overlook the importance of the last stanza of David's last song (vv. 44–50). With his last breath, David sang about God and the nations. His first words to us (1 Sam. 17:46) and his last words (2 Sam. 22:50) are pure passion for the glory of God among all peoples. In the middle, when he was delivered from Saul and established as king, it was the same song, different verse (Psalm 57:5, 9, 11). David's whole life centered on worshiping and exalting the God of all peoples, the God who must be honored and glorified in all the earth, the God who is worthy of the praise and glory of every tongue.

While we will undoubtedly make new friends in heaven, the old ones of earth will be ever precious. When we get to heaven and join the ranks of the redeemed, including the Phu Thai of Laos, we will see one band of rowdy, rugged worshippers. They will all be soldiers, they will all be childlike, they will probably be more enthusiastic than anyone else, and they will be decidedly multicultural. They will be David's mighty men, and it's impossible to find a more culturally diverse band (except the crew at Pentecost) in all the Scriptures. They will be leading the praise, and right in the middle will be David with a sparkle of pure joy in his eye as the angel choir starts singing one of his old songs.

PRAYER FOCUS: *Phu Thai of Laos (Evangelical: 0.40%)*

MAY 22: NO COMMENTARY NEEDED

TODAY'S READING: PSALMS 95, 97–99

How can our hearts not burst for the glory of God among the unreached peoples of earth when we read the Psalms? So blatant is the missionary impulse of David's singing, so repeated is his mentioning of the glory of God among all nations, so insistent is his call to all the *ethne* to receive salvation that only the God of Israel can provide, that many of His psalms need no commentary. Today's readings are of such missionary ilk.

Oh come, let us worship and bow down; let us kneel before the **LORD** *[Jehovah] our Maker. For He is our* **God [Elohim],** *and we are the people of His pasture, and the sheep of His hand. Today, if you will hear His voice: "Do not harden your hearts...." (95:6–8)*

The **LORD** *[Jehovah] has made know His salvation; His righteousness He has revealed in the sight of* **the nations.** *He has remembered His mercy and His faithfulness to the* **house of Israel; all the ends of the earth** *have seen the salvation of our* **God [Elohim].** *Shout joyfully to the* **LORD** *[Jehovah], all the earth... Let the sea roar, and all its fullness,* **the world and those who dwell in it...***for He is coming to judge* **the earth.** *With righteousness He shall judge* **the world, and the peoples** *with equity. (98:2–4, 7, 9)*

The **LORD** *[Jehovah] reigns; let* **the peoples** *tremble! He dwells between the cherubim; let* **the earth** *be moved! The* **LORD** *[Jehovah] is great in* **Zion,** *and He is high above* **all the peoples.** *Let* **them** *praise Your great and awesome name—He is holy. Exalt the* **LORD** *[Jehovah] our* **God [Elohim]** *and worship at His footstool—He is holy. (99:1–3, 5)*

There is hardly a more beautiful or more missionary expression in all the Psalms, maybe all the Scriptures, than this: "Exalt Jehovah our Elohim and worship at His footstool—He is holy." In that sentence, we have the transcendent character of our holy God, we have His covenant name with Israel (implying the promise to bless them that they might be a blessing to all nations), we have the Canaanite name for God, "El" (indicating Jehovah will be every people's God), and we have the invitation to worship (the goal and fulfillment of all saved men). We read this Psalm and pray, give, and go that the Druze of Lebanon will join us in singing: "Jehovah is our Elohim—the Lord is our God!"

David knew who the real King was. He knew the covenant story. He knew the missionary and inclusive heart of God. David knew that the God of Israel (Jehovah) was the only true God (Elohim) of all the peoples. Nothing made David happier than for Jehovah to save from among all peoples, that all knees might bow and that all tongues might praise. David's psalms are great proof that the Bible is a missionary book. Let us in our living be as zealous as David was in his singing to be God's missionary people.

PRAYER FOCUS: *Druze of Lebanon (Evangelical: 0.01%)*

MAY 23: THERE MUST BE A PERSONAL COST

TODAY'S READING: 2 SAMUEL 24; 1 CHRONICLES 21-22; PSALM 30

It's intriguing that the parallel passages of 2 Samuel 24 and 1 Chronicles 21 diverge on the impetus for David's census. There is further intrigue as we're never told why this census was a sin, though it's clear it was because David said so (2 Sam. 24:10; 1 Chr. 21:8). What is clear is that David did not count it as blame to God; he took responsibility for his foolish action. We must conclude that something was amiss in David's motivation which caused God to either remove His restraining hand of wisdom or His protecting hand from the devil's influence. The lesson for us is that when our motivations are awry, even good things become abominable to God and disastrous to God's people.

In David's time a census was usually called for to collect taxes or to collect names for a military draft. Neither reason was popular with the common people, and both could lead the ruler to depend on a resource other than Jehovah. Perhaps at the root of this sin was David shifting trust away from Jehovah to his own treasury and weapons. The ambiguity of the text affords us a third theory. The census error, plague, and dramatic deliverance in 1 Chronicles 21 is immediately followed with the details of all David did to prepare materials for the temple. What if by taking the census David was wanting the people to pay for his responsibility? (They ended up paying all right—with 70,000 lives.) What if David knew he wanted to provide lavishly for the building of the temple and got the idea to tax his people so there would be plenty (and he wouldn't have to give anything from his personal wealth)? Following the misguided census and plague, David began to make provision for the temple. In purchasing the temple site a chastened David said to Ornan, "I will not take what is yours for the LORD, nor offer burnt offerings with that which costs me nothing" (1 Chr. 21:24). It certainly seems David realized he must ensure the worship of Jehovah at personal cost, he must not take what belonged to others to promote the glory of God, and he must make his own sacrifices. So must we. We must make our own personal sacrifices for the global worship of God to go forth.

It is impossible to read any portion of Scripture without some reminder that God is ever inclusive and mindful of all nations. Ornan was a Jebusite, the original inhabitants of Jerusalem, a non-Israelite. It was on the land of a non-Israelite that the temple was built by aliens as the masons, with Sidonians supplying the timber. Putting anecdotal evidence together, I think David took a census so he could have the Israelites pay the bill for an ethno-centric temple, and the Lord became angry that David had drifted from God's sacrificial missionary heart. God said, "Everybody sacrifices and every nation will have a place in my house. A Jebusite will give the land, immigrant aliens will cut the stone, and Lebanese will provide the timber. And one day the Liberian Vai will stand in My courts and lift their voices in praise."

PRAYER FOCUS: *Vai of Liberia (Evangelical: 0.23%)*

MAY 24: DRAWING COSMIC CONCLUSIONS

TODAY'S READING: PSALMS 108–110

"It is not our work to make men believe: that is the work of the Holy Spirit."

D. L. MOODY

Psalm 110 is the Old Testament text most quoted in the New Testament regarding Christology. Jesus, Peter, and Paul all made liberal use of this psalm—and with good reason. In fact, Jesus claimed this psalm was about Him. As we shall see through this brief explanation from Christopher Wright, it is a grand missionary text.

"The synoptic Gospels all record Jesus using this text twice: first as a teasing question about the Messiah…second, at his trial in answer to the high priest's question, 'Are you the Christ?'... Taking their cue from Jesus' own teaching, then, the earliest Christians used the imagery of Psalm 110:1 to describe the present 'location' of the risen and ascended Jesus. Jesus was not just 'absent.' Jesus was already 'seated at the right hand of God.' That is to say, Jesus was already now sharing in the exercise of universal governance that belonged uniquely to YHWH. This exalted claim is found in the preaching of Peter on the day of Pentecost, when he links Psalm 110 to the historically witnessed fact of the resurrection of Jesus and then draws the cosmic conclusion about the lordship of Jesus (Acts 2:32–36).

"For Paul, the double imagery of Psalm 110:1 (the right hand of God, enemies beneath the feet) provided the most powerful way that he could express not only the authority of the risen Christ but the ultimate source of that authority, namely, the fact that Jesus shared the identity of YHWH himself, and therefore shared in his universal rule…these affirmations, of course, underlie Paul's own theology and practice of mission, for it was only out of the conviction that these claims were the sober truth about the one whom he had met on the road to Damascus that he obeyed Christ's mandate to be the apostle to the nations."

Some present at Pentecost who heard Peter preach from Psalm 110 were from the districts of Libya around Cyrene, or the present-day city of Benghazi (Acts 2:10). How desperately they need to hear once more that Jesus is the God who came near; that He has all authority; that before Abraham was, He is; and that all His enemies will be trampled underneath His feet. How urgent the need to have prophetic singers once more lift their voice in eastern Libya proclaiming the name of Jesus as the only One who can make wars cease and peace last forever. May the reality that Jesus sits at the right hand of God with all enemies under His feet call men and women one more time to be apostles where the gospel isn't, where Christ is not yet worshiped. May Psalm 110 live one more time in our day.

PRAYER FOCUS: *Arab, Cyrenaican of Libya (Evangelical: 0.03%)*

MAY 25: THE HOUSE YET BEING BUILT

TODAY'S READING: 1 CHRONICLES 23-29; PSALMS 127

"To stay here and disobey God—I can't afford to take the consequence. I would rather go and obey God than to stay here and know that I disobeyed."

AMANDA BERRY SMITH

David went to great lengths to prepare both the materials and organizational structures for Solomon to build the temple. Solomon was then handed the keys to the Ferrari with the paternal warning and exhortation: "As for you, my son Solomon, know the God of your father, and serve Him with a loyal heart and with a willing mind; for the LORD searches all hearts and understands all the intent of the thoughts. If you seek Him, He will be found by you; but if you forsake Him, He will cast you off forever. Consider now, for the LORD has chosen you to build a house for the sanctuary, be strong and do it" (1 Chr. 28:9–10).

We know from David's own mouth that Jehovah Elohim is the God of all nations. The God of all nations cannot be confined to a building, as Solomon soon declared, but whatever place God deigns to inhabit is certainly meant to receive all peoples of earth. Solomon was directly instructed by his father to build a place where all the nations could bow before the living God. David keenly felt the responsibility to carry on the missionary obedience of his fathers, linking the provision of the people for temple building to God's covenant with Abraham to bless all nations. David's prayer in 1 Chronicles 29 was a beautiful missiological summary. The people gave generously of their wealth so that the God of all the nations might have a local address. David directly tied the provisions for this local address of a global God to the promises God made to Abraham and our fathers. David saw himself and his son as links in that great inheritance. Establishing once again the metanarrative of history, David commanded his people—and us down through the ages: "'Now bless the LORD [Jehovah] your God [Elohim]'" (v. 20). The people got the link David made between the temple of the God of all peoples and the promises of God to their fathers. They bowed and blessed God because *they* were now entrusted to carry on the mission of God, to create space and place where God could be glorified and where all nations could come and worship with them.

So it is today—the house of the Lord yet being built. It is a house of living stones, made up of every tribe, tongue, people, and nation. It is a house that needs pastors and singers, businessmen and intercessors, leaders and followers, senders and goers, young and old, male and female, from every nation to every nation. We stand on the shoulders of the fathers. Not just the patriarchs, not just the apostles, and not just the men and women of God over the last two millennia who burned for the glory of God among all nations. We also stand on the shoulders of the closest spiritual generation to us: our godly and missionary-minded parents, our prayerful and nations-oriented pastors, our disciplers and mentors who taught us to cry over the unreached. They did their part. Let's do ours.

PRAYER FOCUS: *Gujarati, Karana of Madagascar (Evangelical: 0.00%)*

MAY 26: DON'T LOSE SIGHT OF THE MISSION

TODAY'S READING: PSALMS 131, 138-139, 143-145

An endearing aspect of David was his single eye. Psalm 131 is one of the final psalms of ascent, written for those ascending the Judean hills toward the sanctuary or temple. As the pilgrimage drew to a close, David sang, "LORD, my heart is not haughty, nor my eyes lofty. Neither do I concern myself with great matters, nor with things too profound for me" (Psalm 131:1). This from the one who was king, the one who amassed treasure for the temple, the one who fought back enemies. David, with more responsibility and demands than any of us, determined he would push those incessant beggars to the back of his mind to focus on the simple, lowly, single things. Spiritual pilgrimage requires a determination to refuse to fixate on the problematic questions and to trust and obey, to have a single eye. A single eye on what? David's single eye lasered in on a whole heart of praise that magnified Jehovah above all other gods, that magnified the word of God above all other texts, that determined God's word would be heard by the kings of the earth who would likewise praise Him. David was a missionary king speaking and singing forth the praises of Jehovah to peers and paupers, believing that all should and would praise the one true God.

David knew this missionary goal was relentless and boundless. "Where can I go from Your Spirit" (139:7)? There is no position or place that releases us from the single intention that God has for His own glory from all peoples. Our passions are ever to be towards His name being glorified by all nations, by all people groups. Our zeal should always be singly in the employ of the mission of God and we should be against all that opposes God's goal. Hate as a concept is so abused today that we no longer think it appropriate in any form. Yet biblically, God hates. He is so against what is wicked that He will destroy it, including wicked people. The whole unrepentant world is under the wrath of a holy God, and God is only good and loving when He hates what is bad. When we have our zealous surges to destroy racism, pornography, child molestation, injustice, and other vile things, that hate is God-sourced. To be single-eyed is to hate what God hates just as much as it is to love what He loves. Immediately on the heels of saying that he will hate what God hates, David said: "Search me, O God, and know my heart; try me, and know my anxieties; and see, if there is any wicked way in me, and lead me in the way everlasting" (vv. 23-24). Going one step further than inappropriate hate being wicked, it is just as wicked to lack hate against whatever is against God and His purposes. Whatever is against God's passion to be glorified by all peoples must be hated if we are to have a single eye.

May we remember that anger is a central part of God's character: "The LORD is gracious and full of compassion, slow to anger and great in mercy" (145:8). God doesn't just get angry when we sin locally; He gets angry when we sin globally by losing sight of the single eye of mission.

PRAYER FOCUS: *Minangkabau, Orang Negeri of Malaysia (Evangelical: 0.00%)*

MAY 27: BETWEEN THE VIOLENT TIMES

TODAY'S READING: PSALMS 111–118

Missionary methods in our day (from the birth of Jesus to His return) reject the use of force or coercion. As the body of Christ, we are ashamed of any exceptions to this; we repent of them and we disavow them. We are committed in love to die for those we gospelize, not to kill them. The glory of God's people in mission today is to do what Jesus did—die for our enemies, die for the unreached peoples we love, die for the sake of the gospel. But non-violence as principle in spreading God's revelation is true only for our age; it was not true in David's time, nor will it be true when Jesus returns. In David's time, God's glory was demonstrated by winning physical battles against real people of real armies of different nationalities. We might not like it today, but we can't deny that Old Testament witness included physical war. The nations believed God was real when His power was displayed against them forcefully. Likewise, we cannot deny the coercive, physical nature of what happens when King Jesus comes back. There will be a literal judgment of the living and the dead, a literal hell of eternal torment, and every knee forced to bow and every tongue compelled to confess that Jesus Christ is Lord of all peoples and all nations to the glory of God the Father.

In Psalm 111:6, we are told that God "declared to His people the power of His works in giving them the heritage of the nations." This heritage was the physical, practical victory of Israel over the surrounding nations. Military conquest demonstrated that Jehovah is "high above all nations" (113:4) in order to elicit *all-day* and *all-place* praise by *all nations* (vv. 1–3). We see the strange and wonderful juxtaposition of God's forever mercy when the psalmist says: "All the nations surrounded me, but in the name of the LORD I will destroy them" (118:10). Psalm 118 combines the mercy of God and the physical destruction of the nations and prophetically states: "The stone which the builders rejected has become the chief cornerstone. This was the LORD's doing; it is marvelous in our eyes.... Save now, I pray, O LORD..." (118:22–23, 25). The mercy of God in Jesus is not at odds with the judgment of God on nations.

Let me be clear: We abhor any coercion in missionary work from the time of Jesus' birth until He comes again in power and glory. At the same time, we cannot deny that Jehovah used violence in the Old Testament past to prove that He is the only God, and we cannot deny that when Jesus comes back, it will be a great day for those who worship Him from every people and a violently terrible day for those who don't. In these times of mercy between those violent times, we choose active, robust, physical missionary work as Jesus modeled for us. We lay down our lives and lift up our voices in constant invitation with Psalm 117: "Praise the LORD, all you Gentiles! Laud Him, all you peoples! For His merciful kindness is great toward us, and the truth of the LORD endures forever. Praise the LORD."

PRAYER FOCUS: *Soninke of Mali (Evangelical: 0.00%)*

MAY 28: A MISSIONARY PLAN FOR YOU

TODAY'S READING: 1 KINGS 1–2; PSALMS 37, 71, 94

The books of Kings present a history beginning about 970 BC when Solomon came to the throne. Because Solomon was a coregent of David for a season, it is difficult to know exactly when his reign began. The history wraps up during the Babylonian exile with the last recorded event occurring in 561 BC. Within 1 and 2 Kings are strands woven together concerning court life, good kings, bad kings, prophets, and peoples. The metanarrative of missionary primacy remains consistent in Kings, for the condemning of the Northern Kingdom resulted from their undoing of the missionary covenant of God. They systematically undermined the tripartite formula: They took other gods and they refused to be His holy people, so He could not live among them to bless them in order that they bless the nations.

Self-exaltation is ever in conflict with the missionary heart of God. Missionary life is based on serving, not on leading. Adonijah exalted himself and built a consortium of support, knowing that his authority had a different leader in mind (1 Kings 1:5, 13, 27). He was the crown prince and was eager to rule and to see old leadership step down. He was so eager that he staged a coup. Woe to the young missionary leaders whose arrogance and ambition leads them to disrespect and displace their elders, their veterans. Our Lord the King in His wisdom makes His own kings, even if they are not as handsome or the "natural" crown prince. If everything rises and falls on leadership, then disaster for the global work of missions results from young leaders seeking position and title to which God did not appoint them. Let not the nations be lost due to leadership lust. Solomon was enthroned, and David defined manhood as keeping the charge of the Lord and honoring His commandments. Brothers and generals are executed, a high priest removed, and wicked opposers of God's people and plan eliminated (2:13–44). We are to walk in His ways, which include blessing the foreigners and holding those close to home accountable. In a modern context Solomon's succession has two applications for missionary leadership: First, leaders in mission will come and go. God is the One who determines the next leader and He will appoint the leader that will fulfill His missionary plan. Second, to desire that leadership position from a self-exalting posture is to ensure God will appoint someone else and further deal severely with your ambition.

Take courage! The missionary God of all the earth has a missionary plan for you. It may be to go to Mauritania. It may be to pray for Mauritania. It may be to send another to Mauritania. Whether Mauritania, the Maldives, or Mongolia, we can be assured that God intends our little lives to contribute to His grand global glory. We need not strive for regency or recognition. We must not long for leadership or leverage. We should only rest in the comfort that the God who formed us in our mother's womb has something only we can birth for Him. Neither self-exalting nor self-abasing, we receive our unique orders and play our part in God's grand missionary plan. Joy!

PRAYER FOCUS: *Fulani, Pulaar of Mauritania (Evangelical: 0.21%)*

MAY 29: THE A TO K OF MISSIONS

TODAY'S READING: PSALM 119:1–88

Psalm 119 is an acrostic poem. Today's reading (and tomorrow's) will be an alliterated missionary reading of Psalm 119, part declaration and part prayer that we can pronounce over the nations:

• **Aleph**: All those who walk in Your missionary ways will be blessed. All the world is where You have commanded Your people to diligently go. All will be praise when the peoples learn Your righteous judgments.

• **Bet/Vet:** By taking heed to Your missionary Bible, we stay pure. Because Your missionary ways are best for me and best for the world, it is all I will think about.

• **Gimmel:** Give me open eyes to see how the Bible is a missionary book. Grant this stranger on earth understanding on how to fulfill Your missionary plans. Glorify Your name among all peoples through me as I keep Your testimonies, no matter the governmental resistance.

• **Dalet:** Dust clings to me as I declare Your word to all peoples, so Lord, please revive me. Don't let me be ashamed or weary; do let me run with the gospel.

• **Hey:** Hearts, O Lord, are so hard; incline mine to You, that You may use me to help other hearts from every people group hunger for Your holy person. Help me, Lord, never to lose missionary zeal for Your glory among all nations all the way to the end of my life.

• **Vav:** Visit me with mercy, O Lord, that Your salvation might be known in every country and every city. Vector my life that it intersects with kings and peoples of influence that I may speak to them of Your gospel testimonies.

• **Zayin:** Zeal takes hold of me because of the wickedness around the world. Zion is my home, and I long to finish this pilgrimage and sing the song of the Lamb with others from every language, culture, tribe, and tongue.

• **Chet:** Choose for me, O Lord, how I can serve You in this world; if You want me to go or to stay home and send, confirm Your choice for me from Your word, but whatever that is, You will always be my portion.

• **Tet:** Train me, Lord, through Your discipline, for affliction helps me see clearly and refocuses me on the missionary purpose for my life that the Bible so consistently reveals.

• **Yod:** Your hands have made me and fashioned me, O Lord; help me understand Your missionary heart and ways. Yes, I will trust Your faithful affliction. Your tender mercies and Your delightful truth all work together for Your glory among the nations.

• **Kaf:** Keep my heart in Your word and my eyes on Your kingdom, Lord, and let my hope rest in Your promise that all peoples, even the most recalcitrant, will one day worship at Your feet.

PRAYER FOCUS: *Kalmyk-Oirat, Western Mongul of Mongolia (Evangelical: 1.80%)*

MAY 30: THE L-TO-T OF MISSIONS

TODAY'S READING: PSALMS 119:88–176

The Psalms are missionary songs and they sing out the different components of God's covenant, and Psalm 119 is no exception. It declares the comprehensive excellence of God's word. We can in good hermeneutical conscience apply these alliterated prayers and praises to God's missionary purposes for every nation and tribe on earth.

• **Lamed:** Let all the generations of all the geographies praise You, O Lord. Lest we forget, heaven and earth are Yours as are all the peoples, and all nations are Your servants—may all creation and all creatures give You praise.

• **Mem:** Make me wiser than the ancients, devoted to obeying Your word, diligent in seeing Your sweet words lifted in the heart language of every people.

• **Nun:** Nothing but Your word shows me how to walk among the nations. Nations may rise against nations, and nastiness come against me, but Lord, by Your grace I will not stray from Your mission purposes, and by Your help I will be a faithful witness to the unreached to the end.

• **Samech:** Shield me from those who resist what You want to do in all the earth. Save me, Lord, and sear Your statutes into my will that I will ever obey Your call to disciple all peoples.

• **Ayin:** All I know is that Your mercy has saved me, and in mercy You long for unreached peoples to be rescued from sin and death. Act, O Lord, we beg, not command You; You are dishonored in the earth, show Yourself mighty to save.

• **Pey:** Pave the way for us among the unreached by the light of Your word. Precept by precept, set those free who are bound in false religions and ideologies globally.

• **Tsade:** Tsars of industry, economy, education, politics, and religion all conspire against Your gospel, and we are so very small and despised; yet, we will hold on to Your covenantal missionary promises and precepts.

• **Qof:** Keep getting me up early, O Lord, with Your missionary passions; there is time to sleep when this season of exile is over, so keep me energized and focused on the lost.

•**Resh:** Redeem, O Lord, as You have rescued us. Reach down into all peoples and ransom for Yourself a remnant who will ever praise You. Revive, O Lord, and raise up from the dead peoples praise and worship of Your holy name.

•**Shin:** Shepherd us to stand in awe of Your statutes, and let us have the joy of finding great treasures of grace from among every people and tongue. Shalom the peoples of earth who love Your law and give them comprehensive wholeness and peace in Your presence.

• **Tav:** Teach my tongue to tell Your truths to all, and let the focus of all my missionary effort be to point the unreached to the Living Word through the written Word of God. This is my story and this is my song, that Your law is my delight and Your judgments help me.

PRAYER FOCUS: *Berber, Southern Shilha of Morocco (Evangelical: 0.16%)*

MAY 31: GENEROSITY TURNED GREEDY

TODAY'S READING: 1 KINGS 3–4

"We who have Christ's eternal life need to throw away our own lives."

GEORGE VERWER

Because Solomon saw himself as small and needing the Lord's wisdom, his reign had peace on every side and his subjects dwelt safely, each under his vine and fig tree. Further, men of all nations from all the kings of the earth who had heard of Solomon's wisdom came to hear the wisdom of Solomon. This is missions at its centripetal finest: the nations coming to the pristine example so that they might likewise be wise and blessed. Solomon's wisdom excelled that of the wise men of his day because in Solomon's case, God's wisdom was so much better than what was available globally. Those hungry for truth, life, and blessing came humbly to sit at the feet of the one who knew Jehovah.

Solomon's missionary heart was connected to God's generous intention to include all people groups of earth in heavenly blessings. Solomon was given "wisdom and exceedingly great understanding, and largeness of heart like the sand on the seashore" (1 Kings 4:29). Critical to note, generosity of heart is a defining characteristic of Solomon, linked directly to his wisdom, which in turn linked directly to all men of all nations coming to know Jehovah. This generosity of heart was actually on display in the famous story of the two women fighting over one baby. Solomon more than settled a case—he determined who shared his generous heart. That in turn was a reflection of God's generosity. Solomon wanted to know which woman cared more about the life of others than her own personal interests, and this is the source of the missionary spirit. Those who share the desire that others may live, even if that means painful consequences for themselves, are those who have understood God's generous missionary heart. Those who are possessive, those who want life on their terms, those who will not sacrifice that others may live, they share the stingy spirit of the one who comes to steal, kill, and destroy. There really are only two kinds of Christians in the world: those who wisely share the generous heart of God and those who are unwilling to endure pain and grief for the saving of life.

Solomon was told that if he walked in God's ways, kept His statutes, and commandments like David did, then all would be well. Unfortunately, as the record will show, Solomon's generosity turned greedy for personal gratification. The tragic consequence of generosity aging into greed was that this beautiful microcosm of God's rule was lost, and with it a missionary invitation to all the nations. God wants to invite the unreached of Mozambique to submit to His rule. He wants to display the benefits of His rule by His generosity both in us and through us. As soon as we stop passing on God's generosity, His blessings dry up, and we have nothing eternally good to give to unreached peoples. That's not Solomonic wisdom; that's just satanic stupidity.

PRAYER FOCUS: *Makhuwa, Nahara of Mozambique (Evangelical: 0.02%)*

LIVE | DEAD

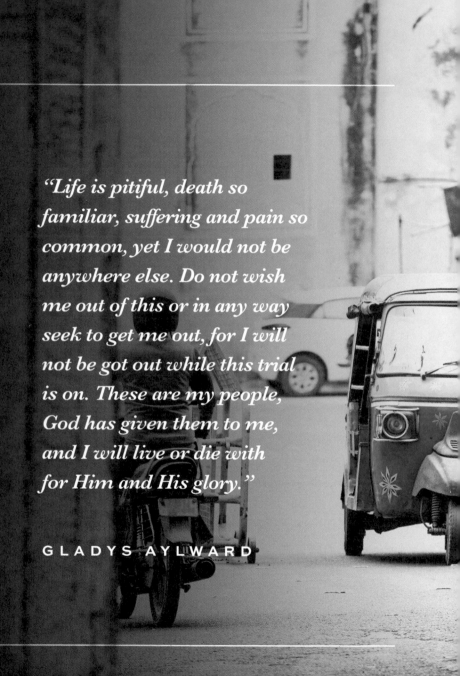

"Life is pitiful, death so familiar, suffering and pain so common, yet I would not be anywhere else. Do not wish me out of this or in any way seek to get me out, for I will not be got out while this trial is on. These are my people, God has given them to me, and I will live or die with for Him and His glory."

GLADYS AYLWARD

JUNI

JUNE 1: SEEK SOLOMON'S COMPANY

TODAY'S READING: 2 CHRONICLES 1; PSALM 72

Second Chronicles continues the record of the monarchy but from the twin positions of being positive (glossing over Solomon's excesses) and of being priestly (focusing mostly on Solomon building and equipping the temple). The book opens with the commentary that God was with Solomon; that Solomon was grateful for God's mercy to his father David; and that Solomon famously requested wisdom and knowledge that he might judge (reign and rule) over God's great people. It is critical we understand why exactly Solomon requested wisdom—and who better to understand the why from than Solomon himself.

Solomon is the author of Psalm 72, and this psalm reprises his original request: "Give the king Your judgments, O God, and Your righteousness to the king's Son" (v. 1). The psalm then builds to verse 17 and its Messianic reference: "His name shall endure forever: His name shall continue as long as the sun. And men shall be blessed in Him; all nations shall call Him blessed." Solomon asked for wisdom to rule Israel, but he did so as the heir of David, and thus, the inheritor of God's promise to David who in turn was an inheritor of the stewardship given to Abraham: blessing of all the nations. David's rule and Solomon's wise reign were simply examples and foreshadowing of the reign of the Messiah, a reign that would intentionally include all people groups of earth. Matthew's opening words in his Gospel, "Jesus Christ, the Son of David, the Son of Abraham," link Jesus to the fulfillment of this double inheritance, stating boldly that Jesus is the king who will reign over all. It is this Jesus who in the Great Commission of Matthew 28 passes on "the missional task to Abraham's spiritual heirs, the Messiah's disciples." Solomon's reign and request cannot be interpreted outside this wider narrative.

Solomon knew that his reign was simply so Jehovah would be glorified by all peoples of earth, that the whole earth be full of His glory. Solomon had no idea how that would happen, so he asked for wisdom. It is poor stewardship to see any responsibility we have been given (captain of a team, president of a class, leader of a small group, father of a family, owner of a business, officer in a company, pastor in a church, any role at any level) outside Solomon's missionary request: O Lord, I don't know how to leverage this responsibility for Your glory in all the earth. Give me wisdom and right judgment, Lord, that I may steward this responsibility, grand or small, for the glory of God among every unreached people and place. Any leadership or responsibility of any scope anywhere in the world has one singular aim: the missionary aim of God being glorified by every tongue. If you have no idea how your current place and position can glorify Jesus among the 4.4 million Tai Man of Myanmar, then you are in good company—Solomonic company. Ask God for wisdom. Ask Him for a generous heart. Ask Him how what you oversee right now can bless all peoples of earth and make way for Messiah's eternal reign.

PRAYER FOCUS: *Tai Man, Shan of Myanmar (Burma) (Evangelical: 0.82%)*

JUNE 2: THE BRIDE MADE BEAUTIFUL

TODAY'S READING: SONG OF SOLOMON

"You want Beautiful Feet? Skip the pedicure! Share the Gospel!"

LIVING WATERS

Paul compared the church to the bride of Christ saying: "Husbands, love your wives, just as Christ also loved the church and gave Himself up for her…that He might present to Himself the church in all her glory…holy and blameless" (Eph. 5:25, 27 NASB). The traditional understanding of the Song of Solomon is that the book is an allegory of God's marriage-like love for His people. "Throughout the ages, it has been read allegorically or metaphorically, rather than literally. Even though God's name is not mentioned, rabbinical tradition saw the book as depicting the relationship between God and Israel. Even Paul uses the image of husband and wife to describe Christ and the church. Some see Christ as calling to the church, 'Arise, my love, my fair one, and come away.' Early Christian interpreters even saw the Song as a way to express their desire for Jesus, and their difficulty in finding him. Or some see it as Christ's love song to the church."

The Song of Solomon is God's song to His bride. It has stanzas filled with longing, stanzas full of joy, and sections of shocking intimacy. But taken together the book reflects the loving, missionary heart of God: Arabian tents (1:5), Egyptian chariots (v. 9), Lebanese lumber (3:9), Syrian mountains (4:8), and Jordanian reservoirs (7:4) are all mentioned. No book of the Bible, no love song of our missionary God ever gets away from the inclusion of all peoples. In fact, what makes God's bride so beautifully desirable is that she is comprised of representatives from every tribe, tongue, people, and nation. Hebrew analogy and comparisons (metaphor and simile) are not based on physical similarity, but intellectual puzzles and pictures. Teeth are compared to sheep because no sheep is missing from the flock, not because teeth look like sheep. Beauty is compared to cities and the banners of armies for what those pictures inspire, not because a woman looks like a city.

When the church lacks representatives from 7,000 unreached people groups, we are not the bride Jesus delights in or longs for. His vision for us, the church in all her glory, the church holy and blameless, is one comprised of men and women of every age, culture, and color from every country, representing every people group, saved, redeemed, and sanctified from every false religion and ideology, made into one beautiful and adorned bride. This is the bride that He sings over, that He woos, that He longs for, that He died for, and that lives for Him. Both bride and Bridegroom anticipate with great longing the wedding day. Jesus is coming back to take us, His bride, to our eternal home. The Song of Solomon focuses us on that great missionary culmination by simply reminding us that God's bride must be beautiful and that she is only beautiful if she is comprised of every people, tongue, and nation.

PRAYER FOCUS: *Brahmin of Nepal (Evangelical: Unknown)*

JUNE 3: A CLASSIC TEXT

TODAY'S READING: PROVERBS 1-3

God is a missionary God and the Bible is a missionary book. As part of the wisdom literature of the Bible, Proverbs points us "to YHWH, the God who is the only hope of…salvation and indirectly then, the story of YHWH's revealing and redeeming acts in which salvation is to be found. A further clue of this perspective is the canonical location of the Wisdom tradition in connection with Solomon and the climax of the Davidic covenant. The texts in 1 Kings that celebrate God's gift of wisdom to Solomon, to the admiration of the nations round about, also include the building of the temple. And we recall that part of Solomon's prayer of dedication that asks God to bless the foreigners who come to pray to Him there. So although the Wisdom literature itself does not mention the exodus, the covenant, the gift of the land, or the building of the temple, the historical narrative binds Wisdom into that tradition through its association with Solomon. Any wisdom that is associated with Solomon must be connected with the Solomonic tradition that God should bless the nations in their interaction with Israel."

Wright points out there is an international ethos concerning Old Testament wisdom literature. First, Israel was at peace with using wisdom material from other nations, editing and purging out false gods and idols as necessary before incorporating the wisdom into the holy Scriptures. Second, not only are aberrant concepts purged from the wisdom of the nations, there are also warnings against false wisdom. Wright draws four missionary implications from Proverbs:

• **Common human concerns.** Wisdom literature provides one of the best bridges for biblical faith to establish meaningful contact and engagement with widely different human cultures around the world.

• **Welcoming the wisdom of the nations.** In the drawing in of the nations' wisdom a foretaste of the ingathering of the nations themselves in eschatological fullness is promised.

• **Critiquing the wisdom of the nations.** Israel approached the wisdom of other nations with the religious and moral disinfectant provided by Yahwistic monotheism.

• **The wisdom bridge is not in itself redemption.** While wisdom may provide a bridge, it also has a built-in self-critique that questions its own adequacy to solve the problems it addresses.

Proverbs is a classic missionary text. The wisdom of the nations is drawn in, filtered, and redeemed as an indicator that Berber men and women are to be included in the family of God. It is in this light that the fear of the Lord is the beginning of missions. The God of all wisdom has placed His truth in all cultures, delighting that these little truths will draw seeking hearts to Himself. Wisdom has been both disseminated and distorted in all cultures. The missionary work is to mine that wisdom out, affirming what is unsullied, redeeming and restoring the marred aspects to biblical truth, and then using those ransomed realities to show that all along Jehovah has been inviting all peoples to Himself.

PRAYER FOCUS: *Berber, Rif of Netherlands (Evangelical: 0.10%)*

JUNE 4: IT'S JUST HARD
TODAY'S READING: PROVERBS 4-6

"God will never do anything with us till he has first of all undone us."

CHARLES SPURGEON

In missionary living we must manage the tension of being in the world (i.e. context/culture) while not being of it. The inclusion of cultural wisdom from other nations (redeemed and refined) makes Proverbs a missionary book, reminding us that in the rescue of others we must keep our heart with all diligence. There are many seductions that would lure missionary hearts away from the purity of God's commands and covenants. Here are the big three:

Seduced by the good will of the authorities. At the end of the day the gospel is problematic to false religions. The gospel demands repentance—turning from idols, false worship, syncretism, and all that exalts itself against Jehovah. For men and women to turn to Jehovah means to turn away from some or many sacred traditions long protected. There are financial and social implications. There is illogical wrath from the guardians of culture and society to be endured. In missionary life we encounter men and women of influence, gatekeepers of society and their people, door openers of opportunity, officials who grant visas and have access to power. The wisdom of Proverbs does not allow the missionary message to be diluted in order to gain favor with authorities.

Seduced by the good will of the populace. At the end of the day we will be loved for the social services we provide and hated for the message we preach. Our goal is not to be hated; yet neither is it to be loved. Our goal is to glorify God by being faithful messengers of the gospel. Jesus sternly warned us that we would be hated for this obedient service (Matt. 24:9). None of us relishes being despised, so the seduction is to change our approach so that we only do what the local population appreciates and we stop doing what they resent. In missions we should indeed meet practical needs, but not as a goal and not as a replacement of the difficult call of the gospel. Missionary lives demand that we resist the call to only be loved and we learn to navigate the tension of being loved for our kind deeds and hated for our truth-telling. The wisdom of Proverbs reminds us that being hated is part of being loved.

Seduced by the prospect of easy work. Missionaries are warned against being sluggards because the work of making disciples is not complicated, it's just hard. Jesus wanted labor workers who knew how to sweat. All missionaries sign up to work hard, but it's one thing to volunteer to labor and another thing to sustain that labor in year 17 and beyond. Most missionaries don't complete their third term; they don't make it past year 7. Our anecdotal observation is that most breakthroughs happen around year 10. Many missionaries cannot sustain the intensity of working hard (especially if fruit appears slowly) so then either go home or live a cozy international life. The wisdom of Proverbs reminds us that missionary work isn't complicated. It's just hard.

PRAYER FOCUS: *Zarma of Niger (Evangelical: 0.10%)*

JUNE 5: TREASURE THE COMMAND

TODAY'S READING: PROVERBS 7-9

The first nine chapters of Proverbs (with the climax in Proverbs 8) are "a picture of the value of wisdom. Wisdom is personified as a woman pleading with men and woman to pursue her." The parallels to Jesus are obvious, for Wisdom in Proverbs is considered pre-created with the Father from the beginning, universal, good for all men and woman globally. Proverbs is an essential missionary text, for its truth both serves and warns all peoples everywhere. A specific missionary lens applied to the general truths in Proverbs allow for these applications.

We should treasure the command to make disciples of all nations. Wisdom tells us to treasure her commands and live, to make Jesus' commands the apple of our eye. Jesus commands us to go. Jesus commands us to preach the gospel everywhere to all people. If that is our single-eyed focus, if that is our treasure, then we will not only treasure the doctrine theoretically, but we will actually live out that command practically and joyfully. "The proper end and tendency of all right doctrine when truly believed, is to produce correct practice.... Oh, when shall the church be purified, or the world converted? Not till it is a settled point, that heresy in practice is the proof of heresy in belief." If we really believe in missions, we will do something profoundly practical about it. To theologically agree that missions is primary *without* primarily giving your time, treasure, or life for God's glory among all peoples is to be a heretic.

To enjoy the sensual luxuries of life while we wait for the Bridegroom to return is adultery. Folly calls us to live an indulgent life with all the trappings of Egyptian linen. Folly seduces us to enjoy the pleasures and conveniences of this world, overspending on ourselves and underspending on the spread of the gospel, delighting ourselves with earthly pleasure, for our husband is not at home and will not come back until the appointed day. The wise know that the Bridegroom's return is imminent. There is neither goodness in nor time for dalliance with anyone or anything other than being ready for His coming. No luxury or fleeting pleasure can compare to the joy of presenting to the returning Bridegroom the gift of redeemed peoples from every tongue.

To fear the Lord is to agree with His opposition to our selfishness. The beginning of wisdom is to not be offended when Jesus puts His finger on our indulgences, to not resist when Jesus asks for more than we are comfortable giving for the sake of His glory among all peoples. "The reason why wicked men and devils hate God is, because they see him in relation to themselves. Their hearts rise up in rebellion, because they see him opposed to their selfishness." Ironically, missions has always elicited anger in the hearts of those who are selfish. The wise recognize that any discomfort when challenged is an indicator that we don't really fear the Lord, that our hearts are rebellious and selfish. God has absolute authority to demand our unselfishness with our treasure and with the apples of our eyes, for He sent His only Son to suffer and die for all nations, all peoples of earth.

PRAYER FOCUS: *Kanuri, Yerwa of Nigeria (Evangelical: 0.01%)*

JUNE 6: HOW TO GET RICH

TODAY'S READING: PROVERBS 10–12

Missionaries work hard. Missionary labor is not complicated; it's just hard. Learning language and culture is hard work. Giving up cultural preferences about time, space, and individuality is hard. Wide sowing of the gospel with little response is hard. Working through the challenges of discipleship is not convoluted, but one does have to choose between hard choices. Missionary hands that are diligent will harvest if they faint not. It might not be quick, but harvest will come after hard work. Missionary work is a collective effort. It's not complicated to send; it's just hard. Missionary sending is the hard choice to send our best. Missionary sending is the hard work of long prayers without much feedback. Missionary sending is the hard work of full days so that funds can be generously sent. Missionary sending and going, missionary living and dying, it's not complicated, just hard.

Missionaries get rich. "The blessing of the LORD makes one rich, and He adds no sorrow with it" (Prov. 10:22). It should be impossible for us to read about the blessing of the Lord without reference to God's promise to bless Abraham. Missionary wealth is in people, not pennies. Disciples are the coin of God's realm and the only currency we carry with us to glory. All other pursuit of wealth adds anxiety. How wealthy are those with nothing in their heavenly pockets but with a line of disciples thronging to hug their necks.

Missionaries are learners, not lecturers. "When pride comes, then comes shame; but with the humble is wisdom" (11:2). Missionary arrogance is damaging to the gospel. We cannot forget that the only thing we must know is Christ crucified. We must determine to be an expert in Jesus. It's the only unique, life-giving component we have in more measure than our local hosts. In every land are indigenous people wiser, stronger, and richer than we are. Missionaries who are not humble fall prey to the messianic delusion that they are mini-Christs deployed to continue His mission. In reality, there is a discontinuity between what Jesus did and what missionaries are to do. There is one Christ, and His work on the cross is done. We are not saviors. We have nothing practical to give that can't be given better and more efficiently by local experts. All we have been entrusted to freely pass on is a message, a hope, an invitation. Missionaries must posture themselves as learners, even by those who reject Christ.

Missionaries are truth tellers. "He who speaks truth declares righteousness" (12:17). Missionaries always tell the truth. There should be no lie in us. It is folly to think truth can be passed on in any life-giving way through un-truthful means. We may in prudence at some time in some way conceal some things, but we never lie. We always tell the truth, but we don't always tell all we know. In cultures that honor deceit, in religions based on falsehoods, we, the truth brokers, must be extra vigilant to have no falsehood in us. Jesus is the truth. We must use truth to point to truth. Elders and leaders in other contexts resent duplicity more than they fear disagreement, so let us have the wisdom to handle difficult questions without deceit.

PRAYER FOCUS: *Arab, Arabic Gulf Spoken of Oman (Evangelical: 0.30%)*

JUNE 7: THE MISSIONARY SPIRIT

TODAY'S READING: PROVERBS 13-15

The missionary spirit is the spirit of investment. The only riches we carry with us when we "shuffle off this mortal coil" will be disciples made. Jesus commanded us to go and make disciples, and if we are not making disciples, there is something wrong with us—at least if we claim to be a follower of Jesus. The Greek of Matthew 28 puts the emphasis on discipleship, literally instructing us to "make disciples wherever we go." That the going centers on unreached peoples is evident from the phrase "of all the nations," but still the emphasis is on making disciples. We are to be faithful ambassadors. Faithful ambassadors must leave home; they bring health by going, not by staying. We can't buy into the lie that investing at home leads indirectly to health among the nations. Real health only comes through the direct investment of our ambassadorial lives among the sickest places and peoples. A good man will leave a missionary legacy to his children's children, namely the legacy of pouring out prayers, riches, and our very lives for those who have never heard the gospel.

The missionary spirit is the spirit of pioneering. Where there are no visionaries, the trough is clean, but much gospel advance comes through the hard-headed wills of pioneer missionaries. Anyone who has lived abroad among fruitful pioneer missionaries quickly realizes that the personas so articulate in our pulpits or gracious in our living rooms have a fiery side. Those missionaries may be sweet single ladies or grey-haired, twinkly-eyed couples or young families with three toddlers, but steel is in their spine. A fighting spirit is required in those who would advance the good news to the bad gates of hell. We like our representatives to have backbone and we realize they need it, but we all tend to squirm at messes in the stall. Put all those hard heads together on the field and it's no wonder missionary attrition happens, primarily because sweet little missionaries can't get along with one another. Pioneers are scrappy people who relish a good fight. Let's help them fight for Jesus, not against each other. Twenty-five million Pashtun need some pretty resilient, rugged missionaries to live among them.

The missionary spirit is the spirit of verbal communication. We must always use words. The gospel is news that must be delivered. We are voices crying in the wilderness. We are witnesses not called to the gospel stand to pantomime, but to clearly point to Jesus and His definitive work on the cross. Yes, soft answers turn away wrath. Yes, wholesome tongues are trees of life. Yes, the lips of the wise disperse knowledge. Yes, joy comes by the answer of the mouth, and how good is a word in season. Yes, the heart of the righteous studies how to answer. None of these injunctions tell us to refrain from speaking; they all instruct us how to speak. Let us be clear, committed heralds and town criers. We are not the solution or the answer. But we know Who is and we must lift up our voice and direct attention to Him.

PRAYER FOCUS: *Pashtun of Pakistan (Evangelical: 0.00%)*

JUNE 8: THE GOAL AND GIFT OF MISSIONS

TODAY'S READING: PROVERBS 16-18

"Oh, that I could spend every moment of my life to God's glory!"

DAVID BRAINERD

The goal of missions is the glory of God. "The LORD has made all for Himself, yes, even the wicked for the day of doom" (Prov. 16:4). As hell grows in unpopularity, so does it grow in proximity. None of the denials by the arrogant can push back against the approach of hell. There is a day of doom, and our theology is apocalyptic: Jesus is coming back soon to judge the living and the dead. Heaven and hell are at stake and they rush upon us. God is not less glorified when He consigns someone to hell than when He allows someone into His holy heaven. The missionary wisdom contained in Proverbs does not allow for the sophistry of twisting God into a monster because He sends the wicked to hell. Because God is beautiful, good, and kind, there must be a hell. God's holiness, righteousness, justice, and glory demand hell for the wicked, and God is just as glorified by hell as He is by heaven. Good missionaries do not dilute hell, nor do they ignore it, but like Jesus they serve it hot and as a warning.

The goal of missions is generations of disciples. "Children's children are the crown of old men, and the glory of children is their father" (17:6). One of the richest men on earth I know is my friend Eli. He has made disciples who have made disciples who have made disciples who are making disciples. Eli is rich in his middle age, crowned with the joy of seeing multiple generations of faith, and in turn, those disciples glory in their spiritual heritage. What Eli has seen and stewarded should be the prayer of and for every missionary: "Lord, grant multiple generations of disciples! We don't care about dollars, projects, institutions, buildings, programs, little plaques, or big ovations. We just want disciples that make disciples. Give us children, grandchildren, great-grandchildren, and great-great-grandchildren in the faith—all for your great-great glory in every unreached people!"

The gift of missions is gospel proclamation. "Death and life are in the power of the tongue" (18:21). Our biblical role is crystal clear. We are announcers, town criers, heralds, watchmen, messengers, voices crying in the wilderness. We are not the Christ, the One to come, the Answer, and neither is any program or ministry on earth. The hope is not in dollars, education, technology, industry, democracy, socialism, or any "ism." We can't legislate morality. We can't bring heaven to earth. We can't usher in the kingdom through social change. We can't solve the problem of sin in human hearts. We can't clean up the earth, seas, or skies without someone quickly sullying them over again. There is only one blessed hope. There is only One who can fix all that has fallen, and our job is to open our mouths and point to His death bringing us eternal life. The missionary mandate is to communicate news: the good news of Jesus' death, resurrection, and return. The greatest gift we give to the nations is to open our mouth and preach the gospel. The life and death of the Maguindanao, all 1,267,000 of them, is in our tongues.

PRAYER FOCUS: *Maguindanao of Philippines (Evangelical: 0.04%)*

JUNE 9: THE REQUIREMENTS OF MISSIONS

TODAY'S READING: PROVERBS 19-21

Missions requires and rewards obedience. "He who keeps the commandment keeps his soul, but he who is careless of his ways will die" (Prov. 19:16). God's commands are wide ranging, yet they are connected to His grand plan for history. God has condescended to be our God if we will be His holy people and He will bless us so that we bless all peoples of earth. Jesus is the key to the blessing passed on through Abraham and David, and those who keep the commandment to bless the nations with Jesus keep their souls. Those who do not bless the nations with Jesus are careless with their ways and they will shrivel up and die. It is not dramatic nor exaggerated to place our missionary responsibility in these drastic terms. The life and death of the people of God, the vibrancy or stagnancy of the "called out" (*ekklesia*) ones, the church, is directly connected to whether or not we keep His commands. There may be many other plans we have, but at the end of the human day, God's goal and counsel will stand. Life and lasting blessing are directly connected to obeying Jesus command to take the gospel global.

Missions requires energy and wisdom. "The glory of young men is their strength, and the splendor of old men is their gray head" (20:29). I used to think that the ideal age for the new missionary recruit was 22. I have recently revised that number to 27. Many young missionaries would do well to be seasoned in their home context, earn a little wisdom the hard way to add to their energy, before landing on the field. When a person has had a pagan boss, they have learned how to be dealt with harshly. They had to go to work the next day to pay the bills. Time in the marketplace adds the wisdom of life to the energy of dreams. I am not saying 27 is a magic number, but I am saying missionary service requires a blend of both energy and wisdom.

Missions requires diligent planning. "The plans of the diligent lead surely to plenty, but those of everyone who is hasty, surely to poverty" (21:5). Missionary praxis has toggled back and forth between Spirit dependence and strategic thinking. Those who advocate Spirit leading to the hurt of strategic planning say that we should "observe what the Spirit is doing and just go where the fish are biting" or "to plan and strategize is to limit what the Spirit wants to do." On the other extreme, those who over rely on strategy tend to make 5-year plans, create 10-step processes, or train and promote one particular model that worked in their context so it must surely work everywhere (with a little tweaking). Good missionaries plan, and they plan on depending on the Spirt. There is enough oil in the dwelling of the wise and there are smart ways to scale city walls. If God can overcome the dumb things we do missiologically, just think what He might do with wise, diligent plans! The wise missionary does not confuse urgency with haste, nor Spirit dependence with the lack of research and preparation. Just think of all the good God will do in the world when we combine great diligence with great dependence on the Spirit!

PRAYER FOCUS: *Arab, Palestinian of Qatar (Evangelical: 0.08%)*

JUNE 10: SECULAR PROVERBS

TODAY'S READING: PROVERBS 22–24

Proverbs 22 begins with the superscription: The Sayings of the Wise. While most proverbs are generally associated with the wisdom of Solomon, the proverbs in chapters 22 to 24, "as well as the outline by which they are arranged, appear also in a book of Egyptian wisdom, called *The Instruction of Amen-em-hotep.*" This book of proverbs is a collection of collections and shows similarities (often word for word) with other non-Israelite wisdom. There are important differences, however. The wisdom teaching of the ancient Middle East had three critical underlying assumptions: that the world is orderly; that human beings are able to understand that order; and that the way to derive principles of wisdom is through personal experience, observation, and adherence to tradition.

Proverbs, then, is the Bible's most secular book in that it draws most heavily on the wisdom of the nations and looks for universal and eternal principles. Secular, trans-national wisdom was not adopted willy-nilly but redeemed through submitting it to the authority of Israel's God, Jehovah, and connecting it to Israel's history and traditions. That history was directly linked to David, Moses, the Patriarchs, and Abraham. Essentially, Proverbs is the wisdom that takes the Abrahamic covenant global. Proverbs gives the practical constructs by which the gospel message must be carried and communicated to all peoples. Reading Proverbs with that lens leads to missionary applications of its wisdom.

"He who loves purity of heart and has grace on his lips, the king will be his friend" (Prov. 22:11). When we communicate the challenging gospel from a pure heart and with gracious lips, we befriend the power brokers of our context who can open doors to a wider hearing. Those who excel in the work of pure, gracious gospelizing will stand before kings. The God of universal wisdom is Jehovah. When Jehovah's ambassadors are faithful in communicating His character and salvation plan to the unreached, He preserves that truth. When Jehovah's truth is fixed on our lips so that our trust is in Him, He gives us counsel and wisdom that we know the certainty of the "words of truth to those who send to you" (vv. 18–19, 21).

A mighty redeemer, souls delivered from hell, and a sure hereafter of hope could easily have been the three main sermon points of Billy Graham, yet they first appear in Proverbs. Jehovah seemingly inserting Himself into the wisdom of the ancients is really His reclaiming of truths that came from Him and issuing them through us to all peoples. Proverbs 24 continues in gospel tone by stating we should deliver those who are drawn toward death and hold back those stumbling to the slaughter. All these salvific comments are echoed in the wisdom text of the ancient Egyptians, and the nations watch how God's people act and speak. How wonderful that this most "secular" book of the Bible was birthed among the peoples of earth, refined by the God of Israel, and preserved for us that we do missionary acts in wise and enduring ways.

PRAYER FOCUS: *Chechan, Nohchi of Russia (Evangelical: 0.01%)*

JUNE 11: MAKE CHURCH MISSIONARY

TODAY'S READING: 1 KINGS 5-6; 2 CHRONICLES 2-3

It's wonderful that the temple was held up by Lebanese lumber. It's wonderful that the temple Solomon dedicated to Jehovah included many construction details and designs common to the temples of that pagan time. God's election of Israel was ever about inclusion of all peoples. Lebanon contributed to the glory of God and as a result was blessed and fed. God's passion for all peoples to be included in His blessing should be at the center of our houses of worship. Whenever God's people gather to praise, there should be prayer for the missing family members from around the world. Those silent Lebanese beams, smothered in gold, held up the roof so that the people of God could petition heaven for His glory to be universally known. So too may God's current pillars—men and women of faith—lift up holy hands on Sundays in temples scattered across this globe.

Jehovah reminded Solomon concerning the temple that if he walked in God's statutes, judgments, and commands, then the promise to David was secured, a promise that the kingdom would include all peoples and that God would dwell among His people. Ritual temple worship was essentially missionary: It kept the elect people of Israel holy, which kept God's powerful presence among them, which gave them the blessing they needed to woo all peoples of earth to come join the party, to come join those Lebanese logs in God's presence.

Jehovah's temple was not just held up by Lebanese lumber—all nations built it. Second Chronicles 2:17 tells us that Solomon numbered all the aliens in Israel and made 70,000 carry stuff, 80,000 cut stone, and 3,600 oversee the work. Hiram sent a skillful man who was half Phoenician as the chief artist, engraver, and skilled worker. Decades before the Phoenicians crafted the beautiful city of Carthage, they beautified God's holy house, built of course on the land of Ornan the Jebusite. It's a wonder we are so blockheaded about God's missionary heart when aliens cut and carried every block of the temple, when the creativity of a Phoenician created the whole artistic design, when Lebanese lumber held up the roof, and when the whole building sat on Jebusite land. Indeed, God's house was always intended to be a house for all peoples.

If God was so intentional that the first temple be so missionary in design, composition, building, and flavor, ought not we be as intentional that the physical composition of our churches be nation-oriented? Should not the warp and woof of our worship times be multinational, even if we live in the heart of the Bible Belt? Some churches accomplish the former by flags, maps, prayer walls, and pictures of unreached peoples. Bravo! Some churches accomplish the latter by having prayer for unreached peoples as part of every gathering, by constantly having missionaries or international Christians in their pulpits, and by repeatedly making their financial giving's priority the nations, and not the needs that are near. There are many creative ways to make our churches and our services missionary, but the principle matter is to be as intentional about making our houses and temples welcoming of all nations just as Jehovah was about His.

PRAYER FOCUS: *Arab, Saudi Hijazi of Saudi Arabia (Evangelical: 0.12%)*

JUNE 12: MIXED MISSIONARY MARRIAGES
TODAY'S READING: 1 KINGS 7; 2 CHRONICLES 4

Both the patron of the temple, Solomon, and the chief architect of the temple, Huram, were a part of mixed marriages. Solomon's main wife was Egyptian and Huram's father was a Phoenician. The temple itself was a mixed marriage, patterned after temples of its time. Always in the center of the biblical story is God's intentional inclusion of all peoples. As a product of a mixed marriage (my mother born/raised in Greece, my father in America), I am glad that God smiles down upon blended races, wanting all combinations of all races around His heavenly throne.

What is common, however, to all who marry into God's family is they check all other gods at the temple door. Though Jehovah's temple was patterned after Syrian temples of the day, it was not Syrian, nor did it make room for Syria's gods. Though Solomon's wife was Egyptian, no false Egyptian idol should ever cross the temple threshold. Though Huram was Phoenician, no evil cultic practice should have any part of Israelite's worship. The nations are welcome, but they must marry in on God's terms, and that pre-nuptial agreement includes forsaking all gods and idols other than Jehovah.

Missionary marriages—the contextualization of the gospel that welcomes all peoples into God's family—is not without guidelines and riverbanks. It's not a syncretistic free-for-all theologically in which God allows any idea or practice to be adopted unscathed into Christian worship. God's gospel is freely offered to all peoples. Yet that gospel is rooted in a specific story and all who would join the Kingdom have to join that story, not reshape or change it. That story is the heart of the Bible and it is missionary. We cannot, must not read the Bible nor live our daily lives outside this one story. We should not breeze through the logistical details of the Scripture without remembering the point of it all: God living with all men, a mixed multitude of every race, joyfully forever. We dare not go from day to day waking up, going to work, returning home, falling asleep, all to repeat tomorrow, outside the story, forgetting why it is we work, sleep, eat, and repeat. King Jesus is coming in glory. King Jesus is coming to destroy all that is wicked. King Jesus will live forever with His mixed-marriage family. Our purpose in this short life is to make that family as big, diverse, variegated, colorful, and wonderful as we possibly can.

Mixed marriages include all relatives, but that doesn't mean there are no family rules, nor that we don't have a family history. We are the children of Abraham. We are spiritual Israel. Our story must merge into and submit to the family story. We can't bring old gods or idols into the temple. If we are going to be authentic family members, then we all have to adopt the history of Israel and God's people as our own. We have to sign the same covenant. When we marry into the family of God, we have to change our name and take up His.

PRAYER FOCUS: *Fulani, Fulakunda of Senegal (Evangelical: 0.01%)*

JUNE 13: WE NEVER STAND ALONE

TODAY'S READING: 1 KINGS 8; 2 CHRONICLES 5

"Prayer is the mighty engine that is to move the missionary work."

A. B. SIMPSON

In Solomon's prayer of dedication for the temple, the Abrahamic and Davidic covenants converge. This prayer enables Matthew, generations later, to open his Gospel by proclaiming Jesus both the Son of Abraham and the Son of David. "It is an implicit fulfillment of the promise to Abraham that foreigners will be attracted to come and invoke the God of Israel for blessing. The motivation offered to God for answering such prayers of non-covenant people is expressly missional—namely, that 'all the peoples of the earth may know your name and fear you, as do your own people Israel' [1 Kings 8:43]. The temple, then, that was so centrally connected to the Davidic covenant in the developing faith of Israel from this point on can be the focus of fulfillment of the Abrahamic covenant. It should be the place of blessing for the representative of the nations." Christopher Wright points out that Solomon's missionary prayer to God at the time of temple dedication is all the more noteworthy because the temple could be construed wrongly to be the particular focus of one people: Israel. When Solomon opened the temple for worship by explicitly asking God to hear the prayers of all peoples and to spread the fame of Jehovah to all nations, he shouted out the missionary heart of God.

In dedicating ourselves to God, whether standing next to Solomon on that glorious day or standing in a modern sanctuary, two critical components emerge. First, we must remember again that God is a missionary God committed to a worldwide goal of redeeming a remnant from every tribe, tongue, and nation. When we stand in His house, we must sense and feel and be energetically aware that the house was intended for all nations. We never stand alone, even if we can't see anyone. If your church is monoracial, your spirit should be yearning for what God sees in your pews: every color and every nation. Second, this missional hope "is turned into a missional challenge to the people that they must be as committed to God's law as God is committed to such a worldwide goal." We live holy lives for the nations. The next time you avert your eyes from something lewd, smile in your spirit and dedicate that obedience to the Fula of Sierra Leone. The next time you write a tithe check from the gross income of your company to the missions program of your church, wave that check before the Lord and in your mind stand with lifted hands next to Solomon asking God that the nations would hear of His fame and come worship. The next time you kneel in prayer over a missionary card or unreached people, remember your prayer is another drop added to the bowl of incense that Solomon contributed to and one day that bowl will be filled and tip over. And we won't be able to continue ministering because the glory of the Lord will fill His filled house.

PRAYER FOCUS: *Fula Jalon of Sierra Leone (Evangelical: 0.0%)*

JUNE 14: RITUAL PRAYERS

TODAY'S READING: 2 CHRONICLES 6–7; PSALM 136

"I have received my all from God. Oh, that I could return my all to God."

DAVID BRAINERD

Solomon's dedicatory prayer of the temple is the highpoint of the Old Testament. There was peace on every border. There was prosperity for every home. There was right relationship nationally with the Lord God of Israel—Jehovah Elohim of Israel. Never was it better for the people of God. They stood at the mountain peak after long, difficult struggles. And it would be downhill from here. But in this precious moment, the people returned to their homes "joyful and glad of heart for the good that the LORD had done for David, for Solomon, and for His people Israel" (2 Chr. 7:10). It is at this zenith that God reminds us that if we humble ourselves, pray, seek His face, and turn from our wicked ways, then He will hear, forgive, and heal, and now His ears will be attentive to the prayers prayed in this place. If Solomon's prayer is inextricably tied to the high point of God's people and His mercy toward them historically, if God says "now, I will hear that prayer," then the content and form of that prayer is instructional for us (see 2 Chr. 6:32–33). The zenith of the prayer at the zenith point of Israel's history reveals the missionary heart of God: That *all peoples of the earth* may know His name and fear Him. This is the purpose of the temple. This is the purpose of Israel. This is the purpose of the church. This is the purpose of you and me. This is the plan of God—that *all peoples of the earth* may know Jehovah Elohim of Israel and fear Him.

The form of Solomon's prayer is also instructive, also missionary if we note its four postures: Solomon stood before the altar of the Lord, he spread out his hands, he knelt down on his knees, and then bowed his face to the ground on the pavement in worship and praise with the people. What is striking about these forms of prayer is that we rarely pray that way and that Muslims pray exactly that way. Ritual Islamic prayers are copies of Byzantine Christian forms of prayer (combination of standing respectfully, lifting hands to heaven, kneeling, and prostrating with forehead pressed to the floor), which are in turn taken right from the Scriptures. Our favorite posture of prayer is sitting. We do our abiding time in our favorite chair with a cup of tea or coffee in our hand. Alternatively, there might be some church leader standing and leading us in prayer, but for the most part the congregation sits with eyes closed. Whatever the setting, today we largely sit to pray. Very infrequently is sitting mentioned as a posture of prayer in the Bible. I'm not saying it's wrong to sit and pray; I'm saying we miss something if we don't *also* stand, lift our hands to heaven, kneel, and prostrate before the presence of the God. It's ironic that Muslims yet pray as Solomon did, somehow more reverent than we are, even if more misguided. A missionary reading of Solomon's dedicatory prayer at the temple can help bring back reverence in our own praying. Today, may someone stand, lift holy hands, kneel, and prostrate before Jehovah for the salvation of the Tamil.

PRAYER FOCUS: *Tamil (Hindu Traditions) of Singapore (Evangelical: 0.8%)*

JUNE 15: THE UNPOPULAR BUT CHOSEN ONE

TODAY'S READING: PSALM 134, 146-150

Picture a classroom of third graders. The class teacher is benevolent but in charge, loved and revered by all the students. In this class sits one girl who doesn't fit in with her classmates. She sits in the back row. She isn't very smart. She is poor. She is socially awkward with no friends. She gets picked on at recess and ignored at lunch. She is tiny for her age, a misfit with no charisma or talent to ever distinguish her from her peers. Now, at the end of every school year this widely loved and feared teacher gives each student a lollipop. The students anticipate the last day of school because that is when the sweet is given and all students receive one. More than just a lollipop, it's a physical token of the teacher's favor and approval. The mystery is who will hand out the lollipops, for the teacher honors just one in the class by entrusting the favored, specially chosen student to make sure each classmate receives a reward. The chosen student always feels honored, lifted up above their peers for the responsibility and honor of distributing the blessing. The lollipops are for all, but the good teacher selects only one student to hand them out.

Thus, God chose Israel. Israel was not chosen because she was strong, wise, big, good, or popular. Israel was the little unpopular girl at the back of history's classroom, the one God chose as His agent to all peoples of the world. God chose Israel to be His special light to all nations. Imagine what that little girl felt when honored by the teacher and entrusted with dispensing the teacher's reward. Certainly, there was the joy of "I was chosen above all the others!" Certainly, there was the joy of the teacher's smile and hug. But that little girl could not, dare not, just stand at the front of the class clutching the lollipops to herself, reveling in being chosen. She must turn with a smile toward her peers and in the joy and confidence of being chosen walk the aisles to hand out lollipops, saying silently with each look to each classmate who received from her hand: "Let us rejoice together, for our teacher is good and mercy endures."

This is exactly what happens in Psalms 134 and 146 to 150. Little chosen Israel lifts up her voice and says, "Let everything that has breath praise the LORD" (150:6). Everything that has breath includes all peoples. This is the story of the Bible, the plan of God. The wonder for Israel is that weak, small, rejected, poor, ignored, and foolish as she was, the great God of heaven smiled down on her and asked her to hand out His salvation blessings. The Psalms record both joys—the joy of being chosen and the joy of brokering God's blessings to the uttermost parts of the world. How foolish it would be for that third-grade girl to receive the honor of being chosen, but not act on what she was honored to do. If she would linger at the front of the class clutching all the lollipops to herself, the beneficence of the good teacher would soon turn to rebuke. We, the Israel of God, have been chosen. What delight and wonder! But if we don't go quickly to Somalia to hand out God's gospel to the Rahanweyn, we, too, will be rebuked.

PRAYER FOCUS: *Rahanweyn of Somalia (Evangelical: 0.0%)*

JUNE 16: ALL HAVE A PART

TODAY'S READING: 1 KINGS 9; 2 CHRONICLES 8

"All the work of Solomon was well-ordered from the day of the foundation of the house of the LORD until it was finished. So the house of the LORD was completed" (2 Chr. 8:16). The beauty of the house of the Lord was the inclusion—all types of peoples and all types of skills. The nations played a part with Hittites, Amorites, Perizzites, Hivites, and Jebusites providing labor. There were men of war and chief officials, and divisions of priests, Levites, and gatekeepers. Every man of every origin did his part and tackled the big job of nation building.

The missionary work of reaching every people group on earth with the gospel must likewise be well-ordered with every man and woman doing their part. Truly the whole church must take the whole gospel to the whole world, and this maxim is true both multi-nationally and multi-vocationally. The whole body of Christ must function in unified missionary purpose no matter geography or gifting. This unified missionary effort is described by Alan Johnson's term *apostolic function*. Imagine a spear made of one alloy, cast in one mold. The spear represents the spiritual body of Christ that God will use to build His church among all unreached peoples. This spear has components that work together for the spear to be a useful weapon in God's hands. The tip of the spear represents the pioneer, visionary missionary, and the spear head represents a team of people the leader needs around them. The front of the spear's shaft represents missionary partnerships with indigenous Christians who raise up all nations to the unreached. The middle contains missionary strategists, leaders who set vision, build global partnerships, and stir the body to stay focused on the lost. The end of the spear, the strongest portion, are the missionary senders: grandmas who pray, businessmen who give, and pastors who raise up and commission. All working together make the spear strong.

Solomon started out so right and so ordered but ended so wrong. When God appeared to Solomon the second time after he finished building the temple, God soberly reminded him that the options were either consecration or expulsion. If Solomon obeyed everything commanded, God would put His name in that temple forever. If Solomon or his sons turned from direct obedience, then they would become proverbs and bywords among *all peoples*. If all the world is a stage and God's relationship with Israel the drama, then the nations of the world are the active audience, eagerly watching how the story unfolds. Everything acted out and recorded in the Bible was done for the nations to view because it's actually about *their* inclusion in Jehovah's house. And if Israel was punished, then the audience of nations would know it was because she left the God of blessing to follow false gods and ignored her one job; therefore, Jehovah brought calamity on her. As the peoples of earth gaze transfixed at the dramatic tragedy playing out before them, they shake their heads and say: "What fools are they who scorn the blessing of Jehovah by disobeying His missionary heart to incur His wrath! How favored are they who obey Jehovah and live in His missionary love, who are well-ordered and speed His light!"

PRAYER FOCUS: *Malay, Cape of South Africa (Evangelical: 0.20%)*

JUNE 17: WE MUST BE

TODAY'S READING: PROVERBS 25–27

We are to open our mouths and tell people about Jesus. Preaching is the verbal explanation of news in a way the hearer can understand. This news is called good news. Faithful missionaries must be adept at "newsification." Proverbs can help us be missionary as Proverbs has much wisdom about the mouth.

We must be faithful messengers (25:13). Faithful messengers are not embarrassed by the message, so they don't try to improve on it. They don't embellish or dilute. Faithful messengers are more concerned that they communicate exactly what their master wanted in the spirit of their master than they are with how the message is received. The overriding loyalty of the messenger is to the master, not to the feelings of the masses.

We must be gentle messengers (v. 15). The gentle tongue can indeed break bones, rocks, hard hearts, and rigid spirits. Gentle doesn't mean weak; gentle is the caress of a mighty ocean tide that meekly returns to shore. It doesn't abuse, assault, or rage, but it can't be stopped either. Gentle missionaries are relentless missionaries, kinder than the hardness they encounter.

We must be discerning messengers (v. 25). The discerning messenger does not confuse the devotion of the deceived with fulfillment. The discerning messenger sees beyond ritualistic religion to thirsty hearts and famished souls. Rejection or rebuffs do not dishearten the discerning messenger, for they see through any apparent strength to the total weariness of spirit that longs for good news and cold water from heaven.

We must be wise messengers (26:4–5). Wise missionaries know when to expose folly and when to let folly expose itself. Wise messengers know that sometimes we shout loudest by saying nothing at all, for the contrast of our restraint to the rebellious raving of the wicked is all the articulation needed.

We must be truthful messengers (v. 24). Good missionaries have no lie in them, no misdirection, no manipulation, no cowardice masquerading as prudence. Those whose assignment is to speak truth with grace can have nothing false about their identity, presentation, or behavior. Our words will only be as powerful as our lives are authentic.

We must be surgical messengers (27:6). Faithful are the wounds of a friend. Missionaries must speak about hell and judgment. Missionaries must tell the ones they love most that they are blind, sick, naked, and poor. Missionaries must be as honest as doctors about the danger of the soul and the pain of the remedy.

We must be considerate messengers (v. 14). If we present gospel truth to the nations in a way that they cannot understand or that is unnecessarily offensive by being selfishly insensitive, then we are to blame for casting pearls before swine. We are foolish if we present truth in an indigestible way. Missionaries have the responsibility to learn the culture, language, and heart of the unreached and to present hard truths.

PRAYER FOCUS: *Sri Lanka Moor of Sri Lanka (Evangelical: 0.0%)*

JUNE 18: THE MISSIONARY ENVIRONMENTALIST

TODAY'S READING: PROVERBS 28–29

"It's not that God has a mission for his Church in the world, but that God has a Church for his mission in the world."

CHRIS WRIGHT

Proverbs 29:13 states that the rich and poor have something in common: Jehovah gives light to the eyes of both. Wisdom and common grace extend to all ranges of economy and to all ethnicities of earth. What makes Proverbs uniquely missionary is that it addresses aspects of the heart, will, mind, and character common to all men everywhere, and it does so with evangelistic intent. In mission work, there is a vital place for those with a passion to care for God's creation.

There is intrinsic value in taking care of God's creation as we were told to do. When we care for creation, "it is not surprising…that those who take seriously, as Christians, our responsibility to embody God's love for creation find that their obedience in that sphere often leads to opportunities to articulate God's love for suffering and lost people." Environmental care is not an end in itself. It is not the goal nor our essential mandate; yet it is our obedience and must be done for the glory of God globally. Our essential commission is to make disciples. Our approach to creation care is to make no secret of the biblical story of the cost Christ paid to redeem all men and all things. The goal is ever the redemption of souls, for humans are the crown of God's creation. Still we cannot deny God's love for *all* that He created nor His plan to renew all things including lakes, forests, mountains, meadows, flora and fauna, seas and oceans. We share a "common humanity, common because we all share the one Maker, God. So rich or poor, slave or free, oppressed or oppressor, we are all alike the work of God's hands. What we do to a fellow human being, therefore, we do to his or her Maker, a profound ethical principle that Jesus reconfigured in relation to himself."

What this practically and ethically means is that in Sudan we need men and women who love God's creation and want to slow its decay. In that love they do not lose sight that men and women are the crown of God's creation and any environmentalism is based on our common humanity which is based on our common Creator. That Creator has history with earth (as described in the Bible) and that Bible describes God's redemption priorities and goals. The best environmentalist must be the most fervent evangelist. The missionary environmentalist is the one who prioritizes the saving of souls, the making of disciples, and the planting of churches by astutely embracing our common humanity, common wisdom, and common responsibility to steward God's creation.

PRAYER FOCUS: *Guhayna of Sudan (Evangelical: 0.0%)*

JUNE 19: OUR SATISFACTION

TODAY'S READING: ECCLESIASTES 1-6

Ecclesiastes is the most pessimistic of all the books in the Bible. It reveals what it feels like to forget the mission of God, to wander from the covenant to bless all peoples, to live an inward middle-class life and wake up in your 40s panicked and unfulfilled. Ecclesiastes is the mourning song of the person who claimed the name of Christ for decades while doing nothing for the cause of Christ globally. Ecclesiastes is the groan of the one who has only fed on the things of earth and become malnourished. No man or woman can bear for long the realization that life is meaningless. The beauty of Ecclesiastes is the purposelessness contrasted with the fear of the Lord. When we fear the Lord by respecting Him, by obeying His command to preach the gospel to all the peoples, we find purpose, meaning, and joy. If your life lacks meaning, it's probably because you're not engaged in God's mission as you should be. The way out of a purposeless life is to find your purpose and part in God's glory being lauded by every tribe, tongue, people, and nation.

Ecclesiastes deals with realities, such as the life we ended up living and not the life we expected to live. Some disappointments in life are due to our own drift, and others to demonic attacks or unfortunate events. "The realities that stem from Genesis 3 are the stark background for the wrestlings of Job and Ecclesiastes: satanic malice, suffering, frustration, meaningless toil, unpredictable consequences, uncertain futures, the twistedness of life and the final mockery of death. Wisdom by itself cannot answer these questions, but it provides a clue where the answer may be found—in the fear of the Lord God himself." If hope for a wasted life is found in the fear of the Lord, then what is that fear exactly? Ironically, part of the answer is linked to the fear of vanity and a fleeting life. Ecclesiastes 6:12 reminds us that life is a shadow, gone before we realize it. Waking up to that reality is a good start. The fear of meaninglessness can lead us to search for purpose, and the search for purpose ends up in God and His mission because God put eternity in the hearts of men, making everything beautiful in its time.

Essentially, the preacher of Ecclesiastes helps us realize that we weren't made for this present earth and that our ultimate satisfaction is in eternity. The recognition of the temporal as unsatisfying only devastates if there is no eternal life. Vanity in all things here and now is great missionary fuel. A deep dissatisfaction with this life can lead to great desire for eternal life and that desire leads us to the Scriptures. Thus, we see our satisfaction (to go home) is inseparably linked to God's satisfaction (representatives of *all* the peoples going home), and our purpose becomes clear: Make disciples of all nations and then we can all go home, all be satisfied. God placed a pessimistic book in His Word to help us remember what His purpose and our satisfaction is: Making disciples of all peoples, including the Alawite of Syria, so we can all go home.

PRAYER FOCUS: *Alawite of Syria (Evangelical: 0.02%)*

JUNE 20: WARNED AND WARMED

TODAY'S READING: ECCLESIASTES 7–12

"I feel now that Arabia could easily be evangelized within the next thirty years if it were not for the wicked selfishness of Christians."

SAMUEL ZWEMER

The Old Testament typically makes rich guys the hero. In the Old Testament, patriarchs (Abraham) and potentates (David) received obvious financial blessing as a sign and means of God's blessing. Ecclesiastes is problematic then, for it pushes back on the prevailing Old Testament trend that God blesses the righteous materially. The reality of Ecclesiastes is that bad things happen to good people. This is true in missionary life. Sometimes horrible things happen to missionaries. Sometimes missionaries are raped, sometimes their children die. Sometimes they are tortured or killed. It's naïve to think that obeying the call to take the precious gospel of grace to all peoples means immunity from trouble or that only the good times will roll.

Though the church is but a few thousand, the largest indigenous church on the Arabian Peninsula is the one in Yemen. I think of the quote by Ion Keith Falconer upon arriving in Yemen in 1885: "I have but one candle of life to burn, and I would rather burn it out in a land filled with darkness than in a land flooded with light." Falconer's candle burned for two years. He died in 1887. In 1921, his mission was expelled, and the first church was not planted until 1961, seventy-four years after his death. Falconer would agree with the writer of Ecclesiastes that everyone will die and that no human has power over death, but he would disagree with the pessimism of the book, for on our side of the Easter story death has no power over those who believe in resurrection. Today, the first little indigenous church in Yemen is said to have been started by a Yemeni led to the Lord by a Yemeni led to the Lord by a Yemeni led to the Lord by a Yemeni led to the Lord by Falconer. Falconer could work hard, see few results, and die in peace, for he knew that life can indeed follow death. Falconer now rejoices in glory and I imagine he welcomes every Yemeni and Iranian believer that enters the heavenly doors.

Ecclesiastes ends with a promise: "Fear God and keep His commandments, for this is man's all. For God will bring every work into judgment, including every secret thing, whether good or evil" (12:13–14). Ecclesiastes warns us and warms us. We are warned that life is short, all men indeed die, and every act will be seen and judged. We are warmed to action, for every little deed matters and it matters after we are dead. Seeds we plant now may fall into the ground and die, but if they die, they will spring up, perhaps long after we are gone, to bear fruit. In this sense, when read with a missionary lens, Ecclesiastes is not depressing, but inspiring. Because reverence of God and obedience to His commands are the critical thing, I'm going to simplify life to a single-eyed focus on the basics: to love God with all my heart and to love His unreached peoples as myself. My short temporal life has no time for anything else and my long eternal life has no other base.

PRAYER FOCUS: *Uzbek, Northern of Tajikistan (Evangelical: 0.22%)*

JUNE 21: INCLUSIVE WITHOUT INCLUSION

TODAY'S READING: 1 KINGS 10–11; 2 CHRONICLES 9

At his best, Solomon represented God's intention for blessing: the nations will see how good it is to serve Jehovah, be struck with divine jealousy and holy hunger, and come ask to be a part of God's family on God's terms. This is what happened with the queen of Yemen. Solomon developed a navy that sailed the Red Sea, so there was access to his news through camel trains and sea trade. The Queen of Yemen heard of Solomon's wealth, wisdom, and order, and desired to come see for herself. Indubitably, there was a business/trade component in her visit, but by her own admission there was something grander (see 2 Chr. 9:8). The Yemeni Queen used the covenant name for God: Jehovah. She further recognized that the throne was Jehovah's and that Solomon is king for Jehovah. The Yemeni queen was missionized and evangelized. She saw the real root of everything was relationship with the God of Israel and that blessing came in being His vassal, His daughter, His tool, His instrument. Yes, she saw the wealth (the result of blessing), but she heard of Solomon in the context "concerning the name of the LORD [Jehovah]" (1 Kings 10:1) and "the half...not told" (v. 7) was linked to the blessings of intimacy with Jehovah. This was Solomon at his best, attracting all the kings of the earth to Jehovah's throne.

At his worst, Solomon represented what happens when we lose the plot. God wants a diverse family, people from every nation around His throne. But it is Jehovah's throne, the throne of rule so pure and holy it cannot share space with any false god. *And* it is Jehovah's rules. Yes, God commissions His people to be a light and invitation to all peoples, but that invitation insists that all peoples come on Jehovah's terms. Solomon became enamored and beguiled by multi-culturalism. His wisdom drove him to the madness of thought that irreconcilable spiritual entities can be united. There is an arrogance to pluralism and universalism, an arrogance that thinks it's enlightened because it's blind and broad in its inclusivity. God's missionary people are inclusive without worshipping inclusion, for they soberly know that Jehovah must be exclusively worshipped. It must be the worship of Israel's God, Jehovah, on Jehovah's absolute terms.

At our missionary best, the people of God live in such a way that our ordered lives confess the beauty of His peace. The spiritual union that we enjoy with God marks us. We beam with His blessing, and the lost are drawn to us. We open our mouths and declare both halves of the reason for the hope that we have. At our missionary worst, we forget that the way is narrow; that the Bible is supra-cultural; that the real test of Christian orthodoxy is how all peoples graft themselves into the story of Jehovah and His people Israel; and that inclusion of all peoples demands exclusion of all their gods. We do the Muslims of the Swahili coast no favors if in loving them we accept their gods. We only are a blessing to the nations, only truly missionary, and only retain our wisdom and Jehovah's blessing by being radically exclusive in our inclusion.

PRAYER FOCUS: *Swahili of Tanzania (Evangelical: 0.8%)*

JUNE 22: ADVICE FROM MOMMA

TODAY'S READING: PROVERBS 30-31

Neither Agur (Prov. 30) nor King Lemuel (Prov. 31) appear to be Israelites. Agur was a Yemeni (Sabean) name, meaning the most religious of the proverbs issued forth from a man of the Arabian Peninsula. Lemuel's wisdom came from his mother, and though we don't know what country Lemuel ruled, it's evident he revered his mother. Through his mother the Bible affords us three missionary applications that tend to run counter to all fallen cultures: abstinence from anything that obscures reason, advocacy for those appointed to die, and appreciation for the vital role women play in life and service.

Abstinence. Momma told her son that it's not for kings to drink wine or princes to drink anything intoxicating. The principle is, leaders need to abstain from anything that obscures reason or causes clouded discernment. Missionaries are to be astute observers and learners of their host culture, but never in a way that abandons their allegiance to the supra-cultural principles of Scripture. The effort to get inside a culture is noble, yet there is value to an external view if that view is submitted to Scripture and stripped of its own cultural bias. Admittedly, this is difficult, but all of us have benefited from a fresh pair of eyes. Becoming so intoxicated with a culture that we take on its unbiblical aspects does missionaries no good and gives God no glory.

Advocacy. Momma told her son to pray for the lost and to preach the gospel to the perishing. One reason missionary prayers are so vital is that so many lost in false religions or ideologies either pray in vain or do not even pray at all. Some groan for deliverance, but are unable to articulate their cry, struck dumb by terror, pain, fear, or bondage. Some are so grieved by religious abuse that prayer itself is repugnant to them. Missionary hearted people pray for those who cannot or do not or will not pray for themselves. If you are from a godly home or a praying church, think of all the advocacy that has risen to the Father on your behalf, then juxtapose that with the 18 million Buddhist Isan of Thailand who perhaps have never heard a prayer ascend to Jehovah on their behalf. Oh, may someone reading these words pray for the speechless and advocate for those who are appointed to die!

Appreciation. Inspires trust. Does good. Seeks. Works. Brings. Provides. Buys. Plants. Girds. Strengthens. Perceives. Holds. Reaches. Fears not. Makes. Supplies. Speaks wisdom. Spreads kindness. Watches. Labors. Excels. Fears the Lord. Different cultures allow different measures of opportunity for women, but God's culture praises and appropriately reveres them. The Bible is clear that God speaks to and through women just as He does men, that God loves and is loved by women just as with men, empowers and trusts women just as He does men. As clearly as the Bible affirms that men and women are different, it also affirms the worth and value of both. The history of missions is the history of women who lived out the verbs above cross-culturally to the glory of God.

PRAYER FOCUS: *Thai, Isan of Thailand (Evangelical: 0.27%)*

JUNE 23: NO DEVIATION ALLOWED

TODAY'S READING: 1 KINGS 12–14

The blessings of God's people lead to blessings for the whole world. Likewise, the brokenness of God's people leads to the brokenness of the world. The tragedy when missionary brothers fight one another is that the unreached around them are no longer the focus of energy and prayer, for emotional attention is spent on civil war. The same is true for churches or Christian organizations; internal squabbling simply means our efforts are not fully united in saving souls. God blessed David and exalted Solomon so that Israel would be a light to the nations, but the united monarchy didn't even last 100 years. Jeroboam splits ten tribes away from Rehoboam, and only five years into Rehoboam's reign the Egyptian king invades Judah and plunders all the gold shields. In short order, Solomon worshipped false gods, Jeroboam stole unity, and Rehoboam became a vassal to Egypt. And it's downhill from there. The kingdom God wanted as a shining example to the nations is still an example—it's just a negative one now.

Critical to the central missionary message of the Bible is the notion that God's passionate desire to be glorified by every tribe, tongue, people, and nation is not up for debate. The question is never if God will be worshiped by every people group, but *how*—whether or not His people will joyfully and wholeheartedly participate in that effort. If we join in, God blesses us and the nations are wooed; if we work against God's missionary plans, God judges us and the nations are warned.

Our warning is that insecurity can often turn our good missionary intentions into disastrous self-preservation—disastrous because self-preservation is so anti the giving heart of God that it cannot but lead us to rebellion. God anointed Jeroboam to do what he did. Ironically, the story of Jeroboam and Rehoboam echo the Moses and Pharaoh story. A new oppressive king meant opportunity, and the people cry out for relief. Rehoboam had a Moses-like opportunity to do good, reform idolatry, receive the blessings of God, and be a light to the nations, while Jeroboam worried about losing his position.[1] What began as a renewed opportunity for the people of God in Israel to glorify Him among all peoples ended in an idolatry even more heinous than that of Judah.

The lesson of today's chapters is that no chosen vessel of Jehovah is allowed to deviate from God's mission without public rebuke and that our insecurity can drive us to disaster. Rehoboam refused servant leadership, scorning the advice of the elders, and lost the kingdom, gold, independence, and chance to sparkle among the nations. Jeroboam refused to let his people worship God in the way God proscribed all nations to observe and lost his life, his dynasty, and any hope of blessing all peoples. The man of God demonstrated that if we do not strictly follow God's specific instructions, we lose our prophetic future and our very lives. Every Christian must reconcile themselves to the reality that Jehovah will use us as an example globally. How much better to be an obedient and blessed participant, and not an insecure, rebellious, idolatrous, self-preserving one.

PRAYER FOCUS: *Arab, Libyan of Tunisia (Evangelical: 0.2%)*

JUNE 24: MISSIONARY FOLLY

TODAY'S READING: 2 CHRONICLES 10–12

Young, zealous missionaries often repeat Rehoboam's folly: the hubristic mistake of despising the wisdom of the elders and discounting the experiences of the previous generation. Rehoboam rejected the advice of the elders, followed the advice of the young men, and did not listen to the people. Chronological snobbery can work in both generational directions, but it is most damaging when the new do not respect the old. Lessons learned the hard way through painful missionary mistakes don't have to be continually relearned at great cost if new missionaries would only listen to the veterans. Age and experience are no guarantee of wisdom, but they sure have a better chance with it than youth and inexperience. This chronological egotism can work broadly as well in which a whole generation of missionaries discount the hard-won truths of eras gone by.

A second missionary folly is the lust to lead and the inability to see less leadership responsibility as a gift. When Jeroboam takes most of the tribes away from Rehoboam, the Lord sends word that this reduction is from Him. What seems like a demotion is actually an opportunity. In missionary terms, the fundamental assignment is to make disciples and plant churches where they don't exist. The natural tendency is to shift from doing that ourselves to telling others how to do it. The reality is that it's difficult to be an effective boots-on-the-ground church planter *and* travel incessantly to mobilize, coach, and teach others to do likewise. If God in His mercy reduces our leadership footprint, it provides the marvelous opportunity to focus on a local context and to make local disciples. In Rehoboam's life this is exactly what happened. Reduced responsibility led to concentration of what was vital at home. Godly people flocked to Jerusalem, and for three years God was glorified. Rehoboam and the kingdom walked in strength and in the righteous ways of David and Solomon. If ever our leadership responsibilities are removed or reduced, let us rejoice and refocus all our energies on making disciples.

Unfortunately for Rehoboam, this refocus lasted only three years. When he had established the kingdom and strengthened himself, he forsook the Lord. A third missionary folly is to depend on the Lord when we are weak and then to turn from Him when we are established and strong. The real evidence of missionary maturity is when we depend on Jesus at all times, especially when things are going well. The tragedy of self-reliance is that it always has negative consequences among the nations. God's people were blessed with His presence in order to be a blessed with His power in order to be a blessing to the nations. When Rehoboam forsook the Lord, the Lord forsook him and put him into the hands of Shishak that he may distinguish God's service from the service of the nations. There are eight million Kurds in Turkey who do not yet know the liberating service of King Jesus. God needs missionaries to live among them, missionaries who will demonstrate how good it is to serve Jehovah, who depend on the Lord when they are small and big, young and old, weak and strong.

PRAYER FOCUS: *Kurd, Kurmanji of Turkey (Evangelical: 0.0%)*

JUNE 25: STAY SMALL

TODAY'S READING: 1 KINGS 15–16; 2 CHRONICLES 13–16

"What we need to be assured of is not that we possess an excellent system of doctrine and ritual, but that the gift of the Holy Spirit is a reality."

ROLAND ALLEN

Abijam's heart was not right before the Lord, not loyal to Jehovah like his ancestor David. David was credited with being loyal to Jehovah except in the case of Uriah the Hittite. The one lapse of David was an offense and betrayal of a non-Israelite. The one time David strayed from God's heart had a central missionary offense; instead of glorifying God among the nations, David did something repugnant and offensive against a Hittite. But the broader review of David's heart as evidenced by his songs and prayers show his passion for Jehovah to be glorified by all nations. It is inescapable then that to walk as David walked before Jehovah is to walk dedicated to God's global glory, and Abijam's disloyalty must have been in part his unconcern for missions, his ethnocentric orientation, and his worship of false gods. This conclusion is verified by the comparative actions of Asa who removed all false worship from the land including all the idols his relatives near and far had introduced. Asa did what was right in the eyes of the Lord as did his father David. The lesson is clear: We are a blessing to all nations when we live as God's holy people, having no gods other than Jehovah so that He may live among us and bless us. Asa and David did this; Abijam did not.

The divided kingdoms are studies in contrasts. Ahab brought Baal home and threw Jehovah out while Asa was threatened by a Sudanese army of one million men, outnumbered two to one. In Asa's case the Sudanese were overthrown before the Lord, and after the Lord saved the weak, the people of Judah made a covenant with Jehovah that referenced the terms their fathers agreed to with God. Those were missionary terms resulting from an Old Testament missionary victory. The Old Testament is the documentation of God using His people to be a light to all nations of the glories of Jehovah. Small, weak armies defeating strong Sudanese armies of a million soldiers demonstrated the glory of God.

We must never forget that all of life is about God's glory, and the smaller we are, the greater God shines when He wins. Asa forgot this essential truth, turned to the Syrians for help, and God reminded him of the big missionary framework for all things: "For the eyes of the LORD run to and fro *throughout the whole earth,* to show Himself strong on behalf of those whose heart is loyal to Him" (2 Chr. 16:9 emphasis added). God's missionary goal is that He would be seen as strong in all the earth among all the nations. God's missionary means is to use those who are small, weak, overwhelmed, and loyal. God chose weak, little Abraham, young, little David, small, little Israel, and frail you and me that He might show Himself mighty among the Gujarati in India. Let's stay small and missionary hearted. That's how we show our loyalty to the God of mission, and that's when He shows Himself mighty in all the earth.

PRAYER FOCUS: *Gujarati, Ugandan of Uganda (Evangelical: 0.0%)*

JUNE 26: THE GLORIOUS CHAIN

TODAY'S READING: 2 CHRONICLES 17

In the up and down histories of Judah and Israel, Jehoshaphat's early reign stands out as a missionary high. This pericope in Chronicles lets us peek at what God intended to be normal. It is a short chapter that conjures up both sadness and joy, for what we see is what could have, should have been.

Here is my paraphrase through a missionary lens: Jehoshaphat was blessed to have a father, Asa, who understood God's mission. When Jehoshaphat came to the throne, he built on what he learned from his father by first making sure no evil thing had access to his heart, home, or homeland. Jehoshaphat didn't just play defense; he aggressively pursued what pleased Jehovah by doing what David did: being zealous for the glory of God among all the nations. Jehoshaphat would have nothing to do with the Baals; all he wanted was the true God to be worshiped by all the peoples of earth. Jehoshaphat studied Jehovah's covenant with Abraham. Jehoshaphat researched Jehovah's covenant with Moses and Aaron. Jehoshaphat marveled at Jehovah's promise to David. Jehoshaphat soberly reminded himself that he was a link in David's chain: One day from his sanctified line the eternal king would come! Jehoshaphat determined to do nothing to break the chain and to do everything to preserve it. This dedication to God's mission in all the earth so delighted Jehovah that the kingdom was established locally and Jehoshaphat was honored and respected broadly. The delight was mutual, for Jehoshaphat took joy in honoring the Lord, making Him famous at home and abroad by sending teachers to every city and cranny of the land so that all the people understood the missionary heart of God and how to be God's missionary people from the missionary book of the law. Because Jehoshaphat honored Jehovah, Jehovah honored the covenant promises made to Eve, Abraham, Moses, and David. The fear of Jehovah fell on all the kingdoms, peace spread, Philistines brought tribute, and Arabs brought presents. The nation and the people grew strong. There were valiant leaders who made disciples who made disciples. Israel was blessed, vibrant, and strong, and the nations around them were blessed with peace because Jehovah was glorified and worshiped.

Jehoshaphat's early reign is a great blueprint for a young pastor, missionary, leader, or marketplace witness. Learn from the men of God who went before you. When you are given responsibility, first secure your defenses, repent and be reformed from all sin, live in holiness, and allow no evil in your home, heart, or ministry. Read the Bible and buy into the missionary heart of God for all nations. Realize you are a link in this glorious chain, that *your* responsibility is to live in this age in such a way that God can visit you with power, bless you, and strengthen you, *so that* you might impact the unreached peoples of earth. Pass this vision to your mighty men. Let the missionary word of God be what you preach and teach. Send your best to the Gulf Bedouin of the UAE and receive from them the greatest treasures God wants: their worship of Jehovah. Let the legacy of your life be disciples from a multitude of unreached peoples around the world.

PRAYER FOCUS: *Bedouin, Gulf of United Arab Emirates (Evangelical: 0.0%)*

JUNE 27: PROPHETS AND PROFIT

TODAY'S READING: 1 KINGS 17–19

Elijah is a powerful illustration of God's missionary passion. How blind we have become to God's incessant revelation of His heart for all nations all through the Scriptures. Just look at what the Bible blatantly points out about Elijah: First, God hid him in Jordan; then God sent him to Lebanon; then God revealed Himself to him in Saudi Arabia; and then God trotted him up to Syria. God constantly commissioned him to the nations, and when Elijah was home, it was to demonstrate that God is superior to all the false gods of all the nations around.

Power encounters are intended to prove that Jehovah is God of all the nations and therefore must be worshiped by all peoples. The priests of Baal sometimes manipulated idols with hidden ropes to awe the unsuspecting. Elijah took the showdown outside to remove any doubt of manipulation. Priests and prophets of Baal and Asherah worked themselves into a tizzy. "But there was no voice, no one answered, no one paid attention" until the God of Israel answered by fire. Elijah made sure that all who watched understood the missionary message. Right before the fire fell, he made known the God of fire was the God of Abraham. Elijah wanted the people of God to remember that to turn their hearts back to God again is to turn their eyes to the nations.

Power encounters in the earth are not just for public awe; they are also for private conviction. When Elijah was hosted in Lebanon, the widow's son died, and when God raised the dead in a humble upper room, the reaction of this gentile mother was, "Now by this I know that you are a man of God, and that the word of the LORD in your mouth is the truth" (17:24). The missionary message found fertile ground, and the God of Israel accepted a Lebanese widow into the family. Ironically, the poor Lebanese widow was from the same country as uptown Jezebel. Jezebel came from Sidon, the Phoenician capital. She brought with her culture, style, panache, and a cosmopolitan confidence that swept the common people into seductive idolatry. Interesting that a private power encounter saw one poor Lebanese woman soften while a public showdown hardened a rich lady of Lebanon. Let's not put all our hopes in the basket of public vindication. Let's remember the God who answered by fire was not in the wind, earthquake or fire, but in the still small voice.

There is one more critical missionary lesson from our reading: the importance of giving to missions from our lack, not just from our abundance. Missionary Elijah asked for support from the poor widow. She didn't know how she or her boy could survive, much less support a missionary, but the missionary had the audacity to say: "Don't fear. Give to missions sacrificially first, and afterward take care of yourself and your son" (see 17:13). She did according to the word of the missionary, and "the bin of flour was not used up, nor did the jar of oil run dry, according to the word of the LORD" (vv. 15–16). Evidently, no one is too poor to be exempted from missions giving. Just as evidently, God loves it when we give to missions sacrificially that when we do, He guarantees our basic needs.

PRAYER FOCUS: *Japanese of United States (Evangelical: 0.50%)*

JUNE 28: WIN, LOSE, OR DRAW

TODAY'S READING: 1 KINGS 20-21

There are spiritual wins, losses, and ties. In the grand missionary goal of God, representatives of all peoples are to be won to worship Jehovah. A sad missionary "tie" would be for the people of God to not win the nations and not lose their faith. A disastrous missionary loss would be for God's people to be won over to the idolatry of the nations. What made Ahab's story a disastrous missionary loss was that in marrying Jezebel, her people were not won to Jehovah, but rather they stirred up Israel to follow false gods. Ahab's epitaph then was descriptive of colossal missionary setback because he "sold himself to do wickedness in the sight of the LORD" (1 Kings 21:25). The double error which provoked Jehovah's wrath was that the Lebanese were not won for the glory of God and Israel was lost to Baal's shameful reign. The tragedy? Ahab's sons, Ahab's house would pay the bill.

How different it could have been. God in mercy often uses bent tools for His greatest works and bald brushes for His most beautiful art. Battles are won by the unlikely so that God will get all the glory. We err crucially when we laud the unlikely for what God did through them, despite them, for His fame among the nations. In Ahab's case, God was still willing to use him to teach the Syrians a glory lesson. God's choice for this glory display were 232 young leaders who He used to overcome 32 cocky kings. These young leaders each killed their own man, and in the sequel the *children* of Israel killed 100,000 Syrian soldiers. The reference to children coupled with the reference to young leaders shows that God used the weak to overcome the strong so that our missionary God would get all the glory. None of the glory is to be shared with His young, inexperienced workers.

In missionary battle, which is ever now about love and souls, not loathing and swords, God expects us to wage total war and take no prisoners. I refuse to lay down any militant analogy, though the risk of misinterpretation is great, for the Bible trusts us to understand the analogy and to fight by loving, serving, and dying to self. In the Old Testament application Ahab not only erred but sinned; he pardoned the one that Jehovah had destined for utter destruction. In God's eyes this was a capital offense. In fact, it was so capital that the neighbor who would not strike the prophet to set up God's illustration was himself eaten by a lion. What seems over the top is intended as a reminder that God is deadly serious about being glorified by all peoples and that we must live seriously for the total glory of God through total war and do our part that all nations hear the gospel via total obedience. Nothing less than a complete, utter devotion to God's passion that all nations be part of His family pleases Him.

PRAYER FOCUS: *Tajik of Uzbekistan (Evangelical: 0.07%)*

JUNE 29: THE POPULARITY CONTEST

TODAY'S READING: 1 KINGS 22; 2 CHRONICLES 18

Alliances with those who are against or neutral about Jehovah's unique glory don't end well. When Jehoshaphat linked with Ahab in a military alliance, it ended with death and disaster, and when he linked with Ahab's son Ahaziah in a commercial venture, it ended in shipwreck. Jehoshaphat's peacemaking with Israel was held against him in the final review of his life, which is further evidence that God wants us to only fight alongside and do business with those who have great passion for all nations to be represented around the throne. Prophetic speech is always missionary speech and missionary speech will always be more unpopular than welcome. Missionary speech connects to the holy truth and the dividing passions of God which always hone in on all peoples of earth bowing before Him. Three types of prophets appear in our reading today *and* in the courts of earth whose conversations ironically mirror the court in heaven.

False prophets saying false things. In the heavenly court God will bring judgment on the missionary failure of Ahab through a lying spirit in the mouth of his prophets. This is exactly what happens: False prophets give false hope that can only lead to death. This is what has happened over again and again. Whether in Nepal, Arabia, Nigeria, or Utah, false prophets have promised nirvana, paradise, prosperity, or purity and delivered their believers to destruction by the billions.

True prophets saying false things. In the beginning of the drama, the false prophets dropped the name of a generalized deity as guaranteeing victory. The deceit graduated to false prophets using Jehovah's name to offer false hope and culminated in a true prophet (Micaiah) going against what he knows to be true in his sarcastic reply to the king. The text offers little explanation, but in the court of heaven God commissioned a messenger to mislead and that destructive misdirection was repeated on earth. God forbid that missionary messengers assigned to truth become agents of falsehood just because the truth is unpopular.

True prophets saying true things. Micaiah spoke the truth of looming judgment, which he knew for sure, for he saw the Lord sitting on the throne and heard how the scenario would play out. Missionaries must be truthful. We must warn of the coming wrath. We must speak unpopular messages to powerful people and even to angry populaces. It was never promised we'd be popular. The popularity missionaries receive at home sometimes leaves them unprepared for the consequences of faithful messaging. The only way to overcome the dissonance is to be more addicted to truth and obedience to the King than to acceptance and respect from the world. We must align ourselves to the long-term right and winner, not the short-term applause. True prophets must say true things and get smacked for it. Prepare yourself as the 1.4 million Moung of Vietnam will not like what we say. But if we really love them and God, we will say it anyway.

PRAYER FOCUS: *Muong of Vietnam (Evangelical: 0.06%)*

"Will you go to His feet and place yourself entirely at His disposal?"

WILLIAM BOOTH

Any king and any tale are judged by whether they stay in covenant with God's goal of ransoming and being worshiped by representatives of every tribe, tongue, people, and nation. This was why Jehoshaphat, when attacked by a coalition from Jordan (Ammonites, Moabites, and Edomites), called out to the God of his fathers. This was why at the end of Jehoshaphat's reign the one indictment against the people was that they had not yet directed their hearts to the God of their fathers. This was why the nations raged and revolted: because Judah forsook the Lord God of their fathers. This was why judgment fell on Jehoram: because he didn't have a heart like David or his father and de-glorified God among the nations.

God is determined to yank our attention through all of Scripture to His glory among the nations. In Jehoshaphat's case it was God being glorified among the peoples of Transjordan through victory. In Jehoram's case it was the Philistines, Arabs, and Sudanese that were used to bring glory to God by defeating a descendent of David who lost his zeal for Jehovah before the nations. The lesson is clear: Make much of Jehovah and He will use you to mediate His glory to all peoples of earth. Or make a mockery of Jehovah and He will use the nations of the world to punish you and glorify His name. The battle for the glory of God among all nations is primarily His. In difficult situations, surrounded by the great multitude of 42 percent of the world that has never heard the gospel, we say with Jehoshaphat that we have no power, nor do we know what to do, but our eyes are on You. It is God's glory and His own battle for His own fame.

When we are overwhelmed by the unreached peoples of earth and don't know what to do, the missionary people of God are told to do three things: **Position ourselves (2 Chr. 20:17)**. Standing still actually means getting close enough to the nations that we can see firsthand what God will do. We still have to go out among them fearless, for Jehovah is with us. **Bow and worship (v. 18).** How critical it is to be a worshiping and submitted people. The posture of submission and complete trust in the God who is sovereignly good is the heart of the missionary spirit. **Stand to praise with voices loud and high (v. 19).** The advance of God's glory among the nations is borne on the high praises, on the fearless public exaltation of who God is and what we believe He will do. If we will but do these things in the overwhelming places and among the intimidatingly lost peoples of earth, like Western Sahara, the Lord wins the battles, He wins the nations to Himself, His fear is on the kingdoms of earth, and our realm is quiet for God gives rest all around.

PRAYER FOCUS: *Berber, Tekna of Western Sahara (Evangelical: 0.0%)*

"I don't think we are in any danger, and if we are, we might as well die suddenly in God's work as by some long, drawn-out illness at home."

ELEANOR CHESTNUT

JULY

JULY 1: REDEMPTIVE JUDGMENT

TODAY'S READING: OBADIAH; PSALMS 82–83

"I will open Africa to the gospel or die trying."

ROWLAND BINGHAM

Just as Old Testament Israel provided a living picture of what it meant for a nation (both an ethnic people and a geo-political state) to live under God's blessing when they pursued God's mission, so Edom provided the foil—the result of when one worked against God's mission. There is debate concerning the date Obadiah was written, but the resistance of Edom to Israel (both northern and southern kingdoms) is consistent. The prophet Obadiah took Edom to task for acting unbrotherly to Jacob (Obad. 1:10) and he pointed out that God will judge all nations who resist His mission and purpose (v. 15). Edom is present-day Jordan, likely the area around Petra (v. 3), and Jehovah's judgment is to make all great powers that resist His people and plan small (v. 2).

The Psalms pick up on God's resistance against those who resist His mission and His chosen people. Psalm 83 is a prayer against the nations who took crafty counsel against Jehovah's people and plan, desiring to wipe them out completely (vv. 3–4). Among the hostile nations listed are Edom, Moab, and Ammon (Jordan), the Ishmaelites (Central Arabia), Philistia (Gaza), Tyre (Lebanon), and Assyria (Iraq) (vv. 5–8). Some call the confederacy against Israel an Arabian tribal confederacy that appears centered on Edom and the Ishmaelites (vv. 5–6). The point is not political, though the modern parallels are evident; the point is that those who resist Jehovah's mission as represented in His elect people will face Jehovah's opposition and that Jehovah's opposition wonderfully and always has redemptive intention. Jehovah's mission is to be glorified by all peoples everywhere and He will use every means for this goal.

As we look at the complex world of the Middle East, let us not confuse politics with prophetic prayers. Obadiah prophesied that judgment would come to Esau, with Jacob and Joseph being a flame to Esau's stubble, and that the kingdom will be the Lord's (Obad. 1:18, 21). The psalmist prayed that God would arise to judge the earth and inherit all nations (Psalm 82:8). That judgment is so they may seek Jehovah's name, so they may know He alone is over all the earth. A missionary understanding of God's judgment on the nations is centered on His redemptive intentions that they seek and know Him. Thankfully, it is the same way God judges us: He removes what is against His mission so that we can worship, obey, be blessed, and be a blessing. The sons and daughters of Ishmael, the inheritors of these prayers, still walk the desert cities of Arabia. There are over six million Yemeni Arab peoples who still need prayer, who have not yet sought or found Jehovah. What joy to be a part of the answer to the prayers of prophets and psalmists from 2,800 years ago. They prayed, so let us preach that Yemeni might enter into Jehovah's praise.

PRAYER FOCUS: *Arab, Yemeni of Yemen (Evangelical: 0.0%)*

JULY 2: POINTERS FROM PROPHETS

TODAY'S READING: 2 KINGS 1–4

Interpreters point out that Elijah was more verbose than Elisha, that Elijah gave more speeches and Elisha did more miracles. Even if Elijah was the verbose one, he ended with a flash of fire: His last public miracle was sitting on a hill and calling fire down from heaven (2 Kings 1:6–14) and his last public act was ascending to heaven in a chariot of fire (2:11). Let's get to the end as passionate for the glory of God among the nations as we started, through word and deed pointing unreached peoples to Jesus. Along the way, Elijah and Elisha give us some great missionary pointers:

Go...do not be afraid of him (1:15). This imperative is somewhat comical as "him" is a lowly captain of fifty who just waded around two fried captains and their cohorts with knees knocking to plead for his life. Let us not forget that we represent the God who answers by fire. We can stand before any captain, prince, king, or principality knowing *their* knees knock in fear, not ours. Missionaries must never forget the awesome power they represent.

Stay under authority (2:6). If we want the mantle of the anointed who have gone before us, we must stay under authority. We can't ask for the blessing and not stay submitted to those God uses to fashion us. Authority is who you run to in times of trouble, not just those above you in the organizational chart. We must remain submitted and attached to both moral and positional authority if we want to receive and steward their spiritual gains.

Dig big ditches and assemble many vessels (3:16; 4:3). Missionaries need to build arks. We need to have the faith to prepare before we can see. Good missionaries believe there will be harvest and in that obedience prepare for the great things God will do, knowing that to whatever degree we prepare, God will fill those ditches and vessels.

Be single-eyed (4:29). There must be a missionary minimalism about us: a single eye on Jesus and His glory among the nations. All else pushed to the side, including good things. We must have a "this one thing I do" mentality, a "consider all things loss" focus, for the surpassing greatness of knowing Christ and making Him known.

Lock yourself in with the dead and the Lord of life (4:32–33). Reminiscent of Jesus putting everyone out of the house, Elisha locked himself in with a dead boy and the Lord of resurrection power. Missionaries need to live embedded with the lost, surrounded by the dead and dying, filled and fueled with the Ever-Living. To be missionary is to intentionally lock yourself in with the lost and with Jesus and to go to work in prayer.

Give what you have, and don't bemoan what you have not (4:42–44). Prefiguring what Jesus told the disciples, Elisha told his disciple to give the 100 men the little bread he had, and they ate and were satisfied. We usually attach this to miracles of physical provision, but it's just as true about the word and knowledge of God. Give what we know of Jesus to the unreached. We might not have much, but we give it—and astoundingly there are leftovers.

PRAYER FOCUS: *Uzbek, Southern of Afghanistan (Evangelical: 0.01%)*

The prophets were not just sent to Israel and Judah; they were also sent to hold other nations accountable for their sins. In the Old Testament period, "nobody at that point was under the impression that they were supposed to go.... What we find rather is the clear promise that it is **God's** intention to bring such blessings to the nations, that **God** will summon the nations to himself in the great pilgrimage to Zion." From this perspective, Elisha reflected the missionary passion of God towards Naaman in the Old Testament inward sense, even though he traveled to Damascus later in the story. The people of God taking the gospel outside Israel is prefigured in the Old Testament but is not yet systematized. All the same, Naaman's story is replete with missionary application.

God uses all nations to glorify His name. Jehovah gave Syria victory, a victory that would soon include the defeat of Israel. The fact that God uses pagan nations for His purposes proves that missions must be centered on the glory of God, not the achievement or employ of missionaries or the church. This was why Elisha didn't come out of the house to greet Naaman, nor go with him to the Jordan. All credit must go to God, not to any agent. God will glorify His holy name among the nations through many agents and agencies.

Business as mission demands an uplifted voice. The Israelite slave girl could be considered a proto-business-as-missionary. I do not overlook the enslavement of a young child, nor do I think she was paid appropriately. I merely point out that God ordained His representative to work in the home of a powerful man and to lift up her voice and announce truth. Today in the Arabian Peninsula, many African and Asian maids work in difficult conditions in influential Arab homes. This is an example for them to not lose sight of the God of glory and to lift up their voices and point to the One who can heal and save.

Salvation requires the abandonment of prior religion. While it is true that missionary messaging requires contextualization, it also demands conversion. Elisha's response to Naaman's requests was not permission to stay in the old religion (2 Kings 5:18–19). Naaman knew it was wrong, which is why, as a brand-new convert of Jehovah, he asked for forgiveness. Elijah merely extended grace for Naaman to grow into what he already knew was right and to forsake what he already knew was idolatrous.

If we wait to share good news, punishment will come upon us. The leprous beggars in the Syrian camp recognized they had an obligation to share good news or face the wrath of a good God. We are nothing special. We are but beggars telling others where to find bread. But if we find bread and don't tell, that's on us and we will pay the price for it. God is so serious that all peoples, including the Shawiye Berber of Algeria, be fed the Bread of Life, that if we don't pass the word about the location of the Bread *quickly*, then "the leprosy of Naaman will cling to us and our house forever" (vv. 26–27).

PRAYER FOCUS: *Berber, Shawiye of Algeria (Evangelical: 0.0%)*

JULY 4: GOD'S MEANS BUT FOR MAN'S MOTIVES
TODAY'S READING: 2 KINGS 9-11

The similarities between Jezebel and Babylon are striking. Both encapsulate the timeless idolatries of money, sex, and power. Ideologies come and go, and kingdoms wax and wane, but all earthly systems center on the acquisition, retention, and abuse of money, sex, and power.

The oft-repeated, definitive description of Jehovah in the Old Testament is the affirmation of a God who is gracious, good, kind, slow to anger, and abounding in love. Jehovah is slow to anger, long overlooking rebellion and wickedness. Jehovah is more loving, patient, and gracious than any human. He is also holier and purer than any human, so there must come a time when His slow-to-anger nature of love must be complemented by His holy wrath. God is zealous for His own name and fame among all peoples—especially His own people—and God still considered the northern kingdom of Israel as His. A tipping point was reached: God's holy anger demanded the destruction of those responsible for dishonoring Him in their elevation of Baal. Jehu was chosen as the instrument of God's judgment; all the sons of Ahab and Jezebel had to go, including those in Judah who married into the idolatrous line. The story of missions is the story of this same Jehovah: good, kind, merciful, compassionate, slow to anger, abounding in love. The story of the nations is the same as Ahab and Jezebel: Every nation has worshiped the idols of sex, money, and power, rather than glorifying Jehovah, and at some point, judgment will fall. These terrible judgments of Jehovah on Old Testament nations are but a shadow of the terror that will descend with finality on all nations at the last day. The missionary message is indeed part warning: Escape the wrath to come.

Most alarming about the vessel of Jehovah's judgment was his motivation. Lauded for the right action, Jehu would be undone for his wrong heart. Yes, Baal worship was evil, but Jehu destroyed it more for his own ends than for God's glory. The destruction of Ahab's line and Jezebel's priests coincided with the destruction of any who would challenge his power. Jehu destroyed Baal from Israel but did not destroy Jeroboam's idols, the golden calves. To remove all Israel's idolatry would necessitate allowing his people to worship Jehovah in Jerusalem only, and Jehu feared that would dilute his power base. He fell into the same trap of all men and nations; he bowed at the altar of power, sex, and money, and ultimately paid the price: his own and the nation's demise.

A simple missionary warning extends from the lives of Jezebel and Jehu: God's means can easily be carried out with man's motives. We can zealously pursue God's global glory with wicked motivations, and wicked motivations tend to center around the timeless lust for the idols of power, money, and sex. If we pursue God's glory among the nations for the wrong reasons, we marry into Jezebel's sensual family and the eschatological fate of Babylon will certainly be ours.

PRAYER FOCUS: *Lezgin of Azerbaijan (Evangelical: 0.10%)*

JULY 5: IF WE FORSAKE JEHOVAH

TODAY'S READING: 2 KINGS 12–13; 2 CHRONICLES 24

The sin of Jeroboam plagued the northern kingdom of Israel throughout its history, leading to its demise. Because he feared losing power, Jeroboam refused to let Israel travel to the temple of Jehovah in Jerusalem and forced his people into idolatry by setting up golden calf idols, forcing them away from the missionary heart of God. This led to disaster, loss of life, blessing, and ultimately exile from the land. Jeroboam's sons and followers maintained this egregious sin and inherited the oppression. Even though Jeroboam and those following broke covenant, the long-suffering heart of God extended patience; as long as there was some missionary activity, there was a stay of execution.

We look at Jeroboam's idolatry and shake our head at his selfish stupidity. We forget it started with his fear of losing power over his people and his cutting them off from the metanarrative. What if Jeroboam's folly today is found in pastors and leaders who do not centralize and prioritize the gospel going to all the unreached peoples of earth? What if Jeroboam's sin today is found in a fear to preach the missionary message, ubiquitous in the Bible, because we want to *keep* our people in our large personality-centered churches and not to *send* them to the uttermost? What if the idolatry of our present day is that we live and preach a non-radical, non-missionary life and make it our chief goal to have more people in our orbit than to launch them to the nations in obedience to the Great Commission? Jeroboam wanted to control his people and the consequence removed them from the missionary covenant. The result: the loss of the blessing, presence, and the protection of God. Maybe Jeroboam's idolatry in our time are attraction-based churches that fixate on gathering large crowds, not missionary churches that passionately live to send.

Joash in the southern kingdom of Judah started a little better than Jeroboam; he at least wanted to care for God's house and collected money for that goal. Pastors and leaders should have no embarrassment that a major part of their stewardship includes the gathering of funds for missionary support so that God's heavenly house would include people praying from all the nations. When Jehoiada died, Joash left the house of Jehovah Elohim of his fathers and wrath descended. It's the same story as the north: Participate in God's missionary heart for all nations and be blessed or depart from God's house and face God's anger. For when we forsake Jehovah and His missionary passion, He forsakes us.

The life and death of a church is connected to its missionary obedience. To stay in harmony with God's covenant with Abraham and David is to be blessed, and to cut others or ourselves off from a prioritization of missions praying, giving, and going is to be cursed. How much better to live for the glory of God among all nations than to wither and die because we resisted, ignored, or diminished God's missionary passion.

PRAYER FOCUS: *Namassej Chandel of Bangladesh (Evangelical: 0.0%)*

JULY 6: MEDDLING MEDDLING

Jeroboam II was an evil king who restored and recaptured land to Israel, strengthening the Northern Kingdom to its greatest extent since the days of Solomon. That a holy God used an evil leader as a result of Jonah's prophesy should not surprise us when we remember that God will always be glorified. Concurrent with Jeroboam II lived King Amaziah of Judah. Amaziah modeled three missionary applications—one positive and two disastrous. For the positive, God used Amaziah to glorify His name by defeating the Edomites in the Valley of Salt. Amaziah raised an army of 300,000 and hired 100,000 more from Israel. God sent a prophetic reminder that it's not about numbers, but about who you partner with. God doesn't need huge numbers to get His will done or be glorified. Let's fixate on what He does need—complete obedience and holy alliances.

On the negative side Amaziah brought home the idols of the Edomites, set them up as his gods, and bowed down to them. At first blush the actions of Old Testament characters seem idiotic: Why worship the gods your God just defeated? But a second look usually reveals that we do the same thing because the human heart is foolish and stubborn. Common practice in ancient days was to respect the gods of conquered peoples in order to win political favor with them. In my view Amaziah was making a political statement first. He defeated Edom militarily and won the war, and then he wanted to win the peace and incorporate Edom into his kingdom. Jeroboam was expanding to the north, so Amaziah thought, "Let me likewise push my influence outward." But what started as a political and cultural concession quickly led to idolatry. Our current Edomite idols may well have political origins. The evangelical community is enamored with political power and personalities and makes compromises in order to win favor and spread influence. Accommodating and excusing immoral behavior in the halls of power in the vain hope of growing our kingdom is to lose our prophetic voice and to incur the anger of God. Political concessions (home or abroad) lead to God's anger, not His glory.

An equal and opposite error is to pick a fight with those God does not want us to attack. If aligning ourselves with the wrong nations and ideologies is damaging, so is fighting the ones God has not ordered us to attack. Amaziah turned his sights on the slights of Jehoash and challenged him to war. Jehoash cuttingly responded (see 2 Kings 14:10). We need to concentrate our energies on winning glory for Jehovah among the nations, not in fighting our brother. It was right for Amaziah to bring glory to God among the Edomites; it was wrong for him to meddle with his neighbor. There is enough work to do for Jesus globally rather than waste our energy meddling with those nearby.

There are many potential distractions to the pursuit of God's glory among all nations and a favorite trick of the enemy is to get missionaries and believers needlessly meddling with one another. May Jesus help us forgo all meddling and focus all energy on loving Him and the lost. Let's not fight one another in Benin; rather, let's fight for the glory of God among the Dandawa.

PRAYER FOCUS: *Dendi, Dandawa of Benin (Evangelical: 0.03%)*

JULY 7: RUNNING AWAY

TODAY'S READING: JONAH

Of all the prophetic books Jonah is unique; it's a narrative, not poetry, exemplifying in many ways that the work of missions is more often problematic than poetic. The irrepressible joy of God expressed by loving all peoples through allowing them to glorify Him bursts forth in this book. The Old Testament norm for missions might be centripetal, but God's heart is centrifugal, ever launching out to search for the one who has not heard.

To run away from God's call to go to the difficult places and peoples of earth is to forfeit the presence of Jehovah. Maybe we look for revival and renewal in the wrong places. Maybe revival tarries because we want it at home delivered on our schedule in our language with our pre-determined settings. Maybe Jehovah's presence hovers over Iraq and we won't be awakened until we go there—through prayers, giving, or physical presence. Many are the sons and daughters of God who legitimately fear Him *and* run away from His missions call at the same time. There's something fishy about that.

The problem with running away from God's missionary mandate is that it hurts the innocent. Whenever we try to preserve ourselves, we damage those closest to us. Whenever we throw ourselves into the sea of God's mercy, it gospelizes those who observe. Some think Jonah died in the belly of the fish. Whether Jonah physically died or not, we know he died to self, fear, and disobedience, even if he was grumpy about it. Jesus keep us from going to the nations, speaking a message of grace while reeking of the whale vomit of bitter obedience. Missionary witness should smile from both the mouth and spirit.

Jonah agreed to be a missionary because he wanted God to judge the Assyrians who terrorized Israel. He realized that everyone needs a chance, but with a 40-day limit and the improbability of repentance among irascible enemies, Jonah was content to go through the motions of warning and then to sit back and enjoy the fireworks. If Jehovah blasted Sodom, just think how He would light up Nineveh! I find the same harsh spirit that wormed its way into Jonah's heart worms its way into mine. There are some days I just want God to smite the nations; I forget He has promised mercy will triumph over judgment.

The appeal in Jonah is a missionary one. We are cautioned to not go out into all the world preaching the gospel because we just want to check off the warning box that the judgment of God will fall—on our schedule. Certainly, the day of judgment comes, but the God of mercy delays it both for the nations and for us. Why Nineveh? It was the largest, most influential city of its day. If Nineveh, the center of global power at the time, repented, so too could and should all nations. Why Nineveh? Because God uses missions to provoke holy jealousy. If the most wicked of the world can fall on their faces and repent, then certainly God's children can follow their example. Missions may well be the last offer from a patient Jehovah to His own. The best hope for revival here at home is to be fully engaged in God's mission abroad.

PRAYER FOCUS: *Ngalong of Bhutan (Evangelical: 0.0%)*

JULY 8: THE DANGER OF SUCCESS

TODAY'S READING: 2 KINGS 15; 2 CHRONICLES 26

Things are bad up north. During Azariah's reign, kings get assassinated in rapid succession in Israel. Things in the south head south, too. Jehovah struck the king with leprosy and sent Rezin and Pekah against Judah. It's so sad because the start was so promising.

Uzziah came to the throne at 16 and sought the Lord all the days of Zechariah. As long as he sought the Lord, God prospered him. In fact, the text says that Uzziah was marvelously helped until he became strong and his fame spread far and wide. With an army of over 300,000, he made war with mighty power. Uzziah had equipment for war. He had farmers, vinedressers, and towers. Uzziah had the world at his feet for one purpose—that Jehovah be glorified by all the nations. Whenever God makes us strong, whenever God makes us known, whenever we are marvelously helped, it is for one purpose—that Jehovah be glorified by all the nations. It is never intended that we adopt what is vile from the nations; rather, we are purposed to live such beautifully holy lives that the nations want to adopt *from us*.

The kings of Israel were not allowed their own private temples, nor were they allowed to enter the holy of holies in the public temple. "The common Near Eastern belief was that the most significant person in the community should also be the one to represent the people before the god. Egyptian kings were considered embodied gods, and had responsibilities for religious rituals.... Mesopotamian and Syro-Palestinian rulers were seen as both vice regents of their patron deities as well as high priests.... Uzziah was trying to act like other kings of the ancient world." And this was where Uzziah went wrong. Rather than leveraging his marvelous help and God-given fame to woo the nations to Jehovah, he was seduced by their ways and arrogantly tried to be both king and priest. Uzziah who started young and teachable became arrogant and presumptuous. Uzziah lost his mentor in Zechariah, found his arrogance, earned his leprosy, and forfeited his authority.

Wonderfully God has called, is calling, and will call many young people into His service. At home or abroad, God will bless those who submit themselves to human authority and seek the Lord. God blesses humble young leaders and exalts them to prominence for only one reason—that they war for His glory among all peoples of earth. It's heady stuff to be marvelously helped by Jehovah, but it's also dangerous. Success and notoriety (which can be leveraged powerfully for the gospel among the unreached) can be astonishingly damaging. As soon as we think God's blessing on one aspect of our ministry means we are qualified to lead in all areas of ministry, we fall into Uzziah's sin of presumption and we speed toward spiritual leprosy. We all need to follow and learn from the Zechariahs near us. By God's grace let us get humbler and more teachable as we age, for it is our only security against presumption.

PRAYER FOCUS: *Fulani, Jelgooji of Burkina Faso (Evangelical: 0.2%)*

JULY 9: UNIVERSAL APPLICATION

TODAY'S READING: ISAIAH 1-4

The Old Testament prophets advance the missionary theme of the Bible in three major ways: "First, they brought something of a covenantal lawsuit against the people of God. In doing this, they often looked beyond the immediate warning of judgment to see a time of restoration. This time of restoration often specifically included the blessings of the nations. Second, the Old Testament prophets viewed the rule of God as encompassing all the earth. The nations are accountable to the moral Judge of the universe even though they had not participated in the historic covenants of the people of Israel.... Third, the prophets foretold the day of a new covenant.... In this new day, God's gracious Spirit would be poured out upon all peoples, resulting in salvation and leading to the eschatological day when all would live in harmony under the kingdom rule of God."

The period of Isaiah's ministry coincided with polytheistic nations (whose theology taught that a god was tied to one place and people) surrounding Israel. The prophets refused to put Jehovah in this category claiming that He ruled over all peoples everywhere. Thus, while pagan, polytheistic thought maintained that certain gods ruled certain lands, "Isaiah anticipated the complaint that the coming Babylonian exile would be regarded as the defeat of Yahweh. But this view would be misguided, taught Isaiah, for the defeat of Judah by Babylon and the subsequent exile of the nation was an expression of Yahweh's judgment on a renegade people who refused to obey their God.... Simply to explain why the nation would suffer such a devastating defeat did not go far enough in vindicating the sovereignty and majesty of Yahweh before all the other nations, much less one's own people. The gods of the nations and their peoples had to face up to the fact that Israel's God should be their God as well."

In this sense Isaiah insisted on a universal application of both condemnation and salvation: All the nations have sinned, rebelled against Jehovah; all the nations must repent; and all the nations will be represented around Jehovah's eternal throne. The first chapters of Isaiah include prophetic missionary and universal themes:

• **Covenantal lawsuit that includes universal redemption:** God's children have rebelled against Him and forsaken the Lord, but God would redeem a remnant that would include Sodom and Gomorrah. Thus, the sins of the nations could be made white as snow along with those of Israel (Isa. 1:3 -4, 9-11, 18).

• **God's global rule:** The day of the Lord will come on all: everything and everyone proud and lofty, whether over Jacob, the Philistines, Lebanon, or Spain. No one will escape the terror of the Lord when He arises to shake the whole earth (2:6, 12-13, 16, 19).

• **The inclusive new covenant:** It will come to pass in the latter days that all the nations will flow to Jehovah. The Lord will purge by the spirit of judgment and burning, and there will be a covering, place of refuge, and shelter from storm and rain (2:2, 4:4-6).

PRAYER FOCUS: *Kampuchea Krom of Cambodia (Evangelical: Unknown)*

JULY 10: NINETY-PERCENT FAILURE RATE

TODAY'S READING: ISAIAH 5-8

"If we are going to wait until every possible hindrance has been removed before we do a work for the Lord, we will never attempt to do anything."

T. J. BACH

The indubitable missionary nature of Isaiah 6 is representative of the whole book: "The whole earth is full of His glory…. Whom shall I send, and who will go for Us…Here I am! Send me" (6:3, 8). From beginning to end, Isaiah resounds with God's missionary heart. "The theme of the nations' involvement with the worship of Yahweh has indeed emerged as a significant one throughout the book of Isaiah, with increasing attention being devoted to it as one moves from chs. 1–39 to 40–66. To an overwhelming degree the texts speak in positive terms of the nations' relation to Yahweh's worship…. **In sum, the nations' worship of Yahweh constitutes a key, insistently underscored component of the future hopes that occupy so large a part of the extant book of Isaiah."**

Isaiah 6 may well be one of the most oft-used missionary texts—and the most truncated. Most preachers stop after the "here am I, send me" response of Isaiah 6:8. But the rest of the chapter is sobering: Nobody will listen, hearts will be dull and healing forfeited, destruction and desolation will follow, judgment through exile is inevitable, and the whole tree will be cut down (vv. 9–13). The reality of Isaiah 6 is that missionary life means more rejection than acceptance and that despite our willingness to proclaim the gospel, the wills of the majority will be counter to the heart of God. Interestingly, the chapter ends with reference to a tithe and the seed being in the stump. Working off the figure of a tithe, we surmise that we are called to a 90-percent failure rate.

Most missionary references to Isaiah 6 do not culminate with the encouragement that we will fail 90 percent of the time, but the context does indicate that more will refuse the message than will hear it. The missionary spirit is a resilient one. In the classic book *In His Steps*, Charles Sheldon mentions Mazzini was correct when he said that "no appeal is quite so powerful in the end as the call: 'Come and suffer.'" The missionary call begins with seeing the Lord and ends with suffering for and with Him in long hours of hard work with frequent rejection.

The other side of suffering a 90-percent failure rate in missions is that we succeed 10 percent of the time. If the tithe is in the stump of the 177,000 Baggara Arabs of Cameroon, that means 17,700 will get saved. We'll take that. If we see a tithe of the 1.7 billion Muslims worldwide come to Jesus, that means 170,000,000 will be added to the family of God. We'll take that! Friend of missions, come suffer a 90-percent failure rate with us. It has a glorious upside.

PRAYER FOCUS: *Baggara, Shuwa Arab of Cameroon (Evangelical: 0.02%)*

JULY 11: WITHOUT EXCUSE

TODAY'S READING: AMOS 1-5

"Jesus is light. He doesn't go to light places. He goes to dark places."

URBANA MISSIONS

A central component of prophetic responsibility is to remind all the earth, all the nations that they are under the authority of the Lord God of Israel. While God said to Israel, "You only have I known of all the families of the earth" (Amos 3:2), this was relayed through Amos *after* he declared the word of the Lord to Syria, Gaza, Lebanon, and Jordan. Amos lived in Judah and *technically* prophesied against the nations in the foreign nation of Israel. Missionary messaging is not all light and fluffy; it must include the reminder that all nations must bow before Jehovah *and* the warning that judgment will fall on those who resist.

Missionary Amos was up north in Israel prophesying during the reign of Jeroboam II (793–753 BC), a time of prosperity in Israel despite the looming Assyrian threat. "Amos spoke harshly about the complacency…and he brought with him a deep intolerance for oppression. He raged against the lavish lives of the rich (4:1–3), the oppression of the poor (5:11–15), and the ostentatious religious ceremony of the oppressors (5:21–24). Even more startling, Amos belittles Israel's precious Exodus heritage. Yes, Israel was chosen from among all the nations, he says, but that just means God will judge Israel more harshly (3:1, 2). Besides, Amos adds, God works among other nations too." Amos' point was that "the God who called Abraham in order to be a blessing to all nations is the God who governs the histories of all nations. The God who called Israel to be his treasured possession and priestly kingdom is the God who can say 'the whole earth is mine'."

Missionary Amos left his homeland and went to another country to declare God's disappointment with many nations. A simple prophet, Amos was offended on God's behalf for the waywardness of all peoples, Israel in particular (for they knew so much and loved so little), and he was provoked that they were not living as their covenant with Jehovah required. A fire burned within Amos and he erupted: "A lion has roared! Who will not fear? The LORD God has spoken! Who can but prophesy" (3:8)? God indeed roars through us, and the prophetic missionary word is universal. No place or people is without excuse. No place or people will escape judgment. No place or people can survive out of covenant obedience to Jehovah. No place or people is blessed, if that blessing is misconstrued to mean we can live contrary to God's covenant and expect to escape His wrath. Amos' missionary prophecy both warned the people of God (that heritage is no guarantee) and wooed the nations (that heritage is no disadvantage). The only recourse for all people is to seek God and live. We are not to seek Bethel—it cannot help us. Our hope is in Jesus, not place or ethnicity, nor in pleasing worship based on poor theology.

PRAYER FOCUS: *Urdu of Canada (Evangelical: 0.0%)*

JULY 12: NO TOLERATION

TODAY'S READING: AMOS 6-9

Amos, a simple shepherd, headed north to the neighboring country on his missionary assignment. The prosperity mixed with complacency irked the black-and-white, intolerant-of-the-selfish prophet, and he raged against the lavish lives of the rich, the oppression of the poor, and the ostentatious religious ceremony of the oppressors. Obvious to Amos, the people of God were not living as God would have them live.

Charles Sheldon wrote the classic novel *In His Steps* about a church community that seriously asks themselves what Jesus would do if He was in their shoes. The book ends with the central protagonist, Reverend Maxwell, giving one last sermon. He very well could be the Amos of our age. "Is it true that the Christian disciples to-day in most of our churches are living soft, easy, selfish lives, very far from any sacrifice that can be called sacrifice? …The Christianity that attempts to suffer by proxy is not the Christianity of Christ. Each individual Christian businessman, citizen, needs to follow in His steps along the path of personal sacrifice to Him…a call for a new discipleship, a new following of Jesus, much like the early, simple, apostolic Christianity, when the disciples left all and literally followed the Master. Nothing but a discipleship of this kind can face the destructive selfishness of the age with any hope of overcoming it…. If our definition of being a Christian is simply to enjoy the privileges of worship, be generous at no expense to ourselves, have a good, easy time surrounded by pleasant friends and by comfortable things, live respectably and at the same time avoid the world's great stress of sin and trouble because it is too much pain to bear it if this is our definition of Christianity, surely we are a long way from following the steps of Him who trod the way with groans and tears and sobs of anguish for a lost humanity."

The missionary message of Amos was simply that the Lord will not tolerate selfish living while the nations of the world perish. To live like Jesus is to live sacrificially, to voluntarily simplify our lives, and to joyfully suffer the loss of all things for gaining Christ and for helping all peoples to gain Him with us. To live any other way is to bring the end of God's blessing upon us, to have the Lord's eyes upon us for harm, not good. In a shocking revelation of God's global intentions, He revealed to Israel that the Sudanese, Philistines (from the eastern Mediterranean), Egyptians, and people of Kir (from present-day Iraq and Iran) all have a place in His plan and heart.

Missionary Amos revealed God's missionary heart—a heart that hates selfish indulgence and loves sacrifice that leads to the gospel going to the ends of the earth. The book of Amos ends with a passage that James will quote in Acts 15 (Amos 9:11–12). God's missional purpose is the Messiah, the Son of David, establishing a kingdom that will and must include all the Gentiles, all the peoples of the earth.

PRAYER FOCUS: *Maba, Mabangi of Chad (Evangelical: 0.01%)*

JULY 13: COMPELLED AND PROPELLED

TODAY'S READING: 2 CHRONICLES 27; ISAIAH 9–12

"I am ready to burn out for God. I am ready to endure any hardship, if by any means I might save some. The longing of my heart is to make known my glorious Redeemer to those who have never heard."

WILLIAM BURNS

Isaiah 11 continues the theme of the eternal ruler from the house of David, the Rod and the Branch on whom the Spirit of the Lord shall rest. This Savior King whom the Gentiles will seek will rule forever and bring the whole world into the comprehensive shalom it has longed for but never found under earthly kings. This holistic and transformative rule will include all nations under its banner. When God's people experience Him, the intended result is global; His worth is so majestic to us, we declare His praise among all the peoples. If the result of our experience of God does not compel and propel us into global mission, it is doubtful whether we have really encountered the God of the Bible.

In the Old Testament, the knowledge of God "is to be proclaimed to the nations, just as much as the good news of its liberations was to be proclaimed to Jerusalem. Or to be more precise, the good news of what God had done for Jerusalem would constitute part of the good news that would go also to the nations." Therefore, what God has done for us must be proclaimed to the 444 unreached people groups of China, including the Uyghur.

To not see God's missionary heart reverberating through Isaiah is to be willfully blind. A further caution, however, is to recognize and even participate in God's missionary work without sharing in His heart. This is a fatal error, for it means we can be like Assyria, God's functional utility, a tool He will discard or break when He is finished using us. When we do the Lord's work for our own gain or fame, we will indeed succeed, but that very success will be our destruction. How much better to be like Jotham who "did what was right in the sight of the LORD [and] became mighty, because he prepared his ways before the LORD his God" (2 Chr. 27:2, 6). The reality is that God blesses His missionary people and His mission-centered churches. But woe to the person or pastor who promotes global mission for his or her own ends (praise, fame, recognition, or funding). Only when we prize sharing in Christ's motives can we truly be trusted to participate in His work. We must get both the why *and* the what pure if we are to truly serve Jehovah.

God seeks churches and households that love the lost, not love the blessing God bestows on them for reaching the lost. God seeks those who sacrificially give for the advance of the gospel because Jesus is worth it, not because Jesus will make it worth it. God wants men and women who commit themselves to love the world in the ways and means that are right in His sight. God forbid a utilitarian approach to missions—that is disastrous for everybody.

PRAYER FOCUS: *Uyghur of China (Evangelical: 0.01%)*

JULY 14: THE INDEFATIGABLE MISSION OF GOD
TODAY'S READING: MICAH

"Oh, that I had a thousand lives and a thousand bodies! All of them should be devoted to no other employment but to preach Christ."

ROBERT MOFFATT

The prophets foretell (speak to what will happen in the future) and forth-tell (speak to what we should be doing in the present), both in the light of God's heart for His own glory among all peoples of the world. Micah is no exception. A contemporary of Isaiah, Micah pointed out that the Messiah would come from the line of David, and his foretelling of all nations *streaming* to the mountain of the Lord in Micah 4:1–3 mirrors that of Isaiah 2:2–4.

I love a phrase that Christopher Wright used when commenting on this Micah passage: "It is **the indefatigable mission of God**—a mission in which he invites our participation—to bring such universal worship of the nations to joyful reality" (emphasis mine). "The indefatigable mission of God" which we are invited to participate in! How marvelously put! And how wonderful that God allows us to join our small strength to His untiring vision, to the priceless vision that all nations will joyfully bow before His throne. Interestingly in ancient times kings employed professional prophets, those who would help him divine what to do on a daily basis through cultic ritual. Micah thundered against this type of prophet who accused him of ecstatic prattling. There is a constant tension between the futurists who speak the probable and those, who despite the apparent facts, call the people of God to the mission of God. We are not missionary logically or pragmatically—we are missionary by obedience. To be missionary is to be full of power by the Spirit of the Lord, to attempt the illogical, to believe for the impossible. The missionary spirit of God in His people resounds with the global and the eternal—our eyes fixed on all the nations and all of time. We do not restrict the King of kings to one people or one period.

Universal and eternal perspective is critical for missionary living, especially when interpreting the message of Micah. If you ask any Christian to quote a verse from Micah, they will almost inevitably quote Micah 6:8, not 4:1–2. While it is *absolutely* correct to do justly, love mercy, and walk humbly with God, we *cannot* interpret those verses as a call to social activism without reference to the missionary theme of the book, the prophetic reminder that God's indefatigable mission is that all nations glorify Him by repenting and believing the gospel. Social justice is a means, not an end. We do justice, love mercy, and walk humbly along the road of mission. Justice, mercy, and humility are how we lift our voices and proclaim the gospel to every unreached people; they are not means in themselves. The goal is not to be just, merciful, and humble; the goal is that every tongue declares Jesus is Lord and every knee bows before the King. It is toward this priceless goal that we must work, untiringly and indefatigably.

PRAYER FOCUS: *Hausa of Cote d'Ivoire (Evangelical: 0.0%)*

JULY 15: FORSAKEN COVENANT

TODAY'S READING: 2 CHRONICLES 28; 2 KINGS 16–17

The story of Ahaz is a microcosm of Israel's story and a harbinger of Judah's future. Ahaz did not do what was right in the sight of the Lord as his father David did; rather he turned to the abominations of the nations. Because he forsook the Lord God of his fathers, disaster struck and death descended. Jehovah brought Judah low because the people were continually and increasingly unfaithful. Turning to other gods was Ahaz's ruin.

The decline seemed to accelerate when Ahaz traveled to Damascus, saw an idolatrous altar, and brought it back to Jerusalem making it central to national worship. The Lord's wrath was provoked, and His protective blessing removed. Second Kings 17 lays out the same sad story but for the northern kingdom of Israel. They feared other gods, they became like the nations around them, and they forsook the covenant God made with their fathers, continually adulterating with the gods of the nations. The forsaken covenant of the fathers is the central missionary theme of the Bible. It's a connected covenant and with any clause removed, it cannot stand: If God will not be our only God, if we are not His holy people, there can be no blessed presence of the Most High among us, and we will not be used to bless all the nations of the earth.

The irony is tragic and obvious. God's missionary people are meant to influence the nations towards Jehovah. When the opposite happens, when the nations missionize God's people to the harm of our intimacy with Jehovah, all is lost—including the very hope of life for the nations. When we stop being missionary subjects, we become missionary objects, and both subject and object descend into the terror of the wrath of God.

How different is God's joy! I recently sat with a beloved friend whom God has used to plant churches in rural America and Southern Sudan. At 65, he and his wife refuse to retire. They refuse to lift their gaze from the glory of God among all peoples, from the priceless vision of souls being saved. He wept as he told me what God has done in Sudan. He wept as he recounted his longing for lost Americans to be saved. He is again planting a church. After six years of constant labor, his church is still small, yet they are committed to support six missionaries. They fulfill their mission commitments, even if that means they go without, and sometimes they do.

One thing I know, this precious couple goes from strength to strength. They have no retirement plan. They spent all their savings on the lost. They are not well known or recognized on earth. But I am convinced they have the awe of heaven. They walk steadfast in the missionary covenant of Abraham and David. They worship no one but Jehovah. They care for nothing but to make Jesus happy. They live for souls to be saved, whether in Illinois or Sudan, for the great glory of God. For every story of rebellion, for every ingrown church, for every lazy Christian, there are numerous other mighty men and women who keep covenant with the God of all the nations—to their own hurt in the present, but to their highest honor in heaven.

PRAYER FOCUS: *Moroccan, Arabic Speaking of Egypt (Evangelical: 0.01%)*

JULY 16: LUCIFER AND MISSIONS

TODAY'S READING: ISAIAH 13–17

Isaiah, who lived during the height of the Neo-Assyrian empire, prophesied against the Neo-Babylonians at the height of their power—200 years into the future! God foretold through His prophets the destiny of nations. The day of the Lord does indeed come on all the nations, and the time comes when all the world is punished for its evil. Our introduction to Lucifer and his fall comes in this missions context as Isaiah compares the pride of the Babylonian king to the pride of Lucifer.

The name "Lucifer" recorded in Isaiah 14:12 is the Latin translation of the Hebrew word *helel*. It means "shining one" and was the name used for the day star Venus. "The planet Venus was an important subject for ancient mythology. It is bright when it rises, but when the sun comes up, Venus becomes invisible like any other star." Isaiah mocked the Babylonian king for making the same foolish error as Lucifer: attempting to rival God, thinking he could shine brighter than the Son, attempting to displace Jehovah as the King of kings, the Sovereign over all nations. Babylon had weakened other nations, desired to sit on the mount of the congregation, and be like the Most High—and all these ambitions had international scope. Demonic desire attempts to usurp Jehovah's global authority and to steal His transnational glory. Any nation, authority, or person that desires to shine in the place of the light will only succeed for a brief moment. Then the Son of Righteousness shall rise and all the pretentions of men will vanish as fleeting as they are foolish. The Lord alone has a hand stretched out over all nations including Assyria, Philistia, the pride of Moab, Damascus, Syria or Israel, and every other frail power.

The rise and fall of nations and the fall of Lucifer from heaven are missionary warnings. No angel, king, or nation is to rule over other nations nor attempt to steal the shining glory of God among all peoples. The metanarrative is that only Jehovah is worthy of praise from every language and people. Only Jehovah is to shine, to rule over all peoples. Any ideology, religion, system, or power that attempts mastery over the nations is in direct rebellion and usurpation of the King of glory. They may shine for a brief morning moment but will be cut down to the ground with its glory despised.

It is interesting that the Hebrew word for Venus (*helel*), which means shining, is so similar to the Arabic word for the crescent moon (*hilal*). Both Venus and the crescent moon (and all that moon symbolizes from the Ishmaelites onward) are pale lights, imitations of that which is the true light come into the world. Neither moon nor planet is a source of light or heat; at best they reflect and at worst they attempt to steal. When the true light dawns, all pretenders immediately vanish. With hope, we look forward to the day when the true light rises in Eritrea. For too long pretenders have claimed authority over the Beja. May God arise and His enemies be scattered and may all those who hate and rebel against His loving rule flee away.

PRAYER FOCUS: *Beja, Hedareb of Eritrea (Evangelical: 0.0%)*

JULY 17: MISSIONARY MESSAGING

TODAY'S READING: ISAIAH 18–22

Concurrent to the fierce king Sargon's rise in Babylon was that of Piankhy in Egypt. Sweeping up from Sudan, Piankhy instituted a dynasty known as "The Black Pharaohs" that overran Egypt and gave hope to smaller nations of the Fertile Crescent that they could rebel against Babylon. With the promise of Egyptian support, the smaller nations of Palestine (Philistia, Moab, and Edom) banded together and invited Judah to join them. Some in Judah looked to this coalition and the promise of Egyptian support as their answer—but Isaiah objected. Some of Isaiah's harshest messages were aimed at either Egypt or those who looked to Egypt for deliverance rather than looking to Jehovah.

In light of this history, Isaiah 18:7 has been precious to all who have lived in Sudan: "In that time a present will be brought to the LORD of hosts from a people tall and smooth of skin, and from a people terrible from their beginning onward, a nation powerful and treading down, whose land the rivers divide—to the place of the name of the LORD of hosts, to Mount Zion." We must look at geo-politics through a missionary lens. Shebna looked at the world around him with fear, and desiring political freedom from Babylon, he suggested the nation turn to the powerful Sudanese Pharaoh. Isaiah looked at the same world, conscious of the same threats, through the lens of the glory and power of God. Rather than bowing to the powers of the day, Isaiah thundered out a missionary message. Isaiah said "go" for we are messengers to the nations. He said when God lifts up a banner, all the nations will see it. Isaiah mentioned God's view of harvest and that it all ends with the nations bowing before the King of glory.

The Sargons of history rotate, one after another, rising and falling; each terrible in their day, each with the same fate: every one of them ultimately bowing before the only true Potentate of time. We should look at the intimidating peoples and princes of our time neither as enemies to be feared nor allies to deliver us from our fears, but as potential worshipers. Before Jehovah all Sargons are very, very small.

Today, we pray for the five million Muslim Amhara of Ethiopia. The Bible will often translate "Cush" as Ethiopia, but historically Cush is present-day Sudan. When Cush was at its zenith, it included some of present-day Ethiopia, so I am sure the Lord doesn't mind if the prophecies of Isaiah are applied to Ethiopia alongside Sudan, Egypt, and Assyria. Truly, may Sudanese, Ethiopians, Egyptians, Iraqis (Assyrians), and Israelis, the great peoples of history and of our time, bring the offerings of their lives and lay them at the feet of Jesus. For this we pray.

And we remind ourselves when under national distress, the answer is not in political or military alliances. The answer is in missionary messaging: Enemies shall become co-worshipers.

PRAYER FOCUS: *Amhara, Wollo of Ethiopia (Evangelical: 0.2%)*

JULY 18: THE TERROR AND JOY OF GOD

TODAY'S READING: ISAIAH 23–27

Isaiah is the most missionary of prophets, for he cannot stop talking about the glory of God among all the nations. The indomitable vector of the Bible is the glory of God. Both nations and persons are invited to find their highest joy in worshiping Jehovah. The invitation is universal as will be the judgment on all those who try and take God's glory rather than freely give it. To scorn that invitation, they face His terrible judgment.

In Isaiah 23 the prophet unloaded his burden against Tyre, Tarshish (Spain), Cyprus, the coastlands (Europe in the Old Testament), Sidon, Sihor, Egypt, Canaan, Chaldea, and Assyria reminding them that the Lord will bring to dishonor all nations that glorify themselves instead of Him and that their wealth will be set apart for the His purposes. Chapter 24 spreads the warning to all the earth and culminates with stating that Jehovah will punish all false gods, including the moon god and the sun god that were worshiped all through Syria and Palestine. Whatever "prophecy" has fallen to in our day, in the Bible it has an irrepressible missions thunder. I suggest a self-proclaimed prophet who does not constantly reference the glory of God among all peoples does not speak for the Master.

The prophetic call for the judgment of all nations that refuse to glorify Jehovah is always accompanied by the prophetic joy of all peoples being invited to Jehovah's embrace. The God who does wonderful things always has and always will do them for *all* peoples of earth. The Lord of Hosts will make a feast for *all* people. He will liberate *all* people and remove the veil that is spread over *all* nations. He will swallow up death forever and wipe away tears from *all* faces. He will take away rebuke from *all* the earth so that all peoples will one day say: "Behold this is our God" (25:9).

The great longing of the Bible is that of all peoples for the Desire of all nations. What makes us most human is the spark of the divine in all of us. The image of God in Jews, Arabs, Indians, Asians, Europeans, Latinos, Americans, Africans, and all races is what we have in common; thus, it is only in the God of the Bible that we can be most united. Other masters have had dominion over us and it has not gone well. Only those who trust in Jehovah are kept in perfect peace with themselves and with one another. We best celebrate the divinity within us by recognizing it in other cultures. We best honor the Father when we unite with all His children from around the world.

The spirit of prophecy continually calls us back to both the terror and the joy of God as relates to all the peoples of earth. There certainly will be a terrible final judgment that spans all the earth and there certainly will be a trumpet blown for a global gathering to feast in unified celebration. All nations will be represented at both events. Let us once again be God's prophetic people and open our mouths and warn all people groups of the judgment to come and win some of each for the joyful feast.

PRAYER FOCUS: *Jew, French of France (Evangelical: 0.0%)*

JULY 19: NO NATIONAL MASCOT

TODAY'S READING: 2 KINGS 18; 2 CHRONICLES 29-31; PSALM 48

"The mission in Acts is about going and gathering, not just going and telling."

ANDY CHAMBERS

Hezekiah became king at 25 and is remembered with honor, for he did what his father David had done, sang David's songs, and led his people to return to Jehovah Elohim of Abraham, Isaac, and Jacob. Coming to terms with God's missionary heart, Hezekiah lived out the reality that covenant violation always has a missionary and international component. Having sullied the temple of God, Israel lost out on intimacy with Jehovah and lost the opportunity for God to live among them and through them to bless all nations. The nations are always involved, for even the consequence of rebellion was that God used invading nations to glorify His holy name. When Hezekiah restored holy worship of Jehovah, it likewise had a missionary and international component. In Hezekiah's rule the restoration of pure temple worship and the return of God's blessing played out in the context and view of the nations. When God's people bring a lot of debris into "the temple," it always negatively affects both us and the nations. Conversely, when we remove the debris from our worship, it also always affects the nations.

The essential error, repeated through the centuries, is to demean God by making Him a tribal deity, a local god, or a national genie. Jehovah has always been and always will be the God of all the earth, the God of all nations. Jehovah never was and never will be an American God. Jehovah does not hold the interest of America over and against the interests of other nations. America as a nation cannot be saved; for only people can repent, not nations. When we make God an American (or Kenyan, Egyptian, or Japanese) God, we commit the same error as the Assyrian Rabshakeh and Sennacherib. "National gods are the ultimate deification of human pride, but they remain constructs, nevertheless.... Indeed that was the identification made by the Assyrian king and his spokesman themselves (2 Kings 18:33–35). Within their worldview, what happened in the sphere of kings and armies reflected what was going on in the sphere of the gods.... The Israelite prophets accepted this worldview at one level but decisively rejected it on another. The international arena was indeed the sphere of divine action (that was the part they agreed on). But far from being an arena packed with clashing gods (that was the part they rejected), only one divine being was active within it—YHWH, the God of Israel."

There is only one God of all the earth, and He is not American. He is the God of all nations and His story is rooted in covenant with Abraham, David, and their spiritual sons. The God of all is, I'm sure, a little perturbed that He is often robed in the red, white, and blue. Some of the debris we bring into our modern temples is nationalism, and that is something very different than missions. God help us. We must neither elevate false gods to any type of rival status with Jehovah, nor turn Jehovah into our national mascot.

PRAYER FOCUS: *Wolof of Gambia (Evangelical: 0.11%)*

JULY 20: WEEP AND WARN

TODAY'S READING: HOSEA 1-7

Hosea is the only prophet who was from Israel; all the others were from Judah. A contemporary of Amos, Hosea's message was unique. While Amos spoke against oppression, injustice, and the greedy rich, Hosea spoke "against the worship of the Canaanite deities, such as Baal and Asherah. These religions stressed rituals that were designed to promote the fertility of the land; among these rituals was sexual intercourse with official cult prostitutes." The Lord asked Hosea to live out His message contextually. Preaching against immorality, Hosea was required to feel the pain of adultery even as he railed against it. A critical missionary lesson from Hosea is that God wants us to deeply share His pain, not just spout His message. The message of missions is that the whole world is under the wrath of a holy God, but to enjoy spreading that message without entering into the pain it causes the God of love is to have the right message with the wrong spirit. Prophets weep; they don't gloat. The prophetic agony is that your words will come true despite your own longing against their fulfilment. To be missionary must include great mourning over the lost.

There is another critical missions component in Hosea. "It is important to remember how surprising the prophets' words were to the people who heard them. They were messages of judgment, holiness, restoration for the Jews and in inclusion for the Gentiles. They were hard for listeners to understand. Even the prophets themselves were amazed. They longed to understand fully what was coming next in God's great plan." The prophets were missionary minded; how can they not be? They must pass on the heart of God, and God's heart is missionary. If you are prophetic without being missionary, you are just a mean cynic. Prophecy's ultimate goal is the glory of God among all nations.

If missionaries must have hard heads and prophets must have thick skins, then a missionary prophet like Hosea would have the grit to press through personal betrayal to express hope of redemption for the nations and their Husband. Imagine the range of emotion in Hosea—he experienced the most bitter pain, yet he held to global hope. Hosea's words in chapter 3 will be artfully used by James in Acts 15 when the church finally codified Gentile inclusion in the gospel. James used the "after these things" prophecy to point to the eschatological return of the Lord and the restoration of Davidic rule as indicative of the necessity to let the Gentiles into the community of faith. Hosea dimly saw it, even if he did not understand the how. Like Hosea, all who would carry God's missionary heart must long for the inclusion of all peoples in the family of God, must be willing to experience both the pain of the Lord at betrayal and the pain of the lost in betraying, and must not be impassioned or unsympathetic heralds. Let us weep as we warn. Let us live what we preach. Let us never forget the prophetic word of God always holds out inclusive hope for all the unreached peoples of earth.

PRAYER FOCUS: *Susu of Guinea (Evangelical: 0.02%)*

JULY 21: FIXATE ON GOD

TODAY'S READING: HOSEA 8–14

"I love to live on the brink of eternity."

DAVID BRAINERD

Hosea's pain came from Israel committing adultery against God, soiling His knowledge and violating their covenant to bring the pure knowledge of Jehovah to nations. Adultery always traumatizes the children, and what spiritual descendants from among the nations can we possibly bless if we cheat on their Father?

Hosea often spoke against the priests, the ones who confused or abused knowledge about God. The priests in Israel were to steward the knowledge of God as a microcosm of what Israel itself was to do. "As the people of YHWH they would have the historical task of bringing the knowledge of God to the nations, and bringing the nations to the means of atonement with God…. Just as it was the role of priests to bless the Israelites, so it would be the role of Israel as a whole ultimately to be a blessing to all the nations." When Israel committed adultery against Jehovah, they became an abomination like the thing they loved. "It was as Israel violated the first three commandments by having other gods, making images for worship, and misusing the name of the Lord that it abandoned the world view of the Pentateuch and adopted the limited worldview of its pagan neighbors…. Hosea 4:7 speaks of Israel exchanging 'their Glory for something disgraceful' meaning an idol…. Only as Israel held a high view of God, such as is taught in the Pentateuch and Psalms, did it maintain any sense of its destiny…of radiating God's glory among the nations." We all become like what we worship/love, and to truly worship the God of all peoples is to become someone who always thinks about all peoples. Sensuality and idolatry always have the effect of removing our attention from the global other to the indulgent self.

If we reverse-engineer an interpretation of Hosea through a missionary lens and apply it to today's context, the logic is straightforward, even if searing. Our destiny as the people of God is to radiate His glory among the nations. We do this by being in love with Him, by enjoying His intimate presence among us, and by actively inviting all peoples of the world to partake in the same joy. We realize that intimacy with Jesus demands and is defined by being His passionate missionary people. Ergo, if we are not fixated on radiating the glory of God to every people, we are not in love with Him; we are only enjoying an idolatrous, self-created version of His intimate presence; He does not really dwell among us; and we are no better than the prostitutes we despise, for our inwardness does nothing to rescue over 58,000,000 Yadav lost in Hinduism in India. Sound shocking? Well, yes. And that's the whole point of Hosea.

PRAYER FOCUS: *Yadav (Hindu Traditions) of India (Evangelical: 0.0%)*

JULY 22: NO HELL, NO GOSPEL

TODAY'S READING: ISAIAH 28-30

Isaiah wrote during the period of Assyrian ascendancy. The northern kingdom of Israel would fall first; Judah in the south would soon follow. God not only allowed Assyria to defeat His people—He expressly willed and empowered it. God's people broke covenant, and instead of being a missionary people, they themselves were missionized, converted to the scandalous practices of those they were to influence for holy good. One such practice was the fiery sacrifices of children to the god Molech. In a valley south of Jerusalem called Hinnom, there was a cultic site called Tophet where babies and young children were burned alive. The prophets, including Isaiah, referred to the fire of Tophet as a symbol of the fiery judgment that God would send on all peoples who rebel against His rule or are unfaithful to Him. Isaiah pictured Tophet as prepared with enough wood to burn the whole empire of Assyria. The Aramaic word for "valley of Hinnom" was *gehinnam*, which translated in Greek is *gehenna* ("hell fire"). Jesus warned about the fiery judgment of hell recalling the judgment Isaiah prophesied over Assyria (Matt. 5:22; Isa. 30:33).

Both hell and heaven are central to the missionary metanarrative of the Bible. Our very understanding of hell's reality is based on God's people breaking covenant to such a horrific degree that they burn their own children alive, on God determining He will judge His people by sending them into exile in Assyria, and on God declaring He would burn evil Assyria in the fires of hell. Yes, hell is real, hot, horrific, and eternal. Jesus warned that hell is torment and agony (Luke 16:19–29) and eternal (Rev. 14:11). Hell is central to the prophetic missionary message, and we do the nations no favors if we pretend hell is not real, not eternal, and not looming. Isaiah declared that the glorious voice of the Lord would be heard right before he prophesied hell fire for Assyria. How dare we remove hell from our messaging when it is so central to what God said both in the Word and through the Word. We are to teach through other tongues precept by precept, line by line, until nations like Lebanon become fruitful fields and the poor among all men rejoice in the Holy One of Israel. Our ears shall hear a word behind us telling us where the way is and not to turn from it, for to turn off the path is to walk towards the fires of hell.

The missionary message speaks clearly and often about the impending reality of an eternal, horrible hell. Secular voices mock and slander us for preaching a literal, eternal hell, but they have no right to edit the Lord's curriculum. As for liberal Christians who would edit of their own accord, they but prove the maxim that intellectual deception follows moral rejection. It is both folly and rebellion to think that we are wiser than God or that God is not good because He created hell and consigns the wicked there. The inverse is the reality: God cannot be good without hell, and without hell there is no gospel message. The most loving thing we can do among the nations is talk about hell more. To talk about hell less or to dilute its eternal horror is not love—it's just sophisticated hate.

PRAYER FOCUS: *Java Banyumasan of Indonesia (Evangelical: 0.2%)*

JULY 23: EVERY LILITH FALLS

TODAY'S READING: ISAIAH 31–34

Isaiah 34 opens with the missionary call for all nations to come near and heed, that all the world would listen to the indignation God has against all nations. Isaiah spoke of the desolation demonic forces wrought when the missionary people of God were long absent. In verse 14 Isaiah mentioned the evil residence of the "night creature" in Edom (southern Jordan today). "Night creature" is a translation of *lilith*, the Mesopotamian name for spirit, and the *lilu* were a group of malevolent demons that attacked babies, mothers in childbirth, and men who slept alone. Both Mesopotamian and Jewish charms have been found invoking protection from these terrifying demons of the night.

The peoples and places yet to be reached with the gospel are difficult, dangerous, and demonic. They are difficult because false ideologies have been entrenched for centuries or millennia without the prayerful presence of God's residential people. They are difficult because they are jungles, deserts, remote, or inner city. They are dangerous because they are often places of war, instability, violence, and lawlessness. They are demonic because demons are real, and they dwell and congregate in real places and terrify those who have lived for generations under the terror of night. It is to these places that the missionary people of God are called to go, live, preach, and shine for the glory of God among all peoples. And which of us is sufficient to take on the demonic powers? And what night creatures will give up the thrones they have tyrannically occupied for so long? What can be done by mere men and women in these spiritual wastelands? Frankly, Isaiah warned that not much will be accomplished "until the Spirit is poured upon us from on high, and the wilderness becomes a fruitful field" (Isa. 32:15).

If one side of missionary folly is to ignore the reality of demonic strongholds over peoples and places, the other is to think we have any intrinsic human capacity to deal with and overcome these powers. Our recourse and hope are in the promised pouring out of the Spirit of God. All our plans, strategies, ministries, language capacity, efforts, intelligence, money, strength, and wisdom are to no avail without the poured-out Holy Spirit. Of the many things that missionaries must be, of primary importance is that we are people of the Spirit and that we live, move, and breathe in the power of the Spirit. Missionaries can only go to the Edoms of our day and evangelize the Kurds of Iran, safe from the terrors of the night, *if* we are under the protection and power of the Spirit of God.

The earth *is* the Lord's, yet demonic rebels hold some of His precious peoples captive. We dare not, we must not enter those lands nor lay our heads in sleep without the help of God's Spirit. Let all missionaries from the moment we wake until the moment we rest ask for a fresh outpouring of the Holy Spirit. Without the Spirit's power, we fail, and with His presence and power, every lilith falls.

PRAYER FOCUS: *Kurd, Central of Iran (Evangelical: 0.11%)*

JULY 24: MISSIONARY LESSONS FROM A MERCENARY

TODAY'S READING: ISAIAH 35-36

Around 700 BC the Assyrians were ascendant, and so it seemed was their god Asshur. Sennacherib had conquered Hamath, Arpad, Sepharvaim, Hena, and Ivah, and none of their gods were able to stand against Assyrian onslaught. Many of the fortified towns of Judah fell and the murderous Assyrians stood howling at the gate of Jerusalem. And in that ominous barking were germs of missionary truth.

First, Sennacherib was correct when he called Judah foolish to trust "the staff of [the] broken reed, Egypt" (Isa. 36:6). When the gospel becomes tied to political or military power, things don't go so well. The church rose until the time of Constantine, then lost its vitality and descended inexorably to the tragedy of the Crusades. When missions work married colonial and/or commercial advance, the divorce was inevitable and messy. Egypt was the balancing superpower of the day and the only realistic hope for Assyrian defeat, but when mission efforts depend on realistic hopes (and not the Holy Spirit, *the* most super of superpowers), God is not pleased, honored, or glorified. Mission efforts must intentionally distance themselves from political power.

Second, Sennacherib bypassed the authorities and addressed the common people in the local language. It was sneaky but effective, for it made the hearts of the populace fear. Missions efforts should not be sneaky but should in all ways be effective. There is a no more effective way of reaching unreached peoples than learning the local heart language and getting the Bible into the common tongue of the common folk. Real missionary work cannot be done through third party interpreters nor discipleship by Google Translate. Hearts must be won and kept by missionaries fluently using the heart language, and that will make the hearts of the populace sing.

Third, missionary apologetics refuses to allow any debate between the God of the Bible and the gods of any other text or tradition to be an equal one. Sennacherib tried to equate Jehovah with all the other conquered gods. But the people of Judah refused to engage in this insulting nonsense; they held their peace. It is not generous to concede the ground of Jehovah's superiority over to other gods. Ontologically, there can only be one God, and that God is only accurately described in the Bible. Missionaries do not get lost in the tall grass of translated names for God, debating, for example, if *Allah* (Semitic origin) is *God* (Germanic). Instead, they hone in on the question: Is Allah (or whichever name is used for God) the God of the Bible? Any description of God other than how He is portrayed in the Bible is false.

Lastly, missionary understanding knows that no matter appearances, King Jesus wins in the end, and that win is universal, over all nations. "They shall see the glory of the LORD, the excellency of our God.... Your God will come with vengeance.... And the ransomed of the LORD shall return, and come to Zion with singing, with everlasting joy on their heads. They shall obtain joy and gladness, and sorrow and sighing shall flee away" (35:2, 4, 10).

PRAYER FOCUS: *Kurd, Kumanji of Iraq (Evangelical: 0.0%)*

Things were rough for Hezekiah and Judah. The Assyrians conquered forty-six cities. They surrounded Jerusalem and took 200,000 into exile. The tribute bankrupted the kingdom, and the king himself was sick and near death. In this context of total disaster, in the supreme moment of his rule, neither he nor his kingdom had the ability to do anything. Sitting among the ruins of Judah, Hezekiah sent word to Isaiah: "It may be that the LORD your God will hear the words…[that] reproach the living God, and will rebuke…. Therefore lift up your prayer for the remnant that is left" (Isa. 37:4). Jehovah answered Hezekiah through Isaiah: "Thus says the LORD: 'Do not be afraid of the words which you have heard, with which the servants of the king of Assyria have blasphemed me. Surely I will send a spirit upon him and…I will cause him to fall by the sword in his own land" (37:5-7). God used Tirhaka, the king of Cush (Sudan) who was pharaoh of the twenty-fifth dynasty and ruled all Egypt, Libya, and much of Philistia, to scare Sennacherib back to Assyria where his own sons killed him in the temple of his false god. Into this vacuum stepped Babylonian envoys as comforters to Hezekiah who unwisely showed them the little that was left, the little that Isaiah promptly declared Babylon would soon take.

It's a dizzying collection of personalities and nations: Hezekiah of Judah, Isaiah the prophet, Merodach-Baladan of Babylonia, Sennacherib of Assyria, Tirhaka of Sudan/Egypt. The threat against Judah will be pushed back (for a time) with the angel of the Lord killing 185,000 Assyrians in one night, but all these names and nationalities are listed for the one reason supplied in Hezekiah's prayer: "You are God, You alone, of all the kingdoms of the earth…. Truly, LORD, the kings of Assyria have laid waste the nations and their lands…. Now therefore, O LORD our God, save us from his hand, that all the kingdoms of the earth may know that You are the LORD, You alone" (37:16, 18, 20).

The deliverance of Judah had one supreme missionary goal—that all the kingdoms of earth may know Jehovah is the only true God. Hezekiah's healing was part of this metanarrative; he was healed and delivered so the nations would know Jehovah is real and powerful, the only God. Any healing or deliverance we experience, privately or personally, is so the nations might know Jehovah is the one true God. Have you been healed? God's intention is that your testimony would lead your Indian physician to Jehovah. Were you delivered from death in a car wreck? God's intention is that His saving intervention be expressed to your Muslim neighbor. Are you overwhelmed, out of strength, nowhere to go, out of resources, at a most critical time in your family, ministry, job, or life? Great! God allowed it so that all the earth may know that He is God alone. Don't waste the crisis. It's a great opportunity for missions, a great opportunity for God's glory to be known in all the earth.

PRAYER FOCUS: *Jew, Russian of Israel (Evangelical: 0.15%)*

JULY 26: EXCHANGE YOUR STRENGTH

TODAY'S READING: ISAIAH 40–43

It was 593 BC in Babylon and the local population was fed up with their absentee co-regents (Kings Nabonidus and Belshazzar). Cyrus the Persian waltzed into town to shouts of joyful welcome, but just before he did, Isaiah prophesied comfort to Israel's exiles. It was the aristocratic elite of Israel and Judah that were taken to Babylon, forced into ethnic "camps," and pressed into forced labor. Almost like being in a refugee camp but having to work for their food by doing menial tasks like digging ditches. "Such social change would have stretched to the limit the exilic community's conviction that Yahweh had elected the Judeans from all the people from the earth." Israel's return home was pictured like a second Exodus, a second chance at covenant, a revival of the promise to Abraham—blessed that all nations of earth be blessed too. Comfort will be spoken over God's people, for the glory of Jehovah shall be revealed and all flesh will see it together.

Some circles see the authorship of Isaiah from chapter 40 on as different from the first 39 chapters because the tone is different. "Second" Isaiah is so full of comfort, hope, and joy over the future. My opinion is there is one author, and my primary reason is the consistent missionary focus of the book, a passion that builds and crescendos in the second half—much like what happens in the Bible itself. The missionary heart of God is evident from Genesis on, building and exploding in the New Testament, culminating in the redeemed of every tongue around the throne in Revelation. The second portion of Isaiah is full of missionary promise, for indeed the Messiah will bring forth justice to the Gentiles and be praised from the ends of the earth, all nations will give glory to Jehovah because God brought His missionary people through water and fire to lift His precious name up; the people of God are to be His witnesses among all nations; and Jehovah will make a way for His people in the wilderness that they may declare His praise (42:1, 10–11, 13, 43:2–3, 9–10, 19).

Hudson Taylor was one such messenger sent to proclaim the praise of Jehovah to the masses in China. After six years in that "wilderness," Taylor's health broke down and he spent five years recovering in England learning how to abide in Jesus. Upon returning to China, a colleague testified that Taylor now lived an "exchanged life." The colleague was referring to Isaiah 40:31: "They that abide in the Lord will exchange their strength." Now Taylor went to bed early so he could rise early to spend two hours abiding in Jesus in the Word and prayer. His preaching had new power, his teaching authority. The China Inland Mission blossomed and gospel water flowed in Chinese deserts. Taylor's exile taught him the lesson of Isaiah: Spend time with Jesus, exchange your pitiful strength for His divine power, and see that power transform nations for the glory of the God of Israel. This is the promise of the Bible. This is the missionary message of Isaiah.

PRAYER FOCUS: *Burakumin of Japan (Evangelical: 0.20%)*

JULY 27: HIDDEN TREASURES

TODAY'S READING: ISAIAH 44-48

"We are a bunch of nobodies trying to exalt Somebody."

JIM ELLIOT

God will pour out His Spirit; thus, His people should not fear, but be His bold witnesses. A missionary-minded God will use all the earth for His purposes in all the earth, even calling wicked Cyrus His anointed one (messiah!), using him to subdue nations so that the treasures of darkness and hidden riches of secret places might be brought into the kingdom.

Cyrus reigned in what is today Iraq. Twenty-five centuries later, the sovereign Lord allowed another "anointed one" to reign in Iraq. Saddam Hussein's reign of terror landed Pastor Jules in a Baghdad prison known to have only one exit—execution. Pastor Jules had been praying for the "treasures of darkness" and upon his arrest was thrown into a tiny, pitch black cell crowded with prisoners. The cell was so dark that the men, though pressed against one another, could not see each another. Overcoming fear for his own life and fear of being a witness, Pastor Jules opened his mouth and over those blind weeks shared the light of the gospel with his new friends. They were Muslims, and they were terrified, too—blind in the cell, blind to hope of life now or eternally. And God gave Pastor Jules the hidden treasures of darkness. As was prophesied for the Egyptians, Sudanese, and Yemeni, these Iraqis made supplication saying, "Surely God is in you, and there is no other; there is no other God" (Isa. 45:14).

The missionary message of God in Isaiah resounds from dark prisons to the uttermost: "Look to Me, and be saved, all you ends of the earth! For I am God, and there is no other.... Listen! ...And now the LORD God and His Spirit have sent Me...with a voice of singing, declare, proclaim this, utter to the end of the earth, say, 'The LORD has redeemed'" (45:22, 48:12, 16, 20). Throughout Isaiah and from the beginning of the Bible to its end, there is one message and one mandate—GO! Go proclaim the saving name of Jesus to all peoples. Go into the heart of darkness. Go to Iraq. Go to Egypt. Go to Sudan. Go to Yemen. Go wherever the church is not. Go wherever Satan has His throne. Go wherever Christ is not worshiped. Go in faith. Go without fear. Just go. And as you go, open your mouth and sing in those dark prisons. As you go, open your mouths to preach that the Spirit of God can open blind hearts. As you go, declare that all nations must submit to the coming King.

Our earth is dark, but full of treasure. What better time to go treasure hunting than now? Our world is bound in fear and shame. What better time to enter their prison fearlessly than now? Our world has lost hope for the future. What better time to sing of the Redeemer, to praise and worship the only One who knows the end from the beginning?

PRAYER FOCUS: *Arab, Bedouin of Jordan (Evangelical: 0.01%)*

JULY 28: THE CRY OF THE CAPTIVE

TODAY'S READING: 2 KINGS 19; PSALMS 46, 80, 135

The psalmist celebrated that Jehovah defeated many nations including the Amorites. "The term 'Amorite' originally meant 'westerner,' indicating people living west of Mesopotamia." The Amorites migrated east from the Mediterranean coast of Syria, and both Babylon and Assyria claimed to be of Amorite descent. The Amorites also moved south and the term "Amorite" eventually became a general label for the peoples of Canaan. Israel's conquest of the Amorites became the highpoint in the invasion and conquest of the promised land. Lest any nations of the West today feel badly that they're not mentioned in the Bible, perhaps we can be included as modern Amorites!

The cry of Psalm 80 is the cry of the captive: "Stir up Your strength, and come and save us! Restore us, O God; cause Your face to shine, and we shall be saved. Visit this vine.... It is burned with fire, it is cut down" (vv. 2–3, 14, 16). The twin realities of history are that the folly of men will always lead them to captivity and the powers of evil will always attack God's own. Life will be pain and struggle whether the cause is internal sin or external assault. The nations will rage and the Lord who is our refuge, strength, help, and courage will utter His voice and melt them. In either case we are commanded to be still and know that Jehovah is God *and* that He will be exalted among the nations. These psalms give the background for Hezekiah's prayer for deliverance, which in turn teaches us how to pray.

Pray the news. Hezekiah took the threatening letter and spread it before the Lord. Hezekiah acknowledged the havoc unleased by and on the nations, praying that God would act in such a way that all the nations of earth would know that Jehovah God is the only true King. In Hezekiah's day, there was relatively little news and much prayer. In our day, we have too much news and too little prayer. Imagine the impact on the nations if the people of God would watch less sensationalized news and spend more time on their knees beseeching the God of heaven to act and save all the distressed peoples of earth! What if for every hour we watched news, we spent an hour watching in prayer.

Pray against evil and for a remnant. God told Hezekiah that his prayers were heard because he prayed "against" Sennacherib. Prayer isn't gentle or gentrified; it is gory and aggressive. We need violent prayers that actively ask God to act and to remove all evil persons and powers that raise their rebellious spirits, words, laws, and ideology against the King of nations. We also need to pray for a remnant of every people to be saved. When we pray against evil persons nationally and internationally, we are not praying against peoples; we are praying that the evil persons who keep their beautiful people out of heaven will be thwarted, judged, and removed, so that every single people group will be represented in God's kingdom. Today, consider taking a one-day fast from the news and spend that time praying for the Muslim Tatar of Kazakhstan.

PRAYER FOCUS: *Tatar of Kazakhstan (Evangelical: 0.09%)*

JULY 29: SERVANT SONGS

TODAY'S READING: ISAIAH 49-53

Abraham was referred to as God's servant. Israel as a nation was referred to as God's servant for the specific task of being a light to the Gentiles and God's salvation to the uttermost peoples of earth. Jesus Himself was understood to be the Servant prophesied in these chapters (Isa. 42:1–4; Matt.12:18–21), the One who will bring salvation to the whole earth, both Jew and Gentile. It is impossible not to see the missions anthem to which these servant songs give full voice (49:1, 13, 23). The servant songs in today's chapters bring three central biblical realities together, for over and again the Bible emphasizes that abiding, apostling, and abandoning are the means toward God's ends.

Abide. The servant songs are full of God's promises of restoration for His people. Isaiah prophesied in a time of decline, backsliding, exile, and sorrow. The compassionate heart of the Father came through prophetic tears, declaring a remnant will survive, promising restoration, extending hope that light will dawn on darkness. Everything started with intimacy with God, and everything failed when that covenant relationship was broken. The prophetic call is always first to repentance, reunion, renewal, and loving relationship with God. It is impossible to read Isaiah without marveling at the tender heart God has for His people, being reminded in wonder that His great goal is to bring us into eternal, intimate union with Himself. Jesus wants to abide with us much more than we want to abide with Him.

Apostle. Intimacy with Jesus has an immediate and inclusive commission—the invitation to others. It is a wicked perversion of heart that ignores the grand heart of God for all peoples. Abraham was blessed so all nations could be blessed. Israel was chosen so all people could be chosen. We are brought into intimacy with Jesus so that all nations might be brought into intimacy with Jesus. Missionary participation is the direct consequence of being intimate with Jesus. If our hearts do not burn for all nations to know Him, we have not truly known Him ourselves.

Abandon. There is no intimacy with Jesus in this life without suffering. If missionary participation is indivisible from intimacy with our master, then suffering for the gospel is indivisible from missions. The servant songs are suffering songs—free salvation costs everything. "Like the Servant, Jesus did not alter His message, and like the Servant, He paid for it with His life." It is terrifying to consider, but what if the turning of Isaiah 53:6 is an ethnocentric selfishness, a desire to monopolize Jesus, and a reluctance to pay the price of salvation going to all peoples? What if the "iniquity of us all" laid on Jesus was our recalcitrance to join Him in His death that all people groups might join us in eternal life? What if a dedication to the mission of God means more suffering at the hands of the selfish church than from the hands of the beloved lost? God have mercy. Missions always costs us—just don't be surprised from where that cost comes.

PRAYER FOCUS: *Mijikenda, Digo of Kenya (Evangelical: 0.05%)*

"Lord, here in your precious Word I give myself, my husband, my children, and all that I have or ever shall possess, all to you. I will follow your will, even to China."

TANNA COLLINS

Isaiah is so delightfully missionary. Our descendants will inherit nations because Jehovah is God of the whole earth. Recently, a young family praying about career missions asked my wife and I about the consequences to their two young girls if they leave home to pioneer the gospel among the unreached. We responded that the best thing anyone can ever do for their children is to take them to the mission field and that those girls will rise up and call their parents blessed, thanking them with tears for obeying Jesus and giving them the inheritance of the nations. What is the consequence of taking our children to the mission field? It is the fulfilment of the promise my mother claimed every day that my sisters and I were in boarding school: "All your children shall be taught by the LORD, and great shall be the peace of your children" (Isa. 54:13). This is a missionary promise in a missionary context.

As is the invitation to come quench our thirst. God promises the sure mercies of David which include the nations. The context of God's word not returning void and His ways being higher than ours are missionary; God slacking our thirst by bringing us into the covenant promise that David's seed would include all nations. The great concerns and questions of life (our children, future, daily bread for the eater and seed for the sower) are answered when we align our hearts and passions for the glory of God among all nations.

Isaiah 56 is a pivotal chapter in the book. It turns its attention to the second temple period, the time under the Persians when the temple was restored. Ironically, it turns out that the priests of that second temple (drawing a half-right conclusion from the lesson of exile) were fastidious to exclude the foreigner. The returnees were punctilious about obeying the ceremonial law, but in that legalism they missed the heart of God. The prophetic anticipation of that error calls out for both the foreigners and the maimed to be welcomed in God's house. Jump to Jesus cleansing the temple. It was Isaiah 56:7 that He quoted. Picture Jesus in a controlled rage. He was furious that in the court of the Gentiles, the dedicated sacred space where all nations were invited to come meet with Jehovah, was now a market and that commercial interests trumped the great passion of God. This blatant, horrific violation of the goal of God so angered Jesus, He flashed His second coming temper on this second temple tragedy: "The sons of the foreigner who join themselves to the LORD, to serve Him, and to love the name of the LORD, to be His servants… and [hold] fast My covenant—even them I will bring to My holy mountain, and make them joyful in My house of prayer.... For My house shall be called a house of prayer for all nations" (vv. 6–7). It's the "mic drop" moment of God made flesh. He said it just days before the cross. He meant it. He lived and died for it, and so should His church. Else we will face His wrath.

PRAYER FOCUS: *Arab, Saudi Najdi of Kuwait (Evangelical: 0.0%)*

JULY 31: ARISE AND SHINE

TODAY'S READING: ISAIAH 59–63

Isaiah was written during the years in which God's people were in decline and oppressed. Land and blessing were lost, exile forced upon them. The powers of the age were other than their own—Assyrian, Babylonian, and Persian, soon to be Greeks, Romans, and a litany of other rulers unfriendly to the gospel. In Persepolis, the capital of Persia, there was a ceremonial hall with an engraving showing a stairway up to the throne of the Persian king. The Persian king was considered the "king of kings" and was depicted as a winged sun, an image portraying universal rule. On the steps ascending the Persian throne were the other kings of the earth, dressed in various ethnic garb, all presenting gifts to the Persian king.

It was in this context that Isaiah thundered: "Arise, shine; for your light has come! And the glory of the LORD is risen upon you.... But the LORD will arise over you, and His glory will be seen upon you. The Gentiles shall come to your light... The LORD will be to you an everlasting light, and your God your glory" (Isa. 60:1–3, 19). In this context the nations of the world are mentioned including Saudi Arabia, Yemen, and the Arab tribes. Oh, hallelujah! I can hardly refrain from dancing when I read Isaiah, for he announced to a forsaken and discouraged people that we are delighted in, wedded to the glorious mission of God, and headed to Beulah land, where the Lord God shines like the sun, reigns in power, and embraces every tribe, tongue, people, and nation to His glorious self (62:4–5).

It is this context—the God of light and glory, shining through His people to win all nations to Himself—that gives us the good news of Isaiah 61, the news we are to spread globally, the assignment Jesus took upon Himself and passed on to us. With Jesus and within this context, we say: "The Spirit of the Lord GOD is upon Me, because the LORD has anointed me to preach...to heal...to proclaim the acceptable year of the LORD, and the day of vengeance of our God" (61:1–2). We can never stray from the biblical priority on the preaching and proclamation of the gospel. The gospel is good news that must be verbalized. Good news only makes sense in the context of bad news (that the day of vengeance is a reality that draws ever near on all people and nations).

Today, if we are to be faithful sons and daughters of light, if we claim to be people of the Spirit, we have but one steady obedience: to open our mouths and declare to all nations that the King is coming in glory and power; to those who bow and worship Him there will be eternal life in His presence; and to all who refuse there will be eternal fiery judgment. Our assignment is not complicated; it's just hard—and beautiful. Let's arise and shine, for our Light has indeed come and the glory of the Lord is risen on all nations.

PRAYER FOCUS: *Hmong Njua of Laos (Evangelical: 0.8%)*

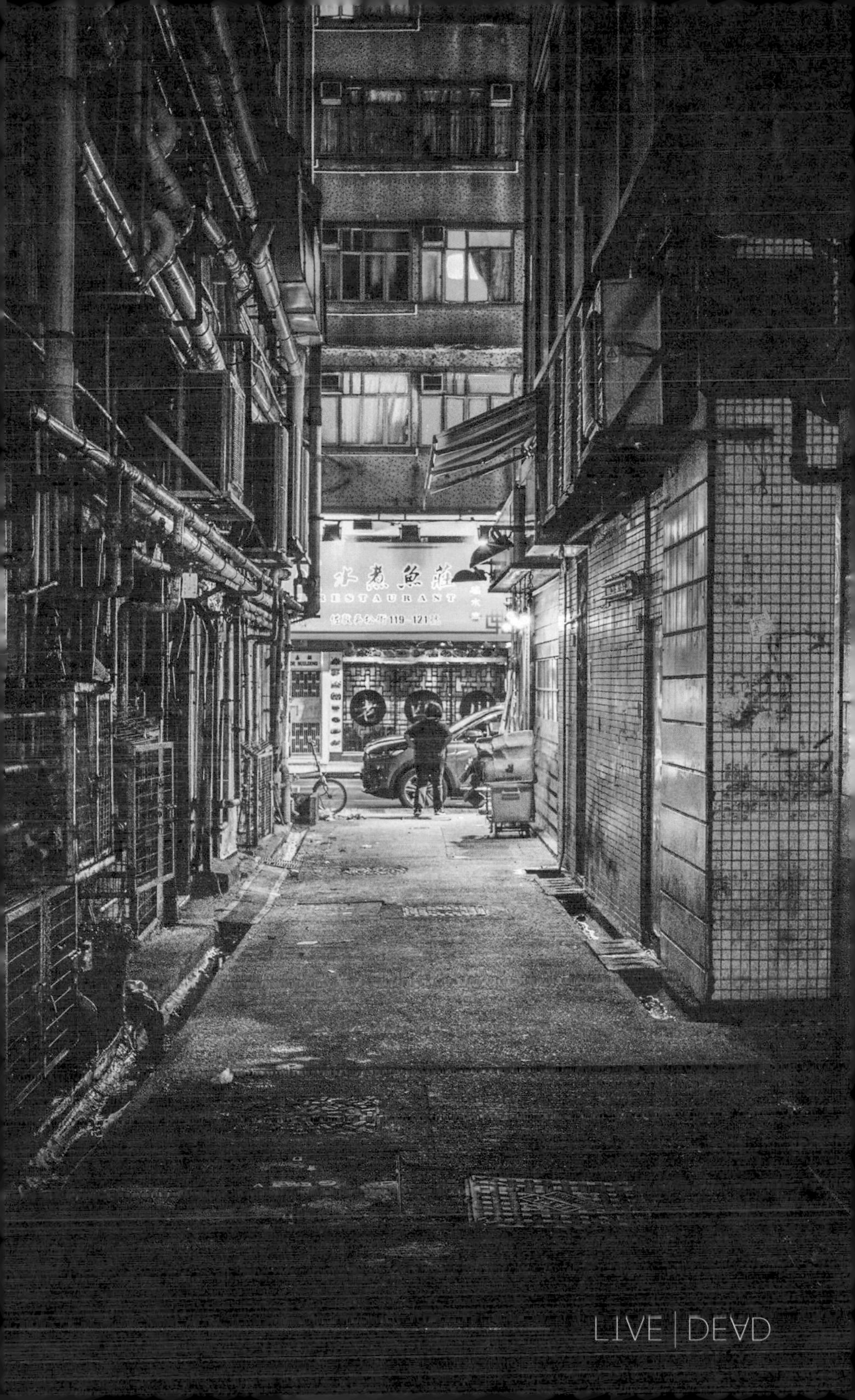
水煮魚莊
RESTAURANT
LIVE | DEAD

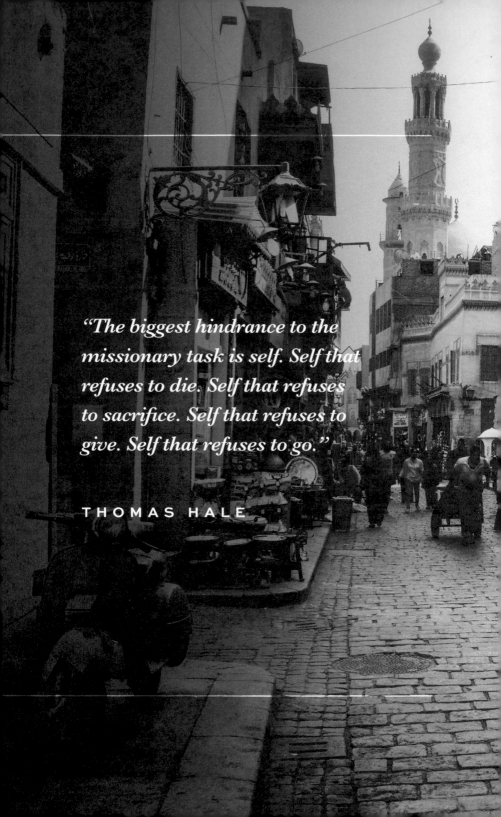

"The biggest hindrance to the missionary task is self. Self that refuses to die. Self that refuses to sacrifice. Self that refuses to give. Self that refuses to go."

THOMAS HALE

AUGUST 1: THE BEGINNING OF THE UNENDING

The book of Isaiah closes much as the Bible does—with both worship and warning. Between 586 and 538 BC, Jerusalem and Judea were largely uninhabited. The exiles returned chastened and sobered saying: "Our holy and beautiful temple, where our fathers praised you, is burned up with fire; and all our pleasant things are laid waste" (Isa. 64:11). The Lord responded: "Heaven is My throne, and earth is My footstool. Where is the house that you will build for Me" (66:1)? Then Isaiah culminates with: "I will gather all nations and tongues; and they shall come and see My glory.... They shall declare My glory among the Gentiles. Then they shall bring all your brethren for an offering to the LORD out of all nations.... All flesh shall come to worship Me" (vv. 18–20, 23). The very last words of the book are then these: "For the worm does not die, and their fire is not quenched. They shall be an abhorrence to all flesh" (v. 24). I can't help but wonder if John the Revelator was reading Isaiah when he was in the Spirit on Patmos.

Because humanity is foolish, we cycle through the same lessons. We seek the Lord and He blesses us. We confuse His blessings with our merits, so we stop worshiping Him and looking to Him for help. In our arrogance we think we are more merciful than God, so we create wicked laws and call them loving. In our hubris we think we can have dirty hearts and clean water, so we become excited about saving the earth while we lose our souls. A repeated error of man (including Christian man) is to think that we can redeem the earth, that we can solve long-term problems of decay through political, social, educational, or civic action. We can't. The world is irrevocably broken and its destiny is destruction by fire. We mourn with the returning exiles; the beauty is lost and we will never get it back. God agrees and tells us His temple is in heaven and all the earth will be burned by fire.

My wife and I love to refresh at a little cottage we built some years ago in Kenya. It's a little memory of and advance hope of Eden. We will garden and steward it alongside our neighbors and friends, but the record of history is unrelenting: Should Jesus tarry, eventually some fallen human or evil will despoil it. The world is fallen and falling to fire. There is but one lasting hope: when the King returns to judge the living and the dead, destroy this world and all sin by fire, and recreates a new heaven and a new earth untainted by evil. Only then is His kingdom in place. Only then is there eternal joy. And in that day all flesh shall worship. In that day He will gather all nations and tongues for His glory. I long for that day. I live for that day. I will die for that day. My hope is in the fiery Lord of heaven and earth. I long for the day He comes in glory to set us all free. The Bible is unvarnished in what that means: eternal fire for the wicked and eternal joy for the redeemed. Brothers and sisters, the Bible calls us to one single-eyed purpose: Let us preach the gospel of the coming King in all the world to every people group, whatever it costs us, and then the end of the beginning will come (Matt. 24:14). And then the beginning of unending Eden for all who have worshiped He who is both our Beginning and our End.

PRAYER FOCUS: *Alawite of Lebanon (Evangelical: 0.0%)*

AUGUST 2: LIFE EXTENSION

TODAY'S READING: 2 KINGS 20-21

It's curious that humans are so reluctant to go to heaven. Hezekiah was told he would die and he prayed for more time on earth, which was granted. It appears the Lord delayed Hezekiah's homecoming so that the extra time could be used for God's missionary purposes: "I will add to your days fifteen years. I will deliver you and this city from the hand of the king of Assyria; and I will defend this city for My own sake, and for the sake of My servant David" (2 Kings 20:6). Hezekiah was allowed to live so that God would get more glory among the nations and so that God's covenant promises to David would not fail. Hezekiah was allowed to live so that the living God would be praised in all the earth.

Whatever life extension we experience is for God's missionary purposes, for His glory among all nations. If your life on earth has been spared, God intends the extra breath to be spent on His sake, on His Davidic (missionary) purposes. This is not revelatory; it's consistent with why we were given breath and brought into the family of God in the first place—that all nations would be blessed in Jesus through us. This is why we were born again. This is why any grace of extended life is benevolently given, not to get rich and show off our treasure to pagans (v. 13), but to spend our treasure on God's fame among all peoples.

It is intriguing that Hezekiah got this so wrong. Rather than using his extra life for God's glory among the nations and spending his treasure on making God famous, it seems Hezekiah's extra time issued the most evil and anti-missionary of all Judah's kings, for Manasseh was born in this time. If the dedication of Solomon's temple was the zenith of God's blessing upon Old Testament Israel, Manasseh was the lowest point. He did "evil in the sight of the LORD according to the abominations of the nations" (21:2). Rather than making Jehovah famous among all peoples, he adopted every wicked, worldly practice. He raised up altars for Baal, worshiped the host of heaven, put pagan altars in God's house and the courts of the Lord, sacrificed his own sons, burning them alive, practiced soothsaying, used witchcraft, consulted mediums, and raised an Asherah pole in the middle of the temple, seducing the people to do more evil than the nations that God had destroyed. Rabbinic tradition says Manasseh ordered Isaiah cut in two. He shed much innocent blood and filled Jerusalem from one end to the other with evil. The whole earth was not filled with the glory of God; rather, the whole filth of the earth despoiled God's once glorious people.

Hezekiah's extra life brought forth an evil son and rejoiced in the luxuries of earth. What a waste. If God in mercy has extended your time on earth, it is so you give Him glory among the nations. If in your relief you concentrate your extended breath on your own nuclear family or in the comforts of earth, you will lapse into the same evil of Manasseh. Shocking as it sounds, God spares us for His global family, not for our nuclear one.

PRAYER FOCUS: *Manya, Mandingo of Liberia (Evangelical: 0.03%)*

AUGUST 3: WEALTH'S WOOING

TODAY'S READING: 2 CHRONICLES 32–33

God delivers for His name's sake. Whenever we're rescued, we must remind ourselves that it's for purposes beyond us and the extension of our small lives on earth. We are always delivered for the great glory of God and His grand global love. Any provision God grants is intended to be applied to the extension of His worship among all peoples. When Sennacherib, at the height of Assyrian power, boasted against the Lord, he was removed and assassinated back home. The text commentary gives the reason: "so that [Hezekiah] was exalted in the sight of all nations thereafter" (2 Chr. 32:23). There were global implications to Hezekiah's deliverance: It was to be a testimony to the nations that Jehovah is God of all the earth and to worship Jehovah is to experience life and blessing, while to speak against Jehovah was to sentence yourself to death. The missionary message every time God delivers His people is that there is life in Jehovah!

Hezekiah became proud and indulgent making treasure for himself instead of spending that treasure on the nations. And the result was evil. In his extra fifteen years of life, Hezekiah produced a son, Manasseh, whom he discipled to live indulgently. How tragic and how common it is for parents to live long lives with the sole intention of providing physical treasure for their children alone and destroying the very ones they love the most by their abundant provision. Parents, love your children enough to spend your treasure on the nations. Parents, love your children enough to teach them the value of work and the joy of giving all away for the glory of God among the unreached. To spend lavishly on your own and sparingly on the other is to bequeath your own evil Manasseh to the world. God didn't protect His only Son with luxury and provision; God sent Him to save the world. Parents, use your treasure to send your children to save the world; in doing so, you just might save their soul and your own.

We know Lord Acton's maxim that power corrupts and absolute power corrupts absolutely. Money has always brought power and we could easily say that wealth corrupts and abundant wealth corrupts absolutely. But all is not lost. Though Manasseh was the most evil of kings and the most spoiled of children, he repented at the end of his life. It took exile in Babylon, but at the end God used a trip overseas to get a greedy, evil man's attention and to turn his heart towards the glory of God.

If you are a wealthy family, why not insure yourself against wealth's wooing to wicked indulgence by spending that wealth on the nations? Spare your own children from the disaster that results when we have abundance without a sacrificial focus on all peoples. I think of two families in Minneapolis raising their families to focus on unreached peoples and places—they are spending their wealth on extending the gospel to Libya and beyond. They will always be wealthy no matter how much (or little) remains in the family coffers. Their kids will ever be rich with treasure no thief can steal or moth destroy.

PRAYER FOCUS: *Bedouin, Sanusi of Libya (Evangelical: 0.0%)*

AUGUST 4: NO FEAR OF JUDGMENT

TODAY'S READING: NAHUM

"Airplanes were invented for missionaries to complete the Great Commission."

LOREN CUNNINGHAM

Nineveh, known as "the bloody city" (Nahum 3:1), was the capital of Assyria, an empire feared for its cruelty and violence. There are archeological remains from Nineveh dated around 4000 BC, and the city is mentioned both during the Accadian period (2500 BC) and the ascendancy of the city state of Asshur (1800 BC). Incorporated into the Assyrian empire in 1360 BC, Nineveh became the capital and for a period the most important world capital of its time. The Assyrian kings devoted much time, labor, and expense to magnificent buildings, including a massive perimeter wall. But the city fell all the same to a Babylonian-Persian alliance in about 612 BC. The fall of Nineveh all but ended the Assyrian empire, and Nahum is both prophecy and rejoicing that God indeed ultimately punished the wicked.

The rise and fall of nations are a missionary motif. God rules in the kingdoms of men, appointing over them who He wills. The rise and fall of nations are all part of God's plan, connected to all the nations worshiping Him alone. Nahum's vindication was set in the larger missions context of God's global glory: "The earth heaves at His presence, yes, the world and all who dwell in it" (1:5). Nahum mentioned both the nations and the gospel. Assyria was no better than Egypt, Sudan, or Libya, for at the end of the day there will be one nation: the multi-ethnic worshipers of the God of Israel. The missionary message of Nahum is that God alone will be worshipped by every tongue of every nation and that His tools for His glory are always judged. Assyria conquered Egypt, the rival superpower of the day. God used Assyria to punish Egypt for her rebellion. God then turned around and used Babylon to punish Assyria, and the cycle continues to this day. God will be glorified in all the world and in His inscrutable wisdom He both uses sinful nations for this end and then judges His very tools. This is a sobering warning for all those who take up missionary assignment.

God will use His missionary people to bring glory to His name in all the earth. Being a tool of God for God brings no security from His judgment; the opposite is true. If God uses you for His glory in all the earth, it is guaranteed that God will judge you. Judgment is not to be feared, for it is a means of life. Judgment is what a surgeon does when he operates on cancer; it is the removal of what kills so that what is good may thrive. When God judges His missionary vessels, He removes what is sinful from them, so that what is true and good may grow and what is for the glory of God may endure. God will use us for His glory among all the nations. God will judge, purify, and discipline us for that assignment in painful and ongoing ways. To bring the good news that mercy triumphs over judgment, it is required that we live that gospel ourselves. God is judge: He will judge His missionaries and He will judge His world.

PRAYER FOCUS: *Brunei Malay, Kedayan of Malaysia (Evangelical: 0.3%)*

AUGUST 5: ABSOLUTE ERADICATION

TODAY'S READING: 2 KINGS 22–23; 2 CHRONICLES 34–35

"Missions is not just for missionaries; God's call is for all."

ANN DUNAGAN

Second Chronicles 34:3 tells us that when Josiah was still young, he sought the God of his father David. Josiah became king at age 8 and began to seek eight years later at 16. That seeking was connected to the God as defined through relationship with David: the God of missions who would rule *all* nations through David's seed. Missionary impulse, participation, and calling starts young—or at least it should. The greatest gifts we can give our children is to hand them missionary biographies as soon as they can read, to model prayer for the unreached as soon as they can talk, and to model sacrificial giving for the glory of God among the nations as soon as they receive an allowance. A missionary orientation to life is too important to defer to adulthood; it must be planted and farmed from infancy.

In 2 Kings 22:13, the word of God was rediscovered and taken to Huldah the prophetess to see if it was really the word of God. I'm not sure what is more shocking—that God's word was lost or that a woman verified it. That God used a woman to verify His word is only shocking because we have strayed from the biblical reality that God's Spirit speaks through men and women equally. No respecter of persons or genders, God pours out His missionary Spirit on and through all flesh. We still have more missionary women than men. God yet speaks through women for His glory among all nations. Huldah commended Josiah: "Because your heart was tender, and you humbled yourself before the LORD when you heard what I spoke…" (v. 19). One mark of men of God is that they hear the Lord when He speaks through women.

Josiah was spoken most highly of and even took his reforms as far as destroying the high places that Solomon had built 300 years previously. Solomon in his "tolerance" made space in Israel for the religions of his wives. Whenever we think we are more merciful or balanced than God, we err grievously. I'm sure Solomon thought he was being progressive, but in actuality he opened the door to the demonic and the decline of God's people. In one sense missionaries must be the most intolerant of all people. Josiah destroyed all idols, false gods, trappings, venues, and opportunities for false religions. His reforms were radical and unsparing—and not just on his home soil. Josiah took his intolerance to the mission field, even cleansing the competing altars Jeroboam set up in the northern town of Bethel. We need to be radically and actively against any form of syncretistic thought or action, no matter how intelligent it appears. We cannot presume to be wiser, more merciful, or more accommodating than our Lord. Jehovah, the God of Israel, must be proclaimed among all the nations, and all the gods of the nations must be absolutely eradicated from any part or place among the people of God. Missionary work is highly inclusive of all ages, both genders, and all peoples, while simultaneously radically intolerant of other religions.

PRAYER FOCUS: *Senoufo, Mamara of Mali (Evangelical: 1.0%)*

AUGUST 6: THE GREAT AND TERRIBLE DAY

TODAY'S READING: ZEPHANIAH

"To know God and to make Him known."

LOREN CUNNINGHAM

Missions is most simply cross-cultural evangelism with a focus on where the gospel has not gone. Since good news must often rectify bad news, the gospel message is both warning and invitation. We must lift our voices and invite/warn all peoples to flee the wrath to come. Zephaniah talks explicitly about the day of wrath, trouble, distress, devastation, desolation, darkness, and gloominess. All this in reference to the great day of the Lord, a day that is near and hastens quickly upon us. Zephaniah warns all nations, including present-day Gaza, Palestine, Jordan, Sudan, and Iraq (2:4–5, 8, 12–13), that they must either worship the God of Israel or perish. In fact, Zephaniah warns that "the Lord will be awesome to them, for He will reduce to nothing all the gods of the earth; people shall worship Him, each one from his place, indeed all the shores of the nations" (2:11). Zephaniah, like all the Bible, is at its core a missionary book. All nations will worship Jehovah. He will be glorified by every people—it's just a matter of how and when. God will gather all the nations either for the fire of His wrath or for their restoration to Himself, so that with a pure language they may *all* call upon the name of the Lord.

In essence, all of history is moving towards the great and terrible day of the Lord, the day when King Jesus comes back in glory to judge the living and the dead. Nothing really matters other than being on the right side of His wrath on that day, mercifully covered from what we deserve by His precious atoning blood. On that day, when the powerful presence of God is released unrestrained on all creation, it will be a day beyond all days—a day unlike any we have ever seen on earth. There have been little foretastes of the power and glory. One such glimpse of the wonder and power of that day happened at a little mission in Los Angeles in 1914 during a three-year revival meeting led by William Seymour. Frank Bartleman was an eyewitness to the revival, the result of which launched a great missionary movement: "The people came to meet God—He was always there. Hence a continuous meeting. The meeting did not depend on the human leader. God's presence became more and more wonderful. In that old building, with its low rafters and bare floors, God broke strong men and women to pieces, and put them together again for His glory. It was a tremendous overhauling process. Pride and self-assertion, self-importance, and self-esteem could not survive there. The religious ego preached its own funeral sermon quickly…God was in His holy temple. It was for man to keep silent."

On that day, there will not be much to say. God will be in His holy temple and all men from all peoples will fall prostrate—some in agony over their folly, some in wonder at their undeserved redemption. In this day then, we must open our missionary mouths to both invite and warn all peoples, including Mauritanians, about the great and terrible day of the Lord.

PRAYER FOCUS: *Soninke of Mauritania (Evangelical: 0.12%)*

AUGUST 7: PRIMAL FEARS

Missionary work is unpopular. Jeremiah was from a small town near Jerusalem and he did not get along well with the established leaders in big city. Jeremiah constantly preached an unpopular message and paid for it through persecution, banishment, and death. What clouds the book of Jeremiah is its chronological confusion; the book's chapters as laid out do not reflect an orderly timeline. What clarifies Jeremiah is its missionary message: "I formed you...I knew you...I sanctified you, I ordained you a prophet to the nations...you shall go to all whom I send you, all the nations" (1:5, 7; 3:17) shall be gathered to the throne of the Lord. Jeremiah begins with the reminder that missionary obedience requires us to overcome three primal fears.

Don't fear unpopularity. Jeremiah's unpopular message was that Jerusalem had "sinned so long and grievously that God was about to destroy the temple, the city, and the land." Jeremiah's prophecy began in 627 BC, right in the middle of King Josiah's reforms. Josiah began to seek the Lord back in 632 BC, so ironically Jeremiah started wailing just when the revival was gaining ground—curious timing for a message of woe. If we will be God's prophets to the nations, then we must reconcile ourselves to unpopularity and to truth speaking that seems out of step with our times. The sober reality is that God sees past external reform, revivalism, and show and into hearts, motives, and trajectories. Spiritually, there is no safety in numbers, and full churches do not automatically equate to fullness of the Spirit.

Don't fear youth. In Hebraic thought, youth was not someone underage but someone without experience. Truth be told, there is hardly anyone with experience in leading unreached peoples to Jesus. Our inexperience in penetrating hostile lands, learning difficult languages, wooing resistant cultures, and thriving in inhospitable climates does not disqualify us from missions service. Truth be told, if the Scripture is true, then the "I know" spirit is counterproductive to world missions. In missions God uses those who do not know, who have not, who cannot—for we are all inexperienced "youth." Too often in ministry in the West, we use God. We know things, have confidence, and present our knowledge to others. We ask God to bless. It's nice when He shows up, but not critical for whether or not He anoints our ministry, as it can happen in our wisdom and strength. That's what we should fear—not our youth, but our "ability" to do ministry without God, our tendency to use Him rather than be used by Him.

Don't fear their faces. God sends His missionaries to peoples who frown on the outside, no matter how they cry within. Missionaries remember that God is with us to deliver, and if we are dismayed before them, God will strike fear in us. Missionaries must have room in their hearts for only one fear: the fear of the Lord. The fear of the Lord refuses any lesser fears a place in our hearts. Fear of the missionary call or the missionary task is a direct insult to God.

PRAYER FOCUS: *Mongolian, Northern of Mongolia (Evangelical: 1.5%)*

AUGUST 8: THE GREAT HINDRANCE

TODAY'S READING: JEREMIAH 4-6

"The church which ceases to be evangelistic will soon cease to be evangelical."

ALEXANDER DUFF

The Lord speaking through Jeremiah says to the shrinking church of our day: "If you will return, O Israel…to Me, and if you will put away your abominations… you shall not be moved" (Jer. 4:1). This makes sense: If Israel repented, God would not punish them, and He would in fact bless them, and if the church in the West repents, God will stop (and reverse) the hemorrhaging. Yet, the text is so much richer and deeper than just blessing to the family of God that repents, for Jeremiah 4 says that if Israel repented, "the nations shall bless themselves in Him, and in Him they shall glory" (v. 2). "In what Jeremiah actually does say, however, it feels as if he almost impatiently brushes that aside as self-evident ('Yes, of course, if **Israel** repents, **Israel** will be blessed') and jumps ahead to a much wider perspective altogether. If Israel will return to their proper place of covenant loyalty and obedience, then God can get on with the job of blessing the **nations**, which is what Israel was called into existence for in the first place." "It becomes clear that true repentance on Israel's part would have far-reaching consequences not merely for Israel but also for mankind in general." Revival in America (or in any nation where the church once strong has started to decline) will have the consequence of all peoples finding life. Missionaries should pray fervently for revival in their homelands—it will bear fruit to their fields.

Fifty-thousand people walk out of church every week in America. That averages to 200,000 every month and 2.4 million leaving the faith of Father Abraham each year. We cry with Jeremiah: "O my soul, my soul! I am pained in my very heart" (v. 19). How do we possibly win the 2.7 million Berber Imazighen of Morocco to Jesus if we keep hemorrhaging 2.4 million of our own every year!? The 2.4 million people leaving the American church each year is not just an affront to God—it's a hindrance to the nations. It is in this context (revival leading to the nations coming to Jehovah) that we are told to break up our fallow ground or face the fury of the Father coming forth like fire (vv. 3 4). Fallow ground is space unused, potential not applied. It is pure evil not to use all our potential for the glory of God among all peoples—and that is true both corporately and personally.

PRAYER FOCUS: *Berber, Imazighen of Morocco (Evangelical: 0.06%)*

AUGUST 9: LIFTING OUR EYES

TODAY'S READING: JEREMIAH 7–9

"A congregation that is not deeply and earnestly involved in the worldwide proclamation of the gospel does not understand the nature of salvation."

TED ENGSTROM

Jeremiah reminds us that the wise and mighty are those who know and glory in the Lord of the whole earth. Often the emphasis of these verses is placed on the character of God (lovingkindness, judgment, and righteous, which are true) to the exclusion of the critical location: all the earth. Lest there be any doubt, the Lord said He will treat all peoples equally, whether Egypt, Judah, Edom, Ammon, and Moab, all from the farthest corners, those in the wilderness, all the nations. Critical to understanding the book of Jeremiah is the guiding reality that Jeremiah was called as a prophet to the nations. Critical to understanding the Old Testament is the framing covenant: that Jehovah will be Israel's God if they will be His holy and obedient people and that He will bless them so they will be a blessing to the nations. These are the parallel rails on which the train of Jeremiah glides. Jeremiah is a missionary prophet who bequeathed us a missionary message from a missionary God.

In this light we must read Jeremiah's warning about both temple and house. Jeremiah, the country bumpkin, not enamored with the big city or the fancy temple, was told to stand outside the temple and warn people not to trust it for help. We can't live like functional atheists (say we believe in God but live however we want) and then come to church to play the religious game. God hated that then, and He hates it now. In fact, He beckons us to sit in history's classroom, go to Shiloh where He first set His name, and see what He will do to all spiritual gamers.

The challenges to public worship in our day are well documented, but Jeremiah pried deeper. Worship of the "queen of heaven" (Jer. 7:17–20) was apparently a family affair conducted in private homes and the ritual centered on a family cultic meal, not a congregational service. We may cringe at how performance now drives our public meetings, but the real problem starts at home. Our cultural hypocrisy is that we indulge in the privacy of our homes what we disavow, yet demand, in public. Our private addiction to entertainment leads us to demand the same on public Sundays. It's not wrong to lift our eyes to Jehovah on the weekends; it's just hollow when we lift those very eyes to the filth from the queen of the heavens beamed into our televisions, computers, and phones at home. What might be most horrific is that we let those queens have the attention of our children for hours every day. We shudder that ancient Israel in their folly appeared to bring child sacrifice into the worship of Yahweh, yet we daily expose our own progeny to the fires and demons of hell.

To be missionary is to lift our eyes to Jehovah and His heart for His glory among all peoples and to train our children to look with us. To train our children to look anywhere else, publicly or privately, makes both Jeremiah and Jehovah weep.

PRAYER FOCUS: *Yao, Muslim of Mozambique (Evangelical: 1.0%)*

AUGUST 10: A CHURCH IN DECLINE

TODAY'S READING: JEREMIAH 10–13

"Resolution One: I will live for God. Resolution Two: If no one else does, I still will."

JONATHAN EDWARDS

I recently visited a campus church of a larger church body. The campus pastor had a sweet spirit and it was evident he loved Jesus and his flock. But my heart wept for him as I sat in the service. Cultural Christianity being what it is, it appeared to me that the people came to be entertained by gifted musicians who were set up to perform no matter how hard they fought to worship. I sensed a disconnect from the video sermon, and despite the warm and sincere invitations of the shepherd, only one or two people responded for prayer as everyone else filed out. There was no mention of missions, but there was a produced plea for funds to complete phase two of the next campus. Hear me, I am not comparing this sincere pastor or flock to the pagan, backsliding people of Judah in Jeremiah's day, but I am saying that the church in America is in trouble.

The plan has always been holy covenant. Jehovah revealed His missionary heart to our fathers, brought them from an iron furnace to be their God and they His people, so He could bless them and through them bless all nations, but they disobeyed. In fact, God considered their non-compliance in missions as a conspiracy to go after other gods. Rather than proclaiming Jehovah to all nations, His people adopted the ways of the nations, broke covenant, and incurred God's wrath. God essentially told them that the mess was their own fault, that He had forsaken His house and left His heritage.

God's intention for His people was that they would glorify Him in all the earth among all peoples—not to devolve to look just like the nations around them. He wanted us to shine for His renown, His praise, and His glory, but we wanted our own. The consequence is that God will ruin great pride. Forgive me for the harsh, admittedly unfair critique of men and women who love Jesus and are only doing what they were mentored to do. I mourn a church that advances either into age or pride, a church that loses its way, a church that glorifies itself more than it seeks to glorify God among all peoples. Yet, I hold to the God who always makes a way and always has a remnant, and our God promises that if we will carefully learn His ways, He will bring us back and have compassion on us.

Admitting that blanket statements are unkind and grief sometimes causes imbalanced words, I stand by the reality that the American church is in decline; and that decline is directly linked to self-glorification at home over God glorification among the nations. There is one way back, one hope: If we will again learn God's missionary ways, He will have compassion on us. If not, we will be destroyed and descend into darkness.

PRAYER FOCUS: *Mon of Myanmar (Evangelical: 0.82%)*

AUGUST 11: WE FORGET TO CRY

TODAY'S READING: JEREMIAH 14–17

"I have always believed that the Good Samaritan went across the road to the wounded man just because he wanted to."

WILFRED THOMASON GRENFELL

Missionary messaging carries a cost, for God requires His voices to not only announce His wrath, but to also represent the agonies of His heart. Jeremiah was the weeping prophet to all nations. He was not allowed to marry or to have children. He was required to give an unpopular message (judgment) as an outcast in both the present and future. And he felt the sting deeply. Yes, the words of God are sweet to us, but they cause us to sit alone with incurable wounds. If we don't walk with a limp, if we have pleased all men, if we have paid no price for God's messaging, if we are not hated for the gospel, then we should question our own obedience, for our hearts are desperately wicked and prone to self-deception. It's impossible to be God's prophetic missionary voice without being resented. It's impossible to proclaim God's looming wrath in the spirit He intends if our tears do not flow night and day.

Missionary reporting and communication do not include enough sorrow. We use statistics for indignation. We show the masses of the unreached and the paucity of missionaries in order to mobilize. We use maps, graphs, and financial reporting to show the inequity of distribution, but we forget to cry. We clinically and logically make a case for those who have never heard, but we forget to cry. We check our emotions at the door and argue from the head, but we forget to cry. We preach motivational sermons about need and God's plea for laborers, but we forget to cry. We point out the tragedy of the billions but forget to weep over the one.

I'm ashamed that in my own life the passage of time has made me more clinical than emotional about the state of the lost. I used to weep over the lost much more than I do now. There were days when I first went to the field, so surrounded by lostness, that I couldn't eat for the stomach-churning agony I felt for my friends and neighbors. There were days when I could hardly speak without voice faltering and tears falling. Now, as Keith Green sang, my eyes tend to be dry, and it's the numbers, not the agony, that can motivate me. Now my pain results more from the social implications of preaching an unpopular message than it does from the agony that the hearer refuses the message and is one step closer to judgment. Now I tend to cry for myself more than I do for the lost.

Jeremiah calls us to return to the primal agony of Jesus weeping over Jerusalem. He calls us to weep for those who reject life, not whimper over our own rejection. He calls us back to the passionate, emotional, agonized, broken heart of God for those who must face His wrath for they have refused His mercy. Jeremiah calls us to a little more missionary weeping and a little less bragging.

PRAYER FOCUS: *Brahmin Hill of Nepal (Evangelical: 0.0%)*

AUGUST 12: CREATION RESPONSIBILITY

TODAY'S READING: JEREMIAH 18–22

"Missions is practicing God's presence until His passion compels us to obey."

ANN DUNAGAN

Jeremiah's definition of balance seems to be equal passion in opposite directions. In the span of just a few breaths Jeremiah erupted: "Oh LORD, You induced me… everyone mocks me…. Because the word of the LORD was made to me a reproach and a derision daily…. But His word was in my heart like a burning fire shut up in my bones…. All my acquaintances watched for my stumbling…. But the LORD is with me as a mighty awesome One…. Sing to the LORD! Praise the LORD! …Cursed be the day that I was born" (Jer. 20:7–11, 13–14). Far from manic, Jeremiah was a living embodiment of the inseparable union and tension of mercy and judgment. Both holiness and love are eternal fires, and both must flow through God's missionaries. As God's handiwork, God's people are fashioned to be the earthen vessels that display the awesome glories of God. The beauty of God is bestowed to be displayed, shared with all peoples everywhere. Israel was formed to be a light to all the nations, as was the church, and if the light in us is polluted darkness, how great is that darkness! The great Artist of heaven has every right then to remake His vessels or repaint His art if they no longer represent His beauty.

The global context of this classic passage in Jeremiah is often overlooked. In Jeremiah 18, the prophet was told to go to the potter's house to learn the lesson of creator rights and creation responsibility. In verse 6, the application was simply and clearly given: Israel was clay in God's hands, and verses 7 and 8 immediately explained why: to be God's prophetic voice to the nations. If, as verse 12 predicted, those blessed with the presence of God and chosen to be His messengers to the nations refused their assignment, it would be the Gentiles who wondered at the grand stupidity of those who exchanged the joys of Jehovah for the folly of idols, becoming a terror to themselves and their friends. The burning heart of the Lord, the artistic intention of the Creator burst forth from His prophet: "O earth, earth, earth, hear the word of the LORD" (22:29). All God's clay is clay designed to bear His glory to all nations, to inherit the promise to David, and to find purpose in God's grand missionary goals.

God created us to announce His holiness, love, and glory among all nations. We have a creation responsibility to present God as He is to all peoples. This responsibility is laced with joy, blessing, life, and fulfilment. If we accept what we were created to do, life will flow in us and from us. If we rebel against our missionary destiny, the Creator is good enough to break us and just enough to make us a terror to ourselves. If we do not learn the lesson of our breaking, the weeping Judge will one day smash us at His righteous gates of refuse (19:1–13). He who falls on this Rock will be broken, but he on whom this Rock falls will be smashed to bits.

PRAYER FOCUS: *Sarnami Hindi, East Indian of Netherlands (Evangelical: 0.3%)*

AUGUST 13: FIRE AND HAMMER

TODAY'S READING: JEREMIAH 23-25

As a prophet, Jeremiah never strayed from his understanding that God ordained him to make much of Jehovah among all nations. Everything must be done with all nations in mind. Everyone must minister, including pastors, with all nations in mind. In fact, God declared He is against those who do not serve with a global view to what He is doing to glorify His name among all peoples. Indeed, Jeremiah predicted a remnant of Israel rescued from exile among the nations, but the context is messianic and includes all the earth. Lest there be any doubt about God's missionary intentions through Jeremiah, the prophet clearly claimed God commissioned him to all nations and even lists by name: Egypt, Palestine, Gaza, Jordan, Lebanon, Europe, Arabia, Central Asia, Iran, and "all the kingdoms of the world which are on the face of the earth" (25:26). Jeremiah shouts to all nations and all peoples that a sword hangs over our heads and that the Lord is about to roar against all the inhabitants of the earth, for He has a controversy with the nations and disaster will go forth from nation to nation.

The challenge for Jeremiah was that he was not the only prophet speaking. Other prophets had much more positive predictions; they spoke of God's favor and delivering power. Jeremiah was a lonely voice saying that God's favor had limits, God's judgment was about to fall, and God's wrath was rightly kindled against all the earth. The gospel without God's immanent wrath is just a spell numbing and blinding to danger. Prophets, pastors, and missionaries must be faithful testifiers of reality, the reality that all men are wicked, all men are doomed, all men will be judged, and there is only one means of escape. It's always been an unpopular message. All those who say "yes" to being a ministerial voice must reconcile themselves to a life of unpopularity.

Jeremiah's contention was that true prophets are distinguished from the false only if they called for moral change in the hearers. If our voice does not call for repentance, reform, consecration, sacrifice, or some measure of stringent Godward change that results in His glory among the nations, then we have not been true to our commission. The God who fills heaven and earth demands that messengers call their hearers to the glory of Jehovah's name among all peoples, which in turn demands they lay down their own dreams. If we have not sacrificed our own indulgent dreams for the *big* dream of God's mission among all peoples, then we are false.

God's word and will is a fire and hammer. God's word is a fire because it burns with one passion: His glory among all peoples. God's word is a hammer because it bangs on one point: His glory among all nations. The adage goes: "If you only have one tool, a hammer, then everything looks like a nail that needs to be hammered." It's a cautionary proverb with positive missionary and biblical application. We have one tool: to burn and bang away with one life towards one passion, the glory of God among all peoples. Only one fire. Only one hammer. Only one life. Only one glory. Let's burn and bang.

PRAYER FOCUS: *Songhai-Koyraboro of Niger (Evangelical: 0.10%)*

AUGUST 14: AN AMERICAN EXILE

TODAY'S READING: JEREMIAH 26-29

According to some chronologies, Jeremiah was 18 when he preached his classic temple sermon. The Lord told Jeremiah not to diminish a word of his judgmental sermon. No guarantee was given that the message would yield repentance, and Jeremiah had the physical disadvantage of being a young country bumpkin. The Lord *did* guarantee that if Jeremiah was ignored, the consequence was that Jerusalem would be made a curse to the nations. As it has ever been and will be, one way or another, God will message the nations through us—either through blessing or cursing.

When we speak the truth of the Lord without diminishing a word, the normal result is the establishment thinks our words of life warrant our death. Missions motivation always disturbs the religious establishment, yet to resist the prophetic voice of the Lord is to do great evil against ourselves. The prophetic voice of the Lord often contradicts popular wisdom. In Jeremiah's day Judah and the neighboring nations sensed a weakness in their rulers as Assyria waned and Babylon rose; rebellion and independence was in the air. Jeremiah told the kings to submit and serve Babylon even as all other voices promoted patriotic defiance. Prophetic voices call us to greater concern about God's glory among the nations than to the national glory of our political home. Proclaiming God as globally glorious is the missionary assignment, and that's hard to do if you're focused on making your own country great again. No godly citizen delights in the decline of his own nation, yet no godly Christian puts the fame of his nation above the glory of God among all peoples.

Jeremiah's message to his own nation is pertinent to America today. America is not a Christian nation; our laws and morality are shameful. America is not blessed above other nations and America is on a slide towards judgment. Outside widespread repentance, America will face the wrath of God—sooner rather than later. God will cause an American exile where our best and brightest serve His purposes overseas among the unreached because as a collective we have refused Him honor at home. We love to quote Jeremiah 29:11 in which God promises that He thinks peace and not evil, and a future and a hope over us. We forget that the context was to those at the beginning of exile, that Jeremiah said they would continue in exile for seventy years, that they needed to settle down, build houses, have children, and serve the nations far from home while God judged and purged their own nation.

Are you disturbed by the godless trajectory of America? Perhaps God's will for you is to use your vocation overseas, to live among the unreached as God's ambassador, to settle there, to bring your children into the world in a foreign land, to be God's prophetic example that He will not be held hostage by any nation, that He will be glorified everywhere by every people. Perhaps God's good future for you and your family is that you spend the decades ahead exiled from your beloved nation, enveloped enthusiastically in His loving plan for the redemption of all the nations beloved to Him.

PRAYER FOCUS: *Kanuri, Yerwa of Nigeria (Evangelical: 0.01%)*

AUGUST 15: WHAT GOD DOES FOR THE RUNT

TODAY'S READING: JEREMIAH 30–31

"I go out as a missionary not that I may follow the dictates of common sense,
but that I may obey that command of Christ."

JAMES GILMOUR

The world has long mirrored Jacob's trouble. God's original covenant with Abraham and sons was simple in its conditions and promises: God would be their God *if* they would be His people. God would live among them and bless them *if* they lived holy lives honoring Him. God's blessing would continue and grow *if* His people passed on that blessing to all the peoples of earth. If any of these conditions were violated, as they were, the covenant was null and void.

Mercifully, the God of the Bible continually devises ways to bring His lost ones home, to save them. Israel broke covenant, did not bless all nations, lost the presence of God, and lost His blessing with the consequence of being sent into exile in chains. Through Jeremiah, Israel was told that God would burst their bonds, give them rest and quiet, glorify them that they be not small, give them the dignity of freedom, be their God, give them grace, and love them everlastingly. All these mercies would be performed in the sight of the nations in a public display of God's glad salvation. God dramatically re-covenants with His chosen before all peoples saying: "Hear the word of the LORD, O nations, and declare it in the isles far off, and say, 'He who scattered Israel will gather him, and keep him as a shepherd does his flock'" (Jer. 31:10).

Why the public display of Israel, both their initial covenant, their punishment, and the new covenant ransom? Because whatever God does *to* His people, He intends to do *through* His people. God's heart has always been for *all* His children. God chose the weakest and most foolish of all His sons to display His glory so that all His variegated brood would marvel: If God did that for the runt, He will surely do it for us! Israelite exceptionalism is simply this: What God does for Israel, He will do for the whole earth, for every people. God's mercy on Israel is advance notice on what He will do for all nations. The Baloch of Oman can read the biblical record and watch the prophetic word be fulfilled with great surges of joy and hope, for what God does to Israel, He does as an announcement of His intentions for the whole earth!

The people of God (whether historic Israel or the church) at rest and at war are exemplary only in what God will do to and through them, not in any way for their own merits or strength. Whenever we are blessed, favored, chosen, anointed, used, empowered, or commissioned by God, we should rejoice with a sober sense of reality and remind ourselves: "I am mercied because I am weak and foolish. I am made an example of, so that the nations may hope. For what God does in wicked, fallen, foolish me, He can and will do in all peoples!"

PRAYER FOCUS: *Baloch, Southern of Oman (Evangelical: 0.0%)*

AUGUST 16: THE ALLS OF GOD

TODAY'S READING: JEREMIAH 32-34

A mother watched her son parade with his colleagues. She beamed with pride saying, "Well, would you look at that? All those fellows are out of step except my boy!" Jehovah must beam with the same parental pride at His prophetic, missionary people who are so out of step with prevailing tendencies. Jeremiah spoke out for national surrender when patriots called for rebellion. Jeremiah spoke out against how big church functioned when numbers seemed to indicate success. Jeremiah spoke out for exile when the populace surged for independence. Then in prison for his pains, Jeremiah bought land just when all the indications of his messages of disaster would come true. God's prophetic, missionary people are ever out of step with the times, so far ahead that we appear to lag behind. Jeremiah anticipated the time when God would restore His people to their land and establish the new covenant. He saw exile coming before pontiff, prophets, and populace were willing to see it, and he saw redemption before any exiled spirit could begin to hope. Jeremiah saw before any person of his day that God would do great things in Egypt, Israel, and among all men, for nothing is too hard for Him.

Nothing is too hard for Jesus. Pakistan is not too hard. It's an easy thing for the God who made the heavens and the earth to save Rajput Muslims. The promise to gather from all countries historically applies to Israel and missiologically applies to all peoples. How sweet is the God of all power who will gather from all nations, shield from His wrath, adopt as His people, grant them one heart and one way, care for their children, guarantee their eternity, and do them good with all His heart and soul (Jer. 32:36-41). All this is an easy thing for the One who made the heavens and the earth by His great power. The omnipotence that Jeremiah prophecies tied to the glory of God in all the earth, among all peoples. We would reserve God's mighty power for our own enhancement; He reserves it for His glory among all peoples.

It's not only God's omnipotence that is intended to play out on the global, all nations stage—it's also His omniscience. When invited to call on Him that we see unknown great and mighty things, that call is answered missiologically as well. God will honor His people before all nations of the earth by establishing His eternal King over all the earth, a kingdom that will include all nations, a host innumerable and a reign unending. God's infinite powers cannot possibly be tamed or restricted to our parochial lives or our particular nation. The *alls* of God were ever intended to awe *all* the nations, *all* the earth, *all* the cosmos. If God applies His infinite power and knowledge to His glory among the nations, then I suppose our finite powers should likewise be applied. Essentially, whatever knowledge or power we possess is for the singular purpose of glorifying Jesus among all peoples.

PRAYER FOCUS: *Rajput (Muslim Traditions) of Pakistan (Evangelical:*

AUGUST 17: ADDITIONAL WORDS NEEDED

TODAY'S READING: JEREMIAH 35-37

"God's call doesn't register in a vacuum; only a person who is committed to doing God's will can receive a call."

THOMAS HALE

The Rechabites are notable for two refusals and one obedience: They refused pollutants and palaces (they would not drink wine or settle in secure buildings) and they steadfastly did what their father told them to do. In these relatively minor matters of obedience they were faithful, and Jeremiah used their example to shame a nation who disobeyed on a grander scale. "This family had rigorously obeyed the arbitrary injunctions of an earthy father. Why could not Judah obey the injunctions of their God Yahweh?" The church has been commissioned to make disciples of all the peoples of earth by our heavenly Father. Why is this not done yet? Why are there still 7,000 unreached people groups? Why have 3.15 billion people never heard a clear presentation of the gospel in their heart language from a Christian witness? Why does 42 percent of the world languish and continue to receive three percent of our missionary attention in finance and people?

Every time we see remarkable examples of faithful obedience—a well-trained animal, a willing child, a professional team, perhaps even the misguided and marginalized who are fully devoted in their error—it should remind us of the grand obedience required of all who bear the name of Christ. Disciples must be made of all the nations, and all smaller obediences must point us to this grand "yes." If the small and misguided can be devoted in their obedience regarding temporal or even foolish things, how much more should the missionary people of God be dedicated to obeying the Great Commission? The great commandments are indivisibly attached to the Great Commission: If we love the Lord our God with all we have, we will love all peoples of the earth enough to proclaim among them how sin can be forgiven and eternal life assured.

God's warnings repeatedly include all nations, as do His invitations, hopes, and prayers that *everyone* will repent and be forgiven. What Jeremiah wrote had the nations in view. How much of our writing is nations-focused? Living as the prophetic and missionary people of God means, in part, that all we do should have global import. It is parochial at best and negligent at worst to not consider every communication tool we employ for the searching, searing love of God for all nations. Modern means of communication empower us to great gospel good if we would shift our content from our petty activities to the grand activity of God in the world. Think of how the gospel might extend to the unreached billions if every believer in America dedicated their Facebook time to facing the nations in dialogue, presenting the book of God to those who have never read it. I'm not saying that prophetic and evangelistic writing will always be well received; many times the powers that be will cast it into the fire. But alongside Jeremiah we can write out the gospel again and "add to them many similar words" (Jer. 36:32).

PRAYER FOCUS: *Tausug, Moro Joloano of Philippines (Evangelical: 0.23%)*

AUGUST 18: MINIMAL SURRENDERS

TODAY'S READING: JEREMIAH 38–40; PSALMS 74, 79

Sometimes surrender is the brave thing to do. Jeremiah told Zedekiah and Judah to give up, to yield to the Chaldeans, and for his pains was thrown in the pit. Sinking down into the miry clay, Jeremiah was rescued by Ebed-Melech, a Sudanese whose name means "Slave of the King." The Bible always has international scope in its riveting suspense. Zedekiah approached Jeremiah privately and Jeremiah told him: If you surrender to the king of Babylon, you will live, so please, obey me and it will go well with you; but if you refuse to surrender, this is the word the Lord has shown me (38:17, 20–21). It was as unthinkable then as it is now that God's will for us could be to give up and give in to an ungodly enemy of another culture, race, and polity. But what if the only hope for one last great awakening in America is if we yield to God's purposes for this nation, though He use another national power to humble us? Can what seems treasonous be our only hope? Soberly, this is what happened to both Israel and Judah 2,600 years ago. Practically, if we are going to escape the last resort of exile, we must make some minimal surrenders.

We must surrender our nationalism. Jeremiah came to terms with the evilness of his nation and the necessity of judgment if anything good from the land was to survive. It's not an easy understanding to reach for those of us who love our nation. The flag we publicly display symbolizes a nation that by law has authorized abortion and homosexual marriage. Perhaps a first step to revival in America sadly includes removing the American flag from our churches as we weep in anguish, confessing the brutal reality of a flag that now represents wicked alongside good. Perhaps we should fly it in places that represent the people, but not in places that represent God. If these lines anger you, that emotion ironically proves that nationalism trumps holiness. Perhaps revival will tarry until we broadly confess we are not a pure nation and not morally better than other nations.

We must surrender our ethnocentrism. Just as an African (Ebed-Melech) rescued a Semite (Jeremiah), we must surrender the right for our own kind to lead us spiritually. We must surrender the idea that we can be revived by God before we are reconciled across the races. There will be no revival in America until our blackness, whiteness, Latino-ness, and all racial whatever-ness are crucified.

We must surrender our familism. Perhaps the most cherished and insidious idol we cling to is family. The family as God ordained it is holy, but the family as an excuse to not go into missions, to not proclaim the gospel to the unreached, that use of family is evil. Perhaps awakening in America and beyond will tarry until we willingly surrender our idea of family to the Father. He sent His only Son to die. Perhaps until we willingly send our sons and daughters to die for the salvation of unreached peoples, God will not send again His Son to revive us.

PRAYER FOCUS: *Arab, Lebanese of Qatar (Evangelical: 0.5%)*

AUGUST 19: THE UNBORN, UNCHALLENGED, AND UNREACHED

TODAY'S READING: 2 KINGS 24–25; 2 CHRONICLES 36

It wasn't just Jeremiah who sunk into the miry clay. Jeremiah prophesied in the days that the kingdom of Judah finally gave up the ghost. The kingdom was established on covenantal grounds, and God's missionary purpose was the heart and soul of the covenant and kingdom. When God's people strayed from this non-negotiable understanding, God sent messengers to remind them of the main thing, "but they mocked the messengers of God, despised His words, and scoffed at His prophets, until the wrath of the LORD arose against His people, till there was no remedy" (2 Chr. 36:16). Second Kings repeats the same sentiment because they had "filled Jerusalem with innocent blood [child sacrifice], which the LORD would not pardon" (24:4).

The Lord of life will not tolerate senseless death whether through abortion or neglect of our missionary commission. Both rebellious sins result in billions dying. The killing of unborn babies and the reluctance to spend ourselves so that the unreached may be born again are equal and connected evils: both would rather that others die, unprotected or unwarned, than be inconvenienced. If we do nothing about the unborn and the unreached, if we do not respond to God's command to fight for life, then we break covenant with Him, scoff at His messengers, and the wrath of God will rise until there is no remedy. With the blood of fifty million unborn on our hands and the blood of 3.15 billion unreached on our heads, surely wrath is nigh, and remedy runs out.

The enemy is most vile in his demonic success when he succeeds in getting us to kill our own. How many future missionaries lie buried in tiny graves? How many unreached will die because a "Christian" nation aborted our own missionaries? A less decried corporate murder, another abortion campaign, is the emasculation of men. Men were born to fight, and the spirit behind homosexuality denies masculinity and seeks to kill the warrior spirit. If the enemy can get us to kill our own children and emasculate our own men, he can sit back in demonic satisfaction as we destroy ourselves and no one lives so that the nations may not die. There are on average seven single missionary women for every one single missionary man. Where are the missionary men? Have we killed them in the cradle of the womb or the cradle of culture, media, and caricature?

What if there is a deeper core to the travesties of abortion and homosexuality? What if the implications are so much bigger than our "rights," "convenience," or "pleasure"? What if these issues are about the nations and the glory of God among all peoples? What if by getting us to kill our children and neuter our men, the devil knows he can hold unreached people captive and death will reign both at home and abroad? Maybe there is yet one last remedy for wrath. Maybe the fate of the unborn, unchallenged, and unreached are all connected. Perhaps as we fight for the abolition of abortion, the warrior masculinity of men, and the glory of God among all peoples, God will have mercy on our land and hold back the winepress of His wrath.

PRAYER FOCUS: *Avar, Dagestani of Russia (Evangelical: 0.01%)*

AUGUST 20: GOD'S AIM ACHIEVED
TODAY'S READING: HABAKKUK

Habakkuk struggled with the violence he saw on the global scale. The Chaldeans originated in the southern part of the Babylonian empire and over time consolidated enough power to overthrow the Assyrians and rule from Babylon. Nebuchadnezzar II was himself a Chaldean, and from the seventh century on, the terms "Babylonian" and "Chaldean" appear to be synonymous. Habakkuk struggled with how God could allow such violence to go unpunished, how a pure God could use such obviously ungodly tools. God answered Habakkuk's timeless question with His eternal answer: "Look among the nations and watch—be utterly astounded! For I will work a work in your days which you would not believe, though it were told you.... For the earth will be filled with the knowledge of the glory of the LORD as the waters cover the sea.... But the LORD is in His holy temple. Let all the earth keep silence before Him" (1:5; 2:14, 20).

As we look over the global landscape, we wonder with Habakkuk about problematic challenges like urbanization, violence, corruption, and materialism. God's answer remains the same. "Whether through the experience of God's saving grace or through exposure to God's righteous judgment, Israel came to know who the true and living God is. And by the same means, ultimately, the nations too will come to know His identity, either in repentance, salvation and worship, or in defiant wickedness and destruction. 'The earth will be filled with the knowledge of the glory of God as the waters cover the sea' (2:14). Such is God's will and purpose. Such is the mission of God."

Habakkuk concisely reminds us of God's aim (which if God be true, and He is) will indubitably be achieved: His glory will cover the heavens *and* the earth will be full of His praise *and* one look from His holy eyes will startle the nations. Whether by death or life, God will be glorified by Bedouins in Saudi Arabia. Whether by the whole nation of Saudi Arabia turning to Jesus or one Saudi family bowing to worship Jesus, God will be glorified.

I finished a one-year fast from reading or viewing world news. It was a tonic to my soul that had become weary with the globally ubiquitous violence and wickedness. I discovered that when an event was significant enough, someone informed me. To some degree, I will engage again, but how sweet to read God's promises about how this ends instead: His glory everywhere to every nation and every people. In that news, "I will rejoice in the LORD, I will joy in the God of my salvation" (3:18). In a world God made, we remember how it all ends. In wrath God will remember mercy, and around His eternal throne all nations will gather whether in holy silence or joyful praise. Look for the Saudis! I hope to be standing next to a passel of them.

PRAYER FOCUS: *Arab, Bedouin of Saudi Arabia (Evangelical: 0.0%)*

AUGUST 21: BATTLE TO THE END

TODAY'S READING: JEREMIAH 41–45

Jeremiah, the "all nations" prophet, exhorted national surrender when patriotism ran high. Jeremiah urged exile when everyone wanted to stay home. When the popular will was to run from home to the apparent safety of Egypt, Jeremiah again went against the grain and stated that flight solves nothing. These chapters of Jeremiah have two essential missionary applications: First, the missionary voice is constantly out of step with what is popular, and second, in this life we cannot run from battle, but we must face our fears.

An upstart named Ishmael murdered the appointed authority, and the people, tired of a litany of national disaster, attempted to manipulate a prophetic endorsement to escape it all: "We will go to the land of Egypt where we will see no war, nor hear the sound of the trumpet, nor be hungry for bread, and there we will dwell" (Jer. 42:14). Collectively, it had been about 500 years of strife (civil and international), and the people of God just wanted to stop fighting. They wanted to withdraw from all conflict, mind their own business, and live in peace. In this age that is not an option. We have no choice but to face our fears, to fight for the glory of God from all nations, or to lift up our voice bearing a message as unpopular on earth as it is fixed in heaven.

Missions is a thing of earth; it will not exist in heaven. Earth is not our home; it is not where we belong. We are pilgrims, strangers, and aliens. There are beautiful things on earth, but they are shadows of the grandeurs of glory. The reason we remain on earth is that God's grand passion to be worshipped by every tongue eternally be fulfilled. As long as we have breath, we speak for the glory of God among all nations. As long as we have strength, we must fight for the glory of God among all peoples.

The uniting theme of this life is that we live and speak for the glory of Jesus among all peoples. Neither this life nor eternal life is centered on us or our glory—all must focus on the magnificent King of kings. Jeremiah's prophetic partner was Baruch who also felt the wear and tear of bearing a prophetic message in a world gone mad. Baruch sought relief from the burden of constant battle for the souls of men, and God told him: "Do you seek great things for yourself? Do not seek them; for behold, I will bring adversity on all flesh…. But I will give your life to you as a prize…wherever you go" (45:5).

It's simple, really—life is war, and it is wartime. As long as we live, we must strain against the popular. We must fight that men and women be saved. Yes, it is exhausting, but we are delusional if we think we can go anywhere that escapes the battle. One way or another we will have to war to the end; either we run to battle or the battle will run to us. The only safe way to navigate the fray is to be sure we fight for the honor of Jesus. If we do anything, including win souls, as a means of seeking great things for ourselves, we have already lost.

PRAYER FOCUS: *Maninka, Western of Senegal (Evangelical: 0.13%)*

AUGUST 22: A COVER FOR OUR COWARDICE

TODAY'S READING: JEREMIAH 46–48

"The Gospel is not an old, old story, freshly told. It is a fire in the Spirit, fed by the flame of Immortal Love; and woe unto us, if through our negligence to stir up the Gift of God which is within us, that fire burns low."

DR. R. MOFFAT GAUTREY

Jeremiah's later prophesies occurred when critical political adjustments were made in the Fertile Crescent. In 605 BC and following, Babylon gained ascendancy over Assyria, conquered Judah, and reached its zenith by 560 BC. For the most part, with minor adjustments, the Middle East was organized with two major powers (Babylon and Egypt) in a face-off, with minor powers aligning with one or the other as was convenient. Not that different from the Middle East of our day, with Iran and Saudi staring at one another over the Persian/Arabian Gulf as other nations carefully chose which bully they will align with.

God used the prophet to remind us that when the dust settles, only One will receive the glory and we don't have to fear because Jehovah will make an end of all nations. God used the Egyptians to push back the Babylonians, the Babylonians to humble Egypt, the Egyptians to punish Gaza, and the Babylonians to judge Moab. It's kind of a judgment free-for-all in which God used various nations, each in turn, as His tool for judgment, even as He does in our day as His tool for missions.

God does not restrict His missions mobilization or empowerment to one nation. All nations are called to participate in the extension of God's glory among all nations. God is sending Egyptian missionaries to Gaza, Iraqi messengers to Jordan, Iranian evangelists to Europe, and workers from every nation to every nation. No nation is exempt from God's mandate, and no country is too poor to send missionaries, just as no country is exempt from sending because they are rich. There is a dangerous strain of thought that says it's more economical for Americans to fund gospel workers overseas than to go ourselves. This thinking is strained and insidious. Lurking in its motivation is the notion that we can pay others to fulfil our obedience, that our sons and daughters are too precious to suffer and die for gospel advance, that other lives are more expendable so we can fund their efforts. How wicked is a philosophy that thinks we can pay others to go to war for us, that we can buy our way out of the summons to dangerous missions.

The Great Commission has not been rescinded for any nation. We rejoice that God is using all nations. We rejoice that God has raised up the Global South, shifted the center of Christianity away from the West, and proved that no one culture or race own His Spirit and mission. But He is yet the Lord of hosts and all must still respond to His war call. We in the West cannot hide behind the false logic of economic stewardship as a cover for our cowardice. We must send our sons and daughters to live and die for King Jesus among the unreached.

PRAYER FOCUS: *Loko, Landogo of Sierra Leone (Evangelical: 0.9%)*

AUGUST 23: EXPOSING PRETENDER GODS

TODAY'S READING: JEREMIAH 49–50

"All the resources of the Godhead are at our disposal!"

JONATHAN GOFORTH

In the first century BC, deities were verified by whether or not their worshipping nations were victorious in battle. The thinking went that if Babylon conquered Israel, then the god of Babylon was mightier than the god of Israel. This time-bound view of the divine was unsettling as nation defeated nation: Assyria replaced Babylon who was replaced by the Neo-Babylonians who were replaced by the Medes and Persians. Jeremiah, prophet to all nations, cut through the nonsense of rotating deities and asserted there is only one true God, His name is Jehovah, and He will eternally rule over all nations.

Jeremiah's prophecies remind us that missionaries should not be private or proud. We are to proclaim to all nations that Jehovah alone is God and that all nations must worship Him. Any nation that appears victorious is merely the hammer of God, a tool of the eternal God to force all nations to worship. There is no place for the missionary to be arrogant or secret (our role as proclaimers precludes being sneaky, duplicitous, confusing, or indirect; we are announcers, not concealers). If we are God's hammer, voice, messenger, tool, or servant, we must remember that without His animating power, we are lifeless, useless, and insignificant.

Jehovah's rule over all nations includes both wrath and ransom. Every nation will be judged, and every nation will have representatives who are redeemed and joined to the family of God. After declaring to Ammon (present-day Jordan) that Jehovah would destroy their pretender god Milcom (Molech), God promised the Jordanians that afterwards He would bring back their captives. After pronouncing desolation on Edom (stretching from Jordan to Basra, Iraq), God promised to preserve their fatherless children alive and care for their widows who will trust in Him. God promised that plunder would be won from the Arabs and that the Iranians, though scattered to every nation, would be restored in the latter days. The God of all nations beautifully promised the same mercy and the same judgment that He guaranteed to Israel to all peoples.

At the end of days, Jehovah alone will be exalted. All pretender gods will be exposed as false. All nations and all men will be judged and humbled, and all will have a remnant who repent, find mercy, and assemble around the throne. Our missionary God will achieve His purpose for human history: the blood-bought redeemed from every people group who will enjoy Him forever. This is the story of the Bible, and to this end we live and serve among the Somali Bantu. They too will be used of God. They too will be judged. They too will be represented in life eternal. All glory to the God of kings, the Lord of nations, the benevolent Ruler of all!

PRAYER FOCUS: *Somali Bantu of Somalia (Evangelical: 0.05%)*

AUGUST 24: JOIN THE GREAT CHOIR

TODAY'S READING: JEREMIAH 51-52

Jeremiah's story ended as it began. His was the lone dissenting voice in a crowd with great plans for themselves and their nations. Not much has changed over the millennia. Men still strive for national greatness, and they still prefer their parochial physical prosperity over the prophetic purposes of God for all peoples. Being true to the missionary heart of God will always mean being out of step with popular sentiment—both in the church at large and in the world which grows increasingly smaller.

Because the Bible is a missionary book from beginning to end, even the major prophets focus on the glory of God and His purposes for all peoples. Whether those peoples are great or small, they all serve the purposes of God. Mighty Babylon was simply a golden cup in the Lord's hand and little Israel was His battle axe. Since the Lord made the whole earth by His mighty power, He easily uses the nations as He will, for His glory and every purpose of the Lord shall be performed. The prophets will not let us forget that God's purpose is redemption and that His definition of redemption includes representatives of every people group eternally secured to be satisfied in Him. God guarantees that every people and nation will be harvested eventually—no matter how strong or evil they are—and that a remnant of every people will be rescued. God's purposes for the nations will triumph and what He does physically and temporally among the nations are merely representative of what He is doing or will do spiritually and eternally. As Israel was an example of what God can do with the weak, Babylon was an example of what God can do with the strong. All nations, all peoples, all men are vessels of Jehovah's glory.

As the missionary people of God, we should take comfort in history. It doesn't matter if we are little or big. It doesn't matter if we are strong or weak. It doesn't matter if we live here or there, if we are young or old, if we are vessels of honor or not. All that matters is that we are used for the glory of God among all nations in this life and that as part of that diverse eternal crowd of glorifiers, we are eternally satisfied in Jesus. Jeremiah's message is that God will be globally glorified among all peoples. We decide on which side of that glory we will stand: Will we stand on the life side, gratified and fulfilled forever, or will we stand on the death side, non-compliant but used anyway?

The dissenting, dissonant voice today, the voice that incessantly calls all men towards God's passion for His glory among all peoples, will be well-surrounded in harmonious heaven. A great choir is being formed. Auditions are lifelong. There is yet ample opportunity to train and employ your voice for that eternal song. It is the song of life, the song of the redeemed. It is the song that feeds us even as we sing it. What joy to start singing now, what joy to sing forever!

PRAYER FOCUS: *Batgama of Sri Lanka (Evangelical: 0.0%)*

AUGUST 25: WEEP WITH GOD

TODAY'S READING: LAMENTATIONS 1-2

The central sadness of Lamentations is the grief of knowing that what God wanted to be a positive blessing to all peoples became a negative lesson. "The book of Lamentations consists of five separate poems on the destruction of Jerusalem in 586 BC. These funeral songs and prayers describe both the horrors of the extended siege… and the destruction itself. No other book captures the despair of seeing Zion destroyed, of seeing the holy city and its temple become a mockery to the nations." Lamentations is attributed to Jeremiah though his name is not mentioned. A witness to the days that Jerusalem finally fell certainly wrote it. The one book of the Bible titled by weeping is about the failure of missions. Israel was intended to be a light to all nations, and its failure made God cry. And God still weeps. Perhaps we should weep with Him.

We should weep over the state of the church. How lonely the halls once filled with eager worshipers. Churches in Europe and America are becoming mosques. Americans go to church less than twice a month on average. Mainline denominations are in decline. The faithful are aging. Some Christians endorse and approve homosexuality. Hell is denied. The Bible is neglected. None of these laments are new, but they are growing. God still weeps. Fire has fallen in the house of God, but not the fire of revival. The Lord has abandoned His sanctuary, and strangers roam His halls. We have performance and narcissism, but no power or nobility. Our eyes fill and fail with tears.

We should weep over the state of the lost: 3.15 billion people of the world in 7,000 unreached people groups who have not had an adequate witness of the gospel in their heart language. Every second or so, somewhere around the world, a soul dies and goes to eternal punishment. Not only are the lost without adequate witness, they also do despicable things to one another. The world grows worse, not better; education and technology help us become crueler and more efficient in both greed and violence. We kill our young and our old. We hate our neighbor. More connected digitally than ever before, we have never been more alone. For these things we weep.

We should weep over the state of missions. Our prophetic voices lie to us. We are no longer challenged to die for the sake of others. We are coached on how to pamper ourselves, live in comfort, and retire in ease. We spend more money on bubble gum and dog food than we do on the cause of global missions. Missionaries that go to unreached peoples on average last about four years before giving up or going home. We should indeed rise up in the night, lift our hands to the Lord, and cry.

Today, there is too much self-congratulation and not enough weeping among us. Lamentations reminds us that a missionary God cries, and so should we. When was the last time you wept over the state of the church, the state of the lost, or the state of missions?

PRAYER FOCUS: *Fur, Forok of Sudan (Evangelical: 0.0%)*

AUGUST 26: NO RHYME, MUCH REPETITION

TODAY'S READING: LAMENTATIONS 3-5

"All roads lead to the judgment seat of Christ."

KEITH GREEN

Hebrew poetry uses little to no rhyme, but it does use repetition of key thoughts and phrases. In poems of lament the usual rhythm is called *qinah*, a five-beat pattern divided into 3 and 2. Lamentations uses an alphabetical acrostic. Each verse starts with a letter of the Hebrew alphabet. Each chapter of Lamentations has 22 verses (the Hebrew alphabet has 22 letters), with the exception of chapter 3 which runs through the alphabet three times for a total of 66 verses. If we read Lamentations 3 with the bifocal lenses of missions and of its natural structure, three critical foci emerge.

Wrath. The context of Lamentations is the failure of God's people to accomplish His mission, thus incurring His wrath. The first acrostic begins with the rod of God's wrath. The wrath of man does not accomplish the righteousness of God, but the wrath of God does. Man has so abused anger that we project onto God our twisted use of anger and forget that anger is part of God's nature. God could not be good if He did not get angry. It is gentle Jesus who whipped up fury in the temple and cursed the fig tree (because they did not fulfil God's mission for them). It is the same God who sent His own people into exile for refusing His mission. God is indeed a God of wrath, but unlike humans who start merciful and end angry, this lament starts with God's anger and ends with the promise that mercy will outlast judgment.

Faithfulness. The second acrostic begins with God's faithfulness and ends with why He does not answer prayer. This refusal of God to answer man's requests outside their obedience reminds us the mission is God's. Because the mission is His, we pray, wait, and obey. Missions is not doing what we want to do, nor asking God to underwrite our strategies. Missions is finding out what God is doing, listening for our orders, and running to His battle. God is faithful even when man is not, and the success of missions does not rest on me or you. God will be glorified among all peoples whether or not we participate. Non-participation in the pursuit of the global glory of Jesus among all nations is our loss, never God's. Missions is not complicated; it's hard. But missions is doable because it rests on God's faithfulness, and any weakling can pray, wait, and obey.

Peoples. The third acrostic begins with reference to the nations and reveals that all nations will be judged and "mercied" just as Israel was. The inspired poet calls down the anger of God asking that his enemies be pursued and destroyed from under the heavens. The beautiful heart of God in this wondrous dance of missions *does* include pursuit and destruction of all peoples, but it *also* includes pursuit, mercy, and eternal life. Wrath is part of the story and inescapably the destiny of some, of many, but it does not have to be for all. Mercy is still great and grace still free, and it is still offered to the Najdi Saudis if only someone will tell them.

PRAYER FOCUS: *Arab, Saudi Najdi of Syria (Evangelical: 0.0%)*

AUGUST 27: FROM VISION TO GLORY

TODAY'S READING: EZEKIEL 1–4

"God, I pray Thee, light these idle sticks of my life and may I burn for Thee. Consume my life, my God, for it is Thine. I seek not a long life, but a full one, like you, Lord Jesus."

JIM ELLIOT

Ezekiel was a young priest taken into exile in Babylon in 597 BC. He appears to have received his prophetic, missionary call five years later around 592–3 BC. A contemporary of Jeremiah, Ezekiel preached the same message of judgment on Judah and the nations. Ezekiel prophesied that the temple would be destroyed, for the national breaking of covenant meant God's glory long since left the building and no godless stones endure forever. What will endure forever and among all nations is the glory of God, which is how Ezekiel begins.

Ezekiel was exiled in the first wave, and his compatriots were consumed with going home. Ezekiel on the other hand was consumed with his vision of God, a vision he cannot adequately express in words. The first missionary lesson of Ezekiel is that a vision of God makes you forget your natural gravitation to the comforts of home and draws you to the fearsome discomfort of the glory of God. The first response of missions is to fall on our face before this glorious God and to listen to His voice. The second missionary lesson of Ezekiel is that we should fear God more than we fear men and that we need to speak His words no matter what it costs us. A reoccurring fallacy in mission is that we will be loved. Fearing God more than fearing man includes reconciling our future to being hated, just like Jesus promised (Matt. 24:9, 14).

The context of a glorious, force-us-to-the-ground power of a vision of God provides the setting for our call to be warning watchmen with foreheads stronger than all our critics. Missions obedience is not centrally about whether anyone listens to us; it is about the glory of God and we as messengers relaying His gospel no matter how we are received. As if God's glory knocking Ezekiel flat once was not enough, it happened again. Ezekiel was told to be a warning watchman and then told to shut up until ordered to speak. What is consistent in our speaking or in our silence is the glory of God.

Some scholars think Paul's reference to the knowledge of the glory of God when explaining his call (2 Cor. 4:4–6) was a quotation of Ezekiel 1. From Ezekiel to Paul to you and me, the process is the same. It all starts with a vision of the glory of God, and it all ends with the glory of God among all nations. The prophetic people of God are always the missionary people of God because they have had visions of the glorious God in all His terrifying beauty. The words of God always follow the visions of God.

PRAYER FOCUS: *Shughni, Shugnan-Rushan of Tajikistan (Evangelical: 0.0%)*

AUGUST 28: SHUDDER AT THE REALITY

TODAY'S READING: EZEKIEL 5-8

"I believe it will only be known on the Last Day how much has been accomplished in missionary work by the prayers of earnest believers at home... I do earnestly covet a volume of prayer for my... work—but oh! for a volume of faith too. Will you give this?"

JAMES FRASER

The prophets gave the people of God the explanation of exile they least wanted to hear: "It was not that YHWH was defeated; on the contrary, he was as much in control as ever. YHWH was still in the business of dealing with His enemies. The question now was, who is YHWH's real enemy? Or more pointed still, *who was Israel's real enemy?* Israel by its persistent rebellion against their covenant Lord had turned YHWH into their own enemy." It is the multiplied disobedience of God's people that makes Him furious and leads Him to a public display of being against His own people, exercising judgment in the sight of the nations. It is the missionary disobedience of His own that infuriates the God of glory. The inclusion of all peoples in His kingdom is something so central to the heart of God that when His children stray from that assignment He takes drastic action. This drastic action underlines that God has no favorite children. "God's impartiality in dealing with the nations, with its correlative truth that there was no favorite status for Israel, is upheld by those prophets closest to exile.... Ezekiel set Jerusalem 'in the midst of the nations', but only to show not some kind of elevation beyond punishment but rather the horrific deformity of the fact they were behaving even worse than the nations that did not know YHWH." No nation can claim a favoritism that exempts it from God's discipline. No matter if you're the first born, the natural child, or the grafted-in, if you stray from God's passion for all His children through selfish, sensual, disobedient living, He will deal with you furiously.

God's fury is connected to His pain. It is staggering to realize that our spiritual adultery can crush God's heart. That the almighty God of glory makes Himself vulnerable to our infidelity is mind-blowing, yet even His fury is intended for us to be a means of knowing Him. To envision a God above pain and above wrath directed at His disobedient loved ones is to make an idol of Him and to miss the heinous reality of what our philandering has done. No person, mission agency, church, or nation is exempt from the wrath of God if we disobey His command to live holy lives that He might use us to woo all nations to Him. Our glorious God is not bound to our idolatrous theology nor to our idolatrous buildings. If we will not be God's missionary people, He will leave us, too. We are in the season where He lifts us through the Spirit by a lock of hair, childish and petulant as we are, that we might see from where we have fallen. Let us shudder at the reality that we could now become God's enemy. Let us remind ourselves that being missionary is how we prove we are His friends.

PRAYER FOCUS: *Shirazi of Tanzania (Evangelical: 0.0%)*

Missions is God-centric. We are not fully missionary until we come to terms with God being more important than the lost, more important than the ministry, more important than the missionary. There is a rebellious core to all men that resists the supremacy of God in all things, including missions. When missions becomes a tool to make us feel good about being little saviors, we have lost the plot. When we are offended by hell, judgment, and the Lord killing the wicked, we have lost the plot. We have essentially forgotten that all things are about our glorious God and that whatever God does is good.

Ezekiel helps us in our missiology because over and again he focused on the glory of God, the weight of the presence of God, and the reality that God is explosively more than we can understand, contain, or explain. The poetic language of Ezekiel is presented with qualifying language such as "the appearance of the likeness of" (Eze. 10:1) because even Ezekiel struggled to articulate the wondrous things that he saw. Even in the struggle to communicate heavenly realities to finite minds, God's passions are present. Ezekiel compared the unacceptable behavior of God's children to the customs of the Gentiles around them, and judgment on God's chosen was strategically intended: "Then they shall know that I am the LORD, when I scatter them among the nations and disburse them through the countries. But I will spare a few of their men from the sword, from famine, and from pestilence, that they may declare all their abominations among the Gentiles wherever they go. Then they shall know that I am the LORD" (12:15–16).

Because God is marvelously, beautifully, and eternally good, it is right that all things (including missions) be about Him. When missions is essentially about the glory of God, the weight of His indescribable presence, it cannot be essentially about how many are judged and go to hell or what happens to His disobedient family. If missions is supremely about God, then it must center on God's well-being, not on man's. And this, of course, offends us and all men. We distort the love of God for man into something that replaces the love of God for God, which is idolatry and vainglory.

Ezekiel's prophetic, missionary, and God-centered visions remind us that all things are about God, He cannot be dishonored, and all things go well. When God is dishonored, He removes His presence and we live in "ichabod"—vainglory, non-glory. Our greatest good is found in glorifying God, living holy before Him, seeking His good. It is hard for self-centered us, but the good of God means His judgments, His punishments, His wrath, and His terror are good. It's hard for stony hearts to hear and think that God loves Himself more than He loves me or the nations. It's hard, for deep within we still want to be the center of God's affections. But we are not. And missions truly begins and new hearts of flesh received when we understand that God is the center of God. And this truth is glorious.

PRAYER FOCUS: *Thai, Northern of Thailand (Evangelical: 0.27%)*

AUGUST 30: GOD IS AT WAR

TODAY'S READING: EZEKIEL 13-15

"It is far easier for churches to give thousands of dollars than to find one of their members who will walk into the slums for a decade."

VIV GRIGG

Ezekiel used the national symbol of Israel, the vine, to show that all creation has a purpose and that if we do not fulfill our created purpose, we will be judged by fire. Israel's purpose was to be a light to the Gentiles, a demonstration of how good and glorious Jehovah is. Ezekiel and all the prophets wrestled with the tragedy that Israel rebelled against her purpose and thus faced God's fire. The covenant was simple, and any violation of it brought judgment and loss. Ezekiel's tension was in the discrepancy between the reality of the consequences of the violated covenant that he prophesied and the lies of those who predicted peace. Through Ezekiel, God said those that espoused peace spoke out of their own heart, followed their own spirit, and spoke nonsense and envisioned lies. The lie was that one can break the missionary covenant of God (to be His blessing to all nations) without consequence. The truth is that those who live unholy, those who are not wholly dedicated to the glory of God among all peoples will face the wind of His fury and the floods of His anger and then they will know that He is the Lord.

Missional reality has not changed from Old Testament to New. Jesus said He did not come to bring peace but a sword. Jesus will come in glory to judge the living and the dead, and most will be judged to fiery hell, for narrow is the way that leads to life and few will find it. Jesus said the kingdom suffers violence and the violent take it by force. The reality is God is at war. He fights for His own glory and He fights against all that is wicked. And when God goes to war, we know who wins. Those who fight against the absolute glory of God by diminishing hell and His judgment are insulting His character. You cannot undermine hell without undermining the glory of God. To diminish hell (disavow eternal punishment and the horribly painful consequences of dishonoring God or breaking His covenant) is to make the same mistake as the false prophets of Ezekiel's day: "Because with lies you have strengthened the hands of the wicked, so that he does not turn from his wicked way to save his life" (Ezek. 13:22). What distinguishes Christian missions from all other efforts is that we tell the truth about hell and heaven, that we love people enough to open our mouths and tell them that God is at war with them, that judgment looms, and that if they do not repent, they will suffer eternally for their foolish rebellion. In this sense, preaching the full gospel is the greatest act of love we can offer the nations, even if we are hated for so loving.

PRAYER FOCUS: *Algerian, Arabic-Speaking of Tunisia (Evangelical: 0.2%)*

AUGUST 31: BEAUTIFUL ONCE AGAIN

TODAY'S READING: EZEKIEL 16–17

The church has no beauty outside of being the covenantal, missionary people of God. The people of God are only attractive when we focus on living for the glory of Jesus among the nations. God chose Israel when she was weak, naked, and infantile, wallowing in her own blood and uncared for. God ransomed an abandoned baby from Canaan's land who had Amorite and Hittite heritage, loved her, and made her attractive so that her fame went out among the nations because of her beauty, for it was bestowed by His splendor. God's intention has ever been to woo the nations through example. What He does with His weak, helpless, ugly, abandoned children, He wants to do to all peoples of earth.

Unfortunately, the church often commits the same ghastly betrayal as did Israel. Ezekiel compared Israel's treachery to the ritual temple prostitution of the day. In a twisted act of religious devotion, the nations around Israel used sexual rituals in their worship. Israel in effect does the same thing with Egyptians, Philistines, Assyrians, and Chaldeans. Israel does the doubly unthinkable: Not only did she cheat on the only One who purely loved, rescued, and married her (that person also happened to be Jehovah), she cheated on Him for the disgusting filth of demonic lovers who never loved her.

We sit in comfortable review 2,500 years after Israel's spiritual adultery, dignified in our horror. We sagely shake our heads at the foolish fornication of a beloved people who traded the splendid love of God for the sordid lust of the nations. But are we any better? The prophetic books of the Bible are intended to both shock and convict us, to shake us into the realization that they describe our reality, not just the heinous acts of history. God has not changed, and unfortunately neither have His people. God still finds us wallowing in our blood, unloved. God rescues and nourishes us and by His splendor makes us beautiful. God does this both to love us and to love all peoples with us, to set us up as a display of His goodness, an example of what He longs to do for all the nations of the world. In our folly, because we are admired by the world, we lose our head and give our hearts to what is vile. The attention flatters and seduces us because we want more, and we cheat on God just like our fathers did. And God warns us that He will deal with us, we who despised Him by breaking the covenant, as we have dealt with Him.

Whenever the people of God do what they do to gain attention, we take steps towards adultery. Our beauty is only real when it remains a reflection of God's splendor, when it serves as an invitation to all peoples that the splendor of God can make them beautiful, too. How amazing that our reconciliation is linked to both our older and younger siblings joining the covenant and to quiet, repentant humility. Despite our serial adultery, there is yet hope, and it combines humility and missions. If the church of God can once again be humble and missionary, we can once again be beautiful.

PRAYER FOCUS: *Kurd, Turkish-Speaking of Turkey (Evangelical: 0.0%)*

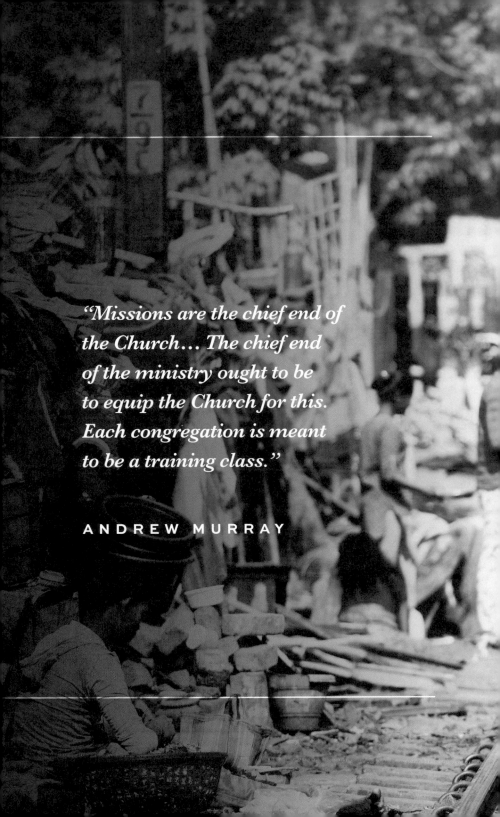

"Missions are the chief end of
the Church… The chief end
of the ministry ought to be
to equip the Church for this.
Each congregation is meant
to be a training class."

ANDREW MURRAY

SEPTEMBER

SEPTEMBER 1: THE JUSTICE OF HELL

TODAY'S READING: EZEKIEL 18-20

"Some are trapped in boxes of pea-sized Christianity, full of myths about missions that rob them of incentive to care about the unreached."

DAVID BRYANT

Because God is the Creator of the whole earth and the Lord of history, He has creator rights to do as He pleases with any nation. Because God is God, His judgments are always right, always justified. "It is one thing to make such affirmations. It is another to defend them before a shocked and smarting people, for whom the fall of Jerusalem proved only that YHWH was incompetent or unfair…. On the contrary, argued Ezekiel… what YHWH had done was utterly justified by the persistent and incorrigible rebellion of the house of Israel. Israel's flagrant sin had left God with no moral alternative but to punish them. Not only must *Israel* be made to know that YHWH had done nothing against Jerusalem 'without cause'…*the nations too* will come to know it, in order that the justice of God's ways may be known on earth."[1]

Ezekiel's point was that justice is central to God's rule over every nation. Ezekiel's view of Israel's history was that God had given them what they deserved in order to protect His own name among the nations. God had revealed Himself to His people in the sight of the nations, and the nations were keen observers of the interaction, for it was exemplary of how things would go for them if they submitted to Jehovah's rule. The Judge of the earth will surely do right, for the character of God is exercised in forgiveness and mercy, extended to all nations, not just Israel. Biblically, the mercy of Jehovah is never a cancellation of hell or judgment but a potential inclusion of all the peoples of earth in His mercy. The Judge of all the earth *will* send all unrepentant sinners to hell (including Israelites) and He *will* invite all repentant sinners to His eternal heaven (including Gentiles). It is in this missionary application of extended mercy that the Judge of *all* the earth does right.

Today's "unfair" cry is that a good God would never eternally punish man in hell. The twin blindness of this thinking is (1) a tainted view of how merciful and holy God is and (2) a twisted view of how evil man is. The Bible clearly states that God is not willing that any should perish and that He takes no delight in the death of the wicked. It clearly states that God is patient beyond all reasonable limits. It clearly states that what God did for Israel He wants to do for all people—and this means both heaven and hell. Biblically, the sting of hell is addressed in this simple way: It's eternally real, but you don't have to go there; in fact, no person from any people needs to suffer there eternally. The mercy of God does not remove the reality of hell; the mercy of God has made a way for all peoples to live eternally blessed in heaven. Because God is just and the Justifier of all peoples, hell is just and justified. In fact, hell proves both the justice and mercy of God. It proves His justice, for it's what we all deserve. It proves His mercy, for He painfully paid for a means of escape. The Judge of all the earth did right.

PRAYER FOCUS: *Bedouin, Gulf of United Arab Emirates (Evangelical: 0.0%)*

SEPTEMBER 2: GOD'S ANGRY NATURE

TODAY'S READING: EZEKIEL 21–22

Anger is part of God's nature—He is just slow to get there. There are some things so intolerable to God that He is committed to eradicating them, and wrath is the energy of God that removes anything wicked from His presence. God could not be good if He let what is bad endure and thrive; thus, the holy goodness of God is the source and justification for His fiery anger. When Jehovah said to His people, "I…will blow on you with the fire of My wrath, and you shall be melted…then you shall know that I, the LORD, have poured out My fury on you" (Eze. 22:21–22), it is a revelation of His goodness. We know the Lord by His tender mercy and by His wrathful judgments. God could not be good if He did not get angry.

The reality that God's judgment of covenant-breaking Israel included Him making them a reproach to all nations and a mockery to all countries indicates the nature of their sin. A big God redeemed little Israel in order to be a light to all nations. Their failure to live in a way that honored God and broadcast His glories to all peoples was so grievous it invoked the fiery anger of God. It is no small thing for the people of God *in any age* to live in such a way that God is dishonored. Dishonoring God at home means He will not use us to spread His fame among the nations. Because we were created to make Him famous among all peoples, dishonoring Him at home is dishonoring Him abroad which is wicked and incurs appropriate wrath.

Zedekiah made an alliance with Egypt to rebel against Babylon and evidently Ammon (present-day Jordan) joined in. Ezekiel prophesied that Nebuchadnezzar would punish both nations, and it was somewhat arbitrary which one was crushed first. Ezekiel's point was that the day of judgment came for both (Israel in Ezekiel 21:25, Ammon in v. 29), and that nothing would remain the same: *All* was overthrown "until He comes whose right it is, and I will give it to Him" (vv. 26–27). All nations will be judged—some for not sending missionaries, some for not receiving them. Ezekiel was missionary both in his prophecies about appropriate angry judgment and anticipatory joy about the Messiah, the joy of all nations, who will one day take His rightful place. He was missionary because both dilemma and deliverance were/are centered on the glory of God among the nations.

God's anger is a last resort. Ezekiel warned that prophet, priest, and prince have all failed. He even said there was no person to stand in the gap at all which was why God consumed with the fire of His wrath. Inversely then, if God finds someone to contend for His purposes in the land, there is hope of judgment averted. The missionary church is the only hope for the pagan nation, both sending and receiving. When we stand in the gap contending for the glory of God among all peoples, God withholds wrath on our own nation and on the nation in which we proclaim. How ironic that the world is only preserved from wrath because of God's missionary people, yet God's missionary people are not welcome in the very lands that by their fidelity they preserve.

PRAYER FOCUS: *South Asian, Bengali-Speaking of United Kingdom (Evangelical: 0.13%)*

SEPTEMBER 3: PEOPLE LEARN THE HARD WAY

TODAY'S READING: EZEKIEL 23-24

Through Ezekiel, God compared Israel and Judah to two sisters who marry the same man. Both sisters became adulterous, and the implication was that the younger sister was even more blameworthy, for she did not learn from the excesses and the judgment of her predecessor. Both sisters belonged to the Lord and both cheated on Him. Not only did the sisters cheat on their Husband, but they were the aggressors in adulterous affairs. They were not seduced but did the seducing. As a result, the Lord alienated Himself from them.

There was a twisted blindness to Israel and Judah's harlotry. Because God chose them in covenant commitment, they wrongly assumed He would never alienate Himself from them. They presumed that even though they sinned, they could stay married. They presumed in some disturbing way that at least in their infidelity they were not as bad as the other nations. It became inconceivable to them that God would ever divorce them. Perverted pride led them to think they could cheat on God cavalierly because He was bound to them regardless of anything they did. It shocked them that God would end the marriage because they serially broke the covenant. Their presumption led to their destruction.

In one sense today's church is the chronological sibling of yesterday's Israel. Jehovah brought us into covenant with Himself. He gave us the assignment to be a light to all the Gentiles. We are to live holy, intimate, consecrated lives with our Husband. Sadly, we have not learned the lesson of our older sister's infidelities, and we face her fate. It is inconceivable to us that God will ever divorce us. It is unthinkable to today's church that God will ever break covenant with us. Perverted pride leads us away from winning the nations to Him to seducing them to ourselves. It is shocking hubris to think that God will only slap the church on our filthy wrists and stay with us regardless of what we do because He has no other options for His glory among all peoples.

God asked Ezekiel to live out what looms over the church. God told Ezekiel that he would lose his wife, the desire of his eyes, and that he could not issue one word of woe. God used the loss of Ezekiel's beloved to show the loss of His bride. Ronald Reagan, when asked why he left the Democratic Party to join the Republicans, answered: "I didn't leave the Democratic party; the Democratic party left me." And so it was with Israel and Judah—God did not divorce them, they divorced Him. They cheated on God by immorally seducing the nations to themselves rather than winning them to Jehovah through purity. We the church, as the younger sister of Israel, now follow suit. We have brought other lovers into our homes, hearts, and churches, and God will not be bound to our immorality. If the church will not be true, God will find another way to glorify His name among the nations.

PRAYER FOCUS: *Arab, Iraqi of United States (Evangelical: 0.20%)*

SEPTEMBER 4: HELL IS A REAL PLACE

TODAY'S READING: EZEKIEL 25-27

"Someone asked, Will the heathen who have never heard the Gospel be saved? It is more a question with me whether we—who have the Gospel and fail to give it to those who have not—can be saved."

CHARLES SPURGEON

God's judgments on the nations are intended to help them know He is the Jehovah. In the missionary metanarrative of the Bible, this means Jehovah is the God of Israel, the God who created all men and all nations to worship Him, and in that worship to find their highest fulfilment. This means that the nations who do not worship the God of Israel will end up worshiping themselves, and in that worship choose God's judgment for themselves—both devastation now and eternal suffering in the hereafter. There is no suffering like eternal suffering. Yes, there is eternal suffering, and yes, the prophetic message is the missionary message that hell is real, and since man was created to be eternal, it is so much wiser if we will receive eternal life by grace. A merciful God sends or allows the little hells of earth to alert us to the certain eternal hell of eternity. Today's chapters in Ezekiel portray the living hell that descends on all who rebel against Jehovah's rule, and the warnings of God's fury are intended to remind us that eternal hell is real and should be avoided. After all, hell is the just idea of a loving God.

Dorothy Sayers objected to the ongoing objection of hell: "[Let] us face the facts. The doctrine of hell is not 'mediaeval': it is Christ's. It is not a device of 'mediaeval priestcraft' for frightening people into giving money to the church: it is Christ's deliberate judgment on sin. The imagery of the undying worm and the unquenchable fire derives, not from 'mediaeval superstition,' but originally from the Prophet Isaiah, and it was Christ who emphatically used it.… It confronts us in the oldest and least 'edited' of the gospels: it is explicit in many of the most familiar parables and implicit in many more: it bulks far larger in the teaching than one realizes, until one reads the Evangelists [gospels] through instead of picking out the most comfortable texts: one cannot get rid of it without tearing the New Testament to tatters. **We cannot repudiate Hell without altogether repudiating Christ.**"

As Ezekiel thundered away in prophetic ire, he did us one great service: He reminds us that God's fiery judgment is real and that the wrath of God looms over every unreached people. Our missionary Bible does not view the unreached people of the world as innocent victims. Our holy God views the unreached people of the world as intentional rebels who insult Him and arrogantly worship themselves. Faithful missionaries must warn those they love that their future is undoubtedly eternal suffering unless they repent and turn from worshipping themselves to worshipping Jehovah, the God of Israel.

PRAYER FOCUS: *Kazakh of Uzbekistan (Evangelical: 0.15%)*

SEPTEMBER 5: THE PROPHETS INSIST

TODAY'S READING: EZEKIEL 28–30

*"The Indian is making an amazing discovery, namely that Christianity
and Jesus are not the same—that they may have Jesus without the system
that has been built up around him in the West."*

E. STANLEY JONES

Tyre (present-day Lebanon) was the center of Phoenician power and the founders of the city-state/empire of Carthage in North Africa. Borrowing from Egyptian thought, the rulers of Tyre set themselves up as mini-gods, which did not broker favor with Jehovah. Tyre had physical things to be proud of: They were "in Eden, in the garden of God," beautiful and full of splendor (Eze. 28:13, 17). Problem was, they were also full of themselves, and there can be only One who fills all things. The missionary message of the Bible is so consistent. What does God do when He encounters pompous people and peoples? He comes against them for His ultimate goals.

I am convinced that we miss out on leveraging God's crucial self-revelation to the nations during times of crisis and disaster. Sovereign God is completely in control of history and nature. When God judges the proud nations and peoples of earth who rebel and resist His glorious rule, we rush to console them without pointing out that the disaster that fell on their heads was directly from God, that God will be glorified in their midst, and that they will know He is the Lord through His terrible judgments so that He will be hallowed among them. Yes, I know this sounds extreme, but it is the missionary message of Ezekiel. All nations, all peoples, all persons who arrogantly resist the lordship of Jesus Christ have one divine pronouncement against them, and it's no different for the Khmer of Vietnam today than it was for Tyre and Sidon 2,500 years ago. Jehovah simply says, "I am against you. I will be glorified in your midst. You will know that I am the Lord. I will execute judgment on you. I will be hallowed in your midst" (see Eze. 28:22). Let us not make the classic, repeated missionary mistake of rushing to bind up the wounds of the nations that God struck in judgment *while* staying silent about the reason for the calamity. Is it really love if we do not explain why God's terrifying judgments were unleashed and they are but precursors?

We don't like the prophets, for they insist we talk about judgment, they insist we call all peoples to repentance, and they insist indeed that love is the motive but looming wrath is the message. We read the Bible with revisionist eyes, taking out what we don't like and putting in what we do. Yes, the motive for Jesus, Paul, and the Apostles was love—it drips from them—but love is not often mentioned in their messaging. Let us take the prophetic, missionary messaging of the Bible seriously and look carefully at what Jesus, Paul, and the Apostles actually preached. Then let us do likewise. There is a reason Jesus repeatedly warned us that His messengers will be hated. One of the great ironies of love is that it drives us to preach repentance and it makes the true lover hated. Woe to us if all men speak well of us, and blessings upon us if we are true and loving enough to warn about the wrath to come.

PRAYER FOCUS: *Khmer of Vietnam (Evangelical: 1.87%)*

SEPTEMBER 6: THE GOAL IS REDEMPTION

TODAY'S READING: EZEKIEL 31–33

God makes the nations "great." He made Egypt beautiful so that all the trees of Eden envied it. God made Egypt fall, delivering her into the hand of "the mighty one of the nations" and casting her down into hell (Eze. 31:11). The God of Israel made the nations shake at the sound of Egypt's fall, troubling and astonishing many peoples so that they trembled for their own lives every moment. God's judgments reveal that all nations who resist His glorious rule will end in hell with their weapons of war, for He will cause His terror in the land of the living.

The judging of all proud, unrepentant nations to hell is the context for the watchman passages of Ezekiel 33. Indeed, we are to warn all nations of God's looming judgment, and if we do not, their blood will be on our head. The judging of all proud, unrepentant nations to hell is the context of God declaring He has no pleasure in the death of the wicked and that His ways are eminently fair. The missionary message is simple: Hell is real, God's people are assigned to warn about hell, God does not want anyone to go to hell, and if anyone does go to hell, it is because God is fair. Woe to us if we complicate God's simple message by failing to articulate it.

As is always true in God's punitive measures, the goal is redemption. "There is…a tremendous universality about Ezekiel's passion for the **knowledge of God.** The one thing that burns throughout his whole book is the certainty that YHWH will be known as God by Israel **and** by the nations. The phrase **'then you (they) will know that I am YHWH'** is virtually Ezekiel's signature—occurring some eighty times in his prophetic memoir…. It means that the nations will come to the decisive and irrevocable knowledge that YHWH alone is the true and living God, unique in His identity, universal in His rule, and unchallenged in His power."

Ezekiel was a missionary prophet because his hope and certainty was that all the nations will know that Jehovah, the God of Israel, is the only true God. In every oracle, this invitation to the nations issued forth from Ezekiel's missionary mouth. To be firm on the reality of hell, to warn all peoples of God's judgment, and to remind all nations that God does not want anyone to eternally suffer in hell is the most loving use of our earthly lives. God's desire that all nations know Him is not a transitory one. It's not a longing for a time-bound relationship for the few short days of earth. It's the eternal heart of heaven longing for all peoples to enjoy full and free relationship with their Creator. If we take nothing else from missionary-minded Ezekiel, let us commit to love enough to warn the Yemeni and all peoples of earth of the danger of eternal death and the promise of eternal life.

PRAYER FOCUS: *Arab, Tihami of Yemen (Evangelical: 0.0%)*

SEPTEMBER 7: NOT FOR OUR SAKE

TODAY'S READING: EZEKIEL 34–36

*"Good spiritual logistics demand that we use every means available to us today
to reach a lost world that desperately needs Christ."*

CLARENCE W. JONES

The prophetic voice is too often consigned to sounding harsh and jarring. That element is certainly present, and sometimes necessary, but prophecy always issues from tender hearts, not mean-spirited ones. God's message through Ezekiel was that He will seek what was lost, save His flock, and establish His Messiah over them, living among them and making them a blessing so there will be "showers of blessing" (Eze. 34:26). All these are tributaries to the meta-current of the Bible: God living with and loving His people and His people living holy lives that are used to bless all nations. This is the context of the hymn we love—not showers of personal dividends, but showers of God's global glory on all peoples of earth.

We forget that Ezekiel was also a priest, that his priestly heart was pastoral, that he agonized over the bad news of death and judgment he must break to those he loved as necessarily antecedent to good news of God's seeking and saving. We forgo the reality that God's seeking and saving is never centered on us, nor restricted to the small group of humans we are most comfortable around. God promises the renewal of His people on this striking premise: "I do not do this for your sake, O house of Israel, but for My holy name's sake, which you have profaned among the nations wherever you went. And I will sanctify My great name, which has been profaned among the nations, which you have profaned in their midst; and the nations shall know that I am the LORD… when I am hallowed in you before their eyes" (36:22–23). The prophetic, pastoral, and missionary heart of God all converge in Ezekiel. Jesus does indeed save us from our sins. O, hallelujah! But shockingly He does not do this for our sake (alone). God saves for His holy name's sake, for His glory among the nations. Ezekiel's one string missionary banjo is strummed again—that the nations shall know Jehovah and that they will know Him when He is hallowed in us *before their eyes.*

How will the grand purposes of God be accomplished in our generation? When we leave all the conveniences of home and all the joys of family to hallow Jehovah in Afghanistan before the very eyes of three million-plus Hazara. What are the showers of blessing we seek after mercy drops have fallen around us? That the family of God would be increased by those who speak Hazaragi because through us the great Shepherd of their souls sought out what was lost, because through us He pastored them and invited them into Messiah's benevolent rule. What is the prophetic, pastoral, missionary convergence? To be clear, as we cry about judgment and wrath, to be hopeful, as we cry out that all God's lost are being sought by Him, and to be humble, as we cry up that God does all this for His sake among all peoples.

PRAYER FOCUS: *Hazara of Afghanistan (Evangelical: 0.03%)*

SEPTEMBER 8: CAN THESE BONES LIVE?

TODAY'S READING: EZEKIEL 37-39

R epeatedly over time critical battles have been fought in narrow spaces. Defending armies strategically chose valleys or mountain passes to make their stand, for a restricted space balanced the field when the attacking army had superior numbers. A balanced field did not mean less casualties but more, for the defended space was so strategic it must be taken at any cost. Ezekiel's famous vision of the valley of dry bones evokes images of the consequences of a fierce battle and the deadly cost paid by its warriors. The fact that the bones were many and dry signifies the attacking force not only overwhelmed the defenders, but that the battle happened long ago. The territory and the battle were lost, seemingly irretrievably. Can these bones live?

Algeria was home to Tertullian and the great church councils of Carthage. Today, it's overwhelmingly Muslim and the bones of the church fathers are dry and bleached in the valleys of time. Can these bones live? Alexandria was home to Athanasius and Origen; now it's a city of approximately 13 million Muslims. Can these bones live? The Arabian Peninsula provided the first worshipers of baby Jesus and the first bishops to the councils of Nicaea and Chalcedon; now it's the cradle of Islam. Can these bones live? Rome, Antioch, Damascus, Ephesus, and Ireland were once home to bishops, revival centers, and missionary sending bases; now they host secularism, paganism, idolatry, and decay. Can these bones live?

The missionary heart never stops believing that God can breathe new life into dry bones, that God can revisit old battlefields with new Spirit, that God can open up graves and cause the dead to rise. The God who can make dry bones live can certainly unite all the peoples of earth under His magnificent rule. There will be one Shepherd over us all. His tabernacle will be among us, and He will be our God and we His people. All this so that the *nations* will know that He is God. The missionary spirit starts with believing that God will bring the dry bones of lost, resistant peoples to the life of His Spirit and that this life is found by the nations in the knowledge of God.

Ezekiel 37 and 38 are apocalyptic (revelatory) chapters in this same understanding: God wants all nations to know Him and He will use all His power and glory to affect His glorious goal. Both resurrection (life from the dead) and apocalypse (death to the living) have the same goal: that the nations would know the Lord. "That the nations may know Me" (38:16) is the goal of all life and death recorded in Scripture as the Lord plainly explains: "Thus I will magnify Myself and sanctify Myself, and I will be known in the eyes of many nations. Then they shall know that I am the Lord" (38:23). Can these bones live? Can the ancient peoples be resurrected to new life in Christ? Surely it is coming, and it shall be done. The first missionary act is to believe that the dead will rise, and that life and death are both wisely wielded to lead all peoples to the knowledge of God.

PRAYER FOCUS: *Bedouin, Tajakant of Algeria (Evangelical: 0.0%)*

SEPTEMBER 9: PARADISE LOST AND FOUND

TODAY'S READING: EZEKIEL 40–42

"No factor of human migration is more significant than that of the Holy Spirit who has decreed all such movement for the sake of mission."

CODY LORANCE

Eternity past was perfect as eternity future will be. Other than the first chapters of Genesis and the last chapter of Revelation, the Bible deals with the ramifications of what went wrong and how God will fix it. In the first Adam all men sinned and in the second Adam all peoples of earth have opportunity for redemption. We are in the "middle-earth" period between the perfections of eternity past and future. The prophetic voice of Ezekiel deals both with the ramifications of the fall and the hope of perfection one day. His vision of the temple is simply a looking and longing for that unending day when all is perfect, beautiful, holy, and orderly again, when all peoples of earth are represented before the King of heaven, home at last.

Missionaries and missionary-minded disciples as prophetic voices are bearers of news. The bad news does not make sense outside the grieved understanding of the loss of perfection in eternity past. The good news does not make sense outside the future hope for perfection eternally. Thus, it is imperative in our message that we offer both the sobriety of paradise lost and the joyful promise of paradise found again and gained. When we sit with those broken by sin, lost in rebellion, crushed by evil, and blinded by lies to communicate the gospel, it must be with both eternities in mind. We must grieve what is lost with the unconverted in order to fully appreciate what is promised. The good news of the gospel starts with the bad news, and God's prophetic, missionary people must be adept at breaking both. We must cry together before we dance together.

If paradise was once lost, you may wonder what will keep us from losing it again. If Adam from the first Eden fell, how will we not follow in that tragic course? What will keep us in the Eden to come? The horrific consequences of the fall gave us one priceless and enduring lesson in the collective. Now we know the difference. Before the fall Adam had no reference for how good perfection was and how bad sin is. Together we now bear the painful scars that help us see the difference between eternal life and eternal death. Because Ezekiel knew what a desecrated, despoiled temple looked like, he had a greater appreciation and longing for a perfected one. Beauty in its purest earthly form is a regret of the lost glory of eternity past and a relish of the coming glory of eternity future. Man has an innate certainty within him that all things are meant to be good, pure, beautiful, and perfect. When we encounter the effects of our fall, it is an acknowledgement that what is broken was once beautifully whole, and one day soon shall again be.

PRAYER FOCUS: *Kayastha (Hindu Traditions) of Bangladesh (Evangelical: 0.0%)*

SEPTEMBER 10: GATEKEEPERS OF GOD'S HOUSE

TODAY'S READING: EZEKIEL 43-45

The primary ministry of the Christian is to the Lord Himself. The primary inheritance and possession of the minister, missionary, or disciple is the Lord Himself. If we flag or fail in this primary understanding, if we do not focus on Him, we lose us and ultimately, we lose the nations. As Adolf Schlatter wrote in 1938, "Do we know Jesus? If we do not know Him, we no longer know ourselves." We can only stay true to ourselves and our missionary calling as the church if we truly know the Lord and stay true to Him. Ezekiel was so struck by the glories of God that he couldn't really explain or articulate what he saw and experienced, but he knew he met Jehovah and that Jehovah was not to be trifled with.

Jehovah sternly reminded Ezekiel: "Let Us have no more of your abominations.... No foreigner, uncircumcised in heart...shall enter My sanctuary, including any foreigner who is among the children of Israel" (Eze. 44:6, 9). We are not "more good" than God. We err in both our exclusion and our inclusion. If we don't really understand God's missionary rules, we pervert our missionary assignment. We did not create the terms for inclusion in God's family and access into His house, nor can we change them. Universalism is an insult and affront to the God who sacrificed His own Son, who is more holy than we could ever be and more merciful than we will ever understand. Any thinking regarding the salvation of man which explicitly or implicitly denies the necessity of Christ's brutal death on the cross is an evil and monstrous insult to the Godhead. In fact, universalism says the Father needlessly killed His own Son. We are gatekeepers of God's house tasked with the fearful responsibility of stewarding who comes in and who stays out. We do the nations no favors (and give our glorious God no respect) when we pervert His eternal laws regarding salvation, the gospel, the cross, and the realities of hell and heaven. The flipside of the inclusive heart of God to include all peoples around His eternal throne is that there is only one way to enter—through the atoning work of Jesus on the cross, all through the blood.

I assume Israel thought they were loving and generous when they found a place for the nations in the temple contrary to God's proscribed way. In reality, that act was heinous and offensive, and they were punished for it with disaster and exile. Because our primary ministry is to Jesus Himself, we must know Him first, best, and accurately. If we don't know how holy He is, we don't know how depraved we are. If we don't know how depraved we are, we won't think clearly about how depraved the nations are. If we don't think clearly about how depraved the nations are, we will try to argue or rationalize them into God's family which ends in disaster for them and us. To attempt to usher a friend or the Cham of Cambodia into heaven contrary to the way God demands is to hate them—and worse to hate Him. If we know Jesus, we know that He is gloriously the only means by which all peoples may be saved.

PRAYER FOCUS: *Cham, Western of Cambodia (Evangelical: 0.01%)*

SEPTEMBER 11: IN THE DESPERATE DEPTHS

TODAY'S READING: EZEKIEL 46-48

❝The Lord is there" are the comforting closing words of Ezekiel (Eze. 48:35). It is ever about God and His fulfilling presence. We need Jesus more than Jesus needs us. In truth, He does not need us at all. He was perfectly content in the unity of the Godhead before the creation of man. We in no sense fill a gap in God's being. God plus nothing is everything; God plus redeemed men and women from every people is everything plus. The whole cosmos being healthy is symbolized by the healing river that flows out of the perfect temple of God. The river that flows from His temple gets deeper the further away it gets—symbolic of God's extended life and missionary heart.

The closing chapters of Ezekiel reinforce God's missionary intentions. Life was never intended for confinement to the temple nor to Israel. Life was ever intended to flow from God's people to all peoples of the earth. God's chosen people and places are ever intended to be rivers, moving, spreading out into the desert, bringing the life of God to every tribe, tongue, and people. The river of life spreading to all nations in healing power is doubly encouraging because its depth increases as its distance from the source increases. Increased depth with increased distance from home is not incidental. The testimony of the missionary is that Jesus becomes sweeter to us the further we flow from home. Shed no tears for missionaries; wherever they go, Jehovah is there. Don't be afraid of leaving the comfort of your church or family to go to the demonized, difficult places of earth. Jehovah is there in a depth that your very spiritual comforts shield you from. Oh, that every Christian would know the joy of launching out into the deep, leaving the safe shoals of the home shore for the great depths of the knowledge of God that often can only be experienced far from home in desperate depths.

We need missions more than missions needs us, for missions launches us into depth. Certainly, God uses human agents to pray, provide for, and proclaim His glorious gospel, but the God who needs nothing honors us by giving us a part. He is not dependent on us at any level. The plans of God will triumph no matter how we respond. What is not in question is God's victory and glory among every people. What is up for answer is whether we will be blessed because we obeyed and participated in what He is doing. We need missions because it thrusts us into the center of God's heart centered on the lost in the deepest evil and darkest places. Thrust into those places (geographical *and* situational) we quickly realize we have no strength and no ability in the flesh to contribute. Overwhelmed we are propelled into the presence of Jesus and find Him sweeter in adversity than we do in affluence. We go to the gates of hell and find "the Lord is there." We launch into the deep only to be overwhelmed by encountering the depth of God. Be not afraid to represent God among the unreached far from home. It may be the only way to move yourself and your family from the shallows.

PRAYER FOCUS: *Jew, English Speaking of Canada (Evangelical: 0.0%)*

SEPTEMBER 12: YOU'RE NOT SPECIAL

TODAY'S READING: JOEL

Not much is known about Joel except that he prophesied at a time when the temple was still standing. Some have that time being the 8th century BC and others during the late Persian period around 300 years later. Whatever the timing, Joel's main warning is the terrible day of the Lord which in the immediate meant a plague of locusts on Israel (horrific to an agricultural society) and in the future the universal day of judgment on all nations.

The day of the Lord in Israel's thinking was a day of their vindication. They did not realize that in calling for justice they were calling judgment down on themselves. It is an error common to all self-righteous men of every age. Fundamental to their/our mistake is the misconception that God chose us because we are inherently special or better. But what if we are chosen for the opposite reason? What if we are chosen precisely because we are not special? Israel was chosen to be God's missionary people, not because they were stronger than all, but because they were weaker than all and because God wanted to use them as an example that He could save and use everyone and anyone. Similarly, the church (the people of God) are not chosen because we are wise, good, or strong, for God descends on the weak and foolish of the world as declaration that the Spirit will descend on all people from all nations.

When God's people forget they were chosen for God's universal ambition to redeem a remnant from every people, they face His wrath, whether that be locusts or apocalypse. When God's people repent of their arrogance, rend their hearts and return to the Lord, He not only forgives and refreshes them with the former and latter rain and His presence in their midst, He also refreshes their memory with His original intention: "And it shall come to pass afterward that I will pour out My Spirit on all flesh" (Joel 2:28)! The pouring out of the Spirit is for the express purpose that the nations be wakened as there are multitudes in the valley of decision.

It was no mistake then at the day of Pentecost when Peter stood and quoted the prophet Joel, that the ones he addressed were Iranians (Parthians, Medes, and Elamites), Iraqi, Kuwaiti, and Syrian (Mesopotamia), Israeli and Palestinian (Judea), Turks (Cappadocia, Pontus, Asia, Phrygia, and Pamphylia), Egyptians, Libyans, Romans, Cretans, and Arabs (Acts 2:9–11) hearing in their own tongues the wonderful works of God. For the message of Joel passed on through Peter was that God has ever wanted to pour out His Spirit on all peoples.

We cannot read Joel without seeing again God's missionary heart for all peoples. We cannot read Joel without a surge of joy that God promised His Spirit will be poured out on *all* flesh, including the Daza of Chad. On that great and terrible day of the Lord, I look forward to hearing worship in the Dazaga tongue. In this great day God looks for Spirit-filled missionaries to lift their tongues where other tongues do not yet praise.

PRAYER FOCUS: *Tubu, Daza of Chad (Evangelical: 0.0%)*

SEPTEMBER 13: THE HISTORY
OF ANSWERED PRAYER
TODAY'S READING: DANIEL 1-3

"Every step in the progress of missions is directly traceable to prayer."

ARTHUR T. PIERSON

When Nebuchadnezzar had a troubling dream no one could answer, Daniel enlisted the help of friends to pray that they would seek mercies from the God of heaven. "Seek mercies from the God of heaven," what a wonderful definition of prayer. Daniel pointed out that it was not his education (three years training and studying), but the God of heaven who reveals secrets and sends mercies—and this the result of prayer.

The fact of the history of missions being the history of answered prayer is a truism missionary David Irwin illustrated well. "In 1983 while in Nairobi, Kenya, I was invited by a...layman to a feast in his house. He also invited an Islamic professor who is an authority on spirits. Over 30 people were present as the professor talked of his control over spirits: 'I can put a spirit of barrenness on a woman and she will never bear a child. I can put a spirit on a man driving an automobile and make him crash and his life will be destroyed. I have that power!'

"I listened for two hours as the man talked about his destructive powers. Something welled up inside me and I began to pray quietly in the Spirit. At the end of the evening I was asked by the host to close in prayer. Politely, as the occasion required, I thanked God for making us His creatures, sustaining us and creating our universe, for giving us life, children, and blessings. I prayed the things that would be common to a Jew, a Christian, or a Muslim. Suddenly these yearnings I'd had for two hours could be contained no longer. I yielded myself to the Holy Spirit and began to pray in a gushing almost uncontrolled way. I was almost embarrassed, because I didn't know what the Spirit was trying to do. He so dominated that all I could do was respond, praying in tongues for 10 or 15 minutes. The young man interpreting for me stepped back because he could not interpret that. A holy hush fell in that house, creating an attitude of reverence in the presence of God. I was so overcome when I finally stopped that I began to weep.

"Sitting at the far end of the table were two very old men with long white beards; they were scholars of Islam, teachers at the mosque. Out of the response to the gentleness of the Spirit and the work of God that night, one of the men stood with tears running down his cheeks and said: 'You know I have read in the Koran all my life about Isa and about the Spirit of God. I would just like to say to you, sir, that tonight we felt the Holy Spirit, and it is like a cleansing to our souls.'"

PRAYER FOCUS: *Tujia of China (Evangelical: 1.0%)*

SEPTEMBER 14: BUT IF NOT

TODAY'S READING: DANIEL 4-6

There were four deportations from Jerusalem to Babylon (605, 597, 586 and 581 BC) with Daniel taken in the earliest one. Some scholars say the opening chapters of Daniel are more about Nebuchadnezzar than Daniel, but it seems they are more about prayer and about God than about any man. Yes, Nebuchadnezzar had earthly power and authority. Yes, Daniel and friends were given knowledge, skill, and understanding. Yes, Daniel worked hard, earned favor, and astoundingly served for over 60 years as a senior civil servant (as a foreigner!) for the superpower of his day. But the opening six chapters of Daniel direct our attention to the God who answered prayer and delivered the faithful representatives of the God of heaven, those who knew when to refuse to bow to the powers on earth, even if it meant fiery furnaces or lion's dens.

"It was May of 1940. The dreaded German Panzar Division had swept across Europe and had the British Army pinned down at Dunkirk. The British and French generals thought that the narrow twisting roads and paths through the Ardennes Forest were too small to allow the mass movement of the large German tanks and machinery. However, German General Heinz Guderian managed to maneuver the large tank force through the Ardennes and was ready to strike. The British commander was able to get a communiqué back to Britain that consisted of just three words, 'but if not!' Those three words sparked a surge of courage, determination and downright grit throughout the British military and the entire civilian population. Those three words brought about the bravest, most unorthodox successful rescue of any army in the pages of history."

Those same three words to a constituency biblically literate enough to know they originated in Daniel also galvanized a nation to pray, with King George calling for prayer from all his citizens. Pray they did. God delivered on the beaches of Dunkirk just as He did at the fiery furnace and the lion's den. Yet, the declaration "but if not" transcends deliverance; it is a stake in the ground, the contention that as long as God is glorified, we will be satisfied whether by life or death.

Missionaries are not guaranteed safety among the peoples of earth, but we are guaranteed the presence of Jesus. We know God is able to deliver us, but if not, we still won't bow. What's the worst that can happen? We go to our heavenly home and God uses what seems gory for His glory among the people He sent us to love, warn, and woo. After all, martyrdom is God's idea, not the devil's. God is the one who sent His only Son to die for the ransom of all peoples. The devil is astute enough to know with Tertullian that "the blood of the martyrs is indeed the seed of the church," so he distracts, divides, seduces, confuses, and pesters us enough to remove our attention from God's mission. The devil tends to revert to making martyrs when his bloodlust overcomes his senses. Those that die for Jesus are neither fools nor heroes; how can they be when God is the One who choses that death? "But if not!" is the cry of the missionary. It is the joy that whether by life or by death God will be glorified among the nations.

PRAYER FOCUS: *Fulani of Cote d-Ivoire (Evangelical: 0.0%)*

The final six chapters of Daniel are prophetic in that they foretold details of the inter-testament period, a period of which the Bible is largely silent, though the Apocrypha is not. In these "silent years," Alexander the Great defeated the Persians and set up Greek colonies across the Middle East. This period of Greek dominance gave us Pericles, Aeschylus, Sophocles, Euripides, Socrates, Plato, Aristotle among others. When Alexander died, his conquered territory was divided among four generals; the two most prominent launched dynasties in Egypt (Ptolemies) and Syria (Seleucids). Jewish nationalists (led by priests who would become kings) overthrew the Greeks in the Maccabean revolt of 166 BC, only to be subdued by the Romans who then controlled Palestine by 63 BC.

"Daniel's visions are the best examples of apocalyptic literature in all the Old Testament. Apocalyptic literature was a particularly Jewish form of writing, fairly common in the centuries after the destruction of Jerusalem in 586 BC. Apocalyptic texts usually presented symbolic visions, with every detail appearing to have a specific hidden meaning, though not always explaining it. The primary purpose of apocalyptic writing was to comfort those who were being persecuted for their faith. Such comfort was found in knowing that all the kingdoms of earth, however powerful they might appear, would one day be crushed and replaced by God's eternal kingdom, in which the faithful would be vindicated (Dan. 2:44, 45, 7:27; 8:25)."

Apocalyptic writing (Daniel and Revelation) can have multiple fulfilments: the time of the visionary, the time of coming persecution, and then ultimate fulfilment on the great, terrible day of the Lord when King Jesus comes back to rule and reign. Over and again in Daniel we are reminded that Jehovah reigns in the kingdom of men, setting those He chooses over the kingdoms for His purposes. The context for Daniel 7 to 9 is the persecution to come from the Greeks and Romans. First, the land of Palestine was a Ptolemaic kingdom, then a Seleucid one. "The Seleucid king Antiochus IV Epiphanes (175–164 BC) sought to establish Greek religion and culture in his realm and to wipe out rival beliefs. He outlawed the Jewish faith, burned all copies he could find of the Jewish Scripture, and in 167 BC sacrificed pigs to Zeus on the altar of the Jerusalem temple. Faithful Jews rebelled [the Maccabean revolt] and in 164 BC were able to cleanse and rededicate the temple, a rededication still celebrated by Jews today, Hanukkah."

The missions implications are simple and profound. The Ancient of Days yet rules from His eternal throne in the kingdom of men. Persecution and trouble are a normal part of gospel advance, but just for a season. At the end the Lord and His people will prevail. If we hold steady, Messiah will come. Let us be resolved that our missions future includes suffering and enduring abominable things, resolved not to doubt the sovereign goodness of God, resolved that God will use our sufferings to display His glory among all nations, and resolved to remember that Jesus comes to His people and on one marvelous day for His people.

PRAYER FOCUS: *Oromo, Jima of Ethiopia (Evangelical: 1.3%)*

SEPTEMBER 16: ONE DAY THE CYCLE WILL END

TODAY'S READING: DANIEL 10–12

"Anywhere provided it be forward."

DAVID LIVINGSTONE

It's ironic that liberal scholars use the accuracy of biblical prophecies to undermine belief in prophecy. Daniel's visions were so precise in chapters 11 and 12 that some say they must have been written after the events. The truth is, God does indeed rule in the kingdoms of men and He knows the end from the beginning. God has a very specific design for history and He helps His greatly beloved know exactly the destiny of nations. What the angelic messenger affirmed to Daniel about the fate of nations the Holy Spirit affirms to us today: God's will for the nations will be done in detail; of this we can have full assurance.

What is that will? That all nations, representatives of every ethnic entity in history will be gathered around the throne worshiping Jesus forever. This beatific vision was and is resisted by demonic powers. The prince of the kingdom of Persia resisted God's will, followed by the prince of Greece, followed by other demonic powers through the centuries, all united in one frantic effort: to thwart God's desire that all nations be represented around the throne. The anti-mission-of-God spirits were active in the Old Testament, resisted Jesus, and howl today. Jesus used imagery from Daniel to accuse oppressive leaders in Jerusalem (Mark 14:62) and John applied Daniel's visions to the Romans in his day (Rev. 13).

Antiochus Epiphanes (meaning "the manifest god") was nicknamed Antiochus Epimanes (meaning "mad"). He represents all the powers of time that want to control the world and reject King Jesus as Lord of all nations. Antiochus spoke blasphemies against the God of gods (Dan. 11:36) and with great wrath tried to establish his own world order and glory—a plan which included the extermination of God's people. Nothing new under the sun. All through history evil powers have used evil men to dominate the world to the exclusion of God's people. The closing words of Daniel are helpful as we endure the latest cycle of demonic rebellion: "[Go] your way till the end, for you shall rest [die], and will arise to your inheritance at the end of days" (12:13).

Daniel's message is the message of the Bible. God is the God of all the peoples of earth and the only One to be gloried. He will redeem to Himself a remnant of every ethnic group. He will be their King and live among them. Other kings and powers will rise and fall, the people of God will live and die, but one day the cycle will end, the King will come, and the dead will rise to our inheritance: an eternal feast for all peoples with the Bridegroom in glory. Let us actively wait for this. Let us live and die in the peaceful assurance that God has definitively determined how it all ends. God does indeed rule in the kingdom of men, and He shall rule forever. We can endure, live, and die in that steadfast hope.

PRAYER FOCUS: *Maninka, Konyanka of Guinea (Evangelical: 0.01%)*

SEPTEMBER 17: TRUE RELIGIOUS FREEDOM

TODAY'S READING: EZRA 1-3

Ezra begins where 2 Chronicles ends: the decree of Cyrus in 538 BC that allowed the Jewish exiles to return to Israel. Originally, Nehemiah was not disconnected from Ezra, and with the likelihood that Ezra (a priest) authored Chronicles, these four books (1 and 2 Chronicles, Ezra, Nehemiah) should be read as a connected narrative. Sheshbazzar led the first return in 538-7 BC, followed by a group led by Zerubbabel (a direct descendent of David). Zerubbabel rebuilt the temple, Ezra rebuilt the community of faith, and Nehemiah rebuilt the city walls. Each met internal opposition and experienced disappointment. Post-exilic hopes were dashed as what began with promise ended in frustration, with the result that eyes were lifted to the only lasting hope: the return of the Messiah and a kingdom that would include all nations. Interestingly, the big lesson of Ezra-Nehemiah is that often life and reform movements end in disappointment and infighting. When faced with broken dreams and crushed hopes, we are to lift our eyes from our little picture to regain the big tapestry view: the King, all nations, and the blessed hope of heaven where all peoples get along because they are focused on glorifying the Lamb.

The Jews were not the only ones Cyrus allowed to go home. An extra-biblical proclamation found in the "Cyrus Cylinder" shows the pluralistic nature of Cyrus' public policy. He felt his power was due to his tolerance (in contrast to Babylonian cruelty) and he said that his god Marduk (he called the "lord of the gods") wanted all sanctuaries of all religions rebuilt. Cyrus changed the name of god depending on whom he was addressing, showing his political and religious dexterity. Thankful as we may be for the religious liberties the powers of our day grant us, let us bear in mind that their agenda does not match ours. The freedom of worship is not to be confused with the mandate to save souls, to confront all ideologies that deny the deity of Christ, and to ransom brands from the burning of false religions. We are "conversionists," commanded to rescue from darkness and bring the nations into the kingdom of the Son of His love (Col. 1:13). A missions temptation is to settle for religious liberty, but we must contend for the preaching of a Jesus-centered gospel. We must insist on calling for repentance and prioritize the saving of souls.

Secular and pluralistic powers will, for the most part, grant us liberty to go home and worship our way, but if we insist on leaving home and demanding that all peoples of the earth worship the God of Israel, they are not so accommodating. The rebuilt temple was to the young as religious freedom is to most of us—a cause for celebration. But the old remember that the temple was intended as a rallying place for all nations. The sages among us will not let us settle for personal religious freedom. We must fight to set captured souls free, and that will mean wrath from pluralists, even as it means glory for God. The Lord will stir up the spirit of kings, and we must yet stir up the 49 million Hindus from their pluralism, preaching Christ alone. This is true religious freedom.

PRAYER FOCUS: *Chamar (Hindu Traditions) of India (Evangelical: 0.0%)*

SEPTEMBER 18: SOMETHING TO SMILE ABOUT

TODAY'S READING: EZRA 4-6; PSALM 137

Reforms in post-exilic Israel ground to a halt, opposition halted the rebuilding, and Haggai and Zechariah were about to insert their prophetic oars. In the meantime, letters were sent back and forth in great tattle-tale bureaucratic fashion, and the Lord proved Himself sovereign even in the paperwork. An officious Persian official in Palestine, Tattenai, took names and intimidated. But when that didn't work, he wrote to the king, only to be surprised that his letter had the opposite effect he intended. Not only was he ordered to allow the work to go forward, but government taxes were to pay the bill!

Not much has changed in 2,500 years. Officials still watch, take names, and intimidate. Missionaries still push past their fears and external threats and put their hand to making disciples, breaking anti-gospel laws. God still intervenes at the highest levels through surprising advocates and unexpected resources. My wife and I landed in Saudi Arabia, a little apprehensive due to the reputation of the kingdom's intolerance for the gospel, but my wife rightly noted: "It's like the land of Oz! We've made it so much bigger in our minds than it actually is." God's missionary people must rise above the intimidating spirits (human and demonic) of our times and territories and in full faith believe that God is sovereign over all officials. We must believe that unlikely support from unlikely influencers is about to be granted. In this light, we should pray for the life of the king of Saudi Arabia and his sons. In this light, truly central to our missionary work is to believe (John 6)! All over our world in the most unlikely places, from Somalia to Saudi to North Korea and beyond, the King of kings still sends His divine decrees to the halls of earthly power: "Let the work of this house of God alone.... Let the cost be paid at the king's expense" (Ezra 6:7–8).

As a result of God's intervention, His people celebrated the Passover with joy with the heart of the Assyrian king towards them. What a wonderful way to take communion! The next time you hold the bread and wine in your hand, look to the God of heaven with joy that He can (and will) turn the hearts of presidents, kings, and dictators toward the people of God to help, establish, fund, and protect them. Communion is a missionary sacrament, reminding us Jesus is King over all the earth, He rules and overrules, He is the grand Sovereign who gives orders from on high that every smaller potentate must enforce and pay for. How glad we can be when we partake of the broken body of Christ, knowing that He broke every chain and He commands the obedience of every minor power!

No power should intimidate the missionary. As plenipotentiaries of the great King, let us stand tall, resist any anti-gospel edicts, and smile into the wind of intimidation and oppression, for we know Who is really in charge. What joy when our majestic God compels the very forces that resist gospel advance to assist the very ones they try to destroy. This is certainly something for us all to smile about.

PRAYER FOCUS: *Madura of Indonesia (Evangelical: 0.01%)*

SEPTEMBER 19: THE CHOICE IN OUR HANDS

TODAY'S READING: HAGGAI

Prophets held out for a transformed remnant who would live in the presence of Jehovah, just like the original covenant. In 520 BC, Zerubbabel led the people of God home. Hopes were high, and the rebuilding of the temple began. They finished the temple foundation but then opposition arose, so their attention turned to fields that laid fallow for decades and homes that needed rebuilding. In the old days, prophets spoke to kings. But with no more kings, there was direct communication to the populace. Haggai stepped up and spoke four messages over four months to the priests and people.

Haggai's first message was about misplaced priorities. The people were building fancy homes while God's house was yet incomplete. The message still needs to be heard today. God decreed that His house will be a house of prayer for all peoples (Isa. 56:7), and that is still 7,000 unreached people groups from happening. Instead, we build up personal wealth, cabins on lakes, campers in driveways, and multimillion-dollar church facilities, while multibillions of people stumble into hell in disrepair. What does God think about us who prioritize the building of elegant homes and church buildings when His house is in such disrepair? Yes, the foundations of God's global house are laid, but 7,000 representative living stones are still missing. It's fairly obvious where we should put our energy and resources.

Haggai's second message was about dashed expectations. This rebuilt temple was modest compared to the old. Haggai drew on Isaiah and Micah to remind God's people of the new Jerusalem from which the King will rule over representatives of all nations. Haggai called the people to work in the hope of what will be, not what was. Zechariah made the same point to the same people at the same time when he exhorted them not to despise the day of small beginnings (Zech. 4:10). We will dream of huge movements of peoples to the Lord and great Pentecost outpourings, even as we faithfully pursue the one Muslim, Hindu, Buddhist, animist, and atheist that Jesus brings to our doors.

Haggai's third message is about covenant faithfulness and purity. If you're not humble and holy, it doesn't matter what you build. The renowned missionary to India, E. Stanley Jones said, "I have found that all real evangelistic work begins in the evangelist. Around the world the problem of Christian work is the problem of the Christian worker…. Christian service cannot rise above the Christian servant." Jesus must be glorified in us to be glorified through us.

Haggai's final message regarded the future hope of God's kingdom ruled by David's heir, the Messianic King. It is certain, yet our choices and participation matter. Haggai asks if we will we work towards what God has willed. Jesus is coming! The Lord can stir up our spirits to build the Lord's house, and He exhorts us to work "for I am with you [and] My Spirit remains among you" (Hag. 2:4–5). God's house will be filled, and there is ample space for more Iranians. What is not yet determined is the part we will play; that choice is in our hands. Jesus is still looking for men and women who love His global house more than their own.

PRAYER FOCUS: *Kurd, Southern of Iran (Evangelical: 0.03%)*

SEPTEMBER 20: STAND OUR SACRED GROUND
TODAY'S READING: ZECHARIAH 1-4

Zechariah, a contemporary of Haggai, was a little more poetic and visionary. Not exclusively focused on the temple, he envisioned a rebuilt nation, a glorious new Jerusalem, and a Davidic king. He referred to both Zerubbabel (from David's line) and Joshua (the priest, called "the branch") with messianic language, symbolism understood to have international and missionary implications. When David's heir was established, *all* nations would be a part of that kingdom.

Zechariah explained to the people that judgment fell due to their failure to keep covenant with Jehovah. In a series of bizarre dreams, God communicated the way forward, the way to not repeat past sins. God spoke through dreams and continues to do so today to seekers around the world. Zechariah's dreams are arranged symmetrically, bookended by a picture of God's four horsemen attentively watching over the nations (dreams 1 and 8). Dreams 2 and 7 refer to past sins that led to exile, and dreams 3 and 6 focus on the rebuilding of a new Jerusalem that will be a beacon to all nations who join God's people in worship. The center of the dream sequence (dreams 4 and 5) concern the key historical figures of that time: Zerubbabel the political leader and Joshua the priest. The point being that neither politicians nor ministers can do anything outside of the Spirit of God (Zech. 4:6).

Zechariah 4 is my favorite chapter of the Bible. I love the image of a weak, chastened people staring across the global landscape wondering how on earth the God of heaven will use them to glorify Himself among all peoples. The answer is quite simple. It centers on grace, faith, and Spirit. When faced with mountains (monolithic religious systems that deny the deity and supremacy of Jesus), we stand our sacred ground and shout grace at them: "Who are you, O great mountain? You shall become a plain before the Messiah's glory!" There is something powerful about shouting grace at giants, about rising up in faith, about not despising our small reality, and about charging in the Spirit. It is the spirit of David that runs towards the challenge crying: "Who are you to defy the Lord God of Israel? You come against me with weapons of terror, but I run at you with the armor of grace that all the world will know there is a God in Israel!"

Pulsating through our veins and spirits as we charge over boundaries and barriers, as we struggle through language learning, as we lean into gale force winds of resistance, as we battle for visas and residence, as we push through heat and fatigue, as we jostle with friends and foes for sure footing, as we engage unreached peoples, as we struggle through sleepless nights, as we absorb the blows of the accusing enemy, as we swing our Bible swords and throw our prayerful spears, as we sow our gospel seed must be the reminder and encouragement: Not by might, not by power, but by My Spirit, says the Lord of hosts.

PRAYER FOCUS: *Kurd, Central of Iraq (Evangelical: 0.01%)*

SEPTEMBER 21: READY TO PARTICIPATE

TODAY'S READING: ZECHARIAH 5–8

A group of Israelites asked Zechariah in December 586 BC if they should stop grieving the destruction of the temple, if it's wrong to grieve if God's Messiah is soon to arrive. Zechariah responded by repeating the ancient missionary challenge: The generation that will see Messiah come is the one that fulfils the covenant and extends Jehovah's blessings to all peoples of earth. Zechariah reversed their question and asked: "Will you become the kinds of people who are ready to receive and participate in God's coming kingdom?"

The answer to Zechariah's question is the same today as it was then. Because God is immutable, there is no possibility of His plan and purposes changing. From the beginning to the end of the Bible, God desires a people that will be holy, so He can live among them and bless them, so they may bless all the nations of the world. This is why God's Spirit has rest when His people go to dark territories, for God is at peace when His glory is extended globally. This is why God sets up earthly kings and eternal kingdom, that both would be branches to bear His glory among all peoples. This is why the prophet foretold the worship of every tongue as "even those from afar shall come and build the temple of the LORD...if you diligently obey the voice of the LORD" (Zech. 6:15). Yes, indeed God is zealous for Zion and surely He will "save [His] people from the land of the east and from the land of the west...and they shall dwell in the midst of Jerusalem. They shall be [His] people and [He] will be their God" (8:7).

The error of Christian Zionists is not that they are wrong about God returning the Jews to their land; the error is to separate physical presence in the promised land from spiritual union with the promises of God. A return to the land is meaningless outside of the Jews returning to their God and thus being a missionary blessing to all nations of earth. There is no enduring guarantee of land without Lordship. There is no legitimate Lordship without missionary impulse. For "just as you were a curse among the nations... so I will save you, and you shall be a blessing" (v. 13). This is the exact verbiage God used with Abraham: You shall be a blessing. To whom? To all the nations for "thus says the LORD of hosts: Peoples shall yet come" (v. 20).

The prophetic message is so consistent: Because you failed to be the holy missionary people of God winning the nations to Jehovah, you were punished and exiled among the nations. When God brings you back to unmerited favor, it is that you extend His blessings to all peoples of the earth, for both exile and restoration center on God being glorified among the nations. If by God's grace you return from the exile and pain of disobedience to the God of all nations, do not think for one moment that restored favor will linger outside a sustained fervor for the glory of your gracious God among all peoples of this earth. In all our inconsistencies and changes, God remains immutable. He never deviates from orchestrating all things for His own fame among all His peoples of earth.

PRAYER FOCUS: *Jew, Eastern Yiddish Speaking of Israel (Evangelical: 0.0%)*

SEPTEMBER 22: FROM SEA TO SEA

TODAY'S READING: ZECHARIAH 9–14

We often isolate the beautiful passages of the coming of Jesus from their prophetic missionary context. Zechariah foretold that King Jesus would come lowly and riding on a donkey, that He would speak peace to nations and His dominion would extend from sea to sea. This beautiful picture of the universal reign of Jesus came squarely after the Lord spoke through Zechariah of the destruction of Tyre, the one who had power in the sea. For two centuries Tyre was the impregnable port of the Persians, their base to extend their empire over the Mediterranean nations. Tyre was an island city, impossible to attack from land. In 332 BC, Alexander the Great's troops built a causeway 300 yards wide and half a mile long to the island. He captured Tyre, sold 30,000 citizens into slavery, and crucified 2,000 of the city-state's leaders.

This gory context of a sea power humbled immediately preceded the prophecy of the Messiah who would come humbly to establish His reign over all nations, who would reign from sea to sea over mixed races of people who, cleansed from abominations, shall be for our God. It is impossible to read the story of Jesus' triumphal entry outside the context of nations being subdued by the Jesus the Great whose causeway to our heart was built with blood and crosses, not with stones and rubble. In fact, Jesus the Great will easily subdue the Greeks and all peoples; He will subdue by saving them, and they shall be like jewels in His crown. I wonder how many in the crowd on Palm Sunday two millennia ago recalled Tyre, Alexander, and peace to all nations. My guess, not many. In the frenzy of their own hopeful excitement, they forgot that "us" must ever mean "all peoples." Let us not make the same mistake when we gather to lift our praise to the coming King. In every church of every land, let praises be lifted inseparable from the understanding that Jesus must be crowned King of all peoples from sea to sea. Those who welcome Jesus enthusiastically for what He can do for *them*, outside the understanding that His blessings are for all nations, are the first to egregiously turn on Him, sell Him for thirty pieces of silver, disappointed that He is a global God, not a personal genie.

Zechariah saw beyond the triumphal entry, past Judas' betrayal, and past the resistance of the nations and the crucifixion to revival among God's people. They will indeed look on Jesus who they pierced, and in that day, a fountain shall be opened for the house of David. Let's remember that God's promise to David was an eternal King, a gentle Shepherd who will bring His people through fire, an awesome Potentate who would return to overcome all nations with glory. In that day, the Lord will be king over all the earth and all the nations shall worship with "holiness to the Lord" engraved on heads and hearts (Zech. 14:20). "Jesus shall reign where'er the sun does his successive journeys run, His kingdom stretch from shore to shore till moons shall wax and wane no more.... Peoples and realms of ev'ry tongue dwell on His love with sweetest song; and infant voices shall proclaim their early blessings on His name."

PRAYER FOCUS: *Eurasian of Japan (Evangelical: 1.5%)*

SEPTEMBER 23: IF WE PERISH, SO BE IT

TODAY'S READING: ESTHER 1-5

Ahasuerus (Xerxes) ironically means "mighty man." The irony is, he was not half as mighty as his father (Darius the Great), nor could he control his wife or counselors. Ahasuerus would famously defeat the Greeks in the battle of Thermopylae in 480 BC, only to lose the war and flee in disgrace. A further irony is that the story does not center on him, nor Haman, nor Mordecai. Nor, astonishingly, does the book mention the name of God. The story revolves around the actions of a woman: Esther. Esther's exploits happened in 483 BC between the return of the exiles. At this time, most Jews still lived in the diaspora where the rules differed from those who lived in the land. Where Ezra and Nehemiah attacked intermarriage, Esther was encouraged towards union with the foreign king. Where Jews in Jerusalem could worship openly, Jews in exile faced more hostility. One of the great lessons for Esther is appropriate for missions today: Faith was not designed to thrive or last hidden; it must stand up fearlessly and face the consequences.

Central to a missionary spirit is the refusal to bow to no one but the king. Mordecai would not bow to Haman, and we must not bow to any authority other than King Jesus. Respect is not to be confused with surrender or agreement. We can respect others' rights to think as they will, but nowhere we are required to affirm that belief nor acquiesce to it. The missionary spirit is the warrior spirit jealous for the glory of God among all peoples, a spirit provoked when King Jesus is insulted and His deity denied, a spirit that cannot stand for the name of Christ to be maligned. Syncretism is still idolatry, and we can contextualize respectfully without ever bowing to false religions or their wicked representatives. When we stand up for Jesus by refusing to bow to idols or ideologies or to compromise with false religions, there is always pushback and consequence, and the palace will not save us from the ramifications. Christianity is antithetical to unending hiding, for we are commissioned to speak up, and if we remain silent, God will bypass us and bring deliverance from another place. The missionary spirit refuses to bow to any but the King and accepts the blows that follow, saying simply and magnificently: "If I perish, I perish."

The missionary life lived in dispersion among the peoples is not to be a hidden presence that only silently leavens through prayer and presence. The missionary life is to be an unbowed present with power proclamation that volunteers to be used as a means of deliverance no matter the cost. The missionary life is not afraid of death; for perish or not perish, the focus is not on us, but on the God of glory and the saving of souls. The missionary life refuses to make self-preservation the goal and is not deluded into thinking powerful friends will shield it from gospel consequences. In this sense Mordecai and Esther were astute missionaries in their day, unbowed, unmoved by the possibility of perishing, not just willing but longing to be used as God's agent of deliverance. If we perish, we perish. It doesn't matter as long as Jesus is glorified and unreached peoples saved.

PRAYER FOCUS: *Arab, North Iraqi of Jordan (Evangelical: 0.2%)*

SEPTEMBER 24: THE BEAUTIFUL, SUBMITTED BRIDE

TODAY'S READING: ESTHER 6–10

A submitted, beautiful bride is irresistible to the king, and the golden scepter of answered prayer is inevitably extended. Queen Esther asked for her life and for the life of her people, a people who were sold, that they be destroyed, killed, and annihilated. When the bride of Christ, beautiful when adorned with submission, approaches the throne of grace and prays for the rescue of unreached peoples, the Lord always extends the glorious scepter of His merciful power. And He does so in wrath, for the Husband King takes any assault on the life of His bride very seriously.

In the Arab world, there is a brave Esther committed to interceding for his people. This man has shielded others who came to faith in Jesus and for his pains has received an unprecedented 900 lashes. Released after his punishment, he refuses to flee the country, for he loves his people too much and his greatest prayer to the King of kings is for his people to be redeemed from bondage, rescued from destruction, saved from eternal death, and plucked from the fires of hell. Will not the Judge of heaven and earth move heaven and earth to grant this request? Will not the glorious scepter of God's power be extended? Will not the King rise in holy wrath to act on behalf of His beloved? He surely will, if we will surely pray.

As a result of Esther's intercession and the king rising up in wrath on behalf of his bride and her people, "the Jews had light and gladness, joy, and honor.... Then many people of the land became Jews, because fear of the Jews fell upon them" (8:16–17). When God's people pray, God arises and His enemies scatter (Psalm 68). When God arises, the righteous are glad, exult before God, rejoice with gladness, and sing praises. Let us lift up a song for Him who rides through deserts, whose name is the Lord and exalt before Him. Responding to the timely intercession of His bride, King Jesus will indeed ride to the spiritually barren peoples of Kazakhstan and all unreached peoples of the world. When the beautifully submitted bride prays, the King arises to save.

The Jewish feast of Purim, still celebrated today, was birthed in prayer for the salvation of a people group. That prayer was prayed by a beautiful, submitted bride. The result was sorrow turned into joy, mourning into dancing, a day of feasting, and gifted delights to one another. The story of Esther is about missionary courage and prayer. If unreached peoples will be snatched from the grave of eternal death, someone will have to take their life in their hands, bear the pain of 900 lashes, and in beautiful submission to the will of the King boldly ask Him to arise in His wrath and scatter His enemies. The ideologies, false religions, and selfish systems that hold all people groups in a death grip are the enemies of the God of all peoples. When the beautiful, submitted bride prays, at cost to herself, the King arises to save. Are we a beautiful, submitted bride? Do we care that our people perish? Are we willing to risk our own life to petition for the lives of our people? A brave Esther in the Arab world bore 900 lashes for his people. Will we not find time to pray for ours?

PRAYER FOCUS: *Uyghur of Kazakhstan (Evangelical: 0.0%)*

SEPTEMBER 25: WE ARE MISSIONARIES EVANGELIZED

TODAY'S READING: EZRA 7–10

God's people are not the only spiritual army with missionary commission. Other faiths and ideologies have global ambition. I have had Muslims weep in their fervent desire to see me embrace Islam, for they truly felt it necessary for my eternal wellbeing. The biblical record, of course, lays out the one way for salvation, and it is Jehovah's way. Jehovah's missionary people are to live so satisfied and so enraptured with Him that the overflow compels us to the peoples of the world, inviting them to join Jehovah's global family, to the shelter from God's wrath under the protection of God's Son.

Ezra's horror at intermarriage with the nations was not racist, but righteous: He knew the plan for God's people was to influence the world towards Jehovah, not to be influenced towards other gods and idols. Intermarriage led to accommodation of other religions, and God's people became a mission field rather than a mission force. Ezra had just returned from exile—the clear punishment on God's people for not being missionary—and here again was the same sin of the fathers, a perversion or prevention of the mission of God. When we mix the world into our worship, our witness is at best warped and at worst wicked, and in that only wrath and weeping in exile await us.

Both missionaries and ministers must be on guard as they seek to contextualize the gospel to culture. While it is appropriate to frame the gospel in ways that can be understood, it is never appropriate to be so influenced by a context that the gospel is defiled in an illicit marriage. There are missionaries who have tried so hard to be relevant that they've lost repentance in their message; in fact, in some cases, the host community believed they had missionized the missionary. What folly it is to congratulate ourselves on being relevant or contextual if that means we have actually removed the stumbling block of the gospel, if we have removed the call to repent, to leave what is false, and to divorce whatever is not of the God of the Bible. It wasn't an easy choice then, and it's not an easy act now.

Our world is not neutral, and we are not the only missionaries out there. We are being evangelized whether we realize it or not. We are wooed, courted, pursued, and romanced. Let us be on guard and not flattered by the attention. Let us not marry into anything that is not the pure family of Jehovah. There are things to which we must say no; there are alliances we cannot and must not make. There are paths we must not travel. Ezra was wise enough to consult God before he married a plan or power. No one likes to be a rubber stamp, least of all the Majesty of heaven, but all too often in missions we develop a strategy and then ask the omniscient Lord to endorse it. If the nations will be won to the Way, we must fast and pray to know the path's details, wed ourselves to it and Him, and live missionary lives impervious to the missionaries who pursue us.

PRAYER FOCUS: *Somali Ajuran of Kenya (Evangelical: 0.08%)*

SEPTEMBER 26: BAND TOGETHER

TODAY'S READING: NEHEMIAH 1–5

Nehemiah arrived in Israel about thirteen years after Ezra; he was the political leader complementing Ezra's spiritual role. Nehemiah's vision was to rebuild the walls of Jerusalem, to protect the nation from ungodly influences. At the same time, Zechariah prophesied that Jerusalem was destined to be a city without walls, surrounded by God's presence and joined by people from all nations. There seems to be a tension between the pastoral defense (let's preserve purity) and the apostolic offense (let's invite all the peoples to join). As with all of God's intended tensions, this union of holiness and harvest is to be managed, not resolved. We can harvest, which requires getting our hands dirty, while keeping our hearts clean. Pastoral care is not wrong as long as it does not become political self-preservation. Pastors, too, must have apostolic hearts; they must compassionately send their best as sheep among wolves. After all, God's heart both loved the Son and sent Him to die. God ordains both suffering and deliverance for us. Paul reminded Timothy of all the persecutions endured *and* the Lord's rescue from them all (2 Tim. 3:11). Practical and spiritual, pastoral and apostolic, they are missionally joined.

Different as Ezra and Nehemiah were, they had striking similarities. They were both super passionate about the purposes of God and both reacted viscerally when those purposes were under threat due to folly of the flock. Like Ezra, Nehemiah reacted to bad news with sitting down, fasting, weeping, and praying. Like Ezra, Nehemiah realized that exile abroad among the nations was punishment for not bringing the nations to Jehovah at home. Like Ezra, Nehemiah was not afraid to ask the principalities of the day for help and received favor from God through earthly king's hands. Two different men with the same passion for the glory of God. How beautiful is our diversity when it's gathered for the glory of Jesus among all peoples! How beautiful when brothers sacrificially give to care for the nations around them; there is an unbreakable bond in that beauty. Moore and Galloway wrote of the bond formed in battle: "In battle our world shrank to the man on our left and the man on our right and the enemy all around. We held each other's lives in our hands and we learned to share our fears, our hopes, our dreams as readily as we shared what little else good came our way."

God uses different forceful personalities to fight for His glory among all peoples. You may be an Ezra or a Nehemiah, or you may be totally unique, but a glory of God is the unity He unleashes on those who band together in their differences for the fame of Jehovah in Laos and beyond. Let's stay holy as we harvest. Let's fight alongside, not against, the strong men and women who share our passion for missions, even if they unleash it differently.

PRAYER FOCUS: *So of Laos (Evangelical: 1.0%)*

SEPTEMBER 27: REFUSE DISTRACTION

TODAY'S READING: NEHEMIAH 6–7

The nations around broken Israel watched as Nehemiah attempted to rebuild Jerusalem's walls. Not liking what they saw, they attempted to get Nehemiah off pace through distraction, fear, and bullying. In our globalized world, the nations are now more able than ever to watch and bully, more determined to get us off point. Nehemiah's reaction to threat is exemplary for missionaries and God's missional people everywhere.

The enemy begins his assault through invitations, opportunities that would take us from focused work to pleasant opportunities. The old adage, "the good is enemy of the best," comes to mind here. Nehemiah saw through the invitation to the harm intended. Some great opportunities will only do us harm. The inability to say "no" has diverted many a missionary. We must have deep within our psyche a single-eyed focus on making disciples among every people, and when good opportunities come our way, we must say with Nehemiah: "I am doing a great work, so that I cannot come down. Why should the work cease while I leave it and go down to you?" (Neh. 6:3). May Jesus help us be so focused on establishing His beautiful church where it doesn't exist that we have the resolve to turn down what turns up—even the good, attractive, and defensible ministry opportunities.

If opportunities don't divert us, the devil devolves to deceit. He slanders. Nehemiah responded succinctly and did not seem to linger in his denial. If the enemy can't get us to physically leave the work, he will attempt to drain our energy from it by dragging us into the court of private opinion and an imagined appeal court. We lay in bed at night going through scenarios, figuring out how to respond, framing arguments, thinking through our justification strategies. We daydream through our work wondering how we can be vindicated. Our emotions are raw and our stomachs in knots, and the work of making disciples suffers. Missionaries and ministers must determine to refute slander at once, turn the page, and focus back on the work.

If slander and infighting don't cripple us, the enemy then tries to terrorize us, sending in his hired guns that we might become afraid and act in a way that is sin. The enemy excels at stretching Goliaths to twice their size. For all the terror of the giant, it was a little stone and little youth that felled him, a boy with no fear and great zeal for the glory of God. The enemy delights at making real opponents of the gospel bigger than they actually are and then bullies like communism seem to fall overnight. The enemy can take the thought of places like Saudi Arabia, Somalia, Yemen, Syria, North Korea, Afghanistan, or Libya and make them seem unassailable, until you arrive and realize they're like the land of Oz. Behind the curtain the giant is anything but. Fear turns small enemies into monsters. Faith sees that all enemies are tiny in the shadow of the Almighty.

As the Bible demonstrates from every page, God is glorified among the nations. Refusing distraction to opportunity, ignoring slander, and fighting for faith over fear, Nehemiah stayed true. If we stay true, He will be glorified in Libya and beyond.

PRAYER FOCUS: *Algerian, Arabic-Speaking of Libya (Evangelical: 0.03%)*

SEPTEMBER 28: MORE OF THE WORD OF GOD

TODAY'S READING: NEHEMIAH 8–10

*"If we want revivals, we must revive our reverence for the Word of God.
If we want conversions, we must put more of God's Word into our sermons; even
if we paraphrase it into our own words, it must still be His Word upon which we
place our reliance, for the only power which will bless men lies in that."*

CHARLES SPURGEON

How beautiful it is when the people of God are attentive to the law. The first seven chapters of Nehemiah do not mention Ezra, but now he enters the scene reading the Scripture in the open square from morning to midday. When Ezra opened the Scriptures to read, the people stood in respect, lifted their heads, shouted "amen," then bowed their heads and worshiped the Lord with their faces to the ground.

Ezra was a scribe. With his friends, he read distinctly from the Scripture and helped the people receive the apostolic sense and understand the meaning. Day by day this reading went on, and we can imagine the sense of shock and awe as God's people were reminded of the big picture. God wants us to be holy. Why? So He can live among us. Why? So He can bless us. Why? So we can bless all the peoples on earth. Why? So they will worship Him. Why? To fulfil prophecy. Why? So the King will come back to reign and restore all things! As the dominoes of biblical understanding fell, how their hearts must have leapt, surging in multiple directions, confessing sins and shame for not being the covenantal missionary people of God, worshiping Him for a second chance. This awakening came from understanding the metanarrative of the Bible and erupted in praise. They stood up and blessed the Lord. One can sense the tremble joy: *We get it! We get it! It's awesome! You chose Abram to bless all peoples, You made a name for yourself in Egypt, You revealed the law in Saudi Arabia, You gave Your people the nations as an inheritance, our fathers sinned and broke the missionary covenant, You justly punished us in exile, for we made a mess of the beautiful mission of God.* Then the people humbly separated themselves from the wicked nations and gave themselves back to God and His law to observe everything He commanded.

It all started with reading the Bible and having a scribe give the meaning, connect the dots, and help the people see the big picture and the end goal. The goal is not "holiness," "judgment," "exile," and "return." We are holy that God might dwell among us that we might be blessed and that every people group be gathered in heaven. Oh, how we need another corporate awakening as in the days of Ezra and Nehemiah. May God lead His people to read, love, and understand His Word. If we get the faintest sense of it, we will again be the missionary people of God He intends.

PRAYER FOCUS: *Bajau, West Coast of Malaysia (Evangelical: 0.0%)*

"Do not think me mad. It is not to make money that I believe a Christian should live. The noblest thing a man can do is just humbly to receive, and then go amongst others and give."

DAVID LIVINGSTONE

Zerubbabel (whose name likely meant "seed of Babylon") was a missionary kid, or at least a third culture kid. His grandfather was Jehoiachin (exiled by the Persians), and now a Persian king-appointed Zerubbabel to be governor of his homeland. Though Zerubbabel was from the royal family of Judah, he was most likely born and certainly grew up in Babylon. Who better to negotiate the tension between cultures than someone familiar with both? Missionary kids, or third culture kids, have the wonderful gift of perspective. Never feel sorry for them. They in turn can be used greatly for the King. Because he was of David's line, because the temple was rebuilt, because the walls of Jerusalem were established, hope began to rise again that the Davidic kingdom would be restored, glory returned, and all the nations affected. But it was not to be. Not yet at least, as Zerubbabel faded into history. As the Old Testament draws to a close, it does so leaving us with the hope and with the longing that Messiah will come.

When the wall was finished, Nehemiah called the Levites from "all their places" to Jerusalem to celebrate the dedication with gladness, thanksgiving, and singing (Neh. 12:27). We can imagine Levites ascending to Jerusalem from the lands all around, singing the psalms of ascent on their way. Many of these psalms date back to David and Solomon, but some were written around the time of Nehemiah and Zerubbabel, like Psalm 126 which praises God for His mighty deliverance of "the captivity of Zion." Since the psalms of ascent appear together, it is likely they were an original collection used as a collective beginning at the second temple period, the time of Nehemiah and Zerubbabel. In fact, it's thought that many of the latter psalms (all the way to Psalm 150) are from the days of the restored temple and the return from exile. This helps us read these psalms in their intended missionary context: "He sends out His command to the earth" (147:15) and "kings of the earth and all peoples; princes and all judges of the earth. Let them praise the name of LORD [Jehovah], for His name alone is exalted; His glory is above the earth and heaven" (148:11, 13).

Nehemiah ends with a reminder of God's missionary intolerance. Nehemiah will not let a Jordanian official access the temple contrary to God's laws, and he will not let his own people marry foreign wives, ripping out his own hair and beard at the provocation. This is but missionary zeal: all peoples are invited into the family and presence of God, but all peoples must approach God in His proscribed way. Thus, we have the two parting shots of the Old Testament before we plunge into the New: The Messiah, the Davidic King, is coming *soon* to set up a kingdom that includes all peoples, but entrance into the Kingdom must be on the King's terms. Come, Lord Jesus! We are ready to bow.

PRAYER FOCUS: *Fulani, Maasina of Mali (Evangelical: 0.01%)*

SEPTEMBER 30: AN APPROPRIATE ENDING
TODAY'S READING: MALACHI

The name Malachi means "my messenger" and was not a proper noun in Hebrew. In other words, an anonymous prophet could very well have written the book of Malachi. Malachi is mentioned nowhere else in Scripture. We're not even certain when he prophesied, though it is likely he did so after the exiled people returned as he referred to them having a governor, not a king. His prophecies are priestly in tone (which probably did not endear him to the priests of the day) and missionary in spirit. In one sense, Malachi was an angry prophet. He was angry that priests were corrupt, angry at familial and national infidelity, angry that man robbed God (for witness among the nations is lost when man is stingy with God's blessings), and angry at those who complain. But in another sense Malachi was full of hope, that on the other side of all this selfish rebellion, God still had His jewels that He would use as His currency, spending them where and how He will to woo the nations to Himself.

A nameless prophet taking up the great missionary theme of the Bible—the name of Jehovah made great among the nations. In this sense Malachi lived out what we should all aspire to: Preach the gospel, die, and be forgotten. There is only one name that shall endure, for "says the LORD of hosts, 'And My name is to be feared among the nations'" (Mal. 1:14). "We can say then, with a broad range of textual support, that a significant part of Israel's eschatological hope in relation to the nations was that ultimately they would bring their worship to YHWH, the one living God of all the earth. And again we must add that such a vision constitutes a major strand within a biblical theology of mission, for it is the indefatigable mission of God—a mission in which He invites our participation—to bring such universal worship of the nations to joyful reality."[2]

The Old Testament ends with the book of Malachi (as the canon has appropriately arranged). Prophetic duty called God's people to repent from sin and saw with increasing clarity that sin would only be dealt with when Messiah came. The prophets increasingly turned their gaze to the horizon of Messianic advent, longing, hoping for the One who would deal with sin and set up a kingdom that included all peoples, a kingdom in which sin would no longer curse us and holiness would define us. We are reminded that God has not changed and He never will. God has the glorified passion to bless all peoples of earth with His majestic presence. He longs to give us what most satisfies us—Himself. He chose a specific person (Abraham) to birth a specific people (Israel) that *all the nations* might be fulfilled in heavenly eternal life. The invitation to life under the rule of the King is extended to all. It's how the Old Testament begins and is constituted. It's how the Old Testament ends. And it's how the New Testament will begin and end. God is a missionary God. The Bible is a missionary book. We are to be His missionary people.

PRAYER FOCUS: *Tuareg, Tamasheq of Mauritania (Evangelical: 0.0%)*

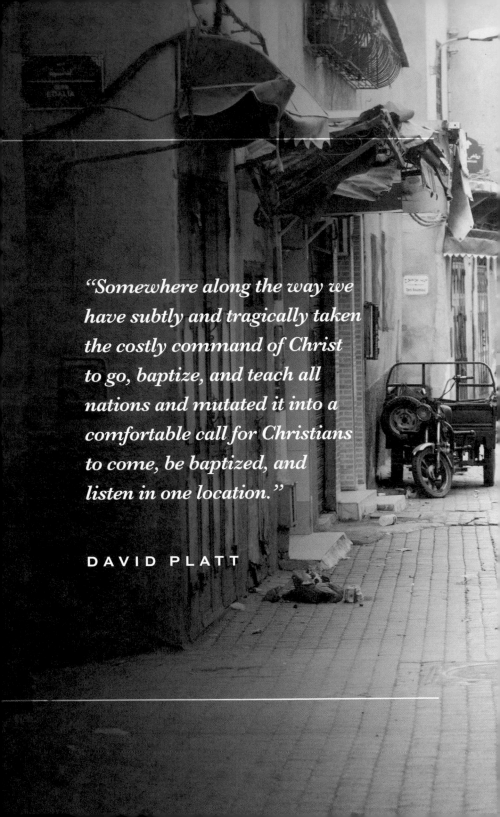

"*Somewhere along the way we have subtly and tragically taken the costly command of Christ to go, baptize, and teach all nations and mutated it into a comfortable call for Christians to come, be baptized, and listen in one location.*"

DAVID PLATT

OCTOBER

OCTOBER 1: STAND AND POINT

TODAY'S READING: LUKE 1; JOHN 1

The Jewish Maccabean revolt (166–160 BC) led to independence from Greek-ruled Syria and ushered in the Hasmonean dynasty, a dynasty of infighting, terrorism, and conflict. Rome, led by General Pompey the Great, invaded Palestine in 63 BC, leaving Roman soldiers stationed in Jerusalem for the next 100 years. In 37 BC Rome allowed Herod the Great to become governor of Galilee and then king of Judea, even though he was technically an Idumean (Edomite) with roots in Jordan. Caesar defeated Pompey and was then assassinated, and in the power struggle that followed Octavian (who took the title Augustus) defeated Anthony and Cleopatra (31 BC). Jesus was born "in the fullness of time" around 5 BC in a land where a Jordanian king served an Italian emperor.

Jesus of Nazareth was born into time and space, a space that included Greeks in the Decapolis, Nabatean Arabs (Herodais, wife of Herod Antipas, an Edomite), Samaritans, Romans, and Lebanese among others. John's Gospel makes it very clear at the beginning that Jesus is the eternal God from outside time and space in whom is life for *all* men, the light for the *whole* world, for as many as receive Him from any nation, He gives the right to become a child of God because they were born of the will of God, not because they were born Jewish! In fact, John opens his reflections on Jesus with a Greek word *logos* and uses it in a way that neither the Jews (divine wisdom) nor the Greeks (universal reason) understood. John says the Word became flesh and lived among His people! In other words, Jesus is God and condescended to live among men, *all* men, not just Hebrews.

Luke, a Greek, wrote to a Greek named Theophilus. He picks up the universal scope of who Jesus is: Jesus will be given the throne of His father David, a direct reference to the Messiah, the One who will rule over all nations as Abraham's promised seed. This international inclusion of all peoples must surely be part of Mary's question, even beyond virgin birth. "Lord, how can it be that *all* peoples are included in Your kingdom?" asked Mary, and she was told, "Nothing is impossible with God" (Luke 1:34–37). When Mary acquiesced to the plan and means of God, she became in effect the first missionary mother: "Let it be, Jehovah. Let my son who is God include all nations in His kingdom, by the overshadowing power of the Holy Spirit." May the missionary spirit of Mary rise all over this world. May mothers of every nation believe in faith that the Spirit of God will overshadow their children to reconcile many sons from every people to glory. May fathers claim over their sons the promises God made to Abraham that all nations will be blessed, believing their sons will herald the Messiah who brings light to all who sit in darkness.

For at the end of the day, all the sons and daughters of the church must stand with John and point all men, especially unreached peoples who have never heard this astounding news, to the Lamb of God who takes away the sin *of the world!*

PRAYER FOCUS: *Kazakh, Qazaq of Mongolia (Evangelical: 0.6%)*

OCTOBER 2: THE BUSINESS OF DYING

TODAY'S READING: MATTHEW 1; LUKE 2

In the Gospels, the King of kings stepped from His heavenly throne and modeled the character of His reign by living among His subjects on earth. The Old Testament may be summarized as revealing the mission of God as focused on establishing an eternal kingdom and including all nations in that kingdom. "The New Testament begins by pointing out that Jesus is 'the son of David, the son of Abraham' (Matt. 1:1), identifying Him both as the heir of the promised eternal Kingdom and as the promised seed of blessing to the nations. This is the historical clarification necessary for understanding the dual Great Commission themes of kingdom authority and all nations (Matt. 28:18–20)." Thus, the opening verse of Matthew is the organizing verse of all Scripture. It summarizes the Old Testament and sets the direction of the New: King Jesus shall reign forever, and in His eternal kingdom will be every tribe, tongue, people, and nation.

Lest there be any doubt, Matthew, writing to Jews, lists five foreign women in the genealogy of Jesus, including the prostitutes Tamar and Rahab, the widow Ruth, the adulterer Bathsheba, and concludes with a young teenager named Mary. Matthew's opening news anticipates the closing call that the good news be preached among all peoples. The people that Jesus will save from their sins are obviously then the peoples of earth, not just one favored nation. The rest of Matthew (and the rest of the Gospels) build on this wonderful anticipation: Jesus is the eternal King who will reign over all the peoples of the earth and of His kingdom there will be end and no stain. God indeed is with us.

Luke's account also leaves no room for doubt that baby Jesus is the King who will reign universally. From the glorious presence of the Lord, the angels announced the good news that shall be great joy to *all* people. God will be glorified, and peace will be made with men of goodwill, irrespective of race or location. We must keep these promises in our heart and never lose sight of the missionary essence of the Bible as we read the New Testament.

Early on, Jesus knew He must be about His Father's business. That business was to die for the sins of the whole world, not to be an impressive young scholar. I can imagine 12-year-old Jesus talking with His elders about the majestic, marvelous plan of God to include all nations in His kingdom. From the beginning of the New Testament, the focus is on God's mission to save all peoples. From the announcement and birth of Jesus, the heavenly, prophetic message heralded that all peoples of earth be saved. From His childhood, Jesus was focused on the Father's business—the redemption of all peoples unto Himself. From Matthew to Revelation, the New Testament has a single eye: King Jesus and His plan to save a remnant from all peoples unto Himself. May we have that same singular vision, hope, and joy.

PRAYER FOCUS: *Berber, Rif of Morocco (Evangelical: 0.01%)*

OCTOBER 3: DOES HE NOT SMILE?

TODAY'S READING: MATTHEW 2

Jewish historian Josephus recorded Herod the Great dying in what we would call 4 BC. Given the reality that Herod killed little boys up to 2 years old, the likely date of Jesus' birth is somewhere between 5 and 6 BC. The medieval creators of our calendar simply miscalculated. What is certain is that from the beginning, Jesus' life and death would center around the nations.

Herod the Great was from present-day Jordan. The wise men from the East were most certainly from Arabia and most likely from Yemen, and their worship anticipated the great throng from east and west that will stream towards the Messiah's throne. The gifts of frankincense and myrrh are resins from plants that grow in Arabia or the Horn of Africa. Jesus and his family flee to Egypt, making the incarnate Lord both a refugee and a third culture kid from the beginning. How the heavens must have rejoiced that the early adopters, the first worshipers of the Messiah, were not Jews, but Arabs, possibly Africans, and the first to receive Jesus were Egyptians.

How empathetically does the risen Lord look down at refugees from Syria (or immigrants from anywhere) who fearfully try to gain a new life and not be forced to return to where they may be harmed! Jesus knows what it's like to flee for one's life, to know no one, to learn a strange language, to have no resources, and to be different from everyone around you, not knowing what tomorrow holds. And does not King Jesus have a special place in His heart for the Arabs as they were the first to give Him gifts? Long before Arabs were deceived into prostrating in vain, they fell down and worshiped Jesus. Does not Jesus smile as He looks down at 100 million Egyptians in nostalgic gratitude, for it was there that he learned to walk, distinguish different foods, watch the palm trees sway, and eat dates with every meal? Does he not smile at the memory of Egyptian wit and humor, the simple joy of silly jokes? Egypt took in the divine Son and gave Him His first home and memories. Will now King Jesus find a place for a multitude of Egyptians in His heavenly house? Will not heaven be brighter for the jolly wit of the sons and daughters of Egypt?

Matthew wrote his account of Jesus primarily to a Jewish audience, and in that light the opening chapters are provocative. It was Arabs who worshipped first and gave the first treasure. It was Egyptians who sheltered first and gave the first nurture. Clearly, the God of Israel is the God of all the earth and all the peoples. The nations have always been central to Christ's heart—and always will be. There are many locally who pretend to worship Jesus, but the Lord of nations prefers the sincere devotion of the foreigner to the feigned allegiance of family. For Jesus knows that home is in heaven and faithful family are those that fall and worship, no matter their color, tribe, location, or status. Be not proud of your earthly lineage. Be quick to join the Yemeni magi in falling at the feet of Jesus. Be quick to open your heart with the Egyptians to the Son.

PRAYER FOCUS: *Mon of Myanmar (Evangelical: 0.82%)*

OCTOBER 4: SHOCKINGLY SHORT LIVES

TODAY'S READING: MATTHEW 3; MARK 1; LUKE 3

The synoptic Gospels indicate that Jesus' ministry did not begin until John the Baptist's had ended. Luke recorded that John began preaching in the fifteenth year of Tiberius. Augustus had adopted Tiberius as his son and co-reigned with him for two years. This puts the possible date for John's ministry around 26 AD, and it certainly means that John the Baptist burned hot and quick. He did not minister long, but he ministered passionately.

John's message was missionary. He appeared announcing the kingdom of heaven was at hand (meaning available and imminent). John made it very clear prophetically that the extent of availability was to all peoples, preaching according to Isaiah's sentiment that forgiveness of sins was available to all men, that *all* flesh would see the salvation of God. In fact, John attacked the Pharisees (zealous laymen) and the Sadducees (professional ministers) alike for their false claim to have Abraham as their father. The whole point of Abraham was the promise that he would be the father of *many nations* and that his seed would bless all peoples. This sentiment and guiding passion was so foreign to the Jewish establishment that John had to shock them into awareness. In so many words John said: "You are so arrogant in your cloistered spirituality; you have missed the whole point. The kingdom of God is for all peoples of the world, and you are doing nothing about it. Repent from this sin of omission and engage in reaching all peoples for the glory of Jehovah, for if you don't, you will be cast out of His kingdom and He will raise up from stones if He must to be tools for missionary advance to all peoples according to His great will" (see Matt. 3:9).

John was a simple prophet and had two simple points. First, the kingdom of God is available to all the peoples of earth, and it is sin not to be busy bringing all the nations to Jehovah. Second, this great responsibility cannot be carried out without the help of the Holy Spirit. Each of the synoptic Gospels mentions this central tenant of John's message. Matthew recorded John saying that Jesus will baptize with the Holy Spirit and fire. Mark recorded John saying that Jesus will baptize with the Holy Spirit. Luke recorded John saying that Jesus will baptize with the Holy Spirit and fire.

The passions of John's short, fiery ministry are simple: The kingdom of Jesus is available to all; we best be busy bringing all the sons of Abraham (the nations) into it; we are going to need the baptism of the Spirit that Jesus alone gives in order to get the job done; it's the same message of Jesus; God so loved the world and He has other sheep; go make disciples of all nations; you will receive power when the Spirit comes upon you, and you will be my witnesses in all the difficult places where the gospel has not gone. Two cousins, two prophets, one God, one gospel. Both John and Jesus had shockingly short lives and ministries, but they burned with passion that all nations, by the power of the Spirit, be included in the Kingdom. So must we.

PRAYER FOCUS: *Magar of Nepal (Evangelical: 0.0%)*

OCTOBER 5: FROM FIRST TO LAST

TODAY'S READING: MATTHEW 4; LUKE 4-5

Some misunderstand missions to be a New Testament development. Others think missions started after Pentecost. But Jesus displayed God's missionary center from the beginning of His ministry. In Matthew 4:8, the devil tempted Jesus with "all the kingdoms of the world and their glory." The devil knows what the prize is and what the battle is over; the supreme war of the cosmos is over worship. Will the nations worship Jesus or the devil? Luke's record says that the devil showed Jesus all the kingdoms of the world and said, "All this authority I will give to you, and their glory" (Luke 4:6), but the condition was devil worship. Missions exists because the worship of Jesus does not. The devil knows the end game, and he tried to abort it from the beginning. Jesus, of course, will have none of the devil's nonsense, and He retorted that only God is worthy of the worship of every tongue.

Establishing the missionary goal by the power of the Spirit, Jesus rooted Himself in Capernaum, which was referred to as the center of "Galilee of the Gentiles" where "a people who sat in darkness have seen a great light" (Matt. 4:15–16). Jesus began His ministry by quoting Isaiah and the liberating promises of God and then illustrated His sermon by citing missionary examples. There were many widows in the famine of Elijah's time, but God sent (missionized) the prophet to a (present-day) Lebanese. There were many lepers, but God used Elijah to cleanse a Syrian. It was not by accident that Jesus' first sermon was a missionary sermon, and it did not unfold without incident. What was the response to the revelation of God's great missionary heart? Destructive wrath that tried to kill Jesus. Jesus was loved for a few short few minutes, but when He started revealing the missionary heart of God, He exposed the miserly heart of God's (supposed) people. How we love sermons that promise our deliverance, but how we resent when Jesus challenges us to be used to deliver the nations. From the first missionary sermon of Jesus, the precedent was followed up systematically. Jesus peripatetically taught, preached, and healed among the people, and His fame spread throughout all Syria. Great multitudes followed Him from Galilee of the Gentiles and the Decapolis and beyond the Jordan. In Luke, when the masses want to clutch Jesus to themselves, He said, "I must preach the kingdom of God to the other cities also, because for this purpose I have been sent" (4:43).

The opening ministry of Jesus resounded with His missionary passion. Even a healing of a Jewish paralytic is turned into missionary messaging: "But that you may know that the Son of Man has power on earth to forgive sins…" (5:24). Jesus established His deity and His universal authority using His favorite title for Himself, Son of Man, which comes from Daniel where the Son of Man is "given dominion, glory, and a kingdom, that all peoples, nations, and languages should serve Him" (7:13–14). God is a missionary God. The Bible is a missionary book. Jesus is a missionary Messiah. From His first sermon to His last summons, Jesus' glorious passion is for all peoples of the earth to worship Him.

PRAYER FOCUS: *Tuareg, Tamajaq of Niger (Evangelical: 0.0%)*

OCTOBER 6: JESUS' MISSIONARY MOTIVATION

TODAY'S READING: JOHN 2-4

The Gospel of John carefully underlines the missionary passion of Jesus from the beginning. John recorded seven miracles, and the first one was culturally kind. Jesus helped a bride and groom evade the shame of being ungenerous hosts to their wedding guests. Jesus valued the honor of His friends more than the religious sensibilities of the elite; he ordered six twenty-gallon containers reserved for ritual washing be used to fuel the wedding festivities. God made flesh, and the first miracle is culturally kind!

His first visit to Jerusalem was missionary driven. John alone recorded Jesus cleansing the temple at the beginning of His ministry. Some think Jesus cleansed the temple twice, while others think John was trying to point out religious opposition. Perhaps John just wanted to remind us that from the beginning Jesus was passionate about His house having space for all nations. Jesus quoted Isaiah 56 as He whipped merchants around, for His house will be a house of *prayer* for *all nations*. The first miracle John recorded was cultural, the first visit to Jerusalem missional, and the first witness universal—it is focused on all the world. God so loved *the world* and He sent His Son into *the world*, not to condemn *the world* but that *the world* might be saved. The light of Jesus came expressly for the dark *world*. John could not be clearer that Jesus' mission was for every people to have salvation opportunity. John 3:36 must ever accompany 3:16: "He who believes in the Son has everlasting life, and he who does not believe the Son shall not see life, but the wrath of God abides on him." The missionary must be faithful to tell *all the world* they are under wrath *and* be faithful to tell *all the world* Jesus offers everlasting life.

John continued to firmly establish the missionary motivation of Jesus from the beginning by detailing the first missions trip. Samaria was at odds with Israel as they opposed the reconstruction of Jerusalem (538 BC). They built their own temple on Mt. Gerizim to their version of the God of Abraham (4th century BC) and rejected the prophets building a case for the Messiah only on the law. In retaliation, the Jews completely destroyed the Samaritan temple (about 2nd century BC) and even considered their drinking vessels unclean (that's why the Samaritan woman was shocked when Jesus asked for a drink). In this missions trip, Jesus did not condone the Samaritan religion. In fact, He debunked both the Samaritan view and the second temple Judaic view by bluntly saying, "Neither on this mountain, nor in Jerusalem…. You worship what you do not know…. But the hour is coming, and now is, when [you] will worship the Father in spirit and truth" (4:21–23). Astonished, the Samaritan woman ran into the city and spoke to the men (!), and they flooded out to see Jesus. This is the *missions* context where Jesus declared the harvest is plentiful—away from home, in hostile territory. It was the Samaritans who were the first people group to declare that Jesus is "indeed the Christ, the Savior of the world" (v. 42). Oh, hallelujah! Jesus is our missionary God, the Savior of the *world*!

PRAYER FOCUS: *Fulani, Adamawa of Nigeria (Evangelical: 0.88%)*

OCTOBER 7: IN SIMPLE FAITH

TODAY'S READING: MATTHEW 8; MARK 2

From the beginning the missionary heart of Jesus clearly demonstrated that His purpose was broader than home, that it included all people, and that He had a passion to rescue even those we are afraid of or despise. He was more than willing to love lepers. He was more than willing to have His roof smashed in so He could love and heal the lame and in that healing demonstrate He had the power to forgive the sins *of the whole earth*. Jesus was more than willing to heal ladies, lackeys of the Romans, and Greeks with legions of demons. Jesus pointedly and intentionally reached out beyond the borders of what the "church" (the religious establishment and popular comfort) thought appropriate. They were scandalized that He associated and loved tax collectors, sinners, and peoples from other nations. Missionary Jesus knew what it was to swim against the tide which would monopolize the gospel, shackling it to the favored family few.

Jesus knew missions mobilization had the twin challenges of unrealistic expectations and deferred obedience. Some were attracted to missions because of the excitement of "cool Jesus" doing fantastic things, gaining notoriety, and receiving praise and welcome in every place. Jesus cut through the idealism and asked if they were willing to follow Him to nowhere. Jesus was (and is) not impressed with those who said this or that must happen in their career or family before they said "yes" to following Him to that nowhere. We want to be something or make ourselves into somebody so we have resources to help Jesus out. Jesus said, "Follow Me and I will make you along the way." Jesus crossed an uncooperative sea to a non-Jewish territory to cast out demons, and for His pains was asked to leave the country. Missionaries must likewise work against the winds and currents of manifold powers that do not want Jesus, the demon destroyer, to set their people free. Jesus knows what it means to face resistance, both natural (difficult climates) and official (leaders who expel). Jesus knows that missions is about casting out demons and that the demonic will strike back.

Of all these early and unmistakable demonstrations of the missionary heart of Jesus, few are as poignant as the Italian soldier who came to pray. It was an unreached person who trusted Jesus more than the household of faith. The centurion recognized in Jesus international authority, and in contrast to the Jews (who demanded Jesus only come to *their* house), the Roman humbly said physical presence was not necessary, just make the command and it shall be done. Jesus loved it. The great missionary heart of Jesus surged and shouted, "YES!" Not only this Italian, but *many* will come from east and west and sit down with Abraham in the kingdom of heaven. How Jesus loves it when unreached peoples express their faith in Him with so much less witness than we have enjoyed. How Jesus rejoices over the many unreached from every people who will likewise in simple faith trust Him!

PRAYER FOCUS: *South Asian, Bengali Speaking of Oman (Evangelical: 0.0%)*

OCTOBER 8: BE WHERE THE PEOPLE ARE

TODAY'S READING: JOHN 5

"Today, 112 years later, 94% of the people in the world recognize the Coca-Cola logo and product. In 112 years, we can reach the world for profit's sake, but we cannot do it for the glory of God in 2,000 years."

DAVID SILLS

Jesus' second visit to Jerusalem (according to John's Gospel) was likely during the feast of Pentecost. The first visit was at Passover, and the next feast was Tabernacles, traditionally associated with Moses receiving the law on Mount Sinai (in Saudi Arabia). This is likely why Jesus referred to the teaching of Moses at the end of chapter 5. It's interesting that Jesus was at the pool of Bethesda; it wasn't an orthodox place to be. In ancient times, there were pools of healing where the lame and sick sought help from gods like Asclepius or Apollo. Why Jesus was strolling through a place pagan in praxis on a calm Sabbath (non-work) day is instructive; He obviously liked to be where people were lost and lame. Jesus showed His divine power and declared it obviously, for His critics had no confusion about His making Himself equal with God. There is a trend in some missionary contextualization to withhold the proclamation of the deity of Jesus until later in the witnessing relationship. There are even some who have removed familial language (Father and Son) from their translations of the Bible. Jesus took no such precautions; they are, in fact, an insult to His worth. Jesus led with His deity. Inflammatory as it was to radically monotheistic Jews of the first century, Jesus declared early and often that He was God.

Why do we soften the deity of Jesus when He made no effort to veil it? We approach the Scriptures trying to prove that Jesus was fully God. Jesus was so sure that He was God and so evident in His claims that He seems to put more energy into proving He was fully man. He just launched His ministry, and He said that "all should honor the Son just as they honor the Father" (John 5:23). This is merely an extension of His introduction by John the Baptist who said, "He who believes in the Son has everlasting life; and he who does not believe the Son shall not see life, but the wrath of God abides on him" (3:36). Neither John nor Jesus began by cloaking Jesus' divinity. Jesus continued, saying that "the dead will hear the voice of the Son of God; and those who hear will live" (5:25) and that He has life in Himself and authority, for He is the Son of Man. Jesus went to pagan places where a great multitude of sick were found. He directly asserted He was God, Lord over all nations. He clearly said that the dead (from any people and place) who hear His voice will *come forth!* Jesus did not hide His divinity, and neither should we. Jesus was not shy about His bringing life to all who are dead, and neither should we be. The missionary spirit announces and broadcasts that Jesus is God, that He has all authority and power, and that He brings life from the dead. The missionary Spirit does not hide the deity of Jesus nor delay its broadcast. Jesus led with His deity; so should we.

PRAYER FOCUS: *Shaikh of Pakistan (Evangelical: 0.0%)*

OCTOBER 9: AVOID SEDUCTION BY NUMBERS

TODAY'S READING: MATTHEW 12; MARK 3; LUKE 6

Ministry constantly tempts us to focus on the multitudes over intimate disciples. All of today's passages refer to the multitudes, and the general sense is that the exuberance of the crowd was more a challenge than a blessing. Mark's Gospel makes a clear distinction between the multitude and the twelve disciples, and Matthew compares Jesus' efforts to limit the spread of His fame to the example of the Messiah in Isaiah 42:1–4. In context, the Messiah was lowly at home because He had the goal of declaring the gospel to the Gentiles in the power of the Spirit.

All God's people are called to be missionary in spirit and function. For some that means to go; for others that means to send. Leaders and laity called to stay home that the gospel may span the globe would do well to learn from Jesus' example. He was never seduced by numbers. He realized that crowds carried contingencies which demanded so much energy that the global mandate became lost. We have so magnified the importance of church growth that we pursue it, even when our size then prohibits us being missional. Jesus resisted the temptation to have a large following and instead focused on discipling a few, for He realized that it's not large ministries that change the world, but it's faithful disciples.

Intentionally making His ministry small, Jesus spent all night in prayer that He might choose twelve faithful, available, teachable men to be with Him. He then trained them to preach, going out into all the world loving their enemies. Jesus knew the enemy would use the tool of popularity to distract us from world mission, *and* He knew when we were on point, we would fill others with rage and they would seek to destroy. To be missionary in focus is to go toward wrath and opposition from both within and without. We will be accused of all kinds of evils when we stand firmly for the priority of the evangelization of the unreached. One of the reasons God uses smaller, nimbler collections of people to spread His fame around the nations is intimacy allows greater agreement. The bigger you are, the more general you must be in theology and the more generous in inclusion. Jesus knew that when you get big, you tend to lose control of focus. He intentionally stayed small, so He could stay true.

It is obviously not either/or. The example of Jesus is that large groups only stay true if founded on smaller gatherings of intimate disciples focused on preaching the gospel in all the world, even to enemies. By all means, let the church continue to grow in size *as long as* that growth is spurred and cultivated in intimate collections of disciples in mission-based relationship. This is after all the point of Jesus in Matthew 12:50: Who are His brothers, sisters, mothers, and fathers? Not those in big groups (necessarily or automatically), but those who do His will. What is His will? That none perish. That every people group is represented around the throne. That we go out in missionary bands and preach the gospel among our enemies. Jesus-oriented mission humbly distances itself from large groups with all the attending distractions and focuses on an intimate band of disciples, raising them up to preach the gospel and change the world.

PRAYER FOCUS: *Iranun of Philippines (Evangelical: 0.0%)*

OCTOBER 10: THE LORD'S GREATEST MISSIONARY PRAYER

TODAY'S READING: MATTHEW 5–7

"Prayer is not a preparation for the battle; it is the battle!"

LEONARD RAVENHILL

The Sermon on the Mount functioned in the New Testament the same way the law functioned in the Old. God chose weak Israel (OT) and the frail church (NT) to issue His invitation to all peoples of earth. The law of Moses and the law of Christ teach us how to live so that we might be worthy of bearing the invitation of God to the ends of the earth. The Sermon on the Mount cannot be understood outside the missionary heart of God. When we live holy lives, God lives among us and blesses us. Blessed, we confidently penetrate all unreached peoples with the gospel, making disciples and planting churches as advanced outposts of the Kingdom. Oceans of ink have been spilt concerning the kingdom of God, and it is necessary to build our understanding on original context. "Teaching His disciples to pray (Matt. 6:9, 10) Jesus adapted a fairly common Jewish prayer called the **Kaddish** that came to be prayed regularly in the synagogues: 'Exalted and hallowed be His great name…and may He cause His kingdom to rule….' This was a prayer for the future kingdom. The Jewish people longed for the ultimate coming of God's reign when He would rule the earth unchallenged and restore justice and mercy in all the world."

The prayer Jesus taught His disciples to pray is a missionary prayer. It is a cry for Jesus to come back again in glory and power. It is a longing for that great day of the Lord when all nations will be gathered around the throne worshiping Jesus. No longer will the nations deny His deity and take Him lightly. Jesus shall descend with a shout, fire in His eyes and sword in His hand, to establish His eternal reign, and no one will dare diminish His unquestioned, unending majesty. Every time we pray the Lord's Prayer let us remember it is the grandest missionary prayer of all. It is our "maranatha," our "come, Lord Jesus, and be hallowed in every language by every tongue." To construe the Kingdom or this prayer in any other advent is to misunderstand the Bible. The reason Jesus went into such detail in this sermon was because "hallowing God's name was a central principle of Jewish ethics: Live even among the Gentiles in such a manner that people will honor God." A holy life always has global purpose—that all the nations may revere the name of Jesus. The law of Moses and the law of Christ are united in spirit and strategy: Live in such a way that God is honored. When God is honored, He tabernacles with us. When God tabernacles with us, we are blessed. When we are blessed, we have the resources to preach the gospel to the ends of the earth. When we preach the gospel to the ends of the earth among all peoples, the end will come, the King will descend, the Kingdom will be established, and all will be right forever.

PRAYER FOCUS: *Persian of Qatar (Evangelical: 0.0%)*

OCTOBER 11: THE MISSIONS-DRIVEN JESUS

TODAY'S READING: MATTHEW 9; LUKE 7

Miracles are missions driven. In the classic healing of the paralytic in Matthew 9:5, Jesus asked, "For which is easier, to say, 'Your sins are forgiven you,' or to say, 'Arise and walk'?" The answer is, it's easier to say "your sins are forgiven" because no one can prove that, except Jesus. "But that you may know that the Son of Man has power on earth to forgive sins.... Arise, take up your bed, and go to your house" (v. 6). Jesus did a miracle to prove He is God. Miracles underline the passion of God to forgive the sins of the repentant of every people group on earth. Miracles are so that gospel news goes into all the land. Miracles show that Jesus is the Son of David and are intended to spread the news in all that country.

Fasting is missions driven. Jesus told His critics "the days will come when the bridegroom will be taken away from them, and then [My disciples] will fast" (v. 15). This is the single best motivation for fasting—we want Jesus to return, we yearn for His return as a hungry body yearns for food, we are hungry for Jesus to come back. Jesus will come back when the gospel of the Kingdom is preached to every people group.

Authority is missions driven. The Roman centurion told Jesus: "For I also am a man placed under authority, having soldiers under me. And I say, 'Go,' and he goes" (Luke 7:8). I wager Jesus thought about this (likely European) soldier when He gave the Great Commission: "All authority has been given to me. Go." It's the same language and spirit. The authority systems of the world are set up for one reason—and it's not global peace. It's peace with God. It's representatives of every nation reconciled to their authority and gathered around the throne. Whatever authority exists on earth is ultimately there to serve God's missionary agenda.

Delays are missions driven. John the Baptist has been misunderstood. John knew exactly who Jesus was—the Lamb of God who would take away the sins of the *world*. When John sent the question to Jesus from prison, he framed it in missionary messianic language: "Are you the Coming One?" Single-eyed, no-nonsense John was about to die, and he wanted to know when the global agenda would kick in. Jesus assured John that all was well, the gospel was being preached, and the goal remained the same. John was great because from beginning to end he understood the global scope of the mission, and with Jesus he was dedicated to it, no matter what anyone thought.

Compassion is missions driven. Jesus went everywhere preaching missions: the Kingdom is coming and it will include all peoples. When Jesus saw the multitudes, He had one singular compassionate reaction: to pray that the Lord of the harvest would send hardworking missionaries into all the earth. We cannot claim to be the compassionate people of God if our deepest prayer and hardest work is not focused on the missionary heart of God—that all unreached peoples everywhere would have access to the gospel because God answered our prayer that He would send missionaries.

PRAYER FOCUS: *Kazakh of Russia (Evangelical: 0.01%)*

OCTOBER 12: HE WILL COME WITH VIOLENCE

TODAY'S READING: MATTHEW 11

Jesus yet commands us to teach and preach. We are to teach the full counsel of God and resist the temptation to end up with a sum zero effect (a neutral, even neutralized, Jesus) by so combining His complementary characteristics that in effect we have a nothing God. We can be so offended at who Jesus actually is that we adjust our message among the nations so that we don't offend anyone or irritate those from other religions.

In explaining John the Baptist's role, Matthew quoted Malachi 3:1 which predicted an Elijah-esque prophet who would prepare the world for the advent of the Messiah. Matthew essentially said John was that Elijah; Jesus will make the same comparison later (17:11-13). Matthew's point was John and Jesus both appear in eschatological context: the coming of the Messiah, the setting up of a kingdom that will include all nations, the fiery judgment on all peoples who resist the rule of King Jesus, and the violent establishment of the Kingdom on that day. We must remember that neither John nor Jesus viewed the Kingdom in terms of something earthly or even as kingdom influence (as many do today). John and Jesus viewed the Kingdom as that literal great day of the Lord when the Messiah comes in wondrous power, coercing all (who have not yet bowed the knee) to worship, slaying all enemies before Him, fire in His eyes and sword in His hand, literal death, literal judgment, literal hell, literal heaven, real, tangible, physical, and violent.

We cannot make the mistake of moralists and liberals who confine Jesus to a gentle iteration of a benign deity that accepts all peoples on their terms. The message of John and the destiny of Jesus is a violent, physical coming of the Messiah to earth, a forcing of all to worship Him, and the establishment of a kingdom will include from all among the Gentiles "a people for His name" (Acts 15:14). Just as John the Baptist was rough and unpolished, just as he met a violent end, so history will unfold before us in violent fashion and will culminate in a violent Jesus ending all violence with the greatest act of violence in history. It is not reverent to remove violence from the character of God or the future actions of Jesus. The kingdom of heaven will come violently, and Jesus will establish it by force. This was why Jesus warned Chorazin, Bethsaida, and Capernaum of judgment and woe and the very fires of hades. Because the King will come with violence.

Yes, Jesus beckons the weary and tired. Glory to His Name! He is gentle and lowly. Praise be to God! We can and will embrace that reality without relinquishing that He is coming to violently judge the wicked, coerce all to worship, and cast those who reject Him to eternal, literal hell. A violent view of Jesus enhances our wonder of His gentleness. A gentle view of Jesus enhances our view of His violence. To have Him as He is, we must have both, and so must the nations. All peoples, including Saudis, must bow in reverent worship at the feet of Him who is both astoundingly gentle and authoritatively violent.

PRAYER FOCUS: *Arab, Arabic Gulf Spoken of Saudi Arabia (Evangelical: 0.10%)*

OCTOBER 13: PESTER THE KING

TODAY'S READING: LUKE 11

"Satan is delighted for us to be satisfied with having given of our time,
contributed significant expense and helping a lot of people
without introducing them to the One who can give eternal hope."

JERRY RANKIN

Your kingdom come. There is no kingdom without a resident King. Jesus asks us to pray that He will return to reign. Only then will the Father's will be done on earth as it is in heaven, when King Jesus comes in power and glory. Prayers of persistence are linked to this model prayer. We should ever be praying for the physical return of King Jesus to this earth. It is this context (praying that King will come back) that we are told to seek and knock. Unabated we are to pester heaven with growing fervor as the day approaches for the return of the King. It is this context in which we ask for the Holy Spirit. Why do we ask for the Holy Spirit? Because when the Holy Spirit is given, we will receive power to be His witnesses in all the earth (Acts 1:8). Why should we be His witnesses in all the earth? So that the King will come (Matt. 24:14). Thus, prayer is not really about us and our needs, bodies, jobs, families, or our wounds; prayer is essentially about the King coming back and the gospel being preached to all nations. The reception of the Spirit is not really about power for me to overcome as an individual in my little sphere; the Spirit is about Jesus overcoming all the enemy's forces that actively resist His mission to return in power and glory.

Because we are so small and focused on ourselves, we naturally interpret anything that happens *to* us as being *about* us. Jesus debunked this when He cast out the mute demon. The mute man spoke and naturally we think the purpose of this demonstration of power centered on the individual. It didn't. Jesus explained, "If I cast out demons with the finger of God, surely the kingdom of God has come upon you" (Luke 11:20). He pointed out that His act to this individual had kingdom, global purposes. It's an arrow in the war for authority over all the earth and all peoples. It's an arrow in the war that will culminate only when the King comes back in power. It's an arrow in the war to gather representatives of all peoples to the King, for in the larger context this personal intervention is all about gathering.

For Jesus, there is no enduring kingdom without the literally present King. He knows we are in the midst of battle, and some ground taken will be lost again. He knows that the blessed are those that obey the King and work towards His will of every nation represented in the Kingdom. He knows that hungry ears want signs, and He calls our attention back to Yemen and Syria (v. 31) as if to say the only sign is the shocker of the King dying for all nations and then re-shocking all satanic powers by rising from the dead. Jesus reminds us that if our eye is singly, missionary-focused on His coming kingdom then our whole body will be full of light. For this we must pray.

PRAYER FOCUS: *Fulani, Pulaar of Senegal (Evangelical: 0.0%)*

OCTOBER 14: SOWING THE WORDS

TODAY'S READING: MATTHEW 13; LUKE 8

Many parables are actually better understood as metaphors or similes—short, concise statements that the hearers immediately understood. The parables of the sower and the tares were exceptions in that they functioned more like allegories which Jesus needed to unpack. The center of both parables is the seed, the word of God; the center of reaching unreached peoples is the word of God. Jesus is explained, in the power of the Spirit, through reference to the Bible. We cannot reach the unreached nor disciple them if we do not have the Bible in their heart language. Faithful Bible translation is at the heart of all missions, and today's Bible passages remind us of some elemental missions principles.

The Word must go everywhere (Matt. 13:1–9; Luke 8:11). Central to missionary praxis is the wide sowing of the word of God. Responsibility of the sower is wide. We are to cast the seed of the word of God on every kind of soil; this is not considered waste. The responsibility of God is to change the soil, which He has done through history and does even now. The missionary must share the gospel broadly, not look or wait for those outwardly responsive. Different levels of fruit are expected and appropriate, but every follower of Jesus is expected to constantly open their mouth (take up their pen, use their gifts) to communicate what the Bible says.

The Word must ever go out (Luke 8:40–45). Right after Jesus shared the parable of the sower, He illustrated His specific intention by taking the disciples on an exciting missions trip to set a non-Jew outside Israel free. Then on the way home, a desperate woman pressed through the crowd to touch Him and He stopped to give her attention. The disciples protested. After all, the dead child of an important man laid languishing. "Master, the multitudes throng and press you" (v. 45). In other words, "Jesus, this is not a good time. It's chaotic and confusing." Jesus' actions throughout demonstrate there is no bad time to share the gospel, that everyone should hear.

Some words take longer to grow than others (Matt. 13:31–32). Slow growth tends to be lasting growth. Rapid expansion has become a bit of a missions idol. We are told to pursue rabbit churches and disciples (those that multiply quickly), and not elephants (those that produce one child every three years). Yes, we want to believe for miracle accelerations and days of Pentecost, but we also want mustard trees, not weeds. Quick growth in and of itself is not helpful, for it does not last.

We will always deal with false words (Matt. 13: 24–30). The Word will always be rejected and offensive, resisted by false words easier to say and hear. Jesus tells us not to be unduly worried, for He will sort it out in the end. He will gather out of His kingdom all things that offend. For now, the missionary task is to ensure that there is nothing offensive to Jesus in our words or life and that we are diligent to get His words into every language by every means.

PRAYER FOCUS: *Susu of Sierra Leone (Evangelical: 0.06%)*

OCTOBER 15: SOWERS SOW

TODAY'S READING: MARK 4–5

"Where the plow does not go and the seed is not sown, the weeds are sure to multiply."

CHARLES H. SPURGEON

The parable of the sower is so critical that Jesus cautions us: If we miss the meaning of it, we will miss the meaning of all parables. Mark 4:14 is the simple key: "The sower sows the word." If we understand nothing else, we must understand that our central assignment is to broadly disseminate the word of God. If we miss that simple, central truth, we will not understand leadership or holism or strategy or evangelism or missions. Let it sink down deeply into our souls and may it soundly penetrate our understanding: Our primary obedience is to broadly proclaim the word of God, sowing to every kind of soil, receptive or not. This essential understanding if missed or diluted will handicap and distort all. The sower sows the Word. Mark 4 and 5 lay out essential missionary necessities. We are to sow, shine, share, scythe, shade, sleep, and send. Jesus was taking the disciples on a missionary trip to a Greek town in a Roman province to cast out demons. "Send" refers both to the casting out of devils and the "go and tell" in which new disciples are expected to multiply by sowing seed themselves (5:19).

In missions to unreached peoples, three encounters typically interact. The insertion point is arbitrary; the encounters are not strictly equal. As referred to above, the primary assignment is to sow seed, to preach and teach the word of God, but that is not always where we begin.

Love Encounters: Missionaries are to share life with their host peoples. We are not to view unreached peoples as targets or projects. We are to love and be loved, we are to serve, we are to bless, we are to lay down our lives in a thousand kind acts for thousands of days in a row. We are to demonstrate that we are a community of love and in that demonstration declare there is a family of God willing and wanting to receive new members.

Power Encounters: As part of their journey, very few Muslims come to faith outside of a dream, healing, miracle, or showdown of one kind or another. In all false religions, the gospel does not just address the forensic realities (guilt/innocence) or the societal implications (shame/honor), but it also addresses the strongman (fear/power). The gospel must declare and demonstrate that Jesus has power over devils, darkness, and death.

Truth Encounters: The gospel as articulated and explained in the Bible must be presented in a way that is understood. Faith still comes by hearing and hearing by the word of God. While love and power encounters are essential, they are not salvific. Men and women have been saved without relationship with Christians and without miracles in their lives, but no one has ever been saved outside of the gospel seed finding good soil in their heart.

The sower sows the Word.

PRAYER FOCUS: *Swahili, Barawani of Somalia (Evangelical: 0.0%)*

OCTOBER 16: THE COLD-WATER CUP

TODAY'S READING: MATTHEW 10

"I never made a sacrifice. Of this we ought not to talk when we remember the great sacrifice which He made who left His Father's throne on high to give Himself for us."

DAVID LIVINGSTONE

Matthew was very interested in the commission of the church, but not just at the end of his Gospel. Chapter 9 culminates with Jesus telling us to ask the Lord of the harvest to send out laborers and chapter 10 begins with Jesus doing what He prayed for. Oh, that all our under-shepherds in every global church would do the same: Pray for God to raise up missionaries and then immediately send out their very best.

The first teaching section in Matthew (Sermon on the Mount) was character based, telling us what kind of missionaries we should *be*, while the second teaching section relates what missionaries should *do*: We should respond to Jesus' call to get intimate with Him and receive His power to cast out demons and heal diseases. We should stay focused on the people group He has assigned to us. We should preach wherever we go that the King is coming back soon, and we should heal the sick, cleanse the lepers, and raise the dead. We should minister without asking or accepting payment and trust the Lord to provide our every need. We should look for persons of peace. We should let God be in charge of how people respond to us. We should be wise and brave and expect persecution. We should not worry under duress but expect God to give us exactly what needs to be said, and we should expect the Spirit to speak through us. We should expect to be betrayed and hated by those close to us, and we should expect to fill up the sufferings of Christ and be hated by all. We should endure until the end and not fear. Missions is not complicated; it's just hard.

The goal is not to be loved, even as we are constantly loving. The goal is to confess Christ before all peoples. The goal is not unity, for Jesus did not come to bring peace but a sword. The goal is to lose our lives in saving others. The goal is not to give a cup of cold water in Jesus' name. One of the most misunderstood verses of Scripture is in this decidedly missionary-oriented passage, for the verb "sent" is where we get our understanding of mission. When Jesus sent the twelve out, the Greek word is *apostolos*, where we get our term "apostle." Real apostles are those that Jesus sends away from home to preach the gospel where the gospel has not been preached. It is in this context we are told that "whoever gives one of these little ones only a cup of cold water in the name of a disciple…shall by no means lose his reward" (v. 42). Bluntly stated, giving a cup of cold water in the New Testament is directly connected to the hospitality and help given to missionary workers (sent-out ones). It has nothing to do with humanitarian wells or social programs. I'm not saying those activities are wrong; I'm just saying they are not urged by this text, nor are they the goal of missions. If you want to be blessed, support missionaries. That's the cold-water cup God rejoices to reward.

PRAYER FOCUS: *Shaikh of Sri Lanka (Evangelical: 0.0%)*

Missions going is predicated on two essential comings. First, we must come to Jesus. In Mark 6:7, before Jesus missionized His disciples, sending them out two by two, He called them to Himself. Interestingly, Luke recorded this with corporate implication, writing: "Then He called His twelve disciples together" (9:1), so secondly, the evangelization of the peoples of the world cannot be sustained outside of coming to Jesus together. We must always come to Him and we must always come together before we go anywhere.

Missions will always be offensive. My wife and I sat with a consular officer from the embassy, sharing with her why we felt God brought us to Saudi Arabia. She listened politely and then told us: "It is my official responsibility to warn you that the consequences of your action could mean five to twenty years in prison." She was not unkind; she just wanted to do her duty and to be sure we knew that missions (meaning preaching repentance and that Jesus is the only Savior) is unpopular and will be offensive. In fact, many will be offended at us. It is important to note Jesus' reaction to others being offended: He went about the villages in a circuit, teaching, and He sent the disciples out two by two to preach that people should repent. We come to Jesus and we come together because if we are faithful, gospel witnesses will be unpopular, and we will need one another to sustain the rejection from others.

Luke's Gospel puts Peter's seminal confession of Christ on the heels of a series of dizzying events. In short order the disciples were sent out on a missions trip, they saw miracles, John was arrested and killed, 5,000 men were fed from one lunch, Jesus walked on water (Peter not so much), and then Jesus popped the priceless question: "Who do you say that I am?" Peter rose from his dip into the waves of unbelief to declare for all of us that Jesus is *the Christ of God* (Luke 9:20). Jesus was pleased and in the next breath reminds us all that the Son of Man is coming in His own glory. This is the third and ultimate coming. First, we come to Jesus. Then we come together so that we can be sent to the nations. Then the Christ, the Son of Man, will come in glory. Of course, as we wait eagerly for that day, God reminds all missionaries and followers that suffering must come before glory. The Christ must suffer, be killed, and be raised from the dead. We must deny ourselves and take up our cross daily. We must follow Him to nowhere, follow Him now, and follow Him with no exit plan. Only after these revelations do we see Jesus in His own light and hear the Father boom, "This is My beloved Son. Hear Him!" (v. 35).

Jesus had only one purpose on earth and the Gospels must be read in His light. We must hear Him say, "Why I came, why you come to Me, why we come together, why I send you out in mission is simply so a redeemed remnant from every people group on earth may come to Me."

PRAYER FOCUS: *Shuikia, Arabized of Sudan (Evangelical: 0.05%)*

OCTOBER 18: ETERNAL FOOD PROGRAMS

TODAY'S READING: JOHN 6

"The best remedy for a sick church is to put it on a missionary diet."

DAVID LIVINGSTONE

Biblically, missions has one supreme end goal: The glory of Jesus through disciples made from every tribe, tongue, people, and nation. Everything else is a means to that end. When feeding programs or social action in missionary activity become ends in themselves or equated in value with the disciple making among every unreached people, then the missionary train comes off the biblical rails. John 6 is a classic foundation for understanding missions rightly. Bluntly, Jesus is not into feeding programs here on earth, not if they become the end and distract from the last day, saved souls, and eternal life. Jesus is into giving eternal *life* to all the peoples of the *world*; He makes this point over and over (see John 6:33, 40, 51). In opposition to the idea that the best feeding happens here and now, Jesus continued harping on "the last day" (vv. 39, 40, 44, 54). John 6 is clear: Jesus is focused on the last day, eternal life, and all nations, and anything we do on earth must serve that purpose.

Miracles don't mean political power. When Jesus made extra food, the politically motivated believers saw the ability to feed an army. A fed army can defeat ruling oppressors, so naturally they wanted to make Jesus king. They wanted to leverage social power for political ends, and Jesus would have none of it, departing to the mountains by Himself. Jesus isn't into big social programs, especially the politically motivated kind. Miracles also don't mean physical guarantees. Jesus is not our genie; He's more concerned about our eternal joy than about our smiles and satisfaction on earth. Jesus is not unconcerned about our physical needs; He's just more concerned about our eternal life. Jesus uses people and programs to feed the hungry but knows these are stopgap measures. If you want to use John 6 as a missionary model for feeding the poor, then by all means pray over your lunch and believe for miracles. But the point is neither a feeding program nor a provisional miracle. The point is eternal life. The point is that only Jesus can give eternal life. The point is that we must be laser-focused on "the last day."

Does this offend you? To prove the point, Jesus asks what we would think if He ascends to heaven. Why does He ask this? Because we are so fixated on physical things and on this present life that He has to physically demonstrate an ascension into glory to show us that our attention *must* be on the saving of souls, the last day, and eternal life. And only the Spirit (not the feeding program) gives this type of life, for the flesh profits nothing and the words that Jesus speaks are spirit and life. Only Jesus has the words of eternal life, so in missions let's be sure we disburse *that* food.

PRAYER FOCUS: ***Druze of Syria (Evangelical: 0.36%)***

OCTOBER 19: A MISSIONS TRIP WITH JESUS

TODAY'S READING: MATTHEW 15; MARK 7

"A nation will not be moved by timid methods."

LUIS PALAU

Scholars debate whether Jesus' excursion to Lebanon (Tyre and Sidon) was a missionary trip or discipleship training. It was both, just as most overseas trips are today. Certainly, Jesus wanted to model and demonstrate the great heart of Father God for all peoples of earth *and* He wanted His disciples to learn something.

At first blush it seems that Jesus was a bit callous towards the importunate mother's cries, but if we understand indirection, we see the great joy of God shining through. First of all, a Lebanese mother recognized Jesus as the Son of David with authority not just over all the nations, but with authority over all demonic powers. How the heart of Jesus must have leapt at this request! In His hometown and country, He constantly faced opposition to both of these essential aspects. Yet here was a foreigner from an unreached people, initiating her request by confessing publicly, "I believe you are the King who will rule over all the peoples of the earth and over all the principalities and powers!" There can be no doubt that the heart of God was smiling, bursting on the inside, eager to heal, deliver, and save. As ever, God works in multiple directions, and so the conversation continued.

Jesus didn't answer her, and here is where discipleship training becomes evident. What would the disciples do? Well, they failed. They urged Jesus to send the irritating woman away. Jesus seemingly complied, but this was merely an escalation of the plot, for in one of the most touching exchanges in the Gospels, this Lebanese mother would not be denied. Instead, she worshiped and whispered, "Lord, help me!" I cannot read these words without crying, and I believe Jesus' eyes had tears. I can't imagine how He restrained both His emotions and His power in this moment. Then one more touching exchange, a twinkle mixed with tears in the eyes of the Master before the glorious answer from the God who came down to earth for encounters just like this—that all nations would be loved and saved.

Jesus then went to the Decapolis and healed the multitudes whereupon they glorified the God of Israel. Jesus was still in Gentile territory, still on a missions trip, when He healed a deaf mute. The crowds were astonished beyond measure and declared, "He has done all things well" (Mark 7:37). Jesus then fed a crowd of 4,000, a complementary feast among the Gentiles as He provided to the Israelites, before He got in a boat and wrapped the missions trip up, and He did this because He had compassion on the crowd of unreached peoples. This is missions at its most glorious: Jesus giving and bringing life to those far from the household of faith, Jesus receiving joy at the faith He finds among the nations, Gentiles recognizing that the God of Israel is the one true God who has included them in eternal life, and missionary disciples having their hubristic prejudice excised along the way. Not much has changed in 2,000 years.

PRAYER FOCUS: *Yao, Muslim of Tanzania (Evangelical: 1.2%)*

OCTOBER 20: FIXATED ON THE WRONG THING

TODAY'S READING: MATTHEW 16; MARK 8

"Nothing so clears the vision and lifts up the life, as a decision to move forward in what you know to be entirely the will of the Lord."

JOHN G. PATON

The feeding of the 4,000 happened in Gentile territory. The disciples didn't get it and Jesus became frustrated with them. The lesson related to the Pharisees and Sadducees doubting Jesus. The religious leaders wanted a sign, the populace wanted bread, and the disciples wanted to understand. Jesus was understandably perturbed with all. Rather than trusting Jesus, the religious elite wanted to put Him on trial. Their destructive, dangerous doctrine revolved around their insistence in putting God on trial—as if God has to prove Himself to others. What frustrated Jesus about the leaders was that they spent more energy on arrogantly vetting God than on obeying His commission. God was not to be judged, He was to be obeyed. What frustrated Jesus about the crowd and the disciples was that their fixation on His power more than His purposes.

From feeding 4,000 in Gentile territory, Jesus led His disciples to the town of Caesarea Philippi, twenty-five miles north of the Sea of Galilee. This city (full of non-Jews) was founded around 332 BC and called Panion (after the Greek god Pan) by 223 BC. After Rome gave the city to Herod the Great, Herod built a temple to Augustus Caesar, and when Herod's son Phillip succeeded him in 4 BC, he changed the city's name to Caesarea. Decades later, Herod II renamed the city Neronias after Nero; then under the Byzantines the city reverted to the name Paneas (like Panion). The point is this, Jesus fed 4,000 on a missions trip among the unreached, and then in a city whose names venerated Pan, Caesar, Nero, and Phillip, He asked His followers who they thought He was.

We disciples tend to be like the blind man at Bethesda. Even when Jesus touches us, it takes us a while to see clearly. Taken together—the Pharisees' bad doctrine, the missions trip, the question of who Jesus is—we see what Jesus was driving at: His purpose, not His power. The point is not that Jesus has all power; the point is that Jesus is the Messiah who came to earth to die for the sins of the whole world. Jesus asked the critical question of His identity in a pagan, idolatrous international city, because all those around Him continued to be blind to the fact that His raging passion and central purpose was to die for the sins of the *world*. It's not about food; it's about unreached peoples! It's not about dying to self to gain the reputation as an ascetic; it's about losing our life *for the gospel's sake*. The gospel is intrinsically universal, inclusive of all nations. What frustrates Jesus to the point of Him telling His own to get behind Him because they think like Satan is our slowness to see that His purpose is that every people group be represented around the throne. It's not about food or power and authority or self-denial. Let's stop frustrating Jesus. Let's see clearly that He has one goal: the gospel going to every people.

PRAYER FOCUS: *Thai, Southern of Thailand (Evangelical: 0.25%)*

OCTOBER 21: JESUS GETS FRUSTRATED

TODAY'S READING: MATTHEW 17; MARK 9

"What we can say for sure is that, at the very least,
God calls every Christian to live with a missionary heart."

DAVID SILLS

In missions, we must have eyes for Jesus only. The transfiguration reminds us that while law (Moses) and prophecy (Elijah) are not to be despised, they are not to be the focus either. We must be careful to look to Jesus, not experiences, and we must be careful to let Jesus frame and interpret our experiences. Peter, endearingly, didn't know what to say (it's endearing because it's so common to us all). The transfiguration is a classic example of the dirt and divinity principle. A bit of Jesus' glory was revealed, and Peter didn't know how to handle it, so he reacted emotionally. The Father corrected him, and us all, reminding us not to be enamored with experiences or rapturous revelations. We are to fixate on Jesus alone.

When we focus on Jesus, He says things we don't like. He refers to Himself as the Son of Man who has to die for the sins of the world. The disciples wanted to understand what just happened, while Jesus wanted them to focus on what will happen. The disciples continued to struggle with the spiritual component of Jesus' messianic mission, and Jesus continued to tell them it meant death and suffering before glory. They just couldn't wrap their heads around it. They were still thinking national and parochial deliverance and missed the grand scope—*all* the nations of the world. Part of this is ignorance, part prejudice, and part faithlessness. Ignorance because it blew their expectations, prejudice because they didn't want to share the Messiah, and faithlessness because they didn't believe Jesus could work through them to cast a demon from a little boy, much less from a Gentile people group. Jesus' frustration with the faithless goes beyond one small encounter with a demonized boy to the greater challenge of demonized peoples spiritually freed by the Messiah globally.

Lest we are too harsh on the disciples, let us bring our own discipleship and faith to reckoning. We can no longer say we're ignorant about God's grand design to redeem all peoples to Himself. That leaves prejudice and faithlessness. Do we really want Arabs and Africans in our heavenly home? Do we really have faith that Jesus can save the Saudi king? Are we more enamored with Moses and Elijah (tradition and charisma) than we are with Jesus going to the cross? Would we rather have things remain as they are and seek internal reform than pay the price of dying to self so that the world might be saved, and does that posture lead us to say ridiculous things? The Father made Moses and Elijah disappear and thundered from heaven that we focus on His beloved Son who came to suffer and die for the sins of the whole world. Jesus thunders through the Gospels that He expects us to have the faith to follow Him to the cross, to lay down our lives for unreached peoples. Jesus gets frustrated when we don't believe His mighty power can use us to set demonized peoples of earth free. Let's not frustrate Jesus.

PRAYER FOCUS: *Zaza-Dimli of Turkey (Evangelical: 0.0%)*

OCTOBER 22: NINETY-NINE BEHIND

TODAY'S READING: MATTHEW 18

*"The Christian is not obedient unless he is doing all in his power
to send the Gospel to the heathen world."*

A. B. SIMPSON

There is a contemporary worship song that celebrates Jesus leaving the ninety-nine to find "me." I find this song sung in lands full of churches ironic. I'm not saying it's untrue in these contexts because every lost soul matters; it's just ironic as the text clearly indicates the shepherd left the many and safe for the dangerous zones (mountains, Matt. 18:12) to find the ones without access. The ninety-nine in the churches sing as if they were the one. We make the same mistake in our hermeneutic of "little ones" with the popular application being children (v. 10). However, Jesus was clearly talking about the lost (v. 11). The little ones in His mind are the lost, the unreached peoples who have wandered away, the one UPG not represented in the fold. By no means am I saying pagans in cities full of churches or cute kids in Kenya or Colombia are lesser souls than unreached peoples. I *am* saying the Bible's attention is ever on the one with no access to the gospel. Jesus repeatedly sought and seeks to yank our attention towards the one in the mountains, the one underrepresented, the one who has never heard, the other sheep, the cities beyond. We do a disservice to God if we make the poor child in a Christian home overseas or the lost pagan who has willingly rejected the gospel one-hundred times the focus of missionary efforts. Jesus says we must leave the ninety-nine; we should not stay among them singing about how we are the one.

It is in this missionary context that Jesus brought up a sinning brother, binding prayer, and compassionate hearts. Notice His transition: "It is not the will of your Father…that one of these little [unreached peoples] should perish. *Moreover* if your brother sins…" (vv. 14–15, italics added). What a strange link and transition to forgiveness and prayer. Unless, of course, *it is sin* to neglect the inconveniently located unreached while you jump around with the found. Jesus seemingly implies that He takes missions so seriously that we have a collective responsibility to keep each other focused, an accountability so serious that those who don't align with God's assignment for the church are to be ostracized. Jesus then goes on to tell us to pray together, and when we gather to pray for the lost (the chapter's context), He is there in the midst. Evidently, leaving the ninety-nine to search for the one and banding together to pray for the lost is the same place — the place where Jesus is. Should we not have compassion on our fellow man, just as Jesus had pity on us? Is not the proper response to being saved more time on our knees and less time jumping around? We can jump around uninterrupted in heaven. For now, let's pray and let's leave the ninety-nine seeking the one, for that is where Jesus is and where He commands us to be.

PRAYER FOCUS: *Pashtun, Northern of United Arab Emirates (Evangelical: 0.0%)*

OCTOBER 23: THE CLAIMS OF JESUS

TODAY'S READING: JOHN 7–8

"The Lord did not tell us to build beautiful churches, but to evangelize the world."

OSWALD J. SMITH

Jesus made His way to Jerusalem again, this time during the Feast of Tabernacles, also called the Feast of Booths. The feast remembered both the Exodus and the end of harvest. Included were elements of thanksgiving for what God had done in providing water in times past and elements of prayer that the fall season would provide enough rain for the spring harvest. During the feast the priests drew water from the pools of Siloam and carried it to the temple where they quoted Scripture and symbolically poured the water out at the foot of the altar to commemorate water from the rock that saved the Israel.

When Jesus cried out at the feast, "If anyone thirsts, let him come to Me and drink…and out of his heart will flow rivers of living water" (John 7:37–38), He was claiming to be the very fulfilment of the feast itself, the very answer to prayer, the very fulfilment of prophecy. John also tells us this water is the Spirit who Jesus gives to those who believe in Him, and lest we forget the purpose of the Spirit poured out, Acts 1:8 tells us it is so the river of Jesus' life may pour from us to all the nations. John 7 is a grand revelation of the missionary heart of God. God has saved us and given us His Spirit, and He wants His Spirit to flow from us to all the nations. As is God's way, when we drink deeply of Jesus, there is so much more of Him than one person or people can contain. He will burst from them and in Spirit life flow to all the nations.

John 8 is a continuation of the narrative of Jesus at the Feast of Tabernacles. The priests not only poured water, they also lit menorahs in the temple, usually in the court of women, casting a brilliant, festive light in all directions. This court sat directly in front of the treasury where Jesus was when He claimed to be the truth that sets all people free. Jesus looked out at the glowing courtyard as He not only claimed to be living water, but the truth, freedom, and most shockingly the I AM that was before Abraham. Jesus made it very clear from that moment that He is God and that His plan includes all peoples. For both realities He was hated and would be killed.

As C. S. Lewis articulately put it in *Mere Christianity*, there is no room for ambiguity: "A man who was merely a man and said the sort of things Jesus said would not be a great moral teacher. He would either be a lunatic—on the level with a man who says he is a poached egg—or else he would be the devil of hell. You must make your choice. Either he was and is the Son of God, or else a madman or something worse. You can shut him up for being a fool, you can spit at him and kill him as a demon, or you can fall at his feet and call Him Lord and God. But let us not come with any patronizing nonsense about his being a great human teacher. He has not left that open to us. He did not intend to."

PRAYER FOCUS: *Turk of United States (Evangelical: 0.5%)*

OCTOBER 24: OUR PRIMARY IDENTITY

TODAY'S READING: JOHN 9–10

The Gospel of John was written almost sixty years after Jesus died, after the epistles, after the formation of the early church, after the first waves of persecution. Not only had Christians been martyred, they also were being cast out of synagogues and shunned in their own society and community. John wrote reminding them that this was nothing new, reminding them that Jesus always divides.

In the first century, the Sadducees had Roman support and were the official religious authorities, but the Pharisees were more popular with the local people. Consider, if you will, the Pharisees as the "Mutaawa" of Jesus' time. In present-day Saudi Arabia there has been an alliance between the royal family and the Wahabi sect of Islam. The Wahabi have functioned to the house of Saud as the Sadducees to the Romans as the recognized religious authorities. The Mutaawa have been the vigilante religious police who volunteer their services to ensure the promotion of virtue and the subjugation of vice. The Wahabi are more formal, the Mutaawa more forceful.

There is a debate as to whether followers of Jesus can remain culturally religious after coming to Jesus, and John 9 helps definitively answer this question. Jesus divides, and to follow Him fully is to ultimately mean ejection from any community that denies His deity. The Jews had agreed that "if anyone confessed that He was Christ, he would be put out of the synagogue" (John 9:22). In the days of Jesus and the days of the early church, to follow Him had religious, cultural, and societal consequences. This by no means implies that followers of Jesus should adopt non-indigenous cultural Christian forms, but it *does* mean one cannot stay a cultural Muslim, for example, *and* follow Jesus. One can stay Arab (humbly proud), stay Saudi (joyful and glad), and follow Jesus, but one cannot stay Muslim, and the non-biblical aspects of being Arab and Saudi must likewise be evacuated (same goes for Americans, Asians, Africans, etc.).

When we come to Jesus, we come to the light of the world! Jesus is Master of all peoples and brings light to the darkness of all religions. He insists on a flock that hears His voice as He leads them out, and whatever and whoever came before are thieves and robber who only kill and destroy. But Jesus calls us out of bondage into abundant life and promises there will be one flock and one shepherd. All peoples of earth must unite in the new tribe called "the church" under the authority of Jesus, and all new believers from everywhere must have their primary identity with this flock. No longer can our primary identity be Arab or Saudi, and it can certainly not include being culturally Muslim. We must be called by the name of Christ and linked spiritually to the people of Christ both militant (alive and active) and at rest (glorified and observant). There is a necessary division that is the consequence of following Jesus. There is a calling out of all that is broken and a uniting with our new people. Once in the hands and tribe of Christ, no other identity or ideology can snatch us away.

PRAYER FOCUS: *Karakalpak, Black Hat of Uzbekistan (Evangelical: 0.0%)*

"Hearing the missionary call has a great deal to do with what you are listening for."

DAVID SILLS

Luke, a Greek, was very careful to point out the intentionality of Jesus to include all the nations in His kingdom. In telling the parable of the Good Samaritan, Jesus made a hero of a non-Jewish enemy to show that His view of love extended beyond the one who was nearby. It felt then as it would today if we used the example in which a pastor and a soccer mom refused to help a woman raped and instead ran away in fear, while the local radical Islamic cleric rescued her.

Luke also stretched his readers when he told the story of Mary and Martha. He pointed out that Jesus endorsed the woman who acted like a man, for it was not for women of that time to act like a male disciple and sit at the feet of Jesus. They were to serve in the kitchen or hover in the background. But Jesus lauded Mary and said she chose the better part, the one thing needed. How important that we remember intimacy is more important than industry. It's not that hard work and active ministry are wrong; it's that they must flow out of intimacy with Jesus and are lesser in value and impact. If we want to change the world, we must first sit at Jesus' feet and feed on Him, for there we are satiated and have something to feed the hungry. However, we cannot slip into the subtle, common error of feeding on Jesus only to have something to give the nations; that turns intimacy into industry and these must be distinct.

A similar distinction must be made with authority. Jesus clearly pointed out that for men and women it is better to be under authority than over it. We are not to rejoice in ministry that gives us power over demons (which He has and which He delights in). We are to rejoice that we will forever be under His blessed rule in His presence where no demons will ever strike again. It is an easy thing to revel in the victories of ministry. When the strength of God flows through us to minister and to overcome evil, it is indeed a joy, but let us not become addicted to that lesser good. Let us remain centered on the greater good of His intimate presence where He has banished all evil. Let us even here chose the better par: The authoritative presence of Jesus over us trumps our authoritative ministry over demons.

Both of these stories are introduced with Jesus sending His disciples out into every city and place He was about to go. What sobriety that Jesus has sent us out as sheep among wolves. I can't help but think that we fight about who will stay home and rule the sheep when Jesus told us to pray that the Lord of the harvest would send us out seemingly defenseless among spiritual predators. It is no accident that these two sentiments of God are next to one another: Pray for laborers, sheep among wolves. It's hard, if not impossible and irresponsible, to go to difficult places defenseless if we are primarily activity oriented. But if have the great good of being under authority and the greatest good of being intimate with Jesus, then it's not only doable, it is a delight.

PRAYER FOCUS: *Nung of Vietnam (Evangelical: 0.15%)*

OCTOBER 26: DELIGHTFUL IN TERROR

TODAY'S READING: LUKE 12–13

"I am on a crusade right now to recruit martyr missionaries for the least reached people groups of the world."

DAVID SITTON

These two chapters in Luke are delightful in their terror. Jesus' passion was unleashed, and we get a glimpse of the God of awe and wonder who is absolutely focused on His glory among all peoples and absolutely intolerant of any and all who do not align themselves to His passions. Gentle Jesus faded as mighty God clarified strong realities in no uncertain terms. We have self-anesthetized our reading of the Gospels by our attempted foolish taming of wild Jesus. We must discipline ourselves to read the text without censoring Christ's ire and emotion.

Here is what the text simply says uncensored: Don't fear the devil; fear God who can both kill you and cast you into hell. If you deny Jesus before men, He will deny you before the angels at the judgment seat. The fool is the one who lays up riches for himself but is not rich toward God. Be ready, for the Son of Man is coming at an hour you do not expect. When the Son of Man comes, the servant who knew His Master's will and did not prepare himself or do according to His will shall be beaten with many stripes. Jesus came to send fire on the earth, and He wishes it were already kindled and is distressed until it is accomplished. We all deserve towers to fall on us, and we are all going to die. If we don't bear fruit, Jesus is going to cut us down; why should we use up ground?

Then in a magnificent distraction, Jesus took a breath from His holy tirade and lavished compassion on a woman who was sick for eighteen years: "So ought not this woman, being a daughter of Abraham, whom Satan has bound…be loosed" (Luke 13:16)? He then resumed His diatribe: "I do not know you.… Depart from Me, all you workers of iniquity. There will be weeping and gnashing of teeth…and yourselves thrust out" (vv. 27–28). And finally, He said, "Go, tell that old fox Herod he can't kill me because I am busy dying for the sins of the whole world" (see v. 32).

Jesus is awesome. He takes our breath away. He just unloaded a torrent of rebuke and correction in rapid fire. Then in the midst of going ballistic, he paused to heal a woman, then He returned to yelling. And it's all about missions! It's a fantastic revelation of God! He is ultra-focused on His mission to redeem a remnant from every tribe, tongue, people, and nation, and He is completely intolerant and enraged against those who do not understand and who will not zealously comply with His purposes. In this vignette, we see God made flesh in the raw beauty of His primary love: all peoples of earth. In that holy fire He warns us: If we know His will and do not align our passions with His, we will be beaten with many stripes and possibly excluded from glory. The Hadrami of Yemen will be represented in heaven with or without us.

PRAYER FOCUS: *Arab, Hadrami of Yemen (Evangelical: 0.0%)*

OCTOBER 27: HATE YOUR FAMILY FOR A MOMENT
TODAY'S READING: LUKE 14-15

The non-missionary Christian is very generous, but unfortunately to the wrong people, or better said, unfortunately not to the right people. Jesus was often criticized for dining with untouchables. He was expected to wine and dine the influential. He used these misunderstandings to underline that the heart of Father God is oriented towards those outside His house. Jesus bluntly said that we should not lavish generosity and hospitality on family and friends, but on those who cannot repay us. We always try to soften the sledgehammer blows of Jesus' truth; even reading that sentence you probably blanched. But Jesus went further and said that if we don't hate our family, take up our cross, and follow Him, we can't be His disciple.

Jesus' time in ministry was a great disappointment to His family. He never acted as they wanted Him to act. He never lavished on them the attention they craved. He never stayed with them when they needed Him most. He was not generous towards them with His time or words as society demanded. Jesus was not mean, rude, or stingy with His family; He was and is just more focused on those outside the house than those in it (as His Father is). This prioritization of the lost in the heart of the Father is unsettling to the found (ask the older son in Luke 15:28), but it can be reconciled if we understand timing. The prioritization of the lost over family, the "hating" of family is simply a recognition of eternity. Those of the household of faith will have forever with Jesus. All that He has is ours. But in this fleeting moment, we are in the last few seconds of time and billions will perish without Him. Jesus loves His family dearly, and He knows that in the blink of the eye, we will joy together forever. So, His passionate focus is not that enduring reality but last-minute rescue and adoption, and He wants us to have that same passion and drive.

The real problem these texts point out is not the words and action of Jesus which call us to bless those who cannot repay and to turn our energy away from family and found. The real problem is the incredible selfishness we have swathed in the concealing clothes that we call family stewardship. How inward are we if we demand all the attention of heaven while all hell breaks loose around us? All Jesus asks is that we get up from our cozy tables, launch ourselves from our La-Z-Boys, and propel ourselves into frenzied action with Him. Jesus has prepared a feast for all He loves, and He is doing one last passionate dash around the neighborhood of earth, frantically looking for any people group that is hungry and alone. His whole purpose is to revel with us forever. Can we begrudge this last lap of invitation? Can we resent that His focus is momentarily on others? Should we not rather leave our own mothers and fathers, our own beloved sons, and run with Jesus to the 2.6 million Pashtun of Afghanistan? Is not the problem with us when we get jealous that Jesus insists that the lost must be found and His house must be filled?

PRAYER FOCUS: *Pashtun, Northern of Afghanistan (Evangelical: 0.01%)*

OCTOBER 28: JUST BE A GOOD STEWARD

TODAY'S READING: LUKE 16-17

"You can't take it [money] with you, but you can send it on ahead."

OSWALD J. SMITH

The point of the potentially confusing parable of the unjust steward is that we are to be resourceful and use all the means available to us for maximum benefit. We will all give an account of our stewardship. One day we will stand before God and He will ask us: "What did you do about my one Great Commission? How did you leverage your life and all your resources for the maximum glory of my Father among all nations?" This question should either terrify or motivate us. If we have not been faithful to make disciples from among all unreached peoples with unrighteous mammon, why would Jesus trust us with true riches?

The haunting question for the wealthy of the world (which includes most every Christian in the West) is if we are serving money or if we are using money to fulfill the Master's commission. We castigate the Pharisees of Jesus' day, willfully forgetting that we who are ministers and missionaries are the Pharisees of our day. We travel land and sea to make converts, yet we are not immune to serving money. The human heart does not change that much, and if the religious leaders and respected spiritual missionaries in the time of Christ were susceptible to the allure of riches, let us not pretend we are immune. It is particularly important for those who live off the sacrificial donations of hardworking men and women to give careful account of our stewardship. Some at home may be at fault for squandering money on themselves, while some on the field may be at fault for squandering the trust of the faithful. It is all too easy to live a comfortable international life, a life that gets credit for being abroad but a life that is not reflective of the sacrifice which empowers it. We all will give an account for our stewardship, and if correction is needed, it must be made now. The time is coming when no changes can be made.

Reverend Larry Griswold gave my wife and I some advice when we were young missionaries. We have referred to it countless times, needing to revisit it now more than ever. Putting his loving hands on our shoulders, he looked right in our eyes and quoted Luke 17:10: "When you have done all those things that you are commanded, say: 'We are unprofitable servants. We have done what was our duty to do.'" The error of missionary senders is to think that our giving removes responsibility to go, and that those who go are special. The error of missionary goers is to think our going removes the responsibility to give, and that we who go are special. Jesus cuts through both levels of nonsense and lovingly but curtly says: "Just do your duty. Just be a good steward. Just use all your life and all your wealth for My glory among all the nations." When the Son of Man comes, may He find many faithful on this earth, those who never stopped giving, never stopped going, never stopped praying, never stopped living (and dying) for His glory among every unreached people.

PRAYER FOCUS: *Berber, Imazighen of Algeria (Evangelical: 0.63%)*

OCTOBER 29: DEALING WITH THE DEAD

TODAY'S READING: JOHN 11

"Will you shed your tears for the souls of the nations?"

WENDI STRANZ

Let us be clear. Every false religion of the world is a demonic death trap. Jesus stands at the doors of those graves, and He does not like death. Jesus groans and weeps over the spiritually dead. Should we not stand with Jesus at the grave and groan? Two evangelists in the early days of the Salvation Army received a difficult assignment in a place of much spiritual death. After repeated futility they wrote William Booth and lamented that they had tried everything and nothing worked. He simply wrote back: "Try tears." Sometimes we just need to stand with Jesus and survey the wreckage of death, crying.

Missions work is not complicated; it's just hard. Someone has to do the difficult, unglamorous labor of rolling away the stones. We cannot look at the amazing movement of Iranians coming to Jesus today without consideration of Robert Bruce who in the 1860s wrote from Iran: "I'm not reaping. I'm not sowing. I'm not even plowing. I'm just gathering rocks from the field." Though the church is but a few thousand, the largest indigenous church on the Arabian Peninsula is in Yemen. We may recognize the famous quote: "I have but one candle of life to burn, and I would rather burn it out in a land filled with darkness than in a land flooded with light." We forget Ion Keith Falconer said these words upon arriving in Yemen in 1885. He only lived there two years, dying in 1887. In 1921, his mission was expelled. The first indigenous church was established until 1961, seventy-four years after Falconer died. None of us harvest without someone long before removing stones. There will be no harvest tomorrow if we are not faithful to move stones today.

Jesus reminds us that if we believe, we will see glory, and His life guarantees that suffering must precede that view. When Jesus groaned at Lazarus' grave, Luke used a word recorded only twice in Scripture, a word with the connotation of "disappointment in lack of trust." I wonder if Jesus groaned not only because a loved one was dead, but also because the living ones did not believe. We must believe that God can raise Muslims, Hindus, Buddhists, animists, secularists, lost family, beloved friends, and unreached peoples *from the dead!* This is our work: to *believe!*

It's easy to fall in love with an idea, map, chart, even a statistic, but discipleship is messy, mentoring draining, and investing in others arduous and unceasing labor. Resurrection is exciting, but the real work is in the loosing and letting go. We cannot microwave discipleship, and the Great Commission will not be fulfilled from our banquet halls or our mission tour vans. We will have to live among the dead, deal with the smell, and unwrap the stinky grave clothes that defile the dead.

PRAYER FOCUS: *Rajbansi (Hindu Traditions) of Bangladesh (Evangelical: 0.0%)*

OCTOBER 30: THE ERRORS OF PRAYER

TODAY'S READING: LUKE 18

Luke's travel narrative is much longer than the accounts in Matthew and Mark and comes to its conclusion in Luke 18. Given the reality that the gospel is a message meant to travel, it's fitting that Jesus taught while he covered territory. It is also fitting that this missionary training of His disciples culminated with teaching on prayer as Jesus revealed two errors in missionary prayer.

Don't stop asking in faith (Luke 18:1–8). To be importunate is to keep on asking even when denied. Thankfully for us we pray to a just judge who is delighted when we approach Him in prayer if we ask according to His will. It is eminently clear from the Bible that the will of God is for the gospel to be preached in all the world among every people group, so asking for that gladdens His heart. The prayer that representatives of every people group will surround the throne is not denied, just delayed. God in His inscrutable wisdom wants us to keep asking for it. Perhaps He knows that if we ask for it often enough, we will eventually start doing something about it.

Don't trust in yourself or your prayer (18:9). The castigation of those who trusted in themselves is in the context of prayer—self-congratulatory and arrogant prayers. Shockingly the inference Jesus makes is that we can't trust in prayer; in other words, we don't pray to prayer. When we pray trusting ourselves, we effectually delude ourselves into thinking the power is in the act of prayer. It is not; that is animism at worst and legalism at best. The power is in God, not in prayer. If power was in prayer, then we could live in any fashion and then pray, and prayer would work. The fact that prayer only "works" when our spirits are right, when we pray the will of God, and when our trust is in God shows us that self-righteous prayer is useless prayer. We don't pray for the nations from the posture of "we are right and they are wrong, so Lord, make them right like us." We pray for the nations from the humility of "oh, Lord, we are a mess and get it all wrong, and our person and our nation are wicked and rebellious, so Lord, have mercy on us all because we are all wrong and only You are right." To ask Jesus to make the nations like us, or like our nation, is to pray self-righteously. God has no intention of making the nations look like me or the church abroad like the church at home. He has every intention of making them look like Him.

Sometimes prayer is just thinly veiled disgust. We don't actually love the Muslim, Hindu, Buddhist, pagan, secularist, or atheist we pray for; we pray for them in the haughty spirit of rejoicing that we're not like them. But we are like them, more than we know. If we are to pray for the nations in a way that quickens the heart of God to answer, let us beat our breast and say: "Lord, have mercy on me, a sinner, and on my wicked and evil nation, and Lord, grant the same mercy to the Bobo Madare of Burkina Faso and beyond."

PRAYER FOCUS: *Bobo Madare of Burkina Faso (Evangelical: 0.01%)*

OCTOBER 31: THE ONE THING WE LACK

TODAY'S READING: MATTHEW 19; MARK 10

All three synoptic Gospels mention the encounter of Jesus and the rich young ruler,[1] and they all have the same point, a point we tend to soften or miss: It is impossible for a rich man to get into heaven. We squirm and do hermeneutical gymnastics to avoid wrestling with what Jesus said. He plainly said it is easier for a camel to go through the eye of a needle than for a rich man to get to heaven. Our gymnastics of discomfort led us to the ridiculous notion that there was a small gate called "Camel" and a camel had to hobble through it—difficult but doable. Nonsense. Jesus bluntly said that a rich man cannot enter heaven. Understanding the "already, not yet" nature of the Kingdom, Jesus did not refer to the generalized authority of Jesus over Christians in the now (real as that must be); He spoke of the Kingdom to come. His repeated default understanding of the Kingdom was the great day of the Lord and following, so He said to the rich young ruler, "You want eternal life and heaven? You can't get there rich. You will have to use all your wealth here on earth, for when you die you won't take a cent with you."

The application: It doesn't matter if you're rich or poor, we all enter heaven penniless. No rich man can enter heaven. It is impossible to take one penny with you, so be sure to spend all your pennies here on earth. What a waste if you reach the end of your life and have money in the bank, money that could have been used for gospel glory. Spend your money as you spend your life—poured out for Jesus. Let's enter the grave spent and broke. If we are so because we gave all to the gospel preached among all unreached peoples, great will be our eternal riches indeed.

Mark 10:45 is the classic text on servant greatness; it's also a missions text. Jesus told His disciples that the Son of Man will win those peoples to Himself by dying for them. Jesus, knowing He will soon send His disciples to be His witnesses, referenced how the Gentiles exercise authority and in effect said: "As you spread out and cover the earth as missionaries, you will see various leadership models. Remember the way that we save the nations is by dying for them, the way that we serve the nations is by giving them the gospel at the cost of our own freedom and life." We cannot divorce this great text from its context: Jesus dying for all the peoples of earth. Servant leadership is predicated on laying down our lives for the unreached of the earth that they may be saved. Even more biblical to say: Servanthood is to go into all the world as missionaries and serve the gospel to all peoples at great cost to ourselves, not to be served at home or entertained at church with no cost to our pocketbook or person. Let's spend all our life and money on seeing representatives of every people group in heaven. It's the one thing we all still lack.

PRAYER FOCUS: *Han Chinese, Teochew of Cambodia (Evangelical: 0.40%)*

LIVE | DEAD

"Some of us are senders and some are goers. Neither is more important than the other. Neither is possible without the other."

DAVID SILLS

NOVEMBER

NOVEMBER 1: THE ELEVENTH-HOUR MISSIONARIES

TODAY'S READING: MATTHEW 20–21

God's heart for His own glory and God's heart of love for people are unified and inseparable passions. Because God created man to be most satisfied when we glorify Him, the best thing for us was this union of our satisfaction and His glorification. Matthew 20 reminds us that the God who desires all peoples to be satisfied in Him is the same God who desires all peoples to be active in bringing glory to His name from all peoples. In other words: All the gospel must be preached to all the world by all the nations. There is no country, no tribe, and no church exempt from the Great Commission. All God's children must be missionary hearted; otherwise, they are illegitimate pretenders.

The parable of the laborers simply reminds us that God is ever wanting (and demanding) all His children be part of the family business. God is about the work of redeeming representatives of every people to Himself and He expects His whole family to share in that work. Dr. Lazarus Chakwera was the general superintendent of the Malawi Assemblies of God. In partnership with Dr. John York, he founded the 11th Hour Institute. Based on this passage in Matthew, Dr. Chakwera made the case that the African church must rise up in mission and deploy its best ministers to take the gospel where the gospel has not gone. He vociferously insisted that the Great Commission both included missionaries from the Global South *and* necessitated their active, equal involvement.

What Dr. Chakwera insisted on for the African church, the Holy Spirit insists on for the globe: All of God's people must be involved in missions. In this eleventh hour of human history we all recognize this is not sterile affirmative action—this is urgent interdependency. The body of Christ will not be able to complete the Great Commission unless all our hands, bodies, wills, resources, personnel, prayers, and sacrifice are laid on the altar. We must be very careful about arrogance on both sides. For those nations who have long labored, we must not resent the entrance of others, proudly remonstrating that we have borne the heat of the day. Nor must we insist that the new harvesters only use our equipment or methods. For those nations new to the field, we must not ignore the hard-learned lessons of missions history, nor think that everything done before we arrived was foolish, nor must we try to emulate systems our cultures or contexts cannot support.

Matthew inserted Jesus' call to serving one another in the double context of His dying for the sins of every people and the raising up of eleventh-hour missionaries. This is no accident, for sacrificial service of our brothers and sisters is a missionary necessity. True service is when God's people lay down their lives for each other, even as they lay down their lives for the nations. If all who are in mission (old and new) will lay down their lives for one another, then truly the Son of David will ride in to save, lowly and riding on donkey. Together the global church is to be that lowly donkey Jesus rides into town on.

PRAYER FOCUS: *Hausa of Chad (Evangelical: 0.01%)*

NOVEMBER 2: ENTERING WITHOUT INVITATION

TODAY'S READING: LUKE 19

In his book *Jesus of Arabia: Christ Through Middle Eastern Eyes*, Andrew Thompson related the story of missionaries on the Arabian Peninsula who handed a Bible open to Luke 19 and the story of Zacchaeus to Arab Muslims. With no knowledge of the gospel, no Christian theology, no context whatsoever, the Arabs were invited by the missionaries to read the story in Arabic.

The Arab men complied and when finished protested in horrified agreement. Here's my paraphrase of the story: "This is terrible! What Jesus did was improper! No one in our culture has the right to invite himself into our homes. Not even the Sultan has the right to invite himself into our homes—he must wait to be invited. The only One who has the authority to invite Himself into our homes is God Himself!" I wonder if the light dawned for those Arab men even as it dawned on the missionaries in a new way. I've read the Zacchaeus story dozens of times, heard it preached dozens more, sung it a dozen times more than that—and never once did I read deity into Jesus' proclamation of "Zacchaeus, you come down, for I'm coming to your house today!" But Arab Muslims did! Semitic men hearing a Semitic story for the first time opened our eyes to something we have missed: Jesus claimed to be God and He claimed to have the authority to invite Himself into anyone's home, anyone's heart, anyone's culture.

For this is the second point we often miss in the Zacchaeus narrative: "Zacchaeus was no mere tax collector. He was a chief tax collector in upper management, the most powerful governmental authority of Jericho in the 'Revenue Department'. He was in charge of a number of men who were assigned to various duties and customs in the surrounding area.... Furthermore, Jericho was a major trade center on the route between Egypt, Palestine, Arabia, and Syria. In other words Zacchaeus is a major player in the Roman government." Not only did Jesus claim to be God with the right to enter any individual's home without invitation, He also claimed to be the God who can enter any nation without invitation, including Rome, the superpower of the day. Sycamore trees and short people may be what we remember, but deity and missions is what our hearts should sing.

The next story Luke recorded was not accidental. After Zacchaeus promised to use his wealth for the purposes of Jesus, Jesus told the story of investing our wealth for the King. Many resented God's demands over their businesses, in effect refusing to dedicate their wealth to see the Kingdom spread from shore to shore. Jesus warned that those who resist His demand to enter their homes and use their business wealth to reach the nations will be brought before Him and slain. Whether our home, donkey, business, or money, if the Lord says He has need of it, we must loose it and let it go that His house become a house of prayer for *all* nations.

PRAYER FOCUS: *Mongol of China (Evangelical: 0.40%)*

The last half of the Gospel of John is devoted to the "Passion Week," the last week of Jesus' life. All four Gospels focus on this week, for it is indeed the purpose of why Jesus came—to die for the sins of world. The world comprised of over 15,000 nations, the world that still has 7,000 nations without a church vibrant enough to reach their own, the world that still needs missionaries from all nations to go with the passion of Jesus to these unreached peoples, never forgetting that passion means suffering. The last half of the Gospel of John details how Jesus suffered that unreached people groups may be saved. Missions has ever included suffering. Jesus will tell us later that we are sent in the same way He was.

In her classic missionary hymn, Margaret Clarkson helps us remember just exactly what the second half of John is all about, what the Bible is all about, and what we should be all about.

So send I you to labor unrewarded, to serve unpaid, unloved, unsought, unknown, to bear rebuke, to suffer scorn and scoffing, so send I you, to toil for Me alone.

So send I you to bind the bruised and broken, over wandering souls to work, to weep, to wake, to bear the burdens of a world a-weary, so send I you, to suffer for My sake.

So send I you to loneliness and longing, with heart a-hungering for the loved and known, forsaking kin and kindred, friend and dear one, so send I you to know My love alone.

So send I you to leave your life's ambition, to die to dear desire, self-will resign, to labor long, and love where men revile you, so send I you, to lose your life in Mine.

So send I you to hearts made hard by hatred, to eyes made blind because they will not see, to spend, though it be blood to spend and spare not, so send I you to taste of Calvary.

John went on to record that "unless a grain of wheat falls into the ground and dies, it remains alone; but if it dies, it produces much grain" (12:24). As for Jesus, so for His church. We must die to self and lay down our lives if the nations are to be spared and saved. Jesus made this super clear in what theologians call a Markan sandwich: The bread on both sides is Mark intentionally recording the cursing of the fig tree and the meat of the sandwich is the cleansing the temple. Fig trees that do not produce figs are cursed, as are temples (churches, denominations, ministries, agencies, Christians, missionaries) that do not produce disciples from all nations.

PRAYER FOCUS: *Arab, Arabic Gulf Spoken of Egypt (Evangelical: 0.0%)*

NOVEMBER 4: TWO CRITICAL FLAWS

TODAY'S READING: MATTHEW 22; MARK 12

*"Any church that is not seriously involved in helping fulfill
the Great Commission has forfeited its biblical right to exist."*

OSWALD J. SMITH

Galilee in Jesus' day was an agriculturally fertile area with a combination of small farms and large private estates. Landowners had huge plantations and hired seasonal workers. Absentee owners were not unusual, and common concern centered on sufficient water for the area and enough housing for the migrant workers. Further, the trade route from Damascus to the Mediterranean skirted the eastern side of the Sea of Galilee, putting Galilee with its agriculture-rich estates and migrant workers along a major international trade route. Jesus will draw on these factors at one time or another in His parables. The parables of Matthew 22 and Mark 12 draw on the context of first century Galilee to show how the people of the King of kings continually insulted Him, abused His messengers, and despised His generosity. Jesus warned His own that the consequences for them was furious destruction and that He was intent on an inclusive calling of those from around the world, from the highways and hedges of the nations. The Jews saw themselves as the untouchable, irreplaceable caretakers of the plans of God, and Jesus shockingly disabused them of that arrogant assumption. He reminds us all that His mission never centers on us and His mission always centers on Jesus and the "others" who will honor the King.

Jesus goes on to point out two critical flaws that undermine His passions in the earth and lead us to being greatly mistaken: We are greatly mistaken when we don't understand the Scriptures and the power of God, nor that Jesus is God of the living. Seeking to trap Jesus, the Sadducees (legal religious authorities) who didn't believe in resurrection made up a ridiculous scenario they think will shame Him. Jesus replied that what was really shameful was to think God was focused on the dead and dying when He is the God of the living, ever pressing forward to an eternity where all nations enjoy Him forever. This is why Jesus again cited that God is the God of Abraham, Isaac, and Jacob—because God promised the patriarchs that from Abraham's seed all nations will come into the Kingdom.

Both Matthew and Mark recorded that Jesus made Himself greater than David; both claims came on the heels of Jesus establishing that the great commandment is to love God and love others. If we understand the Scriptures and the power of God, and if we understand that God is the God of the living, this is earthshaking. In context and rapid succession Jesus established His deity, His right to rule, His intention to include all nations in His kingdom, and His declaration that the greatest obedience is to love Him and to love our neighbors. At once Jesus pulled all things together into His eternal self, encapsulating all Scripture into the simple commission to *love Him by* loving all peoples of the earth.

PRAYER FOCUS: *Oromo, Bale of Ethiopia (Evangelical: 0.07%)*

The Pharisees of Jesus' time were quite respected. At first it was a little shocking for Jesus' followers and listeners to hear His vehement denunciations of these religious and spiritual leaders, for the Pharisees and scribes were generally held in high esteem. A good equivalent in our time would be missionaries, for they are generally respected by the community of faith, sometimes, even if inappropriately, more than local pastors. In that light, Matthew 23 sobers us with seven missionary warnings in which Jesus takes names and calls us some ugly names.

Woe to missionaries who bar the gate to heaven. As we spread the good news of the gospel to all peoples, we better live what we preach. Otherwise our hypocrisy will cause our listeners to reject Christ and go to hell. If we go out into all the world and cause people to choose hell, Jesus bluntly says they will have our company.

Woe to missionaries who pretend to pray and give. Missionaries are trusted with the money of the poor, not just the rich. Even as the Pharisees were trusted to steward the estates of the deceased. If we piously receive funds and cavalierly spend them, while pretending to be spiritual, we will pay for that largess on judgment day.

Woe to missionaries who make demonic disciples. Jesus has no tolerance for sons of hell that make sons of hell. Boarding an airplane and crossing oceans doesn't sanctify us. If demons are repressed within us, the pressure of culture and ministry will release them, and we will demonize others. Jesus can't stand missionaries who are supposed to be full of the Spirit but instead spawn evil.

Woe to missionaries who are blind idiots pretending to see yet focusing on the wrong things. Those commissioned to help all peoples understand principles but instead doggedly focus on obscure applications disgust Jesus and waste His precious time. On the narrow way we are to be big picture, principle-driven, and Spirit-led people.

Woe to missionaries who live the indulgent international life. Jesus is not fooled by missionaries who cry in pulpits and living rooms then live it up overseas with their international comforts. Jesus expects missionaries to live the crucified life, not just preach it.

Woe to missionaries who are dead and decaying from the inside out. There is nothing hidden from the One who sees every fork inserted in our mouths and every image we feed our minds. We who have learned to prize external beauty (eloquence, passion, intelligence) to the scorn of internal holiness are ugly to the Lord.

Woe to missionaries who are as deceptive as snakes. Children of light and messengers of truth can have nothing false about them. When we deceive ourselves or others, Jesus is revolted and to Him we are serpents winding our way to the fires of hell.

Is it shocking to consider that missionaries are guilty of the above indecencies? We often are. God have mercy. Yet, it's not only missionaries who act like Pharisees. God have mercy on us all. We dare not soften these verbal blows of Jesus or evade their warning.

PRAYER FOCUS: *Rajput (Hindu Traditions) of India (Evangelical: 0.0%)*

NOVEMBER 6: THE SIGNS OF THE TIMES

TODAY'S READING: MARK 13

"You must go or send a substitute."

OSWALD J. SMITH

Jesus referred to the "abomination of desolation" in Mark 13:14, and there is some conjecture about what that was/is. Daniel's use of the term was perhaps fulfilled when the Greek (Syrian) Antiochus Epiphanes sacrificed a pig to Zeus in the temple in 167 BC. Jesus perhaps was referring to Jewish patriots slaughtering priests in the temple in 66–70 AD or the Romans sacrificing to their army standards on the temple mount in 70 AD, then building a pagan temple there after another Jewish revolt in 135 AD. Perhaps Jesus was referring to something in the future. It's not super clear, but what is clear are the signs that will precede fulfillment. When His disciples asked Jesus about the timing of the end of human history and the physical, literal, comprehensive, eternal reign of God, He laid out signs, and they are all missions centered.

Nation will rise against nation. War is indeed hell, but wars pave the way to heaven. When we see yet another news story about yet another conflict, let us leaven our sorrow with the joy that we are one step closer to the Prince of Peace, the Son of Man, the King who will include all peoples in His kingdom, coming back in power and glory to kill death once and for all.

The gospel must first be preached to all the nations. We cannot escape the biblical focus on ethnicity. Over and over again, the Bible centers the mission of God as intentionally pursuing representatives from every people. Yes, we must plant churches in cities. Yes, we must plant churches across the generations. Yes, we must plant churches among the poor. Yes, we must plant churches among the influential. But none of these are the repeated focus, biblically, of missions, making disciples, and proclaiming the gospel. The Bible ever and again points us to unreached people groups—the inclusion of every ethnicity globally.

When they arrest you, it is not you who speak but the Holy Spirit; you will be hated by all for His name's sake. Arrest is just a matter of time if we are Spirit empowered. At some point the Herodias of our time will come unglued against the John the Baptist role we must take up. If we want Jesus to come, we must break the laws that restrict the gospel being proclaimed to every person in every tongue, and when we are resented for turning the world upside down, we must lift our heads to heaven, for our redemption draws nigh.

False christs and prophets will arise. We probably don't have more spiritual shenanigans per capita than in days past, but we certainly have the technology to better broadcast their poisonous ideas. What is false is proliferating both within and without the body of Christ. In this tragic proliferation, we take one comfort: We are that much closer to King Jesus coming, and when He comes, the Son of Man will indeed gather from the farthest parts of earth.

PRAYER FOCUS: *Minangkabau of Indonesia (Evangelical: 0.01%)*

Herod the Great's great building projects were crowned by the Temple Mount reconstruction. The temple by the time Jesus was ministering was certainly impressive—at least to others, not to Christ. The disciples called Jesus' attention to the temple, and He called their attention to eschatology, using the looming fall of Herod's temple as a reference point for the fall of all nations and the end of this present evil age. The crux of it all is the missionary mandate presented in Matthew 24:14.

And this gospel: "Gospel" means good news. There must be bad news if the good news is to make sense. God is only good if He sends bad people to hell. The bad news is that all people are bad, thus the whole world is under the wrath of a holy God. The good news is that in Jesus God saves us from sin by saving us from His own wrath. The love of God saves us from the wrath of God for the joys of God.

Of the kingdom: Jesus did not view His kingdom as of this world. He does not view our role as a clean-up crew so that this present world is fit for His rule. He is clear that He will return and burn everything up with fire and the elements themselves will dissolve in the fervent heat. The King will start over, ruling and reigning over a restored (new) heavens and earth. The Kingdom will not be established until the King is in residence physically.

Will be preached: Our biblical role is crystal clear, and the Spirit has found numerous ways to describe our primary assignment: town criers, prophets, ambassadors, announcers, watchmen on the wall, apostles, teachers, preachers, proclaimers, disciplers, and witnesses, *all titles* with the understanding that faith comes by hearing and hearing by the spoken word of God. From stables to stadiums, from ragged to rich, from illiterate to illuminati, our primary role is to open our mouths and herald the Messiah. Everything else we do must empower this primary assignment.

In all the world…to all the nations: The scope is universal. The clear intent is every ethnic group. The indubitable obedience is to send missionaries to every one of the 7,000 UPGs that as of yet do not have an indigenous church able to reach their own and beyond.

As a witness: The Greek word implies being a martyr, paying the price, embracing suffering, living the crucified life, being a faithful witness whether by shutting the mouth of lions or filling them. The gospel has ever gone forth under pressure, and in this last hour that will not diminish, it will increase. More bloody Christian seed must be sown before the final harvest.

And then the end will come: We are missionary because we want to go home, because we long for Jesus to come back and restore all things, because we agree with Paul that to die is gain and that to be with Christ is far, far better. This end is beautiful because it is but the end of the beginning. Next up? The presence of Jesus forever. No death, sin, curse, pain, tears, night, strife, sickness, or evil.

PRAYER FOCUS: *Gilaki of Iran (Evangelical: 0.0%)*

NOVEMBER 8: SERVED BY THE NATIONS

TODAY'S READING: MATTHEW 25

Directly after Matthew 24 and just before Matthew 28, Jesus told three parables that relate to His return, all missionary in nature. First, the wise virgins were those who would not give their oil away at the cost of the light for all. When asked to share their oil, they surprisingly stated: "No, lest there should not be enough for us and you" (Matt. 25:9). Jesus commissioned us to be His light in all the world, to every people. If we spend ourselves so that we have no light left, we offer no service to the world. A central principle of missions is that when it comes to intimacy with Jesus, the Spirit, and Father, no service, no giving of ourselves, no spending or sacrifice is wise if it extinguishes our lamp. If we are to be of any use to the Master and of any use to the lost, we must guard our oil so there is enough for "us and you." Intimacy with Jesus is the only hope for both us and the nations as we wait for His return.

Secondly, the parable of the talents was not about gaining more money, education, or natural talent. In the direct context of preaching the gospel to every nation and making disciples of every nation, "talents" refer to making disciples. Investing our talents means using whatever capacity we have to make disciples. Jesus knows we have different capacities and that some will make more disciples than others. He is good with that; in fact, He set that up. What He is not good with is if we don't make any disciples *at all*. The "good and faithful" pronouncement that will gladden our soul forever is not connected to the number of disciples, but to whether we made as many disciples as we possibly could. The reward for making disciples is more disciples, for the currency of God's realm has ever been and will be *people*. Discipleship is so beautiful that it will go on forever.

Thirdly, when the Son of Man (the Lord of all peoples) comes in His glory, *all the nations* will be brought before Him for judgment, and we see that some will be sheep (enter into heaven) and some goats (sent to hell). The joy is that we are guaranteed some fruit (disciples) from every people group, so we labor in hope and believe for that reward. The agony is that there will be some sent to eternal hell from every nation. What's intriguing is that the judgment of the nations will be linked to how they treated missionaries. Jesus expressed this shocking reality with an explanation regarding the provision of food, drink, shelter, and hospitality, that the righteous are the *nations* that serve *His brethren*.

Two realities have been lost from this text: One is that the service is done to evangelizing missionaries (not the poor), and two is that the nations of the world perform the service (or don't). Logically then, if the nations of the world are the ones to serve the brethren of Jesus, this act must be happening among the nations. The peoples of earth that love on missionaries and receive their message of repentance will be the sheep of God that forever enjoy heaven with our Good Shepherd.

PRAYER FOCUS: *Turkmen, Middle-Eastern of Iraq (Evangelical: 0.0%)*

NOVEMBER 9: WE WEEP WITH THEM

TODAY'S READING: MATTHEW 26; MARK 14

Jesus more than anticipated that the gospel would be preached in the whole world. He authorized it. And He authorized that our attention (all of us from all peoples) be directed on spending extravagantly on Him, for He is more precious than service to the poor. We know from Jesus' life and teaching that to love the poor is a reflection of God, but we also take warning that loving the poor is not more important than loving the Lord. Before we pour ourselves out for the world, we must pour ourselves out extravagantly at Jesus' feet, we must "waste" ourselves on Him. This is the key to the missionary assignment. The way the fragrance of Jesus wafts to every corner of the globe and penetrates the dying stench of every unreached people is by the people of God lavishing attention on Him. This is abiding. This is our first call. This is our joy and the source of our power on earth and our gladness in heaven—the extravagant luxury of extending time with Jesus.

In this first love we all betray Jesus. The true answer to who betrays is all of us. None of us pour on Jesus the affection, obedience, and adoration He alone deserves. None of us break our alabaster box consistently (we are more into sprinkling than immersion when it comes to our daily abandon). The beauty of Jesus is that knowing this, He yet abides with us, yet sheds His precious blood *for many* for the remission of sins. How much Jesus lavishes on us for the meager love we begrudgingly give Him. How foolish our protests of fidelity are to the divine ears and all-knowing heart. We all betray again and again, yet He ever lives and forgives. We speak vehemently while Jesus loves violently, and not just us, but the billions of betrayers around us.

The fate of the nations is mysteriously linked to prayer, but we can't endure in prayer, even in the most desperate and urgent times as we should. The fate of the nations depends on us representing Jesus well, but we make messes that He has to clean up. The fate of nations depends on us standing with Jesus in bold, holy witness, but at all the crucial moments the church forsakes Him and flees, naked and ridiculous, and our speech betrays that we are of Jesus, but not necessarily with Him. When we think how much God has entrusted to us, the intimacy and the responsibility, and how we have betrayed Him, we too must weep bitterly.

The gospel must be preached in all the world by weepers. There is no place for arrogance as we traverse the nations pleading with all peoples to waste themselves on Jesus. We who have been lavished on so extravagantly have betrayed that love so consistently. The cross is to us as much a wonder on our repeated visits as it is to those who stand there astonished for the first time. We weep with them. Our old tears mingling with their new ones, astounded, amazed, and atoned. I cannot stand at the cross weeping with the freshly forgiven without marveling that Jesus has again forgiven foolish, unfaithful me.

PRAYER FOCUS: *Jew, Romanian of Israel (Evangelical: 0.05%)*

NOVEMBER 10: TAKE UP YOUR TOWELS

TODAY'S READING: LUKE 22; JOHN 13

"In much of the world it's spring and not fall. In much of the world,
our workers go with a hoe and not a sickle."

J. PHILIP HOGAN

John's version of the Last Supper is unique from the synoptic Gospels, but not contradictory. John's account focuses on Jesus washing the disciple's feet. Interestingly, foot washing was not part of the Jewish Passover ritual. Jesus instituted something profoundly new, not just because He flipped the leadership/servant script by washing, but because He also crossed an international line, for "even a Jewish slave could not be required to wash his master's feet; such an act was only required of a non-Jewish slave!" Jesus not only demonstrated that leaders must humbly serve, but He also demonstrated that His followers must serve the nations, they must give up their racial prejudices, they must lay down their lives for all peoples, not just for the people they love or the people of their birth. One of the last acts of Jesus' freedom was to live out a cross-racial service and demand it be the norm for all who bear His name. We must wash the feet of the nations, even at cost to our own. Jesus would have His own feet nailed to the cross, as must ours be, for the feet that bear good news are ever bloodied.

When we understand that foot washing was an act Jews only received from non-Jews, we see Peter's objection in John 13:8 in the double angst of status and race. Jesus' answer must then be viewed with the same lens: If we will not serve, we have no part with Him, *and* if we will not cross racial and cultural barriers, we have no part with Him. To share in the missionary heart of Jesus is not an option, it's not an appendage, it's not something for the elite. If we do not share in God's burning passion to love and serve all peoples, we have no part of Him! We must follow His example on both counts. We must come down out of pride and we must come down out of prejudice, and we must carry our crosses that all men might be saved, that all unreached peoples might hear the gospel. The primary way we serve our world today without pride or prejudice is to ensure that every unreached people group hears of the Lord who came down from heaven to wash feet—all of our feet. By this all the world will know that we are His disciples, not by taking care of our friends and peers, but by serving the least, last, and lost. The world will know Jesus when we bend low at their feet to serve them, when we explain the action with tongues that still marvel at the God who died for man.

Our hearts may move us, but our feet must transport us. It is not enough to be stirred emotionally, we must move geographically. We must let our feet take us down the difficult trails that lead to dangerous places, strip away our armor to take up towels, and wash the feet of defiant peoples. Stupefied, they may just consider the invitation of the Savior, for what other God suffers such shame that we might be so clean?

PRAYER FOCUS: *Kabardian of Jordan (Evangelical: 0.04%)*

NOVEMBER 11: FAMOUS LAST WORDS

TODAY'S READING: JOHN 14–17

"The mission of the church is missions."

OSWALD J. SMITH

Final speeches are indicative of first and central passions. Today's text summarizes the heart of Jesus and the points He most wanted His disciples to retain. All fluff cast away, the simple passions of God are laid bare in one last appeal and explanation. To summarize the summary, here are the passages most critical and most consistent with the whole Bible's message: John 15:5, Jesus to the disciples; John 15:16, Jesus to the disciples again; and John 17:18, Jesus to the Father.

He who abides in Me, and I in him, bears much fruit (John 15:5). The word "abide" in Greek, *meno*, is where we get our word mansion, our home, where we spend our time. The word "fruit" in Greek, *karpos*, does not refer to character or the attributes of the Spirit in this context, but to that which is harvested, that which is outside and brought into the barns. Jesus is simply saying those who spend a lot of time with Him will make many disciples. The foundation of discipleship is to help others be like Jesus. If we are to help others be like Jesus, we must be like Jesus ourselves. If we are to be like Jesus, we must spend much time with Him. With His last teaching breath, Jesus simply said, "In order to make many disciples, you must spend much time with Me."

I chose you and appointed you that you should go and bear fruit, and that your fruit should remain [abide] (John 15:16). We have been told in no uncertain terms that we have been chosen and commissioned to go and make disciples, disciples that in turn spend a lot of time with Jesus. There is no ambiguity here, only authorization. Our task on earth is to go and make disciples and to center those disciples on Jesus. We don't have to spend any energy on what we are to do in this life. Over and over we have been told to go and to make disciples. The only question is where. And Jesus answered that for us, too.

As You have sent Me into the world, I have also sent them into the world (John 17:18). There is no confusion for the pure in heart regarding the focus of God and the locus of where we are to go make disciples that abide. Jesus has sent us to the world, the dangerous world, the unreceptive world, the lost world, the world that uses crosses, whips, mocking, stones, and swords to kill disciples, prophets, and ambassadors of Christ and the Son of God. The Father sent the Son to save souls at a dangerous time in a hostile environment. And so Christ sends us—to save souls in dangerous times and in hostile environments.

The only escape from direct obedience to the last (and first) words of Jesus is through either sophistry or stubborn rebellion. It's pretty clear: Spend time with Jesus and make disciples in all the world. It's not complicated: it's just hard.

PRAYER FOCUS: *Gujarati, Kenyan of Kenya (Evangelical: 0.02%)*

NOVEMBER 12: WHAT IS YOUR MONSTROUS EVIL?

TODAY'S READING: MATTHEW 27; MARK 15

Pilate, as the Roman governor of Judea, had the authority to execute when he saw best, and in the past he had no trouble mingling the blood of some Jews in their sacrifices (Luke 13:1). This man was no victim; he was powerful and capable of decisive acts. "Pilate deserves no sympathy for his dilemma in sentencing Jesus. As governor, he was authorized with plenary power by Rome, so his weakness and vacillation should not be mistaken for virtue. Josephus recounts Pilate's effective and indeed ruthless use of that power on a number of occasions. By choosing the path of least resistance in Jesus' case, Pilate was responsible for a monstrous evil: the release of a convicted assassin and the condemning of the righteous Son of God to torture and death."

What's your excuse for not actively working for Jesus and His plan to make disciples of all the nations? What is your path of least resistance, and is it in fact a monstrous evil? What forces do you pretend you must accommodate or cater to when all along you have the power of will to be fully engaged in God's mission? The biblical record of Pilate serves not only to condemn him but to convict us. There are many ways we can excuse ourselves from standing with Jesus. We too wash our hands but not our consciences.

Flogging was used to weaken the accused so that they would die more expediently on the cross. We must never lose the physical brutality inflicted on Jesus, yet the Gospels tend to focus more on the emotional and spiritual pain. Matthew also intentionally mentions that the first person to share in Christ's shame and pain was a Libyan, Simon of Cyrene. Think of it! We are all called to take up our cross and follow Jesus. And the first to do so was not a fellow Jew but a foreign North African. How sweet that memory, that service must be to Simon and all his sons as they even now surround the throne. No doubt Matthew included this detail to remind us of the scope of Calvary—every people, tribe, tongue, and nation redeemed by the blood.

Is it not remarkable that the last person to help Jesus before He was crucified was a Libyan and the first person to believe in Him after He was crucified was an Italian, or at least a Roman? Mark 15.38–39 records: "Then the veil of the temple was torn in two from top to bottom. So when the centurion, who stood opposite Him, saw that He cried out like this and breathed His last, he said: 'Truly this Man was the Son of God!'" Jesus dying on the cross for the sins of the *world* was an event bookended by encounters with representatives from the nations. How beautiful is our missionary God and His missionary Bible! And the veil torn is a thunderous missionary declaration. No more is the Spirit confined to one place in one nation. Henceforth, the Spirit will be unleashed on the world and the Spirit will inhabit human moveable temples who take the gospel to all the nations of the earth.

PRAYER FOCUS: *Lao, Phaun of Laos (Evangelical: 0.80%)*

NOVEMBER 13: THE KINGDOM IS NOT HERE

TODAY'S READING: LUKE 23; JOHN 18–19

The gospel message brings together unlikely enemies. The death of Jesus united an evil Roman with an evil Jordanian. The missionary heart of God will draw some from every nation to Himself in worship, while many from every nation will unite against Him in war. God's people are called to the triumphant promise that Jesus will be the praise of every tongue and to the sober reality that narrow is the path to life and broad the road to destruction and that more tongues of every language will curse the Savior than praise Him. In Christian missions we are triumphant without triumphalism, for we bear with Christ the agony that many will scorn His mercy and chose for themselves His eternal wrath. We cannot forget that the Father takes note of all who demand His Son's death that their favorite Barabbas might live.

One of the most critical clarifications of Jesus during His trial before Pilate was the declaration: "My kingdom is not of this world" (John 18:36). What was a relief to time-bound earthly powers was a consternation to the people of God then and now. The Israelites wanted a political kingdom then, a theocracy ruled by the Messiah. We have within the household of faith some with the same longing, but they couch their theology of dominionism in terms of holism or revival. From the conservative "heaven invading earth" right to the liberal "social gospel" left, it is the same error: the longing that Jesus' kingdom would be of our world, our time, our moment, our way.

Jesus surprises us all by not complying with our theology. Jesus' kingdom will not be established until our crucified and resurrected King comes back in power and glory. Jesus has given power and authority to wicked rulers for a season; they will continue to wield it until the trumpet sounds. This earth, this world, human history is a moral train wreck hurtling towards destruction by fire. The Kingdom is *not* of this earth, not of this world. There will be a restart, a new earth and a new heaven, and only then will the Kingdom be established by the living, ruling, present King.

We should not weep for Jesus; rather, we need to weep for ourselves and this world. This world and all its systems are irretrievably fallen and must be destroyed. The cross was the declarative statement that this world as we know it can never be host to God's kingdom. The cross gives us relief from the fruitless pressure of trying to reform this world to make it God worthy. Jesus died for and to this world, as must we. Our energies must be collected and spent on getting ready for the next world by going out into all this world and preaching the gospel to every nation. The Kingdom is not here and will not be established here. We need not fight one another or squabble over land and authority. We must lift up our eyes to the resurrected King who is coming soon to destroy this earth and make a new one. This is our blessed and only hope, for only when the King comes does the Kingdom come.

PRAYER FOCUS: *Arab, Sudanese of Libya (Evangelical: 0.05%)*

NOVEMBER 14: ALWAYS IN ALL WAYS

TODAY'S READING: MATTHEW 28; MARK 16

All authority (Matt. 28:18). Jesus the King, the crucified Messiah, was proved to be God by His resurrection from the dead. He has been given all authority in heaven and earth. He has forcibly taken the keys of death and hell. There is no earthly authority that trumps Jesus, no law that countermands His, no command that supersedes His orders. Because of the incarnation, crucifixion, and resurrection, Jesus can tell anyone to do anything and He has the absolute pure moral authority to do so. And He does. He orders us to....

Go into all the world, to all the nations (Mark 16:15; Matt. 28:19). The universal authority of Jesus that will be applied universally when He comes back forcibly in power and glory is to be announced globally in every corner of the world, to every unreached people. One day the authoritative King will force worship and obedience, whether from heaven or hell, but He mercifully extends a period of grace for all peoples of every tribe, tongue, people, and nation to choose that their eternal worship ascends in joy from heaven, not in pain from hell. King Jesus orders us to go, to diligently ensure that not only every place, but also every ethnic people, has opportunity to choose to bow. A focus on unreached peoples is not something sociologists made up; it is the passion of the Savior from the creation of language and culture (Gen. 10–11) that every tongue of every people worships Him forever.

Make disciples; preach the gospel to every creature; and teach all things that I have commanded (Matt. 28:19; Mark 16:15; Matt. 28:20). Jesus did not tell us to dig wells, build schools, establish hospitals, change government policies, provide shoes and shelter, or start orphanages as our priority assignment. We can certainly do all those things if, and only if, they empower our clear orders: make disciples by preaching, teaching, and baptizing. We know from the clarity above that disciple making is to be done among all peoples. The mandate is very clear to the people of God, and we are to have a collective single eye: make disciples among every unreached people through preaching, baptizing and teaching *all* things that Jesus has commanded. Whatever platform, mechanism, delivery system that aids that obedience is blessed. Whatever service that slows making disciples among all peoples is to be discarded.

I am with you always (Matt. 28:20). At the end of his life, David Livingstone told a group of university students that it was this promise that sustained him through the years and toil of his exiled life in Africa. Livingstone called it "the promise of a gentleman." When he died, he was found kneeling at his cot in his tent with his Bible open to Matthew 28:20 with his scrawling notation, *the promise of a gentleman.* Indeed, *all* authority has been given to Jesus, so that we may go into *all* the world to make disciples of *all* the people groups teaching them *all* that Jesus commanded, for truly He is with us always in *all* ways.

PRAYER FOCUS: *Nepali, General of Malaysia (Evangelical: 1.8%)*

If the great cloud of witnesses was allowed to interrupt, I'm sure they would have erupted on the Emmaus road. The resurrected Lord, the Son of Man who will rule all nations, the crucified Messiah who just conquered death and made the way possible for all men from every nation to be redeemed, is walking incognito down a dusty road when His companions ask, "Are you the only stranger in Jerusalem, and have You not known the things which are happening there in these days?" And the only One who knew everything must have hidden His divine grin and asked, "What things?"

We were hoping Jesus was He who was going to redeem Israel. At this the angel choirs must have burst forth: "And redeem Somalia! And Ireland! And North Korea! And Libya! And the Maori! And the Pashtun!" And the saints in glory must have laughed delightedly and burst forth exuberantly into the songs of Zion: "Salvation belongs to our God who sits on the throne, and to the Lamb. Worthy are You, for You were slain and purchased men for God from every tribe, tongue, people, and nation!" How heaven must have burst at the seams for joy, while men walked the dusty trails of earth with their heads down.

Jesus did not allow the Gospels to end with our heads down. He burst forth from the grave and He lifted our eyes again to Himself and His glorious purpose. He said, "As the Father has sent Me, so send I you," and He breathes on us and tells us to receive the Spirit (John 20:21-22). He opens our minds so that we can understand the Scriptures that "it was necessary for the Christ to suffer and to rise from the dead the third day…that repentance and remission of sins should be preached in His name *to all nations*" (Luke 24:45-47, emphasis added). The heavenly host must have grinned and broke out into foot stomping, singing all over again. Jesus blessed His disciples and was parted from them, taken up to heaven to join the party. "And they worshiped Him, and returned to Jerusalem with great joy, and were continually in the temple praising and blessing God. Amen" (Luke 24:52-53).

We thus come to the end of the Gospels on this note of joy. We finally get it. Jesus has walked with us when our heads were down. He has held back the rapture of heaven while He smiles upon us, breathes His Spirit into us, and opens up our minds to understand the Scriptures: *He came, He suffered, He died, and He rose that repentance and remission of sins should be preached in His name to all nations.* This is the Bible in a sentence. Here is our explanation, our orders, our joy. Here is our purpose, our life, our suffering, our death, our resurrection, and our glory. What can we do but praise and bless God? What can we possibly do with our short, little lives better than join the mission of God and then on that glorious day when the King comes back enter with the beloved from every nation into the joy of our mutual Lord!

PRAYER FOCUS: *Khasonke of Mali (Evangelical: 0.63%)*

NOVEMBER 16: WE MUST LEAVE HOME

TODAY'S READING: ACTS 1-3

*"If every Christian is already considered a missionary, then all can stay put
where they are, and nobody needs to get up and go anywhere to preach the gospel.
But if our only concern is to witness where we are, how will people
in unevangelized areas ever hear the gospel?"*

GORDON OLSON

After Jesus rose from the dead, He spent forty days filling His disciples with hope and joy regarding the kingdom He would establish when He came back. Being as slow to understand then as we are now, they asked if He was referring to a here-and-now kingdom. Jesus answered by pointing them to the priority of the age of humans: the mission of God—a representative portion of every ethnic group worshiping Jesus eternally. Toward that end Jesus said, "Don't focus on earthly kingdoms. Put all your energy into making disciples of all the nations. Put all your hope on the day when I come back to rule and reign. In order to do this, you will need My Spirit!"

This promise to be witnesses in Jerusalem, Judea, Samaria, and the ends of the earth is perhaps one of the most misinterpreted. We tend to say this verse means we start at home, reach those around us, and then in ever expanding circles take the gospel further out. The fly in that hermeneutical ointment is Acts 1:11 when two men address the disciples as "men of Galilee." None of the disciples were from Jerusalem, Judea, or Samaria, and they certainly did not hail from the uttermost parts of the earth. Jesus was not saying the Spirit would empower them to stay home and then when everyone in their neighborhood was saved to gradually move onward. By contrast, Jesus was saying, "Leave home! Go back to the city where they just tortured and killed Me. Preach where they will want to kill you. Head from there to where you are unpopular and unwanted, and then keep going to the uttermost places of earth in all of which you will be met by curses and crosses." This is why He was clear that they so expressly needed the Spirit: they must leave home and make disciples in the most difficult parts of the earth under duress.

To underline God's unrelenting passion for all peoples, when the Spirit was poured out, it was done so in the context of those from Iran, Iraq, Turkey, Egypt, Saudi Arabia, Greece, and Libya. The Jews thought the Spirit of God had been withdrawn. Peter announced that the Spirit is back, that these are the last days, and that the same Spirit that was in Samson to tear up city gates is now available to us to tear down the gates of hell. The same Spirit that spoke through Samuel, Isaiah, and Jeremiah now speaks through us so that *all* the nations might hear Jesus is God, Lord, and Christ. The power of the Spirit is not so we stay home; the power of the Spirit is expressly given that we leave home and go into all the world so that *whoever* calls on the name of the Lord, all who are far off, as many as the Lord our God shall call shall be saved. Peter answered the "what shall we do?" question by saying: Repent and get working to spread the gospel to the ends of the earth.

PRAYER FOCUS: *Jebala of Morocco (Evangelical: 0.0%)*

NOVEMBER 17: ALL ARE TO BE FILLED

TODAY'S READING: ACTS 4-6

Three times in the first three chapters of Acts, Peter was filled with the Holy Spirit and it affected his mouth. The day of Pentecost was his first experience when he was "filled with the Holy Spirit and began to speak in tongues...[and]standing up... [he] raised his voice and said" (Acts 2:4, 14). Then before the Sanhedrin "Peter, filled with the Holy Spirit, said," and then again Peter and friends "were all filled with the Holy Spirit, and they spoke the word of God with boldness" (4:8, 31). Over and over again, Acts details the work of the Spirit who fills us with power to witness of Jesus. The baptism of the Holy Spirit, as any work of the Spirit does, glorifies Jesus. When Peter spoke, they realized he had been with Jesus. God the Holy Spirit is the executive of missions, and if we are going to reach all nations, we will have to be filled with all of God over and over again. Fillings of the Spirit cannot only be demonstrations of God that He will save from among every ethnicity; they are also demonstrations that we need to be filled and refilled with the Holy Spirit so that we can authoritatively point to Jesus.

When Peter pointed to Jesus, he unfailingly pointed out the universal scope of Christ's claim. Peter told the Sanhedrin bluntly, "Nor is there salvation in any other, for there is no other name under heaven given among men by which we must be saved" (v. 12). Gospel enemies understood the global implication, planning how the gospel would spread no further, so obviously the scope of saving is all men under the heavens. When threatened and released, Peter and John quoted the psalmist who referenced the raging nations and the kings of the earth. The first to give money to church expansion was from Cyprus and the first internal issue was multicultural as Libyan, Egyptian, and Turkish believers elbowed their way not just to the table, but into the very family of God.

Holy Spirit filling is intended to animate our proclamation to all peoples. Daily in the temple and in every house, the apostles did not cease teaching and preaching Jesus as Christ. The longest recorded sermon in Acts was delivered by the first martyr whose job was to wait on tables so that the apostles could concentrate on prayer and the ministry of the Word. The Spirit is not confined to verbal proclamation, of course, for Stephen was chosen to serve tables *because* he was full of the Spirit, yet instructively we know nothing about his service plan. What we do know is that Stephen, full of faith and power, did great wonders and signs, that they could not resist the wisdom and the Spirit by which he spoke, and that he did not cease to speak. The biblical point is simple: *All* men and women are to be filled with the Spirit and to open their mouths and proclaim Jesus. Some from pulpits, some from cash registers, some from soup kitchen counters, some from a pull-up bar, but all are to be filled with the Spirit, speaking the gospel, focused on the nations. As a consequence, the word of God will spread, and disciples multiplied greatly under all heaven.

PRAYER FOCUS: *Han Chinese, Mandarin of Myanmar (Evangelical: 1.4%)*

NOVEMBER 18: GOING FOLLOWS PREACHING

TODAY'S READING: ACTS 7-8

"If God wills the evangelization of the world, and you refuse to support missions, then you are opposed to the will of God."

OSWALD J. SMITH

A man whose job it was to minister to Libyans, Egyptians, and Turks and who would not shut up about the gospel gave the longest sermon recorded in Acts; it is a classic missionary sermon. From beginning to end Stephen made a case that God is the Lord of all the earth, working in every place and among every people, and should be worshiped globally. Stephen hammered away to nationalistic Jews that God has ever worked (and ever will) outside their borders as well as within them.

The sermon in Acts 7 began with a reference to Abraham, the one through whom God would bless all nations, whom God met first in Iraq and then in Syria, telling him to leave his own country and people. God didn't give Abraham a foot of land in Palestine but instead promised that the path to glory led through slavery in Egypt, where Jacob and all the fathers died. The point is piercing: The patriarchs never owned land in Israel and didn't even die there. God obviously is not confined to one place or people. Moses, mighty in word and deed, was born in Egypt and then received revelation in Saudi Arabia where God called the ground holy. Whether the exact location was Saudi Arabia or the Sinai Peninsula, the main point remains it was *outside* Israel, for God is not confined to one place or people. God showed signs and wonders *outside* Israel. God spoke to Moses and gave him the law *outside* Israel. The tabernacle was made and the presence of God descended upon it *outside* Israel. Solomon's temple could not contain God, for heaven is His throne eminently *outside* Israel. On and on Stephen thundered on how God has ever been at work outside one country and one people. For this truth he is stoned, for those who think they own God are ever furious when He reminds them He is the God of glory and the God of the Gentiles, and not our personal, parochial genie.

To emphasize the point, Luke recorded that the effect of Stephen's missionary sermon was persecution and the preaching of the gospel everywhere. We tend to focus on the persecution, but Luke's point was that missionary going always follows missionary preaching. He underlined this by taking us to Samaria, a Gentile city, and then to Samaritan villages, and then to a Sudanese official. The Spirit used Stephen's sermon and sacrifice to stir Saul's sadism so that Samaria, Samaritans, and Sudanese might receive the Spirit. Missionary preaching always leads to missionary going, and it is missionary going that leads to salvations, baptisms, and Spirit fillings, and if we want to see the 7,000 unreached peoples evangelized, if we want to participate in God's glory manifest in all the world as Stephen declared it, we will have to constantly preach missions. We must preach missions to our infants, children, youth, adults, seniors, and ourselves. To not preach missions is to be stiff-necked resistors of the Spirit.

PRAYER FOCUS: *Tharu of Nepal (Evangelical: 0.0%)*

NOVEMBER 19: HIS DEITY IS THE POINT

TODAY'S READING: ACTS 9

*"The greatest missionary is the Bible in the mother tongue.
It needs no furlough and is never considered a foreigner."*

WILLIAM CAMERON TOWNSEND

In 34 AD a fanatic Jew from present-day Turkey meets Jesus in Syria and then spends three years in Arabia sorting it all out before becoming God's chosen instrument to bear Jehovah's name before Gentiles, kings, and the children of Israel. The greatest human missionary of all time was called out of the nations, to be saved in the nations, to be taught in the nations, and to go preach among the nations. Paul would traverse the Middle East, Turkey, Europe, and Greece preaching the deity of Christ as evidenced by the resurrection. Paul immediately began his exaltation of Jesus as the divine Lord after his encounter with Jesus on the Damascus road when in a stunning reversal he went from championing the Jewish position against Christ and Christian to confounding the Jews by proving Jesus is the Christ.

From the beginning, the great missionary Paul was adamant about affirming the deity of Jesus using the simple affirmation of the early believers, *kyrios Iesous* (Jesus is Lord), repeatedly. In fact, Paul used the term *kyrios* over 275 times, almost always in reference to Jesus. "Indeed he probably knew the expression and hated it in the days when he was persecuting those who dared to claim that the crucified carpenter from Nazareth was (God forbid, he thought) the Messiah and (even worse) Lord. It was Paul's encounter with the risen Jesus on the road to Damascus that made him blindingly aware that the phrase was not a heinous blasphemy but the simple truth." There was no doubt in Paul's mind that Jesus was God and he made this simple truth the central point of all his missiology—as should we. Any efforts to remove deity from our texts, our preaching, our witness, our testimony, our language, our prayers, or our proclamation are counter to the example of Paul. It was inflammatory for Paul and it will be for us, but it's still the main point that we must begin and end with no matter the consequence. The gospel is nonsensical and extra-biblical outside the deity of Jesus.

A second critical missionary lesson from the conversion of Paul is the role Barnabas played in bringing Paul into the church and onward into missions. It may be that a primary missionary function is to be the Barnabas who finds the local Paul and encourages that person to shake the world. Most missionaries dream and pray that God would use them to catalyze church planting movements, and Jesus will certainly answer that prayer, but it might very well be through us being a Barnabas, not a Paul. Imagine the effect on the evangelization of unreached peoples if every foreign missionary was a Barnabas who went out and found their Paul!

PRAYER FOCUS: *Fulani, Sokoto of Niger (Evangelical: 0.0%)*

NOVEMBER 20: THE GOSPEL PREACHED PRIORITY

TODAY'S READING: ACTS 10–11

It is well established that no Christian can in good conscience say, "No, Lord" (Acts 10:14), for this is an oxymoronic reaction when the King of all the earth gives an order to one of His own. What is less remembered is that this whole incident revolved around taking the gospel to the nations. Almost twenty years passed since the Spirit was poured out at Pentecost, and Peter, lead vocalist for the revival on that day, still did not fully grasp the scope of God's heart for all peoples. Peter was fine with Jews from every nation under heaven receiving the Spirit, but evidently, he was still clouded about God including all the Gentiles at His heavenly banquet. Peter still had to work through his prejudice and legalistic (nationalistic) tendencies and to confess that "God has shown me that I should not call any man common or unclean" (v. 28).

The point is simple. When we talk about saying "yes, Lord," we tell of the oxymoronic response of Peter who told the King "no" and we must be true to the context of God commanding Peter to abandon his nationalistic hubris and to engage all peoples of the earth with the gospel. If you are not fully leveraging your time and resources for the gospel to go to all the peoples of earth, you are still saying "no, Lord!" It makes no matter how holy, religious, spiritual, or church-immersed you are. Peter was being asked to leave the tribe and culture he was most comfortable with in order to preach Jesus to the nations. To that command of the Lord, we must all say "yes," for Jesus has "commanded us to preach to the people" (v. 42).

Luke intentionally records for us that the first church outside Jerusalem was not only the result of preaching Jesus in persecution but also was planted by men from Cyprus and Libya! The Antioch church was multi-cultural from the beginning, in contrast to the homogeneous mother ship in Jerusalem. This inclusive church must be a credit in part to Barnabas who went to Turkey to bring back Paul and integrate him into the body. It's important to note that Barnabas and Paul were first sent to Jerusalem to carry relief for the Christians who were starving during the famine of 46–47 AD, and this simple precedent establishes three critical missions points regarding social action: (1) We are people who compassionately care; (2) compassionate care is directed to the body of Christ abroad; and (3) compassionate care is not the priority. Paul and Barnabas are apostles of note in the Bible because they preached the gospel where it had not yet been embraced or embedded. This was their priority and it must remain ours, even as we periodically help our global brothers and sisters in times of distress.

When we focus on social action over the saving of souls and making disciples, when we do not intentionally make the effort to include all races and peoples in our churches, when we do not focus our energies and resources on the gospel crossing cultural boundaries despite our personal discomfort, we essentially say, "No, Lord!" Jesus, help us say, "Yes!"

PRAYER FOCUS: *Gera of Nigeria (Evangelical: 1.4%)*

NOVEMBER 21: CALLED AND DOUBLY SENT

TODAY'S READING: ACTS 12–14

Martyrdom in the Bible was neither heroic nor foolish; it was normal and God-decreed in His wisdom and in His time. James was no fool and Peter was no hero. There is no recorded reason why James was struck with a sword that killed him and Peter with a slap that woke him. Life and death are in the hands of the Lord and He employs them both for His glory. What is recorded is that Herod was struck and killed because he did not give glory to God. In missions we cannot be sure if we will be delivered from prison or delivered up to die, but we can be sure that if we try to steal or share any of God's glory because we speak well, it will not end well.

What does bring Jesus glory is a church that reflects heaven in its diversity. The whole mission of God is to redeem a remnant from every people group on earth. Thus, whenever He sees advance outposts of this multi-cultural eternal body, He takes great delight. Antioch, the first church outside Jerusalem, was such a glorious collection. Not only were there prophets (after 400 silent years), these prophets were from all over the place. Barnabas was from Cyprus, Simeon likely a black man from North Africa, Lucius from Libya, Manaen likely a freed slave, and Paul the Turk. Not only was the Antioch church multi-cultural from the beginning, it also was missionary right from the start. Churches that make Jesus glad are multi-cultural and missionary from day one.

It is of note that missionaries are first to be called and second to be doubly sent. Paul and Barnabas were clearly first called by God, then sent by the church and the Holy Spirit, with prayer and fasting as the glue that brought unified purpose and action. How often did Paul and Barnabas need to look back to that moment when they knew God had called them. When the stones struck, the doors slammed shut, the waves assailed, and the enemy tormented, what kept them was that they knew they were called and sent by God and His church. Even so today. Missionaries who are not called and sent do not endure when all hell breaks loose against them and every friend disappoints them. What keeps missionaries in the war is the peace that God Himself has called and sent them, and that the body of Christ has affirmed this call.

Acts 13 revealed a flaw in the early church's logic. They assumed after Pentecost that the gospel would spread naturally to the ends of the earth and all peoples. It doesn't—it spreads intentionally and at a cost. Paul's example shows us four critical aspects of biblical missions. First, the church must send their best. The Antioch church fasted and prayed, and God moved them to send their best leaders, their most spiritual and influential members. Second, preaching the Word is the main activity of missions accompanied by healing and wonders. Third, persecution always follows the preaching of the Word. Fourth, prayerfully indigenous disciples must be made, and leaders raised up and empowered to lead local churches. If we glorify God in this, it doesn't matter when or how we die.

PRAYER FOCUS: *Arab, Dhofari of Oman (Evangelical: 0.4%)*

NOVEMBER 22: WITHOUT THESE WORKS

TODAY'S READING: JAMES

Peter called James "the Lord's brother" (Mark 6:3), and Paul included him among the apostles (Gal. 1:19) and characterized him as one of the pillars of the church (2:9). James was the first apostle to die, but not before he wrote to the "twelve tribes scattered abroad" (James 1:1), primarily to give counsel on how to respond to poverty and suffering.

The book of James has been resented through the ages. Perhaps the most notorious objection coming from Martin Luther who called it "an epistle of straw," a comment he later retracted. Theologians have aptly reconciled James' stance on active faith and works with Pauline and Gospel teaching on grace. Missiologically, the tension is elsewhere namely in our resistance to poverty and persecution. The struggle is mostly taken up by those in the West, for no Christian in Pakistan doubts that following Jesus essentially means being poor and persecuted. The rich and protected Christian abroad is the exception.

We object to the good and perfect gifts God sends down as being poverty and persecution, yet that's the very context of James' writing, living, and dying. James lived in a time when the church was impoverished, hungry, abused, beaten, tortured, hounded, *and* growing! In the difficult, dangerous mess of the volatile first century, a time in which Rome would chew through four corrupt emperors in less than thirty years, James boldly stated that these troubles are ordained from God, good and perfect gifts, and that in such perilous times precious fruit can be brought forth. In his epistle of steel he laid out that perilous, impoverished times give no excuse for the wrath (or folly) of man. The implication for missions is twofold. If you are from a poor country that persecutes Christians, you have no excuse from living a holy life, nor from participating in God's holy passion to take the gospel to all peoples. Rather than your condition being a disadvantage, you have been given a good and perfect gift in the same way the early church was given. If you are from a wealthy country with security and indemnity from most persecution, we have no excuse from living a sacrificial life that takes risks so that souls will be saved from death. We have no exemption from taking up the cross and denying ourselves. In fact, the book of James was written to help us fight against all the internal allowances and external luxuries that prevent us from full participation in God's mission.

James makes pertinent reference to the grandfather of missions, Abraham, by pointing out it was Abraham's radical action, his willingness to sacrifice his son, that won God's favor. James' critical contribution to the biblical theme of missions is that faith is not enough; we must also tame the tongue, resist pride, use wealth for gospel advance, and patiently endure. We must sacrifice and suffer. For missions without these works is dead.

PRAYER FOCUS: *Arain (Muslim Traditions) of Pakistan (Evangelical: 0.0%)*

NOVEMBER 23: LET THE PEOPLE IN

TODAY'S READING: ACTS 15–16

"God has called every Christian to international missions,
but He does not want everyone to go. God calls some to be senders."

DAVID SILLS

Missions involves great dissension. Men and women who leave home and hearth to herald the King in the most difficult places of earth tend to be hardheaded and opinionated. You don't make it in North Korea, Yemen, Libya, or Somalia for years if you're a spiritual or emotional pansy. The trick for missionaries then is to stay soft-hearted and to pick their battles; making sure if they go to blows, it's for the defense of the gospel. Which is what made the Jerusalem council in Acts 15 so tricky, for both sides felt they were defending the gospel.

After testimony, James summarized the consensus of the elders. James was not making an arbitrary decision. He had listened to the give and take, discerned the unified agreement, and articulated it. This truly was an eldership that discerned the way forward together with the Spirit's help. Importantly, James framed the decision in light of Old Testament scripture, quoting Amos 9. The prophet Amos spelled out that when the kingdom of David was reinstated, it would include men and women of every nation. James made the link. It's an astounding moment in the history of missions. The elders of the church affirm what the missionaries out on the extremities have long ago understood, and while councils can't really save anyone or start much, they sure can restrict and inhibit. Thankfully, James and the elders recognized what God was doing and opened the gates for the flood to continue to rush into salvation's house. The boundaries they set under the aegis of the Holy Spirit are just as important. The doors were thrown open, but they were doors with boundaries—it was not a syncretistic free-for-all. What was explicitly forbidden were the religious practices of Roman idolatry. The council welcomed the nations, but they had to come in as the new Israel. They had to leave all false religions, and their allegiance was to be fully and only to Christ and His body. All nations were welcome, but all other religions and false worship were to be checked at the door of Christ. Jesus still says no to some things (and sometimes to some places at certain times). The Spirit is the executive of missions, and He still gives orders and boundaries.

Not everyone is ready for missions or called to go. Paul and Barnabas, long-term friends, could not settle their dispute over John Mark. The text does not vindicate either brother directly, but the fading of Barnabas from the scene would indicate Paul made the right decision. While all should have a missions heart, not all should be missionaries, and the only thing worse than no missionary team members is having the wrong ones. Even in this we must follow the Spirit's lead. Sometimes the best thing for the gospel is for those not ready to not go, lest they do more harm than good. The same Paul who argued for the Gentiles to be let in argued for John Mark to be left out. Both hard arguments seemed to be of the Spirit. We do the nations no favors when we export our problematic, immature people.

PRAYER FOCUS: *Sama, Southern of Philippines (Evangelical: 0.0%)*

NOVEMBER 24: EXPORT JESUS ONLY
TODAY'S READING: GALATIANS 1–3

Galatians is a missionary letter written by missionary Paul to the churches he planted in the Roman province of Galatia (southeast Turkey today). It was most likely written in 49 AD, just before the Jerusalem council mentioned in Acts 15, making it the first letter Paul wrote that became part of the canon. When we remember that the book is a missionary writing to nascent churches, it helps us interpret the book correctly. Paul introduced himself as a missionary, for the word "apostle" in Greek meant a "sent one," one sent to preach the gospel to those who had not heard it and to labor for the mission of God. Everything Paul did, said, and wrote was through this missionary framework. Paul also cited all the brethren with him, as missions work must be done in teams. We do not aim to reproduce individuals; we aim for churches. These communities of faith are to be multinational.

Paul's rebuke of Peter in Antioch was a public correction of a public figure for a public error, an error we still make today. We confuse our cultural view of Christianity with biblical Christianity and thus insist that other nations become like us (nationally) as part of them becoming like Christ (spiritually). When Paul said the gospel to the Gentiles had been committed to him while the gospel to the Jews was committed to Peter, he was not saying there were two gospels; he was saying there was one gospel supra-cultural and no one nation owns it. The context then of being crucified with Christ is a missionary context in which Paul pointed out that God denies the right of one ethnicity to own the gospel—the gospel must own all of us, the gospel must own every culture, the gospel must own every nation.

Essential to missionary fruitfulness then is not only death to self, but also death to nationalism, ethnic pride, and prejudice, and death to our favored form of Christianity. Without falling into syncretism, the missionary seeks to allow gospel truth to be planted in indigenous soil rejoicing that the application of the unvaried truth will be very varied in application. Paul's missionary letter to the Galatians simply reminds us that we received the Spirit by faith and harkens back to the Abrahamic promise guaranteeing all nations will receive the Spirit by faith, too. Not by Sunday School, professional worship, one-hour services, excellent childcare programs, engaging video, recovery classes, not by any of these good things that have helped us all, but by faith.

Because God's promise to Abraham is explicitly fulfilled in Jesus, Paul's point to missionaries is that we better *only* export Jesus, and his point to indigenous believers, they better only import Jesus. To be crucified with Christ is a missionary commitment to be crucified to all but Christ, including cultural Christianity. Naked we must be nailed to our cross, disrobed from the comfort of our cultural Christianity. The application to Christians everywhere is that we have to die to the broken aspects of our culture as much as we do to our flesh. The cross is supposed to stand at the doors of our hearts and cultures as a barrier against anything and everything that is not like Jesus.

PRAYER FOCUS: *Azerbaijani of Russia (Evangelical: 0.2%)*

NOVEMBER 25: REAP WHAT YOU SOW

TODAY'S READING: GALATIANS 4–6

As a new resident of Saudi Arabia, I take great delight in Paul pointing out that Mt. Sinai was in Arabia. What beautiful irony that Moses was restored and called in Saudi Arabia (Midian), that the law the Jews revere was revealed here, that Paul whom the ages emulate was renewed here, that Elijah heard God's voice here. If it took Elijah forty days and nights to get here and while Jesus took a forty-day trip into the wilderness, I can't help but wonder if Immanuel walked down to Arabia and possibly leveled the devil with Scripture on the same mount where He laid down the law.

Paul's missionary letter first established that every people has the Spirit freedom to follow Jesus in culturally submitted ways and assures us that some redeemed cultural variation will exist across the body of Christ. Paul began by insisting that it is beautiful to have many applications of biblical culture, and he ended his missionary letter by insisting we can't make diversity the goal or the idol, "for in Christ Jesus neither circumcision nor uncircumcision avails anything, but faith working through love" (Gal. 5:6). First, Paul smacks us all for not allowing the other to be different, then he smacks us again for making different the goal: "God forbid," he wrote, "that I should boast except in the cross of our Lord Jesus Christ, by whom the world has been crucified to me, and I to the world" (6:14), and then again to his point, "For in Christ Jesus neither circumcision nor uncircumcision avails anything, but a new creation" (v. 15).

If we are boasting in our blackness, we are insulting the cross. If we are arrogant in our whiteness, we are insulting the Christ. If we are internally critical of Arabs, Asian, Americans, Africans, or whoever is different than us, we are insulting the Father of all. As strong as Paul rebuked Peter publicly for not allowing cultural differences, so he rebukes us all through the Spirit for allowing them. The cross sees no color and admits no prejudice, all blood flows red and all pride must be nailed to the tree. Sandwiched in between Paul's two statements that cultural differences avail nothing (5:6 and 6:15) is his list of the fruits of the Spirit. Love, joy, peace, patience, kindness, goodness, faithfulness, gentleness, and self-control are missionary indicators, guidelines for us in cultural interaction. I venture to suggest these Spirit fruits are most sweet when they eaten cross culturally.

In missionary application, Paul warns us that God cannot be mocked, thus we will always reap what we sow. Again, Galatians is a missionary letter written by a missionary to emphasize that all peoples must bow to biblical culture, that all peoples must be born of the Spirit by faith, that there is beauty in all peoples when we share the fruit of the Spirit cross culturally and ugliness when our boast is centered on our culture more than our crucified Christ. If gospel advance marches forward with divisive missionaries leading the way, we will plant divisive churches. But if we do not grow weary in dying to self and culture, we shall reap a unified church if we do not lose heart.

PRAYER FOCUS: *Punjabi of Saudi Arabia (Evangelical: 0.0%)*

NOVEMBER 26: SLAPPING SPIRITUAL FACES

TODAY'S READING: ACTS 17

"God is a God of motion, of movement, and of mission… Mission is not an activity of the church but an attribute of God. God is a missionary God, Jesus is a missionary Messiah, and the Spirit is a missionary Spirit. Missions is the family business."

LEN SWEET

Whenever a Muslim friend tells me Islam and Christianity are compatible, I slap him on the shoulder or knee with a big smile and say, "I am so glad that you believe that Jesus is God!" They immediately protest and then we have a genuine conversation. Paul entered Thessalonica and preached the deity of Jesus, for resurrection proves His deity, it proves Jesus is the Christ, God who came down to save. The gospel message must center on the deity of Jesus. This focus will provoke hostility and charges of turning the world upside down. If only that charge were true of the church today. It is certainly what Paul did wherever he went, including Athens. While Stoics opposed pleasure, Epicureans worshiped it and avoided pain at all costs. Both errant philosophies are still with us in various forms, for some yet worship the body and others neglect it. Paul corrected both errors by preaching Jesus as the God who came in the flesh, died in the flesh, and rose again in the flesh, living in holy pleasure and enduring great pain for glorious good.

What Paul did not do was soft serve the gospel. If you don't understand Middle Eastern indirection, you miss the force of Paul's assault on errant thinking. First of all, Paul's spirit was provoked; he was angry at idolatry. The fact that the philosophers called his reasoning "babbling" showed he was confronting them, not accommodating, as he clearly preached the deity of Jesus, a doctrine new to them. This leads to a trial. In other words, just like in Thessalonica and Berea, Paul preached Jesus as God in Athens and was in hot water, but he did not back down: "I see you blockheads even have an altar to a god you do not know, so I will inform you blockheads of whom you ignorantly worship. Only blockheads think God dwells in temples made from human hands. Only blockheads think He is worshiped with human hands. God has overlooked your blockhead ignorance for a time, but now commands you to repent, and you better do so quickly because Jesus who is God is coming to judge you."

The fact that Paul quoted some Greek poets does not mean non-biblical scriptures can be used to make theological points. Paul based his argument squarely on the nature of Jesus, the God who became flesh in order to show us through the pain of the cross what sanctified pleasure should be. Paul slapped both sets of philosophers across their spiritual faces with the reality that Jesus is God. We have no other way forward in missions. We must affirm both the humanity and the deity of Jesus boldly, winsomely, and unapologetically. The result was that some mocked and some believed as is ever the case when Jesus is proclaimed as God incarnate who died on the cross and rose from the dead. Wherever we go, we must preach Christ crucified and risen from the dead. Wherever we go, we must proclaim that Jesus is God.

PRAYER FOCUS: *Mandingo, Mandinka of Senegal (Evangelical: 0.05%)*

NOVEMBER 27: SHORT-TERM PAIN FOR UNENDING PLEASURE

TODAY'S READING: 1 & 2 THESSALONIANS

Silas and Timothy joined Paul on his second missionary journey to visit the Greek city of Thessalonica, the capital of the Roman province of Macedonia, an important urban center on the road that connected Rome to Byzantium. Paul was unable to stay long as angry men abused both he and his friends and chased them out of the city, heading on to Corinth (via Athens). Worried about the trouble his visit caused and the persecution it engendered, Paul sent Timothy back to check on the nascent church. Finding the disciples weathering the storm, Paul wrote with joy to encourage them on.

In missionary living, eternal hope must overcome our dread of earthly consequences. The missionary message must cause great harm on earth in order to bring great joy in heaven. Missionaries must steel themselves to bear the weight of knowing that suffering must precede glory for all who listen to their message. The men and women in Thessalonica would have to endure great temporal persecution as a consequence of Paul's obedient, bold preaching of the gospel. Paul got to leave town, but everyone else had to stay and suffer. The missionary by definition is a sent one who is not local (an external catalyst). Indigenous believers must endure the temporal ramifications of their decision long after the missionary has gone. The missionary must love the lost so fiercely that he or she is willing to see them suffer because the hope of heaven is so bright. The missionary must never be cavalier, for the consequences of faith are always less severe on the visitor and most severe on the local believer.

Given this essential context of Thessalonians, we better understand Paul's thoughts to the Thessalonians: The joys of heaven are worth the wounds of earth, so let us fix our eyes on the return of the Lord. It is our hope. The Word must be preached boldly even in much affliction as affliction actually helps the gospel to spread. We must be bold to preach the gospel even in much conflict. Wrath will come upon those who resist missions. Our hope, joy, and crown of rejoicing is the coming of Jesus and disciples from difficult places that are in Him when He comes, blameless and holy. For the Lord Himself will descend from heaven with a shout, with the trumpet sound, and the dead in Christ will rise and we shall ever be with the Lord. Therefore, comfort one another with these words. Rejoice always, pray without ceasing, and in everything give thanks. This is the will of God for churches planted among the unreached who suffer because they embrace the missionary message.

Because Paul could see what would be, he was willing to do something that hurt the ones he loved. Which is why he asked for prayer, that the word of the Lord would keep running swiftly and be glorified. More short-term pain for unending pleasure. Jesus, help us be wise and strong enough to give out and receive the former that we all rejoice in the latter.

PRAYER FOCUS: *Garre of Somalia (Evangelical: 0.0%)*

NOVEMBER 28: DIVERSITY AND DYNAMITE

TODAY'S READING: ACTS 18-19

Aquilla, resident of Rome, hailed from the southern Black Sea region of present-day northern Turkey. Paul, chased from Thessalonica and then Athens, was likely relieved to find a brother in Corinth. A few believers accepted the Messiah, including Crispus and his household, and it seems Paul began to struggle internally. Maybe he thought the cycle was starting all over again and wondered in self-doubt if he had the stomach to be beaten himself and have others beaten as well. The Lord spoke to Paul and told him not to fear: "No one will attack you to hurt you; for I have many people in this city" (Acts 18:10). It doesn't seem that Sosthenes (beaten in verse 17) minded taking his turn as he appears later as a co-author of 1 Corinthians.

Paul remained a good while in Corinth, spending some time there before pushing the gospel forward, finding vigorous Egyptian Apollos in Ephesus. How important were multi-national warrior brothers in missionary endeavor! Paul sent half-Greek Timothy back into persecuted Thessalonica; refugee Turkish-Italian Aquilla brought Paul peace in Corinth; Greek Sosthenes took one for the team; and Egyptian Apollos took on the hardheads and refuted them. Each man had a story and a scar or two. Paul was surrounded by his own diverse group of mighty men. As we head out into the nations, it was never intended that we do so from a mono-cultural perspective. Missions is always most robust when its messengers are most diverse.

Acts 19 is a reminder that we are not the only missionaries out there. I remember a survey trip to the completely Islamic islands of the Comoros. Four of us walked shoulder to shoulder down a little path between huts made of zinc sheets. We turned a corner and came to a sudden stop, face to face with four Muslim Arabs, white robed and long bearded, as foreign as we were, who were also walking shoulder to shoulder. All eight of us chuckled as we greeted one another and shook hands, for we each knew exactly why the other was there and what they were doing.

Paul came to Ephesus where "competitive missionary activity is the setting behind the 'itinerant Jewish exorcists' and the 'seven sons of Sceva' (Acts 19:13,14). Impressed by the works of Paul, these missionaries sought to prove their God's superiority over other gods in order to convert people to the synagogue...Yet the evil spirit knew the difference." The difference was that Paul was full of the Spirit and those he discipled had the Holy Spirit come upon them with the evidence of speaking in tongues and prophesying. To go out into the world among the evil spirits of our day will require both diversity and dynamite—the full power of the Holy Spirit, empowerment that cannot be faked. It is a biblical question then, not a denominational one, to ask: "Did you receive the Holy Spirit when you believed?" (v. 2). If not, when you go out into the world, you will end up naked and wounded. We must have ongoing fillings of the Spirit. Perhaps the question for missionaries should be: "Have you received a refilling of the Spirit since you arrived on the field?"

PRAYER FOCUS: *Guwamaa of Sudan (Evangelical: 0.0%)*

NOVEMBER 29: THE PATRON OF PATRONS

TODAY'S READING: 1 CORINTHIANS 1–4

"You have one business on earth: to save souls."

JOHN WESLEY

Paul wrote to the Corinthians (Greece) from Ephesus (Turkey), probably during his third year there, around 55 AD. Paul was in the midst of his third missionary journey and seeing unprecedented levels of fruit. All Asia was hearing the word of God, yet he couldn't forget his friends back in Europe. Corinth was located on a trade route and was rich and immoral. The church Paul planted on his second missionary journey was diverse and starting to fragment, so Paul wrote to remind them that salvation is based on Christ alone, not on human wisdom or personalities.

Corinthians clearly establishes that missionary methodology must center on preaching the gospel. In an age where missions is becoming everything but verbal proclamation, let us allow the Spirit to clearly speak from the text without hermeneutical gymnastics diluting what Jesus clearly wants us to do: "Christ did not send me to baptize, but to preach the gospel…. For the message of the cross is foolishness to those who are perishing, but to us who are being saved it is the power of God…. It pleased God through the foolishness of the message preached to save those who believe…. We preach Christ crucified…Christ the power of God and the wisdom of God. And I, brethren, when I came to you, did not come with excellence of speech or of wisdom declaring to you the testimony of God. For I determined not to know anything among you except Jesus Christ and Him crucified…. My speech and my preaching were…in demonstration of the Spirit and of power, that your faith should not be in the wisdom of men but in the power of God. But we speak the wisdom of God…. These things we also speak, not in words which man's wisdom teaches but which the Holy Spirit teaches…. The wisdom of this world is foolishness with God…. We are fools for Christ's sake."[1] Here Paul addressed two essential problems in Corinth: worldly wisdom and worldly power. In the Greco-Roman system of patronage, power was derived on who you knew, not on a system of equal access to services. Patrons had connections who could grant favors. Clients pledged their loyalty to patrons, giving patrons more power as they had more people at their beck and call. Wisdom was based on logic, persuasion, sophistry, rhetoric, and charismatic communication. Paul stood against both concepts, objecting not to the realities of power and wisdom, but to where the world said they were sourced.

It is true that power and favor come from whom you know, and Paul's point was that any patron other than the Lord Jesus Christ is limited. It is true that wisdom is communicated through words, and Paul's point was that wisdom is not in clever words, but in gospel truth. As missionaries go out to all nations, let us not unwittingly fall back into Corinthian error. Let us be consumed with knowing Jesus, loyal to the Patron of patrons. Let us be consumed with gospel truth, not slick campaigns or marketing. Jesus is both our power and wisdom. The strong, wise missionary never veers from that simplicity.

PRAYER FOCUS: *Arab, Palestinian of Syria (Evangelical: 0.5%)*

NOVEMBER 30: TAKING ISSUES HEAD ON
TODAY'S READING: 1 CORINTHIANS 5-8

Evidently, a delegation of Corinthians visited Paul in Ephesus bringing a letter of concerns from the church plant back home. What a messy church plant it was: incest, lawsuits, prostitution, food offered to idols. Paul wrote back addressing each issue. His transition to a new topic usually indicated by his saying, "Now concerning." Cross-cultural church planting is indeed messy.

Several missions points are clear from Corinthians. First of all, didactic teaching is central to our approach. Discovery Bible Study is in vogue, but we must take seriously the clear pattern of Paul who point by point addressed specific issues with pointed opinion. Second, short-term pain through discipline and judgment is preferred to a sloppy grace approach that never deals with difficult issues head on. There are times in which brothers need to be turned over to Satan for the destruction of their flesh so that their eternal souls might be rescued. An overreaction to paternalistic and colonial approaches in missions history has led some missionaries to abdicate their clear biblical responsibilities to rebuke and correct. Let us not avoid one abuse by careening to the extreme and being afraid to confront in love. Do you not know that the saints will judge the world and angels? Our inability or insecurity to correct in grace and judge in love does not remove the biblical responsibility to do so. Third, to live as we are called does not refer to staying in demonic false religions as some social science-oriented missiologists errantly advocate. The second half of that verse revealed Paul saying, "So I ordain in all the churches." He was clearly talking to people of varied economic or marital status who were in the church, associated with the church, and belonging to the church.

Paul also took immorality head on, addressing the obvious wrongs by providing the overarching principle: We are to glorify God in our body and in our spirit. The clear abuse of this is sexual sin, while the less obvious abuse is either the neglect or the worship of our physical body. Simply stated, missionary Paul told his converts that their body was to be used to glorify God. It is not enough that our body not de-glorify God by sexual sin; our bodies must actively glorify God by healthy living. When was the last time you prayed that God would glorify Himself in your mortal, physical body? The body is for the Lord and the Lord for the body, and the Lord will raise our physical bodies on that glorious day. Pastors, Christians, missionaries, and new converts are expected to glorify God with their physical bodies. We can falter in this assignment in two directions. First, we can work hard at physical exercise and healthy eating because we revel in the glory that others give us. This does not glorify God; this is self-glorifying the body. Second, we can neglect the body by lack of exercise, indulgence, laziness, or eating too much or too little. This does not glorify God; this is the body glorifying self by destroying itself prematurely. God's glory is besmirched if we make our bodies the attraction, and not the gospel, or if our bodies break down so we can't remain in context to further preach the gospel.

PRAYER FOCUS: *Thai Islam Central of Thailand (Evangelical: 0.0%)*

"All the money needed to send and support an army of self-sacrificing, joy-spreading ambassadors is already in the church."

JOHN PIPER

DECEMBER

DECEMBER 1: WE ARE TO IMITATE
TODAY'S READING: 1 CORINTHIANS 9–11

"I alone cannot change the world, but I can cast a stone across the waters to create many ripples."

MOTHER TERESA

We must not forget or diminish biblical context when interpreting and applying Scripture. Most Christians would be very familiar with our mandate to "endure all things," be "a servant to all," and "become all things to all men" (1 Cor. 9:12, 19, 22). What we tend to forget or diminish is that Paul's missionary message to the church he planted is in the context of insisting nothing hinder the gospel going forward to all peoples and of the necessity to preach the gospel to all peoples and by some means save some of every people. All that Paul talked about in 1 Corinthians 9 he did "for the gospel's sake" (v. 23). By all means let us endure, serve, and relate to all people, but if we are to be biblical, we do all this purely for the gospel to advance to all peoples for the glory of God. Endurance, service, and understanding divorced from the effort to take the gospel to all peoples is diluted obedience (at least as regards 1 Corinthians). This is why we run; the prize we discipline ourselves towards is the gospel saturating the earth.

The example of our fathers is recorded for our admonition. To take heed lest we fall into temptation is to watch that we don't fall *from* the selfless pursuit of adding all peoples to the body of Christ *to* the selfish indulgence of our own particular body. We must not slip from the missions underpinning of all Paul's correction to the Corinthian church. When he wrote that all must be done (or left undone) for the glory of God, it was for the direct purpose to give no offense to Jew or Greek that we might please all men in all things *that they may be saved.* The imitation of Paul was in this very explicit context of a missionary writing to a missionary church plant, telling them not to live selfish, sensual lives. Rather, they were to live and die in such a way that men and women of every tribe, tongue, people, and nation be saved! Jesus came to seek and save the lost, saying "yes" and "no" according to what served that goal. Paul said "yes" and "no" according to what would serve the goal of all nations represented in heaven worshiping Jesus around the throne. We are to imitate them. We are to determine what we say "yes" or "no" to by what makes the greatest impact on gospel advance to all the nations.

In this context of selfless living for the salvation of all men, Paul gave instruction for taking communion. We are to take the bread and cup in remembrance of Jesus. We are to keep taking the bread and cup until Jesus comes again. If we take communion without remembering that Jesus died for the sins of the *whole* world or without remembering that He is coming back to rule as King over the *whole* world, or without aligning our hearts again to this purpose of the cross, then we partake in an unworthy manner and are guilty of the body and blood of the Lord.

PRAYER FOCUS: *Arab, Lebanese of Turkey (Evangelical: 0.10%)*

DECEMBER 2: LOVE AND MISSIONS NEVER FAIL

TODAY'S READING: 1 CORINTHIANS 12-14

"The Church must send or the church will end."

MENDELL TAYLOR

The people of God have consistently taken their eyes from the high goal of the mission of God for a more comfortable parochial application. We love the references in 1 Corinthians 12 to differences and diversity when we can apply them at the local level to the different members of our nuclear family or to the diverse races within our culturally isolated church. These are not untrue applications, but they were not what Paul was talking about. Paul said that by one Spirit we were all baptized into one body whether Jews or Greeks. Paul's first point is that the body of Jesus (the church) must be defined by having members of every people group. The hand, ear, toes, and nose to which he referred are Arabs, Africans, Asians, Europeans, Latins, and Americans of every tongue and culture. Let's begin up high with the grand view of diversity that God demands as central for His people, never losing sight of a multi-cultural church even as we recognize apostles, prophets, teachers, miracle workers, helpers, administrators, and all. Let's not forget that "apostle" means "sent one" and is the basis for our concept of missionary. An apostle (missionary) is one sent to make disciples and plant churches where there are none. In this sense Paul's question in verse 29 makes sense: Are all missionaries? Of course not! But all should love, hope, and have faith.

Our beloved 1 Corinthians 13 is a reminder to all missionaries and all the people of God that if we do not love, we are nothing. If the worst kind of suffering is eternal suffering, then the best kind of love is that which rescues from eternal suffering and assures eternal joy. We must be careful that what we profess as love is not carefully concealed hate. For if we educate, clothe, feed, nourish, and rescue practically but never open our mouths to warn of God's wrath and tell of God's ransom, then we have not loved, we have done nothing. Love suffers long abuse and rejection and is kind enough to keep proclaiming the gospel to resistant peoples. Love does not envy the easier life that some friends live back at home, does not parade itself as better than the ones who send, does not seek to be recognized as brave or exceptional, is not provoked when forgotten but rejoices in declaring truth to the unreached. Love bears all the burdens of learning language and new cultures, believes that the hardest fundamentalist can be saved, hopes that God will send revival on the most resistant nations, and endures the difficulties that always accompany gospel advance. Love never fails, and neither does missions, for we know that at the last when Jesus stands again on the earth, that all tongues and tribes will welcome Him back.

PRAYER FOCUS: *Baloch, Southern of United Arab Emirates (Evangelical: 0.0%)*

DECEMBER 3: LONGING FOR OUR HEAVENLY HOME

TODAY'S READING: 1 CORINTHIANS 15–16

Paul wrote to the Gentile Greek Christians in Corinth, "I am not worthy to be a missionary, but by the grace of God I am what I am, laboring by God's grace so that the gospel is preached among the nations" (see 1 Cor. 15:9–11). Corinthians is a missionary letter with a missionary message, a message that centers on the deity of Jesus and the age to come. Over and over the missionary Paul pointed to the looming wrath of God, the merciful love of God, and the coming eternal reign of God that will be inclusive of all peoples.

Our missionary Bible ever directs our attention to the age to come, that great and glorious day of the Lord when King Jesus returns to judge the living and the dead, to destroy all evil, and to set up His glorious kingdom. We are not to fixate on this shadowy life with all its flaws and wickedness; instead, we fix our eyes on the soon coming King and strain our ears for the trumpet blast. We are not to worry about death, for the dead do indeed rise to life eternal. We will rise incorruptible, powerful, and honorable, and we shall bear the image of the heavenly Man. We will all be changed in a moment, in the twinkling of an eye. The missionary message we declare across this broken world to every broken culture is that the awful realities of this life need not despair us, that the partial beauty of now cannot satisfy, that we were made for the world to come.

If we will preach this missionary message of eternal life with authority, if we with authenticity will ask, "O Death, where is your sting?", then we must live with a certain estrangement from this world and a great anticipation of heaven. A necessary condition of the missionary heart is a beatific longing for heaven. If we shake with the glad desire for Jesus to come that we might live forever in His glorious presence, our message is authenticated. If we are to preach repentance with power, we must also hold out the hope of heaven with palpable joy. What makes us steadfast and immovable is that, even with the constant instability here on earth, nothing changes regarding God's promise of eternal life in His glorious heaven.

Missionary Paul let the Corinthians know he might pass by but not stay, for his eyes were always on the open doors despite the many adversaries. In a few breaths, Paul mentioned Galatia, Ephesus, Achaia, and Asia. The gospel must ever go forth to the uttermost peoples and places. It was the ambition of Paul. Why? So that we can all go home and be with Jesus. The missionary heart has no time for banal pleasantries as its focus is on paradise for all willing to repent. The missionary heart ever pursues the next unreached people and place because it longs for its heavenly home.

PRAYER FOCUS: *Persian of United States (Evangelical: 0.3%)*

DECEMBER 4: CRITICAL MESSAGING

TODAY'S READING: 2 CORINTHIANS 1-4

Most missionary work is painful. At least in the short term. Paul planted a church in Corinth that descended into debauchery and division. Strong letters and confrontational visits followed, leading some scholars to think 2 Corinthians is a compilation of several shorter letters as the tone shifts from a warm beginning to a harsh ending. Whatever the book's composition, what is certainly applicable is that missionary messaging must include both the glad and sad, the gentle and harsh. We are not faithful to the missionary heart of God if we do not preach all His counsel or carry our cross.

A central reality of missionary messaging is that the sufferings of Christ will abound. The context of abounding comforts are abounding afflictions. If we do not disciple the nations to expect and endure persecution, we cripple their capacity to thrive in Jesus. If we do not model endurance, courage, and fearless faith in persecution, we have no moral authority to ask them to suffer. Over and again I have seen missionaries model fear, protecting their bodies, freedom, or visas at the expense of their example. We cannot flee a country and ask new believers to stay. We cannot protect our longevity and ask new believers to risk their lives. It is ridiculous to teach and preach that to follow Jesus is to abound in calamity *and* comfort if we are not willing to suffer, if we leave town or avoid meeting with colleagues at the first squeeze of pressure. Paul could call others to suffering because he knew what it was like to be burdened beyond measure and to carry around the sentence of death.

A second difficult reality of missionary messaging and living is that we all betray and will be betrayed. We must decide to "pre-forgive." We are not ignorant that one of Satan's favorite devices is to allow unforgiveness, to cause division when missionaries hurt and betray other missionaries or locals and vice versa. It was in the context of missionary hurt, betrayal, and disappointment that Paul said God always leads us in His triumph in Christ and that we can be the sweet fragrance of Christ. How? By recognizing the devil's weapon of unforgiveness and turning it against him, by being like Jesus in how often and sincerely we forgive. What testimony it is to the unreached when they see loving forgiveness among the people of God. Those who know they need forgiveness seek with longing a community that will truly forgive.

A third critical component of missionary messaging is that nothing should be veiled; we should not walk in craftiness, never be deceitful, and always manifest truth. We preach Christ who commands light to shine. Missionaries who attempt to veil their message, identity in Christ, purpose for existence, or relationship to the body of Christ do not represent Jesus well. We are proclaimers, not concealers. The excellent power of God is best seen in us when we are hard pressed, crushed, persecuted, carrying about the dying of the Lord Jesus, and delivered to death for Jesus' sake, the very things cloak-and-dagger missions seeks to avoid at nearly any cost.

PRAYER FOCUS: *Tatar of Uzbekistan (Evangelical: 0.15%)*

DECEMBER 5: THE COMPELLING LOVE OF CHRIST

TODAY'S READING: 2 CORINTHIANS 5-9

The Spirit is a guarantee of our heavenly home for which we earnestly groan. Missions is the earthly growl of longing for that day when we *all* get to heaven (*all* meaning representatives of every tribe, tongue, people, and nation). According to Paul, missionary living, Christian living is always focused on the last day and the coming of King Jesus, which is why we persuade men and women of all peoples to repent. This is why the love of Christ compels us, this is why we are ambassadors for Christ with Christ pleading with us. Let us remember that the Bible's promise of being a new creation is a missionary promise bounded and blessed in the context of all nations given invitation to eternal life.

The construction of "the love of Christ compels us" in Greek grammatically allows for triple application. It could mean that the love we have for the lost compels us to mission. It could mean that the love we have for Jesus compels us to mission. It could mean that the love Jesus has for the lost compels us to mission. Because the grammatical construction is flexible, context must help us discern the intended meaning. The first two options we discard, for we quickly find there are many days we do not love the lost and sadly on some days we do not love Jesus as we ought. Besides, God's mission is too important to depend on the fickle love of man. The third option is true because only God's love never wanes and because the text is universal in scope: we persuade men, Jesus died for all, if anyone is in Christ. How thankful we must be that the motivation for mission is God's unfailing love, not man's fickle, feeble emotion. Woe to the missionary who ventures forth armed only with their personal love for the lost.

Missionary living is holy living, living that gives no offense and has no liaisons with darkness. Missionary practice does not allow or encourage local believers to stay in the demonic filth of false religions but calls unapologetically with the Spirit and Scripture: "Come out from among them and be separate" (2 Cor. 6:17). It is the weakest of strawmen to twist this call to holy living into non-contextualized or imperial missions. To be indigenous has never meant independence or sequestered living from the global body of Christ. Paul will go on to exhort the interdependence of the body practically, as financial giving is based in spiritual unity.

It is intriguing to note the exchange between the missionary, mission-sending church, and new church plant. The new church plant sent an offering to the saints and the saints back home sent their prayers and love, with both services extended with cheerfulness and thankfulness. When missions is construed and constructed as a one-way street where the physically rich but spiritually anemic West sends its controlling funds and diluted prayers to the Global South, it is denuded of power. When missions is truly bi-lateral and multi-directional, it is as much about receiving the strength and wisdom of others as it is about giving our meager offerings abroad. In this reciprocity is both great power and great joy.

PRAYER FOCUS: *Tai Dam of Vietnam (Evangelical: 0.06%)*

DECEMBER 6: LESSONS FROM THE LETTER

TODAY'S READING: 2 CORINTHIANS 10-13

Remembering that 2 Corinthians is a missionary letter, written by a missionary to an ornery church he planted among an unreached people, there are some definite missionary lessons to be drawn from this passage.

Spiritual warfare is primarily about fighting for unreached peoples to be saved. The individualized West excels at personalizing Scripture, even when authorial intent was collective. Dealing with rascally Corinthians, Paul referred to pulling down strongholds, casting down arguments, and bringing every thought into captivity as what was needed to be done to confront the wrong thinking of a whole demographic in Gentile society. We have turned those verses into support for our personal holiness; Paul used them in terms of the gospel fight to ransom and correct a whole sector of the Gentile population. We reach the Akdam of Yemen by pulling down the stronghold of Islam, by casting down the arguments of works-oriented salvation, and by bringing every thought about Jesus not being divine into captivity under His Lordship. Absolutely apply these verses to keeping your thoughts pure, but do so while you fight to ransom the unreached from demonic ideologies.

Spiritual authority is for edification, not for leadership, strategy, or decision making. We absolutely need leadership, strategy, and accountability, but biblically this is not the main purpose of being trusted with authority. Humans love to make authority about positional leadership. The Bible centers authority on edification. The real leaders in a missionary society are those that most broadly edify. Missionary statesmanship is not to hold positional power over local brothers and sisters; rather, it is for broad edification.

The missionary spirit ever has its eyes on the regions beyond. Paul told the Corinthians he was eager to preach in the regions beyond them, not because he was frustrated with them but because this is the impulse of our missionary God. Who has not heard? This question burns in the heart of missionaries and in any missions organization that has any biblical fidelity and Spirit obedience. This burning ambition must be fulfilled collectively. Stewardship (language learning, relational equity, discipleship process) does not lend itself in our day to missionary tourism, but as a group we are ever relentless for the peoples that have never heard.

Church-based support is still the norm. Paul is our example both for tent making and for support taking from sending churches. We laud him for being bi-vocational, but that was his infrequent practice. As long as there are churches, there should be missionaries sent and funded by them.

A little bit of weakness is what makes us strong. Grace sufficient and strength made perfect in weakness are missionary promises to those who determine to take the gospel where it has not been preached and as a consequence are buffeted by Satan. Paul just finished listing all his missionary qualifications and balanced them with the crown jewel of weakness. Sufficient grace and perfected strength are best evidenced when we are sent as missionaries helpless in our natural strength to live among the millions of an unreached people. It is there, surrounded by the lost, reproached, sick, underfunded, persecuted, distressed, for Christ's sake, that we will be strong.

PRAYER FOCUS: *Akdam, Arabized Blacks of Yemen (Evangelical: 0.0%)*

DECEMBER 7: OUR MISSIONARY FOUNDATION

TODAY'S READING: ROMANS 1–3

Paul wrote his epistle to the Romans from Corinth at the end of his third missionary journey around 56 AD. Perhaps all the messed-up theology of the Corinthians helped Paul to concisely and precisely unpack the gospel in this theological gem. Encountering bad thinking gives us opportunity to clarify and articulate what the Bible teaches. Paul opened this letter by reminding his readers that he was called to be a missionary, set apart to spread the gospel of God in all the earth. He opened this marvelous letter with a phrase he then repeated three times in some form, a phrase which is, in fact, the heart and soul of the epistle: obedience to the faith among all nations. If we understand nothing else about Romans, we must understand that this "faith among all nations" theme is the fire that fuels the burning of Paul's theology. Paul's missionary heart beat with God's missionary heart that there would be men and women from all nations who put their trust in the Lord Jesus Christ.

Paul delighted that the faith of the believers from Rome was spoken about in the whole world. Paul viewed himself as a debtor to the Greeks and barbarians. It didn't matter if the unreached Gentiles were rich or poor, educated or ignorant, Paul keenly felt that he *owed* them gospel preaching; he felt this about the denizens of Rome as well. Yes, Romans is a theological wonder, but let us not forget that essential theology is missiology—the whole heart of God burns for His glory among all peoples and the gospel is the power of God for salvation to *everyone* who believes. To know and love God has the inescapable conclusion that we must love the nations and give our lives that every people group be represented in heaven. Written over our hearts must be the mantra: *All glory to Jesus from all nations.*

Because all false religions suppress the truth, using partial truths to strengthen their lies, the wrath of God will be revealed from heaven. Missionary messaging bluntly reminds the world that "indignation and wrath, tribulation and anguish" (Rom. 2:9) wait for every person from every tribe of every age that does evil—and that damns everyone. Missionary messaging also offers hope that "glory, honor, and peace" (v. 10) are available to every race and people group, for there is no partiality with God. Missions is the great source of all racial unity and blessed multi-culturalism, and it is only in the gospel that we truly avoid all prejudice. Outside the gospel all efforts at racial equality are weird. Missionary service is the best cure for racial prejudice, bar none.

Paul established in the first three chapters of Romans that the current game is all men are sinners and under wrath, and justly so, and that the end game is all nations obedient to Jesus. There is no one righteous, not one. All have sinned, yet all can be forgiven, for there is no difference. Jesus, both just and justifier, is the God of the Jew and Gentile. Romans gives us our theological missionary foundation, God's great heart for all peoples, and our eschatological promise, *all* the nations will be obedient.

PRAYER FOCUS: *Turkmen of Afghanistan (Evangelical: 0.0%)*

DECEMBER 8: ALL OF US TOGETHER

TODAY'S READING: ROMANS 4-7

"It's amazing what can be accomplished if you don't worry about who gets the credit."

CLARENCE W. JONES

Whenever Abraham is mentioned as father, it is in reference to God promising him that he would be the father of many nations, that in his seed *all* the nations of the earth will be blessed. When David is referenced, it is in view of his seed being the Messiah (God made man) who will rule over all nations. This is why Matthew began his Gospel linking Jesus to Abraham and David, and this is why Paul, after establishing that all have sinned but all peoples can be represented in heaven, now points to faith as being the key for all peoples of the world. Paul oozes missions throughout Romans.

Not wavering at the promises of God, being fully convinced that what God has promised He is able to perform are direct missionary realities. Paul mentioned again Abraham being the father of many nations and underlined that Abraham had faith that God was able to bring all peoples to Himself despite extraordinary physical challenges. We should read Romans 4 to 7 with the clear light of context: No matter the physical challenges, let us have *faith* that God will bring representatives of *all peoples* to Himself. They will come, Jew and Gentile, just as we come—by faith in Jesus.

Paul emphasized in Romans the universality of the gospel, using the plural to denote all the peoples of earth: *We* have peace with God; *we* glory in tribulations; while *we* were still sinners Christ died; *we* shall be saved from wrath; for when *we* were enemies, *we* were reconciled; *we* also rejoice in God; death spread to *all* men; the grace of God...abounded to *many*; and *many* will be made righteous (Rom. 5:1, 3, 8–12, 15, 19). The plurality and universality Paul intentionally established should be how we read Romans. We are not supposed to read or understand this beautiful theology outside Paul's clear intention that it speaks for all men of every tribe and tongue.

Sin not having dominion over "you" is not a personal promise then (though we certainly can and should apply it that way); it is a corporate missionary promise. Sin will not have dominion over Algerians! Sin will not have dominion over Somalis! Sin will not have dominion over North Koreans! Jesus is the Savior of the *world*, and the death of Jesus on the cross has the power to save men from every tribe. There is no people group of earth who sin and who Satan will so terrorize that they are not well represented in heaven. Sin shall *not* have dominion over the peoples of earth, and Jesus shall reign. Yes, slaves of God under His beautiful and unending dominion of all peoples must certainly start in individuals. Each man and woman must be personally delivered. Thanks be to God through Jesus Christ *our* Lord that the beautiful and diverse body of God will be assembled one by one into a holy nation, with every one of Abraham's colorful children represented.

PRAYER FOCUS: *Berber, Imazighen of Algeria (Evangelical: 0.63%)*

DECEMBER 9: BECAUSE THE SPIRIT GROANS

TODAY'S READING: ROMANS 8-10

"People who don't believe in missions have not read the New Testament.
Right from the beginning Jesus said the field is the world.
The early church took Him at His word and went East, West, North and South."

J. HOWARD EDINGTON

Commenting on the groaning recorded in Romans 8:18–27, G. D. Watson writes: "It is as if God inspired the whole material world, and all the animals and fishes and birds and the human bodies and souls, with one gigantic longing and prayer for the coming of Jesus, and the fulfilment of God's purpose in redemption." In Romans' first seven chapters, Paul made the case that the gospel is for the whole earth, for all peoples without exception. Now he points out that all creation longs, groans, pants for the fulfilment of God's purpose in redemption, namely Jesus returning to be worshipped by every tribe, tongue, people, and nation. In other words, every rock and mountain, every forest and glade, every stream and ocean all pulsate with the missionary heart of God. The earth will not be renewed until the nations are reached.

Romans 8 also references the groaning of the Holy Spirit. "The Holy Spirit can see with infinite knowledge every detail to the uttermost extent concerning the fall of man and the curse on man and on creation, and He can see the infinite merit of the death of Christ, and also the infinite extent of the glory that is to come, and hence, being a Divine person and knowing everything with absolute clearness, He works in us, not according to our vision and knowledge, but according to God's infinite purpose and glory, and so His intercession and prayer in us is on the lofty scale of Divine measurement, and must be beyond our ability to understand and express: and so the apostle says that He makes intercession for us with groanings that cannot be uttered. If the prayer that the Holy Spirit prays through us was nothing more than our human thoughts and desires, then it could be expressed or uttered; but because it is an infinite prayer to the Godhead for an infinite glory, it lies beyond all our ability to express in words. …[The] Holy Spirit groans…for the absolute consummation of every plan and every purpose and every work that belongs to the Son of God." What is the work that belongs to the Son of God? To purchase men to God from every tribe, tongue, people and nation. To build a worshiping church comprised of every tribe, tongue, people, and nation. It is to this end that the Spirit groans through us.

It is to this end that the great missionary promises of Romans 8 are addressed. Given that God the Spirit Himself groans for the saving work of Jesus to be accomplished, then *all* things will indeed work towards this glorious good. Given that God the Spirit Himself prays from within us that every unreached people will be offered eternal life, we know that in every missions endeavor we will be more than conquerors and nothing will ever separate us from the love of God. Because the Spirit groans we believe. Because the Spirit groans we preach. Because the Spirit groans we send.

PRAYER FOCUS: *Ansari of Bangladesh (Evangelical: 0.0%)*

DECEMBER 10: WALK PROPERLY

TODAY'S READING: ROMANS 11–13

"I will lay my bones by the Ganges that India might know there is one who cares."

ALEXANDER DUFF

Let us not forget the missionary purpose of living sacrificial lives and being unconformed to this world, transformed by renewed minds. The purpose is that both Jew and Gentile might be saved. This goal—all people groups, the fullness of the Gentiles—is the "good and perfect and acceptable will of God" (Rom. 12:3). In view of God's mercies on all people, Paul urged the Romans to live in such a way that the perfect will of God would be completed.

This is why we serve one another, because we are a body comprised of Indians, Asians, Arabs, Tartars, Latins, Europeans, Africans, and Americans. Being patient in tribulation, blessing those who persecute us, weeping with those who weep, and associating with the humble without being wise in our own opinion are all missionary skills. All these obedient actions are needed in the pursuit of Jew and Gentile being saved so that when *the world* is reconciled, we all might partake of life from the dead! We read Romans thinking of Paul as a master theologian, but let us not forget he was essentially a passionate missionary. Romans is a burning missionary treatise focused on God fulfilling His grand mission of obedient worshipers from every people group. Paul called Christians of every age to live in such a way as to expedite this grand ambition of God.

We are to live out the love of God for one another—that is, the global one another, not just the one another we married or that looks/speaks/talks/acts/thinks like us. Because the love of God is for the world, our "one another love" must be for the world, the others of the world, the others who have not yet heard of the love of God. The author who tells us to owe nothing but love framed himself as a debtor to both Jew and Greek with the love he owed them being the preaching of the gospel. To love like Paul loved is to love like Jesus loved, which is to love unreached peoples by preaching repentance to them for the glory of God. We do this knowing the time of our salvation is nearer than when we first believed. In the Bible, "salvation" is completed on the last day, the day when King Jesus comes back in power, glory, and wrath to judge the living and the dead. On that day those under the blood will have the death judgment pass over them and they will be saved from the wrath of God. We walk properly, putting on the Lord Jesus, making no provision for the flesh, for the day of wrath is at hand.

To walk properly is to walk after Paul as he walked after Christ. It is to walk in holiness for the steadfast purpose of loving the world to safety. That love will cost us everything. It will cause us to walk away from home and comfort and towards the heathen and the cross. It will take us down dusty trails and through urban jungles. It will take us to loneliness and trial. It will take us ultimately to glory, to the joy of "all Israel" being saved.

PRAYER FOCUS: *Han Chinese, Teochew of Cambodia (Evangelical: 0.4%)*

DECEMBER 11: THE TRAGEDY OF ROMANS

TODAY'S READING: ROMANS 14-16

"God will not lead you where He will not provide for you."

DAVID SILLS

Paul presented the law of love in the missionary context of all the Gentiles being saved and glorifying God. What we eat or don't eat, what we celebrate or don't celebrate, what we wear or don't wear is directly tied to the glory of God among all peoples. Why else did Paul explain living and dying unto the Lord in terms of *every tongue* confessing, or our confession among the Gentiles, or the Gentiles rejoicing *with* the people of God, or all the Gentiles praising the Lord, or King Jesus being the hope of *all* the Gentiles? The God of hope fills us with joy by the power of the Spirit because all peoples have found hope in Christ, because the offering of the Gentiles is acceptable, and because in mighty signs and wonders by the power of the Spirit of God, the gospel was fully preached from the Middle East (Jerusalem) to Europe (Illyricum).

How tragic that the missionary center of Romans has been neglected! We should never be able to read a chapter from this great theological work without seeing how every part of the book drips with God's passion for all peoples. It is from the book of Romans that missionary Paul most loudly shouted his life purpose: *I made it my aim to preach the gospel where Christ has not been named!* Paul's purpose in writing Romans (and the Spirit's intention in preserving it for us) was to be sure we have a passion for all peoples to be justified by faith. That's why Paul planned to head to Spain. If we are to apply the full message of Romans, we must ask ourselves where the gospel has not gone and what we will do about it. Any other application of this book is suspect.

It is evident from the closing chapter of Romans that Paul's readers were with him in application as well as spirit. Phoebe was part of the church plant in Cenchrea; Aquila and Priscilla were fellow church planters with Paul in Corinth beloved by all the churches of the Gentiles; Epaenetus was firstfruits from Achaia; Mary labored much; Andronicus and Junia went to prison with Paul; Urbanus was a fellow church planter as were Tryphena and Tryphosa; Persis labored much in the Lord; and on and on the missionary list goes. Names and persons now lost to us, all who shared the missionary heart of Paul, all who shared his ambition to keep preaching Christ where Christ had not yet been named.

Paul ends Romans with one last reminder of what the book is all about, what is "now made manifest, and by the prophetic Scriptures made known to all the nations, according to the commandment of the everlasting God, for obedience to the faith" (16:26). The God who alone is wise, to whom be glory through Jesus Christ forever, has commanded that all nations will be obedient to the faith. Amen. So be it. It shall be done. Let's do it.

PRAYER FOCUS: *Fulani, Adamawa of Chad (Evangelical: 0.10%)*

DECEMBER 12: RAISING WRATH

TODAY'S READING: ACTS 20–23

Trouble in missions does not automatically mean that we have done something wrong. The biblical default seems to be the other way around—we are actually not doing anything right unless things go wrong! Paul was repeatedly warned that trouble was in the forecast, but he already knew this as the Holy Spirit had already testified that in every city chains and tribulations awaited. Humans tell us that in missions we should avoid trouble; the Spirit says trouble is our norm. Humans criticize missionaries for taking risks that could be avoided; the Spirit rebukes us for avoiding risks that should be taken. Paul traveled to Jerusalem and was arrested in 57 AD. Those were tumultuous times, for Nero was emperor. In 59 AD, Paul appealed to Nero who ordered the death of his own mother that very year. If we follow Paul as he followed Jesus, we will take risks going to and staying in dangerous places in dangerous times. Appealing to matricidal Nero is not in the risk-avoidance game plan.

Paul was arrested on the charge of bringing a Gentile into the inner court of the temple. The outermost court of the temple was called the court of the Gentiles and non-Jews were allowed there, while the inner courts had signs warning that to bring a non-Jew into those restricted areas was to face the death penalty. Paul, of course, didn't break that law. He didn't need to, for Jesus' death already tore the veil, signifying the Holy Spirit was unleashed on the world and there was no difference in God's eyes between Gentile and Jew. It was the religious cowards who were behind the times. They wanted to bottle up God for themselves, something Jehovah has never allowed or smiled upon. As soon as the church attempts to contain the God of the nations, lock Him in while locking others out, things go very poorly for those handling the locks. These days we don't hang "keep out" signs on our temples, just on our wallets and children. After being arrested Paul asked to address his opposition. Things went well at first as Paul established his Jewish credentials in a familiar language mentioning his acceptable religious pedigree. His credibility earned Paul a hearing, even when he talked of Jesus as Lord. All was calm until it wasn't, at which point the crowd rose up in fury, tore off their clothes, and insisted Paul had no right to live. The turning point and Paul's crime? "Then Jesus said to me, 'Depart, for I will send you far from here to the Gentiles'" (Acts 22:21). It was Paul's obedient response to missions that made his peers vow to kill him.

Isn't it curious that missions raises such wrath among the religious establishment? Not just 2,000 years ago. In our time missionaries are welcomed as long as they tell good stories and don't speak too prophetically to the home crowd. Let the missionary voice establish credentials, speak the local slang, tell a few jokes, and stand on affirming ground, and all will be well. But as soon as the missionary voice calls out for the prioritization of the church to be singularly on the unreached, the mood shifts and the church says: "This fellow is not fit to speak in our pulpit."

PRAYER FOCUS: *Bouyei of China (Evangelical: 0.17%)*

DECEMBER 13: JEHOVAH IS NOT OURS

TODAY'S READING: ACTS 24-26

"Christ wants not nibblers of the possible, but grabbers of the impossible."

C. T. STUDD

People thought Paul a plague and a causer of dissension because he steadfastly urged the people of God that the priority of God was on the lost, on the regions beyond. Paul countered that he only believed all things written in the Law and the Prophets; his point being that the whole Bible establishes that missions is the priority of the church. Paul essentially said, "It is not my intent to offend anyone. I'm just doing what all the Scripture tells us all to do." Missions being priority of the church and the message of the Bible causing consternation to the spiritually comfortable is no excuse for the frustrated missionary to be inflammatory or provocative. Let us do and speak what is right and biblical without being wrong or carnal in how we do it. Paul was never unnecessarily abrasive.

When Paul gave a review of his own life and ministry, he framed them essentially on his hope in the promise of God made to "our fathers" (Acts 26:6), a direct reference to God's promise to Abraham. For this hope (that the resurrected Jesus was indeed the promise to Abraham) Paul was accused by the Jews. The problem was neither Messiah nor resurrection; the problem for the Jews was Gentile inclusion. Paul was empathetic, for he himself struggled against what God wanted to do in all the earth until he got knocked off his horse on the Damascus road and God told him that he was to go to the Gentiles.

There are equal and opposite errors regarding the gospel and all peoples. On one side the Jews did not want to share "their" Jehovah. They had to be forcefully taught that Jehovah did not belong to them; they belonged to Him, as do all peoples. That error exists today in a subtler form, for now we don't actively exclude but neither do we actively include. The flipside error is to think that any people can participate in the gospel outside association with Israel, the unique people God historically chose. Paul's mandate was to invite the Gentiles into an inheritance among those Jews sanctified by faith. The subtle error on the Gentile side is to think that Jehovah is now "ours." But this too is idolatry. We all (Jew and Gentile) are His with equal access, for light must go and reside in both Jew and Gentile. Yet, Jehovah biblically is indeed called the God of Israel, not the God of Babylon, the God of Rome, the God of China, nor the God of America. Jehovah certainly is Lord and Potentate of all, but historically He chose Abraham and sons. We join that story, fully adopted, equal rights, joint heirs of the promises *but* grafted in with the natural branches. Let our grafting in inspire humility even as we revel in equality.

PRAYER FOCUS: *Beja, Bedawi of Egypt (Evangelical: 0.0%)*

DECEMBER 14: COMING IN LIKE ELIJAH

TODAY'S READING: ACTS 27–28

"Death alone will put a stop to my effort!"

DAVID LIVINGSTONE

Rich Mullins wrote these great lyrics: "Well, if they dressed me like a pauper or if they dined me like a prince, if they lay me with my fathers or if my ashes scatter on the wind, I don't care. But when I leave I want to go out like Elijah, with a whirlwind to fuel my chariot of fire." I love the imagery: going out in a blaze of fire. That's what we see with Paul.

It is thought Paul died around 64 AD with the last stretch including two years of prison in Caesarea, shipwreck on Malta, and two years of house arrest in Rome. A physically worn-down Paul still had the raging fire missiologically. He was true to the end, living and standing for the same things he always had, not one spark of his desire for all people groups to be saved diminished. Paul arrived in Rome and after three days called leaders together to solemnly testify of the kingdom of God, persuading them concerning Jesus from the law and prophets, from morning to evening. Some accepted his teaching and some rejected it, and Paul's volcano erupted one more time: "Therefore let it be known to you that the salvation of God has been sent to the Gentiles, and they will hear it" (Acts 28:28). Isn't it interesting the last recorded words of Jesus according to Luke are "repentance and remission of sins should be preached…to all nations" (Luke 24:47) and the last recorded words of Paul are "let it be known…that the salvation of God has been sent to the Gentiles, and they will hear it"? Luke, a Greek historian and physician, both professions that require attention to detail, was careful to point out the fire in the life and death of Jesus and Paul: the unwavering passion for the glory of God among every unreached people.

When I die, I want to go out like Jesus and Paul: I want my last thoughts and words to be about Jesus and His glory among all peoples. As I age, I want the passion in me that Christ be honored by every tongue to wax, not wane. As my body breaks down, I want my heart to gear up in prayer and hope that every people will be represented around the throne. As my mind slows, I want my spirit to quicken with the joyful anticipation that the salvation of some from every people is nearer now than when I first believed. When it comes time to take that last breath, grant it, Lord, that my final, temporal strength yet reflects Your unchanged passion as I rattle out: "Jesus, You are worthy, for You have redeemed men to God from every tribe, tongue, people, and nation!" Then let my first heavenly breath sing on: "Yes, Lord Jesus! You are worthy!" Let my first sight be of Arabs, Africans, Asians, Latinos, Americans, Europeans, and all the peoples of earth worshiping You. On that day let all that is within me burn with a refined holy fire. Let my earthly match whimper out and then let Your eternal breath blow it into unending flame. When I come in, oh Lord, I want to come in like Elijah.

PRAYER FOCUS: *Afar of Ethiopia (Evangelical: 0.08%)*

DECEMBER 15: WE LABOR AND FIGHT

TODAY'S READING: COLOSSIANS; PHILEMON

"I want to be where there are out and out pagans."

FRANCIS XAVIER

Paul most likely wrote the letters to Philemon and the Colossians from Rome around 62 AD. Many of the people mentioned in Philemon are also mentioned in Colossians. Paul led runaway slave Onesimus to faith while in chains and appealed to his missionary colleagues to receive Onesimus back as a brother. Paul referred to Philemon as a fellow laborer and soldier. Laborers are those who sweat, work hard, and have little respect for the lazy. Soldiers are those who fight, endure, live with pain, and have no respect from those who run from battle. Missionaries then are both laborers and soldiers, which can make them hard to live and work with. Philemon evidently was sharing his faith and loving the lost, but at the same time overbearing with his own, just like some pioneer missionaries today. Put a bunch of missionaries together and you have a bunch of hardheads. Put a young missionary on a team with grizzled veterans and you have sent a young lion into a den of Daniels. Paul's admonishment to missionaries is that we stay kind to our own even as we work and war for the lost.

Paul never visited Colossae (100 miles east of Ephesus), but the gospel had been preached there. Paul's letter dealt with the heresy that mixed Judaism with an early form of Gnosticism, concluding Jesus was super-human but not truly God, greater than man but not able to save; thus, men must go through mediating angels to arrive at deeper spirituality. To this nonsense Paul penned his majestic Christological response: Jesus is the image of the invisible God. Jesus created all things. Jesus is before all things. In Jesus all things consist. Jesus is the head of the church. Jesus has preeminence in all things. All the fullness of God is in Jesus. Jesus reconciles all things to the Father. In Jesus are hidden all the treasures of wisdom and knowledge. In Jesus dwells all the fullness of the Godhead bodily. Jesus is the head of all principality and power. Jesus is our life. The central missionary point of Colossians is that Jesus is very God of very God, and missionary Paul made this very clear in his missionary letter. If we are to take, write, and speak the gospel among the unreached, we must explicitly teach that Jesus is God and broker no dilution in word, thought, or honor to His deity.

Colossians and Philemon align with the missionary theme of the Bible: The gospel "has come to you, as it has also in all the world" (Col. 1:6) and "was preached to every creature under heaven" (v. 23). "God willed to make known…the riches of [His] glory… among the Gentiles: which is Christ in you, the hope of glory. Him we preach, warning every man and teaching every man" (vv. 27–28) that "there is neither Greek nor Jew…but Christ is all and in all" (3:11), so pray for us "that God would open…a door to speak the word…to make it manifest" (4:3–4). If we read Colossians as Paul wrote it, we should leap to our feet and run to the nations shouting from the rooftops that Jesus is the God of glory.

PRAYER FOCUS: *Mahratta of India (Evangelical: 0.0%)*

DECEMBER 16: THREE MISSIONARY I'S

TODAY'S READING: EPHESIANS

It's likely Paul wrote Ephesians and Colossians at the same time and thought the Ephesian church needed to hear some of the same truth as the Colossians. Paul briefly visited Ephesus on his first missionary journey and spent two years there on his third. He wrote to them as a missionary: "Paul, an apostle [a missionary] of Jesus Christ by the will of God...."

Missionary Intercession. We see in Ephesians what prayers for our brothers and sisters globally should contain: that the Father of glory may give them the spirit of wisdom and revelation in the knowledge of Him; that the eyes of their understanding may be enlightened to the hope of His calling, the glory of His inheritance, and the exceeding greatness of His power; that according to the riches of His glory they would be strengthened by His Spirit in the inner man; that Christ may dwell in their hearts through faith; that they would be able to know the love of Christ which passes knowledge and be filled with all the fullness of God; and that their church would give Jesus glory to all generations forever. If your missionary assignment is to pray for the gospel advance among all peoples, you can do no better than to pray the missionary prayers Paul prayed for the Ephesians.

Missionary Identity. Paul reminded the Ephesians that though they were once strangers and aliens from the commonwealth of Israel, they have now been brought near by the blood of Christ. The well-known references to Jesus being our peace and breaking down the dividing wall of separation are missionary in context, promising Gentiles equal access with Jews to one Father, that they are fellow citizens of the household of God and fellow heirs through the gospel. The wonderful reference to Jesus being the cornerstone is a missionary reference. Paul was saying the house of God is being built with living stones from every tribe, tongue, culture, and people, and it is Jesus which brings us all together. Jesus is our missionary peace and our missionary cornerstone.

Missionary Imitation. Paul told us to walk in love as Christ has loved us, imitating God. Missionary work is not for the immature in Christ. We don't send missionaries to the field so they grow up, or because they don't fit in at home, or because they have addiction issues that we think Africa or Arabia will wring out of them. If those that walk in sin have no place in the kingdom of Christ, they certainly have no place on the missionary field. We cannot walk as or with fools. Missionaries must have enough strength of character to submit to one another in the fear of the Lord. They must know how to fight against sin and Satan, not against authority or associates, and they must have the dignity of ambassadors in chains. This does not describe the immature in faith. God sent His brilliant Son. The Son sent brilliant Paul. Let's imitate them and send as missionaries the ones we would most dearly want to keep at home. We don't really love the nations if we don't send them our brilliant best.

PRAYER FOCUS: *Bugis of Indonesia (Evangelical: 0.01%)*

DECEMBER 17: THREE SACRED LOVES

TODAY'S READING: PHILIPPIANS

Paul wrote Philippians from prison, most likely in Rome, between 61–63 AD. Philippians is a deeply personal letter showing how much Paul loved Jesus, the people, and the church. If we are to be biblical missionaries, we must share these same sacred loves.

Love Jesus. We know well that Paul's stated ambition was to preach Christ where He had not been named, but Paul's sacred ambition was much more enduring. He wanted to be with Jesus and to know Jesus. Paul knew that to die was to gain Christ and he considered this so much better. Paul was driven by the understanding that Jesus wanted all nations to hear the gospel before He returned in glory, so for Paul the quickest way to his deepest desire was to labor as a missionary. To be a missionary was not Paul's satisfaction—Jesus was. To live a long life was not Paul's hope—being with Jesus was. Let it be our longing to be in the eternal presence of Jesus that drives us to the presence of our enemies. Let us indeed count all things loss compared to the surpassing greatness of knowing Jesus.

Love People. Paul longed for his multi-cultural friends and disciples with the affection of Jesus Christ, and he stayed around on earth for their good. He called his friends beloved and longed for, his joy and his crown. Paul also loved the lost and in imitation of Jesus humbled himself that every tongue had a chance to confess Jesus as Lord. How often we take critical Bible concepts and untie them from their missions mooring! We are to humble ourselves in love so that unreached peoples confess Jesus as Lord. Why are we to work out our own salvation and not complain? So that in love we shine as lights in the world. When we love people, we don't care what happens to us; all we care about is that the gospel is preached, and in that loving act we will rejoice. Missionaries must not view the lost as statistics or trophies.

Love the Church. We are sometimes better at loving the lost than we are the found. We tend to have more patience with unrepentant sinners than struggling saints. Today it's even considered advanced to think "beyond church." Post-modernism is skeptical about organization and hierarchy and thinks naively that we can embrace the organic life of the church while ignoring the cumbersome organizational aspects. Paul was under no such illusion and wrote to the saints with their bishops and deacons. If we are going to plant churches, we must love the church, mess included. Christ through Paul implores us to love one another, even the messy parts. To rejoice always, be gentle with all men, be anxious for nothing, and pray about everything was a missionary request for two squabbling sisters in the church Paul planted and loved. Missionaries deeply love the church that sent them in order to just as deeply love the church they are sent to establish.

PRAYER FOCUS: *Mazanderani, Tabri of Iran (Evangelical: 1.14%)*

DECEMBER 18: FROM AN OLD LION TO A YOUNG LION

TODAY'S READING: 1 TIMOTHY

"Don't bother to give God instructions, just report for duty."

CORRIE TEN BOOM

First and 2 Timothy and Titus are addressed to pastors, not churches like the rest of the epistles. Timothy was half Greek, half Jewish, and was led to Jesus by Paul in Lystra (present-day Turkey) on his first missionary journey. Timothy then joined Paul and Silas on the second missionary journey, traveling with them to Greece. Paul then sent Timothy on missionary assignments to Thessalonica and Corinth before assigning him to pastor in Ephesus. The book of 1 Timothy then is an old missionary writing to a new missionary, an old lion passing on what is critical about a missionary heart and life to the young lion.

Teach. Counter to the wisdom of our day which insists new believers must discover truth, Paul pounded into missionary Timothy his missionary responsibility to impart truth and correct error. Timothy was to control what doctrine was taught, preserving sound doctrine as a glorious gospel trust even if that meant turning some over to Satan so they learn not to blaspheme. Doctrine matters; it's a good thing. Timothy was to instruct the brethren in how they should live and act. Paul used even stronger verbiage saying, "These things command and teach" (1 Tim. 4:11). Timothy was to give attention to exhortation and to take heed to doctrine, continuing in teaching so that he might save both himself and those who hear him. Timothy was to guard the doctrine that accords with godliness, correcting anyone who teaches otherwise. Timothy was to give commands. Good missionary practice centers on strong, clear teaching and correcting. Let us rise to this biblical injunction.

Model. Strong, authoritative missionary or pastoral teaching only has moral authority if the life of the teacher is blameless. Paul, by no means perfect, realized his life was a pattern for those who would believe. Every minister must live an exemplary life, including showing how to suffer and how to receive God's mercy. Paul expected Timothy to conduct himself in the house of God in a blameless manner. Paul expected young Timothy to be an example to all in conduct, love, spirit, faith, and purity, pursuing righteousness, godliness, faith, love, patience, and gentleness. Yes, we must teach with power and conviction, but that truth will only be palatable and powerful if we live blameless lives.

Fight and Pray. To pray is to fight, for we advance against the powers of hell on our knees. Paul tells Timothy to wage the good warfare by first of all making supplications, prayers, intercession, and giving of thanks for all men. Paul desired that men pray everywhere, lifting up holy, fighting hands without wrath or doubting, guarding what is committed to their trust not by prattling, but by praying. Missionaries are wired to act, but those who act without praying are merely actors. The real missionary action figures, the real warriors of the faith over time have always been those who fought first from their knees.

PRAYER FOCUS: *Arab, Saudi Najdi of Iraq (Evangelical: 0.0%)*

DECEMBER 19: BE FORCEFUL

TODAY'S READING: TITUS

Titus was an uncircumcised Greek whom Paul left in Crete to oversee the work of church planting on that island. Titus helped Paul relate to the Corinthian church and through this letter was being tasked with two essential missionary activities post the initial indigenous church being established: the appointing of elders and the halting of false teaching.

Plural Eldership. A critical missionary mistake is to establish a new church that is over-reliant on one person or family. The church was not designed to have a singular voice. The Spirit is never contained or interpreted by only one person, and church governance is never healthy if all power is concentrated in one individual. When missionaries only know one person, disciple that one, trust the reports of that one, and empower (teaching, funding, relationship) only that one, they set that person and church up for disaster. Plural eldership not only protects the church-to-be; it protects the leader. None of us were designed to rule over others; all of us were designed to have robust accountability constraining and protecting us. Paul expected Titus to appoint a plurality of spiritual leaders, and this must be our standard in the church at home and abroad.

Plural eldership is not antithetical to apostolic leadership. Paul himself is an obvious example as is the instruction he gave Titus throughout this epistle (Paul empowered Titus to make some unilateral, forceful decisions). However, God never intended any of us to be without covering, without boundaries, without other leaders who can correct and protect us from ourselves and the blind spots we have. As missionaries, let us love the new churches we plant and the new leaders we raise up enough to correct and protect them by refusing to install systems or expectations that lead to ecclesiastical monarchies.

Sound Doctrine. Paul began this missionary letter by reminding Titus that truth leads to godliness and that the word of God is manifest by preaching. Paul demonstrated that missionary work demands pointed teaching and the defense of sound doctrine (especially at the pioneering, catalytic stage). Leaders are, by sound doctrine, both to exhort and convict those who contradict. Some mouths must be stopped. We should rebuke some sharply that they become sound in the faith. We should speak the things that are proper for sound doctrine. We should speak, exhort, and rebuke with all authority. We should do all this avoiding foolish disputes and rejecting divisive men when they don't listen to admonition. Missionaries have the mandate to teach and preach sound doctrine forcefully. Let no current embarrassment of universal truth lead us to adopt methods that subtly suggest truth is in the individual.

Forceful leadership and submitted accountability, forceful teaching and genuine humility have this in common: They are both based in Christ's character and example. Jesus gave Himself for us, in kindness and love, according to great mercy, lavishing unmerited grace. Missionaries are indeed to be forceful leaders who are great in kindness, love, mercy, and grace.

PRAYER FOCUS: *Bedouin, Fezzin of Libya (Evangelical: 0.0%)*

DECEMBER 20: SUFFERING CERTAINLY GLORIOUSLY

TODAY'S READING: 1 PETER

*"Our God of Grace often gives us a second chance,
but there is no second chance to harvest a ripe crop."*

KURT VON SCHLEICHER

Peter wrote to Gentile Christians in present-day central and western Turkey, including the provinces that today border Armenia, Syria, and Lebanon (Pontus and Cappadocia). He likely wrote around 64 AD, right about the time Nero escalated his persecution of Christians. Peter opened the book by calling himself a "sent one," for the apostolic fathers seriously applied their missionary orders to take the gospel to all the world. Egyptian theologians contend this letter might have been written from Cairo, as at that time Babylon (1 Peter 5:13) was the name of the fort the Persians built on the Nile after they invaded Egypt in the fifth century BC. Regardless the location, it is a missionary letter to the converted peoples of Turkey telling them persecution is normal and we can endure it in a way that glorifies Jesus.

Heavenly Eyes. We are pilgrims; we don't belong here. We are sojourners; we are just passing through. We have an inheritance incorruptible waiting for us, reserved in heaven. Salvation is assured now, but not fully received until that crowning day. Peter reminded those in pain that they were kept by the power of God through salvation ready to be revealed at the last time. He reminded them to rest their hope fully on the grace that would be brought when Jesus returns. We stay in our hurtful earthly homes, for our eyes are on heaven, and we know if we leave our contexts of trial, then our earthly family will have even less opportunity to hear the gospel and live with us forever with our heavenly family.

Collective Endurance. A favorite trick of the enemy is to make us think we are alone, that no one has suffered as we have, that no one understands. Peter reminded his readers to rejoice when we partake of Christ's sufferings, for He suffered more, He suffered first, He understands. Peter reminds us to feel blessed when we suffer as a Christian, for the Spirit of glory and of God rests upon us. Peter reminds us that we resist the devil firmly because the same sufferings are experienced by the brotherhood. In this sense, let us not be the weak-in-faith link. Let us hold the line with the brotherhood.

Living Above Reproach. The chosen generation, royal priesthood, holy nation, and special people are, in the context of Peter's writing, by the mercy of God, unreached people in present-day Turkey who are called to proclaim the praises of Him who called them out of their false religion into God's marvelous light. We, from all nations, are to live with incorruptible beauty, being of one mind, compassionate, tenderhearted, courteous, and absorbing evil. Missionary living is winsome, not abrasive. We can be prophetic without being punks, holy without being haughty. We are going to suffer, so let's do so gloriously.

PRAYER FOCUS: *Tamang of Nepal (Evangelical: 0.0%)*

DECEMBER 21: JESUS THE ENGINEER

TODAY'S READING: HEBREWS 1-6

Hebrews was certainly written in the second half of the first century as we have a letter by Clement to the church in Corinth around 95 AD that quotes it extensively. Hebrews itself quotes extensively from the Old Testament, uses Jewish methods of interpretation common in the synagogues of the day, and is a masterful description of the salvation obtained by Christ's priesthood and sacrifice. The Jewish author of Hebrews "describes Jesus as the author of pioneer salvation (Heb. 2:10), the source of our eternal salvation (Heb. 5:9) and the mediator of complete salvation for all who come to God through Him (Heb. 7:25). New Testament salvation is as utterly Christ-shaped as Old Testament salvation is YHWH-shaped." Hebrews makes it very clear that Christ-shaped salvation must include representatives of every people as it promises that Jesus tasted death for everyone, many sons will be brought to glory, and that Jesus is the author of salvation to all who obey Him.

The crescendo of Hebrews 6 occurs when God shows that the immutability of His counsel, the immutable promises in which it is impossible for God to lie, and the consolation, hope, and refuge before us are mission promises. The author quotes Genesis 22:17 and the promise to Abraham which is the guarantee that all nations of the world will be blessed through Jesus, Abraham's seed. It is this covenant with Abraham which gives us the foundation for the hope we have as an anchor of the soul, both sure and steadfast. Not only is our salvation sure, so is the salvation of representatives of all nations. It is impossible for God to lie about this. And Jesus not only guarantees the result, He also does the work to ensure His promise. Thus, He has been counted worthy of more glory than Moses. What relief that Jesus both guarantees a full, free salvation and also engineers it.

David Brainerd recorded a wonderful example of this wonderful reality taken from his missionary work among American Indians: "I never saw the work of God appear so independent of means as at this time. I discoursed to the people, and spoke what, I suppose, had a proper tendency to promote convictions. But God's manner of working upon them appeared so entirely supernatural and above means that I could scarce believe he used me as an instrument, or what I spake as means of carrying on his work. It seemed, as I thought, to have no connection with, nor dependence upon means in any respect. Although I could not but continue to use the means which I thought proper for the promotion of the work, yet God seemed, as I apprehended, to work entirely without them. I seemed to do nothing, and indeed to have nothing to do, but to 'stand still and see the salvation of God.' I found myself obliged and delighted to say, 'Not unto us,' not unto instruments and means, 'but to thy name be glory.' God appeared to work entirely alone, and I saw no room to attribute any part of this work to any created arm."

PRAYER FOCUS: *Baloch of Pakistan (Evangelical: 0.0%)*

DECEMBER 22: THE POWERS THAT POWER US

TODAY'S READING: HEBREWS 7–10

*"Prayer alone will overcome the gigantic difficulties
which confront the workers in every field."*

JOHN R. MOTT

The power of an endless life (Heb. 7:16). It's amazing what you *will* do if you are not afraid of dying and what you *will not* do if you keep your eyes on the prize of eternal life. Missions only makes sense to those who believe that living forever is real and that living forever with Jesus is far preferable to living forever burning in hell. If eternal life is real, then dying is the charade. The devil would have us think that physical death is the end, so we better live it up now. The Lord would have us rejoice that death is the beginning of our forever, so we deny ourselves now that we might live it up forever. When missionaries have no fear of death, they operate in the power of an endless life. *Nothing* makes God's representatives shudder, slink away, or shut up when they live in the reality of forever. When the absolute worst thing the bad guys can do to missionaries or believers is to send them to eternal life with Jesus, it's easy to see why the children of God can live in fearless power.

The power of prayer (7:25). The most astounding revelation of the activity of our ascended Lord Jesus is that He spends His time praying for us. Jesus uses His everlasting life and power to pray. Jesus ascended to prepare a place for us by praying! With everything that Jesus could be doing right now, He chooses to spend His time praying for us. It's hard to comprehend, but Jesus is our primary prayer partner. If omnipotent Christ prays in heaven, how much more should all feeble humans pray on earth. The best thing we can do for the advance of the gospel, whether as senders or missionaries on the field ourselves, is pray. A critical missionary error is to think that prayer is only the work of the sender. Prayer must be the first work of the goer.

The power of confession (10:23–25). How we prove that we're not Christians is with our mouth. The Roman emperor Trajan and governor Pliny corresponded about how to discern if someone was a Christian: "If the accused makes it clear he is not a Christian by offering to our gods, he is to be pardoned," Trajan wrote. In other words, words of public worship prove our allegiance. If we belong to Jesus, we must hold fast to that confession publicly. We must open our mouths and declare we belong to Jesus and He is God. Hebrews is repetitively clear that we can belong to Jesus and then forfeit that status through willful disobedience and insulting the Spirit of grace. To live by faith is connected to believing Jesus is coming back to judge and enduring so that we can receive the promise.

The missionary spirit remembers we will live forever and thus lives with the power of endless life. The missionary spirit observes that Jesus spends His eternal time praying and resolves to do likewise. The missionary spirit is acutely aware that faith necessitates public confession that we belong to Jesus for the joys of what is before them in heaven.

PRAYER FOCUS: *Kabardian, East Circassian of Russia (Evangelical: 0.02%)*

DECEMBER 23: RUN YOUR LEG WELL

TODAY'S READING: HEBREWS 11–13

"When he landed in 1848 there were no Christians here;
when he left in 1872 there were no heathen."

SAID OF JOHN GEDDIE

The Bible repeatedly asks two great faith resolutions from us: first, that we will trust Jesus to save us through His grace and not by our works, and second, that we will trust Jesus to save men and women from every tribe, tongue, people, and nation in the very same way that He saved us. The story of the Bible and the witness of those before us are that God can be trusted on both accounts, personal and global. God is a missionary God precisely because He is worthy of our faith in these two monumental promises. He is able to save us to the uttermost and He is able to save from the uttermost parts of the earth. In this faith brave men and women, of whom the world was not worthy, were tortured, mocked, scourged, chained, imprisoned, sawed in two, slain, and wandered around destitute, afflicted, and tormented.

The writer of Hebrews, like all of his/her fellow human writers of Scripture, cannot get away from the centrality of Abraham. By faith Abraham obeyed to go out to Syria, Palestine, and Egypt—all places he would not inherit in this life. By faith Abraham, when he was tested, gave up his only begotten son, his only earthly hope. In Abraham God recognized the same missionary obedience and spirit as was in the eternal heart of the Trinity. Jesus, trusting the Father, left home for no immediate temporal inheritance. The Father gave up His only begotten Son. The missionary spirit sourced in God and exemplified in Abraham is yet needed in our world today. God is still looking for those who will look like Him by leaving home with no temporal guarantees of success and who will bear the agony of separation from children or aging parents. The price the great cloud of witnesses paid was worth it because they saw by faith the promises of God. They believed God could grant them eternal life and they saw dimly but firmly the eternal life that is on offer for all.

Hebrews is not written in a biblical vacuum. A redeemed Jew writing to redeemed Jews understood the metanarrative. We live holy lives so God will live among us and bless us to bless all nations. The "therefore" of Hebrews 12:1 is connected to the great theme of history. Because God promised to live among us and through us to bless all peoples of earth, and because those who have gone ahead of us had such faith this would happen one day, they endured unimaginable things. *Therefore*, let us throw aside every weight and run with perseverance our leg of the race, looking to Jesus, the author and finisher of *our* faith (see vv. 1–2). The "our" of the faith includes representatives of all God's created peoples as does the joy set before Jesus. Does it not make Jesus glad that His death on the cross made a way for *all peoples* to be saved? We are running a relay race united to the body of Christ across time and space by God's missionary heart, and we must run our leg well.

PRAYER FOCUS: *Kawahia, Fezara of Sudan (Evangelical: 0.0%)*

DECEMBER 24: PREACH IN POWER UNRESTRAINED

TODAY'S READING: 2 TIMOTHY

Second Timothy is considered Paul's last epistle before his death in Rome. Writing around 67 AD, Paul encouraged Timothy to be a faithful missionary pastor, enduring in the face of opposition from false teachers. Timothy was also encouraged to carry on gospel ministry and to train up others who will carry on the work when he was gone.

Paul was clear about his assignment right to the end. He reminded Timothy: "I was appointed a preacher, a missionary, and a teacher of the Gentiles" (2 Tim. 1:11). Paul's point was that Timothy, too, was appointed a preacher, missionary, and teacher who should not fear, who should not be ashamed of the testimony of Jesus, and who should not shirk suffering for the gospel's sake. We are fearless, unashamed, and willing to suffer because we know whom we have believed and are persuaded that He is able to keep what we have committed to Him until that day. What day? The day of the Lord when Jesus comes back to judge us regarding whether we obeyed Him and glorified Him to the ends of the earth among all peoples by preaching, missionizing, and teaching.

Let us be under no illusion about Paul's last words to Timothy which are of first importance to us. Paul understood the Scriptures and the intention of God to be glorified by every people group. Paul gave his life to this and expected his disciples to do the same. What Timothy heard and saw in Paul among many witnesses, he was to pass on to faithful men who would then teach others. The hard-fighting warrior, the hard-running competitor, and the hardworking farmer are all in the context of Timothy being instructed to live and die in missionary focus as Paul did. Missionary-oriented Christianity is the biblical expectation for all men and women of all vocations from all nations across all time. Timothy was a pastor, yet Paul urged him to live and die for the glory of God among the nations. All Timothy's fighting, running, and laboring was to be focused on Jesus being glorified by every tongue. Timothy was to remind and charge all he discipled that they were to focus on this grand goal and not get pulled down into silly disputes. The defense of good doctrine and the call to holy living are for this purpose: that we might in unrestrained power make Jesus famous among the nations.

Paul closed his life with one last reminder of two missionary essentials: First, persecution is normal and all who desire to be missionary hearted like Jesus will suffer. Second, preaching is primal and when Jesus comes we will be judged according to whether or not we were faithful preachers of the Word and whether or not we did the work of evangelism among the nations.

If we summarize half of Acts, Romans, Corinthians, Galatians, Ephesians, Philippians, Colossians, Thessalonians, Timothy, Titus, Philemon, and possibly Hebrews, it would simply be these final words of Paul: "The Lord stood with me and strengthened me, so that the message might be preached fully through me, and that all the Gentiles might hear" (4:17). Amen.

PRAYER FOCUS: *Zhuang, Zuojiang of Vietnam (Evangelical: 0.14%)*

ECEMBER 25: A CHRISTMAS GIFT FROM JESUS

TODAY'S READING: 2 PETER, JUDE

t is likely Jude, the half-brother of Jesus, wrote his epistle at the same time as 2 Peter due to the common language shared in Jude verses 4–9 and 2 Peter 2:1–3:3. We're t sure who borrowed from whom, but it's clear the message is common. Jude wrote Christians who were being led astray by false teachers. The missionary implications of Jude are two-fold: First, we must speak up against false teaching and proactively show our disciples what is wrong or errant. Missionary work is not passive, nor does it rely on the self-discovery of the seeker or disciple. Missionaries teach and preach, exhort, rebuke, and counsel. Missionaries save with fear, pulling out of the fire. Second, we don't converse arrogantly or presumptuously with the devil. We let the Lord do that particular rebuking. Succinctly, those who make disciples have the spiritual authority to rebuke their disciples, even cross culturally, but Jesus alone has the authority to rebuke the devil. Let's do our job relieved and content that God will always do His. He is able to keep us from stumbling.

Peter refers to the "like precious faith" (2 Peter 1:1) shared across the multi-cultural body of Christ. To truly participate in the body of Christ means we need each other, and the rebuke mentioned above must be a two-way street. We must be corrected by the cross-cultural body of Christ; we desperately need it. Peter, in addressing false teaching, exemplified this reality. Peter needed Paul to rebuke him. The Gentiles needed Peter's correction. Globally, Christians don't get an accurate understanding of Jesus without the perspectives of other redeemed cultural lenses. Think of the travesty if the Bible was only interpreted by Americans! Think of the beauty, depth, and wisdom when the God-given insight of all cultures combines to study the Scripture under the aegis of the Holy Spirit!

Peter was crystal clear that the Lord would keep His promises, namely that Jesus will come again soon in power and glory to rule and reign over all the peoples of this earth. The heavens will pass away with a great noise, and the earth and the works in it will be burned up. The reason the Bible focuses us on souls from every unreached people group is because everything else physical will be destroyed. A missionary understanding keeps us from falling in love with this world and keeps us fixed on hastening the day of King Jesus coming back. The only reason Jesus delays patiently is that more might find salvation. God's missionary people live with the tension of longing for Jesus to come back for the joy set before us and the terror of what that means for those who have never heard, or who have heard and not repented. We urge Jesus to come quickly even as we plea for a little more time for the lost. Maybe our Christmas gift from Jesus is a little more time for a few more souls to be saved.

PRAYER FOCUS: *Somali of Yemen (Evangelical: 0.03%)*

DECEMBER 26: THIS IS HOW WE LOVE

TODAY'S READING: 1 JOHN

By and large the apostles were martyred outside of Jerusalem and Israel. John, son of Zebedee, was perhaps the only sent one not martyred, though he too died outside of Israel. He wrote 1 John to Christians in Asia Minor around 85 AD just before he was exiled on the island of Patmos. We should read this epistle understanding that a missionary wrote it to a missionary church plant.

Like all those the Spirit used to author books of the Bible, John clearly showed that the heart of Jesus is for all the peoples of earth. John wrote to Gentiles, not Jews. He pointed out that Jesus was their Savior as well as the Savior of the Jews and that the gospel should not stop in Turkey, but it must keep going to the uttermost parts of the earth. It's always the "keep going" part Christians struggle with most. The Jews were happy to be God's special treasure but not keen on sharing the spiritual wealth. John rejoiced with the believers in Asia Minor that Jesus was their saving Advocate, but reminded them they must share, for Jesus is Savior of *the world*. We must be conscious of our propensity to revel selfishly in Jesus being ours. We must remember Jesus globally is *ours* and He is the Savior of the *whole* world. Gospel love must keep spreading.

In this light John wrote of Jesus being manifested to take away sins. John told his readers that the world does not know us and in fact hates us, so both resistance and redemption play out on the global stage. We know love because Jesus laid down His life for us—as part of the whole world. John said then that we also ought to lay down our lives for the brethren. The implication is impossible to miss: Jesus laid His life down to save from among every people all who would repent, and this is love. If we are to love, we must lay our lives down that some from among every people might receive forgiveness of sins. We can't separate John's teaching about love from Jesus laying down His life for all peoples. John's not talking about loving our immediate family; he's talking about every unreached people on earth.

John framed the blessings of God in the context of obeying His commandments and doing the things pleasant in His sight, with the accompanying help of the Holy Spirit. Jesus commanded us to go into the whole world and make disciples of every people, promising us the Holy Spirit as our power and wisdom. First John is in perfect harmony with the gospels and the full Bible narrative, emphasizing that this expected corporate obedience is simply love. Missions is loving our brothers in Afghanistan and beyond. For in this the love of God was manifested to us—that God sent His only begotten Son into the world that we might live through Jesus. And in this we manifest our love to God—that we send our only begotten children into God's world that Jesus might raise the unreached from the dead. The missionary spirit sends. This is how we love the brethren; this is how we love our world.

PRAYER FOCUS: *Aimaq of Afghanistan (Evangelical: 0.0%)*

DECEMBER 27: THE PULL FOR PREEMINENCE

TODAY'S READING: 2 & 3 JOHN

Missions is centered in a robust Christology. John wrote his second epistle to a lady leading a house church, likely in Asia Minor, and his third to Gaius, most probably a member or leader in another church in Asia Minor. To the lady, John bluntly said that those who do not abide in the doctrine of Christ do not have God the Father. He said that anyone who claims to be of the faith yet considers Christ as anything but fully God and fully man is to be shunned, not even greeted. There is no place in Christian mission for the cloaking, diluting, veiling, softening, hiding, or mistranslating the deity of Jesus. John simply said that anyone who undermines the deity of Jesus or collaborates with those who do is evil. If we get one thing right in mission, if there is one message we cannot afford to corrupt, it is the proclamation of the deity of Jesus, the preaching that God became flesh and dwelt among us, died for our sin, and was resurrected from the dead.

John had no greater joy than knowing his children walk in this truth. Understanding John's high Christology and missionary example, we can be sure that walking in truth for John centered on loving the Lord Jesus and loving to make Him known. Evidently, Diotrephes had taken over the church and turned it from being a Christ- and mission-centered church into one centered on himself. Diotrephes stopped the church from supporting itinerant missionaries seemingly because he wanted God's glory for himself and God's gold for his followers.

Is it any different in our churches today? Do the leaders of our churches lead the body in such a way as to enshrine themselves as head, with Christ reduced to figurehead? Do the leaders in our churches spend more money on buildings and salaries or on speeding the gospel to the ends of the earth? It's easy to ask the question of others, but we must all stand in front of the mirror and ask it of ourselves: Do I live that I might be preeminent or is Jesus really my glory and the obvious Sovereign of my life? Do I spend more on myself than I spend on the gospel going to the nations? Do I give myself the best portion and pompously fling some crumbs toward the starving unreached? Beloved, do not imitate what is evil, but imitate our good God who gave at great cost that all peoples of earth might repent.

As a missionary, I keenly feel the deceptive pull at my heart for preeminence. There is an ugly, twisted evil in me that wants to be known for making Christ known. Because we missionaries are so enthusiastically and sincerely affirmed, we are in the most danger of delusion, and the same is likely true for pastors and ministers. We who live by the gospel should be conscientiously careful that we live truly *for* the gospel. We who live on the generous sacrifice of hardworking saints must be the most sacrificially generous of all. Missionaries of all people should support other missionaries around the world. Missionaries of all people should recoil with the most horror when anyone but Jesus is praised.

PRAYER FOCUS: *Bania of India (Evangelical: 0.0%)*

DECEMBER 28: THIS IS WHY

TODAY'S READING: REVELATION 1–5

Four broad schools of interpretation have influenced how we understand Revelation. "Preterists" apply the book to John's lifetime and the persecution of Domitian. "Historicists" view the book as describing the events from the ascension of Christ to His return. "Futurists" think the book refers mainly to the end times and the events that immediately precede Christ's coming. "Idealists" maintain that Revelation is not a specific description of future events, but a symbolic picture of the cosmic conflict between the kingdom of God and the forces of evil.

In my view, Revelation is not granted to us that we make specific timelines for future events, for wise men are not dogmatic about the details and dates of their eschatology. Wise men and women read the apocalyptic sections of Scripture to be reminded and assured that God is sovereignly good and in complete control of all (including the future) and that King Jesus is coming soon. The word "apocalypse" comes from the Greek word *apokalypto*, which literally means "unveiling." Revelation 1:1 then should be understood as the unveiling of Jesus: both Jesus revealed and Jesus revealing. When we read Revelation with a hunger to know more of Jesus and His glorious plan for the nations of the world, we emerge from that reading worshipful and awe-filled, not befuddled and afraid.

The cosmic conflict view of Revelation (that culminates when Jesus returns) has the most grounds for sure footing. The conflict is about glory: Who gets it, why they get it, and from whom they get it? The Bible rightly culminates in pointing out that Jesus will get all the glory from all the nations, from all the people groups of earth. Various churches are described in Revelation 1 to 3 and all given rewards if they overcome, but the focus of Revelation is not on the bride, but the Bridegroom. Who is worthy of glory? "You are worthy, O Lord, to receive glory and honor and power; for You created all things, and by Your will they exist and were created" (Rev. 4:11). Why is God worthy of glory and from whom? "You are worthy to take the scroll and to open its seals; for You were slain, and have redeemed us to God by Your blood out of every tribe and tongue and people and nation" (5:9).

Revelation simply reminds us that Jesus is worthy of glory and He will receive it from representatives of every tribe, tongue, people, and nation. This is the story of the Bible. This is the heart and mission of God. This is what we were born for. This is what is worth living and dying for. This is what happens when time surrenders: Jesus glorified, worshiped, and enjoyed forever by members of every tribe, tongue, people, and nation. This is why we say that God is a missionary God and that the Bible is a missionary book. This is why we must all be His missionary people and calibrate all our mind, soul, and strength to the priceless missionary vision: Jesus, the endless praise of every people group, every tongue, and every creature.

PRAYER FOCUS: *Gujar (Muslim Traditions) of Pakistan (Evangelical: 0.0%)*

DECEMBER 29: THE NUMBER MUST BE COMPLETED

TODAY'S READING: REVELATION 6–11

The middle chapters of Revelation detail twenty-one plagues described in three sets: Seven seals, seven trumpets, and seven bowls. The plagues and judgments are terrible and awesome, and they serve to remind the reader and the world that the age of the cross (where Christ and His Christians turn the other cheek) will soon end and the age of the crown (where King Jesus rules with absolute power and authority) is coming to a start. "For six thousand years this world has been under the usurpation of the enemies of God, and with all the boasted civilizations, improvements, and education and the multiplied religions in the world, the human race has constantly degenerated and the humans grown more obdurate, proud, self-willed, until the race culminates in bowing down to Antichrist and worshiping the great beast in the place of God. This will be the climax to the history of sin and natural human character, and the time will then be perfectly ripe for the Son of God, as a Divine warrior, to return with omnipotent righteousness and with a sharp sword proceeding out of His mouth, in order that He might destroy His enemies and assume absolute command of the world which He has bought with His own blood."

The central theme of the Bible is that the world Jesus bought with His own blood is organized and ornamented by ethnicity, by people groups of all colors and cultures. As human history crescendos, John looked into heaven and saw "a great multitude which no one could number, of all nations, tribes, peoples, and tongues, standing before the throne and before the Lamb…crying out with a loud voice, saying, 'Salvation belongs to our God who sits on the throne, and to the Lamb'" (7:9–10). John saw that in that day there will be no heat, nor hunger, just living fountains of water with every tear wiped from our eyes. To that great day we all groan and ask, "When?" The answer to that question is as straightforward as it is difficult. Revelation 6:9–11 tells of the slain martyrs under the altar who have been killed for the word of God and for their testimony. They cry with a loud voice: "How long?" The Divine response is: "Not yet." We must wait a little longer, until the number of their fellow servants who would be killed as they were is completed.

All human history draws close to an end. With great relish we anticipate the day when representatives of all peoples of earth are gathered tearless around the throne. With great sobriety we realize that more martyrs must first plant their bloody seed in the ground, slain for the words of testimony about Jesus that come from their mouths. A good and sovereign God has decreed that suffering precedes glory. If our death or the death of my sons or my friends will hasten that day and "complete the number," then Lord, let Your will be done soon that Your kingdom come quickly. If more martyrs are required to hasten that day, then what are we waiting for? Loving, selfless acts that hasten the dawn of endless peace and joy are not tragedies; they are joys.

PRAYER FOCUS: *Sayyid of Bangladesh (Evangelical: 0.0%)*

DECEMBER 30: IN THE LIGHT OF FOREVER

TODAY'S READING: REVELATION 12–18

The Bible's final book cannot stop repeating the grand theme of all Scripture, the very sum of history, the passionate heart of God. To fixate on plagues and pestilences is to miss the point. The attention of heaven is on God's determined plan to glorify Himself through the praise of every people group. In the light of forever—God most glorified by man being most satisfied in Him—judgments and martyrdoms make cosmic sense. They are still fear-inspiring, they still are emotionally devastating, they still cause pain, but we can embrace them, for we see in the clear light of what they usher in, that they are worth it, small prices to pay for the great gain they afford. We *still* overcome by the blood of the Lamb and by the word of our testimony *and* by not loving our lives even unto the death. These are not words for the past or for other cultures far from us; these are words for us in the here and now. Mankind is so evil and rebellious there is no way forward outside God's judgments and gospel martyrdom. The church today is both embarrassed about her God's judging of the wicked and confused about Her children's dying at the hands of the wicked. We want the end to come, but not desperately enough to pay the modest price (all things considered). We must embrace both judgment and martyrdom before we get to the end of the beginning and enjoy a new beginning with no end. Let us not be so shortsighted that we cannot see the insignificant price compared to the glories of the other side.

G. D. Watson wrote of the four ages of man. He called the first age (from Adam to the flood) the age of conscience. Without law, church, or special revelation, man was given the chance to govern themselves and made a terrible mess of it. The second act is the age of law, both moral and ceremonial, with Israel as the chosen custodian (from Moses to Christ). This, too, proved a spectacular failure, demonstrating that character cannot be changed by force or instruction. The third age is the gospel age, the space between the two advents of Christ. We have our conscience and the moral law like those before us, yet we also have incarnate God and the Holy Spirit. We have the church, sacraments, and endowed authority to evangelize every people. Yet, all is not well. We still live in a fallen world, we still are under duress from temptation and attack, and we still struggle with sin. The wicked men wax worse, and darkness shall increase until Jesus comes. The end of the Bible gives us great hope that the beginning of the unending age is just about to start. With a clear mind we look out at the wickedness that will cause martyrs and martyrs' blood that will cry out for judgment. We welcome these horrors, not because we are twisted, but because Scripture helps us see what is beyond them: life forevermore in the presence of Jesus, surrounded by every joyful tribe and every worshiping tongue.

PRAYER FOCUS: *Jat (Hindu Traditions) of India (Evangelical: 0.0%)*

DECEMBER 31: HOW TIME WILL END

TODAY'S READING: REVELATION 19–22

"Untold millions are still untold."

JOHN WESLEY

A stunning missionary Bible climaxes with our Missionary God returning to rule and reign with great power and glory over all the nations for all of time. When King Jesus comes back, He will be awe-inspiring and terrifying. He comes to judge and make war. His eyes will be fire and His robe will be splattered with the blood of the enemies and nations He has struck. He will rule with a rod of iron (absolute authority); heaven has no room for democracy. He *Himself* treads the winepress of the fierceness of God's wrath, for Jesus has a violent, terrible side of His goodness, a side that will send the devil and wicked to hell to be tormented night and day forever. Yes, this is Jesus, our King and Lord. He would not be good if He was not violently dedicated to the absolute eradication and punishment of all evil. We must never forget that we will stand one day trembling before the throne of Him. Thanks be to God! The blood of Jesus saves us from the wrath of God!

The Bible intentionally focuses on nations. Even in its closing chapters, the inspired Word directs our attention to the broad inclusion of grace. In the explanation of the New Jerusalem, it says: "And the nations of those who are saved shall walk in its light, and the kings of the earth shall bring their glory and honor into it…. The leaves of the tree of life were for the healing of the nations" (Rev. 21:24; 22:2). Even the last chapter of the Bible announces that the plan of God includes all the peoples of earth. Satan has known this all along, which is why in his demented fury he has tried so hard through all the ages to bring entire people groups with him to hell. The reason our good and glorious warrior King confines and punishes the devil is so that he "should deceive the nations no more" (20:3). We make too much of ourselves when we think we are the object of the devil's primary attention. He has grander ambitions than dragging you and me to hell. He fights to take down entire people groups. Which is why a focus on unreached peoples as the priority of missions is not a fad or passing strategic whim. From the beginning God has made this His loving aim—*all peoples*. The devil has thus attacked this great love of God consistently, battling in the heavens and earth to forever bind the ethnic peoples God created for His glory and their joy. Spiritual warfare is not centrally about me or you and our personal little wounds or worries; it's about unreached peoples. If you want to join the cosmic fight, come battle for the unreached. If you want to hit Satan where it hurts him most, come in this last hour and glorify Jesus by snatching the unreached from the fires of hell.

This is how time will end, in the beauty God designed from the beginning: "The tabernacle of God is with men, and He will dwell with them…and be their God" (21:3). The promises to Abraham and David will be fulfilled, all nations with their eternal King.

PRAYER FOCUS: *Awan of Pakistan (Evangelical: 0.0%)*

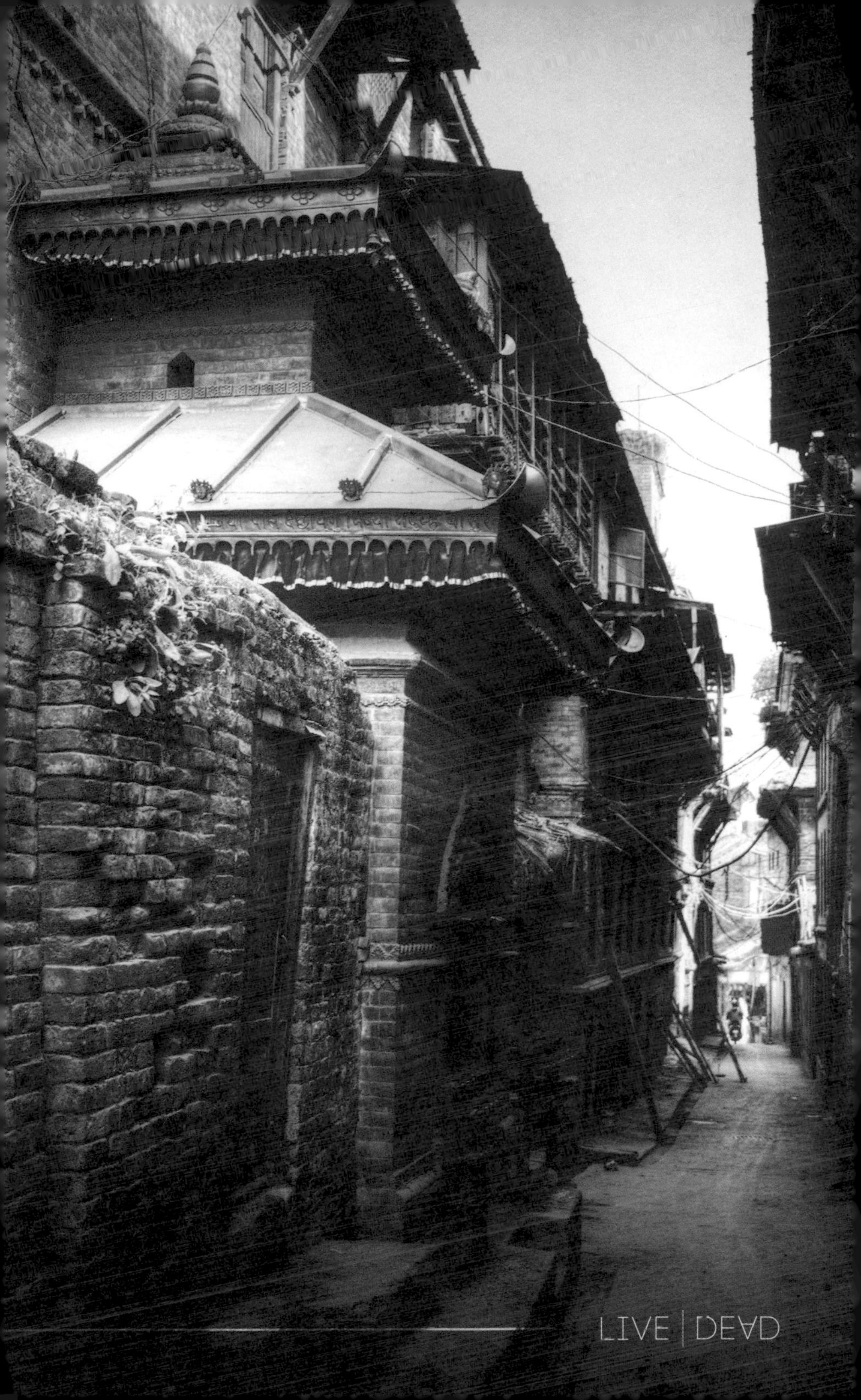
LIVE | DEAD

ENDNOTES

1   Walter C. Kaiser, Jr., *Mission in the Old Testament: Israel as a Light to Nations* (Grand Rapids, MI: Baker Academic, 2000), 10.

2   Ibid, 15.

3   Ibid, 16.

4   Ibid.

5   "Jubilo! The Emancipation Century." https://jubiloemancipationcentury.wordpress.com/2015/03/04/the-blood-drawn-with-the-lash-shall-be-paid-by-another-drawn-with-the-sword-lincolns-view-of-the-war-as-the-lords-judgement-for-slavery/ (accessed December 6, 2019).

6   *The Chronological Study Bible* (Nashville: Thomas Nelson, 2008), 8.

7   Kaiser, 17.

8   *The Chronological Study Bible*, 21.

9   Kaiser, 18–20.

10   See pages 177–184 in John Piper's *Let the Nations Be Glad! The Supremacy of God in Missions* (Grand Rapids: Baker, 1993).

11   "Bildad." https://en.wikipedia.org/wiki/Bildad. "Zophar." https://www.britannica.com/biography/Zophar (accessed January 1, 2019).

12   *The Chronological Study Bible*, 902.

13   "Missio Dei in the Book of Job." http://www.galaxie.com/article/bsac166-661-02 (accessed December 6, 2019).

14   In this devotional, I will often refer to peoples and places by their current geographical names and contexts, knowing that this is anachronistic as various peoples have lived in these places over time. For example, Temites do not necessarily equate directly to Saudi Arabians, nor Job from Uz (likely in Edom, located in what we now call Jordan) to current Jordanians. My point is to emphasize that God intends to receive global, not parochial, glory.

15   *The Chronological Study Bible*, 910.

16   "From Mesopotamia there are at present four known documents that are superficially similar to the book of Job: *Man and His God; I Will Praise the Lord of Wisdom; The Babylonian Theodicy; and Dialogue Between a Master and His Slave*." Ibid.

17   *The Chronological Study Bible*, 925.

18   "Palestine, 3." https://www.internationalstandardbible.com/P/palestine-3.html (accessed January 7, 2019).

19   As described by Horace J. Wolf, commenting on Genesis 22:22 in the *International Standard Bible Encyclopedia*. https://biblehub.com/topical/b/buzite.htm (accessed January 7, 2019).

20   Shinar, Ellasar, Elam, Sodom, Gomorrah, Admah, Zeboiim, Zoar, the Rephaim, the Zuzim, the Emim, the Horites, Seir, El Paran, En Mishpat, Amalekites, and Amorites.

21   *The Chronological Study Bible*, 22.

22   The definition of vassal is "a holder of land by feudal tenure on conditions of homage and allegiance."

23   The definition of suzerain is "a sovereign or state having some control over another state that is internally autonomous."

24   *The Chronological Study Bible*, 23.

25   In mathematics, the Pythagorean theorem is fundamental relation in geometry among the three sides of a right triangle. It states that the square of the hypotenuse (the side opposite the right angle is equal to the sum of the squares of the other two sides. The theorem can be written as an equation relating the lengths of the sides a, b and c, often called the "Pythagorean equation": $a^2 + b^2 = c^2$, where c represents the length of the hypotenuse and a and b the lengths of the triangle's other two sides.

26   Olaudah Equiano, *The Interesting Narrative and Other Writings* (New York: Penguin Books, 2003), 44.

27   "Saadia Gaon's tenth century Arabic translation of the Hebrew Bible substitutes "Havilah" with "Zaila" in present day Somalia. Zaila was the dominion of the Harla up until the sixteenth century. Benjamin Tudela, the twelfth century Jewish traveler, claimed the land of Havilah is confined by Al-Habash on the west. In 1844, Charles Forster argued that a trace of the ancient name *Havilah* could still be found in the use of *Aval* for what is now known as Bahrain Island." "Havilah." https://en.wikipedia.org/wiki/Havilah (accessed January 10, 2019).

28   *The Chronological Study Bible*, 44.

29   Christopher J. H. Wright, *The Mission of God: Unlocking the Bible's Grand Narrative* (Downers Grove, IL: IVP Academic, 2006), 273–275.

30   Ibid.

31   Ibid, 269–270.

32   Ibid, 273.

33   John G. Paton, *Thirty Years with South Sea Cannibals* (Chicago: Moody Press, 1964).

— FEBRUARY —

1   Wright, 93.

2   Ibid, 95.

3   Ibid, 270.

4   Kaiser, 21.

5   Ibid.

6   Wright, 76.

7   *The Chronological Study Bible*, 87.

8   "Missions Is Answered Prayer." The Voice of the Martyrs. http://www.globalprn.com/wp-content/uploads/Missions-is-Ansered-Prayer.pdf (accessed February 2, 2019).

9   October 17 entry from Oswald Chamber's *My Utmost for His Highest* (New York: Dodd, Mead & Co., 1935).

10   "If you will obey me fully and keep my covenant, then out of all the nations you will be my treasured possession. Although the whole earth is mine, you will be to me a kingdom of priests and a holy nation" (Exo. 19:5–6).

11   Kaiser, 22–23.

12   *The Chronological Study Bible*, 94–95.

13   John V. York, *Missions in the Age of the Spirit* (Springfield, MO: Logion Press, 2001), 27–28.

14   John Owen, *Communion with God* (Carlisle, PA: The Banner of Truth Trust, R.K.J. Law, 1991), 42.

15   Wright, 45.

16   Carl E. Braaten, "The Mission of the Gospel to the Nations," *Dialogue 30* (1991), 27.

17   Wright, 334–335.

18   Ibid, 88.

19   Ibid, 470–471.

20   *The Chronological Study Bible*, 106.

21   Wright, 362.

22   *The Chronological Study Bible*, 112.

23   Wright, 331.

24   Walter Vogels, *God's Universal Covenant: A Biblical Study* (Ottawa: Ottawa University Press, 1986), 48–49.

25   *The Chronological Study Bible*, 125.

26   Ibid, 129.

27   Owen, 58–59.

28   *Se'irim* is the literal translation for "demons" in Leviticus 17:7. It is interesting that the goat is now linked with devil worship today.

29   Leviticus 19:3–4, 10, 12, 14, 16, 18, 25, 28, 30–31, 33.

30   Wright, 373–375.

31   Ibid, 462.

32   "The Jewish Holidays: A Simplified Overview of the Feasts of the LORD." https://www.hebrew4christians.com/Holidays/Introduction/introduction.html (accessed February 16, 2019).

33   Levitt and Parsons point out that the first four feasts (all in the spring) reveal that Jesus was crucified on Passover, buried during Unleavened Bread, raised on First Fruits, and sent the Holy Spirit at Pentecost.

34   *The Chronological Study Bible*, 141.

35   "Power tends to corrupt and absolute power corrupts absolutely." From "Lord Acton Quote Archive." Acton Institute. https://acton.org/research/lord-acton-quote-archive (accessed February 16, 2019).

36   Scholars are divided as to when exactly the Exodus occurred; the early and late dates differ by over 100 years.

37   *The Chronological Study Bible*, 147.

38   Wright, 459.

39   William Borden is remembered for walking away from family wealth and for writing the pithy exhortations: "No reserves. No retreats. No regrets."

40   Numbers 4:15, 24, 31.

41   *The Chronological Study Bible*, 154.

42   York, 29.

43   Historically, Cush is the area now known as northern Sudan.

44   Aaron and Miriam spoke against Moses because he married a darker skinned Sudanese, a black woman.

45   Giants, perhaps even some strange mix of fallen angels and men.

— MARCH —

1   *The Chronological Study Bible*, 174.

2   York, 31.

3   Terrence E. Fretheim, *Exodus* (Louisville: John Knox Press.,1991), 212.

4   John I. Durham, "Exodus," *Word Bible Commentary 3* (Waco, Texas: Word, 1987), 263.

5   Wright, 226.

6   John Goldingay, *Old Testament Theology (Volume 1): Israel's Gospel* (Downers Grove, IL: Intervarsity Press, 2003), 471.

7   Ibid.

8   *The Chronological Study Bible*, 177.

9   Kaiser, 24.

10   Leith Anderson. Sermon heard at Missio Nexus Missions Conference, Orlando, FL, on September 22, 2018.

11   "People of God." Lyrics by Wayne Watson. Singspiration Music. 1982.

12   "Stand Up! Stand Up for Jesus!" Lyrics by George Duffield. Public Domain.

13   *The Chronological Study Bible*, 189.

14   The word "Deuteronomy" is derived from Latin and means "second law," and the "second law" refers to the second sermon which is the bulk of the book (chapters 5–28). Deuteronomy follows

a treaty format common in the ancient Near East, especially among the Hittites: a preamble (with the history), the agreement (including blessings and cursings), and the closing (calling on witnesses to preserve the document). Moses' three sermons in Deuteronomy follow the same essential outline. *The Chronological Study Bible*, 190.

15   Wright, 463.

16   Ibid, 386.

17   Ibid.

18   Wright, 329.

19   Ibid, 458.

20   Greg Beggs serves as the Assemblies of God World Missions (AGWM) Africa Regional Director.

21   In Romans Paul "quotes [Deuteronomy 32's] final doxology, calling on the nations to praise God with his people (Deut. 32:43), in his exposition of the multinational nature of the gospel and its implications for the need of cross-cultural acceptance and sensitivity between Jewish and Gentile Christians (Rom 15:7-10)." Wright points out that it was Paul who "recognized that the fulfillment of God's purposes for Israel could never be complete without the ingathering of the nations as well." Wright, 343.

22   Ibid, 344.

23   York, 33–37.

24   Paul York, *A Biblical Theology of Missions* (Springfield, MO: Africa's Hope, 2008), 47–52.

25   John F. Walvoord and Roy B. Zuck, *The Bible Knowledge Commentary* (Wheaton, IL: Scripture Press Publications, 1985), 326.

26   *The Chronological Study Bible*, 246.

27   Ibid, 250.

28   Ibid, 257.

29   Ibid, 262.

— APRIL —

1   Baal wasn't considered particularly smart, but he was considered brave and strong and a foe that could storm back. *The Chronological Study Bible*, 268.

2   Harry S. Truman said, "It is amazing what you can accomplish if you do not care who gets the credit."

3   I do not denigrate the great graces of itineration; I merely point out the great dangers.

4   *The Chronological Study Bible*, 274.

5   Ibid, 281.

6   Paul York, 64.

7   John V. York, 38.

8   *The Chronological Study Bible*, 293.

9   Ibid, 302.

10   Walter Brueggemann, *First and Second Samuel* (Louisville: John Knox Press, 1990), 132.

11   Richard Bauckham, *The Bible and Mission: Christian Mission in a Postmodern World* (Carlisle, UK: Paternoster. 1998), 37.

12   *The Chronological Study Bible*, 314.

13   Her "enduring house" reference to David in 1 Samuel 25:28 anticipated one of the most seminal passages of the Old Testament when in 2 Samuel 7, God promised David a dynasty from which Messiah will come.

14   George Peters, *A Biblical Theology of Missions* (Chicago: Moody, 1972), 115–116.

15   It's not a bad rule of thumb for every song we sing in worship to include a stanza on God's heart for the nations.

16   Some examples from today's selected psalms: 6:10; 8:1, 9; 9:5, 8, 11, 17, 19–20; 10:16; 14:2, 7; 16:2–3; 19:1–3; 21:8, 10.

17   From the hymn "Jesus Shall Reign Where'er the Sun" by Isaac Watts.

18   "The priests were the ones responsible for maintaining genealogical records, which explains why the genealogies that are preserved tend to be most complete when they describe the priestly families…. These [genealogies] serve as a sort of historical shorthand to bridge the generations from the first man, Adam (1 Chr. 1:1), to the first king, Saul (9:35–44), after which the historical narrative begins." *The Chronological Study Bible*, 959.

19   *The Chronological Study Bible*, 438.

20   Wright, 498.

21   *The Chronological Study Bible*, 962.

22   Ibid.

23   For the story of Ishbosheth, see 2 Samuel 2:8–11, and for the story of Mephibosheth, see 2 Samuel 6:9–13.

24   *The Chronological Study Bible*, 968.

— MAY —

1   *The Chronological Study Bible*, 347.

2   Kaiser, 25–26.

3   According to the commissions at the end of the gospels, fundamental missionary activity is to make disciples of all peoples teaching them to obey everything Jesus taught (Matt. 28:18–20), to preach the gospel in all the world to every creature (Mark 16:15), to proclaim repentance and forgiveness of sins to all the peoples of earth (Luke 24:47–48), to be sent as the Father sent Jesus (John 20:21), and to be witnesses in the power of the Spirit away from home in ever expanding difficulty and distance (Acts 1:8–11).

4   Kaiser, 34.

5   Ibid.

6   Paul York, 77-78. York lists 2, 9, 18, 22, 33, 45–49, 57, 65, 67, 68, 72, 76, 77, 79, 82, 83, 86, 87, 94–100, 102, 103, 105, 108, 114, 117, 118, 126, 138, 139, 144–146, 150 as the psalms that specifically deal with God's salvation plan for the nations.

7   Wright, 104.

8   Ps. 33:6–9; Jer. 10:10–12; Ps. 24:1, 89:11; Deut. 10:14; Ps. 33:10–11; Isa. 40:22–24; Ps. 33:13–15; Ps. 33:4, 119:60; Isa. 45:19; Ps. 145:9, 13, 17; Ps. 36:6; Isa. 45:22; Ps. 67:4; Ps. 56:8–10.

9   Wright, 169.

10   *The Chronological Study Bible*, 375.

11   In most Bible translations YHWH is translated "Lord" and Elohim translated "God."

12   Kaiser, 30.

13   Ibid, 31.

14   Kaiser links this physical blessing to the spiritual: "The same power and presence of God that had brought material increase was now available for the spiritual increase that would visit all the nations and peoples on earth. The psalmist was not just mouthing empty words or hyping pious-sounding concepts that no one expected anyone to do anything about it. The psalmist and the revealing word of God expected the people of Israel to experience a real change in their lives He wanted them to be the agents through which the blessing of God would come to all the peoples on earth. That was the only way they could join in the refrain and fulfil the prayer and wish that 'all the peoples might praise' God as their God too." Kaiser, 33.

15   Some gates were set at right angles to the city walls so that attackers had to not only penetrate the gate, but then in close quarters turn a sharp corner to face defenders before them in narrow spaces, giving the defender the advantage. These gates were designed to have defenders raining projectiles down on the heads of the attackers from open space above. Often, this outer gate led to a main gate with four such successive chambers.

16   Wright, 478–479.

17   Ibid, 477.

18   Ibid.

19   Marvin E. Tate, "Psalms 51-100," *Word Biblical Commentary 20* (Dallas: Word, 1990), 159.

20   Wright.

21   Ibid, 451.

22   Walter Brueggemann, *Theology of the Old Testament: Testimony, Dispute, Advocacy* (Minneapolis: Fortress, 1997), 324.

23   *The Chronological Study Bible*, 388.

24   David put it this way: "I have not sat with idolatrous mortals, nor will I go in with hypocrites. I have hated the assembly of evildoers, and will not sit with the wicked... That I may proclaim with the voice of thanksgiving, and tell of all Your wondrous works... In the congregations I will bless the Lord" (Psalm 26:4–5, 7, 12).

25   *The Chronological Study Bible*, 398.

26   Wright, 113–115.

27   Not forgetting Ananias and Sapphira (Acts 5:1–11).

28   *The Chronological Study Bible*, 404.

29   "All these strands are woven together and unified by theological comments that interpret the history. The interpretations evaluate the different kings and kingdoms in terms of the requirements found in the book of Deuteronomy. For instance, 2 Kin. 17, which explains in some detail why God allowed the northern kingdom to be destroyed, uses thoughts and even specific expressions from Deuteronomy." *The Chronological Study Bible*, 404.

30   Bluntly, the text says in 2 Kings 17:22–23 that the people persisted in sin, exalting themselves, until Jehovah removed His presence from them.

31   Each of the twenty-two stanzas begins with one of the twenty-two letters of the Hebrew alphabet (starting with the "A" or "aleph" and ending with "T" or "tav"), and each line of the stanza begins with that letter. For example, all the lines of the first stanza ("Aleph") begin with the "a" sound, which in Hebrew can be a silent letter. Psalm 119 is giving us the "A to Z," or in the case of the Hebrew, the "A to T," concerning the excellencies of God's Word.With the addition of a strategic dot some Hebrew letters can change sounds. For example, "*shin*" with the dot at end is pronounced "sh" but with the dot at the beginning is "s": שׁ(right dot) is shin (e.g. **sh**op) and שׂ (left dot) is *sin* (e.g. **s**our).

32   "'The wise' was the term given to a class of people known across the ancient Near Eastern world. These were people renowned for their knowledge, sought out for their advice and guidance. At a popular level they seem to have been consulted rather like a Citizen's Advice Bureau... And the Israelites were well aware of this fact. Indeed, they admired the wisdom of other nations, even in the process of praising their own. So, for example when the historian records that Solomon's wisdom surpassed that of various named wise men of other countries, it only makes sense as a compliment if the latter were justly renowned for their great wisdom. The point was not to vilify the wisdom of other nations but to acknowledge its great reputation in order to exalt Solomon's as even greater... It is remarkably clear that Israel was quite prepared to make use of wisdom materials from those other nations, to evaluate and where necessary edit and purge them in light of Israel's own faith and then calmly incorporate them into their own sacred Scriptures." Wright, 442–443.

— JUNE —

1   Wright, 233.

2   Betty Berghaus, "A Christian Manner and Mission." Westminster Presbyterian Church. https://www.wpcdurham.org/a-christian-manner-and-mission/ (accessed May 9, 2019).

3   *The Chronological Study Bible*, 499–501.

4   Wright, 448.

5   Ibid, 445–446.

6   *The Chronological Study Bible*, 462.

7   Charles Finney, "Lectures to Professing Christians." https://jesus.org.uk/wp-content/uploads/2018/04/finney_lectures_to_professing_christians.pdf (accessed June 1, 2019).

8   Ibid.

9   *The Chronological Study Bible*, 895.

10   "Israel's version of wisdom teaching is somewhat distinct, though. The basic assumptions of wisdom were quite secular. They spoke of worldly matters and had little to say about God. Wisdom

was sought through human experience, not through prayer or any direct revelation. Israel's sages, not quite comfortable with such a focus, sought to incorporate God more fully. As a result, Israel's central theme was 'The fear of the Lord is the beginning of wisdom' (Prov. 9:10). Devotion and obedience to God were seen as prior to and more important than the human quest for wisdom." Ibid.

11   "Perhaps the real test of theological authenticity is the capacity to incorporate the history of Israel and God's people and to treat it as one's own." Andrew Walls, *Understanding Insider Movements: Disciples of Jesus within Diverse Religious Communities* (Kindle Locations 7327–7358), William Carey Library, Kindle Edition.

12   Wright, 347.

13   Ibid, 386.

14   Alan Johnson coined the term to describe how a missionary among unreached peoples can function when he or she doesn't feel like a super apostle, and Alan generously allows us to use it to refer to the well-ordered synthesis of roles in the overall mission of God.

15   "While the law and the prophets are so solidly founded on the core history of Israel, the Wisdom literature draws its theology and ethics from a more universal, creation based moral order. This too has missional implications. In approaching people of other cultures, faiths, and worldviews, we nevertheless share a common humanity and (whether they acknowledge it or not) a common Creator God. Particularly where our missional engagement operates at a cultural and societal level, addressing issues of ethical, social, economic, and political concern, we should not be surprised to find areas of common cause with people who would not identify with the biblical story of redemption. It is to that story that we hope ultimately to bring them... The biblical wisdom tradition shows us that there is as certain universality about biblical ethics simply because we live among people made in the image of God, we inhabit the earth of God's creation, and however distorted these truths become in fallen cultures, they will yet find an echo in human hearts." Wright, 419.

16   Ibid, 450.

17   Ibid, 449.

18   "God has placed within the human heart an inherent desire for more than just the earthly.... Consequently, material things, secular activities, and the pleasures of this earth will never fully satisfy." Donald C. Stamps, Editor, *The Full Life Study Bible* (Grand Rapids, MI: Zondervan Publishing House, 1992), 949.

19   Wright, 447.

20   Sheba was a kingdom that originated at the southwestern tip of the Arabian Peninsula (Yemen) and spread north to current day southern Jordan.

21   Her kingdom was impressive in its own right, apparently "sophisticated, having large urban centers, irrigation systems, and a myriad of trade connections throughout the Near East and southern Asia." *The Chronological Study Bible*, 513.

22   Solomon's wives were never required to worship Jehovah which seemed enlightened. But it was actually disastrous, for it led Solomon to embrace a deadly inclusion so that at the end of his life he not only tolerated but worshiped Ashtoreth of the Sidonians; Milcom and Molech, the abomination of the Ammonites; and Chemosh the abomination of Moab.

23   The same word is used in both texts: se'aqa is the technical term for the cry of protest or pain out of a situation of injustice, cruelty, or violence. Wright, 272.

24   "Clearly he did not want to be seen to be suggesting the worship of any other god but YHWH, and indeed the text hints that Jeroboam may have been claiming the mantle of Moses in having delivered the tribes from the oppression of Solomon and son. Nevertheless, he reconstructed the whole religious apparatus of his state so that the cult of YHWH was clearly under his patronage.

So the narrative subtly implies that while the name at the top of every page still said 'YHWH', the table of contents was very much of Jeroboam's own making. YHWH had been fashioned like a god made by human hands. The living God was being commandeered and crafted through state propaganda to serve the needs of national security—a form of idolatry that did not perish with Jeroboam." Ibid, 155–156.

— JULY —

1   Edom was a direct descendant of Esau.

2   "The Ishmaelites were the first known power from the central Arabian desert. An Ishmaelite tribal confederacy reached its greatest power during the Late Assyrian period. The first reference to them comes from the 8th-century records of Tiglath-Pileser III, describing his campaigns in Syria. The Ishmaelites sent tribute of camels to this Assyrian king after his campaign against them in 738 B.C.... Another Assyrian king, Sargon II received tribute from a variety of Ishmaelite tribes in 716 B.C. The Ishmaelite tribes evidently lived along the trade routes used to transport incense and controlled the trade of incense and aromatic goods...the term "Ishmaelite" disappeared at the end of the 7th century B.C. Many of the splinter tribes however, continued to exist, including the Arab tribes in central Arabia." *The Chronological Study Bible*, 373.

3   Reminds me of the Rich Mullins song: "But when I leave I want to go out like Elijah." "Elijah." Lyrics by Rich Mullins. https://genius.com/Rich-mullins-elijah-lyrics (accessed June 25, 2019).

4   "God was the rightful ruler of the whole earth, not just Israel. The prophets knew they were to speak to the nations." Paul York, 105.

5   "Missions to the nations, from the Old Testament perspective, is an eschatological act of God, not (yet) a missionary sending agenda for God's people." Wright, 503.

6   Babylon is called the "Mother of Harlots" in Revelation 17:1–6.

7   Naaman the Syrian coming to faith in Jehovah and Elisha representing Jehovah in Damascus.

8   *The Chronological Study Bible*, 609.

9   John V. York, 53–54.

10   Kaiser, 52.

11   "Universal" as in available to all nations and peoples, not as in a liberal soteriological sense where someone can be saved outside of faith in Jesus Christ.

12   Christopher T. Begg, "The Peoples and the Worship of Yahweh in the Book of Isaiah," *Worship and the Hebrew Bible*, edited by M.P. Graham, R.R. Marrs, and S.L. McKenzie (Sheffield, U.K.,: Sheffield Academic Press, 1999), 35–55.

13   Charles M. Sheldon, *In His Steps* (New York: Grosset & Dunlap, 1935), 88.

14   *The Chronological Study Bible*, 579.

15   Wright, 467.

16   *The Chronological Study Bible*, 579.

17   Charles M. Sheldon, *In His Steps* (New York: Grosset & Dunlap, 1935), 236–240.

18   Wright, 92.

19   Ibid, 489.

20   *The Chronological Study Bible*, 866.

21   Wright, 153–154.

22   *The Chronological Study Bible*, 589.

23   Paul York, 122.

24   Wright, 330–331.

25   John V. York, 47.

26   *The Chronological Study Bible*, 872–873.

27   Author's translation. "Wait" in the Septuagint is *meno*, the Greek word "abide" used in John 15 and elsewhere. "Renew" in the Hebrew is literally "exchange."

28   *The Chronological Study Bible*, 1024.

29   Ibid, 891.

30   Deuteronomy 23:1–3 does indeed forbid foreigners and those with defects.

31   *The Chronological Study Bible*, 1042.

— AUGUST —

1   Possibly the time of the Genesis 10:11 reference.

2   *The Chronological Study Bible*, 699–700.

3   Frank Bartleman, *Azusa Street: The Roots of Modern Day Pentecost* (New Kensington, PA: Whitaker House. 1982), 56, 58.

4   *The Chronological Study Bible*, 688–689.

5   Ibid, 689.

6   Ibid, 690.

7   Wright, 241.

8   J. A. Thompson, *The Book of Jeremiah, New International Commentary on the Old Testament* (Grand Rapids: Eerdmans, 1980), 213.

9   *The Chronological Study Bible*, 710.

10   Ibid, 730.

11   Ibid, 705–6.

12   Wright, 122.

13   *The Chronological Study Bible*, 811.

14   Ibid, 815, 818.

15   "The gospel carries the knowledge of God among the nations. Paul understood himself to be God's apostle to the nations, entrusted with the task of taking this gospel of the knowledge of the living God to the nations that knew him not. But he clearly saw this personal mission of his as entirely dependent on the prior mission of God, that is, God's own will to be known. It was not the case that Paul chose to have a mission to the nations on behalf of Israel's God. It was that the God of Israel chose Paul for his mission to the nations." Wright, 122.

16   Ibid, 96.

17   Ibid, 97–98.

— SEPTEMBER —

1   Wright, 98–99.

2   Nathan MacDonald, "Listening to Abraham – Listening to YHWH: Divine Justice and Mercy in Genesis 18:16–33," *Catholic Biblical Quarterly* 66 (2004), 25–43.

3   Dorothy Sayers, *A Matter of Eternity* (Grand Rapids, MI: Eerdmans Publishing Co., 1973), 86.

4   Wright, 100–101.

5   Adolf Shlatter, *Do We Know Jesus?* (Grand Rapids, MI: Kregel Publications, 2005), 19.

6   Universalism meaning other roads to salvation than through penal substitutionary atonement.

7   Likely because Joel referenced the Greek and referenced the earlier prophesies of Isaiah 2:4 and Micah 4:3.

8   *The Chronological Study Bible*, 1031.

9   David Irwin, excerpt from a sermon as quoted in *Mountain Movers* magazine (Springfield, MO: Gospel Publishing House, December 1984), 10.

10   Tim Throckmorton, "But If Not," *Circleville Herald*, https://www.circlevilleherald.com/comment/columns/but-if-not/article_9501e7de-5131-5f24-b78e-69e48586969f.html   (accessed August 19, 2019).

11   *The Chronological Study Bible*, 1060.

12   Ibid, 1059–1060.

13   "The book of Daniel offers readers of all generations an insight into God's promise and a pattern at work in history. The pattern reveals how humans and their kingdoms become violent beasts when they glorify their power and don't acknowledge God as their true King. But Daniel's visions also hold out a promise, that one day God will confront the beast, rescue his world and his people, and bring his Kingdom." Tim Mackie, *Read Scripture: Illustrated Summaries of Biblical Books* (Portland, OR: The Bible Project, 2018), 56.

14   The setting was the rise of the Persian empire: an empire that extended from Cyrus to his son Cambyses (replaced by his brother) to Darius (a general for Cambyses), and from Darius' son Xerxes to Xerxes' son Artaxerxes. In this time, the religiously tolerant Persians allowed the Jews to go home.

15   E. Stanley Jones, *The Christ of the Indian Road* (London: Hodder and Stoughton, 1925), 27.

16   Mackie, 78.

17   "Jesus Shall Reign Where'er the Sun." Lyrics by Isaac Watts. http://www.lutheran-hymnal.com/lyrics/tlh511.htm (accessed September 4, 2019).

18   Mackie, 30.

19   Harold G. Moore and Joseph L. Galloway, *We Were Soldiers Once...and Young* (New York: HarperPerennial, 1992).

20   *The Chronological Study Bible*, 1012.

21   Wright, 489.

— OCTOBER —

1   John V. York, 26.

2   *The Chronological Study Bible*, 1137.

3   Again, this title Son of Man originated in Daniel 7 and is connected to the Ancient of Days and the Messiah who is Lord over all the nations.

4   *The Chronological Study Bible*, 1117.

5   Ibid.

6   Which does not insult the Godhead and undermine the gospel by removing familial or filial language.

7   Sleep refers to grace and trust in mission adversity.

8   Matthew 10:1, 5–12, 15–39.

9   Mark 7:26 calls her a Greek, a Syro-Phoenician by birth.

10   The Greek-speaking cities of Syria on the eastern side of the Sea of Galilee.

11   "Philippi" was added to distinguish it from the Caesarea on the Mediterranean.

12   *The Chronological Study Bible*, 1152.

13   The priests quoted scriptures such as Isaiah 12:3 and 44:3, Zechariah 14:8, and Ezekiel 36:25–27.

14   The etymology of the word "neighbor" is "the one who lives nearby."

15   Luke 12:5, 9, 20–21, 40, 47, 49–50; 13:4, 6–9.

16   *The Chronological Study Bible*, 1178.

17   Matt. 19:16–30; Mark 10:17–31; Luke 18:18–30.

— NOVEMBER —

1   Mark E. Moore, *The Chronological Life of Christ* (Joplin, MO: College Press, 1996), 484.

2   Margaret Clarkson, "So Send I You," https://propempo.com/story-behind-so-send-i-you-margaret-clarkson/ (accessed September 30, 2019).

3   *The Chronological Study Bible*, 1202.

4   Daniel 9:27, 11:31, 12:11.

5   Herod the Great's Temple Mount reconstruction likely refurbished the temple according to the plan of the second temple but much more extravagantly.

6   There was a hand washing ritual called *rihaz*.

7   *The Chronological Study Bible*, 1219.

8   Ibid, 1231.

9   Dominion theology holds to the belief that the kingdom is here and now, and we are the super anointed or dedicated ones who will so live and serve in the earth that it will be overwhelmingly Christian.

10   Wright, 107.

11   *The Chronological Study Bible*, 1283.

12   The comment originally appeared in Luther's 1522 *Preface to the New Testament*, but Luther himself removed the comment for subsequent editions.

13   Paul in his letter to believers in Roman Turkey referenced Arabia, Syria, Turkey, and Judea, and the calling to preach to the Gentiles twice.

14   Mt. Horeb is another name for Mt. Sinai.

15   "By the 1st century A.D. the council of the Areopagus had regained much of its former authority. The assembly to which Paul preached was again the chief governing body in Athens, a position it would keep until the advent of Christian domination in the 4th century A.D." *The Chronological Study Bible*, 1290

16   My paraphrase of Acts 17:22–31.

17   *The Chronological Study Bible*, 1299.

18   Ibid, 1300.

19   Preaching meaning the verbal declaration of sin, Savior, and salvation.

20   1 Cor. 1:17–18, 21, 23–24; 2:1–2, 4–5, 7, 13; 3:19; 4:10.

— DECEMBER —

1   George D. Watson, *God's Eagles: Or, Complete Testing of the Saints* (Salem, OH: Schmul Publishing Co. Inc., 1989), 84.

2   Ibid, 95–96.

3   This was this was the same year Nero compelled senators to fight in the stadium.

4   "Elijah." Lyrics by Rich Mullins. https://www.kidbrothers.net/lyrics/elijah-s.html (accessed November 6, 2019).

5   *The Chronological Study Bible*, 1360.

6   Ibid, 1361.

7   Col. 1:15–19; 2:3, 9–10; 3:1–4.

8   *The Chronological Study Bible*, 1371.

9   No indigenous church among unreached peoples is established if extraction is the normal policy for helping believers under duress. It is the most natural reaction in the world to remove our loved ones from pain, but it may not be the wisest or the most loving in the long term. If we really love the church, if we really want to see indigenous churches established among every people, then we will have to be part and party to decisions that encourage those being persecuted to stay where the pain is and endure. Further, we will have to model what we exhort. Peter, nowhere in his letter to beloved Christians, exhorted them to leave or flee. Rather, he counseled them to keep their eyes on heaven, endure with the brotherhood, and live above reproach.

10   *The Chronological Study Bible*, 1390.

11   Wright, 120.

12   Jonathan Edwards, *Life and Diary of David Brainerd* (Pantianos Classics, 1749), 145.

13   *The Chronological Study Bible*, 1398.

14   Hebrews 2:1, 3; 3:12, 13; 4:1, 11; 6:4–6; 10:26–29, 38.

15   *The Chronological Study Bible*, 1377.

16   Ibid, 1386.

17   Ibid, 1409.

18   Watson, 187–8.

19   A warning to all who think that authority and organization are intrinsically oppressive, for without them man descends into depravity.

LIVE | DEAD

The Live Dead Journal ▶

◀ Live Dead The Journey

Live Dead The Story ▶

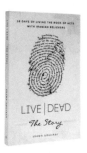

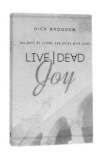

◀ Live Dead Joy

The Live Dead Journal:
Her Heart Speaks ▶

Live Dead Life ▶

◀ Live Dead India:
The Common Table

This Gospel ▶

◀ Leading Muslims to Jesus

Live Dead Together ▶